The Wiley-Blackwell Handbook of Adulthood and Aging

Blackwell Handbooks of Developmental Psychology

This outstanding series of handbooks provides a cutting-edge overview of classic research, current research and future trends in developmental psychology.

- Each handbook draws together 20–30 newly commissioned chapters to provide a comprehensive overview of a sub-discipline of developmental psychology.
- The international team of contributors to each handbook has been specially chosen for its expertise and knowledge of each field.
- Each handbook is introduced and contextualized by leading figures in the field, lending coherence and authority to each volume.

The *Blackwell Handbooks of Developmental Psychology* will provide an invaluable overview for advanced students of developmental psychology and for researchers as an authoritative definition of their chosen field.

Published

The Wiley-Blackwell Handbook of Adulthood and Aging
Edited by Susan Krauss Whitbourne and Martin J. Sliwinski

The Wiley-Blackwell Handbook of Infant Development, 2nd Edition
Edited by Gavin Bremner and Theodore D. Wachs

The Wiley-Blackwell Handbook of Childhood Social Development
Edited by Peter K. Smith and Craig H. Hart

The Wiley-Blackwell Handbook of Childhood Cognitive Development, 2nd edition
Edited by Usha Goswami

The Blackwell Handbook of Adolescence
Edited by Gerald R. Adams and Michael D. Berzonsky

The Science of Reading: A Handbook
Edited by Margaret J. Snowling and Charles Hulme

The Blackwell Handbook of Early Childhood Development
Edited by Kathleen McCartney and Deborah A. Phillips

The Blackwell Handbook of Language Development
Edited by Erika Hoff and Marilyn Shatz

Forthcoming

The Wiley-Blackwell Handbook of Developmental Psychology in Action
Edited by Rudolph Schaffer and Kevin Durkin

The Wiley-Blackwell Handbook of Adulthood and Aging

Edited by Susan Krauss Whitbourne and Martin J. Sliwinski

A John Wiley & Sons, Ltd., Publication

Contents

Notes on Contributors

Jason C. Allaire is an Associate Professor of Psychology at North Carolina State University. He earned his PhD in Lifespan Developmental Psychology at Wayne State University (Institute of Gerontology) and completed his postdoctoral training at The Pennsylvania State University. His research interests center on examining the changes in cognition that occur during the latter portion of the lifespan and how these changes impact the ability of older adults to function in their everyday lives.

Anne Ingeborg Berg, PhD is an Assistant Professor and Licensed Psychologist at the Department of Psychology, University of Gothenburg, Sweden. The focus of her research has mainly been directed at various aspects of well-being in old age, with particular interest in the identification of prerequisites of life satisfaction and cognitive health.

Kira S. Birditt is an Assistant Research Professor at the Institute for Social Research at the University of Michigan. She has a PhD in Human Development and Family Studies from The Pennsylvania State University. Her research focuses on the negative aspects of social relationships and their implications for well-being across the lifespan.

Rosemary Blieszner is the Alumni Distinguished Professor of Human Development and Associate Director of the Center for Gerontology at Virginia Tech. Her research focuses on family and friend relationships, life events, and psychological well-being in adulthood and old age. She is coeditor of *Older Adult Friendship* and *Handbook of Families and Aging*, coauthor of *Adult Friendship, Spiritual Resiliency in Older Women*, and *Spiritual Resiliency and Aging*, and author of numerous journal articles and book chapters.

Cory Bolkan is an Assistant Professor of Human Development at Washington State University Vancouver where she teaches courses in Gerontology and Adult Development. Her previous research has explored self and personality processes in older adults to understand the relationship between mental and physical health, as well as health behaviors. In addition, she is currently working on research projects related to psychosocial aspects of late-life depression and the depression care delivery system.

Susan Turk Charles is an Associate Professor in the Department of Psychology and Social Behavior at the University of California, Irvine. Her work focuses on how emotional experiences vary across the adult lifespan, as well as how emotional experiences relate to physical health processes.

Adam Davey is an Associate Professor of Public Health at Temple University where he directs the Doctoral Program in Health Ecology and is a member of the Biostatistics Research Support Center. His more than 100 publications include *Statistical Power Analysis with Missing Data: A Structural Equation Modeling Approach* and *Caregiving Contexts: Cultural, Familial, and Societal Implications*. Current research focuses on exceptional survival (Georgia Centenarian Study) and patterns of cognitive change (Maine-Syracuse Longitudinal Study).

Colin A. Depp is an Assistant Clinical Professor in the Department of Psychiatry at the School of Medicine of the University of California, San Diego.

Judith Dirk is currently a postdoctoral researcher at the IDeA Center (Individual Development and Adaptive Education of Children at Risk) in Frankfurt, Germany. She obtained her PhD in 2010 from the University of Geneva where she was working on age- and task-related differences in interindividual and intraindividual variability in cognitive performance across the lifespan. Her current research focuses on children's daily performance fluctuations, methodological aspects in the study of variability, and ambulatory assessment.

Barry A. Edelstein is a Professor of Clinical Psychology at West Virginia University. His scholarly work focuses on assessment of older adults, older adult decision making, and older adult anxiety.

Sarah Eisel received her BA from the University of South Florida, majoring in psychology, with a minor in gerontology. She is currently involved in research that examine the effects of diet and antioxidants on long-term memory, as well as the interaction between nicotine and alcohol.

Elliot M. Friedman is an Associate Scientist in the Institute on Aging at the University of Wisconsin-Madison. His background is in health psychology with a specific interest in Psychoneuroimmunology. He has numerous publications on social, behavioral, and psychological predictors of biological processes related to health, particularly inflammation, in middle-aged and older adults.

Lindsay A. Gerolimatos is a PhD student in Clinical Psychology at West Virginia University. She is currently working on her master's thesis examining health anxiety in older adults. Her primary research interests include anxiety in older adults with a secondary interest in assessment. She earned her BSc in Human Development from Cornell University in 2009.

Denis Gerstorf is a Professor of Developmental Psychology at Humboldt University, Berlin, Germany, and also holds an Adjunct appointment at the Department of Human Development and Family Studies at The Pennsylvania State University. He is a lifespan developmental psychologist with a general research interest in better understanding differential development across adulthood and old age. He is the recipient of the 2010 Springer Early Career Achievement Award in Research in Adult Development and Aging from Division 20 of the American Psychological Association.

Christine E. Gould is a doctoral candidate at West Virginia University. She is currently completing her predoctoral clinical internship at the Veterans Affairs Palo Alto Health Care System. She will continue as a postdoctoral fellow in the Special Fellowship Program in Advanced Geriatrics at the Geriatric Research Education and Clinical Center (GRECC).

Eileen Kranz Graham is a recent graduate from Brandeis University's PhD program for Social and Developmental Psychology. She is currently on faculty at Mt Holyoke College as Visiting Assistant Professor and is continuing her research on personality and other psychosocial factors that contribute to maintaining cognitive health in older adulthood.

Scott M. Hofer is a Professor of Psychology and Harald Mohr MD and Wilhelma Mohr MD Research Chair in Adult Development and Aging at the University of Victoria, Canada. He codirects an international Integrative Analysis of Longitudinal Studies on Aging (IALSA) research network for the coordinated analysis and synthesis of longitudinal research on aging-related change and variation in cognition, health, and personality.

Karen Hooker is a Professor of Human Development and Family Sciences and Founding Director of the Center for Healthy Aging Research at Oregon State University. Her work on personality and aging is widely published in journals and books and she is currently Principal Investigator on an Integrative Graduate Education and Research Traineeship Program funded by the National Science Foundation.

Derek M. Isaacowitz is an Associate Professor of Psychology at the Volen National Center for Complex Systems at Brandeis University. His research focuses on links between attention and emotion in adulthood and old age. This work has been funded by the National Institute on Aging and has appeared in journals such as *Psychological Science*, *Developmental Psychology*, and *Psychology and Aging*.

Dilip V. Jeste, MD is the Estelle and Edgar Levi Chair in Aging, Director of the Sam and Rose Stein Institute for Research on Aging, and Distinguished Professor of Psychiatry and Neurosciences, University of California, San Diego. He is the recipient of multiple honors and awards, and federal research grants. He has published 10 books and over 600 articles in peer-reviewed journals and books. He is a member of the Institute of Medicine of the National Academy of Sciences, and is editor-in-chief of the *American Journal of Geriatric Psychiatry*, and is in the ISI list of the "world's most cited authors."

Boo Johansson, PhD is a Professor of Geropsychology at the Department of Psychology, University of Gothenburg, Sweden. He was affiliated with the Institute of Gerontology, Jönköping University 1975–2001. He also holds an adjunct position at The Pennsylvania State University. His research interests since the 1970s have mainly been directed toward various aspects of cognitive and mental health. His scientific publications are largely based on data from population-based longitudinal studies of older individuals and twin pairs followed until their death.

Leslie I. Katzel, MD, PhD is an Associate Professor of Medicine in the Division of Gerontology, Department of Medicine, University of Maryland School of Medicine, and Baltimore Veterans Affairs Medical Center (BVAMC); and Clinical Director of the BVAMC Geriatric Research Education and Clinical Center (GRECC). He has extensive experience in human clinical investigation and in the oversight of clinical research.

Margie E. Lachman is the Minnie and Harold Fierman Professor of Psychology at Brandeis University, where she is also director of the Lifespan Developmental Psychology Lab and the Lifespan Initiative on Healthy Aging. She is the editor of two books, *Multiple Paths of Midlife Development* (1997) and the *Handbook of Midlife Development* (2001). She is a co-investigator on the National Study of Midlife in the United States (MIDUS).

Richard B. Lipton, MD is a Professor and Vice Chair of Neurology, Professor of Epidemiology and Population Health at the Albert Einstein College of Medicine, where he also directs the Einstein Aging Study. He has a long-standing interest in the factors that contribute to cognitive decline in older adults, including both normative aging as well as Alzheimer's disease and other dementias.

Vanessa M. Loaiza is a graduate student in the cognitive psychology program at Colorado State University. Her research focuses on the functioning of working memory across the lifespan. She is particularly interested in underlying processes supporting working memory performance that are intact or deficient with increasing age, and how these processes are differentially responsible for relations between working memory and higher order cognition.

David P. McCabe (1969–2011) was an assistant professor of psychology at Colorado State University. He will be remembered for his research that encompassed a wide range of topics pertaining to memory performance and accuracy across the lifespan, with a particular focus on age-related changes in working memory, conscious recollection, and metamemory. He used both experimental and individual differences methods to investigate age-related changes in controlled processing underlying higher order cognition.

Cathy L. McEvoy is a Professor of Aging Studies at the University of South Florida. Her research focuses on aging and memory, with an emphasis on the implicit, or unconscious, processes underlying recall and recognition. Her research has been funded by the National Institute on Aging and the National Institute of Mental Health.

Victor Molinari, PhD, ABPP (Clin.) is a Professor in the Department of Aging and Mental Health Disparities of the Florida Mental Health Institute at the University of South Florida. He is a member of the National Advisory Council on Aging, and has served on the American Psychological Association's (APA) Committee on Aging and as past president of APA's Society of Clinical Geropsychology.

Nicky J. Newton is a doctoral candidate in psychology at the University of Michigan. She received her BA degree (2004) in psychology from the University of California, Berkeley, and her MA degree (2007) in psychology from the University of Michigan. Her work has appeared in *Psychology of Women Quarterly*, and she was a cocontributor to *The Handbook of Gender Research in Psychology* (2010).

Jennifer R. Piazza received her PhD from the University of California, Irvine, and is currently a postdoctoral fellow at The Pennsylvania State University. Her work examining mental and physical health across the lifespan has been published in books and journals, including *The Journals of Gerontology: Psychological Sciences* and *Psychology and Aging.*

Andrea M. Piccinin is an Associate Professor in the Department of Psychology, University of Victoria, Canada. Her research focuses mainly on cognitive function in later life from a life-span individual differences perspective – on normal patterns as well as on the impact of disease and other characteristics and risk factors. She codirects the collaborative international network, Integrative Analysis of Longitudinal Studies on Aging (IALSA), which provides extensive opportunities for coordinated analysis and replication of developmental research from a within-person perspective.

Nilam Ram is an Assistant Professor of Human Development and Family Studies at The Pennsylvania State University with specialty in longitudinal methods. He works to develop intraindividual analytic techniques and study designs that maintain a focus on the individual while still tackling issues of aggregation and generalizability.

Philippe Rast is currently a postdoctoral fellow at the University of Victoria in the Centre on Aging. He received his PhD in psychology in 2008 from the University of Zurich. His research focuses mainly on the identification and explanation of individual differences in learning, on metamemory, and memory performance across the adult lifespan.

Kerri S. Rawson is a doctoral candidate in the School of Aging Studies at the University of South Florida, where she also completed her MS in Medical Sciences: Aging and Neuroscience. Her research focuses on the role of stress and immune system functioning on the cognitive performance of older adults.

Karen A. Roberto is a Professor and Director of the Center for Gerontology and the Institute for Society, Culture, and Environment at Virginia Tech. Her research focuses on the intersection of health and social support in late life. She is the author or editor of 10 books, including *Resilience in Aging: Concepts, Research, and Outcomes* (2011, with B. Resnick & L. Gwyther) and *Pathways of Human Development: Explorations of Change* (2009, with J. Mancini).

Carol D. Ryff is a Professor of Psychology and Director of the Institute on Aging at the University of Wisconsin-Madison. She also heads the MIDUS (Midlife in the US) national longitudinal study. Her research centers on the role of positive psychosocial factors as protective influences on health vis-à-vis the challenges of aging and social inequality. Explicating the biological processes through which such protective influences occur is a key objective in these studies.

Florian Schmiedek is a Researcher at the Max Planck Institute for Human Development in Berlin, Germany.

Daniel L. Segal is a Professor and Director of Clinical Training at the University of Colorado, Colorado Springs. His research interests include the assessment of psychopathology among older adults, suicide resilience, and expression and impact of personality disorders across the lifespan. He is a Fellow of the Gerontological Society of America, an associate editor for the *Clinical Gerontologist*, and he serves on the editorial boards of three journals (*Behavior Modification, Clinical Case Studies*, and *Journal of Clinical Psychology*).

Ilene C. Siegler, PhD, MPH is a Professor of Medical Psychology and Psychology & Neuroscience, Duke University and Adjunct Professor of Epidemiology at the University of North Carolina at Chapel Hill. She received the 2007 Developmental Health Award from Divisions 20 and 38 of the American Psychological Association, and was a member of the National Advisory Council on Aging from 2000–03. She directs the UNC Alumni Heart Study from the Duke Behavioral Medicine Research Center.

Dean Keith Simonton is the Distinguished Professor of Psychology at the University of California, Davis. He studies genius, creativity, leadership, talent, and aesthetics. His more than 400 publications include 12 books. Honors include the William James Book Award, the George A. Miller Outstanding Article Award, the SPSP Theoretical Innovation Prize, the Sir Francis Galton Award for Outstanding Contributions to the Study of Creativity, and the Rudolf Arnheim Award for Outstanding Achievement in Psychology of the Arts.

Martin J. Sliwinski is a Professor of Human Development and Family Studies and director of the Center for Healthy Aging at The Pennsylvania State University. He received his doctorate in Neuropsychology from City University of New York and his BA in Interdisciplinary Studies from Georgetown University. His areas of research interest include early detection of preclinical dementia, health influences on cognition and well-being across the adult lifespan, and methodological issues in the developmental sciences.

Brent J. Small is a Professor of Aging Studies at the University of South Florida. His work focuses on cognitive aging in preclinical Alzheimer's disease, the influence of context factors (e.g., diet, mental activities) on cognitive functioning, and the application of advanced statistical methods to longitudinal data. His research has been funded by the National Institute on Aging and the National Cancer Institute.

Jennifer Tehan Stanley is a postdoctoral fellow in the Emotion Lab at Brandeis University. She received her doctorate in Experimental Psychology, with a focus on Cognitive Aging from Georgia Institute of Technology. Her research interests relate to socioemotional functioning in adulthood. She is especially interested in how contextual factors influence age differences in emotion recognition and interpersonal functioning.

Gregory M. Steinbrenner, MS is an Exercise Physiologist and Clinical Research Associate in the Geriatrics, Research, Education, and Clinical Center at the Baltimore VA Medical Center. He has extensive experience in the assessment of functional performance in people with chronic diseases and in the implementation of exercise rehabilitation strategies to restore functional deficits and improve quality of life.

Joshua R. Steinerman is an Assistant Professor of Neurology at the Albert Einstein College of Medicine and Montefiore Medical Center, Bronx, New York, where he founded the Center for Healthy Brain Aging to integrate his clinical practice with community-based research in cognitive technology.

Abigail J. Stewart is the Sandra Schwartz Tangri Distinguished University Professor of Psychology and Women's Studies at the University of Michigan, where she is Director of the ADVANCE Program, and Associate Dean of the Graduate School. Her current research examines educated women's lives and personalities; women's movement activism both in the US and globally; gender, science, and technology among graduate students, postdoctoral fellows and faculty; and institutional change in the academy.

Ipsit V. Vahia is a junior faculty member at the Stein Institute for Research on Aging at the University of California, San Diego, and staff psychiatrist at Sun Valley Behavioral Medical Center in Imperial, California. He serves on the editorial board of the *American Journal of Geriatric Psychiatry* and was recipient of a 2008 Junior Investigator Award from the International College of Geriatric Psychoneuropharmacology. He is currently working on several research projects related to successful aging.

Mo Wang is an Associate Professor of Psychology at the University of Maryland, College Park. His research focuses on older worker employment and retirement, and has appeared in prestigious academic journals, such as *American Psychologist, Psychology and Aging, Journal of Applied Psychology, Personnel Psychology*, and *Academy of Management Journal*. He currently serves as an associate editor for *Journal of Applied Psychology*. He also edited *The Oxford Handbook of Retirement* (2011).

Elvina Wardjiman is a graduate of the University of Michigan, where she received an honors degree in Psychology. While at Michigan, she became extensively involved in research through the Institute for Social Research and wrote her thesis on the role of personality on daily interpersonal tensions and salivary cortisol. She is currently applying her research skills to market research and plans to pursue a graduate degree in the future.

Stacey B. Whitbourne received her PhD in Social and Developmental Psychology from Brandeis University in 2005. She is a Research Health Scientist with the Massachusetts Veterans Epidemiology and Research Information Center (MAVERIC), a research service of the VA Boston Healthcare System; she is an Instructor of Medicine at Harvard Medical School and an Associate Epidemiologist with Brigham and Women's Hospital, Boston, MA.

Susan Krauss Whitbourne is a Professor of Psychology and Director, Office of National Scholarship Advisement at the University of Massachusetts Amherst. She is the author of over 130 refereed articles and book chapters and 15 books (many in multiple editions and translations); her most recent work is *The Search for Fulfillment*. She is the recipient of a 2011 Presidential Citation from the American Psychological Association, and her research covers a wide range of topics in the psychology of aging.

Richard Zweig is an Associate Professor of Psychology at the Ferkauf Graduate School of Yeshiva University. He is coauthor of *Personality Disorders in Older Adults: Emerging Issues in Diagnosis and Treatment* and the recipient of two federal grants to train students in geropsychology. He has written and presented on the assessment and treatment of personality-disordered older adults, depression and suicide in the elderly, and geropsychology training.

Preface

Susan Krauss Whitbourne and Martin J. Sliwinski

The study of adult development and aging is a rapidly expanding field that is drawing increased attention throughout psychology and the other social sciences. As you will learn in this volume, "aging" is a decades-long process that covers the entire developmental period from late adolescence through the last years of life. Many of the chapters in this volume cover changes throughout the entire period of adulthood, although due to the nature of the field itself, our contributors have tended to give greater attention to the middle and later adult years.

For readers who are unfamiliar with the topic and are using this volume to gain an overview of the area, we would advise that you browse through the chapters in the order in which they appear. We have organized the chapters so that we begin with a solid theoretical overview, a grounding in current demographics, and then a review of the major areas of research formulated broadly within the biopsychosocial perspective. Our contributors were asked to provide a general overview of their specific topics and, within these topics, to focus on their particular areas of investigation. Readers with expertise in the area of adult development and aging will benefit from these overviews, but should be particularly interested in the state-of-the-art approaches that our contributors have succinctly summarized.

Although we represent different orientations within the field, both of us share a broad-based view that changes within the individual must be examined in a multidimensional, multifaceted manner. We agree with conceptualizations of development in the later years of adulthood that approach aging not as a linear, progressive, process of decline but instead believe that development is characterized by plasticity. This means that changes with age can be modified by factors within the individual and those within the individual's context. Contemporary research in the field increasingly emphasizes the ways that aging individuals can prevent and compensate for changes that, in the past, were seen as immutable. Many of the contributors to this volume present concrete examples of this principle.

Part I of this volume begins with an overall theoretical orientation provided by Elliot Friedman and Carol Ryff, who explicitly present the biopsychosocial model and lays out the concept of successful aging, a theme that later contributors also address. In the following chapter, Susan Whitbourne and Stacey Whitbourne present the latest demographic information concerning the aging population within the United States and throughout the world. They present this data in terms of overall trends as well as according to demographic variations. Prevalence data for major diseases and health conditions are also covered in this chapter. Social context forms the organizing theme of the chapter by Dennis Gerstorf and Nilam Ram, who examine factors that shape well-being in late life. They present a heuristic model that provides a multilevel framework which connects regional and individual-level factors that regulate risk and resilience in older age. They argue that late life offers a naturally occurring "stress test," which provides a novel lens through which to observe how these macrolevel and microlevel processes influence trajectories of well-being. Scott Hofer, Philippe Rast, and Andrea Piccinin survey developmental research methods, which represent a particular challenge for psychologists who study aging. Their discussion highlights central issues that fall at the interface among theory, design, and analysis. In particular, they address contemporary methodological challenges to the field that involve distinguishing normative versus nonnormative changes, disentangling multiple time-dependent processes, and the role of contextual factors(such as those discussed in Chapter 3) on modeling individual change.

Part II of the volume spans the areas of physical functioning and health. Leslie Katzel and Gregory Steinbrenner, building on the theoretical perspective of successful aging, review the literature on aging-related changes in physical strength and cardiovascular capacity. Their review focuses on the distinction between normal aging and disease, and also points to the importance of distinguishing between cross-sectional and longitudinal studies. They also show how compensation for normal aging and disease are possible through exercise, hence addressing the book's theme of plasticity in later life. The relationship between personality and health is the subject of Ilene Siegler and Adam Davey's chapter, which presents data from the University of North Carolina Alumni Heart Study (UNCAHS). In the UNCAHS, follow-ups of college students through their forties revealed striking relationships between college personality and midlife health. Their review of studies of centenarians show the importance of examining behavioral correlates of health at different age periods.

The chapters in Part III focus on cognitive functioning, traditionally an area that has a central place in the research on adult development and aging. Judith Dirk and Florian Schmiedek, in their chapter on processing speed, critically review the current state of our understanding of the most ubiquitous finding from the field of cognitive aging: age-related slowing. They provide a thorough critique of the extant literature, identifying several major limitations in our understanding of age-related changes in processing speed. Then they introduce contemporary approaches to quantitative modeling of response time variability as an approach to isolating and explaining the mechanisms underlying age-related slowing. Their chapter concludes by reviewing how these modeling approaches can connect with neurobiological process that underlie cognitive slowing. David McCabe and Vanessa Loaiza cover the topic of working memory, which, along with processing speed, have been identified as "cognitive primitives" that could potentially explain age-related differences on a broad range of higher order cognitive abilities. They identify several key questions for understanding aging and working memory, and relate these to major contemporary theoretical frameworks. Examining age effects across all areas of memory systems, Brent Small, Kerri Rawson, Sarah Eisel, and Cathy McEvoy provide a comprehensive review of the most recent findings on aging-related changes in semantic and episodic memory function. They identify a number of challenges that affect how we interpret results from cross-sectional and longitudinal studies for understanding memory and aging. They discuss the importance of considering cohort and retest effects for establishing the timing of aging-related memory changes. They conclude by discussing the highly relevant question of whether aging-related memory loss can be remediated, and review some recent studies that examined the effects of cognitively stimulating activities, physical activities, and dietary factors on memory loss. Jason Allaire's contribution on everyday cognition presents a contrast to the findings of laboratory studies on cognition. Allaire points out that understanding "cognition in context" can have more real-world relevance to the functional capabilities of older adults than performance on "acontextual" laboratory-based assessments. He discusses approaches to measuring everyday cognition and how these approaches relate to important, real-world outcomes, such as instrumental functioning and mortality.

In Part IV, we include work in the area of personality and aging. Nicky Newton and Abigail Stewart provide a comprehensive view of personality development from the standpoint primarily of Erikson's psychosocial theory. Their chapter includes an in-depth analysis of development in the areas of identity, intimacy, generativity, and ego integrity as well as discussion of suggested expansions of Erikson's theory. Going beyond the notion of personality as an individual difference variable, they also examine development in relation to social roles, drawing from both empirical and narrative studies. Moving into socioemotional theory, Jennifer Stanley and Derek Isaacowitz discuss a wide range of findings on emotion and aging. Reviewing the literature ranging from self-report questionnaires to experimental data, they examine evidence in favor of important theoretical perspectives in the area including the "paradox of well-being," and socio-emotional selectivity theory. They point out that, consistent with the overall theme of the volume, there are important individual differences in approaches to aging. Nevertheless, their conclusions emphasize the generally "positive story" about aging and emotion as well as the ability of many older adults to compensate for age-related losses in other areas of functioning. Examining the link between personality and cognition, Eileen Graham and Margie Lachman review the emerging body of research connecting personality traits within the Five Factor Model and intelligence. They also show ways in which these relationships vary according to age, with different patterns of correlations for younger than for older adults. Included in their analysis are findings relevant to personality action constructs (PACs) and age differences in sense of control and self-efficacy. They also review the areas of stress, anxiety, identity, and coping, all of which are highly relevant to studies of older adults. From their perspective, personality is a resource that can help individuals navigate the changes in health, physical functioning, and cognition in later life.

The chapters in Part V cover "abnormal" aging, focusing on a range of psychological disorders. In their chapter on affective disorders and aging, Jennifer Piazza and Susan Turk Charles provide a "developmental lens" for viewing anxiety and mood disorders.

Although, as they point out, these disorders are less prevalent in older adults, psychologists need to be aware of how their symptoms appear because they may look very different than they do in younger adults with these disorders. These differences make diagnosis a challenge for mental health professionals. Moreover, these conditions overlap with other disorders such as dementia, and with each other as well. Consistent with the book's theme, they provide a biopsychosocial analysis of psychopathology in later life. Joshua Steinerman and Richard Lipton focus exclusively on Alzheimer's disease and dementias stemming from different physical conditions, including vascular dementia. They describe prevalence data from the perspective of early detection, arguing that dementia is underidentified during its prodromal or preclinical phases. They present a staging model for Alzheimer's disease and argue for the importance of refining early classification as therapeutic development shifts from symptom management toward preventive intervention that can delay onset of clinical symptoms. Their discussion also highlights common and uncommon symptoms of dementia, as well as pharmacologic and nonpharmacologic treatments and preventive measures. Examining personality disorders in later life, Daniel Segal, Richard Zweig, and Victor Molinari also address issues raised by Piazza and Charles regarding difficulties in diagnosis and symptom overlap, problems that are particularly pronounced in the case of personality disorders. Tying in the findings on aging and personality development, they present evidence supporting the maturational model which proposes that aging is associated with change in adaptive abilities that tie into changes in symptom expression of these disorders. As indicated in the psychopathology chapters thus far, there is a need for improved assessment and diagnosis, the topic examined by Christine Gould, Barry Edelstein, and Lindsay Gerolimatos. They present a multifaceted approach to assessment that takes into account the developmental dimension in evaluating adults of different ages. Using a case report, they also illustrate how, ideally, clinical assessment takes place in a way that incorporates developmental principles. Although the chapter has a clinical emphasis, it also provides useful information for assessments conducted within research settings.

In Part VI, our contributors turn to social processes and aging. Continuing the theme of motivation and aging, Cory Bolkan and Karen Hooker examine a "six foci" model of personality and aging that places heavy emphasis on goals and self-regulation. Individuals navigate the later years, according to these authors, in order to achieve their goals; an understanding of these goals helps provide an understanding of the reasons behind an individual's behavior. Moreover, sociocultural factors influence the way these goals are conceptualized and implemented. Aging stereotypes in particular influence the way that individuals set their goals by causing individuals to develop negative expectations, which in turn influence their performance. Rosemary Blieszner and Karen Roberto examine specific types of social relationships in adulthood, including romantic partnerships and friendships. They provide a lifespan development perspective on dyadic relationships, examining the links among relationships, health, and well-being. They also provide insights into friendships, a relatively understudied area within the field of adult development and aging. Expanding from dyadic to intergenerational relationships and aging, Kira Birditt and Elvina Wardjiman review the literature on parent–child relationships throughout adulthood, including research on intergenerational exchanges and caregiving. In contrast to the typical view of parent–child relationships in later life as being unidirectional, Birditt and

Wardjiman show the bidirectional nature of these interactions. A life course perspective on retirement is represented in Mo Wang's chapter on the topic, emphasizing the importance of context, life history, and timing. Wang also discusses methodological issues in the study of retirement, pointing to the problems involved in cross-sectional studies that do not follow participants prospectively from preretirement to postretirement phases, and to the need for quantitative, meta-analytic studies.

Finally, Part VII returns to the theme of successful aging. Boo Johannsen and Anne Berg provide an in-depth and comprehensive review on the literature that falls under the rubric of "terminal decline." They adopt a rigorously and unique developmental perspective in their approach to terminal decline, considering both time from birth and time from death. Their discussion of alternative time metrics for charting developmental trajectories dovetails with the chapter by Hofer, Rast, and Piccinin, and provides a concrete example of the complexity entailed in disentangling multiple time-dependent processes, both conceptually and methodologically. They conclude by describing the need for an integrative model for understanding changes in cognitive function and well-being that the biopsychosocial approach demands. Successful aging is examined by Colin Depp, Ipsit Vahia, and Dilip Jeste, who trace theories of healthy or optimal aging from the first use of the term in 1961 through present empirical studies that attempt to quantify this key concept. They review quantitative and qualitative research to provide an operational definition, analyzing the multiple components of optimal aging including wisdom and spirituality. Interventions such as dietary restriction, physical activity, cognitive interventions, and "antiaging" interventions present intriguing applications of knowledge about the factors that contribute to successful aging. Instead of "lifespan" as a measure of successful aging, both at the individual and population levels, they suggest considering the term "healthspan." We end the volume with Dean Keith Simonton's contribution on creative productivity in later life. He points out that previous work in this area has not taken sufficient account of factors such as career age (when a creative person begins a career) and is subject to the problems of aggregation error. Concluding that the age decrements in productivity do exist nonetheless, Simonton points out that there are still ample examples of highly productive older creators whose work far outshine those of younger individuals, or even themselves when they were younger.

We believe that we have assembled an outstanding array of contributors to the vital and vibrant field of adult development and aging. It is our hope that having got a taste of what the psychology of aging has to offer, our readers will embark on their own creative ventures, expanding the scope and range of research and theory on this ever-fascinating topic.

PART I

Foundations

1

Theoretical Perspectives

A Biopsychosocial Approach to Positive Aging

Elliot M. Friedman and Carol D. Ryff

A Historical Introduction

The topic of successful human aging has engaged many great minds, including the Roman orator Cicero (43 BCE/1923), who observed, "It is not by muscle, speed, or physical dexterity that great things are achieved but by reflection, force of character, and judgment; in these qualities, old age is usually not only not poorer, but is even richer" (Chandler, 1948). Similarly, Plato associated old age with calm and freedom (Griffin, 1949). Nearly two millennia would pass before positive aging would emerge as a topic of scientific inquiry. Such work began in the 1940s with a group of scholars at the University of Chicago who were interested in personal and social adjustment in old age (Burgess, 1960; Cavan, Burgess, Havighurst, & Goldhamer, 1949; Pollak, 1948). The Kansas City Studies of Adult Life (Williams & Wirths, 1965) continued the Chicago tradition and offered a conception of successful aging based on four dimensions: the amount of activity in which the individual was engaged, the ability to disengage, satisfaction with life, and maturity or integration of personality. Two additional components were later added: a balanced exchange of energy between the individuals and the social system, and a stable social system. Few of these ideas were accompanied by tools for empirical assessment.

In the decades that followed, life satisfaction became the most frequently investigated dimension of successful aging (for reviews see Cutler, 1979; Larson, 1978). The construct included components of zest versus apathy, resolution and fortitude, relationships between desired goals and achieved goals, self-concept, and mood tone (Neugarten,

Havighurst, & Tobin, 1961). Others elaborated the meaning of successful aging to include happiness, adjustment, affect balance, morale, subjective well-being, and optimal interplay between the individual and the environment (Fozard & Popkin, 1978; Herzog, Rodgers, & Woodworth, 1982; Lawton, 1977; Stock, Okun, & Benin, 1986). Some of these initiatives grew out of a specific focus on old age, while others were imported from different domains and applied to the later years.

Limitations of these early approaches were noted, such as the lack of guiding theory (Ryff, 1982, 1989a) which resulted in related problems (i.e., elusive definitions of constructs, assessment instruments lacking evidence of validity) (Sauer & Warland, 1982). Despite the emphasis on positive aging, much research was conducted with tools designed to assess ill-being (e.g., anxiety, depression, worry, anomie, loneliness, somatic symptoms; for reviews, see Lawton, 1977, 1984). Even on the positive side, much successful aging research utilized dependent variables that could characterize optimal functioning *at any age*, which, in turn, meant that the unique challenges and opportunities of growing old were neglected. Clark and Anderson (1967) drew attention to the challenges of aging by describing "adaptive tasks," which included having an awareness of aging and a sense of instrumental limitations, redefining one's physical and social life space, substituting alternative sources of need satisfaction, reassessing the criteria for evaluation of self, and reintegrating values and life goals. On the opportunity side of aging, Ryff (1989a) drew on multiple theories of psychosocial development (Bühler, 1935; Bühler & Massarik, 1968; Erikson, 1959; Jung, 1933; Neugarten, 1968, 1973) to advance an approach to well-being that incorporated such constructs as personal growth, purpose in life, and self-acceptance, all of which could potentially improve with age.

Other advances in successful aging research focused on psychological processes of selection, optimization, and compensation (Baltes & Baltes, 1990). Illustrated largely in the context of cognitive function, selection referred to the restriction of one's life world to fewer domains of functioning, given age-related loss in adaptive potential. Optimization referred to engaging in behaviors that enrich and augment general reserves (e.g., cognitive reserve) and maximize chosen life directions and associated behaviors. Compensation resulted from restrictions in range of plasticity and adaptive potential, combined with the use of new strategies (e.g., external memory aids, when internal memory mechanics are insufficient).

Adopting a broader, less discipline-bound formulation, Rowe and Kahn (1998) defined successful aging to include three elements: absence of physical illness or disability, high levels of cognitive function and physical functioning, and active engagement with life. Little empirical research accompanied their formulation, although recent research with older Canadians showed that only one of the three criteria was empirically viable (Weir, Meisner, & Baker, 2010). That is, the majority of older Canadians maintained connections with their community (active life engagement), but with increasing age, many experienced disease-related disability and impaired physical functioning.

This brief introductory overview underscores diverse formulations of successful aging evident in gerontological research over the past 70 years, with some having more lasting impact than others. That the ideal of positive aging evolves through time is meaningful and appropriate, to the extent that new versions build on what has gone before by refining core conceptualizations and strengthening empirical underpinnings. With such evolution in mind, we posit that two overarching criteria are critical to theoretical and empirical formulations of successful aging. First, normally occurring changes in the aging mind and body must be incorporated – that is, the formulation must be explicitly *developmental*, while also giving notable attention to individual differences in the timing of such change. Although lifespan developmental criteria have been previously prominent in psychological formulations of successful aging (e.g., Baltes & Baltes, 1990; Ryff, 1982), they have been curiously absent in formulations of physical aging. The Rowe and Kahn (1998) criteria of successful aging, in fact, neglect the reality that over the course of aging most older persons will develop multiple medical conditions. Comorbidity is thus part of normal aging and, as such, should be considered in formulating optimal later life functioning – something recognized half a century ago by Clark and Anderson (1967). Others have begun to endorse a conception of successful aging in which disease and functional limitations coexist, along with compensatory psychological or social mechanisms (Young, Frick, & Phelan, 2009).

A second key criterion is that the inherent interplay between biological, psychosocial, and social aspects of aging (Ryff & Singer, 2009) must be recognized – that is, formulations of successful aging must be fundamentally *biopsychosocial*. Our call for greater emphasis on a biopsychosocial approach is intended to address the neglect of biological processes in most prior formulations of positive aging, whether about psychological functioning or physical health. In this regard, we seek to connect the field of gerontology to a long and growing tradition in health research, which emanates from dissatisfaction with traditional medical models (Engel, 1977). Our intent is to build on advances in this literature, including those emerging from psychoneuroimmunology (Lutgendorf & Costanzo, 2003) and psychoneuroendocrinology (Campeau, Day, Helmreich, Kollack-Walker, & Watson, 1998; de Kloet, 2003). Combined with recognition of the wide heterogeneity among aged persons, we see the route to understanding why some age well and others do not as occurring via integrative models built on diverse combination of risk and protective factors (biological, psychological, social).

What follows is organized in four main sections. We first provide an overview of biopsychosocial approaches to health that we believe have useful import for the field of aging. Second, we address what it means to live well in later life, despite the emergence of medical comorbidities. Third, we consider what it means to live well in the face of social inequality. With both of these topics, we give primacy to psychological and social strengths, which are important not only for quality of life and positive subjective experience, but also because they are increasingly linked to biological regulation, brain activity, and unfolding trajectories of morbidity and mortality. Given the cascade of mechanisms and processes situated around these phenomenological experiences, which define the human condition, we conclude with consideration of interventions designed to promote psychosocial well-being.

Biopsychosocial Approaches to Health

Decades ago, psychiatrist George Engel proposed the adoption of a biopsychosocial model as an alternative to the dominant biomedical model (Engel, 1977). Engel recognized the extraordinary power of the biomedical model to identify "biochemical defects" within the body and to guide the development of treatments for these defects, but he called for physicians to pay more attention to the psychological and social aspects of illness and the patient. He believed that while many of the causes of and treatments for psychiatric conditions likely involve specific biological processes within the brain, important other aspects of treating psychiatric conditions – environmental factors associated with mental illness, cultural and psychological factors influencing a person's decision to seek treatment, physician–patient communication, a patient's willingness and ability to follow treatment recommendations – require that physicians become familiar with the social and psychological contexts of their patients' lives. Engel called for the integration of the biopsychosocial perspective into the training of medical students, and he himself brought biopsychosocial training to the medical curriculum at the University of Rochester where he taught.

Engel's goal of fundamentally changing the practice of medicine has not been extensively adopted; the biomedical model continues to dominate medical education and practice. Thus his exhortation to the medical community remains as pertinent now as it was 30 years ago (Alonso, 2004; Borrell-Carrio, Suchman, & Epstein, 2004). The biopsychosocial model has been incorporated into medical practice in a limited number of ways (Bitton et al., 2008; Finestone, Alfeeli, & Fisher, 2008; Griffith, 2009; Koppe, 2010; McCabe et al., 2010; McCollum & Pincus, 2009; Widerstrom-Noga, Finnerup, & Siddall, 2009), but its largest impact has been in providing the framework for a generation of basic science researchers and as a conceptual foundation for research disciplines favoring an integrative perspective on biological processes relevant to health, such as psychosomatic medicine (Fava & Sonino, 2010; Novack et al., 2007), psychoneuroimmunology (Lutgendorf & Costanzo, 2003), and psychoneuroendocrinology (Campeau et al., 1998; de Kloet, 2003). Psychoneuroimmunology (PNI) is the study of how the immune system is affected by social and psychological experiences and the biological pathways, including brain regulation, by which these influences impinge on immune function. Psychoneur-oendocrinology (PNE) is the study of neural and hormonal responses to social and psychological experiences. Psychosomatic medicine integrates the basic sciences of PNI and PNE with a focus on clinical outcomes and potential interventions to improve health. Many of the same biological systems and social and psychological processes feature in research in all of these fields, so for the sake of parsimony we will not dwell on conceptual or empirical distinctions among them. Rather, using PNI as an organizing framework, we aim to present a broad overview of research that exemplifies a biopsychosocial perspective and, as such, may inform integrative approaches to successful aging.

Long before PNI became a formal area of research, the physiologist Hans Selye characterized a set of physiological changes that routinely occurred in animals after exposure to stressors ranging from cold and surgical injury to sublethal doses of a variety of drugs. These changes included a rapid decrease in the size of tissues related to the immune system, such as lymph nodes and the thymus gland (Selye, 1936). Subsequent efforts showed that adrenal hormones mediated the effects of Selye's stressors on immune cells and tissues (Dougherty, 1952), and to this day adrenal hormones remain central elements of research focused on the biological effects of social and psychological experiences. Other seminal lines of research that led to the development of PNI as a discipline included links between personality characteristics and autoimmune disease (e.g., Solomon & Moos, 1964); between impaired immune function and extremes of negative mood, such as bereavement (Bartrop, Luckhurst, Lazarus, Kiloh, & Penny, 1977) or depression (Irwin, 2002); and the demonstration that the immune system could be trained to respond to nonimmunological stimuli through Pavlovian classical conditioning (Ader & Cohen, 1975). There was also a rapid expansion of PNI research that followed the identification of mechanisms by which the brain and major hormone systems communicated with and received communications from the immune system (see Ader, 2007, for overview).

The embedding of the immune system in a larger network of biological systems provides a plausible biological route by which social and psychological experiences can affect immune processes and resistance to illness. We now focus on a line of PNI research that may serve as an exemplar of biopsychosocial integration that is relevant for aging: inflammation. Inflammation as an adaptive process is a cascade of events that is triggered by damage to tissues or by the detection of a potentially infectious agent, such as a bacterium, and an optimal inflammatory response is critical for tissue repair and healing. The term *inflammation* is also used to describe a family of proteins that mediate the inflammatory response and help to promote tissue repair and healing, including tumor necrosis factor alpha (TNFa), interleukin-6 (IL-6), and C-Reactive Protein (CRP). And while elevations in these proteins in the context of infection or injury is important for healing, elevations in these same proteins in the blood in the absence of injury or infection is associated with increased risk of future morbidity and mortality (Abraham et al., 2007; Blake & Ridker, 2003; Ershler, 1993; Ferrucci et al., 1999; Stork et al., 2006). Inflammation is of specific interest for researchers in the field of aging because some inflammatory proteins increase with age, and these increases are not fully explained by the onset of chronic disease conditions (Ershler, 1993).

Importantly, circulating levels of inflammatory proteins are associated with social, psychological, and biological processes. At the level of social experience, a subordinate position in the social hierarchy, for example, as measured by low income, education, occupational status, or subjective social status, is linked to higher circulating levels of inflammatory proteins, and this association is evident across the life course (Alley et al., 2006; Demakakos, Nazroo, Breeze, & Marmot, 2008; Friedman & Herd, 2010; Gruenewald, Cohen, Matthews, Tracy, & Seeman, 2009; Morozink, Friedman, Coe, & Ryff, 2010). There is also evidence for developmental influences on the link between social status and inflammation. Children who grow up in low socioeconomic conditions – living in a rented home, having a parent with a low status occupation – are more likely to have higher circulating levels of inflammatory proteins once they grow to adulthood (Danese et al., 2009; Miller & Chen, 2007; Miller, Chen, et al., 2009).

At the level of the individual, social relationships are associated with variations in inflammation. Consistent with studies linking isolation from social communities with increased mortality risk (Berkman et al., 2004; House, Landis, & Umberson, 1988), middle-aged and older adults who are socially isolated also have higher circulating levels of inflammatory proteins than those who are more socially integrated (Loucks, Berkman, Gruenewald, & Seeman, 2005, 2006). Perturbations to important social relationships, such as marital conflict, are associated not only with increases in circulating levels of inflammatory proteins but also with impairments in adaptive inflammatory responses to tissue damage (Gouin et al., 2010; Kiecolt-Glaser et al., 2005; Robles & Kiecolt-Glaser, 2003). Older adults often face the challenge of caring for a spouse or family member with chronic illness, and one component of that challenge is isolation from social networks and consequent loneliness. Studies of caregivers have shown not only that they have higher levels of inflammatory proteins in circulation (Lutgendorf et al., 1999), but also that the rate at which inflammatory proteins accumulate in the blood with age is higher compared to noncaregivers (Kiecolt-Glaser et al., 2003). Moreover, the relatively steeper rate of increase does not always resolve once the burden of caregiving is removed (Kiecolt-Glaser et al., 2003), suggesting a lasting change in the biological regulation of inflammation. Complementing these adverse associations is a growing literature on positive social factors and their links to lower levels of inflammation. Among adult women with late-stage gynecologic cancer, those who reported having high quality social relationships had lower levels of IL-6 both in the blood and at the site of the tumor (Costanzo et al., 2005). In a sample of community-dwelling older women, we found that higher ratings of social well-being predicted lower circulating levels of IL-6 (Friedman, Hayney, Love, Singer, & Ryff, 2007).

The production of inflammatory proteins is regulated by a number of other biological systems, most notably the hypothalamic-pituitary-adrenal (HPA) axis and the adrenal hormone cortisol as well as the sympathetic branch of the autonomic nervous system; cortisol in particular is robustly anti-inflammatory. Recent studies have shown that the regulation of inflammation by the HPA axis and the sympathetic nervous system (SNS) is altered by social and psychological experiences acting at cellular and genetic levels. One study compared parents caring for a child with cancer with parents of healthy children and found that the stressed parents had higher circulating levels of inflammatory proteins than parents with healthy children. Importantly, analyses of cell function in culture showed that a synthetic version of cortisol had less of an inhibitory effect on production of inflammatory proteins in cells from stressed parents compared to controls (Miller, Cohen, & Ritchey, 2002), suggesting that the chronic stress of having and caring for a child with cancer altered the ability of the HPA axis to regulate inflammation. More recent studies have shown that social isolation and loneliness are associated with patterns of gene expression that are consistent with greater production of inflammatory proteins, including reduced expression of genes for receptors that make cells more sensitive and responsive to cortisol (Cole, 2009).

These different lines of research converge on an integrative biopsychosocial approach to the regulation of inflammation. Social adversity, in the form of low social status, is associated with higher levels of cortisol as well as patterns of hormonal dysregulation (Cohen et al., 2006; Hajat et al., 2010; Kunz-Ebrecht, Kirschbaum, & Steptoe, 2004). As noted above, low social status is associated with higher levels of inflammatory proteins across the life course. Studies of gene expression related to inflammatory proteins show that adverse social environments, including backgrounds of low socioeconomic status (SES), are associated with patterns of expression, including loss of sensitivity to the anti-inflammatory effects of cortisol, that favor higher circulating levels of inflammatory proteins (Chen et al., 2009; Miller, Chen, et al., 2009). In children with asthma, the association between social status and inflammatory processes appear to be partially mediated by psychosocial factors. Low SES children from stressful and threatening family environments had cells that produced higher levels of inflammatory proteins than children from less threatening environments (Chen et al., 2006). Conversely, cells from asthmatic children who perceived support from their parents produced lower levels of inflammatory proteins than cells from children with less supportive parents (Miller, Gaudin, Zysk, & Chen, 2009). Thus, social factors and chronic stressors are linked to dysregulation of hormone systems that regulate inflammation, and impairments in these regulatory systems can result in chronically elevated levels of inflammation. The impact of social environments on inflammatory processes may be mitigated or exaggerated by the presence or absence of psychosocial resources, such as supportive social networks.

The regulation of inflammation is one of a number of examples of biopsychosocial models that are relevant for successful aging. The length and regulation of telomeres on chromosomes is another model in which social processes and psychosocial resources are linked to biological processes that have implications for aging (Epel et al., 2004). In each of these instances, biological processes related to health and aging are patterned by social environments and psychological strengths and liabilities as well as the ways in which they interact with one another. Accurately reflecting the composition of the literature, most studies mentioned to this point have focused primarily on factors that predict increased risk of disease and mortality. Given our emphasis on successful aging, we turn in the next sections to an explicit consideration of the role of positive influences in mitigating the potential adverse outcomes in two domains of aging: living with medical comorbidities and social inequalities.

Living Well with Later Life Comorbidity

Consistent with our view that theoretical and empirical formulations of successful aging must incorporate developmental changes in mind and body that occur with age, in this section we consider age-related declines in physical health and functional capacities and the challenges such declines pose for notions of what it means to age successfully. The absence of physical disease or disability is one of the three criteria for successful aging set out by Rowe and Kahn (1987, 1998). Other models of successful aging similarly highlight the prevention or delay of disease and disability as a central component of aging successfully (Depp & Jeste, 2006). According to a recent report from the 1998 Medical Expenditures Panel Survey, however, almost 50% of women and 40% of men in the United States have at least one chronic medical condition and over 20% of adults have two or more. Among those 65 years old or older, 62% have two or more conditions (Anderson & Horvath, 2004), a number that is projected to increase substantially in coming years (Vogeli et al., 2007). Living with medical comorbidity has thus become the norm for older adults. Indeed, fewer than 19% of participants aged 65–99 years from the Alameda County Study (Strawbridge, Wallhagen, & Cohen, 2002) and fewer than 12% of respondents over the age of 65 from the Health and Retirement Study (McLaughlin, Connell, Heeringa, Li, & Roberts, 2010) met the criteria for successful aging formulated by Rowe and Kahn, largely because of disease and/or physical impairments.

These numbers stand in stark contrast to older adults' views of their own aging. In one study of approximately 200 community-dwelling adults over the age of 60 in Southern California, only 15% were free of physical illness, but 92% of the sample considered themselves to be aging successfully (Montross et al., 2006). Similarly, among the older adults from the Alameda County Study, half (50.3%) agreed with the statement "I am aging successfully (or aging well)" in spite of the presence of chronic disease conditions (Strawbridge et al., 2002). We therefore agree with many others (McLaughlin et al., 2010; Strawbridge et al., 2002; Young et al., 2009) that the absence of physical disease or disability is too strict a criterion for successful aging. Rather, a biopsychosocial perspective on aging successfully highlights compensatory processes that enable a high quality of life in the context of physical decline, and illumination of such processes comes from a number of quarters, one being studies of exceptional longevity.

Although living longer is not equivalent to aging successfully, long life is generally viewed as one component of successful aging. Longevity is substantially influenced by genetic endowment – heritability studies suggest that as much as 50% of individual variability in length of life can be attributed to genetic influences – and a number of genes related to both longevity and various aspects of successful aging have recently been identified; in some cases longevity is predicted by interactive relationships among two or more genes (Glatt, Chayavichitsilp, Depp, Schork, & Jeste, 2007; Jazwinski et al., 2010). This also means that at least half of individual variability in longevity is attributable to nongenetic influences, including demographic and psychosocial factors. The Georgia Centenarian Study, begun in 1988, has followed a cohort of over 200 centenarians and octogenarians as they age. Although most of the oldest study participants had at least one disease condition, most commonly cardiovascular disease, they were typically living full and engaged lives in independent settings (Poon, Clayton, et al., 1992). Inquiries into characteristics of centenarians have found strong evidence of strengths: positive subjective ratings of health, a strong predictor of morbidity and mortality at all ages (Idler & Benyamini, 1997; Idler & Kasl, 1995), and quality of life, which, in turn, are associated with a variety of demographic and psychosocial resources, such as education, conscientiousness, and social support (Poon et al., 2010). Educational attainment in particular was related to better cognitive functioning in study participants (Davey et al., 2010), and cognitive resources are a key component of managing daily life among centenarians (Poon, Martin, et al., 1992). Moreover, analyses of events across the course of participants' lives suggested cumulative effects of both negative and positive experiences, particularly those occurring earlier in life (Arnold et al., 2010), as well as greater happiness in those that hold positive feelings about their past experiences (Bishop et al., 2010). Exceptional longevity is thus a product of genetic, demographic, and psychosocial processes, and good quality of life in very old age is less likely to involve the avoidance of disease than successful adaptation to disease.

Research on centenarians has also shed new light on cognitive decline and dementia, signature concerns of aging adults. While rates of dementia typically rise with age, a recent meta-analysis showed that the rate of increase slows and then plateaus in adults in their eighties and nineties (Ritchie & Kildea, 1995). Moreover, while specific genes, such as ApOE4, markedly increase the risk of Alzheimer's disease (AD) in middle-aged adults, the association with AD in older adults is significantly weaker, suggesting potential interactions between genetic susceptibility and other factors in predicting risk of AD in older adults (Breitner et al., 1999). Particularly intriguing are results from the Nun Study, a longitudinal study of aging and AD in over 600 Catholic nuns who were 75–100 years old at intake. In addition to submitting to annual examinations, the nuns agreed to donate their brains at death. The nuns had diverse backgrounds and life experiences, and in old age while some were virtually incapacitated by dementia, others showed no signs of cognitive impairment. On average, postmortem neurological examinations showed that neuropathology was associated with assessments of cognitive performance and functional limitations (Tyas, Snowdon, Desrosiers, Riley, & Markesbery, 2007). However, examination of specific cases also revealed moderate to severe AD-related neuropathology in the *complete absence* of any clinical signs of dementia; these nuns remained active and scored high on annual tests of cognitive performance right up until their deaths (Snowdon, 1997, 2003).

Such findings join other studies in showing that neuropathology and dementia are not inevitable consequences of getting older (Morris, 1999; Ritchie & Kildea, 1995). Moreover, they point to potential compensatory processes by which the presence of neuropathology does not result in cognitive decline or dementia. Compensatory processes within the brain may play a role in preserving function (Mattson & Magnus, 2006), but there may also be a role for demographic and psychosocial processes. Nuns with greater linguistic ability earlier in life – assessed from autobiographies written when the nuns were 22 years old – showed less cognitive decline and had reduced risk of AD later in life (Riley, Snowdon, Desrosiers, & Markesbery, 2005; Snowdon et al., 1996). A companion study showed that those nuns who expressed more positive emotions in their writing lived significantly longer than those with less (Danner, Snowdon, & Friesen, 2001), although links to cognitive decline or AD dementia have not been reported.

We end this section with a consideration of studies explicitly focused on the role of psychosocial strengths in preventing morbidity and mortality as well as probing how such effects might occur. The Rush Memory and Aging Project is a longitudinal study of 1,200 older adults living in communities in and around Chicago that includes assessment of chronic medical conditions, cognitive function, personality, depressive symptoms, social networks, and positive psychological functioning using the Purpose in Life subscale from Ryff's scales of psychological well-being (Ryff, 1989b). All were free of dementia at the start of the study. Two recent prospective studies examined links between well-being at baseline and subsequent outcomes by comparing participants with scores in the 90th percentile on purpose in life against those with scores in the 10th percentile. In one study, those participants with high purpose in life scores were 2.4 times less likely to develop Alzheimer's disease over the course of a 7-year follow-up period than those with the lowest scores (Boyle, Buchman, Barnes, & Bennett, 2010). A second study found that those high in purpose in life had a mortality risk over a 5-year follow-up period that was 57% the risk for those with scores in the 10th percentile (Boyle, Barnes, Buchman, & Bennett, 2009). It is important to emphasize that these studies were prospective and rigorous, controlling for a variety of potential confounds, including age, gender, health, depression, and personality. The results suggest that a strong sense of life purpose may be protective against age-related dementia and mortality. Finally, our work examined the extent to which psychological well-being might be associated with reduced biological risk of morbidity and mortality in aging adults with existing medical conditions. Circulating levels of inflammatory proteins like IL-6 and CRP are prospectively related to morbidity and mortality in both healthy adults and those with diagnosed disease conditions, particularly in elderly people (Blake & Ridker, 2003; Cesari et al., 2003; Stork et al., 2006). In this analysis, we showed that greater burden of medical comorbidities were associated with declines in well-being and increases in IL-6 and CRP. However, among middle-aged and older adults with greater well-being – higher scores on purpose in life and positive relations with others – increases in disease burden were associated with much smaller increases in inflammation compared to adults with lower well-being (Friedman & Ryff, 2010).

In summary, as the population of the United States ages, medical comorbidities are increasingly the norm, and theories of successful aging must account for the realities of biological decline. Studies of exceptional longevity make it clear that even a substantial burden of medical conditions is not an inevitable barrier to leading a full and engaged life. They also highlight numerous instances where neuropathology is not accompanied by loss of cognitive function or mental health. And newer studies suggest that a strong sense of life purpose in aging adults may reduce biological risk associated with myriad diseases and delay the onset of cognitive decline and mortality. All of these studies are cogent illustrations of the biopsychosocial perspective, where risk factors and strengths interact with one another to predict outcomes, and social or psychological strengths may mitigate the adverse outcomes associated with biological decline.

Living Well in the Face of Inequality

A large and growing literature shows systematic linkages between a person's standing in the socioeconomic hierarchy and health (Adler et al., 1994; Matthews & Gallo, 2011). The current challenge in such research is filling in the mechanisms and processes that account for these connections. Among the possible pathways under consideration are psychosocial factors, such as vulnerability to psychological distress (Gallo & Matthews, 2003) as well as exposure to traumatic events, chronic stress, and daily hassles (Almeida, Neupert, Banks, & Serido, 2005; Gallo, Bogart, Vranceanu, & Matthews, 2005; Hatch & Dohrenwend, 2007). Positive psychosocial resources, such as social support from others as well as self-esteem, sense of control, and optimism, have also been examined as intervening influences in the link between SES and health (Lachman & Weaver, 1998; Marmot et al., 1998; Matthews, Gallo, & Taylor, 2010; Uchino, 2006).

Understanding how inequalities in health come about has also led to a developmental emphasis, which addresses factors in early life that create risk for health problems among low SES children (Chen, Matthews, & Boyce, 2002), as well as life course approaches, which examine long-term profiles of social status and health (Alwin & Wray, 2005). In studies of adulthood and later life, the idea of cumulative disadvantage over time has been of interest (House, Lantz, & Herd, 2005; Mirowsky & Ross, 2008; Ross & Chia-Ling, 1996). It suggests that SES discrepancies in health progressively worsen over the life cycle, presumably due to the confluence of multiple factors (e.g., stress exposure, coping strategies, health behaviors). Comprehensive analyses (cross-sectional and longitudinal) with population-based samples, in fact, show that socioeconomic disparities in health are small in early adulthood, and then increase through midlife and early old age, although they lessen in later life, possibly due to selective attrition (House et al., 2005).

Despite the pervasive emphasis on negative processes that underlie health inequality, there is growing recognition that some from disadvantaged backgrounds are able to avoid adverse health outcomes. For example, Werner's (1995) classic study of children growing up in extreme poverty showed that some were notably resilient. She identified multiple protective factors to account for these outcomes: those within the individual (e.g., being bright, outgoing, active); those within the family (e.g., having close bonds with at least one nurturing, competent parent); and those in the community (e.g., receiving support from peers and elders). Resilience has also been of interest in later life, although with less explicit linkage to socioeconomic standing (Staudinger, Marsiske, & Baltes, 1995). Our objective herein, given the overarching focus on successful aging, is to highlight emergent findings in adulthood and later life that show how psychosocial strengths can serve as buffers against the forces of inequality (Hatch, 2005). Many are based on findings from the MIDUS (Midlife in the US) national study (Brim, Ryff, & Kessler, 2004).

Lachman and Weaver (1998) examined sense of control as moderating influence between income and poor health. Respondents with lower income had lower perceived mastery and higher perceived constraints as well as poorer health. For all income groups, higher perceived mastery and lower perceived constraints were related to better self-rated health, greater life satisfaction, and lower depressive symptoms. However, control beliefs played a moderating role: Participants in the lowest income group with a high sense of control showed levels of health (self-rated health, functional limitations, acute symptoms) and well-being (life satisfaction, depressive symptoms) comparable to that of high income groups. Thus, among those who perceived that they had high mastery and limited constraints, economic disadvantage was not inevitably linked to poorer health.

A further study from MIDUS focused on the challenges of inequality related to ethnic minority status (Ryff, Keyes, & Hughes, 2003), which also confers increased risk for ill health (Braveman, Egerter, & Williams, 2011). Surprisingly, the results showed that ethnic minority status was a *positive* predictor, compared to majority status, of most aspects of eudaimonic well-being (e.g., environmental mastery, personal growth, purpose in life) after adjusting for numerous factors. Such outcomes suggest that certain aspects of well-being may possibly be honed by the adversities and challenges of inequality. The idea of finding meaning and purpose in adversity is not new – it was Victor Frankl's (1992) response for explaining how some were able to survive the horrors of Nazi concentration camps. The growing literature on posttraumatic growth (Tedeschi & Calhoun, 2004; Tedeschi, Park, & Calhoun, 1998) similarly invokes the emergence of strengths in the aftermath of trauma.

That adverse experiences can foster resilience was recently bolstered by findings from a multiyear national longitudinal sample (Seery, Holman, & Silver, 2010). Those with a history of some lifetime adversity reported better health and well-being, not only compared to people with a high history of adversity, but also compared to those with no history of adversity. There are parallel formulations in physiology, where Dienstbier (1989) described a kind of "toughness" shown by some in response to intermittent stressors. It included a pattern of arousal (i.e., low SNS activity, combined with strong, responsive challenge-induced SNS – adrenal – medullary arousal, with resistance to brain catecholamine depletion and suppression of pituitary adrenal-cortical responses) that works in interaction with effective psychological coping, to comprise positive physiological reactivity. The emphasis on resistance to catecholamine depletion (SNS activity), combined with rapid return of cortisol levels (HPA axis activity) to normal operating range following stress exposure, and thereby maintenance within optimal operating ranges of other biomarkers (inflammatory processes, cardiovascular risk factors) offers a provisional formulation of what might constitute optimal physiological response to adversity. Mechanisms of resilience at the biological level have also been elaborated by Charney (2004), who focuses on neurochemical response patterns to acute stress assessed in laboratory contexts.

More investigations that explicate the interplay between psychosocial strengths, real-life adversity, and biological processes are needed. To that end, we conclude this section with a summary of our recent findings (Morozink et al., 2010) from the MIDUS study showing that psychological well-being is a moderator of links between educational status and the inflammatory protein IL-6. As predicted, the analyses showed that greater educational attainment was linked with lower levels of IL-6, after adjusting for multiple controls. However, psychological well-being interacted with education to predict IL-6, such that adults with less education but higher levels of purpose in life, environmental mastery, self-acceptance, positive relations with others, and positive affect had lower levels of IL-6.

In summary, research on social inequalities in health increasingly reflects a biopsycho-social approach that integrates multiple levels of inquiry – socioeconomic status, psychosocial vulnerabilities and resources, and biological mechanisms. Our emphasis has been to highlight the role of psychosocial strengths in the face of inequality – qualities such as self-esteem, sense of control, optimism, social support, coping strategies, and psychological well-being – all of which constitute protective resources vis-à-vis the life challenges associated with inequality. The scientific objective is to understand the biological mechanisms through which these effects occur; hence our descriptions of physiological toughness and the biology of resilience. Our recent findings documenting the protective influence of psychological well-being on risk for increased inflammatory risk among low-educated adults illustrates the biopsychosocial integration needed to explicate why some are able to live well in the face of inequality.

Interventions to Promote Psychosocial Well-Being

We have repeatedly emphasized the potential health benefits associated with positive psychosocial factors, including in later periods of life when chronic conditions and comorbidity become realities, as well as in contexts of socioeconomic inequality. Given this emphasis, a fundamental question is whether psychosocial strengths can be cultivated. To the extent that protective resources can be promoted, they could potentially be made available to ever larger segments of society. Fortunately, work in interventions for treatment of psychological disorders suggests this is possible. Specifically, "well-being therapy" (WBT), developed by Fava and colleagues, has helped to prevent relapse among individuals suffering from mood and anxiety disorders (Fava, 1999; Fava, Rafanelli, Cazzaro, Conti, & Grandi, 1998). The intervention, provided in combination with cognitive behavioral therapy (CBT), was initially effective in preventing relapse of major depression over a 2-year period (Fava, Rafanelli, Grandi, Conti, & Belluardo, 1998). Subsequent work showed that these effects persisted over 6 years (Fava et al., 2004). Other related studies showed the effectiveness of the CBT-WBT sequential combination in treating generalized anxiety disorder (Fava et al., 2005).

What is well-being therapy? Fava and Ruini (2003) describe the key components of the intervention, which is based on Ryff's (1989a) multidimensional model of psychological well-being. The goal of therapy is to improve patients' experiences of well-being in hopes of preventing relapse in the residual phase of mood and anxiety disorders. It is a short-term (8 week) therapeutic strategy involving the use of structured diaries kept by patients, combined with interaction with the therapist about diary entries. Clients are required to record positive experiences from their daily lives, however fleeting. The focus in therapy sessions is then on helping clients sustain such experiences, rather than prematurely interrupting them by maladaptive cognitions. The fundamental idea behind the therapy is that recovery from mood and anxiety disorders requires the capacity to experience well-being (Fava, Ruini, & Belaise, 2007). That is, eliminating the symptoms of distress is, in and of itself, insufficient to achieve full recovery; the client must also be able to participate in positive psychological experience.

Because well-being therapy has been shown to be effective in preventing relapse of psychological disorders, it is now being adapted for use in preventive contexts as well. Ruini, Belaise, Brombin, Caffo, and Fava (2006) developed an intervention protocol, derived from well-being therapy, for students in school settings. Pilot research showed that the intervention resulted in a reduction in psychological symptoms and an increase in psychological well-being. We submit that community interventions designed to instill and enhance experiences of well-being among elderly people may also constitute promising future directions in promoting successful aging. That is, because research shows that well-being constitutes an important moderator of later life morbidity and mortality, and because clinical findings show that the promotion of well-being helps prevent relapse of psychological disorders, we see notable promise for interventions designed to nurture psychological well-being among older adults.

Summary and Conclusions

The overarching objective of this chapter has been to call for a new approach to successful aging that is explicitly developmental – that is, deals with changes that occur mentally and physically as individuals move across later life, and is explicitly biopsychosocial in approach – that is, seeks to understand the interplay of biological, psychological, and social factors that underlie why some age well and others do not. We began with a historical overview of how successful aging has been formulated from the middle of the last century to the present. To make the case for what we see as needed refinements, we then distilled the history of the biopsychosocial approach to health and illustrated its use in explicating the interplay between biological systems, primarily those dealing with inflammatory processes, and socioeconomic factors as well as psychosocial factors. Examples came from early development in childhood as well as aging. Because most of that literature has emphasized negative, vulnerability factors (low SES, stress, psychological disorders), we then shifted to a focus on the role of psychosocial strengths in helping to explain why some older individuals are able to live well, despite increased chronic conditions, which define normal aging. The scientific nexus between these psychosocial moderators and inflammatory processes was emphasized. A second context for illustrating positive psychosocial factors pertained to why some individuals who lack socioeconomic advantage are nonetheless doing well in terms of mental and physical health outcomes. Their resilience vis-à-vis the challenge of inequality were examined, again with a focus on how psychosocial strengths relate to intervening inflammatory processes.

Our recurrent emphasis on the positive side of the psychosocial ledger led to an important question: Namely, are these factors modifiable? Can they be promoted? We briefly reviewed recent intervention strategies to treat individuals with mood and anxiety disorders using "well-being therapy." Because these strategies have been shown to be effective in preventing relapse, they are now used in educational contexts with children, in hopes of engendering skills that nurture and sustain experiences of well-being and that will last into adulthood and later life. Given our overview of recent evidence that well-being delays onset of later life morbidity, promotes length of life, and is linked with reduced inflammatory processes, even in the face of increased chronic conditions, we thus issued a call for community interventions that are designed to engender greater experiences of psychosocial well-being among community elders. The underlying assumption, which rests at the core of our biopsychosocial formulation of successful aging, is that seeking, savoring, and sustaining well-being offers benefits, not only for how one feels subjectively, but also for healthy regulation of underlying biological systems. In effect, positive aging has become fundamentally a mind/body enterprise.

References

Abraham, J., Campbell, C. Y., Cheema, A., Gluckman, T. J., Blumenthal, R. S., & Danyi, P. (2007). C-reactive protein in cardiovascular risk assessment: A review of the evidence. *Journal of the Cardiometabolic Syndrome, 2*(2), 119–123.

Ader, R. (Ed.). (2007). *Psychoneuroimmunology* (4th ed.). San Diego, CA: Academic Press.

Ader, R., & Cohen, N. (1975). Behaviorally conditioned immunosuppression. *Psychosomatic Medicine, 37*(4), 333–340.

Adler, N. E., Boyce, T., Chesney, M. A., Cohen, S., Folkman, S., Kahn, R. L., et al. (1994). Socioeconomic status and health: The challenge of the gradient. *American Psychologist, 49*, 14–24.

Alley, D. E., Seeman, T. E., Ki Kim, J., Karlamangla, A., Hu, P., & Crimmins, E. M. (2006). Socioeconomic status and C-reactive protein levels in the US population: NHANES IV. *Brain, Behavior, and Immunity, 20*(5), 498–504.

Almeida, D. M., Neupert, S. D., Banks, S. R., & Serido, J. (2005). Do daily stress processes account for socioeconomic health disparities? *Journals of Gerontology: Series B: Psychological Sciences and Social Sciences, 60B*, 34–39.

Alonso, Y. (2004). The biopsychosocial model in medical research: The evolution of the health concept over the last two decades. *Patient Education and Counseling, 53*(2), 239–244.

Alwin, D. F., & Wray, L. A. (2005). A life-span developmental perspective on social status and health. *Journals of Gerontology: Series B: Psychological Sciences and Social Sciences 60B,* 7–14.

Anderson, G., & Horvath, J. (2004). The growing burden of chronic disease in America. *Public Health Reports, 119*(3), 263–270.

Arnold, J., Dai, J., Nahapetyan, L., Arte, A., Johnson, M. A., Hausman, D., . . . Poon, L. W. (2010). Predicting successful aging in a population-based sample of Georgia centenarians. *Current Gerontology and Geriatrics Research* doi: 10.1155/2010/989315

Baltes, P. B., & Baltes, M. M. (Eds.). (1990). *Successful aging: Perspectives from the behavioral sciences.* New York: Cambridge University Press.

Bartrop, R. W., Luckhurst, E., Lazarus, L., Kiloh, L. G., & Penny, R. (1977). Depressed lymphocyte function after bereavement. *Lancet, 1*(8016), 834–836.

Berkman, L. F., Melchior, M., Chastang, J. F., Niedhammer, I., Leclerc, A., & Goldberg, M. (2004). Social integration and mortality: A prospective study of French employees of Electricity of France-Gas of France: The GAZEL Cohort. *American Journal of Epidemiology, 159*(2), 167–174.

Bishop, A. J., Martin, P., MacDonald, M., Poon, L., Jazwinski, S. M., Green, R. C., et al. (2010). Predicting happiness among centenarians. *Gerontology, 56*(1), 88–92.

Bitton, A., Dobkin, P. L., Edwardes, M. D., Sewitch, M. J., Meddings, J. B., Rawal, S., et al. (2008). Predicting relapse in Crohn's disease: A biopsychosocial model. *Gut, 57*(10), 1386–1392.

Blake, G. J., & Ridker, P. M. (2003). C-reactive protein and other inflammatory risk markers in acute coronary syndromes. *Journal of the American College of Cardiology, 41*(4 Suppl. S), 37S–42S.

Borrell-Carrio, F., Suchman, A. L., & Epstein, R. M. (2004). The biopsychosocial model 25 years later: Principles, practice, and scientific inquiry. *Annals of Family Medicine, 2*(6), 576–582.

Boyle, P. A., Barnes, L. L., Buchman, A. S., & Bennett, D. A. (2009). Purpose in life is associated with mortality among community-dwelling older persons. *Psychosomatic Medicine, 71*(5), 574–579.

Boyle, P. A., Buchman, A. S., Barnes, L. L., & Bennett, D. A. (2010). Effect of a purpose in life on risk of incident Alzheimer disease and mild cognitive impairment in community-dwelling older persons. *Archives of General Psychiatry, 67*(3), 304–310.

Braveman, P., Egerter, S., & Williams, D. R. (2011). The social determinants of health: Coming of age. *Annual Review of Public Health, 32*(1), 381–398.

Breitner, J. C., Wyse, B. W., Anthony, J. C., Welsh-Bohmer, K. A., Steffens, D. C., Norton, M. C., et al. (1999). APOE-epsilon4 count predicts age when prevalence of AD increases, then declines: The Cache County Study. *Neurology, 53*(2), 321–331.

Brim, O. G., Ryff, C. D., & Kessler, R. C. (Eds.). (2004). *How healthy are we?: A national study of well-being at midlife.* Chicago: University of Chicago Press.

Bühler, C. (1935). The curve of life as studied in biographies. *Journal of Applied Psychology, 43,* 653–673.

Bühler, C., & Massarik, F. (Eds.). (1968). *The course of human life.* New York: Springer.

Burgess, E. W. (1960). *Aging in Western societies.* Chicago: University of Chicago Press.

Campeau, S., Day, H. E., Helmreich, D. L., Kollack-Walker, S., & Watson, S. J. (1998). Principles of psychoneuroendocrinology. *Psychiatric Clinics of North America, 21*(2), 259–276.

Cavan, R. S., Burgess, E. W., Havighurst, R. J., & Goldhamer, H. (1949). *Personal adjustment in old age.* Oxford: Science Research Associates.

Cesari, M., Penninx, B. W., Newman, A. B., Kritchevsky, S. B., Nicklas, B. J., Sutton-Tyrrell, K., et al. (2003). Inflammatory markers and cardiovascular disease (The Health, Aging and Body Composition [Health ABC] Study). *American Journal of Cardiology, 92*(5), 522–528.

Chandler, A. R. (1948). Cicero's ideal old man. *Journal of Gerontology, 3,* 285–289.

Charney, D. S. (2004). Psychobiological mechanisms of resilience and vulnerability: Implications for successful adaptation to extreme stress. *American Journal of Psychiatry, 161*(2), 195–215.

Chen, E., Hanson, M. D., Paterson, L. Q., Griffin, M. J., Walker, H. A., & Miller, G. E. (2006). Socioeconomic status and inflammatory processes in childhood asthma: The role of psychological stress. *Journal of Allergy and Clinical Immunology, 117*(5), 1014–1020.

Chen, E., Matthews, K. A., & Boyce, W. T. (2002). Socioeconomic differences in children's health: How and why do these relationships change with age? *Psychological Bulletin, 128*(2), 295–329.

Chen, E., Miller, G. E., Walker, H. A., Arevalo, J. M., Sung, C. Y., & Cole, S. W. (2009). Genome-wide transcriptional profiling linked to social class in asthma. *Thorax, 64*(1), 38–43.

Cicero (44 BCE/1923). *Cato major de senectute.* Cambridge, MA: Loeb Classical Library, Harvard University Press.

Clark, M., & Anderson, B. G. (1967). *Culture and aging.* New York: Charles C. Thomas.

Cohen, S., Schwartz, J. E., Epel, E., Kirschbaum, C., Sidney, S., & Seeman, T. (2006). Socioeconomic status, race, and diurnal cortisol decline in the Coronary Artery Risk Development in Young Adults (CARDIA) Study. *Psychosomatic Medicine, 68*(1), 41–50.

Cole, S. W. (2009). Social regulation of human gene expression. *Current Directions in Psychological Science, 18*(3), 132–137.

Costanzo, E. S., Lutgendorf, S. K., Sood, A. K., Anderson, B., Sorosky, J., & Lubaroff, D. M. (2005). Psychosocial factors and interleukin-6 among women with advanced ovarian cancer. *Cancer, 104*(2), 305–313.

Cutler, N. E. (1979). Age variations in the dimensionality of life satisfaction. *Journal of Gerontology, 34,* 573–578.

Danese, A., Moffitt, T. E., Harrington, H., Milne, B. J., Polanczyk, G., Pariante, C. M., et al. (2009). Adverse childhood experiences and adult risk factors for age-related disease: Depression, inflammation, and clustering of metabolic risk markers. *Archives of Pediatric and Adolescent Medicine, 163*(12), 1135–1143.

Danner, D. D., Snowdon, D. A., & Friesen, W. V. (2001). Positive emotions in early life and longevity: Findings from the Nun Study. *Journal of Personality and Social Psychology, 80*(5), 804–813.

Davey, A., Elias, M. F., Siegler, I. C., Lele, U., Martin, P., Johnson, M. A., et al. (2010). Cognitive function, physical performance, health, and disease: Norms from the Georgia Centenarian Study. *Experimental Aging Research, 36*(4), 394–425.

de Kloet, E. R. (2003). Hormones, brain and stress. *Endocrine Regulations, 37*(2), 51–68.

Demakakos, P., Nazroo, J., Breeze, E., & Marmot, M. (2008). Socioeconomic status and health: The role of subjective social status. *Social Science & Medicine, 67*(2), 330–340.

Depp, C. A., & Jeste, D. V. (2006). Definitions and predictors of successful aging: A comprehensive review of larger quantitative studies. *American Journal of Geriatric Psychiatry, 14*(1), 6–20.

Dienstbier, R. A. (1989). Arousal and physiological toughness: Implications for mental and physical health. *Psychological Review, 96,* 84–100.

Dougherty, T. F. (1952). Effect of hormones on lymphatic tissue. *Physiological Reviews, 32*(4), 379–401.

Engel, G. L. (1977). The need for a new medical model: A challenge for biomedicine. *Science, 196* (4286), 129–136.

Epel, E. S., Blackburn, E. H., Lin, J., Dhabhar, F. S., Adler, N. E., Morrow, J. D., et al. (2004). Accelerated telomere shortening in response to life stress. *Proceedings of the National Academy of Science USA*, *101*(49), 17312–17315.

Erikson, E. H. (1959). Identity and the life cycle: Selected papers. *Psychological Issues*, *1*, 1–171.

Ershler, W. B. (1993). Interleukin-6: A cytokine for gerontologists. *Journal of the American Geriatrics Society*, *41*(2), 176–181.

Fava, G. A. (1999). Well-being therapy: Conceptual and technical issues. *Psychotherapy and Psychosomatics*, *68*, 171–179.

Fava, G. A., Rafanelli, C., Cazzaro, M., Conti, S., & Grandi, S. (1998). Well-being therapy: A novel psychotherapeutic approach for residual symptoms of affective disorders. *Psychological Medicine*, *28*, 475–480.

Fava, G. A., Rafanelli, C., Grandi, S., Conti, S., & Belluardo, P. (1998). Prevention of recurrent depression with cognitive behavioral therapy. *Archives of General Psychiatry*, *55*, 816–821.

Fava, G. A., & Ruini, C. (2003). Development and characteristics of a well-being enhancing psychotherapeutic strategy: Well-being therapy. *Journal of Behavior Therapy and Experimental Psychiatry*, *34*(1), 45–63.

Fava, G. A., Ruini, C., & Belaise, C. (2007). The concept of recovery in major depression. *Psychological Medicine*, *37*(3), 307–317.

Fava, G. A., Ruini, C., Rafanelli, C., Finos, L., Conti, S., & Grandi, S. (2004). Six-year outcome of cognitive behavior therapy for prevention of recurrent depression. *American Journal of Psychiatry*, *161*(10), 1872–1876.

Fava, G. A., Ruini, C., Rafanelli, C., Finos, L., Salmaso, L., Mangelli, L., et al. (2005). Well-being therapy of generalized anxiety disorder. *Psychotherapy and Psychosomatics*, *74*(1), 26–30.

Fava, G. A., & Sonino, N. (2010). Psychosomatic medicine: A name to keep. *Psychotherapy and Psychosomatics*, *79*(1), 1–3.

Ferrucci, L., Harris, T. B., Guralnik, J. M., Tracy, R. P., Corti, M. C., & Cohen, H. J., et al. (1999). Serum IL-6 level and the development of disability in older persons. *Journal of the American Geriatrics Society*, *47*(6), 639–646.

Finestone, H. M., Alfeeli, A., & Fisher, W. A. (2008). Stress-induced physiologic changes as a basis for the biopsychosocial model of chronic musculoskeletal pain: A new theory? *Clinical Journal of Pain*, *24*(9), 767–775.

Fozard, J. L., & Popkin, S. J. (1978). Optimizing adult development: Ends and means of an applied psychology of aging. *American Psychologist*, *33*(11), 975–989.

Frankl, V. E. (1992). *Man's search for meaning: An introduction to logotherapy* (I. Lasch, Trans.) Boston, MA: Beacon Press (Originally work published 1959).

Friedman, E., & Ryff, C. D. (2010). Chronic disease co-morbidity and inflammation in aging adults: Moderation by psychological well-being. *Brain, Behavior, and Immunity*, *24* (Supplement 1), S31. doi: 10.1016/j.bbi.2010.07.102

Friedman, E. M., Hayney, M., Love, G. D., Singer, B. H., & Ryff, C. D. (2007). Plasma interleukin-6 and soluble IL-6 receptors are associated with psychological well-being in aging women. *Health Psychology*, *26*(3), 305–313.

Friedman, E. M., & Herd, P. (2010). Income, education, and inflammation: Differential associations in a national probability sample (The MIDUS study). *Psychosomatic Medicine*, *72*(3), 290–300.

Gallo, L. C., Bogart, L. M., Vranceanu, A.-M., & Matthews, K. A. (2005). Socioeconomic status, resources, psychological experiences, and emotional responses: A test of the reserve capacity model. *Journal of Personality and Social Psychology*, *88*(2), 386–399.

Gallo, L. C., & Matthews, K. A. (2003). Understanding the association between socioeconomic status and physical health: Do negative emotions play a role? *Psychological Bulletin, 129*(1), 10–51.

Glatt, S. J., Chayavichitsilp, P., Depp, C., Schork, N. J., & Jeste, D. V. (2007). Successful aging: From phenotype to genotype. *Biological Psychiatry, 62*(4), 282–293.

Gouin, J. P., Carter, C. S., Pournajafi-Nazarloo, H., Glaser, R., Malarkey, W. B., Loving, T. J., et al. (2010). Marital behavior, oxytocin, vasopressin, and wound healing. *Psychoneuroendocrinology, 35*(7), 1082–1090.

Griffin, J. J. (1949). Plato's philosophy of old age. *Geriatrics, 4*, 242–255.

Griffith, K. A. (2009). Biological, psychological and behavioral, and social variables influencing colorectal cancer screening in African Americans. *Nursing Research, 58*(5), 312–320.

Gruenewald, T. L., Cohen, S., Matthews, K. A., Tracy, R., & Seeman, T. E. (2009). Association of socioeconomic status with inflammation markers in black and white men and women in the Coronary Artery Risk Development in Young Adults (CARDIA) study. *Social Science & Medicine, 69*, 451–459.

Hajat, A., Diez-Roux, A., Franklin, T. G., Seeman, T., Shrager, S., Ranjit, N., et al. (2010). Socioeconomic and race/ethnic differences in daily salivary cortisol profiles: The multi-ethnic study of atherosclerosis. *Psychoneuroendocrinology, 35*(6), 932–943.

Hatch, S. L. (2005). Conceptualizing and identifying cumulative adversity and protective resources: Implications for understanding health inequalities. *Journal of Gerontology: Social Sciences, 60B*, S130–S134.

Hatch, S., & Dohrenwend, B. (2007). Distribution of traumatic and other stressful life events by race/ethnicity, gender, SES and age: A review of the research. *American Journal of Community Psychology, 40*(3), 313–332.

Herzog, A. R., Rodgers, W. L., & Woodworth, J. (1982). *Subjective well-being among different age groups.* Ann Arbor: University of Michigan, Institute for Social Research, Survey Research Center.

House, J. S., Landis, K. R., & Umberson, D. (1988). Social relationships and health. *Science, 241* (4865), 540–545.

House, J. S., Lantz, P. M., & Herd, P. (2005). Continuity and change in the social stratification of aging and health over the life course: Evidence from a nationally representative longitudinal study from 1986 to 2001/2002 (Americans' Changing Lives Study). *Journals of Gerontology: Series B: Psychological Sciences and Social Sciences, 60* (Special Issue 2), S15–S26.

Idler, E. L., & Benyamini, Y. (1997). Self-rated health and mortality: A review of twenty-seven community studies. *Journal of Health & Social Behavior, 38*(1), 21–37.

Idler, E. L., & Kasl, S. V. (1995). Self-ratings of health: Do they also predict change in functional ability? *Journals of Gerontology: Series B: Psychological Sciences and Social Sciences, 50*(6), S344–S353.

Irwin, M. (2002). Psychoneuroimmunology of depression: Clinical implications. *Brain, Behavior, and Immunity, 16*(1), 1–16.

Jazwinski, S. M., Kim, S., Dai, J., Li, L., Bi, X., Jiang, J. C., et al. (2010). HRAS1 and LASS1 with APOE are associated with human longevity and healthy aging. *Aging Cell, 9*(5), 698–708.

Jung, C. G. (1933). *Modern man in search of a soul* (W. S. Dell & C. F. Baynes, Trans.). New York: Harcourt, Brace & World.

Kiecolt-Glaser, J. K., Loving, T. J., Stowell, J. R., Malarkey, W. B., Lemeshow, S., Dickinson, S. L., et al. (2005). Hostile marital interactions, proinflammatory cytokine production, and wound healing. *Archives of General Psychiatry, 62*(12), 1377–1384.

Kiecolt-Glaser, J. K., Preacher, K. J., MacCallum, R. C., Atkinson, C., Malarkey, W. B., & Glaser, R. (2003). Chronic stress and age-related increases in the proinflammatory cytokine IL-6. *Proceedings of the National Academy of Science USA, 100*(15), 9090–9095.

Koppe, H. (2010). Two HEADSSS are better than one – a biopsychosocial screening tool for use when treating other doctors. *Australian Family Physician, 39*(5), 329–331.

Kunz-Ebrecht, S. R., Kirschbaum, C., & Steptoe, A. (2004). Work stress, socioeconomic status and neuroendocrine activation over the working day. *Social Science & Medicine, 58*(8), 1523–1530.

Lachman, M. E., & Weaver, S. L. (1998). The sense of control as a moderator of social class differences in health and well-being. *Journal of Personality and Social Psychology, 74*(3), 763–773.

Larson, R. (1978). Thirty years of research on the subjective well-being of older Americans. *Journals of Gerontology: Series A: Biological Sciences and Medical Sciences, 33*, 109–125.

Lawton, M. P. (1977). Morale: What are we measuring? In C. N. Nydegger (Ed.), *Measuring morale: A guide to effective assessment* (pp. 6–14). Washington, DC: Gerontological Society.

Lawton, M. P. (1984). The varieties of well-being. In C. Z. Malatesta& C. E. Izard (Eds.), *Emotion in adult development* (pp. 67–84). Beverly Hills, CA: Sage.

Loucks, E. B., Berkman, L. F., Gruenewald, T. L., & Seeman, T. E. (2005). Social integration is associated with fibrinogen concentration in elderly men. *Psychosomatic Medicine, 67*(3), 353–358.

Loucks, E. B., Berkman, L. F., Gruenewald, T. L., & Seeman, T. E. (2006). Relation of social integration to inflammatory marker concentrations in men and women 70 to 79 years. *American Journal of Cardiology, 97*(7), 1010–1016.

Lutgendorf, S. K., & Costanzo, E. S. (2003). Psychoneuroimmunology and health psychology: An integrative model. *Brain, Behavior, and Immunity, 17*(4), 225–232.

Lutgendorf, S. K., Garand, L., Buckwalter, K. C., Reimer, T. T., Hong, S. Y., & Lubaroff, D. M. (1999). Life stress, mood disturbance, and elevated interleukin-6 in healthy older women. *Journals of Gerontology: Series A: Biological Sciences and Medical Sciences 54*(9), M434–M439.

Marmot, M. G., Fuhrer, R., Ettner, S. L., Marks, N. F., Bumpass, L. L., & Ryff, C. D. (1998). Contribution of psychosocial factors to socioeconomic differences in health. *Milbank Quarterly, 76*(3), 403–448.

Matthews, K. A., & Gallo, L. C. (2011). Psychological perspectives on pathways linking socioeconomic status and physical health. *Annual Review of Psychology, 62*(1), 501–530.

Matthews, K. A., Gallo, L. C., & Taylor, S. E. (2010). Are psychosocial factors mediators of socioeconomic status and health connections? *Annals of the New York Academy of Sciences, 1186*(1), 146–173.

Mattson, M. P., & Magnus, T. (2006). Ageing and neuronal vulnerability. *Nature Reviews. Neuroscience, 7*(4), 278–294.

McCabe, M., Althof, S. E., Assalian, P., Chevret-Measson, M., Leiblum, S. R., Simonelli, C., et al. (2010). Psychological and interpersonal dimensions of sexual function and dysfunction. *Journal of Sexual Medicine, 7* (1 Pt 2), 327–336.

McCollum, L., & Pincus, T. (2009). A biopsychosocial model to complement a biomedical model: Patient questionnaire data and socioeconomic status usually are more significant than laboratory tests and imaging studies in prognosis of rheumatoid arthritis. *Rheumatic Disease Clinics of North America, 35*(4), 699–712.

McLaughlin, S. J., Connell, C. M., Heeringa, S. G., Li, L. W., & Roberts, J. S. (2010). Successful aging in the United States: Prevalence estimates from a national sample of older adults. *Journals of Gerontology: Series B: Psychological Sciences and Social Sciences, 65B*(2), 216–226.

Miller, G., & Chen, E. (2007). Unfavorable socioeconomic conditions in early life presage expression of proinflammatory phenotype in adolescence. *Psychosomatic Medicine, 69*(5), 402–409.

Miller, G. E., Chen, E., Fok, A. K., Walker, H., Lim, A., Nicholls, E. F., et al. (2009). Low early-life social class leaves a biological residue manifested by decreased glucocorticoid and increased proinflammatory signaling. *Proceedings of the National Academy of Science USA, 106*(34), 14716–14721.

Miller, G. E., Cohen, S., & Ritchey, A. K. (2002). Chronic psychological stress and the regulation of pro-inflammatory cytokines: A glucocorticoid-resistance model. *Health Psychology, 21*(6), 531–541.

Miller, G. E., Gaudin, A., Zysk, E., & Chen, E. (2009). Parental support and cytokine activity in childhood asthma: The role of glucocorticoid sensitivity. *Journal of Allergy and Clinical Immunology, 123*(4), 824–830.

Mirowsky, J., & Ross, C. E. (2008). Education and self-rated health: Cumulative advantage and its rising importance. *Research on Aging, 30*(1), 93–122.

Montross, L. P., Depp, C., Daly, J., Reichstadt, J., Golshan, S., Moore, D., et al. (2006). Correlates of self-rated successful aging among community-dwelling older adults. *American Journal of Geriatric Psychiatry, 14*(1), 43–51.

Morozink, J. A., Friedman, E. M., Coe, C. L., & Ryff, C. D. (2010). Socioeconomic and psychosocial predictors of interleukin-6 in the MIDUS national sample. *Health Psychology, 29*(6), 626–635.

Morris, J. C. (1999). Is Alzheimer's disease inevitable with age?: Lessons from clinicopathologic studies of healthy aging and very mild Alzheimer's disease. *Journal of Clinical Investigation, 104*(9), 1171–1173.

Neugarten, B. L. (1968). *Middle age and aging.* Chicago: University of Chicago Press.

Neugarten, B. L. (1973). Personality change in late life: A developmental perspective. In C. Eisodorfer& M. P. Lawton (Eds.), *The psychology of adult development and aging* (pp. 311–335). Washington, DC: American Psychological Association.

Neugarten, B. L., Havighurst, R. J., & Tobin, S. S. (1961). The measurement of life satisfaction. *Journal of Gerontology, 16,* 134–143.

Novack, D. H., Cameron, O., Epel, E., Ader, R., Waldstein, S. R., Levenstein, S., et al. (2007). Psychosomatic medicine: The scientific foundation of the biopsychosocial model. *Academic Psychiatry, 31*(5), 388–401.

Pollak, O. (1948). *Social adjustment in old age: A research planning report. (Social Science Research Council Bulletin., No. 59.).* Oxford: Social Science Research.

Poon, L. W., Clayton, G. M., Martin, P., Johnson, M. A., Courtenay, B. C., Sweaney, A. L., et al. (1992). The Georgia Centenarian Study. *International Journal of Aging and Human Development, 34*(1), 1–17.

Poon, L. W., Martin, P., Bishop, A., Cho, J., da Rosa, G., Deshpande, N., et al. (2010). Understanding centenarians' psychosocial dynamics and their contributions to health and quality of life. *Current Gerontology and Geriatrics Research.* doi: 10.1155/2010/680657.

Poon, L. W., Martin, P., Clayton, G. M., Messner, S., Noble, C. A., & Johnson, M. A. (1992). The influences of cognitive resources on adaptation and old age. *International Journal of Aging and Human Development, 34*(1), 31–46.

Riley, K. P., Snowdon, D. A., Desrosiers, M. F., & Markesbery, W. R. (2005). Early life linguistic ability, late life cognitive function, and neuropathology: findings from the Nun Study. *Neurobiology of Aging, 26*(3), 341–347.

Ritchie, K., & Kildea, D. (1995). Is senile dementia "age-related" or "ageing-related"? Evidence from meta-analysis of dementia prevalence in the oldest old. *Lancet, 346*(8980), 931–934.

Robles, T. F., & Kiecolt-Glaser, J. K. (2003). The physiology of marriage: Pathways to health. *Physiology and Behavior, 79*(3), 409–416.

Ross, C. E., & Chia-Ling, W. (1996). Education, age, and the cumulative advantage in health. *Journal of Health & Social Behavior, 37*(1), 104–120.

Rowe, J. W., & Kahn, R. L. (1987). Human aging: Usual and successful. *Science, 237*(4811), 143–149.

Rowe, J. W., & Kahn, R. L. (1998). *Successful aging*. New York: Pantheon Books.

Ruini, C., Belaise, C., Brombin, C., Caffo, E., & Fava, G. A. (2006). Well-being therapy in school settings: A pilot study. *Psychotherapy and Psychosomatics, 75*(6), 331–336.

Ryff, C. D. (1982). Successful aging: A developmental approach. *The Gerontologist, 22*, 209–214.

Ryff, C. D. (1989a). Beyond Ponce de Leon and life satisfaction: New directions in quest of successful aging. *International Journal of Behavioral Development, 12*, 35–55.

Ryff, C. D. (1989b). Happiness is everything, or is it? Explorations on the meaning of psychological well-being. *Journal of Personality and Social Psychology, 57*(6), 1069–1081.

Ryff, C. D., Keyes, C. L. M., & Hughes, D. L. (2003). Status inequalities, perceived discrimination, and eudaimonic well-being: Do the challenges of minority life hone purpose and growth? *Journal of Health & Social Behavior, 44*(3), 275–291.

Ryff, C. D., & Singer, B. H. (2009). Understanding healthy aging: Key components and their integration. In V. L. Bengtson, M. Silverstein, N. Putney& D. Gans (Eds.), *Handbook of theories of aging* (pp. 117–144). New York: Springer.

Sauer, W. J., & Warland, R. (1982). Morale and life satisfaction. In D. A. Mangen& W. A. Peterson (Eds.), *Research instruments in social gerontology: Vol. 1. Clinical and social psychology* (pp. 195–240). Minneapolis: University of Minnesota Press.

Seery, M. D., Holman, E. A., & Silver, R. C. (2010). Whatever does not kill us: Cumulative lifetime adversity, vulnerability, and resilience. *Journal of Personality and Social Psychology, 99*(6), 1025–1041.

Selye, H. (1936). A syndrome produced by diverse nocuous agents. *Nature, 138*, 32.

Snowdon, D. A. (1997). Aging and Alzheimer's disease: Lessons from the Nun Study. *Gerontologist, 37*(2), 150–156.

Snowdon, D. A. (2003). Healthy aging and dementia: Findings from the Nun Study. *Annals of Internal Medicine, 139*(2), 450–454.

Snowdon, D. A., Kemper, S. J., Mortimer, J. A., Greiner, L. H., Wekstein, D. R., & Markesbery, W. R. (1996). Linguistic ability in early life and cognitive function and Alzheimer's disease in late life. Findings from the Nun Study. *Journal of the American Medical Association, 275*(7), 528–532.

Solomon, G., & Moos, R. (1964). Emotions, immunity, and disease. *Archives of General Psychiatry, 11*, 657–674.

Staudinger, U. M., Marsiske, M., & Baltes, P. B. (1995). Resilience and reserve capacity in later adulthood: Potentials and limits of development across the life span. In D. Cicchetti & D. Cohen (Eds.), *Developmental psychopathology. Volume 2: Risk, disorder and adaptation* (pp. 801–847). New York: Wiley.

Stock, W. A., Okun, M. A., & Benin, M. (1986). Structure of subjective well-being among the elderly. *Psychology & Aging, 1*, 91–102.

Stork, S., Feelders, R. A., van den Beld, A. W., Steyerberg, E. W., Savelkoul, H. F., Lamberts, S. W., et al. (2006). Prediction of mortality risk in the elderly. *American Journal of Medicine, 119*(6), 519–525.

Strawbridge, W. J., Wallhagen, M. I., & Cohen, R. D. (2002). Successful aging and well-being: Self-rated compared with Rowe and Kahn. *Gerontologist, 42*(6), 727–733.

Tedeschi, R. G., & Calhoun, L. G. (2004). Posttraumatic growth: Conceptual foundations and empirical evidence. *Psychological Inquiry, 15*(1), 1–18.

Tedeschi, R. G., Park, C. L., & Calhoun, L. G. (Eds.). (1998). *Posttraumatic growth: Positive changes in the aftermath of crisis*. Mahwah, NJ: Erlbaum.

Tyas, S. L., Snowdon, D. A., Desrosiers, M. F., Riley, K. P., & Markesbery, W. R. (2007). Healthy ageing in the Nun Study: Definition and neuropathologic correlates. *Age Ageing, 36*(6), 650–655.

Uchino, B. N. (2006). Social support and health: A review of physiological processes potentially underlying links to disease outcomes. *Journal of Behavioral Medicine, 29*(4), 377–387.

Vogeli, C., Shields, A. E., Lee, T. A., Gibson, T. B., Marder, W. D., Weiss, K. B., et al. (2007). Multiple chronic conditions: Prevalence, health consequences, and implications for quality, care management, and costs. *Journal of General Internal Medicine,* 22 Suppl. 3, 391–395.

Weir, P. L., Meisner, B. A., & Baker, J. (2010). Successful aging across the years: Does one model fit everyone? *Journal of Health Psychology, 15*(5), 680–687.

Werner, E. E. (1995). Resilience in development. *Current Directions in Psychological Science, 4,* 81–85.

Widerstrom-Noga, E. G., Finnerup, N. B., & Siddall, P. J. (2009). Biopsychosocial perspective on a mechanisms-based approach to assessment and treatment of pain following spinal cord injury. *Journal of Rehabilitation Research and Development, 46*(1), 1–12.

Williams, R. H., & Wirths, C. G. (1965). *Lives through the years: Styles of life and successful aging.* Oxford: Atherton Press.

Young, Y., Frick, K. D., & Phelan, E. A. (2009). Can successful aging and chronic illness coexist in the same individual? A multidimensional concept of successful aging. *Journal of the American Medical Directors Association, 10*(2), 87–92.

2

Demography of Aging

Behavioral and Social Implications

Susan Krauss Whitbourne and Stacey B. Whitbourne

Each day, news headlines discuss the growth of the 65 and older population as one of the most significant changes to affect the social, political, and cultural climate of the world. These changes have broad implications at a global scale for issues such as economic policy and healthcare. From a psychological standpoint, these changes will affect the way that individuals think and feel about themselves as they grow older. The individual's vocational opportunities and family relationships will also be affected by the growth of the aging population.

The purpose of this chapter is to provide a broad overview of demography to form the basis for understanding the biological, psychological, and sociocultural phenomena described in subsequent chapters. We will cover changes within the United States and the rest of the world along with projections into the mid and late 21st century. In addition, we will summarize demographic trends relevant to social demography and health, including implications for financing of retirement and health care in the United States.

Divisions by Age of the Over-65 Population

As a backdrop to understanding the aging of the population, we first need to describe the age groupings used to classify older adults. Although age is an imperfect index of an individual's functioning, demographers have no better alternative than chronological age as the basis for calculating population statistics.

The Wiley-Blackwell Handbook of Adulthood and Aging, First Edition. Edited by Susan Krauss Whitbourne and Martin J. Sliwinski. © 2012 Blackwell Publishing Ltd. Published 2012 by Blackwell Publishing Ltd.

Traditionally, 65 years of age is viewed as the entry point for "old age." Within the 65 and older population, however, there are important distinctions. Individuals who are 65 years old face different issues than those who are 85 years old. In general, at increasingly older ages, individuals are less physically fit, have more chronic health conditions, and have experienced more cognitive changes. They also have more economic constraints and fewer social opportunities.

To capture these differentiations, gerontologists make the distinction among young-old (ages 65 to 74), old-old (ages 75 to 84), and oldest-old (ages 85 and older). Despite the dangers of placing too much credence in a number, gerontologists find these rough age groupings to have some value. In fact, gerontologists urge researchers not to group all people 65 and older together because of the differences among these groups in a number of areas of functioning. Unfortunately, many of the statistics we will present do not have this fine-grained distinction, so it is important to keep this fact in mind.

The demarcations of young-old, old-old, and oldest-old were developed some years ago, prior to the rapid current and projected growth of the over-85 population. Those over the age of 100, the "centenarians," are rapidly increasing in number both within the US and around the world. The newest term to emerge in gerontology is the very highest age category, known as "supercentenarians," those who are 110 and older. Typically, the oldest person in the world at any given time is between the ages of 114 and 116. Jeanne Louise Calment, the oldest documented living human, was 122 at the time of her death. Supercentenarian will probably retain its definition as 110 and over, at least for the foreseeable future, given the upper limits on life span of about 120 years.

Demographic Terms and Concepts

Having provided this background about the age categories within the older adult population, we now define concepts used in research on adult development and aging to characterize important social factors or indicators.

Sex and gender

The term "gender" refers to the individual's identification as male or female. It is generally considered distinct from a person's biological sex, which refers to the individual's genetic makeup. Both sex and gender are important in the study of adult development and aging. Physiological factors relevant to sex influence the timing and nature of physical aging processes, primarily through the operation of sex hormones. For example, the sex hormone estrogen is thought to play at least some role in affecting a woman's risks of heart disease, bone loss, and possibly cognitive changes.

Social and cultural factors relevant to gender are important to the extent that the individual assumes a certain role in society based on being viewed and self-identifying as a male or female. Opportunities in education and employment are two main areas in which gender influences the course of adult development and becomes a limiting factor for women. Although progress has certainly occurred in both domains over the past several decades, women continue to face a more restricted range of choices and the prospects of lower earnings than men (U.S. Department of Commerce Economics and Statistics Administration, 2011). Furthermore, these differences are important to consider when studying the current generation of older adults who were raised in an era with more traditional gender expectations.

Race and ethnicity

The 2010 US Census defined race on the basis of a person's self-identification. Following the tradition begun with the 2000 Census, the 2010 Census also included categories based on national origin and allowed individuals to select more than one racial category. These changes from previous methods of categorizing race were intended to capture more realistically the way that Americans define themselves according to race and ethnicity. US Census figures currently report data for the major groupings of Black or African American, American Indian and Alaska Native, Native Hawaiian and Other Pacific Islander. Hispanic origin is considered an ethnicity, not a race.

Though race and ethnicity reflect social influences, there may also be differences in functioning in adulthood among different racial and ethnic groups that reflect biological factors such as genetic risks. People who have inherited a risk factor that has been found to be higher within their race or ethnicity are more likely to be at risk for developing that illness during their adult years.

The impact of racial and ethnic differences in risk factors may also depend on the distinct cultural lifestyle characteristic of their tradition or background. For example, people at risk for a disease with a metabolic basis (such as inability to metabolize fats) will be more likely to develop that disease depending on the prevalence of high fat foods in their culture's traditional cuisine, especially if they maintain those traditions in their own homes.

Social and cultural aspects of race and ethnicity may also alter an individual's development in adulthood through the structure of a society, particularly when there are systematic biases against people seen as belonging to that social grouping. For example, in the US, health problems are higher among the African American population than among the White population. Differences in health may be attributed in part to lack of opportunities for education and well-paying jobs. In addition, systematic discrimination is also believed to take a toll on health by increasing the levels of stress experienced by African Americans (Green & Darity, 2010).

Socioeconomic status

An individual's socioeconomic status (SES), or "social class," is defined according to the values assigned to level of education, prestige level of occupation, or a weighted combination of the two. People with higher levels of education tend to have occupations that are higher in prestige, and so some researchers use level of education alone as the index of SES.

Income levels are not necessarily associated with socioeconomic status. High-prestige jobs (such as teachers) are often associated with mid- or even low-level salaries. However, as a proxy for or in addition to SES, some researchers use income as the basis for analyzing social class differences in health and opportunities.

Age Demographics in the United States

A quick snapshot of the US population according to age and sex appears in Figure 2.1. The age–sex structure provides a useful way of looking at the population. A "young" population is shaped like a pyramid, an "old" population is depicted by an upside-down pyramid, and a population considered stable is shaped like a rectangle. From the figure, the "bulge" in the middle of the population is clear, reflecting the Baby Boom generation of people born between 1945 and 1964. As this bulge continues to move upward throughout the 21st century, this generation will have a continued impact on the nature of society, particularly in the way people view aging (Whitbourne & Willis, 2006).

In 1900, people over the age of 65 years made up about 4% of the American population (constituting 3.1 million people). By 2009, this number increased more than 13-fold to 39.6 million. Those 65 and older now represent 12.9% of the total US population (U.S. Bureau of the Census, 2011c). As shown in Figure 2.2, beginning in 2010 with an estimated 40.2 million adults 65 and older, this number is projected to more than double to 88.5 million by the year 2050 to become 20.2% of the total US population (U.S. Bureau of the Census, 2009). A disproportionate rise in the population 85 years and older will also occur. Perhaps most impressive is the estimate in the growth in the number of centenarians. In 1990, an estimated 37,306 people over the age of 100 lived in the United States. By 2010 this number was estimated at 79,000, and by 2050 there are estimated to be 601,000 of these exceptionally aged individuals (U.S. Bureau of the Census, 2008).

The major explanation for these large increases in the 65 and older population can be accounted for by the movement of the Baby Boomers through the years of middle and later adulthood. It is important to consider not just that there are high numbers of these individuals, but also that they are expected to live longer into their eighties, nineties, and hundreds, increasing the numbers of oldest-old individuals in society.

Increases in the aging population reflect the vast advances that have taken place in the average length of life. Life expectancy is defined as the average number of years lived by people born within a similar period of time. To calculate life expectancy, statisticians take into account death rates for a particular group within the population, and use these figures to project how long it will take for all members of that group to die.

Life expectancy from birth rose overall from 62.9 years in 1940 to 77.9 years in 2007 (Xu, Kochanek, & Tejeda-Vera, 2009). Many factors have contributed to increases in life expectancy, including reduced death rates for children and young adults. People are also living longer once they reach the age of 65, at which point the life expectancy becomes 83.5 years of age (Centers for Disease Control and Prevention, 2010a).

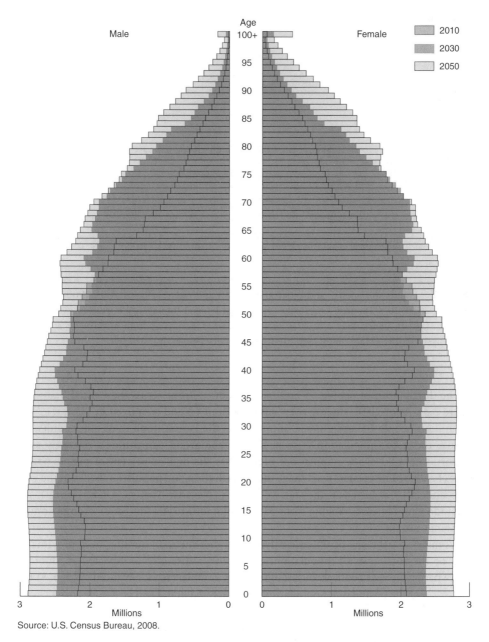

Source: U.S. Census Bureau, 2008.

Figure 2.1 Age and sex structure of the population of the US: 2010, 2030, and 2050. Source: U.S. Census Bureau, 2008. Originally appeared in Vincent, G. K., & Velkoff, V. A. (2010). *The next four decades. The older population in the United States: 2010 to 2050. Current Population Reports.* Retrieved from http://www.census.gov/prod/2010pubs/p25-1138.pdf.

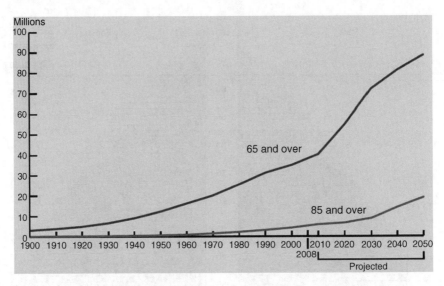

Figure 2.2   Population age 65 and older and age 85 and older: selected years 1900–2008 and projected 2010–2050. Source: Originally appeared in Federal Interagency Forum on Age-Related Statistics. (2010). *Older Americans 2010: Key indicators of well-being*, from http://www.agingstats. gov/agingstatsdotnet/Main_Site/Data/2010_Documents/Docs/OA_2010.pdf.

The distribution of people 65 and older is not uniform across the United States (see Figure 2.3). As of 2010, slightly over half of persons 65 and over lived in 11 states. With 4.1 million people 65 and older, California has the largest number of older adults, but because the state's population is so large, this age group constitutes a relatively small proportion (11%) of the population. Florida has the highest percent of people 65 and older (17.2%). The greatest percentage increases in the aging population between the years 1998 and 2010 occurred in the states of Alaska, Nevada, Arizona, Utah, Georgia, and Colorado with increases ranging from 31% (Colorado) to Alaska (52%) (Administration on Aging, 2010).

Women over the age of 65 currently outnumber men, amounting to approximately 58% of the total over-65 population. This gender disparity is expected to diminish somewhat by the year 2050, as the last of the Baby Boomers reach advanced old age. At that time, 55% of the 65 and older population in the United States will be female and 45% will be male (U.S. Bureau of the Census, 2010d).

Changes are also evident in the distribution of White and minority segments of the population. In 2008, whereas 20% of the over-65 population was made up of members of racial and ethnic minorities, this number will rise to 41% by the year 2050 (Federal Interagency Forum on Age-Related Statistics, 2010). The Hispanic population of older adults is expected to grow at the fastest rate, increasing from approximately 6 million in 2003 to over 18 million by 2050 (He, Sangupta, Velkoff, & DeBarros, 2005). Detailed projections are shown in Figure 2.4 for 2010 to 2050 by specific racial group.

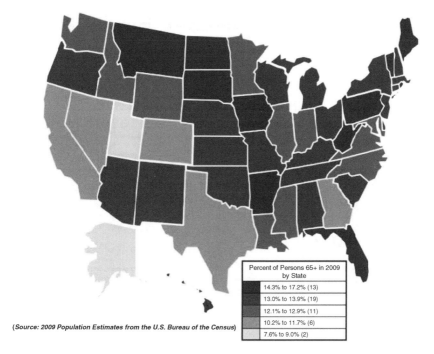

Figure 2.3 Persons 65 + as a percentage of the total population. Source: Originally appeared in Administration on Aging. (2010). *A profile of older Americans: 2010*, from http://www.aoa.gov/AoAroot/Aging_Statistics/Profile/2010/index.aspx.

Aging Around the World

Data from around the globe confirm the picture of an increasingly older population in the 21st century. In 2010, there were 531 million people worldwide over the age of 65. This number is predicted to triple to 1.55 billion by the year 2050 (U.S. Bureau of the Census, 2010b). China currently has the largest number of older adults (106 million), but Japan has the highest percentage of people 65 and older (20%) (Kinsella & He, 2009).

World population statistics are often reported in terms of "developed" and "developing" countries. Developed countries include all those in Europe, North America, Japan, Australia, and New Zealand plus some nations formerly in the Soviet Union. All other nations of the world are classified as developing. Developing countries are characterized by agrarian-based economy, along with lower levels of health care, education, and income.

As shown in Figure 2.5, the rate of growth of the 65 and older population living in developing countries will peak by 2020 in the next decade, far exceeding the rate of growth in developed countries (Kinsella & He, 2009). The larger proportion of the aging population in the world will place a strain on the economies and health care systems of all nations, but particularly the developing nations which do not have well-developed health and social support infrastructures.

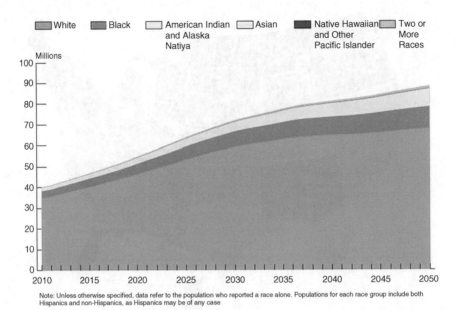

Figure 2.4   Projected population aged 65 and over by race for the United States 2010 to 2050. Source: Originally appeared in Vincent, G. K., & Velkoff, V. A. (2010). *The next four decades. The older population in the United States: 2010 to 2050. Current Population Reports.* Retrieved from http://www.census.gov/prod/2010pubs/p25-1138.pdf.

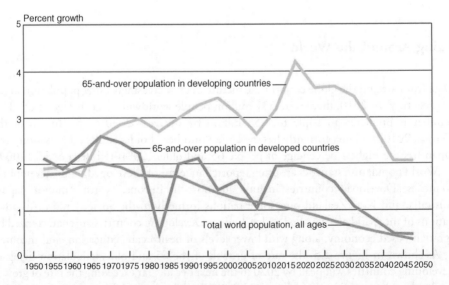

Figure 2.5   Average annual percent growth of older population in developed and developing countries. Source: Originally appeared in Kinsella, K., & He, W. (2009). *An aging world 2008: International Population Reports P95/09-1*, from http://www.census.gov/prod/2009pubs/p95-09-1.pdf.

Social Demography

In this section, we cover the demographic data relevant to an understanding of the social and economic characteristics of the aging population. Although our focus is on older adults, we also review data relevant to young and middle adulthood, as this information sets the stage for understanding psychosocial issues discussed in later chapters.

Marriage and family living situations

In the year 2010, 120.7 million adults were married and living with their spouse, a number that represents 53% of the US population age 18 and older. Among the entire population 18 and older, the percentage of those who have ever been married is far higher—approximately 73% of the population (U.S. Bureau of the Census, 2011b). The median age of marriage, 26.1 for women and 28.2 for men, has steadily risen over the past decades (U.S. Bureau of the Census, 2010c), as has the proportion of unmarried and never married adults (Goodwin, McGill, & Chandra, 2009). Among all adults 18 and older, over half of Whites (56%) are married. Asian Americans (62%) are most likely to be currently married and living with a spouse, and Blacks (34%) the least (U.S. Bureau of the Census, 2010a).

Among people 65 and older in the United States, there are a higher percentage of men (75%) than women (44%) married and living with a spouse. Consequently, women over the age of 65 are almost twice as likely (40%) as men (19%) to be living alone (Administration on Aging, 2010). This leaves older women at greater risk for the disadvantages associated with single status, including fewer financial resources and less access to care and social support.

Living in a stable relationship prior to or instead of marrying is referred to as cohabitation. Since the 1960s, there has been a steady increase in the number of couples who choose this lifestyle. In 1960 an estimated 439,000 individuals in the United States reported that they were cohabiting with a person of the opposite sex. By 2006 this number was estimated at about 6.2 million (U.S. Bureau of the Census, 2010e). Around 50 to 60% of all marriages are now preceded by cohabitation (Stanley, Amato, Johnson, & Markman, 2006); looking at the data on couples who cohabitate, approximately 28% of women 44 and under who cohabitate eventually marry their partner (National Center for Health Statistics, 2010).

Along with a rise in the overall numbers of couples who cohabitate, there is a parallel increase in the number of cohabiting adults with children under the age of 15. In 1960 this number amounted to 197,000, but by 2009 had increased greatly to the present level of approximately 2.6 million (U.S. Bureau of the Census, 2010a).

As of the 2000 US Census, 594,000 people (1 in 9 of all unmarried couple households) identified themselves as living with a member of the same sex, with nearly equal numbers of male–male and female–female partnerships. The largest percentage (1.6%) of same-sex partners involved people of two or more races. San Francisco, Seattle, and Portland, Oregon, were the cities with the highest numbers of same-sex partnerships. It is estimated that 34% of lesbian couples and 22% of gay male couples who live together have children (Simmons & O'Connell, 2003).

Approximately 10% of the adult population in the United States is divorced (U.S. Bureau of the Census, 2011b). Taking into account all marriages that end in divorce, the average length of first marriage prior to divorce is about 8 years (Kreider, 2005). Divorce statistics also show important variations by race. Black women between the ages of 25 and 44 have higher divorce rates than White or Hispanic women (National Center for Health Statistics, 2010). Research on children of divorced parents suggests that for women, but not men, parental divorce is a stronger indicator of a lack of commitment and confidence in the marriage (Whitton, Rhoades, Stanley, & Markman, 2008).

In the United States, approximately 18% of all marriages are second marriages, and 4% are third marriages. The average duration of a second marriage that ends in divorce is slightly longer than that of a first marriage—8 years for men and 9 years for women (Kreider, 2005). The probability of a second marriage ending in divorce after 10 years is .39, slightly higher than that of the ending of a first marriage, which is .33 (Bramlett & Mosher, 2002).

When a marriage ends in the death of a partner, the survivor is faced with enormous readjustments in every aspect of life. Even when there is time to prepare, adjustment to widowhood is a difficult and painful process. In the United States, currently there are approximately 14.3 million widowed adults aged 18 and older; 75% of these are 65 and older. The majority (80%) of the over-65 widowed adults are women. By the age of 85 and older, the majority of women are widows (73%), more than double the rate for men (35%) (U.S. Bureau of the Census, 2011b). The highest rate of widowhood is among Black women 85 and older, among whom the large majority (87.5%) have lost their spouses (He et al., 2005).

Despite population trends toward more single-parent and cohabiting families, the large majority of households in the United States (77%) consist of people living together as a family. In the United States, the average household size is 2.57 people. Households with married couples constitute 49.9% of all households (U.S. Bureau of the Census, 2011b).

Approximately 4.1 million women in the United States give birth each year. In the United States in 2009, 76% of all children were born to mothers between the ages of 20 and 34 years old (National Vital Statistics System, 2011). In 2009, the number and rate of births continued to fall from its high point reached in 2007, reflecting the downturn in the economy. The exception to this overall trend was among women in their forties who may have felt that despite the poor economic times, they could not wait longer to have a child (Hamilton, Martin, & Ventura, 2010).

There are approximately 56 million grandparents in the United States (Fields, O'Connell, & Downs, 2006); as of 2010, about 11% (7.5 million) live with their under-18-year-old grandchildren. Of grandparents living with grandchildren, 22% are responsible entirely for their basic needs (U.S. Bureau of the Census, 2010c). This situation, referred to as a "skip generation family," may occur for a variety of reasons, including substance abuse by parents, child abuse or neglect by parents, teenage pregnancy or failure of parents to handle children, and parental unemployment, divorce, AIDS, or incarceration.

Work and retirement

The labor force includes all civilians in the over-16 population who live outside of institutions (prisons, nursing homes, residential treatment centers) and have sought or are actively seeking employment. In 2010 the total civilian noninstitutionalized population over the age of 16 amounted to 237.8 million people and, of these, nearly two thirds (65%) were in the labor force. Reflecting the downturn in the US economy beginning in late 2008, the percentage employed in 2010 was 90%, down from 96% just 3 years earlier. This means that 59% of those in the labor force were occupying jobs (Bureau of Labor Statistics, 2011a).

Although Whites, Blacks, and Asians have similar labor force participation rates, the unemployment rates are higher for Blacks or African Americans (16.0%) than for Whites (8.7%) or Asians (7.5%). People with a college education are far less likely to be unemployed (4.7%) than people with a high school education or less (14.9%) (Bureau of Labor Statistics, 2011b). However, education alone does not account for earning potential. Even when controlling for education, Black and Hispanic workers typically have lower earnings than do Whites, a disparity particularly pronounced among men. For example, in 2008, among men with a bachelor's degree and higher, Black men earned 71% of the income of Whites, and Hispanic college graduates earned 78% of the income of White men. This disparity remains approximately the same even at the advanced graduate degree levels (Center for Medicare and Medicaid Services, 2010).

Employment rates rise steadily after the early twenties to reach a peak of 83% by the age of 45–49 years; by 70–74 years of age, the percentage in the labor force drops to 18% (Bureau of Labor Statistics, 2011a). Projections are that by the year 2018, the size of the 55 and older workforce will rise from 18.1 at present to 23.9 (as a percentage of the total workforce) (Bureau of Labor Statistics, 2010a). The highest income is earned by men in the 45 to 64 age group; for women, the highest income was earned by those who were 55 to 64. Virtually all of those 75 years and older (92.6%) have ended their full-time participation in the nation's workforce (Bureau of Labor Statistics, 2010b). However, many remain employed on a part-time basis; nearly half of all men and 61% of all women 70 years and older engage in some paid work (He et al., 2005).

Women comprise 46.8% of the labor force (U.S. Department of Labor, 2011). The labor force participation of women with young children rose steadily between 1984 and 2004, dipped in the mid 2000s, and once again is on the increase, reflecting the economic necessities associated with the economic downturn after 2008. As of 2010, 77.5% of mothers with children aged 6 to 17 were employed and 63.6% of mothers with children less than 6 (Bureau of Labor Statistics, 2011c).

Despite their increasing involvement in the labor force, women still earn less than men, a fact referred to as "the gender gap," expressed as a proportion of women's to men's salaries. As of late 2010, full-time employed women earned 81.2% of the median income for men. The gender gap is highest among Whites (81.1%) and lowest among Blacks (96.2%). The gender gap is particularly pronounced among women in the 55 to 64-year-old age group, who earn 74% of the income of men in the same age bracket (Bureau of Labor Statistics, 2010b).

Educational levels within the United States vary considerably by age group. In general, there has been an increasing trend over the past 40 years for older adults to have higher levels of education. As of 2009, 14% of adults 65–74 and 11% of those 75–84 earned at least a bachelor's degree. This trend is certain to continue, as is evident from the fact that the 25 to 34-year-old age bracket now includes the highest percentage of college graduates of all adult age groups (22.8%) (Center for Medicare and Medicaid Services, 2010).

As already discussed, the large majority of individuals 75 and older are no longer in the labor force; the drop-off in employment occurs gradually, beginning in the sixties. Once they have reached age 65 and are retired, many workers in the US are eligible for retirement benefits through Social Security. As of 2010, 34 million retired workers were receiving Social Security benefits. The average monthly Social Security benefit for a retired worker through 2008 was $1,170 (Harrington, Carrillo, Blank, & O'Brian, 2010). By the end of 2009, 37% of the income of Americans 65 and older came from Social Security. The remaining percentages of income come from earnings (30%), assets such as interest income (13%), and either private (9%) or government employee (9%) pensions (Social Security Administration, 2010a).

In the year 2009, $548 billion were paid out in benefits to retired workers (Social Security Administration, 2010b). Social Security is almost entirely a pay-as-you-go program, meaning that today's workers pay into the system that pays today's retirees, although there is a Social Security Trust Fund that contains significant assets. Most of the funding (83%) of Social Security comes from payroll taxes on current workers, and 76% of these revenues go out directly in retirement benefits (Social Security Administration, 2009).

Long-term care

With the growth of the older population, demographic data are increasingly becoming vital in planning for both public and private funding for long-term care. Although there is a relatively small percentage overall of people 65 and older living in nursing homes, the percentage of older adults who are institutionalized increases dramatically with age. As of 2007, the percentages of Medicare recipients residing in long-term care facilities rises from 1.3% for persons 65 to 74 years to 3.8% for persons 75 to 84 years and 15.4% for persons 85 + (Federal Interagency Forum on Age-Related Statistics, 2010). The occupancy rates of nursing homes are declining in the US from 85.5% in 2004 to 83.7% in 2009 (Social Security Administration, 2011).

Nearly two thirds of nursing homes in the United States fall into the category of "for-profit" facilities, meaning that they seek to have their revenue exceed their expenses. Nonprofit facilities, which include primarily those run by religious organizations, constitute the second largest group (26.5%), and government-owned facilities, primarily those run by the Veterans Administration, compose the remainder (6%). Therefore, most nursing homes are run like a business with the goal of making a profit. Perhaps because they are less oriented toward the "bottom line," not-for-profit nursing homes have higher quality ratings than their for-profit counterparts (Comondore et al., 2009). Related to this issue is the payment mode of residents. When nursing homes have more private pay patients, they are able to provide better care because the rates for these patients are higher than the reimbursement rates that facilities receive from governmental subsidies.

The most common primary diagnosis of nursing home residents when admitted to a nursing home is cardiovascular disease, and the strongest predictors of admission to a nursing home are inability to carry out basic activities of daily living, cognitive impairment, and prior nursing home admission (Gaugler, Duval, Anderson, & Kane, 2007). The greatest form of disability is loss of cognitive skills associated with Alzheimer's disease (Schultz et al., 2002). Given that Alzheimer's disease is found in nearly half of all nursing home residents (45% in 2008), this means that difficulties in carrying out daily living skills are a significant problem for these individuals. In fact, 56.8% of nursing home residents are chairbound, meaning that they are restricted to a wheelchair. Despite the large number of residents with Alzheimer's disease, only 5% of nursing homes have special care units devoted specifically to their care (Harrington, Carrillo, & Blank, 2009).

Mood and anxiety disorders are present in nearly 20% of all older adults living in these settings (Sahyoun, Pratt, Lentzner, Dey, & Robinson, 2001). Over half (65.2%) of residents receive psychotropic medications, including antidepressants, antianxiety drugs, sedatives and hypnotics, and antipsychotics (Harrington et al., 2009). In addition to increased functional limitations compared with older adults living in their own homes, nursing home residents also have more depressive symptoms and lower self-rated quality of life (Karakaya, Bilgin, Ekici, Kose, & Otman, 2009).

In 2009, total state and federal expenditures for nursing homes were estimated to amount to $144 billion (Social Security Administration, 2011). Medicaid is the largest source of funding in the US for medical and health-related services for those in need of assistance. In 2009 it provided health care assistance amounting to a total of $373.9 billion. Together Medicare and Medicaid (federal and state) financed $876.2 billion in health care services in 2009, which was 35% of the nation's total health care bill of $2.5 trillion (private and public funding combined) (U.S. Bureau of the Census, 2011a). There is considerable variation by state in the amount spent on long-term care; Louisiana has the highest percent in the United States at 26.6% (Kaiser Family Foundation, 2010).

About two thirds (64%) of residents had their nursing home expenses paid for by Medicaid in 2009, slightly over one fifth (22%) pay for nursing homes themselves through their own funds or other forms of insurance, and the remainder (14%) have their nursing home expenses paid for by Medicare (Social Security Administration, 2011). Although quality control is intended to provide comparable care to all residents, those who are paying for their own nursing homes are afforded a greater range of facilities, better accommodations, and higher staff-to-patient ratios compared to those who are funded through Medicaid (Donoghue, 2006).

Clearly, given the expense of long-term care and, from a psychological point of view, the impact of quality of care on the individual, the growth of the aging population has tremendous implications. Consequently, considerable efforts in the field of gerontology are devoted to maximizing the functioning of older adults living independently in their communities.

Mortality and Health Statistics

We turn next to mortality and health statistics, which provide important information about the ultimate quality of life of individuals throughout the years of adulthood. Mortality data provide an important perspective for understanding population demographics, given that the number of people in the population within a given age range depends on the death rates for that age group. An understanding of mortality data is also helpful in gaining a perspective on health and factors related to health and aging.

In 2007, there were 2,423,712 deaths in the United States (Xu, Kochanek, Murphy, & Tejeda-Vera, 2010). This translated to an overall death rate, per 100,000, in the population of 803.6, meaning that 803.6 people died for every 100,000 in the population. However, this number does not tell the whole story, since deaths are more likely to occur in older age groups. The death rate among people aged 65–74 is 2,011, meaning that of 100,000 people aged 65–74, about 2,000 died. The death rate skyrockets to 12,946 among people 85 years and older. These numbers represent the age-specific death rate, which is the number of deaths per 100,000 of a particular age group.

Therefore, the overall number of 803.6 deaths per 100,000 in the United States is misleading because it does not control for the fact that more deaths occur in a smaller proportion of the population. A statistical correction must be applied to the overall death rate in order to take this into account. Applying this correction leads to the age-adjusted death rate, a weighted sum based on each age group's death rate and size within the population. Using this formula, the age-adjusted death rate in the United States becomes 760.2. The age-adjusted death rate of 760.2 in 2007 was substantially less than the prior year's rate, which was 776.5. These statistics have led public health agencies to conclude that the United States became "healthier" in 2007 compared to 2006.

The age-adjusted death rate provides a number that controls for the age distribution of a population and thus enables comparison of the relative health of nations. Based on estimates from the World Health Organization, the unhealthiest countries are located in sub-Saharan Africa (World Health Organization, 2009). The majority of deaths in these African countries are due to infectious or parasitic diseases, with the highest rates occurring in Zimbabwe due to HIV/AIDS. Cardiovascular disease, in contrast, has the highest age-adjusted death rates in Kazakhstan, Ukraine, and Afghanistan, all of whose rates are far higher (600 to 700) than any state in the United States, including those with the highest cardiovascular death rates.

Improvements in health-related behaviors contributing to lower mortality rates from the major causes of death relate to what health experts call compression of morbidity, a reduction in disability prior to their death (Manton, 2008). This concept is comparable to the commonly held desire to "die with your boots on."

There are, however, large disparities within segments of the population in age-specific mortality rates. According to 2007 statistics (Xu et al., 2010), White females have the lowest age-adjusted mortality rate (647.7); non-Hispanic Black men have the highest (1210.9) followed by non-Hispanic White men (906.8). These discrepancies seem to follow regional variations (Kindig, Seplaki, & Libby, 2002) with the highest rates of mortality in the "stroke belt" of the Southeastern US, where the rate of mortality from stroke is substantially higher than the rest of the country. It appears that these regional inequities in death rates are largely accounted for by variations due to race; when race and Hispanic status are factored into the calculations, the death rates in the Southeast actually become reduced to levels lower than in some Northeast states. However, the Midwest "advantage" remains, as does the high death rate in Nevada.

Marital status and education are two significant predictors of mortality. The age-adjusted death rate for those who never married is substantially higher than for those who were ever married, even taking into account the higher mortality of those who are widowed and divorced. The advantage holds for both men and women across all age groups of adults aged 15 and older (Xu et al., 2010). Educational status is also related to mortality rate. At all age groups, those with a college education or better have lower mortality rates.

These findings on education are in accordance with the well-established relationship between social status and mortality (Adler et al., 1994). Since the mid-19th century, men in laboring and trade occupations are known to have higher death rates than those of the professional class (Macintyre, 1997). Data from the Whitehall II Study, a longitudinal investigation of health in over 10,300 civil employees in Great Britain, elucidate the causes of this phenomenon. Men in lower employment grades have higher risk of coronary heart disease compared with men in higher employment grades (Marmot, Shipley, Hemingway, Head, & Brunner, 2008). Men and women from Whitehall II in lower socioeconomic positions had a 1.60 times higher risk of death compared with those in higher socioeconomic positions (Marmot et al., 2008). People in lower socioeconomic classes are also more likely to suffer from communicable diseases, exposure to lead, and work-related injuries (Pamuk, Makuc, Heck, Reuben, & Lochner, 1998). These results also apply to women from lower socioeconomic classes (Langford & Johnson, 2009).

Trends in mortality rates are associated not only with the level of occupation but also the pattern of jobs a person holds throughout adulthood. The risk of mortality is lower in men who move from manual to professional or managerial-level occupations (House, Kessler, Herzog, & Mero, 1990; Moore & Hayward, 1990). Men who hold a string of unrelated jobs have higher rates of early mortality than those with stable career progressions (Pavalko, Elder, & Clipp, 1993).

Across all countries studied by the World Health Organization, the poor are over four times as likely to die between the ages of 15 and 59 as are the nonpoor (World Health Organization, 2009). People with incomes below the poverty level are exposed to other risk factors as well. For example, low-income men are almost twice as likely to smoke as are men in the highest income groups (Schoenborn, Vickerie, & Barnes, 2003).

Major diseases and associated risk factors

Cardiovascular disease is the number one killer in the United States, resulting in 33% of all deaths in the year 2007 (Xu et al., 2010). However, given that deaths occur disproportionately in the population, with over half of all deaths occurring in people 75 years and older, heart disease is the number one killer because it is the number one killer among the oldest segment of the population.

Worldwide, coronary heart disease was the leading cause of death in 2002, amounting to 7.2 million deaths or nearly one third of all deaths around the globe. Another 5.5 million people per year die from cerebrovascular disease. The countries with the highest death rates from cardiovascular disease as of 2009 were Russia, Bulgaria, Hungary, and Romania; the United States ranked 13th and Canada ranked 26th in the world (Lloyd-Jones et al., 2010).

Degree of physical activity is an important influence on cardiovascular risk. The majority of adults at highest risk for heart disease (i.e., those 75 and older) are the least likely to exercise. Only about 36% of people 65 to 74 and 16% of those 75 and older engage in vigorous leisure activity (National Health Interview Survey, 2009).

Smoking is an additional risk factor both for cardiovascular disease and cancer, among other chronic diseases. Approximately one fifth of all adults in the United States are current smokers. The rates of current smokers decrease across age groups of adults to 10% of those 65 and older (National Health Interview Survey, 2009). It is very possible that the smoking rates decrease not only because older adults are less likely to smoke but also because the nonsmokers are more likely to survive.

Body weight is another major risk factor for cardiovascular and other chronic diseases. An analysis of 57 longitudinal studies conducted in Western Europe and North America showed a causal relationship between high BMI and mortality due to vascular disease (Whitlock et al., 2009). According to the CDC, there have been dramatic increases in overweight and obese adults in the United States over the past 20 years. Currently, 30.3% of the United States population is considered obese by government standards. According to the Organization for Economic Co-operation and Development (2007), this is the highest percentage in the world. High intake of "bad" cholesterol (LDL) foods in particular is the component of obesity that places individuals at greater risk for developing cardiovascular disease and stroke (Erqou et al., 2009). Conversely, high levels of the "good" cholesterol (HDL) are related to lower risk of cardiovascular disease (Cooney et al., 2009).

Variations in stroke rates by race/ethnicity, social class, and poverty have emerged as issues of national concern in the United States. The Southeast is considered the "stroke belt" of the United States, with 8 to 12 states in this region having substantially higher stroke mortality than the rest of the country. The three states comprising the "stroke buckle" are North Carolina, South Carolina, and Georgia. The high rates of stroke are attributed in part to diets in this region that are based on high consumption of sodium, monounsaturated fatty acids, polyunsaturated fatty acids and cholesterol, and the low consumption of dietary fiber.

In 2009, it was estimated that nearly 1.5 million Americans received a diagnosis of cancer (not including skin cancer or noninvasive cancers) and that about 10.5 million are living with the disease. The lifetime risk of developing cancer is about 1 in 2 for men and 1 in 3 for women (American Cancer Society, 2009). Skin cancer is the most prevalent type of cancer in the United States, with an estimated 1 million new cases occurring each year. Lung cancer accounts for 30% of the deaths in men and 26% in women.

In addition to a person's lifestyle and history of disease, variations due to race and ethnicity are observed among certain types of cancers. Skin cancer is more likely to develop in people with fair skin that freckles easily, while Black people are less likely to develop any form of skin cancer. Other cancers varying according to race include uterine cancer (more prevalent among Whites), and prostate cancer (more prevalent among Blacks). Stomach cancer is twice as prevalent in men and is more common in Black people, as is colon cancer. Rectal cancer is more prevalent among Whites.

It is estimated that 10 million Americans have been diagnosed with diabetes, and there may be as many as 5 million people who have the disease but have not received a diagnosis. Diabetes is estimated to afflict 10.3 million people 60 years of age and older, approximately 21% of adults in this age category. The CDC estimates that having diabetes doubles the risk of death compared with other people in one's own age group (Centers for Disease Control and Prevention, 2010b). While Type 1 diabetes was once considered a children's disease, higher rates of Type 2 diabetes in children have increased at an alarming rate. Such findings will have important health implications for future generations of older adults.

According to the World Health Organization, the number of people suffering from diabetes worldwide is approximately 171 million in 2010, a number that is projected to double by 2030. Approximately 3.2 million deaths per year are due to complications of diabetes. The United States is third following India and China in the number of people who suffer from diabetes, but the rise in cases is greater in the developing countries (World Health Organization, 2010).

Chronic obstructive pulmonary disease (COPD) is the fourth leading cause of chronic illness and death and the fifth in the world in terms of the burden of disease (Global Initiative for Chronic Obstructive Lung Disease, 2009). COPD's prevalence increases with age, such that the disease is estimated to affect about 25% of those 75 and older (Iyer Parameswaran & Murphy, 2009).

The World Health Organization estimates the prevalence of Alzheimer's disease worldwide of people over 60 as 5% of men and 6% of women (World Health Organization, 2001). The incidence rates of new cases is less than 1% a year for those aged 60 to 65 or possibly as high as 6.5% in those 85 and older (Kawas, Gray, Brookmeyer, Fozard, & Zonderman, 2000). A commonly quoted figure regarding the number of people in the United States with Alzheimer's disease is 5–5.5 million people, representing a rate of over 12% of the over-65 age groups and 50% or higher of those over 85 years of age. The media and other sources have projected this number to soar into the mid-21st century, reaching a staggering 14 million individuals who will suffer from the disease by 2050 unless a cure is found (Alzheimer's Association, 2010).

However, it is necessary to look more carefully at these statistics, which, according to other estimates, are overly high. First, the estimates originate from a nonpeer-reviewed publication of the privately funded Alzheimer's Association. Their projection is based on a study of 856 US residents living in 42 states ranging in age from 71 and older. US prevalence statistics were extrapolated from the figures in this sample (Plassman et al., 2007). This approach of generalizing from a relatively small sample has characterized much of the Alzheimer's prevalence research and thus has led to disputes among researchers about the validity of this estimate. Others have arrived at an estimated prevalence of about half the media number at 2.3 million (Brookmeyer, Corrada, Curriero, & Kawas, 2002; Hy & Keller, 2000). Furthermore, norms for diagnostic tests for the disorder vary by education and age, so estimates of its prevalence in the oldest-old and the less well educated might result in inflated figures (Beeri et al., 2006).

Particularly important when evaluating statistics on the prevalence of Alzheimer's disease is whether the data refer specifically to dementia due to Alzheimer's disease only or whether they include vascular dementia. Approximately 20% of cases of dementia are due to cerebrovascular disease (Knopman, 2007). The proposition that misdiagnosis may inflate prevalence statistics was supported by findings from the Honolulu Aging Study showing that dementia symptoms may be caused by one of a large variety of brain lesions (White, 2009).

Despite the presence of significant physical changes, health conditions, and psychological disorders, older adults view themselves and their situations in a positive light. This fact is borne out by the findings of the National Health Interview Survey, which tracks the incidence of serious psychological distress. Survey after survey in this series consistently reports lower rates of serious distress within the past year for adults 65 and older (2.3 in 65 and older vs. 2.8 in those 18 to 24) (Pratt, Dey, & Cohen, 2007). These results are not limited to the United States. A large-scale investigation of nearly 7,500 adults in Australia aged 20 to 64 showed lower rates of anxiety and psychological distress among the older age groups (Jorm et al., 2005). It is important to remember that despite the presence of chronic physical health conditions and the experience of psychological disorders among many in the older adult population, the majority cope successfully with the changes associated with the aging process.

Summary

The demographics of adult development and aging have a variety of implications for understanding the biological, psychological, and sociocultural changes associated with the aging process. As shown in this chapter, there are important distinctions within the adult population according to age, gender, race or ethnicity, social class, and nationality.

As the Baby Boom generation of people born between 1945 and 1964 reaches the age of 65 and beyond they will come to represent 20.2% of the total US population. Data from around the globe confirm the picture of an increasingly older population in the 21st century. The rate of growth of the 65 and older population living in developing countries will peak by 2020, exceeding the rate of growth in developed countries, causing a strain on the economies and health care systems of all nations.

Over half (53%) of people aged 18 and older in the US are married; approximately 10% of the adult population is divorced, with the average length of first marriage 8 years. Among those 65 and older, men are more likely to be married and living with a spouse. The majority (75%) of widowed individuals is 65 and older, and most are women.

With the growth of the older population, demographic data are important in planning public and private retirement pensions as well as funding for long-term care. The impact of quality of care on the individual has tremendous implications for the aging population. Therefore, psychological interventions and social policies that can help older adults maintain independent living in the community is a topic of increasing importance.

Mortality data provide an important perspective for understanding population demographics and health and factors related to health and aging. There are large disparities within segments of the population in age-specific mortality rates according to factors such as marital status, education, race, and social class. Lower levels of physical activity, smoking, and high body weight are all risk factors associated with increased risk of death due to cardiovascular disease, currently the number one cause of death. However, other chronic diseases, including cancer, diabetes, COPD, and various forms of dementia also present significant risk factors and are themselves associated with social factors and lifestyle.

Despite the presence of social stressors and chronic illness, the incidence of mental health disorders among the older adult population is relatively small and they are less likely to report significant distress.

An understanding of the demography of adult development and aging is essential to gaining perspective on changes associated with the aging process. As will be shown in later chapters, there is great diversity within the aging population. Thus researchers who investigate psychological changes in later life should attend to and be sensitive to these important variations.

References

Adler, N. E., Boyce, T., Chesney, M. A., Cohen, S., Folkman, S., Kahn, R. L., & Syme, S. (1994). Socioeconomic status and health: The challenge of the gradient. *American Psychologist, 49*, 15–24.

Administration on Aging. (2010). A profile of older Americans: 2010. Retrieved from http://www.aoa.gov/AoAroot/Aging_Statistics/Profile/2010/index.aspx

Alzheimer's Association. (2010). 2010 Alzheimer's disease facts and figures. Retrieved from http://www.alz.org/national/documents/report_alzfactsfigures2009.pdf

American Cancer Society. (2009). Estimated new cancer cases for selected cancer sites by state, US, 2009. Retrieved from http://www.cancer.org/acs/groups/content/@nho/documents/document/cff2009estcst4pdf.pdf

Beeri, M. S., Schmeidler, J., Sano, M., Wang, J., Lally, R., Grossman, H., & Silverman, J. M. (2006). Age, gender, and education norms on the CERAD neuropsychological battery in the oldest old. *Neurology, 67*(6), 1006–1010.

Bramlett, M. D., & Mosher, W. D. (2002). Cohabitation, marriage, divorce, and remarriage in the United States. *National Center for Health Statistics. Vital and Health Statistics 23*(22).

Brookmeyer, R., Corrada, M. M., Curriero, F. C., & Kawas, C. (2002). Survival following a diagnosis of Alzheimer disease. *Archives Neurology, 59*(11), 1764–1767.

Bureau of Labor Statistics. (2010a). Occupational outlook handbook, 2010-11 edition. Retrieved from http://www.bls.gov/oco/oco2003.htm#Labor%20Force

Bureau of Labor Statistics. (2010b). Usual weekly earnings of wage and salary workers fourth quarter 2010. *News Releases*. Retrieved from http://www.bls.gov/news.release/pdf/wkyeng.pdf

Bureau of Labor Statistics. (2011a). Employment status of the civilian noninstitutional population by age, sex, and race. Retrieved from http://bls.gov/cps/cpsaat3.pdf

Bureau of Labor Statistics. (2011b). Employment status of the civilian noninstitutional population by educational attainment, sex, race, and Hispanic or Latino ethnicity. Retrieved from http://bls.gov/cps/cpsaat7.pdf

Bureau of Labor Statistics. (2011c). Labor force participation rates among mothers. Retrieved from http://bls.gov/opub/ted/2010/ted_20100507.htm

Center for Medicare and Medicaid Services. (2010). National health expenditure data. Retrieved from http://www.cms.hhs.gov/nationalhealthexpenddata/

Centers for Disease Control and Prevention. (2010a). Life expectancy. Retrieved from http://www.cdc.gov/nchs/fastats/lifexpec.htm

Centers for Disease Control and Prevention. (2010b). National Diabetes Fact Sheet. Retrieved from http://www.cdc.gov/diabetes/pubs/estimates05.htm

Comondore, V. R., Devereaux, P. J., Zhou, Q., Stone, S. B., Busse, J. W., Ravindran, N. C., ... Guyatt, G. H. (2009). Quality of care in for-profit and not-for-profit nursing homes: Systematic review and meta-analysis. *British Medical Journal, 339*, b2732.

Cooney, M. T., Dudina, A., De Bacquer, D., Wilhelmsen, L., Sans, S., Menotti, A., ... Graham, I. M. (2009). HDL cholesterol protects against cardiovascular disease in both genders, at all ages and at all levels of risk. *Atherosclerosis, 206*(2), 611–616. doi: 10.1016/j.atherosclerosis.2009.02.041

Donoghue, C. (2006). The percentage of beds designated for Medicaid in American nursing homes and nurse staffing ratios. *Journal of Health and Social Policy, 22*(1), 19–28.

Erqou, S., Kaptoge, S., Perry, P. L., Di Angelantonio, E., Thompson, A., White, I. R., ... Danesh, J. (2009). Lipoprotein(a) concentration and the risk of coronary heart disease, stroke, and nonvascular mortality. *Journal of the American Medical Association, 302*(4), 412–423. doi: 10.1001/jama.2009.1063

Federal Interagency Forum on Age-Related Statistics. (2010). Older Americans 2010: Key indicators of well-being. Retrieved from http://www.agingstats.gov/agingstatsdotnet/Main_Site/Data/2010_Documents/Docs/OA_2010.pdf

Fields, J., O'Connell, M., & Downs, B. (2006, August). *Grandparents in the United States, 2001*. Paper presented at the annual meeting of the American Sociological Association, Montreal Convention Center, Montreal, Quebec, Canada.

Gaugler, J. E., Duval, S., Anderson, K. A., & Kane, R. L. (2007). Predicting nursing home admission in the U.S: A meta-analysis. *BMC Geriatrics, 7*, 13. doi: 1471-2318-7-13

Global Initiative for Chronic Obstructive Lung Disease. (2009). *Global strategy for the diagnosis, management, and prevention of chronic obstructive pulmonary disease*. Gig Harbor, WA: Medical Communications Resources, Inc.

Goodwin, P., McGill, B., & Chandra, A. (2009). Who marries and when? Age at first marriage in the United States: 2002. *NCHS Data Brief, No. 19, June*.

Green, T. L., & Darity, W. A., Jr. (2010). Under the skin: Using theories from biology and the social sciences to explore the mechanisms behind the black-white health gap. *American Journal of Public Health, 100 Suppl. 1*, S36–S40. doi: 10.2105/AJPH.2009.171140

Hamilton, B. E., Martin, J. A., & Ventura, S. J. (2010). Births: Preliminary data for 2008. *National Vital Statistics Reports, 58, No. 16*.

Harrington, C., Carrillo, H., & Blank, B. W. (2009). Nursing facilities, staffing, residents, and facility deficiencies, 2003 through 2008. Retrieved from http://www.pascenter.org/nursing_homes/nursing_trends_2008.php

Harrington, C., Carrillo, H., Blank, B. W., & O'Brian, T. (2010). Nursing facilities, staffing, residents, and facility deficiencies, 2004 through 2009. Retrieved from http://www.pascenter. org/nursing_homes/nursing_trends_2009.php

He, W., Sangupta, M., Velkoff, V. A., & DeBarros, K. A. (2005). *65+ in the United States: 2005. Current population reports special studies. U.S. Census Bureau, Current population reports, P23-209.* Washington, DC: U.S. Government Printing Office.

House, J. S., Kessler, R. C., Herzog, A. R., & Mero, R. P. (1990). Age, socioeconomic status, and health. *Milbank Quarterly, 68*, 383–411.

Hy, L. X., & Keller, D. M. (2000). Prevalence of AD among whites: A summary by levels of severity. *Neurology, 55*(2), 198–204.

Iyer Parameswaran, G., & Murphy, T. F. (2009). Chronic obstructive pulmonary disease: Role of bacteria and updated guide to antibacterial selection in the older patient. *Drugs and Aging, 26*(12), 985–995. doi: 10.2165/11315700-000000000-00000

Jorm, A. F., Windsor, T. D., Dear, K. B., Anstey, K. J., Christensen, H., & Rodgers, B. (2005). Age group differences in psychological distress: The role of psychosocial risk factors that vary with age. *Psychological Medicine, 35*(9), 1253-1263.

Kaiser Family Foundation. (2010). State health facts. Retrieved from http://www.statehealthfacts. org/savemap.jsp?typ=4&ind=180&cat=4&sub=47

Karakaya, M. G., Bilgin, S. C., Ekici, G., Kose, N., & Otman, A. S. (2009). Functional mobility, depressive symptoms, level of independence, and quality of life of the elderly living at home and in the nursing home. *Journal of the American Medical Directors Association, 10*(9), 662–666. doi: 10.1016/j.jamda.2009.06.002

Kawas, C., Gray, S., Brookmeyer, R., Fozard, J., & Zonderman, A. (2000). Age-specific incidence rates of Alzheimer's disease: The Baltimore Longitudinal Study of Aging. *Neurology, 54*(11), 2072–2077.

Kindig, D. A., Seplaki, C. L., & Libby, D. L. (2002). Death rate variation in US subpopulations. *Bulletin of the World Health Organization, 80*(1), 9–15. doi: 10.1590/ S0042-96862002000100004

Kinsella, K., & He, W. (2009). An aging world 2008: International population reports P95/09-1. Retrieved from http://www.census.gov/prod/2009pubs/p95-09-1.pdf

Knopman, D. S. (2007). Cerebrovascular disease and dementia. *British Journal of Radiology, 80 Spec No 2*, S121–S127. doi: 10.1259/bjr/75681080

Kreider, R. M. (2005). Number, timing, and duration of marriages: 2001. *Current Population Reports P70-97*. Washington, DC: U.S. Bureau of the Census.

Langford, A., & Johnson, B. (2009). Social inequalities in adult female mortality by the National Statistics Socio-economic Classification, England and Wales, 2001-03. *Health Statistics Quarterly, 42*, 6–21.

Lloyd-Jones, D., Adams, R. J., Brown, T. M., Carnethon, M., Dai, S., De Simone, G., . . . Wylie-Rosett, J. (2010). Heart disease and stroke statistics – 2010 update: A report from the American Heart Association. *Circulation, 121*(7), e24–e215. doi: 10.1161/CIRCULATIONAHA.109.192666

Macintyre, S. (1997). The Black report and beyond: What are the issues? *Social Science and Medicine, 44*, 723–745.

Manton, K. G. (2008). Recent declines in chronic disability in the elderly U.S. population: Risk factors and future dynamics. *Annual Review of Public Health, 29*, 91–113. doi: 10.1146/annurev. publhealth.29.020907.090812

Marmot, M. G., Shipley, M. J., Hemingway, H., Head, J., & Brunner, E. J. (2008). Biological and behavioural explanations of social inequalities in coronary heart disease: The Whitehall II study. *Diabetologia, 51*(11), 1980–1988. doi: 10.1007/s00125-008-1144-3

Moore, D. E., & Hayward, M. D. (1990). Occupational careers and mortality of elderly men. *Demography, 27,* 31–53.

National Center for Health Statistics. (2010). Marriage and cohabitation in the United States: A statistical portrait based on Cycle 6 (2002) of the National Survey of Family Growth. Series 23, Number 28. Hyattsville, MD: Vital and Health Statistics.

National Health Interview Survey. (2009). Early release of selected estimates based on data from the January-March 2009 National Health Interview Survey. Retrieved from http://www.cdc.gov/nchs/data/nhis/earlyrelease/earlyrelease200909.pdf

National Vital Statistics System. (2011). Births: Preliminary data for 2009. Retrieved from http://www.cdc.gov/nchs/data/nvsr/nvsr59/nvsr59_03.pdf

Organization for Economic Co-operation and Development. (2007). Table 1321. Percentage of the adult population considered to be obese. Retrieved from http://www.oecd.org/document/62/0,2340,en_2649_34489_2345918_1_1_1_1,00.html

Pamuk, E., Makuc, D., Heck, K., Reuben, C., & Lochner, K. (1998). *Socioeconomic status and health chartbook. Health, United States, 1998.* Hyattsville, MD: National Center for Health Statistics.

Pavalko, E. K., Elder, G. H., & Clipp, E. C. (1993). Work lives and longevity: Insights from a life course perspective. *Journal of Health and Social Behavior, 34,* 363–380.

Plassman, B. L., Langa, K. M., Fisher, G. G., Heeringa, S. G., Weir, D. R., Ofstedal, M. B., . . . Wallace, R. B. (2007). Prevalence of dementia in the United States: The aging, demographics, and memory study. *Neuroepidemiology, 29*(1–2), 125–132. doi: 10.1159/000109998

Pratt, L. A., Dey, A. N., & Cohen, A. J. (2007). Characteristics of adults with serious psychological distress as measured by the K6 Scale: United States, 2001-04. *Advance data from vital and health statistics, No. 382.* Hyattsville, MD: National Center for Health Statistics.

Sahyoun, N. R., Pratt, L. A., Lentzner, H., Dey, A., & Robinson, K. N. (2001). *The changing profile of nursing home residents: 1985-1997. Aging trends; No.4.* Hyattsville, MD: National Center for Health Statistics.

Schoenborn, C. A., Vickerie, J. L., & Barnes, P. M. (2003). Cigarette smoking behavior of adults: United States, 1997-98 *Advance Data from Vital and Health Statistics; no 331.* Hyattsville, MD: National Center for Health Statistics.

Schultz, S. K., Ellingrod, V. L., Moser, D. J., Kutschner, E., Turvey, C., & Arndt, S. (2002). The influence of cognitive impairment and psychiatric symptoms on daily functioning in nursing facilities: A longitudinal study. *Annals of Clinical Psychiatry, 14*(4), 209–213.

Simmons, T., & O'Connell, M. (2003). Married-couple and unmarried-partner households: 2000. Retrieved from http://www.census.gov/prod/2003pubs/censr-5.pdf

Social Security Administration. (2009). Fast facts and figures about Social Security, 2009. Retrieved from http://www.ssa.gov/policy/docs/chartbooks/fast_facts/2009/fast_facts09.pdf

Social Security Administration. (2010a). Fast facts and figures about Social Security, 2010. Retrieved from http://www.ssa.gov/policy/docs/chartbooks/fast_facts/2010/fast_facts10.pdf

Social Security Administration. (2010b). Status of the Social Security and Medicare programs. Retrieved from http://www.ssa.gov/OACT/TRSUM/index.html

Social Security Administration. (2011). Social Security basic facts. Retrieved from http://ssa.gov/pressoffice/basicfact.htm

Stanley, S. M., Amato, P. R., Johnson, C. A., & Markman, H. J. (2006). Premarital education, marital quality, and marital stability: Findings from a large, random household survey. *Journal of Family Psychology, 20*(1), 117–126.

U.S. Bureau of the Census. (2008). Projections of the population by selected age groups and sex for the United States: 2010 to 2050. Retrieved from http://www.census.gov/population/www/projections/summarytables.html

U.S. Bureau of the Census. (2009). 2008 national population projections tables and charts. Retrieved from http://www.census.gov/population/www/projections/tablesandcharts.html

U.S. Bureau of the Census. (2010a). America's families and living arrangements: 2009. Retrieved from http://www.census.gov/population/www/socdemo/hh-fam/cps2009.html

U.S. Bureau of the Census. (2010b). International data base. Retrieved from http://sasweb.ssd.census.gov/idb/worldpopinfo.html

U.S. Bureau of the Census. (2010c). U.S. Census Bureau reports men and women wait longer to marry. Retrieved from http://www.census.gov/newsroom/releases/archives/families_households/cb10-174.html

U.S. Bureau of the Census. (2010d). U.S. Interim projections by age, sex, race, and Hispanic Origin: 2000-2050. Retrieved from http://www.census.gov/population/www/projections/usinterimproj/

U.S. Bureau of the Census. (2010e). Unmarried and single Americans week: Sept. 19–25, 2010. Retrieved from http://www.census.gov/newsroom/releases/archives/facts_for_features_special_editions/cb10-ff18.html

U.S. Bureau of the Census. (2011a). The 2011 statistical abstract. Retrieved from http://www.census.gov/compendia/statab/cats/education.html

U.S. Bureau of the Census. (2011b). America's families and living arrangements: 2010. Retrieved from http://www.census.gov/population/www/socdemo/hh-fam/cps2010.html

U.S. Bureau of the Census. (2011c). Annual estimates of the resident population by sex and five-year age groups for the United States: April 1, 2000 to July 1, 2009 (NC-EST2009-01). Retrieved from http://www.census.gov/popest/national/asrh/NC-EST2009-sa.html

U.S. Department of Commerce Economics and Statistics Administration. (2011). Women in America: Indicators of social and economic well-being. Retrieved from http://www.whitehouse.gov/sites/default/files/rss_viewer/Women_in_America.pdf

U.S. Department of Labor. (2011). Quick stats on women, 2009. Retrieved from http://www.dol.gov/wb/stats/main.htm

Vincent, G. K., & Velkoff, V. A. (2010). The next four decades. The older population in the United States: 2010 to 2050. *Current Population Reports.* Retrieved from http://www.census.gov/prod/2010pubs/p25-1138.pdf

Whitbourne, S. K., & Willis, S. L.(Eds.). (2006). *The baby boomers grow up: Contemporary perspectives on midlife.* Mahwah, NJ: Erlbaum.

White, L. (2009). Brain lesions at autopsy in older Japanese-American men as related to cognitive impairment and dementia in the final years of life: A summary report from the Honolulu-Asia Aging Study. *Journal of Alzheimer's Disease, 18,* 713–725.

Whitlock, G., Lewington, S., Sherliker, P., Clarke, R., Emberson, J., Halsey, J., . . . Peto, R. (2009). Body-mass index and cause-specific mortality in 900 000 adults: Collaborative analyses of 57 prospective studies. *Lancet, 373*(9669), 1083–1096. doi: 10.1016/S0140-6736(09)60318-4

Whitton, S. W., Rhoades, G. K., Stanley, S. M., & Markman, H. J. (2008). Effects of parental divorce on marital commitment and confidence. *Journal of Family Psychology, 22*(5), 789–793. doi: 10.1037/a0012800

World Health Organization. (2001). The world health report 2001. Mental health: New understanding, new hope. Retrieved from http://www.who.int/whr2001/2001/main/en/index.htm

World Health Organization. (2009). Disease and injury country estimates. Retrieved from http://www.who.int/healthinfo/global_burden_disease/estimates_country/en/index.html

World Health Organization. (2010). Diabetes. Retrieved from http://www.who.int/dietphysicalactivity/publications/facts/diabetes/en/

Xu, Z., Kochanek, K. D., Murphy, S. L., & Tejeda-Vera, B. (2010). Deaths: Final data for 2007 *National vital statistics reports* (Vol. 58, No. 19). Hyattsville, MD: National Center for Health Statistics.

Xu, Z., Kochanek, K. D., & Tejeda-Vera, B. (2009). Deaths: Preliminary data for 2007 *National vital statistics reports* (Vol. 58, No. 1). Hyattsville, MD: National Center for Health Statistics.

3

Late Life

A Venue for Studying the Mechanisms by Which Contextual Factors Influence Individual Development

Denis Gerstorf and Nilam Ram

Theoretical accounts of developmental contextualism propose that individuals live in contexts and that those contexts shape fundamental aspects of human ontogeny across life through the affordances and limitations they place on development (P. B. Baltes, 1987; Bronfenbrenner, 1979; Elder, 1974; Lawton, 1982; Lerner, 1991; Magnusson & Cairns, 1996; Riley, 1987; Sampson, Raudenbush, & Earls, 1997; Verbrugge & Jette, 1994). The general idea is that microlevel and macrolevel contextual factors mold the nature and course of developmental processes occurring at the individual level. Consistent with these views, empirical research has produced a substantial body of evidence that, net of individual factors, contextual-level characteristics (e.g., socioeconomic disadvantage, neighborhood violence) are indeed linked with individuals' functional health, well-being, development, and mortality (Argyle, 1999; Balfour & Kaplan, 2002; Kawachi & Berkman, 2003; Krause, 2003; Marmot & Wilkinson, 1999; Ross & Mirowsky, 2001; Sampson, Morenoff, & Gannon-Rowley, 2002; Silver, Mulvey, & Swanson, 2002).

In this chapter, we consider further how the dialogue between theory and method informs how context may be integrated into our study of lifespan development (see also Gerstorf & Ram, 2009; Gerstorf, Ram, Fauth, Schupp, & Wagner, 2009; Nesselroade & Ram, 2004; Ram & Gerstorf, 2009; Ram, Gerstorf, Fauth, Zarit, & Malmberg, 2010; Ram & Nesselroade, 2007). To provide the conceptual backdrop, we first review central features of context typically associated with differences in individual development. Second, we propose that the final life phase (terminal decline at the end of life) provides a

The Wiley-Blackwell Handbook of Adulthood and Aging, First Edition. Edited by Susan Krauss Whitbourne and Martin J. Sliwinski. © 2012 Blackwell Publishing Ltd. Published 2012 by Blackwell Publishing Ltd.

particularly useful crucible for studying the mechanisms and pathways by which contextual factors influence individual development. This reasoning is based on the idea that late life constitutes the "ultimate stress test" in individuals' entire lifespan – thereby highlighting between-person differences and the contexts and mechanisms that may be contributing to those differences. To illustrate, we use emerging empirical evidence from studies of terminal decline in well-being. In a final step, we consider how contextual factors may serve as "risk regulators" (Glass & McAtee, 2006) that up-regulate or down-regulate the mechanisms and behavior patterns that put individuals at risk for or protect against terminal decline. Generally, we consider how risk regulators at a variety of different levels of analysis interact with individual regulatory systems to affect late-life development in well-being. We conclude by highlighting the potential, as well as some of the distinct challenges, of the developmental-contextual research agenda.

Contextual Influences on Development

Lifespan psychological and sociological perspectives have long suggested that individuals live in contexts that create both opportunities for and constraints on individual developmental pathways (P. B. Baltes, 1987; Elder, 1974; Magnusson & Cairns, 1996; Riley, 1987; Verbrugge & Jette, 1994). Many perspectives, including social disorganization theory (Faris & Dunham, 1939), human ecology (Bronfenbrenner, 1979), environmental gerontology (Lawton, 1982), or environmental psychology (Wohlwill, 1970), highlight the importance of ecological factors for development. For example, social disorganization theory (Faris & Dunham, 1939; Sampson et al., 1997) proposes that the characteristics of disadvantaged neighborhoods (e.g., poverty and residential instability) contribute to attenuated institutional strength, limited network interactions, diminished neighborhood attachment, and low levels of informal social control – factors that, in turn, contribute to individual-level outcomes such as increased risks for victimization and compromised mental health (e.g., depression and psychiatric disorders). In a related vein, notions of environmental gerontology highlight the critical role of both physical and social environments for the maintenance of functioning into late life (M. M. Baltes, 1996; Wahl & Lang, 2004). As a classic example, Lawton's (1990) environmental docility hypothesis suggests that such environmental features become increasingly important as personal competencies decline.

Making liberal use of these perspectives, we outline how four components of context (i.e., economic, service, social, and physical characteristics) common to most notions of developmental contextualism may be linked to individual-level development. We note that the distinctiveness of these components is primarily heuristic (rather than truly empirically based) and acknowledge that a given characteristic or indicator variable may be rightfully included within more than one component. Further, the nomenclature and specific definitions of what "socioecological context" is differs between the various disciplines of study, and important distinctions are often made between specific geographic or cultural features of the environment (e.g., communities vs. neighborhoods). Thus, with the "broad-strokes" approach we pursue here, the four-component structure is being used to describe a full range of contexts, from microlevel (apartment or proximal living environment) to macrolevel (e.g., neighborhood, city, or county; for overview, see Leventhal & Brooks-Gunn, 2000; Robert, 1999; Sampson et al., 2002; Wahl & Lang, 2004). Using select empirical findings for illustration, we use these four components to highlight generally that characteristics of the residential area people are living in are important for individual-level outcomes. Later we shall examine in more detail how these features of context are connected to individuals' development.

Central Features of the Context

Economic characteristics

Among the most frequently studied indicators of context differences (e.g., between neighborhoods, communities, countries) are average income, gross domestic product, rate of unemployment, extent of welfare arrangements and financial aids, level of poverty, and gross tax revenue. Clearly, outside of a few utopic communities, living environments differ in their local economics, often to a great extent. The structure and distribution of wealth in a home, neighborhood, community, tract, province, or country appears to shape and have profound implications for the progression of individuals' daily life. Drawing an example from investigations of childhood development, the effects of median tract income on children's reading and math abilities appear to be due, in part, to quality of schooling or the availability of and access to child care and services (for discussion, see Dearing et al., 2009). Local economic realities provide affordances or place constraints on development. In a similar vein, regions with low average income and high rates of unemployment are typically faced with the challenges associated with a shortfall in business tax revenue on the one hand and an excess of welfare expenses on the other hand. In turn, those poor economic structures impose limitations on investments into the provision of regional-level services and institutions, including the support for social programs or the availability and accessibility of health and long-term care facilities (e.g., fees and ancillary costs) that directly or indirectly influence individuals' health. More generally, economic markets and conditions at the regional level essentially shape the configurations of the other three components of context discussed in more detail below.

Service characteristics

Many of the developmental contextual perspectives mentioned above discuss the importance of the service environment and particularly the role that institutions (e.g., quantity, quality, density, availability, affordability, and accessibility) play in accommodating people's living needs and promoting people's healthy development (Leventhal & Brooks-Gunn, 2000). For example, communities often differ in the density and quality of institutions that provide health services. Communities with a dense system of high-quality health care may provide residents with more opportunity to maintain functional health and well-being in the face of debilitating diseases as compared with individuals living in communities with widely available health-care facilities. Greater numbers of doctors, registered nurses, hospital beds, or ambulatory care facilities per capita may allow for more robust provision of care. For example, some communities (e.g., wealthy ones) may differentially allow for, draw, and foster institutions (e.g., gyms and health promotion programs, public transportation, or senior citizens centers) that provide the wide variety of services that directly or indirectly affect resident's health and well-being (Browning & Cagney, 2003).

Social characteristics

A third category of commonly discussed and studied aspects of context are the social features of individuals' living, working, or leisure environments and mechanisms broadly tied to processes of social cohesion and collective efficacy (see Bandura, 1986; Sampson et al., 1997; Thompson & Krause, 1998). For example, residential instability, various forms of incivility (e.g., criminal victimization), or high levels of social mistrust are all factors that undermine the development or maintenance of social integration, positive affiliations with others, and a generally supportive and engaging community culture. The resulting lack of social ties and support may either have direct or indirect implications for health and well-being through mechanisms that play on individuals' ambitions, attitudes, and motivations, or via processes of informal social control such as monitoring, supervision, and the availability of role models (see Berkman, Glass, Brisette, & Seeman, 2000; Cohen & Wills, 1985; Cacioppo, Hughes, Waite, Hawkley, & Thisted, 2006; House, Landis, & Umberson, 1988; Seeman, 2001). The social features of environments can be operationally defined as social ties, role models, violence and crime, discrimination, social cohesion, or collective efficacy.

Physical characteristics

A fourth broad category of contextual factors that moderate, afford, or restrict individual health and well-being encompass the physical features of environment (Lawton, 1982). Physical factors include noise and pollution, sanitation, extent and accessibility of green space, and so forth (see Krause, 1996). For example, the disablement process model (Verbrugge & Jette, 1994) proposes that features of the built environment can make a profound difference in whether or not individuals' functional limitations become a disability. To illustrate, a woman with limitations in lower-body functioning (e.g., being able to walk only a couple of steps consecutively) may still be able to leave her house on a regular basis when she is living on the ground floor, but not when she is living on the sixth floor without an elevator (see also Clarke & George, 2005).

The above conceptual arguments map onto a series of empirical reports documenting that neighborhood-level characteristics such as socioeconomic disadvantages or violence are indeed linked with individual-level physical and psychological health variables, reflecting more physical health problems, less active lifestyles, reports of lower levels of well-being, and increased mortality hazards (Aneshensel et al., 2007; Krause, 1996; Yen, Michael, & Perdue, 2009). However, the great bulk of these studies has focused on outcomes in early phases of life such as childhood or adolescence and often has been cross-sectional in nature. We propose that key insights can be gained from examining how context factors relate to between-person differences in end-of-life development and senescence.

A "Stress Test" Paradigm for Examining Mechanisms

To achieve a better understanding of the mechanisms through which contextual factors influence individuals' development, we need "variance." Specifically, we need a venue where differences in individuals' behavior, experience, and attributes are expressed and can be readily observed.

To borrow an illustrative example from the Tour de France, the ordering of riders vying for the overall crown is usually decided during the steep climbs in the Pyrenees and Alps. As the racers describe it, these are the days that "explode the field" – the particular stages of the race when athletes push and are pushed to ride as hard as they can, uphill. The environment (here, the mountain roads) affords some riders an opportunity to excel, whereas it highlights the limitations of, or completely crushes, others. Between-person differences in the outcomes provide an indication of the mechanisms that contribute to riders' forward movement (e.g., lung capacity, blood-oxygen capacity, team organization, iron will, doping). Another example is the diagnosis of heart disease. Here, individuals are typically subjected to an exercise "stress test" wherein their cardiovascular reactivity and regulation is observed as their bodies are pushed towards their physiological limits (e.g., walking or running on a treadmill). Such paradigms have also been used in the examination of differences in cognitive plasticity. For example, in their "testing-the-limits" paradigm, Kliegl, Smith, and Baltes (1990) pushed individuals to the limits of their mental (learning) capacity so as to better measure and understand the mechanisms contributing to differences or "inequalities" in cognitive function and plasticity.

The general idea of these experimental paradigms is to produce a situation where between-person differences stand out in "bas-relief" and can be more easily observed. Differences in cardiovascular function are not so apparent when individuals are resting or going about their daily lives. Under "stress" conditions, in contrast, differences in functionality become readily apparent, can be diagnosed, and subsequently treated. Following this logic, we propose that stress test paradigms may also be useful in the study of developmental contextual processes. Natural experiments wherein individuals' adaptive capacities are being pushed to their limits should provide superb opportunities to observe differences (i.e., variance) and identify possible underlying mechanisms and pathways.

Late Life as the Ultimate "Stress Test"

Studies of late life and terminal decline suggest that impending death may provide a natural "testing-the-limits" paradigm for studying mechanisms of change. Conceptually, developmental changes during adulthood and old age result from primary or normal forms of aging, secondary or pathological aspects of aging, and tertiary or mortality-related processes of aging (Birren & Cunningham, 1985; Busse, 1969). Acknowledging that developmental change at the end of life reflects a combination of these three mechanisms, notions of terminal decline (Kleemeier, 1962) suggest that, as people approach death, mortality-related processes may rise to the forefront and become the major force underlying late-life development. The accumulation of mortality-related burdens and systemic dysfunction (e.g., in physical and/or cognitive health) should "stress" individuals' adaptive and regulatory systems – making it increasingly difficult for them to maintain health and well-being. In essence, approaching death serves as an absorbing state or "whirlpool" that drags individual functioning down. As this occurs and individuals fight against the "drag of the current," differences in capacity and development become increasingly visible. Some individuals can remain afloat, some can swim against the current, while others are dragged down quickly. The differences between individuals should become more pronounced – and thus provide the variance in trajectories of change essential for identifying and studying the mechanisms that contribute to development. At the same time, late life provides a kind of homogeneity. By definition, terminal decline will go on until expiration. All individuals' lives end in death. As such, late life provides an opportunity to study developmental mechanisms that are common across persons – much in the same way that childhood does (as an inverse phenomena). Although somewhat pessimistic in moral principle, late-life change processes in health and well-being may offer a unique opportunity to observe and understand some of the specific mechanisms that contribute to development.

Late-Life Development in Well-Being: An Emerging Example

Throughout adulthood and old age, average levels of well-being appear to remain relatively stable (Diener, Lucas, & Scollon, 2006). In recent years, however, evidence has accumulated that toward the very end of life well-being is prone to terminal decline (Berg, Hassing, Thorvadsson, & Johansson, 2011; Diehr, Williamson, Burke, & Psaty, 2002; Gerstorf, Ram, Estabrook et al., 2008; Gerstorf, Ram, Röcke, et al., 2008; Mroczek & Spiro, 2005; Palgi et al., 2010). In our own work, for example, we (Gerstorf, Ram, Mayraz, et al., 2010) used data from now deceased people in nationally representative samples in Germany, the UK, and the US to show that, on average, well-being was relatively stable over age, but declined rapidly when viewed in relation to impending death. These national-level replications are in line with conceptual notions of terminal decline – that the end of life is typically foreshadowed by a phase of precipitous decline. As such, late-life well-being provides an "ultimate stress"-based research paradigm for studying the mechanisms of development.

Inherent in the conceptual notion of terminal decline is that two phases of late-life change can be distinguished: a preterminal age-dominated phase of relative stability or minor decline, and a terminal, mortality-dominated, phase of precipitous decline (Kleemeier, 1962; Riegel & Riegel, 1972; Siegler, 1975; for overviews, see Bäckman

& MacDonald, 2006; Berg, 1996). Despite these conceptual notions having been around for decades, the literature lacks specificity regarding when the onset of terminal decline is expected to occur. For example, Birren and Cunningham (1985) proposed that a "cognitive and social slipping" may occur some "months to years" prior to death (p. 21).

Recently, researchers have been using multiphase growth modeling to locate the prototypical point of inflection – where precipitous terminal decline kicks in – empirically. For example, in studies of terminal decline in cognitive abilities, Sliwinski et al. (2006) and Wilson and colleagues (Wilson, Beckett, Bienias, Evans, & Bennett, 2003; Wilson, Beck, Bienias, & Bennett, 2007) located the transition from preterminal to terminal phases of decline within a window occurring between 2 and 6 or even 8 years prior to death (see also Sliwinski, Hofer, Hall, Buschke, & Lipton, 2003; Thorvaldsson et al., 2008). Applying similar methods to data on individuals' well-being, we have located the prototypical point of inflection as occurring between 3 and 5 years prior to death (see Gerstorf, Ram, Mayraz, et al., 2010). Before the transition, well-being is characterized by relatively little decline (e.g., in the national German data, 0.26 SD decline per 10 years). After the transition into the terminal phase, however, the average rate of decline steepens by a factor of three or more (e.g., in the German data, 1.31 SD decline per 10 years). The prototypical individual's well-being declines nearly a full standard deviation over the last 4 years of life.

These findings suggest that mortality-related mechanisms or other progressive processes leading towards death (e.g., deteriorating health) overwhelm the regulatory and motivational mechanisms that usually keep well-being stable and become the prime drivers of late-life decline in well-being. As expected, the severity of the decline occurring with impending death highlights the fragility and inefficiency of individuals' self-regulation capabilities and processes (see P. B. Baltes & Smith, 2003). Following this reasoning, individuals are getting pushed to their limits (or pulled down), but probably some people are in situations or have the capacity to stay afloat better than others. We propose that highly valuable information about the mechanisms of change is contained in the between-person differences in the decline people experience throughout the last years, and particularly in the timing of the terminal decline phase (after which, by definition, there is no recovery). To draw an analogy, one objective in the cardiovascular stress tests used to diagnose heart disease is to determine the inflection point at which individuals' heart rate suddenly shifts in response to increased workload. Valuable information about the mechanisms underlying stroke risk is contained in how between-person differences in the point of inflection in heart rate are related to between-person differences in the structure of the cardiovascular system (i.e., the context), particularly the extent of arterial blockage. Positive relationships among between-person differences in the point of inflection and such arterial blockage would provide support for the hypothesized mechanism of change.

Few investigations have attempted to empirically extract between-person differences in the onset of terminal decline, partly because the type of data needed have not been available. More specifically, the above reports noted prototypical transitions at the population level using the very strict assumption that the location of the inflection point does not vary across individuals. In other words, all persons were assumed to transition into terminal decline at exactly the same point in time. Relaxing this presumably unrealistic assumption requires extensive within-person change data. Using data obtained from 400 individuals who each provided 12 or more annual data points over 25 years, we were able to estimate between-person differences in the onset of terminal decline (see Gerstorf, Ram, Estabrook, et al., 2008). As expected, there were considerable between-person differences in where the estimated transition point was located. While individuals, on average, transitioned to the terminal phase at roughly 4 years before death, some individuals entered earlier (e.g., 6 or 8 years prior to death), others entered later (e.g., 2 years prior), and still others did not show any evidence of ever entering the terminal phase. These latter individuals likely did not experience the transition because they died earlier than expected, presumably of some "random" accident.

In sum, there are substantial between-person differences in how late-life well-being progresses. The stressors that accompany late life (e.g., loss of friends, loss of muscle mass, decline in health) are like or even exceed the mountain stages of the Tour de France. They "explode the field" and contribute to heterogeneity. Some individuals maintain their well-being, whereas others take a precipitous fall. The individual and contextual factors associated with this heterogeneity can provide some important clues and information about possible mechanisms of change. Thus a central goal is to identify the particular individual and contextual differences that are related to between-person differences in the timing and progression of terminal decline.

Contextual Influences on Late-Life Development in Well-Being

Why is it that the end of life constitutes a venue for studying how contextual factors, processes, and mechanisms operate to influence individual development? We have argued above that late life represents an ultimate stress test for individuals' adaptive and regulatory systems (see also P. B. Baltes & Smith, 2003). As a consequence, between-person differences are particularly pronounced in the final phases of life. This should make it easier to identify and study the factors and mechanisms that affect development. For illustration purposes, we have used emerging empirical evidence from late-life development of well-being. In the following, we draw from tenets of lifespan psychology to highlight that, in addition to the stress test reasoning, there are also strong theoretical arguments as to why late life provides a special opportunity to study the influence of contextual factors on development. P. B. Baltes (1997), for example, has argued that late life is characterized by an ever-increasing need for cultural resources and supportive environments to compensate for and adjust to the age-related increases in the biogenetic incompleteness of human life, which is manifested in health constraints and many other ailments. That is, to maintain the status quo as they age, individuals need more and more cultural resources. Unfortunately, the mechanisms by which those cultural resources help balance the continued loss also lose their efficiency with age. So the more the cultural resources are needed, the less efficient and helpful they are. Thus, the consequences of differences in the availability of cultural resources become exaggerated – a useful variance for identifying and studying context effects.

In a similar vein, Lawton's environmental docility hypothesis (1990) posits that environmental features are particularly important for the "needy" population segments (for discussion, see Subramanian, Kubzansky, Berkman, Fay, & Kawachi, 2006; Wight, Cummings, Karlamangla, & Aneshensel, 2009). Among older adults, for example, the cessation of participation in work environments means that the conditions of and social interactions in the residential environment (e.g., neighborhood) become more salient and significant (Cantor, 1975). Similarly, age-related increases in physical frailty and decreased mobility often result in greater feelings of vulnerability to and salience of environmental threats (Pearlin & Skaff, 1995; for discussion, see Bierman, 2009). For example, individuals' functional limitations, which are most prevalent near the end of life, may necessitate a greater dependency on the affordances provided by community resources and services. Individuals with access to those resources may continue to survive and do well, whereas those without may be prone to severe and quick decline. Together, all these theoretical views suggest that typical late-life declines make the person-context system that manifests at the very end of life particularly prone to displaying individual differences.

Empirically, cross-sectional evidence from adult samples provides some preliminary evidence that community effects are among the mechanisms that contribute to development and decline in well-being. For example, Shields, Price, and Wooden (2009) reported from an Australian data set that neighborhood effects accounted for approximately 3% of between-person differences in reports of life satisfaction (for similar reports from the UK, see Propper et al., 2005). Based on the above views of P. B. Baltes (1997) and Lawton (1990), we would expect contextual effects to be considerably more important during the end of life, particularly with respect to when terminal decline begins and the rate at which well-being decline proceeds. Individuals late in their lives should be particularly susceptible to the "life-lines" provided or not provided through sociocultural effects and mechanisms.

As a first step toward empirically addressing such conceptual notions, it would be necessary to quantify the contribution of community characteristics to between-person differences in late-life health and well-being. Multilevel variance decomposition techniques can be used to obtain a rough quantification of the extent to which individuals' environments shape late-life development. For example, using data from now deceased participants in a nationally representative sample from Germany, we were able to disentangle differences in late-life development that could be attributed to individual factors from differences attributable to county-level differences (as one instantiation of macrolevel community characteristics; see Gerstorf, Ram, Goebel, et al., 2010). Specifically, information about the geographic location of individuals' residences was used to construct a three-level growth model (occasions nested within individuals nested within regions/counties) to examine differences in individuals' developmental trajectories. Results indicated that regional differences accounted for a striking 8% of the variance in both current levels of well-being and rates of decline in well-being. We note that our models covaried for key individual-level correlates (age at death, gender, education, and household income), indicating that the effects of regional residency characteristics go beyond those provided by crucial individual characteristics (omitted variables notwithstanding). Our results suggest that a sizeable portion of individual differences are not due to differences between persons per se, but in reality reflect differences among the contexts (e.g., residential areas) where people live and die.

Such findings are important because they provide a rough quantification of the extent to which individual late-life development in a central aspect of quality of life is shaped by the structure of opportunities and constraints in one's living environment (and presumably the policies that determine those structures). Individual-level correlates of levels of well-being typically account for relatively minor portions of the variance, with education or personality characteristics of extraversion and neuroticism rarely exceeding effects of 4% (see meta-analysis by DeNeve & Cooper, 1998, Table 6). The size of our regional residency effect is instead comparable to that of individuals' health (10%: DeNeve & Cooper, 1998, Table 14). The effect size for regional characteristics on the rate at which well-being is changing is even more striking because correlates of (well-being) change are typically rare and often of minor size.

The evidence that regional differences indeed exist in terminal decline of well-being provides an important first step toward highlighting what might be gained from more in-depth study of contextual effects and mechanisms in late life. The next steps are to identify further which specific regional factors contribute to the noted between-person differences in order to better understand how macrolevel characteristics contribute to or regulate individuals' health and well-being (i.e., "get under the skin," Seeman, 2001).

Identifying Contextual Risk Regulators for Late-Life Development in Well-Being

What are the key regional factors that may help or hinder the fulfillment of personal needs? Unfortunately, it is not a straightforward matter to explore the role that the economic, service, social, and physical characteristics of context outlined above play in creating or regulating between-person heterogeneity in late-life development. Such complexities are well acknowledged in the social and behavioral sciences (see discussions on the fundamental causes of disease: House et al., 1990; Land & Yang, 2006; Link & Phelan, 1995). For example, social-contextual factors such as poverty, racial discrimination, or war typically do not "cause" detrimental outcomes in a strict sense (e.g., as a necessary and sufficient cause). Propagating or inhibiting factors can be located at multiple levels (e.g., at the societal level, at the household level) and the mechanisms that "connect" them to individual's lives are likely multifaceted, complex, and indirect.

Acknowledging the many intricacies involved in identifying the causal pathways by which contextual factors affect health, Glass and McAtee (2006) have begun using the concept of risk regulators. Adapting their framework to the study of late life, *risk regulators* are defined as characteristics or features of context that operate at a system level to propagate or inhibit (up- or down-regulate) the mechanisms that contribute to individual-level risks. Such context-level regulators do not act as protective or risk factors per se, but instead provide affordances for the adaptive and regulatory mechanisms that protect against and delay the onset of terminal decline or as constraints that increase exposure to or intensity of the maladaptive and disruptive mechanisms that promote functional decline and pathology.

In the following, we explore the concept of risk regulators and discuss how contextual features may propagate or inhibit terminal decline. Specifically, we consider how regional-level, national-level, and historical risk regulators, in interaction with individuals' adaptive and regulatory systems (and processes occurring at other levels), affect late-life development in well-being. We acknowledge at the outset that studying the mechanisms by which risk regulators operate is complicated by the fact that there is little opportunity to experimentally manipulate the conditions leading up to and surrounding individuals' deaths without severe moral dilemma. However, society has created and continually creates natural experiments. Some individuals are, through governmental policy or other decisions, provided with opportunities and/or resources, whereas others are not. These disparities/inequalities can be viewed as quasi-experimental designs. We explore here how these "manipulations" of contextual risk regulators may moderate development and allow for identification and study of the mechanisms through which risk regulators affect people's lives.

A Model of Risk Regulators and Late-Life Development in Well-Being

Underlying our application of the risk-regulator concept is the idea that there are individual differences in how late-life development proceeds. As indicated in the bottom portion of Figure 3.1, some individuals experience terminal decline early, some later, some with precipitous decline, some with less severe decline, and some not at all (and all the possible combinations of those trajectories). For simplicity, we build on assumptions that individuals whose "personal needs" are met and maintained have a better chance of preserving their well-being all the way until death (following from e.g., P. B. Baltes, 1997; Lawton, 1990). Specifically, when individuals have all the resources they need, their adaptive and regulatory systems keep them functioning well and aging successfully (i.e., no or delayed onset of terminal decline).

Note that in this scenario, there are two ways in which individuals' developmental trajectories may be affected. More distally, when resources are low (i.e., personal needs are not met), the adaptive and regulatory mechanisms do not have the proper "inputs" and cannot proceed smoothly (i.e., they become maladaptive or disorganized). As a consequence, functioning and development suffer. More proximally, the adaptive and regulatory mechanisms may themselves become compromised, disorganized, or fall into maladaptive patterns of early or severe terminal decline. While this is an extremely simplistic version of all the elements that foster (or inhibit) the emergence of developmental sequences, it highlights the separation of two general concepts – resources and processes. *Resources* encompass "things" that can be assigned a value – abilities, qualities, and other features of the individual that can be measured at a specific point in time. These are the "individual-level variables" in our models. Adaptive and regulatory *processes* instead encompass all the transformations that take a person from one state to another (Ford & Lerner, 1992). These are the mechanisms (e.g., self-regulation process) through which resources (e.g., self-regulatory abilities) play out over time – the "arrows" that we quantify with parameter estimates. We make this distinction because it maps heuristically onto how, in practice, risk regulator models may be tested empirically.

Context is depicted across multiple levels that span from individuals' immediate proximal environment (i.e., exact geographic location at any given moment, who they

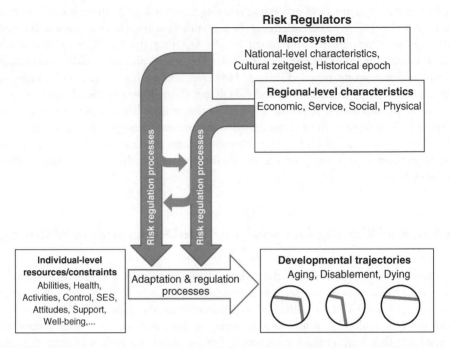

Figure 3.1 Working model of the contextual influences on late-life developmental trajectories. Underlying our model is the assumption that individual-level outcomes of aging, disablement, and dying processes are shaped by a configuration of individual-level and context-level characteristics and the way these factors operate and interact one another. We build on assumptions that individuals whose "personal needs" are met and maintained have a better chance of preserving their functioning all the way until death. Specifically, when individuals have all the resources they need, their adaptive and regulatory systems keep them functioning well and aging successfully (i.e., no or delayed onset of terminal decline). However, processes of adaptation and regulation are not only shaped by individual resources and constraints, but also by risk-regulation processes revealed by contextual factors at the regional level and those residing at even higher levels (e.g., macro-system). Created by Denis Gerstorf and Nilam Ram.

are conversing with) to the general social environments (e.g., cultural zeitgeists, historical epochs). Features or characteristics of these contexts (e.g., the economic, service, social, and physical features) are quantified as "context-level variables" (e.g., regional-level unemployment rate, neighborhood-level sidewalk and green space). "Context effects" manifest through a wide variety of mechanisms, many of which are unknown. These are the processes through which contextual features (the risk regulators) regulate lower-level processes. This may happen at multiple levels. For example, national-level or macrosystem (Bronfenbrenner, 1979) policies may regulate or influence the mechanisms by which regional-level governments can provide resources to their constituents. More proximal to individual development, household-level features (e.g., ramps vs. stairs) may regulate individual-level adaptation and regulation processes (e.g., locomotion within or around the home) by providing affordances for or putting constraints on those processes. That is, the contextual features (risk regulators) facilitate or inhibit the processes through which resources affect people's behavior.

Risk regulators: Regional-level characteristics

Earlier, we outlined four major components of context (i.e., economic, service, social, and physical characteristics) common to most notions of developmental contextualism that may be linked to individual-level development. Specifically, these frameworks suggest that the economic, service, social, and physical characteristics of people's residential environments can promote or constrain the adaptive and regulatory mechanisms and systems that contribute to individuals' maintenance and quality of life.

Regions differ in economic structure and resources. Impoverished regions are often characterized by an abundance of stressors that constrain individuals' mobility and pursuit of healthy daily routines. The accumulation of stress and limitations on the availability of compensatory resources over the long term may then corrode the adaptive and regulatory mechanisms (mental and physical health) of residents, thereby making them more vulnerable to late-life decline in well-being (Ellen, Mijanovich, & Dillman, 2001). In contrast, people living and dying in more affluent environments may not experience chronic exposure to stress, and can often rely on the structural provisions offered in the community. Thus they are more likely to be able to maintain well-being into the last phases of life, even though functional limitations will increasingly challenge their adaptive capabilities.

Both the quantitative and qualitative characteristics of regional institutions and services (e.g., local welfare arrangements, public health service, ambulatory care nursing availability) can be linked to late-life well-being. For example, inadequately structured public transportation services may place additional strain on individuals' adaptive capabilities. In contrast, placement of retail stores near residential living areas and provision of barrier-free and highly walkable sidewalks can facilitate individuals' adaptive and regulatory function and thus positively affect their quality of life and well-being. Federal and state governments often use communities, boroughs, or counties as units for the allocation of resources that may have substantial implications for the lives of their residents (e.g., communal family police; number of senior citizens' centers; and health promotion programs). Through taxes and legislation, boroughs and counties constitute a policy action unit that can provide health-promoting public goods for local residents, such as subsidized health care, municipal centers, and other local services and amenities (Kim, Subramanian, Gortmaker, & Kawachi, 2006). As a result, quantity and quality of services differ across regional settings in ways that may influence residents' development in late (and early) life (Subramanian et al., 2006).

Interactions of regional-level and individual-level characteristics

Deliberately interpreting and applying the Glass and McAtee (2006) framework in a manner that maps onto a multilevel modeling framework, risk regulators do not influence developmental outcomes directly, but they work by up- or down-regulating the processes through which individual resources and abilities influence the course of individual development. That is, the economic, service, social, and physical contexts in which people are living and dying facilitate, compensate for, or impose constraints on individuals' adaptive and regulatory systems. This interplay between adaptive and regulatory mechanisms and contextual factors is particularly highlighted in Lawton's (1990) environmental docility notion. Applied to the current context, Lawton's proposal was that contextual risk regulators have particularly strong effects when individual regulatory systems are fragile and vulnerable. Thus, rather than affecting individual-level outcomes directly, they interact with the individual systems. For example, regional-level structural disadvantage might not affect the course of development directly, but would rather exacerbate differences among persons – by providing or not providing means to do well in the ultimate stress test. To illustrate, we highlight two examples of how context-level risk regulators and individual-level regulatory systems may interact in shaping late-life well-being decline.

A first scenario for such cross-level interaction effects is that in more wealthy areas, risk regulators such as local welfare arrangements, public health services, public transportation, or financial aids provide resources and facilitate the mechanisms that compensate for and buffer the effects of scarce individual resources such as low income. As a consequence, disparities in the progression of late-life well-being may be less pronounced in structurally advantaged regions. In contrast, differences between individuals' trajectories may be profoundly exacerbated in structurally poor areas. Within these poorer settings, individuals with greater individual-level resources or abilities may know of, have access to, and be able to utilize additional resources outside the community, so as to compensate for scarce regional resources. Their resource-poor peers may be more strongly affected by any constraints imposed by the relative inaccessibility of regional-level resources. Results from our own empirical analyses (Gerstorf, Ram, Goebel, et al., 2010) are in line with these considerations. In particular, we found that regional risk regulators of wealth amplified the differences in developmental trajectories attributed to individual regulatory systems variables. Such findings have profound societal implications, for example, by highlighting that it is particularly the most vulnerable segments of society that suffer from the most detrimental effects (e.g., strongest decline among the least advantaged sociodemographic strata in the least privileged regions). Next steps would be to explore how targeted intervention programs can alleviate such cumulative disadvantage (see Dannefer, 2003; Marmot & Wilkinson, 1999).

Another scenario for such moderator effects revolves around the possibility that individuals with the same level of functional competency, but who live in different regional contexts, may develop in a dramatically different manner. For example, regions with few economic resources may not be able to repair dilapidated sidewalks or install elevators. As a consequence, individuals in these areas who have even the slightest worry of falling may become "disabled" – unable to complete their daily tasks because of the environmental constraints. In contrast, individuals living in relatively wealthy regions are afforded mobility across well-maintained sidewalks and by making use of working elevators – and remain "disability-free" because they are still able to complete their daily living tasks. It is the interaction between context and individual that accounts for differential behavioral outcomes (e.g., whether or not elderly people hesitate to go out for a walk, to meet friends and neighbors, and see the doctor; see Wen, Hawkley, & Cacioppo, 2006).

A key point here is that there are contextual-influence mechanisms working on individual-level mechanisms. For example, the social facets of the environment include level of social cohesion and collective efficacy. These are variables that describe specific characteristics of the environment. They influence individuals' lives through a variety of mechanisms including collective provision of social support, affiliation, identity formation, and so on. In turn, these processes up-regulate or down-regulate individual-level adaptive and regulatory processes such as maintenance of continuity and adaptive problem solving – processes that contribute to stability or vulnerability to decline in well-being.

National and Historical Characteristics

As per the multilevel modeling framework used to articulate and test such models, risk regulators moderate individual-level processes. Of course, the modeling framework allows for additional levels of analysis and additional layers of moderation. The underlying idea is that (risk) regulation processes at both the contextual and the individual level can be shaped by factors residing at even higher levels of context (e.g., macrosystem; for overview, see Figure 3.1).

National and cultural-level characteristics

For example, economic characteristics at the national level may influence or regulate the mechanisms driving the developmental trajectory of individuals' well-being. Wealthier nations typically have higher average levels of well-being (Easterlin, 2005), and some studies report that national-level changes in wealth and economic structure are accompanied by changes in average levels of well-being (Inglehart, Foa, Peterson, & Welzel, 2008; see, however, Diener & Oishi, 2000; Kahneman & Krüger, 2006). If true, a case could be made that national level characteristics moderate individual-level adaptation and regulation processes. For example, inequalities in well-being decline may be more pronounced in nations without public insurance systems for long-term healthcare as compared to nations that have such systems, particularly because those in the low to middle income range are at increased risk of losing financial resources in long-term care.

Following our assertion that between-person differences will be particularly pronounced late in life, we would generally contend that more nuanced differences in the amount of specific resources and the structure of the institutions that distribute those resources will manifest profoundly when specifically examining late life. Building on the models laid out by cross-cultural and cross-national research on well-being (for overview, see Oishi & Schimmack, 2010), global studies of late life will be useful in establishing and understanding the factors that regulate risks and the mechanisms by which national-level characteristics "get under the skin" (Seeman, 2001). In particular, examining whether or not individuals living in different nations follow substantially similar trajectories into death would shed light onto the pervasive or culturally bound nature of particular sociocultural processes that regulate individuals' adaptation and regulation. For example, the mechanisms invoked by obligatory health insurance, and how those mechanisms affect individual-level functioning, may differ substantially from the mechanisms at play under a voluntary system.

Historical time

Contexts are located within a place in history and are operated on by enduring time-related processes. Thus another level of analysis can be brought into the risk regulator framework. The regional- and individual-level processes that contribute to individual development may also be moderated by *historical time*. That is, risk regulators may become more or less relevant from decade to decade. One of the most prominent proposals relevant to historical changes in late life development is James Fries's notion of compression of morbidity (1980). The basic argument is that positive secular trends such as advances in medical technology and health care (i.e., the service environment, broadly defined) have helped to delay the onset of chronic diseases and shorten the period of morbidity, low functioning, and disability at the very end of life. Generally consistent with the notion, empirical evidence indicates that disability hazards are indeed lower for later-born cohorts (Crimmins, Hayward, & Saito, 1996; Graham et al., 2004; Manton, Gu, & Lowrimore, 2008, Robine, Romieu, & Michel, 2003). However, such reports have (almost) exclusively relied upon comparing birth cohorts at a similar range of chronological ages. We argue that a more direct test of the notion requires moving from examinations of age-related change to examinations of terminal decline. To the best of our knowledge, the timing of the transition to terminal decline and the rate of that decline have not been compared between nonoverlapping cohorts based on their year of birth or year of death.

In our own work, we have just started to move in this direction. As a first step, we have used longitudinal data from the Seattle Longitudinal Study to compare terminal decline trajectories in five cognitive abilities between earlier-born (1886–1913) and later-born (1914–1948) cohorts (see Gerstorf, Ram, Hoppmann, Willis, & Schaie, 2011). Interestingly, our mortality-related findings provided very little evidence for the positive secular trends often reported from age-related analyses, according to which the later-born cohorts are typically favored (Bowles, Grimm, & McArdle, 2005; Finkel et al., 2007; Schaie, Willis, & Pennak, 2005; Zelinski & Kennison, 2007). In contrast, the later-born cohort in our analyses experienced steeper mortality-related decline on four of the five abilities examined. We conclude that pervasive mortality-related processes overshadow and minimize cohort differences in cognitive functioning and change that were apparent earlier in life, probably because survival at the end of life becomes increasingly more "manufactured" (Olshansky, Hayflick, & Carnes, 2002). We note, however, the exploratory nature of our analyses, requiring further inquiry to substantiate these initial findings. It is an open question, for example, if and how well-being decline late in life is also steeper among later-born cohorts. Similarly, our operational definition of the compression of morbidity hypothesis focused on differences in rates of late-life decline. A more direct operational definition of the notion would focus on cohort differences in the onset of the steep end-of-life deteriorations, implemented via multiphase models of change (Gerstorf, Ram, Estabrook, et al., 2008). In the context of the present discussion, these results highlight that risk regulators and regulatory systems do not necessarily operate in the same manner in different historical epochs and in different phases of the lifespan.

In sum, working from the idea that late life provides a particularly useful crucible of "ultimate stress," we have explored how regional-level and individual-level characteristics may contribute to terminal decline in well-being. Specifically, we have considered how the conceptual models surrounding risk regulators and the associated contextual influences on individuals' late-life development can be tethered to the multilevel modeling analytic framework. In Figure 3.1, we have proposed a model that separates five distinct elements. Specifically, we consider three types of *variables/constructs* (represented as boxes in the Figure): (a) the individual-level outcomes of developmental trajectories represent the dependent variables, (b) the individual-level characteristics of individual resources and constraints represent Level-1 independent variables, (c) the context-level characteristics of risk regulators represent Level-2 independent variables. To quantify the relations among those variables, we consider two sets of *parameters/processes* (represented as arrows in the Figure). First, we examine individual-level processes of adaptation and regulation that can be rendered operational by the Level-1 associations between (a) and (b) – how individual-level resources and constraints shape individual-level developmental trajectories. Second, we examine interaction effects between individual processes and context characteristics that are operationally defined by moderation of the Level-1 associations – how individual processes of adaptation and regulation are shaped by contextual risk regulators. We very much hope that the explicit distinction and representation of variables, processes, and their interactions allows for an easier and more thorough empirical test of how contextual factors influence individual development.

Summary and Outlook

In this chapter, we have argued that late life represents a prime venue for studying the mechanisms by which contextual factors influence individual development. Our proposition was that such a conjoint consideration promises to benefit our understanding of how and why late-life processes progress and how factors that reside at levels beyond the individual operate. To do so, we first briefly reviewed a long tradition of research on the importance of economic, service, social, and physical features of the environment for individual functioning and development. We then used emergent evidence on well-being at the end of life to illustrate that late life constitutes a testing-the-limits situation for people's adaptive capacity. Because the pervasive nature of impending death brings a sharp end to the possibilities afforded by the system of self-protective processes, it should be easier to study between-person differences along with their antecedents, correlates, and consequences. Finally, drawing from research in other domains (Glass & McAtee, 2006), we have developed a working model of the contextual embedding of late-life well-being trajectories. Here we argue that contextual factors operate as risk regulators that up- or down-regulate behaviors and experiences, which in turn serve as risk factors for and protective factors against late-life decline. For illustration purposes, we have considered risk regulators at regional levels, in interaction with individual regulatory systems, and at further levels of analysis.

In closing, late-life well-being is often shaped by resources and constraints that are more distal to and not fully captured by individual-level measures typically included in studies of well-being correlates. More mechanism-oriented research is most certainly warranted to identify the specific contextual affordances and limitations that are of greatest importance when individual resources are declining most rapidly. Pursuing the line of research sketched in this chapter will help to identify and explain the unique and shared contributions of factors and processes operating at individual, regional, and national levels onto how well-being progresses late in life. In turn, these insights will inform social policy not only geared towards alleviating the imbalance between personal needs and environmental resources that arise at the end of life, but also positive development more generally in a key ingredient of quality of life, from childhood through adulthood and into late life.

References

Aneshensel, C. S., Wight, R. G., Miller-Martinez, D., Botticello, A. L., Karlamangla, A. S., & Seeman, T. E. (2007). Urban neighborhoods and depressive symptoms among older adults. *Journals of Gerontology: Social Sciences, 62B*, S52–S59.

Argyle, M. (1999). Causes and correlates of happiness. In D. Kahnemann, E. Diener, & N. Schwarz (Eds.), *Well-being: The foundations of hedonic psychology* (pp. 353–373). New York: Sage.

Bäckman, L., & MacDonald, S. W. S. (2006). Death and cognition: Synthesis and outlook. *European Psychologist, 11*, 224–235.

Balfour, J. L., & Kaplan, G. A. (2002). Neighborhood environment and loss of physical function in older adults: Evidence from the Alameda County Study. *American Journal of Epidemiology, 155*, 507–515.

Baltes, M. M. (1996). *The many faces of dependency in old age*. New York: Cambridge University Press.

Baltes, P. B. (1987). Theoretical propositions of life-span developmental psychology: On the dynamics between growth and decline. *Developmental Psychology, 23*, 611–626.

Baltes, P. B. (1997). On the incomplete architecture of human ontogeny: Selection, optimization, and compensation as foundation of developmental theory. *American Psychologist, 52*, 366–380.

Baltes, P. B., & Smith, J. (2003). New frontiers in the future of aging: From successful aging of the young old to the dilemmas of the fourth age. *Gerontology, 49*, 123–135.

Bandura, A. (1986). *Social foundations of thought and action: A social cognitive theory*. Englewood Cliffs, NJ: Prentice Hall.

Berg, A. I., Hassing, L. B., Thorvadsson, V., & Johansson, B. (2011). Personality and personal control make a difference for life satisfaction in the oldest-old: Findings in a longitudinal population-based study of individuals 80 and older. *European Journal of Ageing, 8*, 13–20.

Berg, S. (1996). Aging, behavior, and terminal decline. In J. E. Birren & K. W. Schaie (Eds.), *Handbook of the psychology of aging* (4th ed., pp. 323–337). San Diego, CA: Academic Press.

Berkman, L. F., Glass, T., Brisette, I., & Seeman, T. E. (2000). From social integration to health: Durkheim in the new millennium. *Social Science and Medicine, 51*, 843–857.

Bierman, A. (2009). Marital status as contingency for the effects of neighborhood disorder on older adults' mental health. *Journals of Gerontology: Series B: Psychological Sciences and Social Sciences, 64B*, S425–S434.

Birren, J. E., & Cunningham, W. (1985). Research on the psychology of aging: Principles, concepts, and theory. In J. E. Birren & K. W. Schaie (Eds.), *Handbook of the psychology of aging* (2nd ed., pp. 3–34). New York: Van Nostrand Reinhold.

Bowles, R. P., Grimm, K. J., & McArdle, J. J. (2005). A structural factor analysis of vocabulary knowledge and relations to age. *Journals of Gerontology: Series B: Psychological Sciences and Social Sciences, 60B*, P234–P241.

Bronfenbrenner, U. (1979). *The ecology of human development: Experiments by nature and design.* Cambridge. MA: Harvard University Press.

Browning, C. R., & Cagney, K. A. (2003). Moving beyond poverty: Neighborhood structure, social processes, and health. *Journal of Health and Social Behavior, 44*, 552–571.

Busse, E. W. (1969). Theories of aging. In E. W. Busse & E. Pfeiffer (Eds.), *Behavior and adaptation in late life* (pp. 11–32). Boston: Little & Brown.

Cantor, M. H. (1975). Life space and the social support systems of the inner-city elderly of New York City. *Gerontologist, 15*, 23–27.

Cacioppo, J. T., Hughes, M. E., Waite, L. J., Hawkley, L. C., & Thisted, R. A. (2006). Loneliness as a specific risk factor for depressive symptoms: Cross sectional and longitudinal analyses. *Psychology and Aging, 21*, 140–151.

Clarke, P., & George, L. K. (2005). The role of the built environment in the disablement process. *American Journal of Public Health, 95*, 1933–1939.

Cohen, S., & Wills, T. A. (1985). Stress, social support, and the buffering hypothesis. *Psychological Bulletin, 98*, 310–357.

Crimmins, E. M., Hayward, M. D., & Saito, Y. (1996). Differentials in active life expectancy in the older population of the United States. *Journals of Gerontology: Social Sciences, 51B*, S111–S120.

Dannefer, D. (2003). Cumulative advantage/disadvantage and the life course: Cross-fertilizing age and social science theory. *Journals of Gerontology: Series B: Psychological Sciences, 58*, S327–S337.

Dearing, E., Wimer, C., Simpkins, S. D., Lund, T., Bouffard, S. M., Caronongan, P., Kreider, H., & Weiss, H. (2009). Do neighborhood and home contexts help explain why low-income children miss opportunities to participate in activities outside of school. *Developmental Psychology, 45*, 1545–1562.

DeNeve, K. M., & Cooper, H. (1998). The happy personality: A meta-analysis of 137 personality traits and subjective well-being. *Psychological Bulletin, 124*, 197–229.

Diehr, P., Williamson, J., Burke, G. L., & Psaty, B. M. (2002). The aging and dying processes and the health of older adults. *Journal of Clinical Epidemiology, 55*, 269–278.

Diener, E., Lucas, R. E., & Scollon, C. N. (2006). Beyond the hedonic treadmill: Revising the adaptation theory of well-being. *American Psychologist, 61*, 305–314.

Diener, E. & Oishi, S. (2000). Money and happiness: Income and subjective well-being across nations. In E. Diener & E. M. Suh (Eds.), *Culture and subjective well-being* (pp. 185–218). Cambridge, MA: MIT Press.

Easterlin, R. A. (2005). Feeding the illusion of growth and happiness: A reply to Hagerty and Veenhoven. *Social Indicators Research, 75*, 429–443.

Elder, G. H., Jr. (1974). *Children of the Great Depression.* Chicago: University of Chicago Press.

Ellen, I. G., Mijanovich, T., & Dillman, K. N. (2001). Neighborhood effects on health: Exploring links and assessing the evidence. *Journal of Urban Affairs, 23*, 391–408.

Faris, R. E., & Dunham, H. W. (1939). *Mental disorders in urban areas: An ecological study of schizophrenia and other psychoses.* Chicago: University of Chicago Press.

Finkel, D., Reynolds, C. A., McArdle, J. J., & Pedersen, N. L. (2007). Cohort differences in trajectories of cognitive aging. *Journals of Gerontology: Series B: Psychological Sciences and Social Sciences, 62B,* 286–294.

Ford, D. L., & Lerner, R. M. (1992). *Developmental systems theory: An integrative approach.* Newbury Park, CA: Sage.

Fries, J. F. (1980). Aging, natural death, and the compression of morbidity. *New England Journal of Medicine, 303,* 130–135.

Gerstorf, D., & Ram, N. (2009). Limitations on the importance of self-regulation in old age. *Human Development, 52,* 38–43.

Gerstorf, D., Ram, N., Estabrook, R., Schupp, J., Wagner, G. G., & Lindenberger, U. (2008). Life satisfaction shows terminal decline in old age: Longitudinal evidence from the German Socio-Economic Panel Study (SOEP). *Developmental Psychology, 44,* 1148–1159.

Gerstorf, D., Ram, N., Fauth, E., Schupp, J., & Wagner, G. G. (2009). Between-person disparities in the progression of late-life well-being. In T. C. Antonucci & J. S. Jackson (Eds.), *Annual Review of Gerontology and Geriatrics: Vol. 29, Life course perspectives on late-life health inequalities* (pp. 205–232). New York: Springer.

Gerstorf, D., Ram, N., Goebel, J., Schupp, J., Lindenberger, U., & Wagner, G. G. (2010). Where people live and die makes a difference: Individual and geographic disparities in well-being progression at the end of life. *Psychology and Aging, 25,* 661–676.

Gerstorf, D., Ram, N., Hoppmann, C. A., Willis, S. L., & Schaie, K. W. (2011). Cohort differences in cognitive aging and terminal decline in the Seattle Longitudinal Study. *Developmental Psychology, 47,* 1026–1041. DOI: 10.1037/a0023426

Gerstorf, D., Ram, N., Mayraz, G., Hidajat, M., Lindenberger, U., Wagner, G. G., & Schupp, J. (2010). Late-life decline in well-being across adulthood in Germany, the United Kingdom, and the United States: Something is seriously wrong at the end of life. *Psychology and Aging, 25,* 477–485.

Gerstorf, D., Ram, N., Röcke, C., Lindenberger, U., & Smith, J. (2008). Decline in life satisfaction in old age: Longitudinal evidence for links to distance-to-death. *Psychology and Aging, 23,* 154–168.

Glass, T. A., & McAtee, M. J. (2006). Behavioral science at the crossroads in public health: Extending horizons, envisioning the future. *Social Science and Medicine, 62,* 1650–1671.

Graham, P., Blakely, T., Davis, P., Sporle, A., & Pearce, N. (2004). Compression, expansion, or dynamic equilibrium? The evolution of health expectancy in New Zealand. *Journal of Epidemiology & Community Health, 58,* 659–666.

House, J. S., Kessler, R. C., Herzog, A. R., Mero, R. P., Kinney, A. M., & Breslow, M. J. (1990). Age, socioeconomic status and health. *The Milbank Quarterly, 86,* 383–411.

House, J. S., Landis, K. R., & Umberson, D. (1988). Social relationships and health. *Science, 241,* 540–545.

Inglehart, R., Foa, R., Peterson, C., & Welzel, C. (2008). Development, freedom, and rising happiness. *Perspectives on Psychological Science, 3,* 264–285.

Kahneman, D., & Krueger, A. B. (2006). Developments in the measurement of subjective well-being. *Journal of Economic Perspectives, 20,* 3–24.

Kawachi, I., & Berkman, L. F. (2003). *Neighborhoods and health.* New York: Oxford University Press.

Kim, D., Subramanian, S. V., Gortmaker, S. L., & Kawachi, I. (2006). US state- and county-level social capital in relation to obesity and physical inactivity: A multilevel, multivariate analysis. *Social Science and Medicine, 63,* 1045–1059.

Kleemeier, R. W. (1962). Intellectual changes in the senium. *Proceedings of the Social Statistics Section of the American Statistical Association, 1,* 290–295.

Kliegl, R., Smith, J., & Baltes, P. B. (1990). On the locus and process of magnification of age differences during mnemonic training. *Developmental Psychology, 26,* 894–904.

Krause, N. (1996). Neighborhood deterioration and self-rated health in later life. *Psychology and Aging, 11,* 342–352.

Krause, N. (2003). Neighborhoods, health, and well-being in late life. In H.-W. Wahl, R. Scheidt, & P. Windley (Eds.), *Annual Review of Gerontology and Geriatrics* (vol. 23, pp. 223–249). Berlin, Germany: Springer.

Land, K. C., & Yang, Y. (2006). Morbidity, disability, and mortality. In R. H. Binstock & L. K. George (Eds.), *Handbook of aging and the social sciences* (6th ed., pp. 42–59). San Diego, CA: Elsevier.

Lawton, M. P. (1982). Competence, environmental press, and the adaptation of older people. In M. P. Lawton, P. G. Windley, & T. O. Byerts (Eds.), *Aging and the environment* (pp. 33–59). New York: Springer.

Lawton, M. P. (1990). Residential environment and self-directedness among older people. *American Psychologist, 45,* 638–640.

Lerner, R. M. (1991). Changing organism-context relations as the basic process of development: A developmental contextual perspective. *Developmental Psychology, 27,* 27–32.

Leventhal, T., & Brooks-Gunn, J. (2000). The neighborhoods they live in: The effects of neighborhood residence on child and adolescent outcomes. *Psychological Bulletin, 126,* 309–337.

Link, B. G., & Phelan, J. (1995). Social conditions as fundamental causes of disease. *Journal of Health and Social Behavior, 35*(extra issue), 80–94.

Magnusson, D., & Cairns, R. B. (1996). Developmental science: Toward a unified framework. In R. B. Cairns, G. H. Elder, & E. J. Costello,(Eds.), *Developmental science* (pp. 7–30). New York: Cambridge University Press.

Manton, K. G., Gu, X., & Lowrimore, G. R. (2008). Cohort changes in active life expectancy in the US elderly population: Experience from the 1982–2004 National Long-Term Care Survey. *Journals of Gerontology: Series B: Psychological Sciences and Social Sciences, 63B,* S269–S281.

Marmot, M., & Wilkinson, R. G. (1999). *The social determinants of health.* Oxford: Oxford University Press.

Mroczek, D. K., & SpiroIII, A. (2005). Change in life satisfaction during adulthood: Findings from the Veterans Affairs Normative Aging Study. *Journal of Personality and Social Psychology, 88,* 189–202.

Nesselroade, J., & Ram, N. (2004). Studying intraindividual variability: What we have learned that will help us understand lives in context. *Research in Human Development, 1,* 9–29.

Olshansky, S. J., Hayflick, L., & Carnes, B. A. (2002). Position statement on human aging. *Journals of Gerontology: Series A: Medical and Biological Sciences, 57A,* B292–B297.

Oishi, S., & Schimmack, U. (2010). Culture and well-being: A new inquiry into the psychological wealth of nations. *Perspectives on Psychological Science, 5,* 463–471.

Palgi, Y., Shrira, A., Ben-Ezra, M., Spalter, T., Shmotkin, D., & Kavé, G. (2010). Delineating terminal change in subjective well-being and subjective health. *Journals of Gerontology: Series B: Psychological Sciences, 65B,* 61–64.

Pearlin, L. I., & Skaff, M. M. (1995). Stressors and adaptation in late life. In M. Gatz (Ed.), *Emerging issues in mental health and aging* (pp. 97–123). Washington, DC: American Psychological Association.

Propper, C., Jones, K., Bolster, A., Burgess, S., Johnston, R., & Sarker, R. (2005). Local neighborhood and mental health: Evidence from the UK. *Social Science and Medicine, 61,* 2065–2083.

Ram, N., & Gerstorf, D. (2009). Time-structured and net intraindividual variability: Tools for examining the development of dynamic characteristics and processes. *Psychology and Aging, 24,* 778–791.

Ram, N., Gerstorf, D., Fauth, B., Zarit, S. H., & Malmberg, B. (2010). Aging, disablement, and dying: Using time-as-process and time-as-resources metrics to chart late-life change. *Research in Human Development, 7,* 27–44.

Ram, N., & Nesselroade, J. R. (2007). Modeling intraindividual and intracontextual change: Rendering developmental contextualism operational. In T. D. Little, J. A. Bovaird, & N. A. Card (Eds.), *Modeling contextual effects in longitudinal studies* (pp. 325–342). Mahwah, NJ: Erlbaum.

Riegel, K. F., & Riegel, R. M. (1972). Development, drop, and death. *Developmental Psychology, 6,* 306–419.

Riley, M. W. (1987). On the significance of age in sociology. *American Sociological Review, 52,* 1–14.

Robert, S. A. (1999). Socioeconomic position and health: The independent contribution of community socioeconomic context. *Annual Review of Sociology, 25,* 489–516.

Robine, J. M., Romieu, I., & Michel, J. P. (2003). Trends in health expectancies. In J. Robine, C. Jagger, C. D. Mathers, E. M. Crimmins, & R. M. Suzman (Eds.), *Determining health expectancies* (pp. 75–101). Chichester, UK: Wiley.

Ross, C. E., & Mirowsky, J. (2001). Neighborhood disadvantage, disorder, and health. *Journal of Health and Social Behavior, 42,* 258–276.

Sampson, R. J., Morenoff, J. D., & Gannon-Rowley, T. (2002). Assessing "neighborhood effects": Social processes and new directions in research. *Annual Review of Sociology, 28,* 443–478.

Sampson, R. J., Raudenbush, S. W., & Earls, F. (1997). Neighborhoods and violent crime: A multilevel study of collective efficacy. *Science, 277,* 918–924.

Schaie, K. W., Willis, S. L., & Pennak, S. (2005). An historical framework for cohort differences in intelligence. *Research in Human Development, 2,* 43–67.

Seeman, T. (2001). How do others get under our skin? Social relationships and health. In C. D. Ryff & B. H. Singer (Eds.), *Emotion, social relationships, and health* (pp. 189–210). New York: Oxford University Press.

Shields, M. A., Price, S.W., & Wooden, M. (2009). Life satisfaction and the economic and social characteristics of neighborhoods. *Journal of Population Economics, 22,* 421–443.

Siegler, I. C. (1975). The terminal drop hypothesis: Fact or artifact? *Experimental Aging Research, 1,* 169–185.

Silver, E., Mulvey, E. P., & Swanson, J. W. (2002). Neighborhood structural characteristics and mental disorder: Faris and Durham revisited. *Social Science and Medicine, 55,* 1457–1470.

Sliwinski, M. J., Hofer, S. M., Hall, C., Buschke, H., & Lipton, R. B. (2003). Modeling memory decline in older adults: The importance of preclinical dementia, attrition, and chronological age. *Psychology and Aging, 18,* 658–671.

Sliwinski, M. J., Stawski, R. S., Hall, R. B., Katz, M., Verghese, J., & Lipton, R. B. (2006). On the importance of distinguishing pre-terminal and terminal cognitive decline. *European Psychologist, 11,* 172–181.

Subramanian, S. V., Kubzansky, L., Berkman, L., Fay, M., & Kawachi, I. (2006). Neighborhood effects on the self-rated health of elders: Uncovering the relative importance of structural and service-related neighborhood environments. *Journals of Gerontology: Psychological and Social Sciences, 61B,* S153–S160.

Thompson, E. E., & Krause, N. (1998). Living alone and neighborhood characteristics as predictors of social support in late life. *Journals of Gerontology: Psychological and Social Sciences, 63B,* S354–S364.

Thorvaldsson, V., Hofer, S. M., Berg, S., Skoog, I., Sacuiu, S., & Johansson, B. (2008). Onset of terminal decline in cognitive abilities in individuals without dementia. *Neurology, 71,* 882–887.

Verbrugge, L. M., & Jette, A. M. (1994). The disablement process. *Social Science and Medicine, 38,* 1–14.

Wahl, H.-W., & Lang, F. R. (2004). Aging in context across the adult life course: Integrating physical and social environmental research perspectives. In H.-W. Wahl, R. Scheidt, & P. Windley (Eds.), *Annual Review of Gerontology and Geriatrics* (vol. 23, pp. 1–33). Berlin, Germany: Springer.

Wen, M., Hawkley, L. C., & Cacioppo, J. T. (2006). Objective and perceived neighborhood environment, individual SES, and psychosocial factors, and self-rated health: An analysis of older adults in Cook County, Illinois. *Social Science and Medicine, 63,* 2575–2590.

Wight, R. G., Cummings, J. R., Karlamangla, A. S., & Aneshensel, C. S. (2009). Urban neighborhood context and change in depressive symptoms in late life. *Journals of Gerontology: Psychological and Social Sciences, 64B,* S247–S251.

Wilson, R. S., Beck, T. L., Bienias, J. L., & Bennett, D. A. (2007). Terminal cognitive decline: Accelerated loss of cognition in the last years of life. *Psychosomatic Medicine, 69,* 131–137.

Wilson, R. S., Beckett, L. A., Bienias, J. L., Evans, D. A., & Bennett, D. A. (2003). Terminal decline in cognitive function. *Neurology, 60,* 1782–1787.

Wohlwill, J. F. (1970). The emerging discipline of environmental psychology. *American Psychologist, 25,* 303–312.

Yen, I. H., Michael, Y. L., & Perdue, L. (2009). Neighborhood environments in studies of health of older adults: A systematic review. *American Journal of Preventive Medicine, 37,* 455–463.

Zelinski, E. M., & Kennison, R. F. (2007). Not your parents' scores: Cohort reduces psychometric aging effects. *Psychology and Aging, 22,* 546–557.

4

Methodological Issues in Research on Adult Development and Aging

Scott M. Hofer, Philippe Rast, and Andrea M. Piccinin

The study of development, and particularly of adult development and aging, presents many challenges and has contributed a rich history of substantive and methodological debates and advances. The resulting innovative developmental designs, improvements in measurement for detecting within-person change, and statistical advances in dynamic modeling and population inference conditional on mortality and attrition are meeting many of these concerns. Central to progress in research on development and aging is a focus on within-person change and variation. In the first part of this chapter we highlight several of the conceptual distinctions that are essential considerations for the interface of theory, design, and analysis. Next, we discuss current issues, innovations, and challenges in the measurement and modeling of intraindividual and interindividual change. We then discuss some recent applications using these approaches, and some of the challenges and potential emphases for future research on adult developmental and aging-related processes.

Conceptual Issues at the Interface of Theory, Design, and Analysis

Normative and nonnormative developmental and aging-related change

Normative developmental processes are those which are strongly age-graded and occur in all or nearly all individuals. Nonnormative processes are those which occur in only a subset of the population and that are not necessarily associated with chronological age (Baltes &

The Wiley-Blackwell Handbook of Adulthood and Aging, First Edition. Edited by Susan Krauss Whitbourne and Martin J. Sliwinski. © 2012 Blackwell Publishing Ltd. Published 2012 by Blackwell Publishing Ltd.

Nesselroade, 1979). Good examples of this distinction and its utility in research in adult development and aging are available in the area of cognitive aging. In terms of theories of cognitive aging, the most prominent normative accounts of cognitive aging are common process theories such as the generalized slowing hypothesis (e.g., Birren & Fisher, 1995; Myerson, Hale, Wagstaff, Poon, & Smith 1990; Salthouse, 1988, 1996) or the common cause hypothesis (Baltes & Lindenberger, 1997; Lindenberger & Baltes, 1994). The general slowing hypothesis is based on results from a considerable number of studies that find age differences in a variety of other cognitive functions to be substantially accounted for by individual differences in speed of processing. Similarly, in terms of the common cause hypothesis, a general conclusion from many studies (see Hofer, Berg, & Era, 2003 for review) is that the majority of age-related variance in cognitive abilities is accounted for by age-related differences in a broad variety of sensory–motor functioning (though most notably in visual and auditory acuity).

Nearly all of the support for these findings is based on cross-sectional studies and analysis of between-person age differences. There are, of course, a number of alternative explanations for such findings, including operational confounds associated with peripheral sensory loss; cohort and individual differences in socioeconomic status, health, and nutrition; mortality and health-related decline in older populations (i.e., terminal decline); and inferential problems that result from analysis of between-person age differences. In addition to the numerous confounds associated with inference regarding aging-related change from cross-sectional data, a major problem with these normative theories is that potentially confounding or explanatory variables are often not included in the model. Among the most prominent nonnormative factor is that of health. Health conditions are considered to be nonnormative because the majority of individuals will not experience these events, although the risk for particular health conditions and comorbidity in the population increases with age. From this perspective, including heterogeneous types of health-related and physiological changes within and across individuals as explanatory variables is likely to be a more fruitful approach than making inferences based on chronological age only (e.g., MacDonald, DeCarlo, & Dixon, 2011).

Ergodicity: Expectations for understanding within-person aging-related change based on between-person age differences

Most of the research that has supported general factor theories of cognitive aging, such as the general slowing, common cause associated with sensory acuity and cognition, and dedifferentiation hypotheses, has been cross-sectional and therefore based on the analysis of individuals of differing ages. The assumption has been that between-person age differences provide an appropriate representation of within-person age changes. Much of what we take as established empirical findings (e.g., the centrality of speed) is grounded in analyses that depend upon the untested assumption of ergodicity (Molenaar, 2004, 2008).

Testing such theories using within-person designs is critical given the numerous limitations for understanding developmental and aging processes using between-person age comparison (Molenaar, 2004; Sliwinski & Hofer, 1999). For example, longitudinal studies have shown a disassociation between cross-sectional and longitudinal speed mediation effects (e.g., Hultsch, Hertzog, Small, McDonald-Miszczk, & Dixon, 1992). Sliwinski and Buschke (1999) showed that within-person declines in speed do not mediate within-person declines in memory function, although they observed the typical speed mediation effect at the between-person level of analysis. The reliance on cross-sectional, between-person information is a major shortcoming that must be remedied for theoretical and methodological progress in aging research (Hofer & Sliwinski, 2001; Hofer, Flaherty, & Hoffman, 2006; Kraemer, Yesavage, Taylor, & Kupfer, 2000; Sliwinski & Hofer, 1999).

Reactivity in longitudinal studies

On a variety of performance and functional assessments, individuals perform better with repeated testing. This phenomenon is known as retest, practice, exposure, learning, or reactivity, and has been reported in a number of longitudinal studies of aging (e.g., Ferrer, Salthouse, Stewart, & Schwartz, 2004; Hultsch, Hertzog, Dixon, & Small, 1998; Rabbitt, Diggle, Smith, Holland, & McInnes, 2001; Schaie, 1988, 1996). However, the overlapping temporal dimensions of retest and aging directly confound estimates of long-term change (e.g., Sliwinski, Hoffman, & Hofer, 2010b). A further complication is that individuals are likely to differ from one another in terms of amount of gain due to retesting or learning in systematic ways related to level of ability, cohort, age and test-specific learning, such as learning content and strategies.

Conditional population inference

In longitudinal aging studies, at each new wave of testing the sample becomes less representative of the population from which it originated, and generalizations from the sample of continuing participants to the initial population become difficult to justify (Nesselroade, 1988; Vaupel & Yashin, 1985). Whereas some forms of nonparticipation can logically permit inference to a single population, in the case of mortality, inference is impossible because individuals have left the population of interest. In this case, inferences must be defined as conditional on the probability of surviving and/or remaining in the study (e.g., Hofer & Hoffman, 2007; Kurland, Johnson, Egleston & Diehr, 2009). In addition, the incomplete data mechanism in studies of aging is not likely to be "missing at random," the major assumption of these standard incomplete data methods, because aging-related outcomes are known to be related to mortality and study nonparticipation (e. g., Cooney, Schaie, & Willis, 1988; Rabbitt, Watson, Donlan, Bent, & McInnes, 1994; Riegel, Riegel, & Meyer, 1967; Siegler & Botwinick, 1979; Streib, 1966), which can be as high as 50% from occasion to occasion.

In age-heterogeneous samples, whether data collection is cross-sectional or longitudinal, unambiguous inference to between-person differences in level of aging-related processes is not possible in the aggregate sample because initial sample selection is confounded with population mortality and other sources of heterogeneity. In the case of longitudinal follow-up, however, individual and population change processes can be evaluated and interpreted. Inference regarding aging-related changes requires the estimation of population parameters that are conditional on morbidity, mortality and other attrition processes. (e.g., Diehr & Patrick, 2003; DuFouil, Brayne, & Clayton, 2004; Harel, Hofer, Hoffman, Pedersen, & Johansson, 2007; Kurland et al., 2009).

Analytic Approaches for Understanding Within-Person Change and Variation

In longitudinal studies, a variety of statistical approaches can be used for the estimation of change and the interaction of change processes related to health and psychosocial indicators. Analyses can be based on complementary statistical models that include latent growth curve models, piecewise latent growth curve models, within-person coupled change, growth mixture models, or other models of change.

Random coefficients (latent growth curve) models: Estimating initial status and rate of change

Latent growth curve modeling (i.e., random coefficients or multilevel models) is commonly used for analysis of longitudinal data. Repeated measurement designs yield at least two levels of analysis: The Level 1 model summarizes individual level outcome data at three or more occasions in terms of "true" initial level of performance (intercept), slope (improvement or rate of change), and error (residual) parameters. The Level 2 model estimates fixed (i.e., average) and random (i.e., individually varying) interindividual and intraindividual differences and can include predictors of individual/group differences in Level 1 parameters (i.e., intercept, slope). Detailed descriptions of these methods are available elsewhere (e.g., Ferrar & McArdle, 2003; McArdle, 1988, McArdle & Epstein, 1987; McArdle & Hamagami, 1992; Raudenbush & Bryk, 2002; Singer & Willett, 2003; Snijders & Bosker, 1999; Verbeke & Molenberghs, 2000). Conceptually, growth curve analysis involves estimating within-individual regressions of performance on time and on expected predictors of these individual regression parameters.

In these models, a level and a slope parameter are generally specified for change relative to a particular time metric. A common choice is to define the level as the initial point of measurement in a longitudinal data set whereas the slope parameter captures the rate of change over time. Especially in models with higher order terms or interactions (including all models with predictors of slope variance) the choice of the centering influences the interpretation of the parameters (cf. Biesanz, Deeb-Sossa, Papadakis, Bollen, & Curran, 2004). The intercept or initial level should be carefully chosen to reflect the hypotheses tested in this context.

It is necessary to consider sample age heterogeneity in all cross-sectional or longitudinal models. Unlike traditional single-cohort longitudinal designs, a majority of longitudinal studies sample individuals that vary substantially in age (and birth cohort membership) at each wave in the study, and the range of these between-person, cross-sectional, age differences tends to exceed the range of within-person, longitudinal, age changes over the course of data collection. Earlier in the development of growth curve analysis, when balanced data were required, the cross-sectional and longitudinal aspects of the data were separated by including initial between-person age differences as a covariate of estimated trajectory intercepts and slopes based on time defined as study wave or elapsed time from the first wave. As methods for dealing with missing data improved, these age-heterogeneous samples were seen as an opportunity to virtually "accelerate" longitudinal designs (e.g., McArdle & Bell, 2000; Mehta & West, 2000), by representing time as the different ages available in the study, rather than as time since the inception of the study. As software has developed to handle extremely sparse data matrices, there has been a significant shift toward using age, rather than time, as the basis upon which to represent change. Without the continued inclusion of baseline age differences, however, the resulting model produces estimates that represent a mix of the cross-sectional and longitudinal effects.

It is important to test explicitly for "convergence" of these between-person and within-person fixed (i.e., average) effects, as indicated by whether or not between-person age is a significant predictor of intercept and/or slope in an age-based model (Sliwinski, Hoffman, & Hofer, 2010a). In general, the time-in-study model conditional on initial between-person chronological age may be the best choice as baseline model for several reasons, both substantive and methodological. For example, age-based models typically require polynomial functions to account for the curvilinearity of overall change, whereas time-in-study models do this parsimoniously in terms of between-person age moderation of linear slopes. When between-person age is not included as a covariate in the age-based model, age differences and age changes are inappropriately aggregated and birth cohort effects (which are often assumed to be negligible) are ignored.

For random effects models using chronological age as the time basis, it is important to keep in mind the variance component shrinkage due to the extrapolation beyond individual data (i.e., random effects will be estimated closer to the population mean; e.g., Raudenbush & Bryk, 2002, Ch. 5). With greater age heterogeneity than study duration, the population mean will be dominated by the cross-sectional information. In addition, the confounding of between-person age differences and within-person age changes in longitudinal models muddles the potential for inference to increasingly selective, and thus conditional, "aging" populations. Selectivity of participants must be accounted for because between-person sampling will be based on the proportion of the population who are alive (population mortality selection) and healthy but will also drop out from the study due to health and mortality causes. Inference to aging populations must, therefore, be conditional on survival, and may be more directly obtained using between-person age differences and survival age (or time-to-death) as conditional predictors in a time-in-study longitudinal model (e.g., Johansson et al., 2004; Hoffman, in press).

Modeling change across alternative temporal metrics

It is often useful to consider alternative ways of clocking time, such as distance to death, or time elapsed since a health or life event (e.g., retirement, death of spouse, cardiac event; see, e.g., Alwin, Hofer, & McCammon, 2006; Hofer & Sliwinski, 2006; Hoffman, in press; Piccinin, Muniz, Matthews, & Johansson, 2011; Sliwinski & Buschke, 2004; Sliwinski, Hofer, & Hall, 2003; Sliwinski, Hofer, Hall, Bushke, & Lipton 2003; Thorvaldsson, Hofer, & Johansson, 2006). Structuring time as an event-defined process permits direct interpretation of the average trajectory and individual differences in change relative to a common underlying within-person process. We can evaluate statistically whether alternative or multiple temporal axes account better for between-person individual differences in change in cognitive outcomes than more typical time-in-study or age-conditional metrics (using information criteria: Akaike, AIC, or Bayesian, BIC; see Hoffman, in press). As mentioned above, the selection of where on the time axis the intercept (i.e., level) is chosen may be critical and must be adapted to the research goals.

Related to fitting alternative temporal structures, different trajectories of change can be fit over different temporal intervals using piecewise linear growth curve models. In the basic latent growth curve approach, linear and quadratic slope parameters can be used to describe performance across repeated measurements, and individual differences are parameterized as deviations from these slopes. In contrast, piecewise growth curve models permit the estimation of multiple slope factors for distinct periods of measurement, such as before and after diagnosis, as well as correlated rates of change across these distinct periods (e.g., Jones & Meredith, 2000). With advancing age, the probability of suffering from cardiovascular or other events, which can have an immediate effect on cognitive functioning, are increasing. We need to be able to model these abrupt changes and relate them to exogenous variables.

Mixture models of growth processes

Recent developments in growth mixture modeling permit the identification of subpopulations that exhibit distinct multivariate patterns of change. Like latent class models, mixture models assume that the sample is composed of members from more than one population. In such analyses, the emphasis is less on individual differences and more on general group trends that capture individual-level change. Growth mixture models (e.g., Muthén, 2001) can be used to ascertain qualitative characteristics that distinguish growth subgroups within a population using individual and group variables. The effect of covariates on the latent class portion of the model can be examined to provide potentially useful information on the characteristics of the individuals assigned to each class.

Population inference in the context of mortality and attrition

Population mortality and related changes in health are the primary causes of selection in cross-sectional samples and attrition in longitudinal studies on aging. Mortality is a natural population dynamic and is accessible only in longitudinal studies. Incomplete data resulting from mortality, morbidity, and other causes must be considered in the statistical analysis and interpretation of findings from studies of aging. While state-of-the-art techniques for treating incomplete data have been developed (e.g., Schafer, 1997; Schafer & Graham, 2002) and are in relatively wide use, the application of these methods to longitudinal samples in late life remains problematic, both conceptually and computationally. Naive use of maximum likelihood estimation for longitudinal analysis (assuming missing at random; i.e., missingness is related to included covariates and previously measured outcomes) relies on the notion of a single, accessible population (e.g., Kurland et al., 2009). The cross-sectional and longitudinal sources of population selection should be considered and modeled by including between-person age differences at the first occasion and survival age differences (or time-to-death from the first occasion) to permit conditional inferences to defined populations of aging individuals (e.g., Hofer & Hoffman, 2007).

Estimating the effects of repeated testing

Statistical procedures have been proposed to directly model retest effects (i.e., Ferrer et al., 2004; McArdle, Ferrer-Caja, Hamagami, & Woodcock, 2002; Rabbitt et al., 2001), requiring modeling of both between-person age differences and within-person changes over time, with limitations if the age-structure closely approximates the time-in-study intervals. A recent innovation in the estimation of practice effects is based on specifying a piecewise linear growth curve model (Ferrer et al., 2004; McArdle et al., 2002; Rabbitt et al., 2001). However, estimation of separate parameters related to exposure to test (i.e., number of repeated occasions) requires an age-based modeling approach in conjunction with a specification of "test exposure" interpreted as retest gains (e.g., Hoffman, Hofer, & Sliwinski, in press; Thorvaldsson, Hofer, Hassing, & Johansson, 2008). As discussed above regarding the age-based approach, there is potential for confounding of effects due to between-person differences and within-person changes and this is particularly the case when both within-person age changes and test exposure are based on essentially the same temporal metric (e.g., widely spaced test intervals).

Methodological Applications in Developmental and Aging Research

The assumption often made in studies of aging-related change is that between-person differences provide an appropriate representation of within-person changes. Longitudinal studies of long-term change have an important role in confirming or disconfirming theories and hypotheses of aging, and permit the direct analysis of influences that have been demonstrated only as "tenable" by cross-sectional analysis of individual differences.

Evidence for correlated rates of change in longitudinal studies on aging

Multivariate latent growth curve models are quite flexible and permit direct assessment of correlated level and rates of change across variables (e.g., Hofer et al., 2009; Johansson et al., 2004; Sayer & Willett, 1998; Sliwinski, Hofer, & Hall, 2003; Wilson, Yan, Bienias, & Bennett, 2006). The structure of individual differences in change provides a basis for understanding the relative independence or interdependence of aging-related processes within the population. Such models should include time-invariant and time-varying covariates and their interactions representing individual differences in chronological age, context, or health status to account for potential confounds that may bias associations among change processes. For example, sample age heterogeneity could lead to inflated associations among rates of change if, on average, older adults change more rapidly than younger adults (Hofer & Sliwinski, 2001; Hofer, Flaherty, & Hoffman, 2006).

Longitudinal evidence does not tend to support the single-mechanism or common factor theories of cognitive aging that have been so successful in accounting for results from between-person cross-sectional age comparisons (e.g., Verhaegen & Salthouse, 1997). Longitudinal studies do provide some evidence that cognitive change across domains is correlated at both the between-person and within-person level (Sliwinski & Buschke, 1999; Sliwinski, Hofer, & Hall, 2003). However, the within-person effects are relatively weak or moderate (e.g., Anstey, Hofer, & Luszcz, 2003; Hultsch et al., 1992; Johansson et al., 2004; Wilson et al., 2006; Zimprich & Martin, 2002) compared to cross-sectional results of shared age-related variance, and do not support the strong theoretical claims that a common aging factor drives most of the cognitive loss experienced by aging adults. Indeed, the most important predictors of cognitive change to date have been variables that measure disease status and progression (e.g., Haan, Shemanski, Jagust, Manolio, & Kuller, 1999; Hall, Lipton, Sliwinski, & Stewart, 2000; Rubin et al., 1998). One reason for why common-factor models work better in accounting for cross-sectional data than longitudinal data is that cross-sectional designs are confounded with mean trends and do not permit sensitive assessment of the myriad of dynamic and progressive processes that can cause aging-related decline (e.g., Hofer & Sliwinski, 2001; Hofer, Sliwinski, & Flaherty, 2002; Kraemer et al., 2000).

When interpreting correlated rates of change, it is important to consider the aggregation of potential subgroups of individuals and to use appropriate statistical models (include covariates and interactions; account for incomplete data due to mortality/attrition). For example, Sliwinski, Hofer, and Hall (2003) estimated correlations among measures of memory, speed, and verbal fluency in the Einstein Aging Study, including, for the individuals with incident dementia only, the data obtained prior to the diagnosis. Between-person correlations among rates of change were moderate and consistent (.56 –.61), but were attenuated (.34–.48) when individuals with preclinical dementia were removed. In individuals with eventual dementia diagnosis, individual differences in rates of change were close to zero when a disease process model (time-to-diagnosis) was applied to model change. This demonstrates how aggregation of heterogeneous groups of individuals (e.g., those with and without dementia) can lead to inappropriate inferences regarding high correlations among rates of change. In addition, change over time and multivariate associations among rates of change are likely to be related to individual characteristics, such as education and occupational status, which provide the context for health and risk behaviors.

Coupled within-person processes

In longitudinal studies on aging with widely spaced assessments, short-term variations in functioning are assumed to be small relative to long-term changes. Indeed, if short-term

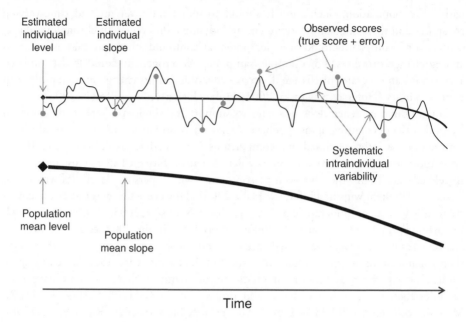

Figure 4.1 Hypothetical observed scores vs individual/population slope over time. Figure reproduced from Hofer & Piccinin (2010) by permission of Oxford University Press.

temporal variability is moderate to high, then single assessments produce imprecise estimates of an individual's characteristic level of cognitive functioning. This has major implications for estimates of individual change. Figure 4.1 shows how a repeated series of measurements can be decomposed into population average level and slope, individual deviation from level and slope, and systematic variation (time-varying) about the individual-level slope as distinct from random error (although in most designs this is indistinguishable from systematic variation). Although the typical focus on long-term change has not featured short-term variation, or has modeled such phenomena as nuisance parameters, short-term intraindividual variability can be an interesting outcome in itself. Sufficient empirical evidence now exists to establish intraindividual cognitive variability as a substantial source of systematic performance variability between persons (Almeida & McDonald, 1998), in younger individuals (e.g., Hofer et al., 2009) but perhaps especially in older adults (Eizenman, Nesselroade, Featherman, & Rowe, 1997; Horn, 1972; Martin & Hofer, 2004; Nesselroade, 2001, 2004; Sliwinski, Smyth, Hofer, & Stawski, 2006), and encourages greater emphasis on within-person dynamic models (e.g., Siegler, 1994).

Longitudinal designs with widely spaced intervals also permit formulation and empirical test of hypotheses about the processes influencing intraindividual variation. In the context of such studies, the focus is on associations among occasion-specific residuals after accounting for individual and population trajectories. Such within-person correlations address the occasion-to-occasion dynamics of within-person change and permit a window on the structure of intraindividual variability and short-term change. It is to be expected that different intervals will yield different patterns of variability and will result from different influences on the "system" or individual. For example, we might consider sampling moment-to-moment (attentional lapses); within-test (fatigue, practice); within-session (fatigue, order effects, motivation); within-day (time of day effects); across days or weeks (environmental perturbations, physical health, practice); or across months or years (characteristic change trajectory; e.g., Martin & Hofer, 2004). Considerations of temporal sampling is a central aspect of study design, as different intervals will yield different patterns of variability, and will feature results from different influences on the "system" or individual.

Evidence for distinct patterns of change: Growth mixture models

Rather than conceptualizing individual differences in change over time as varying continuously about a single population slope, mixture models are used when individuals can probabilistically belong to discrete groups that may be distinguished by qualitatively different growth trajectories. Growth mixture models (Muthén, 2001) can be used to ascertain qualitative characteristics that distinguish growth subgroups within a population using individual and group variables. Similar to latent class models, growth mixture models assume that the sample is composed of members from more than one population that exhibit distinct patterns of change.

The use of growth mixture models has particular relevance to aging studies. Using individual response patterns in a longitudinal setting with repeated measurements to define trajectories, growth mixture models (a) identify homogeneous groups of individuals or trajectory classes, (b) assign each participant a probability of belonging to a particular trajectory class, and (c) use class membership information to estimate the influence of individual characteristics on trajectory shape. Other forms of cluster analysis have been used to identify patterns of individual differences and trajectories in gerontological studies (Aldwin, Spiro, Levenson, & Cupertino, 2001; Maxson, Berg, & McClearn, 1996, 1997; Smith & Baltes, 1997) but many of these have been cross-sectional in design. Smith and Baltes (1997) applied cluster analysis to Time 1 assessments of intellectual, personality, self-related, and social functioning in the Berlin Aging Study (BASE; N = 516). Nine subgroups were obtained, with four exhibiting positive patterns of functioning that were associated with being younger and male. Maxson et al. (1996, 1997) investigated the survival probabilities for five subgroups identified by cluster analysis in the Gothenburg H-70 study. They found that disability in any one domain (cognitive performance, physical health, functional capacity, subjective well-being, and social contacts) had a greater impact on subsequent functioning and mortality than general level of performance across all areas. Aldwin et al. (2001) clustered physical and psychological health trajectories and found that high increasing physical health symptoms were associated with higher hostility, anxiety, overweight, and smoking behavior, whereas individuals with low health problem trajectories were typically emotionally stable, educated, nonsmokers, and thin.

Use of design-based approaches for distinguishing retest from change

While retest effects are often regarded as a critical limitation of longitudinal designs (e. g., Salthouse, 2009), learning gains related to repeated test exposure are an aspect of nearly all processes under study (e.g., memory). The challenge is in separating gains from repeated test exposure from changes due to other processes. As discussed earlier, a number of methods have been applied that essentially make corrections using between-person age differences relative to naive performance. However, as retest effects most likely vary across individuals as well as within individuals over time, the assumptions of these approaches are unlikely to hold. As a consequence, the between-person comparisons become poor approximations and are confounded with cohort effects (Hoffman, Hofer, & Sliwinski, 2011).

Recently, Sliwinski, Hoffman, and Hofer (2010b) addressed retest effects in a longitudinal design based on measurement bursts. This type of design uses a mix of very closely spaced retest intervals to model practice effects and longer, for example, 6-month intervals to model age-related changes (Nesselroade, 1991). The authors applied an exponential learning function in order to address changes in the asymptotic performance between the measurement bursts, indicating longitudinal change, and changes within the bursts, indicating retest effects. The pairing of multiburst designs and informative measurement models allowed separation of short-term from long-term developmental processes which operate across two different time scales. This approach is a promising step toward disentangling developmental changes from retest effects.

Learning as an indicator of individual status and subsequent change

The ability to learn is of central importance for the development of individuals and continued adaptation to changing environmental demands in adulthood and old age. That is, learning may be considered to be at the core of development and necessary for adaptive processes which become increasingly important in older age (e.g., Freund, 2008). Hence from a developmental perspective it is important to understand how these individual differences in learning relate to other variables as well as to understand what variables contribute to learning.

A focus on learning is further motivated by the hypothesis that individual differences in the ability to learn might also account for individual differences in cognitive aging, less in an explanatory sense, but rather as a parallelism of development taking place in a different time frame. Several researchers have speculated that learning might represent "microdevelopment," that is, development within a short time frame, as opposed to "macrodevelopment," which typically covers development over longer time spans (Yan & Fischer, 2002). Similarly, Lindenberger and Baltes (1995) speculated that the mechanisms underlying learning might be similar to those underlying cognitive development, thus turning the study of learning into a showcase of examining cognitive development. This idea was corroborated by Zimprich et al. (2004) who used retest gains within the first occasion of a longitudinal study to predict long-term change. The authors showed that short-term practice gains in processing speed were positively associated with long-term (6-year) changes in processing speed in a sample of older adults.

In order to examine individual differences in learning and to relate these differences to concomitant variables, the learning process must be formalized. Learning typically follows a nonlinear trajectory: If performance is diagrammed as a function of the number of practice repetitions, the so-called learning curve emerges, which follows a gradually increasing, negatively accelerated, trajectory (see Ritter & Schooler, 2001). Nonlinear functions appear to capture these properties appropriately, and may be defined by three psychologically interpretable parameters: initial recall, learning rate, and asymptotic performance. These parameters can be defined as latent variables in a latent growth curve model where the factor loading matrix is structured according to the first order derivatives of the function chosen to capture the fixed and random effects (see Browne & Du Toit, 1991). This technique also allows the incorporation of concomitant variables and the simultaneous estimation of variances and covariances between predictors and learning parameters. This approach has seen a rising popularity in recent years (Rast & Zimprich, 2009; Grimm & Ram, 2009, Ghisletta et al., 2010) but is still rare compared to the investigation of learning using averaged data (e.g., Poreh, 2005).

Studies using this approach to investigate different types of learning have shown that, for example, performance in verbal learning varies considerably across persons. Reliable individual differences can be found in the initial performance, the learning rate, and the asymptotic performance (Zimprich, Rast, & Martin, 2008; Zimprich & Rast, 2009; Rast & Zimprich, 2009). Zimprich et al. (2008), for example, used a hyperbolic function which explained 84% of variance in the five manifest indicators of verbal learning in the Zurich Longitudinal Study on Cognitive Aging (ZULU). Asymptotic performance and learning rate were significantly, but negatively correlated, showing that those with a higher asymptotic performance tended to have a slower rate of learning, that is, they needed more trials to achieve their maximum performance. The authors were able to show that learning is a restricted process, that is, higher learning rates are at the expense of asymptotic performance in the sense that those who learn faster reached their upper maximum earlier compared to those who started slower but ended at a higher asymptotic performance. This result was unprecedented, but has been confirmed in later studies, as well as with nonverbal material (Rast, in press; Rast and Zimprich, 2009, 2010: Zimprich & Rast, 2009).

In order to explain these individual differences in learning, a number of explanatory variables have been investigated in the context of verbal and nonverbal learning: age, processing speed, educational level, verbal knowledge, and working memory. Most of these variables, except for age, had a positive influence on initial performance (Rast & Zimprich, 2009). In addition, higher levels of working memory and education positively affected the asymptotic performance, and higher scores in verbal knowledge and speed of information processing were positively associated with the learning rate (Rast & Zimprich, 2010; Rast, 2011; Zimprich et al., 2008). This means that learning is differentially affected by a number of variables and that the age of the respondent does not determine the performance in the three parameters. In all studies, the learning parameters exhibited substantial individual differences, implying that individual learning trajectories should not be collapsed across individuals, because this would discount relevant information.

Modeling nonnormative processes: Aging-related change in the context of health

The finding that health or cognitive performance declines on average across the adult lifespan is not very informative about the processes leading to such changes. However, there is substantial variability within and across individuals in development and aging processes. In some people, decline is relatively modest while in others it is serious enough to merit a clinical diagnosis at some point in time. This variability, both between and within individuals, provides a basis for describing and understanding patterns and processes of change across the lifespan. If we are able to understand why some people develop and age more successfully than others, we can start building theories about development and aging which can form the basis for interventions to face this challenge. Hence the recommended focus for researchers should be on the identification and explanation of within-person change and variation and individual differences in the variety of different functions and capabilities across the adult lifespan.

The rate of aging across multiple systems may differ among individuals, implying the existence of different patterns of age-related change. A useful distinction can be made between "common cause" and "common outcome" as it is entirely possible that a common cause can lead to different outcomes and that different causes can lead to common outcomes. For example, different aging-related and/or disease-related processes may influence multiple systems within an individual. Age-related environmental influences (e.g., loss of spouse) or health-related changes may be unique to each individual although different causative "aging" influences may appear to have a common outcome in the population (e.g., Hofer et al., 2003; Sliwinski, Hofer, & Hall, 2003). This heterogeneity and increasing disease risk with age are perhaps the main sources of the difficulty in differentiating aging-related changes from changes associated with disease processes. Additionally, changes in health may result from a complex interaction of lifespan influences, including formal education, occupational status, behavioral risk and health factors, and genetic risk factors for cardiovascular and other disease.

Recent work has demonstrated that some of what were considered normative cognitive aging effects is actually attributable to nonnormative processes (e.g., preclinical dementia; Sliwinski, Lipton, Buschke, & Stewart, 1996). Nonnormative processes might be very important determinants of cognitive aging, especially in very old age (> 80 years), as recent longitudinal evidence has shown that cognitive loss is strongly linked to disease onset in the case of preclinical Alzheimer's disease, and that cognitive function is relatively stable prior to that time (Hall et al., 2000; Rubin et al., 1998; Sliwinski, Hofer, and Hall, 2003). Haan et al. (1999) have shown that cognitive decline tends to occur primarily in individuals at risk for disease (e.g., AD, cardiovascular disease), and that cognition is relatively stable in individuals without such diseases. In all of these studies, disease was studied in its preclinical state – meaning that affected individuals were asymptomatic during the initial study period.

Sliwinski, Hofer, and Hall (2003) found that representing cognitive loss as a function of disease progression (indexed by time to diagnosis, disease-based) provided a much better fit to the data than did representing cognitive change as a function of chronological age (age-based). This result is noteworthy because cognitive loss in the preclinical cases was more closely linked to disease progression than to chronological age. Although between-person heterogeneity and covariation in age-based rates of change in memory, speed, and verbal fluency were high in the preclinical cases, the variances and covariances in dementia-based rates of decline were essentially zero. Refitting the multivariate change model for the preclinical cases using time to diagnosis instead of chronological age as the predictor resulted in much better model fit, evidence of disease-based accelerating cognitive loss, and attenuated correlations among different types of cognitive functions for disease-based rates of change. The heterogeneity in rates of age-based decline and their large covariances are due to a misalignment of individuals with respect to the causal process producing their cognitive loss. The lack of correlated rates of cognitive change in the disease-based model should not be viewed as evidence against a single prominent cause driving cognitive loss in the preclinical cases. Rather, the low variance and covariance components for change signify homogeneity in disease progression. These results suggest that the rate of dementia-based cognitive loss is well predicted by progression of the dementia and less so by chronological age. Recent findings from longitudinal studies lend support to the limited impact hypothesis (Luszcz, 1998; Salthouse, 1991), which states that cognitive aging trends in the population are driven by a restricted subset of aging individuals who experience abrupt and drastic decline, while the majority of aging individuals remain cognitively stable during a given time period.

By definition, normative causes of cognitive loss occur in most individuals as they age. However, there is compelling evidence for the operation of processes that cause cognitive loss in a restricted (but not trivial) subset of aging individuals. The development of preclinical dementia (Haan et al., 1999; Hall et al., 2000; Rubin et al., 1998; Sliwinski, Hofer, & Hall, 2003), and the progression of subclinical cardiovascular disease (Haan et al., 1999), and respiratory dysfunction (Albert, Jones, Savage, & Berkman, 1995) have all been demonstrated to substantially impact rates of cognitive decline. Moreover, these processes, though increasing in prevalence and severity with age, are not strongly correlated with chronological age in cross-sectional analysis. The identification of normative changes may depend on the prior identification of nonnormative changes.

Besides the catastrophic impact of dementia on cognition, a long list of other diseases in late life (e.g., Nilsson & Söderlund, 2002) may compromise cognitive functioning (e.g., Hassing et al., 2002; Tilvis et al., 2004) and thereby everyday life. These other diseases are likely to have more modest effects, except when they contribute to the risk of dementia. Diabetes, cardiovascular disease and cerebrovascular events are all prominent risk factors for dementias. The more complex morbidity patterns and the increased probability of death with age provide a challenging situation in which to identify normal age changes and the impact of disease-related, pathological changes. Indeed, distinguishing between primary and secondary aging (e.g., Birren & Cunningham, 1985) becomes more difficult in late life because physiological changes lead to greater propensity for disease-related changes. Comorbidity increases with age (Nilsson & Söderlund, 2002), which compounds the difficulty of evaluating the relative importance of specific health-related changes such as those related to diabetes, hypertension, stroke, depression, and hearing loss (e.g., Hassing et al. 2002; Hassing, Grant, et al., 2004; Hassing, Hofer, et al., 2004). Additionally, health status and health habits have been shown to partially mediate sex differences in cognitive functioning (Jorm, Anstey, Christensen, & Rodgers, 2004). Although the functional consequences of diseases other than dementia generally are less obvious, a number of diseases may restrict overall physical functioning. For example, functional limitations in lower and upper body functioning due to musculoskeletal problems become more prevalent with age. Impaired sensory functioning represents another important class of impairments that is likely to compromise everyday life.

Approaches to measuring and modeling change in health, including those used in health psychology, epidemiology, and medicine, vary across and within disciplinary boundaries. Health is a multidimensional concept derived from indicators drawn from various domains, including physiological parameters, functional health, diagnoses, indices, ratings, and quality of life. The concept of healthspan, the portion of the lifespan spent in relatively good health, as distinct from a decline phase prior to death, underlies much of gerontological and lifespan developmental research. Decisions regarding the appropriate measurement of health (e.g., disease, health indicators, disability, impairment) are critical for modeling health-related changes and healthspan, and these models of health-related change, in turn, are necessary for understanding of aging-related changes more generally (i.e., cognitive, psychosocial, functional).

Integrative Data Analysis: Within-Person Change in the Context of Cohort, Country, and Culture

A key challenge facing development of theories about processes of aging is to describe and explain changes that occur within aging individuals and how these processes are modified by different contexts. This process orientation is underdeveloped in current theories because many studies have treated "aging" as a between-person characteristic. There are now numerous longitudinal studies on aging that permit formulation and empirical test of hypotheses about the processes influencing intraindividual change and variation. In addition, recent applications of intensive measurement designs are permitting greater resolution of sources of intraindividual variation and change and will likely be useful to identify both short-term and long-term processes and individual change points related to aging and health-related processes (e.g., Horn, 1972; Walls, Barta, Stawski, Collyer, & Hofer, 2011).

Some of the critical tasks in cumulating scientific evidence, and in advancing the field along the lines described above, requires comparison across independent scientific studies. Differences in measurement often make it difficult to gauge differences across studies that sample from different historical periods, birth cohorts, or countries. Indeed, measurement differences can be magnified in cross-cultural or cross-national data where additional variation is inevitably introduced due to differences in language, administration, and item relevance. However, most studies permit comparison at the construct level. A major step in comparing results across studies involves identifying comparable variables and establishing evidence for measurement equivalence (e.g., Bontempo, Grouzet, & Hofer, 2011).

The science of development and aging can be greatly advanced by cross-study comparison, coordinating the analysis and measurement harmonization across studies.

Analyses can incorporate individual and study-level characteristics to account for disparities across studies differing in birth cohort and nationality. We believe that direct and immediate comparison and contrast of results across independent studies, based on the open availability of analysis protocol, scripts, and results, will provide the most solid accumulation of knowledge based on cross-validated evidence. Various collaborations, developed with different structures and levels of linkage among investigators and data, are summarized in Piccinin & Hofer (2008).

There are clearly many benefits to collaborative endeavors related to longitudinal studies on aging, most notably the opportunity for simultaneous evaluation of longitudinal data to test, replicate, and extend prior findings on aging (Hofer & Piccinin, 2009, 2010). Given the key aim of cross-study comparison and research synthesis, harmonization of variables and statistical models are critical aspects, as are the evaluation of alternative models on the same data to permit direct comparison of results across models and the determination of why results might differ. Longitudinal research by itself is challenging, and coordinating analyses across studies more so given the diversity of study designs, samples, and variables. These challenges are not insurmountable, however, and there is great promise for new collaborations that integrate recent theoretical perspectives for within-person aging (with emphasis on both health and aging), developments in statistical analysis of within-person data, and the remarkable number of completed and ongoing longitudinal studies on aging.

Acknowledgment

This chapter was supported by the Integrative Analysis of Longitudinal Studies of Aging (IALSA) research network (NIH/NIA AG026453). Parts of the chapter were supported by a grant from the Swiss National Science Foundation (SNSF-131511) to the second author.

References

Albert, M. S., Jones, K., Savage, C. R., & Berkman, L. (1995). Predictors of cognitive change in older persons: MacArthur studies of successful aging. *Psychology and Aging, 10,* 578–589.

Aldwin, C. M., Spiro, A. III, Levenson, M. R., & Cupertino, A. P. (2001). Longitudinal findings from the normative aging study: III. Personality, individual health trajectories, and mortality. *Psychology and Aging, 16,* 450–465.

Almeida, D. M., & McDonald, D. (1998). Weekly rhythms of parents' work stress, home stress, and parent-adolescent tension. In A. C. Crouter & R. Larson (Eds.), *Temporal rhythms in adolescence: Clocks, calendars, and the coordination of daily life* (pp. 53–67). San Francisco: Jossey-Bass.

Alwin, D. F., Hofer, S. M., & McCammon, R. (2006). Modeling the effects of time: Integrating demographic and developmental perspectives. In R. H. Binstock & L. K. George (Eds.), *Handbook of the aging and the social sciences* (6th ed., pp. 20–38). San Diego, CA: Academic Press.

Anstey, K. J., Hofer, S. M., & Luszcz, M. A. (2003). A latent growth curve analysis of late life cognitive and sensory function over eight years: Evidence for specific and common factors underlying change. *Psychology and Aging, 18,* 714–726.

Baltes, P. B. & Lindenberger, U. (1997). Emergence of a powerful connection between sensory and cognitive functions across the adult life-span: A new window to the study of cognitive aging? *Psychology and Aging, 12,* 12–21.

Baltes, P. B., & Nesselroade, J. R. (1979). History and rationale of longitudinal research. In J. R. Nesselroade & P. B. Baltes (Eds.), *Longitudinal research in the study of behavior and development* (pp. 1–39). New York: Academic Press.

Biesanz, J. C., Deeb-Sossa, N., Papadakis, A. A., Bollen, K. A., & Curran, P. J. (2004). The role of coding time in estimating and interpreting growth curve models. *Psychological Methods, 9,* 30–52.

Birren, J. E., & Cunningham, W. (1985). Research on the psychology of aging: Principles, concepts and theory. In J. E. Birren & W. Schaie (Eds.), *Handbook of the psychology of aging* (2nd ed., pp. 3–34). New York: Van Nostrand Reinhold.

Birren, J. E., & Fisher, L.M. (1995). Aging and speed of behavior: Possible consequences for psychological functioning. *Annual Review of Psychology, 46,* 329–353.

Bontempo, D. E., Grouzet, F. M. E., & Hofer, S. M. (2011). Measurement issues in the analysis of within-person change. In J. T. Newsom, R. N. Jones, & S. M. Hofer (Eds.), *Longitudinal data analysis: A practical guide for researchers in aging, health, and social sciences.* New York: Routledge.

Browne, M. W., & Du Toit, S. H. C. (1991). Models for learning data. In L. Collins & J. L. Horn (Eds.), *Best methods for the analysis of change* (pp. 47–68). Washington, DC: American Psychological Association.

Cooney, T. M., Schaie, K. W., & Willis, S. L. (1988). The relationship between prior functioning of cognitive and personality dimensions and subject attrition in longitudinal research. *Journal of Gerontology: Psychological Sciences, 43,* P12–P17.

Diehr, P., & Patrick, D. L. (2003). Trajectories of health for older adults over time: Accounting fully for death. *Annals of Internal Medicine, 139,* 416–420.

DuFouil, C., Brayne, C., & Clayton, D. (2004). Analysis of longitudinal studies with death and dropout: A case study. *Statistics in Medicine, 23,* 2215–2226.

Eizenman, D. R., Nesselroade, J. R., Featherman, D. L., & Rowe, J. W. (1997). Intraindividual variability in perceived control in an older sample: The MacArthur Successful Aging Studies. *Psychology and Aging, 12,* 489–502.

Ferrer, E., & McArdle, J. J. (2003). Alternative structural models for multivariate longitudinal data analysis. *Structural Equation Modeling, 10,* 493–524.

Ferrer, E., Salthouse, T. A., Stewart, W. F., & Schwartz, B. S. (2004). Modeling age and retest processes in longitudinal studies of cognitive abilities. *Psychology and Aging, 19,* 243–259.

Freund, A. M. (2008). Successful aging as management of resources: The role of selection, optimization, and compensation. *Research in Human Development, 5,* 94–106.

Grimm, K. J., & Ram, N. (2009). A second-order growth mixture model for developmental research. *Research in Human Development, 2–3,* 121–143.

Ghisletta, P., Kennedy, K. M., Rodrigue, K. M., Lindenberger, U., & Raz, N. (2010). Adult age differences and the role of cognitive resources in perceptual-motor skill acquisition: Application of a multilevel negative exponential model. *Journal of Gerontology: Psychological Sciences, 65B,* P163–P173.

Haan, M. N., Shemanski, L., Jagust, W. J., Manolio, T. A., & Kuller, L. (1999). The role of APOE ε4 in modulating effects of other risk factors for cognitive decline in elderly persons. *Journal of the American Medical Association, 282,* 40–46.

Hall, C. B., Lipton, R. B., Sliwinski, M. J., & Stewart, W. F., (2000). A change point model for estimating onset of cognitive decline in preclinical Alzheimer's disease. *Statistics in Medicine, 19,* 1555–1566.

Harel, O., Hofer, S. M., Hoffman, L. R., Pedersen, N., & Johansson, B. (2007). Population inference with mortality and attrition in longitudinal studies on aging: A two-stage multiple imputation method. *Experimental Aging Research, 33*, 187–203.

Hassing, L. B., Grant, M. D., Hofer, S. M., Pedersen, N. L., Nilsson, S. E., Berg, S., McClearn, G., Johansson, B. (2004). Type 2 diabetes mellitus contributes to cognitive change in the oldest old: A longitudinal population-based study. *Journal of the International Neuropsychological Society, 4*, 599–607.

Hassing, L. B., Hofer, S. M., Nilsson, S. E., Berg, S., Pedersen, N. L., McClearn, G. E., & Johansson, B. (2004). Comorbid Type 2 diabetes mellitus and hypertension acerbates cognitive decline: Evidence from a longitudinal study. *Age and Ageing, 33*, 355–361.

Hassing, L. B., Johansson, B., Berg, S., Nilsson, S. E., Pedersen, N. L., Hofer, S. M., & McClearn, G. E. (2002). Terminal decline and markers of cerebro- and cardiovascular disease: Findings from a longitudinal study of the oldest-old. *Journals of Gerontology: Psychological Sciences and Social Sciences, 57B*, P268–P276.

Hofer, S. M., Berg, S., & Era, P. (2003). Evaluating the interdependence of aging-related changes in visual and auditory acuity, balance, and cognitive functioning. *Psychology and Aging, 18*, 285–305.

Hofer, S. M., Flaherty, B. P., & Hoffman, L. (2006). Cross-sectional analysis of time-dependent data: Problems of mean-induced association in age-heterogeneous samples and an alternative method based on sequential narrow age-cohorts. *Multivariate Behavioral Research, 41*, 165–187.

Hofer, S. M., Gray, K. M., Piccinin, A. M., Mackinnon, A. J., Bontempo, D. E., Einfeld, S. L., Hoffman, L., Parmenter, T., Tonge, B. J. (2009). Correlated and coupled within-person change in emotional and behavior disturbance in individuals with intellectual disability. *American Journal on Intellectual and Developmental Disabilities, 5*, 307–321.

Hofer, S. M., & Hoffman, L. (2007). Statistical analysis with incomplete data: A developmental perspective. In T. D. Little, J. A., Bovaird, & N. A. Card (Eds.), *Modeling ecological and contextual effects in longitudinal studies of human development* (pp. 13–32). Mahwah, NJ: Erlbaum.

Hofer, S. M., & Piccinin, A. M. (2009) Integrative data analysis through coordination of measurement and analysis protocol across independent longitudinal studies. *Psychological Methods, 14*, 150–164.

Hofer, S. M., & Piccinin, A. M. (2010). Toward an integrative science of life-span development and aging. *Journals of Gerontology: Psychological Sciences and Social Sciences, 65B*, P269–P278.

Hofer, S. M., & Sliwinski, M. J. (2001). Understanding ageing: An evaluation of research designs for assessing the interdependence of ageing-related changes. *Gerontology, 47*, 341–352.

Hofer, S. M., & Sliwinski, M. J. (2006). Design and analysis of longitudinal studies of aging. In J. E. Birren & K. W. Schaie (Eds.), *Handbook of the psychology of aging* (6th ed., pp. 15–37). San Diego, CA: Academic Press.

Hofer, S. M., Sliwinski, M. J., & Flaherty, B. P. (2002). Understanding aging: Further commentary on the limitations of cross-sectional designs for aging research. *Gerontology, 48*, 22–29.

Hoffman, L. (in press). Considering alternative metrics of time: Does anybody really know what "time" is? In G. Hancock and J. R. Harring (Ed.), *Advances in longitudinal methods in the social and behavioral sciences*. Charlotte, NC: Information Age Publishing.

Hoffman, L., Hofer, S. M., & Sliwinski, M. J. (2011). On the confounds among retest gains and age-cohort differences in the estimation of within-person change in longitudinal studies: A simulation study. *Psychology and Aging*, epub ahead of print.

Horn, J. (1972). State, trait and change dimensions of intelligence. *British Journal of Educational Psychology, 42*, 159–185.

Hultsch, D. F., Hertzog, C., Dixon, R. A., & Small, B. J. (1998). *Memory changes in the aged*. New York: Cambridge University Press.

Hultsch, D. F., Hertzog, C., Small, B. J., McDonald-Miszczk, L., & Dixon, R. A. (1992). Short-term longitudinal change in cognitive performance in later life. *Psychology and Aging, 7,* 571–584.

Johansson, B., Hofer, S. M., Allaire, J. C., Maldonado-Molina, M., Piccinin, A. M., Berg, S., Pedersen, N. L., Gerald, E., McClearn, G. E., (2004). Change in memory and cognitive functioning in the oldest-old: The effects of proximity to death in genetically related individuals over a six-year period. *Psychology and Aging, 19,* 145–156.

Jones, C. J., & Meredith, W. (2000). Developmental paths of psychological health from early adolescence to later adulthood. *Psychology and Aging, 15,* 351–360.

Jorm, A. F., Anstey, K. J., Christensen, H., & Rodgers, B. (2004). Gender differences in cognitive abilities: The mediating role of health state and health habits. *Intelligence, 32,* 7–23.

Kraemer, H. C., Yesavage, J. A., Taylor, J. L., & Kupfer, D. (2000). How can we learn about developmental processes from cross-sectional studies, or can we? *American Journal of Psychiatry, 157,* 163–171.

Kurland, B. F., Johnson, L. L., Egleston, B. L., & Diehr, P. H. (2009). Longitudinal data with follow-up truncated by death: Match the analysis method to research aims. *Statistical Science, 24,* 211. doi: 10.1214/09-STS293

Lindenberger, U., & Baltes, P. B. (1994). Sensory functioning and intelligence in old age: A strong connection. *Psychology and Aging, 9,* 339–355.

Lindenberger, U., & Baltes, P. B. (1995). Testing-the-limits and experimental simulation: Two methods to explicate the role of learning in development. *Journal of Human Development, 38,* 349–360.

Luszcz, M. A. (1998). A longitudinal study of psychological changes in cognition and self in late life. *The Australian Educational and Developmental Psychologist, 15,* 39–61.

MacDonald, S. W. S., DeCarlo, C. A., & Dixon, R. A. (2011). Linking biological and cognitive aging: Toward improving characterizations of developmental time. *Journals of Gerontology: Psychological and Social Sciences, 66B,* i59–i70.

Martin, M., & Hofer, S. M. (2004). Intraindividual variability, change, and aging: Conceptual and analytical issues. *Gerontology, 50,* 7–11.

Maxson, P. J., Berg, S., & McClearn, G. (1996). Multidimensional patterns of aging in 70-year-olds: Survival differences. *Journal of Aging & Health, 8,* 320–333.

Maxson, P. J., Berg, S., & McClearn, G. (1997). Multidimensional patterns of aging: A cluster-analytic approach. *Experimental Aging Research, 23,* 13–31.

McArdle, J. J. (1988). Dynamic but structural equation modeling of repeated measures data. In J. R. Nesselroade & R. B. Cattell (Eds.), *The handbook of multivariate experimental psychology* (Vol. *2,* pp. 561–564). New York: Plenum Press.

McArdle, J. J., & Bell, R. Q. (2000). Recent trends in modeling longitudinal data by latent growth curve methods. In T. D. Little, K. U. Schnabel, & J. Baumert (Eds.), *Modeling longitudinal and multiple-group data: practical issues, applied approaches, and scientific examples* (pp. 69–107). Mahwah, NJ: Erlbaum.

McArdle, J. J., & Epstein, D. (1987). Latent growth curves within developmental structural equation models. *Child Development, 58,* 110–133.

McArdle, J. J., Ferrer-Caja, E., Hamagami, F., & Woodcock, R. W. (2002). Comparative longitudinal structural analyses of the growth and decline of multiple intellectual abilities over the life span. *Developmental Psychology, 38,* 115–142.

McArdle, J. J., & Hamagami, F. (1992). Modeling incomplete longitudinal and cross-sectional data using latent growth structural models. In L. M. Collins and J. L. Horn (Eds.), *Best methods for the analysis of change* (pp. 275–303). Washington, DC: American Psychological Association.

Mehta, P. D., & West, S. G. (2000). Putting the individual back into individual growth curves. *Psychological Methods, 5,* 23–43.

Molenaar, P. C. M. (2004). A manifesto on psychology as idiographic science: Bringing the person back into scientific psychology, this time forever. *Measurement: Interdisciplinary Research & Perspectives, 2,* 201–218.

Molenaar, P. C. M. (2008). Consequences of the ergodic theorems for classical test theory, factor analysis, and the analysis of developmental processes. In S. M. Hofer & D. F. Alwin (Eds.), *Handbook of cognitive aging* (pp. 90–104). Thousand Oaks, CA: Sage.

Muthén, B. (2001). Latent variable mixture modeling. In G. A. Marcoulides & R. E. Schumacker (Eds.), *New developments and techniques in structural equation modeling* (pp. 1–33). Hillsdale, NJ: Erlbaum.

Myerson, J., Hale, S., Wagstaff, D., Poon, L. W., & Smith, G. A. (1990). The information-loss model: A mathematical theory of age-related cognitive slowing. *Psychological Review, 97,* 475–487.

Nesselroade, J. R. (1988). Sampling and generalizability: Adult development and aging research issues examined within the general methodological framework of selection. In K. W. Schaie, R. T. Campbell, W. Meredith, & S. C. Rawlings (Eds.), *Methodological issues in aging research* (pp. 13–42). New York: Springer.

Nesselroade, J. R. (1991). The warp and woof of the developmental fabric. In R. Downs, L. Liben, & D. Palermo (Eds.), *Visions of development, the environment, and aesthetics: The legacy of Joachim F. Wohlwill* (pp. 213–240). Hillsdale, NJ: Erlbaum.

Nesselroade, J. R. (2001). Intraindividual variability in development within and between individuals. *European Psychologist, 6,* 187–193.

Nesselroade, J. R. (2004). Intraindividual variability and short-term change. *Gerontology, 50,* 44–47.

Nilsson, L-G., & Söderlund, H. (2002). Aging, cognition, and health. In M. Naveh-Benjamin, M. Moscovitch, & H. L. Roediger, III (Eds.), *Perspectives on human memory and cognitive aging: Essays in honour of Fergus Craik.* Philadelphia: Psychology Press.

Piccinin, A. M., & Hofer, S. M. (2008). Integrative analysis of longitudinal studies on aging: Collaborative research networks, meta-analysis, and optimizing future studies. In S. M. Hofer & D. F. Alwin (Eds.), *Handbook on cognitive aging: Interdisciplinary perspectives* (pp. 446–476). Thousand Oaks, CA: Sage.

Piccinin, A. M., Muniz, G., Matthews, F., & Johansson, B. (2011). Terminal decline from within and between person perspectives, accounting for incident dementia. *Journal of Gerontology: Psychological Sciences, 66,* 391–401.

Poreh, A. (2005). Analysis of mean learning of normal participants on the Rey auditory–verbal learning test. *Psychological Assessment, 17,* 191–199.

Rabbitt, P., Diggle, P., Smith, D., Holland, F., & McInnes, L.M. (2001). Identifying and separating the effects of practice and of cognitive ageing during a large longitudinal study of elderly community residents. *Neuropsychologia, 39,* 532–543.

Rabbitt, P., Watson, P., Donlan, C., Bent, N., & McInnes, L. (1994). Subject attrition in a longitudinal study of cognitive performance in community-based elderly people. *Facts and Research in Gerontology, 1994,* 29–34.

Rast, P. (2011). Verbal knowledge working memory and processing speed as predictors of verbal learning in older adults. *Developmental Psychology, 47,* 1490–1498.

Rast, P., & Zimprich, D. (2009). Individual differences and reliability of paired associates learning in younger and older adults. *Psychology and Aging, 24,* 1001–1006.

Rast, P., & Zimprich, D. (2010). Individual differences in a positional learning task across the adult lifespan. *Learning and Individual Differences, 20,* 1–7.

Raudenbush, S. W., & Bryk, A. S. (2002). *Hierarchical linear models: Applications and data analysis methods* (2nd ed.) Newbury Park, CA: Sage.

Riegel, K. F., Riegel, R. M., & Meyer, G. (1967). A study of the drop-out rates in longitudinal research on aging and the prediction of death. *Journal of Personality and Social Psychology, 4*, 342–348.

Ritter, F., & Schooler, L. J. (2001). The learning curve. In N. Smelser & P. B. Baltes (Eds.), *International Encyclopedia of the Social and Behavioral Sciences* (pp. 8602–8605). Oxford: Elsevier.

Rubin, E. H., Storandt, M., Miller, J. P., Kinscherf, D. A., Grant, E. A., Morris, J. C., & Berg, L. (1998). A prospective study of cognitive function and onset of dementia in cognitively healthy elders. *Archives of Neurology, 55*, 395–401.

Salthouse, T. (1988). The role of processing resources in cognitive aging. In M. L. Howe & C. J. Brainerd (Eds.), *Cognitive development in adulthood* (pp. 185–239). New York: Springer-Verlag.

Salthouse, T. (1991). Mediation of adult age differences in cognition by reductions in working memory and speed of processing. *Psychological Science, 2*, 179–183.

Salthouse, T. A. (1996). The processing-speed theory of adult age differences in cognition. *Psychological Review, 103*, 403–428.

Salthouse, T. A. (2009). When does age-related cognitive decline begin? *Neurobiology of Aging, 30*, 507–514.

Sayer, A. G., & Willett, J. B. (1998). A cross-domain model for growth in adolescent alcohol expectancies. *Multivariate Behavioral Research, 33*, 509–543.

Schafer, J. L. (1997). *Analysis of incomplete multivariate data.* New York: Chapman and Hall.

Schafer, J. L., & Graham, J. W. (2002). Missing data: Our view of the state of the art. *Psychological Methods, 7*, 147–177.

Schaie, K. W. (1988). Internal validity threats in studies of adult cognitive development. In M. L. Howe & C. J. Brainard (Eds.), *Cognitive development in adulthood: Progress in cognitive development research* (pp. 241–272). New York: Springer-Verlag.

Schaie, K. W. (1996). *Intellectual development in adulthood: The Seattle Longitudinal Study.* New York: Cambridge University Press.

Siegler, I. C., & Botwinick, J. (1979). A long-term longitudinal study of intellectual ability of older adults: The matter of selective subject attrition. *Journal of Gerontology, 34*, 242–245.

Siegler, R. S. (1994). Cognitive variability: A key to understanding cognitive development. *Current Directions in Psychological Science, 3*, 4–5.

Singer, J. D., & Willett, J. B. (2003). *Applied longitudinal data analysis: Modeling change and event occurrence.* Oxford: Oxford University Press.

Sliwinski, M., & Buschke, H. (1999). Cross-sectional and longitudinal relationships among age, memory and processing speed. *Psychology and Aging, 14*, 18–33.

Sliwinski, M., & Buschke, H. (2004) Modeling intraindividual cognitive change in aging adults: Results from the Einstein Aging Studies. *Aging, Neuropsychology and Cognition, 11*, 196–211.

Sliwinski, M. J., & Hofer, S. M. (1999). How strong is the evidence for mediational hypotheses of age-related memory loss? A commentary on Luszcz and Bryan. *Gerontology, 45*, 351–354.

Sliwinski, M. J., Hofer, S. M., & Hall, C. (2003). Correlated and coupled cognitive change in older adults with and without clinical dementia. *Psychology and Aging, 18*, 672–683.

Sliwinski, M. J., Hofer, S. M., Hall, C., Bushke, H., & Lipton, R. B. (2003). Modeling memory decline in older adults: The importance of preclinical dementia, attrition and chronological age. *Psychology and Aging, 18*, 658–671.

Sliwinski, M. J., Hoffman, L., & Hofer, S. M. (2010a). Evaluating convergence of within-person change and between-person age differences in age-heterogeneous longitudinal studies. *Research in Human Development, 7*, 45–60.

Sliwinski, M. J., Hoffman, L., & Hofer, S. M. (2010b). Modeling retest and aging effects in a measurement burst design. In P. C. M. Molenaar & K. M. Newell (Eds.), *Individual pathways of change: Statistical models for analyzing learning and development* (pp. 37–50). Washington, DC: American Psychological Association.

Sliwinski, M., Lipton, R. B., Buschke, H., & Stewart, W. F. (1996). The effect of pre-clinical dementia on estimates of normal cognitive function in aging. *Journal of Gerontology: Psychological Sciences, 51B*, P217–P225.

Sliwinski, M. J., Smyth, J., Hofer, S. M., & Stawski, R. (2006). Intraindividual coupling of daily stress and cognition. *Psychology and Aging, 21*, 545–557.

Smith, J., & Baltes, P. B. (1997). Profiles of psychological functioning in the old and oldest old. *Psychology and Aging, 12*, 458–472.

Snijders, T., & Bosker, R. (1999). *Multilevel analysis: An introduction to basic and advanced multilevel modeling.* Thousand Oaks, CA: Sage.

Streib, G. F. (1966). Participants and drop-outs in a longitudinal study. *Journal of Gerontology, 21*, 200–209.

Tilvis, R. S., Kahonen-Vare, M. H., Jolkkonen, J., Valvanne, J., Pitkala, K. H., & Strandberg, T. E. (2004). Predictors of cognitive decline and mortality of aged people over a 10-year period. *Journals of Gerontology: Biological and Medical Sciences, 59*, M268–M274.

Thorvaldsson, V., Hofer, S. M., Hassing, L., & Johansson, B. (2008). Cognitive change as conditional on age heterogeneity in onset of mortality-related processes and repeated testing effects. In S. M. Hofer & D. F. Alwin (Eds.), *Handbook on cognitive aging: Interdisciplinary perspectives* (pp. 284–297). Thousand Oaks: Sage.

Thorvaldsson, V., Hofer, S. M., & Johansson, B. (2006). Ageing and late life terminal decline: A comparison of alternative modeling approaches. *European Psychologist, 11*, 196–203.

Vaupel, J. W., & Yashin, A. I. (1985). Heterogeneity's ruses: Some surprising effects of selection on population dynamics. *American Statistician, 39*, 176–185.

Verbeke, G., & Molenberghs, G. (2000). *Linear mixed models for longitudinal data.* New York: Springer-Verlag.

Verhaeghen, P., & Salthouse, T. A. (1997). Meta-analyses of age-cognition relations in adulthood: Estimates of linear and nonlinear age effects and structural models. *Psychological Bulletin, 122*, 231–249.

Walls, T. A., Barta, W., Stawski, R. S., Collyer, C., & Hofer, S. M. (2011). Timescale-dependent longitudinal designs. In B. Laursen, T. D. Little, & N. Card (Eds.), *Handbook of developmental research methods* (pp. 46–64). New York: Guilford Press.

Wilson, R. S., Yan, L., Bienias, J. L., & Bennett, D. A. (2006). Cognitive decline in old age: Separating retest effects from the effects of growing older. *Psychology and Aging, 21*, 774–789.

Yan, Z., & Fischer, K. W. (2002). Always under construction: Dynamic variations in adult cognitive microdevelopment. *Human Development, 45*, 141–160.

Zimprich, D., Hofer, S. M., & Aartsen, M. J. (2004). Short-term versus long-term changes in processing speed. *Gerontology, 50*, 17–21.

Zimprich, D., & Martin, M. (2002). Can longitudinal changes in processing speed explain longitudinal age changes in fluid intelligence? *Psychology and Aging, 17*, 690–695.

Zimprich, D. & Rast, P. (2009). Verbal learning changes in older adults across 18 months. *Aging, Neuropsychology, and Cognition, 16*, 461–484.

Zimprich, D., Rast, P., & Martin, M. (2008). Individual differences in verbal learning in old age. In S. M. Hofer & D. F. Alwin (Eds.), *The handbook of cognitive aging: Interdisciplinary perspectives* (pp. 224–243). Thousand Oaks, CA: Sage.

PART II

Physical Changes and Health

5

Physical Exercise and Health

Leslie I. Katzel and Gregory M. Steinbrenner

Concept of Successful Aging

"Successful aging," as defined by Rowe and Kahn (1987), includes three main components: low probability of disease and disease-related disability, high cognitive and physical
functional capacity, and active engagement with life. This contrasts with "usual aging,"
where adverse lifestyle, preventable diseases, poor control of medical conditions and poor
management of risk factors for disease accelerate the effects of aging on health and function
which leads to "accelerated aging." Usual aging characteristics are therefore modifiable.
The concept of successful aging proposed by Rowe and Kahn formed the basis for the
MacArthur Foundation Research Network on Successful Aging (Berkman et al., 1993).
The overall findings of the MacArthur foundation studies support the importance of
potentially modifiable environmental and behavioral factors in determining the risk of
disease late in life (Rowe & Kahn, 1997).

The proportion of older adults who age successfully differs from study to study, due in
part to different definitions of successful aging and characteristics of the population sampled.
Depp and Jeste (2009) recently reviewed 28 studies of successful aging that used a variety of
definitions of successful aging. Overall they reported that 36% of older community dwelling
adults were successful agers. They concluded that factors that correlated with the various
definitions of successful aging were age (young-old); nonsmoking; absence of disability,
arthritis, and diabetes; increased physical activity; more social contacts; better self-rated
health; absence of depression and cognitive impairment; and fewer medical conditions.
Exercise is one of the cornerstone lifestyle factors in successful aging. In this chapter, we will
examine the beneficial effects of exercise and physical activity on health in older adults. There

The Wiley-Blackwell Handbook of Adulthood and Aging, First Edition. Edited by Susan Krauss Whitbourne
and Martin J. Sliwinski.   © 2012 Blackwell Publishing Ltd. Published 2012 by Blackwell Publishing Ltd.

is strong scientific evidence regarding the importance of physical activity and exercise to health across many domains (Fulton, Simons-Morton, & Galuska, 2009). We will also highlight and summarize data on functional performance and metabolic profiles of older athletes who many consider to exemplify "successful" aging.

Age-Associated Change in Peak/Maximal Aerobic Capacity (VO₂max)

VO_2max, the rate of maximal oxygen consumption during exhaustive exercise, is the best physiologic measure of functional capacity. The VO_2max is typically measured during a maximal effort treadmill test in which subjects exercise to voluntary exhaustion. During the tests oxygen (O_2) consumption, carbon dioxide (CO_2) production, and respiratory minute ventilation are measured breath-by-breath using a metabolic cart. VO_2max is achieved by obtaining a plateau in oxygen consumption, despite an increase in workload. If a subject is unable to achieve the criteria for the VO_2max (American College of Sports Medicine, 2010), a VO_2peak is obtained. Often the VO_2max is not directly measured, but calculated from the metabolic equivalents (METs) derived from standard equations using the speed and grade achieved during the test (American College of Sports Medicine, 2010). In healthy populations, the measured VO_2max is highly correlated with the estimated METs. However, the estimated METs are far less accurate in older populations with medical comorbidities. Older subjects may have balance problems or other issues that require them to hold on to the railing of the treadmill during the test. This can lead to a lower measured VO_2peak than one would predict from the equations. Cycle ergometers are another modality used for exercise testing. Typically when subjects are cycling their values are substantially lower (−10 to −15%) than those obtained on a treadmill. In addition, some subjects have difficulty cycling because of problems with coordination and inexperience.

The VO_2max is the product of cardiac output and arteriovenous oxygen difference (a-vO_2) at exhaustion. Mathematically, this is expressed by the Fick equation: $VO_2 =$ cardiac output (Qt) $\times$ (CaO_2 − CvO_2) where Qt = cardiac output and (CaO_2 − CvO_2) is the difference in O_2 content between arterial and mixed venous blood (Bassett & Howley, 2000; Guyton & Hall, 2000, pp. 220–222). Cardiac output increases during exercise through changes in both heart rate and stroke volume. In young adults, intense exercise can elicit a 15-fold increase in VO_2, a 10-fold increase in minute ventilation, a 5-fold increase in cardiac output, and a 3-fold increase in systemic O_2 extraction. In healthy adults, maximal cardiac output limits aerobic exercise capacity.

VO_2max declines with age (Katzel, Sorkin, & Fleg, 2001; Kitzman & Taffet, 2009; Rosen, Sorkin, Goldberg, Hagberg, & Katzel, 1998; Talbot, Metter, & Fleg, 2000). Cross-sectional studies performed in healthy men and women indicated that the rate of decline is approximately 1% per year or an absolute change of −0.5 ml/kg/min per year. The decline in VO_2max might be accelerated in those above 70 years, resulting in a curvilinear relationship between VO_2max and age (Fleg et al., 2005; Schwartz & Kohret, 2009). Figure 5.1 shows the conceptual model where the age-associated decline in VO_2max reflects the contributions of primary aging (biologic aging), secondary aging (lifestyle) and tertiary aging (disease).

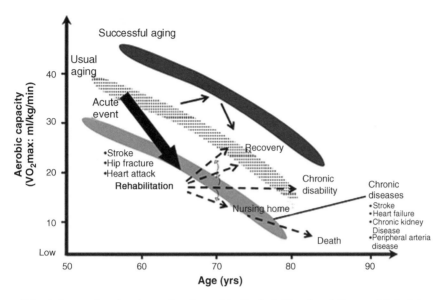

Figure 5.1 Aging vs. functional capacity. Created by Leslie I. Katzel and Gregory M. Steinbrenner

Comparison of older master athletes and their sedentary peers

Older athletes generally exemplify "successful" aging. They have a significantly higher VO_2max, lower percentage body fat, and more favorable cardiac risk factor profiles than their sedentary peers (Fleg & Goldberg, 1990; Rogers, Hagberg, Marint, Ehsani, & Holloszy, 1990; Yataco, Busby-Whitehead, Drinkwater, & Katzel, 1997). In our laboratory and in similar studies conducted elsewhere, the VO_2max of 60–70-year-old male aerobically trained competitive distance runners is often >50 ml/kg/min, which is ~60% higher than their healthy overweight sedentary peers (25 to 30 ml/kg/min) and triple that of older adults with serious medical comorbities such as stroke, congestive heart failure or peripheral arterial disease, who often have VO_2peak below 15 ml/kg/min. Given that VO_2max declines by about 1% per year in healthy populations, the older aerobically trained athletes have a VO_2max that generally exceeds the VO_2max of sedentary individuals in their twenties. Functionally, master athletes outperform untrained sedentary individuals who are 30 to 40 years younger. With improved training techniques, the most elite master athletes have achieved race times that would have enabled them to win Olympic medals at the first Olympiad competition in 1896 (see Table 5.1).

Is the decline in VO_2max with aging attenuated in athletes?

Cross-sectional studies.   It has been hypothesized that continued vigorous aerobic training attenuates the age-associated reductions in VO_2max. Indeed, a number of cross-sectional studies suggest that the rate of decline in VO_2max with aging is attenuated in master athletes

Table 5.1   Secular effects of improved training methods in master athletes (Tanaka & Seals, 2007).

Running events	1896 Olympic winning time (from the first Olympic games in Athens)	Current age-group records that surpass 1896 Olympic times and age at which these records were achieved
100 m (s)	12.0	11.7 (61 years)
200 m (s)	22.2	22.1 (46 years)
400 m (s)	54.2	53.9 (63 years)
800 m (min:s)	2:11.0	2:10.4 (60 years)
1500 m (min:s)	4:33:2	4:27:7 (60 years)
Marathon (h:min:s)	2:58:50	2:54:5 (73 years)

(Buskirk & Hodgson, 1987; Hagberg, 1985; Heath, Hagberg, Ehsani, & Holloszy, 1981; Lakatta, 1993; Pollock, Foster, Knapp, & Schmidt, 1987; Rogers et al., 1990); that is, the slope of the change of VO_2max with aging is less steep in athletes than in their sedentary counterparts. By contrast, several other studies report a greater cross-sectional decline in VO_2max with age than in sedentary individuals (Pimentel, Gentile, Tanaka, Seals, & Gates, 2003; Tanaka et al., 1997). This greater slope results in a convergence between VO_2max in athletes and sedentary individuals at oldest age. How do we reconcile these differences? Subject selection and criteria used to select subjects in both the athlete and sedentary populations can substantially impact on the results. For example, one needs to know if the population has been screened for coronary artery disease, silent myocardial ischemia, hypertension, and other medical comorbidities known to impact on fitness. Another factor to consider is how the data is expressed and how the rate of change is described. If the athletes have higher absolute values, when the decline is expressed as a percentage change, they would of course be expected to have a smaller percentage change. Therefore, one needs to look at the absolute slopes. Another issue is that athletes and their sedentary counterparts differ in weight and body composition. Some advocate expressing VO_2max in terms of lean body or fat free mass (Fleg & Lakatta, 1988; Kitzman & Taffet, 2009). When one does that, the rate of decline of VO_2max with age is less marked. In our opinion, the major factor explaining the disparity among the various studies is attributable to subject selection biases inherent in cross-sectional studies; the oldest individuals are selected from a smaller pool of potential subjects free of comorbid disease than are younger and middle-aged individuals.

Longitudinal studies.   One must distinguish between the results of the cross-sectional and longitudinal studies in this area of research. Cross-sectional studies can underestimate the true slope of the age-related decline in aerobic capacity seen in longitudinal studies (Dehn & Bruce, 1972; Marti & Howald, 1990; Schroeder et al., 2007; Trappe, Costill, Vukovich, Jones, & Melham, 1996). As noted above, this is largely due to selection biases inherent in cross-sectional studies; the oldest athletes are selected from a smaller, more elite pool of potential subjects than are younger and middle-aged athletes. Some longitudinal studies demonstrate an attenuation in the age-related decline in VO_2max in athletes who continue to engage in vigorous endurance exercise (Rogers et al., 1990; Rosen et al., 1998). In a widely cited study, Rogers et al. (1990) estimated that the 5.5% per decade age-related decline in VO_2max of master athletes is approximately 50% of the rate of decline seen in age-matched sedentary men. Kasch and colleagues reported no significant change in VO_2max in 13 moderately trained middle-aged men who continued to run an average of 25 miles per week over the 10 years of follow-up (Kasch, Wallace, & Van Camp, 1985; Kasch, Wallace, Van Camp, & Verity, 1988). Other longitudinal studies, however, report more pronounced declines in VO_2max with aging (Kasch et al., 1985; Trappe et al., 1996). Pollock and colleagues reported 10- and 20-year longitudinal changes in VO_2max in 21 well-trained competitive runners (mean age of 52 ± 9 years at entry) (Mengelkoch et al., 1997; Pollock et al., 1987; Pollock et al., 1997). At 10 years of follow-up, on average the VO_2max declined by 8%. However, at 20 years of follow-up (mean age 70 ± 9 years), there was an accelerated decline in VO_2max; the mean VO_2max declined by an additional 20%, or -2% a year between the 10- and 20-year visits (Mengelkoch et al., 1997; Pollock et al., 1997). When stratified by training intensity at time of 20-year follow-up over the final 10 years of follow-up, the VO_2max declined by 17% in the nine men who continued to train at a high intensity, by 18% in the 10 men who continued to train at a moderate intensity, and by 36% in the two men in the low intensity group. Trappe reported a 32% decline in VO_2max over 22 years of follow-up (-1.5% per year) in 10 master runners (Trappe et al., 1996).

We previously reported in a longitudinal study of master athletes (Katzel et al., 2001) that the rate of the age-related decline in aerobic capacity was triple that predicted in the initial cross-sectional study, whereas in the sedentary men, the longitudinal and initial cross-sectional analyses provided similar estimates of the rates of the age-associated declines in VO_2max. This divergence of baseline cross-sectional and longitudinal follow-up regression lines in the athletes most likely reflected secular changes in their training regimens, as athletes who were able to maintain a higher intensity training regiment had significantly less of a decline in VO_2max than athletes who could no longer maintain a high level of training. Collectively, these longitudinal studies demonstrate significant variability in the rate of decline of VO_2max with aging, which is most likely attributable to: (a) differences in the initial age and VO_2max in the populations studied; (b) differences in the ability of the athletes to maintain a high level of training; and (c) the development of disease.

Mechanisms underlying the age-associated decline in VO_2max

The age-associated decline in VO_2max reflects a reduction in maximal cardiac output (central factors), reduced skeletal muscle mass, increased body fat, reduced peripheral blood flow, and reduced peripheral O_2 extraction. Age-related changes in muscle fiber type and muscle histochemistry, including declines in synthesis rate of mixed muscle proteins, myosin heavy chain, and mitochondrial protein, result in decreased activities of the oxidative mitochondrial enzymes cytochrome c oxidase and citrate synthase (Short, Vittone, Bigelow, Proctor, & Nair, 2004). These changes contribute to declines in muscle oxidative capacity and mitochondrial function, respectively. The decline in muscle mass and alterations in muscle histochemistry that occur with "healthy" aging are accelerated in the presence of comorbid medical conditions and physical deconditioning.

It is well established that there is an age-associated decline in maximal heart rate in both athletes and sedentary individuals (Lakatta, 1993); generally the maximal heart rate declines by approximately 1 beat per minute per year after age 20. Cross-sectional studies by Ogawa and colleagues suggest that the decline in VO_2max with age is primarily related to a decline in maximal cardiac output that results from decreases in both maximal heart rate and stroke volume (Ogawa et al., 1992). Longitudinal studies by Hollenberg emphasize the primary importance of both declining pulmonary forced expiratory volume (FEV 1) and declining maximal exercise heart rate in accounting for the aging-associated decline in VO_2max (Hollenberg, Yang, Haight, & Tager, 2006).

The Dallas Bed Rest study provides insight into the contribution of changes in central cardiac function and peripheral changes to the change in VO_2 max with aging (McGavock et al., 2009; McGuire et al., 2001a, 2001b; Saltin et al., 1968). In 1966, five healthy 20-year old men underwent a physiological evaluation of the effects of 3 weeks of bed rest followed by 8 weeks of intensive endurance training on their cardiovascular function (Saltin et al., 1968). Follow-up studies of these men were performed 30 years later in 1996 (McGuire et al., 2001a, 2001b), and 40 years later in 2006 (McGavock et al., 2009). In 1996, 3 weeks of bed rest caused >30% decline in VO_2max due to declines in cardiac output. Follow-up in 1996 demonstrated that 3 weeks of bed rest in 1966 caused a greater deterioration in cardiovascular and physical work capacity than did 30 years of aging in these five men. The maximal oxygen uptake declined at age 50 in 1996 as expected but unexpectedly did so primarily via a decrement in the peripheral oxygen extraction. There was no decline in maximal cardiac function over the three decades of aging, as there was an increase in maximal stroke volume to compensate for the decline in maximal heart rate. They estimated physical inactivity accounts for as much as 40% of the age-related decline in maximal oxygen uptake. In 1996 they put the subjects in an exercise training program and noted a 16% increase in VO_2max. They found that the mechanism of recovery of aerobic power predominantly involved a peripheral adaptation to training evidenced by increased arterial venous difference in O_2 (AV-DO_2max) at maximal exercise, with no change in maximal cardiac output.

The men were restudied 10 years later in 2006. Now at 60 years of age, they found that VO_2max declined by 17% from age 50 to 60 versus 8% from age 20 to 50. Therefore the annual decline in VO_2max was triple that seen from age 20 to 50. The decline in maximal oxygen uptake in these five individuals after age 50 was secondary to a decline in both cardiac output max and AV-DO_2max. The decline in maximal aerobic capacity after age 50 was variable and was highly dependent upon changes in muscle mass, habitual physical activity, and development of disease. The reduced capacity for increasing maximal stroke volume and maximal cardiac output (central cardiac reserve) in the face of declining peripheral oxygen extraction may explain the accelerated decline in VO_2max after the age of 50.

It is certainly attractive to attribute much of the age-associated decline in VO_2max in the athletes to changes in training regimens, rather than primary aging per se. Several studies have reported a correlation between the change in training intensity quantified by either the change in distance run or running pace versus the change in VO_2max over time (Jackson et al., 1995; Marti & Howald, 1990; Pollock et al., 1997). For example, in the study by Pollock, over the second 10-year follow-up interval the change in VO_2max was correlated with the change in running pace ($r = .56$) (Pollock et al., 1997). One could contend that individuals with a lower VO_2max cannot train at as high an intensity, or for as long a duration, as those with a higher VO_2max. In addition, age-associated declines in muscle mass, decreased peripheral blood flow during exercise, and decreased O_2 extraction by muscle, contribute to the age-associated decline in VO_2max (Jackson et al., 1995).

In our longitudinal studies of master athletes, the athletes who decreased their training due to injuries or disease experienced the largest declines in their VO_2max, general >40%. They now had values similar to their lean sedentary peers. This 40% decline in VO_2max we observed in the athletes who were no longer training aerobically is worse than expected, but is consistent with results of other studies that have examined the effects of deconditioning on VO_2max (Schulman et al., 1996). Prior studies in our laboratory demonstrate that 3 months of voluntary cessation of endurance exercise by older athletes can result in a decline of >10% in VO_2max (Schulman et al., 1996). Kasch et al. (1985) concluded that two-thirds of the decline in VO_2max with age in an untrained person is due to disuse. Indeed, even in highly trained athletes, there is a curvilinear deterioration in performance that accelerates above the age of 75. This curvilinear change may represent primary aging effects.

Age-Associated Change in Strength and Power

A large number of studies have also examined age-associated changes in strength and power (Bean et al., 2003). Overall, these studies demonstrate that strength declines in both men and women starting in the fourth decade, and at a rate of about 8–10% decline per decade in both men and women. Power, however, declines more rapidly with age than does strength. The loss of strength and power results in decreased physiological reserve that can impact on the ability of older adults to perform a variety of tasks encountered during daily life such as rising up from a chair, carrying a bag of groceries, or opening a jar. Factors that contribute to the age-associated decline in strength include: (a) loss of muscle fibers (greater loss of type II fast twitch than type I); (b) decline in oxidative and glycolytic capacity; (c) loss of muscle mass (particularly cross-sectional area); and (d) loss of motor units (progressive denervation of muscle fibers). Clinically, loss of strength and muscle mass (sarcopenia) may result in frailty, a syndrome characterized by weakness, weight loss, muscle wasting, exercise intolerance, frequent falls, immobility, and incontinence (Fried et al., 2001). The definition of frailty employed by clinicians and investigators varies, but there is general agreement that the primary characteristic of frailty is decreased physical reserve. Markers of frailty include declines in lean body mass, ability to respond to stressors, endurance, balance, and walking performance/physical activity. Studies demonstrate that frailty is associated with increased risk for functional decline, hospitalization, and death (Gill, Gahbauer, Han, & Allore, 2010). Exercise and nutritional and pharmacological interventions to prevent and treat frailty remain an active area of investigation.

Aging, Physical Activity, and Cardiovascular Risk Factors

It is well established that there is a small age-related increase in fasting plasma glucose in healthy nondiabetic individuals on the order of 1 mg/dl per decade (Shimokata et al., 1991). This small increase in fasting glucose levels is accompanied by a much larger 10 mg/dl increase per decade in 2-hour postprandial glucose levels during a standard glucose tolerance test. These higher postprandial glucose levels are accompanied by an increase in plasma insulin levels, rather than a reduction in insulin secretion, consistent with a decrease in insulin sensitivity. Data from the Lipids Research Clinics (Heiss et al., 1980) published prior to the widespread treatment of hyperlipidemia demonstrate that there are age-associated increases in triglycerides (TG) that may exceed 80mg/dl and 40 mg/dl in low-density lipoprotein cholesterol (LDL-C). The rise in TG parallels an increase in total body fat.

A number of mechanistic studies have examined the metabolism of LDL in young and older subjects. An analysis by Miller (1984) demonstrated that the LDL apo B fractional catabolic rate decreased with age, whereas the LDL production rate did not change with age. The age-related rise in LDL was attributed to an acquired defect in the LDL receptor function. Similar findings subsequently were reported by Ericsson et al. (1991), who suggested that there might be an age-associated reduction in hepatic LDL receptor expression. The increase in TG appears to be due to both an increased rate of production, and decreased clearance. These metabolic studies did not control for differences in body composition and physical activity among age groups, factors which may elevate plasma free fatty acid concentrations and glucose and insulin concentrations and result in increased hepatic production of TG in older subjects.

Results from studies in master athletes demonstrate that they have lipoprotein lipid concentrations and fasting and postprandial glucose and insulin levels during an oral glucose tolerance test (OGTT) comparable to healthy lean younger individuals (Fleg & Goldberg, 1990; Yataco et al., 1997), suggesting that high intensity physical activity may protect against age-related declines in glucose tolerance in insulin sensitivity and increase TG and LDL-C. Attribution of the superior lipoprotein lipids and glucose and insulin profiles to regular aerobic exercise is complicated by the fact that older athletes have a significantly lower percentage body fat than their sedentary peers. In multiple regression analyses, the differences in obesity contributed the most to the difference in TG and HDL-C concentrations between older athletes and their sedentary counterparts, while the differences in VO_2max accounted for a smaller, but statistically significant percentage of the variance in these lipoproteins (Goldberg et al., 2000; Yataco et al., 1997). These cross-sectional studies are supported by results of intervention studies in our laboratory and elsewhere (see below) that demonstrate that exercise and weight loss have additive or potentially synergistic beneficial effects on lipoprotein and glucose metabolism. We would contend that many of the purported age-related changes in lipoprotein and glucose metabolism concentrations reflect interactions between primary age-related changes and the effects of obesity, physical inactivity, diet, and other lifestyle habits (i.e., secondary aging). We are not aware of any long-term longitudinal intervention studies that examined the effects of aerobic exercise training on metabolic risk factors and subsequent cardio-vascular events.

Exercise and biomarkers for cardiovascular disease in older adults

The discussion in this chapter has focused on widely recognized traditional risk factors for coronary heart disease. Many older individuals have metabolic abnormalities that promote atherosclerosis that are not routinely measured. These risk factors include elevated lipoprotein (a) (or Lp [a]), elevated apolipoprotein (apo) B, small dense LDL particles (the atherogenic LDL pattern B phenotype), oxidized LDL, hyperinsulinemia, high sensitivity C-reactive protein (hsCRP), homocysteine, and other markers of inflammation. The clinical utility of these and other biomarkers in providing incremental benefit in predicting coronary vascular disease risk beyond the routine measures is an area of active investigation (U.S. Preventive Services Task Force, 2009). Exercise, with concomitant weight loss, has been shown to have beneficial effects on these risk factors. It is becoming increasing clear that the burden of subclinical disease increases in older adults (Kuller et al., 2000; Newman et al., 2003). The measurement of structural markers of arterial vulnerability (carotid intimal-medial thickness and assessment of coronary artery calcium among others) and functional markers of arterial vulnerability (brachial artery reactivity assessment of endothelial function, arterial stiffness, and ankle-brachial blood pressure index [ABI]), similarly provide incremental benefit in predicting cardiovascular disease (CVD) risk in the elderly and help identify older individuals who might benefit from risk factor intervention.

Physical Activity, Exercise, Aging, Coronary Heart Disease, and Death

Physical exercise is an independent factor decreasing both morbidity and mortality. Increased physical activity is associated with decreased incidence of coronary heart disease, hypertension, noninsulin-dependent diabetes mellitus, colon cancer, and increased longevity, and may decrease the risk for dementia and other diseases (Fulton et al., 2009). For this section of the chapter we will focus on the large body of observational epidemiological studies demonstrating a reduction in mortality and coronary heart disease in a variety of populations.

One of the classic studies published more than 40 years ago by Morris and colleagues reported that London conductors (ticket takers) on double-decker buses who traversed up and down the stairs during their workday had lower rates of coronary heart disease and a

50% reduction of death rates than the sedentary bus drivers who did not have these occupational levels of activity (Morris, Kagan, Pattison, & Gardner, 1966). A frequently cited study of 17,000 male Harvard University alumni by Paffenbarger et al. assessed the relationship between remote and recent leisure-time physical activity to coronary heart disease rates and death (Paffenbarger & Hyde, 1984; Paffenbarger, Hyde, Wing, & Hsieh, 1986; Paffenbarger, Wing, & Hyde, 1981). They reported that the age-adjusted incidence of CHD was inversely proportional to the self-reported energy expenditure. Overall, men expending fewer than 2,000 kcal per week had a 64% higher risk for CHD than men expending more than 2,000 kcal per week. This increased risk persisted even after adjustment for other CHD risk factors and other confounders. Importantly there did not appear to be additional risk reduction by expending more than 2,000 kcal per week. Paffenbarger and colleagues further noted that regular physical activity was associated with an increase in average life expectancy. At age 80, they estimated a gain of approximately two years if exercise was begun in young adulthood, but only a gain of 0.4 years if exercise was begun between the ages of 75 and 79. A subsequent follow-up conducted several years later on this population also indicated that there appeared to be a threshold of benefit at 2,100 kcal per week for CHD endpoints (Sesso, Paffenbarger, & Lee, 2000). However, they found that for men with multiple coronary risk factors, a greater level of total physical activity, >4200 kcal per week, was required to reduce risk for CHD endpoints. This has important public health implications on policy that guides individuals on the minimal desirable and or optimal amounts of physical activity.

The studies described above have examined the relationship between physical activity and a variety of health outcomes. Fewer studies have examined the relationship between objective measures of physical fitness, assessed by treadmill testing and health outcomes. Physical fitness can be measured more objectively than physical activity, which is typically quantified by questionnaire data, and hence might provide better insight into mechanisms underlying cardioprotective effects of physical activity and exercise. We will briefly review several key studies.

Blair and colleagues have performed a number of studies examining physical fitness and risk of all-cause mortality in men and women who received preventive medical examinations at the Cooper Clinic in Dallas. In these studies, all subjects performed exercise treadmill tests and METS were estimated from the treadmill settings. In a study published in 1989 involving >13,000 subjects followed for a mean of 8 years (Blair et al., 1989), Blair reported that after statistical adjustment for age and a number of risk factors, all-cause mortality declined across fitness quintiles from 64 per 10,000 person years in the least fit men to 18.6 per 10,000 person years in the most fit men. There were also reduced rates of mortality from cancer in the higher fit individuals. A subsequent study from the Cooper Clinic (Blair et al., 1996) involving a larger cohort of >32,000 subjects focused on the interactions between fitness and cardiovascular risk factors and all-cause mortality. They found that higher fitness levels were protective against commonly measured risk factors such as smoking, high blood pressure, or elevated cholesterol levels. For example, men in the highest tertiles of fitness who were nonsmokers had a death rate of about 20 deaths per 10,000 person years, whereas nonsmokers in the lowest fitness tertile had a death rate of about 35 deaths per 10,000 years. By contrast, smokers in the lowest fitness tertile had a death rate of about 50 deaths per 10,000 person years. The results clearly demonstrated the protective effect of fitness levels in the presence of cardiovascular risk factors. It is difficult to attribute causality in these observational studies. Blair and colleagues hypothesized that changes in fitness levels would impact on all-cause mortality. They performed an analysis of 9,777 men who had two evaluations at the Cooper Clinic (Blair et al., 1995). They stratified subjects as to whether they were unfit at both examinations, fit at both examinations, or went from unfit at the first examination to fit at the second examination. The overall all-cause mortality rate for men unfit at both visits was 122 per 10,000 man years. Men who were fit at both visits had a substantially lower mortality rate of 39.6 per 10,000 man years. Men who improved their fitness levels had a mortality rate, intermediate between the two other groups, of 68 per 10,000 man years. They estimated that for each minute increased time on the treadmill, there was an 8% reduction in mortality. One potential flaw of this study is the impact of regression to the mean when one employs categorical analyses; a small shift in performance by men near one of the threshold boundaries for fitness would put them in a different category. Nevertheless, the results suggest that improving fitness and maintaining higher levels of fitness are protective and reduce mortality.

Recently, investigators at the Cooper Clinic examined whether higher cardiorespiratory fitness attenuates the mortality risk associated with obesity in 13,155 adults with hypertension (McAuley et al., 2009). Fitness was quantified as the duration of a symptom-limited maximal treadmill exercise test, and subjects were stratified as being in one of three groups: low (lowest 20%), moderate (middle 40%), and high (upper 40%). The moderate fit group had a reduction of about 42% in all-cause mortality compared to the low fit, with a greater 57% reduction noted in the high-fit group compared to the low-fit group. Of note, high-fit obese men had similar all-cause and cardiovascular mortality as their high-fit, nonobese counterparts. This suggests that high levels of fitness may in part protect against the adverse metabolic effects of obesity.

Lakka and colleagues at the Kuopio Research Institute of Exercise Medicine assessed fitness via cycle ergometry with measurement of aerobic capacity using a metabolic cart in 1,453 men aged 42 to 60 years and followed them on average for 4.9 years to examine the impact of physical activity and fitness on risk of acute myocardial infarction (Lakka et al., 1994). Subjects in the highest third of physical activity had a 69% reduction in risk for acute MI compared to the lowest third. Similarly, individuals in the highest third of fitness level had a 74% reduction in risk for acute MI compared to the lowest third, supporting the notion that both higher levels of leisure-time physical activity and fitness are inversely associated with risk for MI. Recently, investigators from the Kuopio Research Institute published a study (Laukkanen et al., 2010) focusing on fitness and risk for cancer. They followed a substantially larger number of subjects than in the prior study, 2,268 men, on whom they had performed treadmill tests with measurement of VO_2max. The men were followed on average for 16.7 years. They reported that men with a $VO_2max >$ 33.2 ml.kg/min (highest tertile) had a 27% decreased risk of cancer incidence and 37% reduced risk of cancer mortality than men with $VO_2max < 26.9$ ml/kg/min (lowest tertile). This reduction was largely due to decreased risk of lung cancer. Higher levels of physical activity were also associated with a 37% decreased risk of cancer. The mechanisms underlying the decreased cancer risk associated with increased physical activity and fitness remain to be determined.

A study by Kokkinos et al. (2008) examined the association between peak METs achieved during a clinical exercise test and mortality in 6,749 black and 8,911 white male veterans, mean age of 59 years, with and without cardiovascular disease. Over a mean follow-up of 7.5 years, peak METs achieved was the strongest predictor of risk for mortality. In continuous analyses, the adjusted risk was reduced by 13% for every 1-MET increase in exercise capacity. When stratified by fitness level, compared with those who achieved <5 METs, the mortality risk was approximately 50% lower for those with an exercise capacity of 7.1 to 10 METs, and 70% lower for those achieving >10 METs. Race and prevalent cardiovascular disease did not significantly impact on inverse relationship between fitness and all-cause mortality. The authors subsequently performed a subgroup analysis of 1,727 males with high-normal blood pressure (Kokkinos et al., 2009). The overall findings were similar to those described for the total population. Over a mean follow-up period of 9.8 ± 6.0 years, the peak METs achieved was inversely associated with all-cause mortality, independent of traditional cardiovascular risk factors. They estimated that for each 1 MET increase in VO_2max, the adjusted mortality risk was reduced by 13%. When stratified by fitness level, their analyses demonstrated a threshold level of 4 METs (14 ml/kg/min) to reduce mortality risk. Mortality risk was reduced by 30% for those who achieved 4.1–6.0 METs, 61% for those who achieved 8.1–10 METs, and additional reductions for those who exceeded 12 METs. The threshold level thus appeared to be lower for those with high-normal blood pressure than for the total population.

Lastly, a recent meta-analysis by Kodama et al. (2009) pooled the results from 33 studies that collectively included >100,000 subjects. They analyzed their fitness data either as continuous variables based on VO_2max indexed in METs, or by categorical analyses of low, intermediate, and high fitness levels. Their results were very similar to those of Kokkinos. They reported that a 1 MET higher level of VO_2 max was associated with 13% and 15% decrements in risk of all-cause mortality and coronary heart disease, respectively. In categorical analyses, individuals with low fitness, which they described as <7.9 MET, had a substantially higher risk of all-cause mortality and coronary heart disease deaths compared with those with intermediate (7.9 to 10.8 METS), and high fitness (>10.9 METs). The authors concluded that a minimal VO_2max of 7.9 METs may be the threshold for significant prevention of all-cause mortality and coronary heart disease. Although not emphasized in the article, there is a discussion that these fitness values are for individuals 40 years of age, and the fitness cut-point values have to be age- and gender-adjusted. At age 60 years, the numbers for men are 7 METS for men and 5 METS for women. Based on 1 MET equaling 3.5 ml/kg/min, 7 METS would represent a VO_2max of 24.5 ml/kg/min for men, and 5 METS, 18.5 ml/kg/min for women aged 60 years. The threshold values for a minimal VO_2max are substantially higher than those observed by Kokkinos.

In interpreting these studies, it is important to recognize that there is a genetic component to physical fitness that may account for 40% of the variation among individuals (Rankinen & Bouchard, 2008). The genetic factors that contribute to fitness, or low fitness, may also influence cardiovascular risk factors, body composition, and other metabolic determinants. Athletes presumably have genetic factors that contribute to their high level of fitness. Some have speculated about a low-fitness phenotype that is in part genetically determined (Church, 2009) that would be comprised in "metabolic disadvantaged" individuals with intrinsically low fitness and low oxidative capacity, that have increased fatigability. These characteristics would predispose them to being sedentary, resulting in increased CVD and metabolic risk. From a public health perspective, identifying and targeting these individuals for aggressive intervention would be of particular health benefit. Nevertheless, the presence and influence of genetic factors on fitness and metabolism does not in any way alter the overall conclusion that high levels of physical fitness are protective against cardiovascular disease, cancer, and all-cause mortality.

Exercise, Physical Activity, and Dementia

A number of studies have examined whether physical activity is protective against dementia. We review three studies. Abbott and colleagues examined the relationships between miles walked per day and risk for dementia in older "physically capable" men aged 71 to 93 years enrolled in the Honolulu Heart Study (Abbott et al., 2004). They found that overall, after adjusting for age, men who walked the least (<0.25 miles per day) experienced a 1.8 fold excess risk for dementia compared to men who walked more than 2 miles per day. In the Nurses Health Study, higher levels of physical activity were strongly associated with higher levels of cognitive function and less cognitive declines (Weuve et al., 2004). There appeared to be dose-response effect, with women in the highest energy quintiles having less cognitive decline than those in the lowest quintile. Other studies have focused on leisure time activities and risk of dementia (Verghese et al., 2003). Reading, playing board games, dancing, and playing musical instruments were associated with decreased risk for dementia.

Exercise, Aging, and Disability

It is well known that the age-adjusted death rates have been decreasing over the past 120 years in Western society, resulting in an overall increase in life expectancy. By contrast, maximal lifespan is unchanged. This results in a rectangularization of the survival curves. That is, the survival curve is shifting to the right and changing in shape from a sigmoidal pattern to a rectangular pattern, resulting in a compression of mortality. A major ongoing issue is whether the additional years gained in longevity are healthy years, or represent additional years of impaired function and disability. Thirty years ago Fries (1980) proposed the compression of morbidity hypothesis. This hypothesis posits that preventive lifestyle behaviors such as regular physical activity in conjunction with other improvement in health behaviors (smoking cessation, better diet, etc) (secondary aging) and better medical care will postpone disability (broadly defined) by at least as much as it does mortality, therefore compressing the time interval between disability and the later onset of death. Stated slightly differently:

the Compression of Morbidity paradigm holds that if the average age at first chronic infirmity is postponed, and if this postponement is greater than increases in life expectancy, then average cumulative lifetime morbidity will decrease, squeezed between a later onset and the time of death. (Fries, 2005, p. 164)

Collectively, the available data supports the compression of morbidity hypothesis. We will briefly review several studies.

One approach to testing the Fries hypothesis is via analysis of longitudinal trends in self-reported health and disability. An examination of the National Long-Term Care Survey, National Health Interview Survey, and other survey data by Fries (2005) indicated that since 1982, disability declined by about 2% a year, while mortality declined by 1% a year, consistent with a compression of morbidity. Moreover, the decline in disability appeared to be accelerating. The study estimated that those with few health risks have only one-fourth the disability of those who have more risks, and the onset of disability is postponed from 7 to 12 years. An examination of Freedman and colleagues' (Freedman, Martin, & Schoeni, 2002) national survey data also demonstrated declines in any disability (−1.55% to −0.92% per year), instrumental activities of daily living disability (−2.74% to −0.40% per year), and functional limitations. Some have cautioned (Parker & Thorslund, 2007) that the measurement instruments are imprecise and that while disability measures often show improvement, there can be a simultaneous increase in the burden from chronic disease and related functional impairments that require the increased use of healthcare resources.

Given the potential for healthy lifestyle to decrease morbidity and mortality, the specific question arises as to whether chronic physical activity decreases disability. Given the model of older athletes as exemplifying successful aging, Fries and colleagues (Chakravarty, Hubert, Lingala, & Fries, 2008) performed a 21-year longitudinal study of self-reported disability in runners (initial mean age of 59 years) and age-matched healthy controls. Multivariate analyses showed that runners had a significantly lower risk of developing disability than the controls, and also had about half the death rate of the controls. Furthermore, they noted that both the disability and survival curves continued to diverge between groups. Even with the inherent issue of self-selection bias, this study supports the hypothesis that chronic physical activity is associated with decreased mortality and reduced disability in later life.

Effects of exercise training on cardiovascular risk factors in older individuals

Increased physical activity is recommended as a means to reduce cardiovascular risk factors. Vigorous exercise improves cardiovascular fitness indexed as VO_2max, reduces visceral adiposity and has salutary effects on lipid profiles, insulin, sensitivity, glucose metabolism, and blood pressure (Katzel et al., 1995), thereby reducing major components and risk associated with the metabolic syndrome. Exercise intervention studies performed in our laboratory and elsewhere generally demonstrate that older individuals who participate in a 3–6-month-long structured aerobic exercise intervention can on average increase their peak/VO_2max by at least 15% (Katzel et al., 1995; Spina, 1993). In general, older and younger individuals have the same relative improvement in peak/VO_2max with aerobic training. These findings are not limited to healthy older adults. We and other have reported substantial improvements in peak VO_2 with aerobic exercise training in older adults with substantial medical comorbidities including peripheral arterial disease (Gardner, Montgomery, Flinn, & Katzel, 2005), congestive heart failure (Gerovasili et al., 2009), hemiparetic stroke (Luft et al., 2008), and Parkinson's disease (Skidmore, Patterson, Shulman, Sorkin, & Macko, 2008). The magnitude of the improvement in peak VO_2 is dependent upon a number of factors including the baseline characteristics of the subjects, their age, and the specific training regiment, that is, time, intensity, and duration of the training. High intensity aerobic training appears to be more effective in increasing VO_2max than duration-based interventions. However, the potential for increased injuries and increased dropout rates with more intense training is apparent. The setting of the intervention is also important as a number of studies have examined compliance to center-based versus home-based interventions. New training paradigms including adaptive physical activity hold promise for improving fitness, balance, and quality of life in older adults (Michael et al., 2009).

Much of the metabolic benefit attributed to vigorous aerobic exercise training is likely due to the accompanying weight loss. Endurance training produces small but significant decrements in percentage body fat and fat mass in older adults, including decrements in intra-abdominal fat as assessed by CT scan. In middle-aged and older women and men aerobic exercise results in significantly improved lipoprotein concentrations, as well as improved glucose tolerance, decreased insulin resistance, and lower blood pressure. The book chapter by Schwartz and Kohret (2009) provides a comprehensive discussion on exercise and cardiovascular risk factors. Typically in healthy older adults following 6 months of endurance training, LDL-C levels are lowered by 5–10%, TG levels are lowered by 10–20%, and HDL-C levels are increased by 5–10% (Katzel et al., 1995). Cross-sectional studies suggest that there is a dose response between the intensity of exercise training and improvement in HDL-C levels with aerobic exercise training. Endurance training has modest effects on blood pressure (3 to 5 mm decrement in both systolic and diastolic blood pressure) and fasting glucose. Several analyses suggest that the blood pressure lowering effect of low and modest intensity exercise is comparable, and perhaps even superior to high-intensity training. On a percentage basis, probably the largest improvements in traditional cardiac risk factors occur in measures of insulin resistance where postprandial insulin levels during an oral glucose tolerance test decline by 30–60%. Aerobic training with weight loss yields substantially larger beneficial effects on metabolic function than aerobic exercise training alone (Katzel et al., 1997). Aerobic exercise training improves nontraditional risk factors including multiple markers of inflammation, endothelial function, and heart rate variability. The effect of aerobic exercise on bone density is modest and endurance training may be more effective at preventing bone loss than improving bone mass/density. The effect of resistive training on lipoprotein values is modest. Resistive training has more pronounced effects on glucose metabolism and bone health.

Guidelines and Recommendations for Physical Activity and Exercise

In 2008, the Department of Health and Human Services published the 2008 Physical Activity guidelines for Americans (Physical Activity Guidelines Advisory Committee, 2008). The specific guidelines for older adults from the report include:

- All older adults should avoid inactivity. Some physical activity is better than none, and older adults who participate in any amount of physical activity gain some health benefits.
- Older adults should determine their level of effort for physical activity relative to their level of fitness.
- Older adults with chronic conditions should understand whether and how their conditions affect their ability to do regular physical activity safely.
- For substantial health benefits, older adults should do at least 150 minutes a week of moderate-intensity, or 75 minutes a week of vigorous-intensity aerobic physical activity, or an equivalent combination of moderate- and vigorous-intensity aerobic activity. Aerobic activity should be performed in episodes of at least 10 minutes, and preferably, it should be spread throughout the week.
- When older adults cannot do 150 minutes of moderate-intensity aerobic activity a week because of chronic conditions, they should be as physically active as their abilities and conditions allow.
- For additional and more extensive health benefits, older adults should increase their aerobic physical activity to 300 minutes a week of moderate-intensity, or 150 minutes a week of vigorous-intensity aerobic physical activity, or an equivalent combination of moderate-and vigorous-intensity activity. Additional health benefits are gained by engaging in physical activity beyond this amount.
- Older adults should also do muscle-strengthening activities that are moderate or high intensity and involve all major muscle groups on 2 or more days a week, as these activities provide additional health benefits.
- Older adults should do exercises that maintain or improve balance if they are at risk of falling.

Thus, there is compelling data that increased physical activity and fitness are associated with decreased cardiometabolic risk, cognitive impairment, and disability. The goal should be a complete lifestyle intervention toward achieving and maintaining an optimal weight in conjunction with regular aerobic physical activity, which is likely to not only result in the greatest improvements in cardiometabolic risk factors, but also reduce the effects of accelerated aging and increase the likelihood of "successful aging."

Acknowledgment

This work was supported by the Department of Veterans Affairs and Veterans Affairs Medical Center Baltimore Geriatric Research, Education and Clinical Center (GRECC) and by The National Institute on Aging (NIA) Claude D. Pepper Older Americans Independence Center P30-AG028747.

References

Abbott, R. D., White, L. R., Ross, G. W., Masaki, K. H., Curb, J. D., & Petrovitch, H. (2004). Walking and dementia in physically capable elderly men. *Journal of the American Medical Association, 292,* 1447–1453.

American College of Sports Medicine. (2010). General principles of exercise prescription. In *ACSM's guidelines for exercise testing and prescription* (8th ed., pp. 152–82). Philadelphia: Lippincott Williams and Wilkins.

Bassett, D. R., & Howley, E. T. (2000). Limiting factors for maximum oxygen uptake and determinants of endurance performance. *Medicine and Science in Sports & Exercise, 32,* 70–84.

Bean, J. F., Leveille, S. G., Kiely, D. K., Bandinelli, S., Guralnik, J. M., & Ferrucci, L. A. (2003). Comparison of leg power and leg strength within the InCHIANTI study: Which influences mobility more? *Journals of Gerontology: Series A: Medical and Biological Sciences, 58,* 728–733.

Berkman, L. F., Seeman, T. E., Albert, M., Blazer, D., Kahn, R., Mohs, R., ... McClearn, G. (1993). High, usual and impaired functioning in community-dwelling older men and women: Findings from the MacArthur Foundation Research Network on Successful Aging. *Journal of Clinical Epidemiology, 46,* 1129–1140.

Blair, S. N., Kampert, J. B., Kohl, H. W., III, Barlow, C. E., Macera, C. A., Paffenbarger, R. S., & Gibbons, L. W. (1996). Influences of cardiorespiratory fitness and other precursors on cardiovascular disease and all-cause mortality in men and women. *Journal of the American Medical Association, 276,* 205–210.

Blair, S. N., Kohl, H. W. III, Barlow, C. E., Paffenbarger, R. S., Gibbons, L. W., & Macera, C. A. (1995). Changes in physical fitness and all-cause mortality. A prospective study of healthy and unhealthy men. *Journal of the American Medical Association, 273,* 1093–1098.

Blair, S. N., Kohl, H. W. III, Paffenbarger, R. S., Clark, D. G., Cooper, K. H., & Gibbons, L. W. (1989). Physical fitness and all-cause mortality. A prospective study of healthy men and women. *Journal of the American Medical Association, 262,* 2395–2401.

Buskirk, E. R., & Hodgson, J. L. (1987). Age and aerobic power: The rate of change in men and women. *Federation Proceedings, 46,* 1824–1829.

Chakravarty, E. F., Hubert, H. B., Lingala, V. B., & Fries, J. F. (2008). Reduced disability and mortality among aging runners: A 21-year longitudinal study. *Archives of Internal Medicine, 168,* 1638–46.

Church, T. (2009). The low-fitness phenotype as a risk factor: More than just being sedentary? *Obesity, 17* (Suppl. 3), S39–S42.

Dehn, M. M., & Bruce, R. A. (1972). Longitudinal variations in maximal oxygen intake with age and activity. *Journal of Applied Physiology, 33,* 805–807.

Depp, C. A, & Jeste, D. V. (2009). Definitions and predictors of successful aging: A comprehensive review of larger quantitative studies. *Focus, 7,* 137–150.

Ericsson, S., Eriksson, M., Vitols, S., Einarsson, K., Berglund, L., & Angelin, B. (1991). Influence of age on the metabolism of plasma low density lipoproteins in healthy males. *Journal of Clinical Investigation, 87,* 591–596.

Fleg, J. L., & Goldberg, A. P. (1990). Exercise in older people: Cardiovascular and metabolic adaptations. In W. R. Hazzard, R. Andres, E. L. Bierman, & J. P. Blass (Eds.), *Principles of geriatric medicine and gerontology* (2nd ed., pp. 85–1000). New York: McGraw Hill.

Fleg, J. L., & Lakatta, E. G. (1988). Role of muscle loss in the age-associated reduction in VO$_2$max. *Journal of Applied Physiology, 65*, 1147–1151.

Fleg, J. L., Morrell, C. H., Bos, A. G., Brant, L. J., Talbot, L. A., Wright, J. G., & Lakatta, E. G. (2005). Accelerated longitudinal decline of aerobic capacity in healthy older adults. *Circulation, 112*, 674–682.

Freedman, V. A., Martin, L. G., & Schoeni, R. F. (2002). Recent trends in disability and functioning among older adults in the United States: A systematic review. *Journal of the American Medical Association, 288*, 3137–3146.

Fried, L. P., Tangen, C. M., Walston, J., Newman, A. B., Hirsch, C., Gottiener, J., . . . McBurnie, M. A. for the Cardiovascular Health Study Collaborative Research Group. (2001). Frailty in older adults: Evidence for a phenotype. *Journals of Gerontology: Series A: Medical and Biological Sciences, 56*, M146–M157.

Fries, J. F. (1980). Aging, natural death, and the compression of morbidity. *New England Journal of Medicine, 303*, 130–135.

Fries, J. F. (2005). Frailty, heart disease, and stroke: The compression of morbidity paradigm. *American Journal of Preventive Medicine, 29* (5 Suppl. 1), 164–168.

Fulton, J. E, Simons-Morton, D. G., & Galuska, D. Physical activity. (2009). An investment that pays multiple health dividends. *Archives of Internal Medicine, 169*, 2124–2127.

Gardner, A. W., Montgomery, P. S., Flinn, W. R., & Katzel, L. I. (2005). The effect of exercise intensity on the response to exercise rehabilitation in patients with intermittent claudication. *Journal of Vascular Surgery, 42*, 702–709.

Gerovasili, V., Drakos, S., Kravari, M., Malliaras, K., Karatzanos, E., Dimopoulos, S., . . . Nanas, S. (2009). Physical exercise improves the peripheral microcirculation of patients with chronic heart failure. *Journal of Cardiopulmonary Rehabilitation and Prevention, 29*, 385–391.

Gill, T. M., Gahbauer, E. A., Han, L., & Allore, H. G. (2010). Trajectories of disability in the last year of life. *New England Journal of Medicine, 362*, 1173–1180.

Goldberg, A. P., Busby-Whitehead, M. J., Katzel, L. I., Krauss, R. M., Lumpkin, M., & Hagberg, J. M. (2000). Cardiovascular fitness, body composition, and lipoprotein lipid metabolism in older men. *Journals of Gerontology: Series A: Medical and Biological Sciences, 55*, M342–M349.

Guyton, A. C., & Hall, J. E. (2000). *Textbook of Medical Physiology* (10th ed.). Philadelphia: Saunders.

Hagberg, J. M. (1985). Effect of training on the decline of VO$_2$max with aging. *Federation Proceedings, 44*, 343–347.

Heath, G. W., Hagberg, J. M., Ehsani, A. A., & Holloszy, J. O. (1981). A physiological comparison of young and older endurance athletes. *Journal of Applied Physiology, 51*, 634–640.

Heiss, G., Tamir, I., Davis, C. E., Tyroler, H. A., Rifkand, B. M., Schonfeld, G., . . . Frantz, I. D., Jr. (1980). Lipoprotein-cholesterol distributions in selected North American populations: The lipid research clinics program prevalence study. *Circulation, 61*, 302–315.

Hollenberg, M., Yang, J., Haight, T. J., & Tager, I. B. (2006). Longitudinal changes in aerobic capacity: Implications for concepts of aging. *Journals of Gerontology: Series A: Medical and Biological Sciences, 61*, 851–858.

Jackson, A. S., Beard, E. F., Wier, L. T., Ross, R. M., Stuteville, J. E., & Blair, S. N. (1995). Changes in aerobic power of men, ages 25–70 yr. *Medicine and Science in Sports & Exercise, 27*, 113–120.

Kasch, F. W., Wallace, J. P., & Van Camp, S. P. (1985). Effects of 18 years of endurance exercise on the physical capacity of older men. *Journal of Cardiopulmonary Rehabilitation and Prevention, 5*, 308–312.

Kasch, F. W., Wallace, J. P., Van Camp, S. P., & Verity, L. A. (1988). Longitudinal study of cardiovascular stability in active men aged 45–65 years. *Physician and Sportsmedicine, 16*, 117–124.

Katzel, L. I., Bleecker, E. R., Colman, E. G., Rogus, E. M., Sorkin, J. D., & Goldberg, A. P. (1995). Effects of weight loss vs aerobic exercise training on risk factors for coronary disease in healthy, obese, middle-aged and older men. *A randomized controlled trial. Journal of the American Medical Association, 995,* 1915–1921.

Katzel, L. I., Bleecker, E. R., Rogus, E. M., & Goldberg, A. P. (1997). Sequential effects of aerobic exercise training and weight loss on risk factors for coronary disease in healthy, obese middle-aged and older men. *Metabolism, 46,* 1441–1447.

Katzel, L. I., Sorkin, J. D., & Fleg, J. L., (2001). A comparison of longitudinal changes in aerobic fitness in older endurance athletes and sedentary men. *Journal of the American Geriatrics Society, 49,* 1657–1664.

Kitzman, D., & Taffet, G. E. (2009). Effects of aging on the cardiovascular system. In J. B. Halter, J. G. Ouslander, M. E. Tinnetti, S. Studenski, K. P. High, & S. Asthana (Eds.), *Hazzard's geriatric medicine and gerontology* (pp. 883–896). New York: McGraw Hill.

Kodama, S., Saito, K., Tanaka, S., Maki, M., Yachi, Y., Asumi, M., ... Sone, H. (2009). Cardiorespiratory fitness as a quantitative predictor of all-cause mortality and cardiovascular events in healthy men and women: A meta-analysis. *Journal of the American Medical Association, 301,* 2024–2035.

Kokkinos, P., Doumas, M., Myers, J., Faselis C., Manolis, A., Pittaras, A., ... Fletcher, R. D. (2009). A graded association of exercise capacity and all-cause mortality in males with high normal blood pressure. *Blood Pressure, 18,* 261–267.

Kokkinos, P., Myers, J., Kokkinos, J. P., Pittaras, A., Narayan, P., Manolis, A., ... Singh, S. (2008). Exercise capacity and mortality in black and white men. *Circulation, 117,* 614–622.

Kuller, L. H., Velentgas, P., Barzilay, J., Beauchamp, N., O'Leary, D. H., Savage, P. J. (2000). Diabetes mellitus: Subclinical cardiovascular disease and risk of incident cardiovascular disease and all-cause mortality. *Arteriosclerosis, Thrombosis, and Vascular Biology, 20,* 823–829.

Lakatta, E. G. (1993). Cardiovascular regulatory mechanisms in advanced age. *Physiological Reviews, 73,* 413–467.

Lakka, T. A., Venalainen, J. N., Raurama, R., Salonen, R., Tuomilehto, J., & Salonen, J. T. (1994). Relation of leisure-time physical activity and cardiorespiratory fitness to the risk of acute myocardial infarction in men. *New England Journal of Medicine, 330,* 1549–1554.

Laukkanen, J. A., Pukkalac, E., Rauramaab, R, Mäkikallio, T. H., Toriolaf, A. T., & Kurla, S. (2010). Cardiorespiratory fitness, lifestyle factors and cancer risk and mortality in Finnish men. *European Journal of Cancer, 46*(2), 355–363.

Luft, A. R., Macko, R. F., Forrester, L. W., Villagra, F., Ivey, F., Sorkin, J. D., ... Hanley, D. F. (2008). Treadmill exercise activates subcortical neural networks and improves walking after stroke: A randomized controlled trial. *Stroke, 39,* 3341–3350.

Marti, B., & Howald, H. (1990). Long-term effects of physical training on aerobic capacity: Controlled study of former elite athletes. *Journal of Applied Physiology, 69,* 1451–1459.

McAuley, P. A., Sui, X., Church, T. S., Hardin, J. W., Myers, J. N., & Blair, S. N. (2009). The joint effects of cardiorespiratory fitness and adiposity on mortality risk in men with hypertension. *American Journal of Hypertension, 22,* 1062–1069.

McGavock, J. M., Hastings, J. L., Snell, P. G., McGuire, D. K., Pacini, E. L., Levine, B. D., & Mitchell, J. H. (2009). A forty-year follow-up of the Dallas Bed Rest and Training study: The effect of age on the cardiovascular response to exercise in men. *Journals of Gerontology: Series A: Medical and Biological Sciences, 64,* 293–239.

McGuire D. K., Levine, B. D., Williamson, J. W., Snell, P. G., Blomqvist, C. G., Saltin, B., & Mitchell, J. H. (2001a). A 30-year follow-up of the Dallas Bedrest and Training Study: I. Effect of age on the cardiovascular response to exercise. *Circulation, 104,* 1350–1357.

McGuire D. K., Levine, B. D., Williamson, J. W., Snell, P. G., Blomqvist, C. G., Saltin, B., & Mitchell, J. H. (2001b). A 30-year follow-up of the Dallas Bedrest and Training Study: II. Effect of age on cardiovascular adaptation to exercise training. *Circulation, 104*, 1358–1366.

Mengelkoch, L. J., Pollock, M. L., Limacher, M. C., Graves, J. E., Shireman, R. B., Riley, W. J., . . . Leon, A. S. (1997). Effects of age, physical training, and physical fitness on coronary heart disease risk factors in older track athletes at twenty-year follow-up. *Journal of the American Geriatrics Society, 45*, 1446–1453.

Michael, K., Goldberg, A. P., Treuth, M. S., Beans, J., Normandt, P., & Macko, R. F. (2009). Progressive adaptive physical activity in stroke improves balance, gait, and fitness: Preliminary results. *Topics in Stroke Rehabilitation, 16*, 133–139.

Miller, N. E. (1984). Why does plasma low density lipoprotein concentration in adults increase with age? *Lancet, 1984*(1), 263–266.

Morris, J. N., Kagan, A., Pattison, D. C., & Gardner, M. J. (1966). Incidence and prediction of ischaemic heart-disease in London busmen. *Lancet, 1966* (2), 552–559.

Newman, A. B., Arnold, A. M., Naydeck, B. L., Fried, L. P., Burke, G. L., Enright, P., . . . Tracy, R. for the Cardiovascular health Study Research Group. (2003). "Successful aging." Effect of subclinical cardiovascular disease. *Archives of Internal Medicine, 163*, 2315–2322.

Ogawa, T., Spina, R. J., Martin, W. H., Kohrt, W. M., Schechtman, K. B., Holloszy, J. O., & Ehsani, A. A. (1992). Effects of aging, sex, and physical training on cardiovascular responses to exercise. *Circulation, 86*, 494–503.

Paffenbarger, R. S. Jr, & Hyde, R. T. (1984). Exercise in the prevention of coronary heart disease. *Preventive Medicine, 13*, 3–22.

Paffenbarger, R. S., Hyde, R. T., Wing, A. L., & Hsieh, C. C. (1986). Physical activity, all-cause mortality and longevity of college alumni. *New England Journal of Medicine, 314*, 605–613.

Paffenbarger, R. S. Jr., Wing, A. L., & Hyde, R. T. (1981). Chronic disease in former college students. XVI. Physical activity as an index of heart attack risk in college alumni. *American Journal of Epidemiology, 108*, 161–175.

Parker, M.G., & Thorslund, M. (2007). Health trends in the elderly population: Getting better and getting worse. *Gerontologist, 47*, 150–158.

Physical Activity Guidelines Advisory Committee. (2008). *Physical activity guidelines advisory committee report, 2008.* Washington, DC: U.S. Department of Health and Human Services.

Pimentel, A. E., Gentile, C. L., Tanaka, H., Seals, D. R., & Gates, P. E. (2003). Greater rate of decline in maximal aerobic capacity with age in endurance-trained than in sedentary men. *Journal of Applied Physiology, 94*, 2406–2413.

Pollock, M. L., Foster, C., Knapp, J. L., & Schmidt, D. H. (1987). Effect of age and training on aerobic capacity and body composition of master athletes. *Journal of Applied Physiology, 62*, 725–731.

Pollock, M. L., Mengelkoch, L. J., Graves, J. E., Lowenthal, D. T., Linmacher, M. C., Foster, C., & Wilmore, J. H. (1997). Twenty-year follow-up of aerobic power and body composition of older track athletes. *Journal of Applied Physiology, 82*, 1508–1516.

Rankinen, T., & Bouchard, C. (2008). Gene-physical activity interactions: Overview of human studies. *Obesity, 16* (Suppl. 3), S47–S50.

Rogers, M. A., Hagberg, J. M., Marint, W. H. III, Ehsani, A. A., & Holloszy, J. O. (1990). Decline in VO$_2$max with aging in master athletes and sedentary men. *Journal of Applied Physiology, 68*, 2195–2199.

Rosen, M. J., Sorkin, J. D., Goldberg, A. P., Hagberg, J. M., & Katzel, L. I. (1998). Predictors of age-associated decline in maximal aerobic capacity: A comparison of four statistical models. *Journal of Applied Physiology, 84*, 2163–2170.

Rowe, J. W., & Kahn, R. L. (1987). Human aging: Usual and successful. *Science*, *237*, 143–149.

Rowe, J. W., & Kahn, R. L. (1997). Successful aging. *Gerontologist*, *37*, 443–440.

Saltin, B., Blomqvist, G., Mitchell, J. H., Johnson, R. L., Wildenthal, K., & Chapman, C. B. (1968). Response to exercise after bed rest and after training: A longitudinal study of adaptive changes in oxygen transport and body composition. *Circulation*, *37/38* (Suppl. VII), VII-1–VII-78.

Schroeder, T. E., Hawkins, S. A., Hyslop, D., Vallejo, A. F., Jensky, N. E., & Wiswell, R. A. (2007). Longitudinal change in coronary heart disease risk factors in older runners. *Age and Ageing*, *36*, 57–62.

Schulman, S. P., Fleg, J. L., Goldberg, A. P., Busby-Whitehead, J., Hagberg, J. M., O'Connor, F. C., . . . Lakatta, E. G. Continuum of cardiovascular performance across a broad range of fitness levels in healthy older men. *Circulation*, *94*, 359–367.

Schwartz, R. S., & Kohret, W. M. (2009) Exercise: Physiologic and functional effects. In J. B. Halter, J. G. Ouslander, M. E. Tinnetti, S. Studenski, K. P. High, & S. Asthana (Eds.), *Hazzard's geriatric medicine and gerontology* (pp. 1381–1396). New York: McGraw Hill.

Sesso, H. D., Paffenbarger, R. S. Jr., & Lee, I. M. (2000). Physical activity and coronary heart disease in men. The Harvard Alumni Health Study. *Circulation*, *102*, 974–980.

Shimokata, H., Muller, D. C., Fleg, J. L., Sorkin, J., Ziemba, A. W., & Andres, R. (1991). Age as independent determinant of glucose tolerance. *Diabetes*, *40*, 44–51.

Short, K. R., Vittone, J. L., Bigelow, M. L., Proctor, D. N., & Nair, K. S., . . . (2004). Age and aerobic exercise training effects on whole body and muscle protein metabolism. *American Journal of Physiology – Endocrinology and Metabolism*, *286*, E92–E101.

Skidmore, F. M., Patterson, S. L., Shulman, L. M., Sorkin, J. D., & Macko, R. F. (2008). Pilot safety and feasibility study of treadmill aerobic exercise in Parkinson disease with gait impairment. *Journal of Rehabilitation Research and Development*, *45*, 117–124.

Spina, R. J., Ogawa, T., Kohrt, W. M., Martin, W. H., Holloszy, J. O., & Ehsani, A. A. (1993). Differences in cardiovascular adaptations to endurance exercise training between older men and women. *Journal of Applied Physiology*, *75*, 849–855.

Talbot, L. A., Metter, E. J., & Fleg, J. L. (2000). Leisure-time physical activities and their relationship to cardiorespiratory fitness in healthy men and women 18–95 years old. *Medicine and Science in Sports & Exercise*, *32*, 417–425.

Tanaka, H., Desouza, C. A., Jones, P. P., Stevenson, E. T., Davy, K. P., & Seals, D. R. (1997). Greater rate of decline in maximal aerobic capacity with age in physically active vs. sedentary healthy women. *Journal of Applied Physiology*, *83*, 1947–1953.

Tanaka, H., & Seals, D. R. (2008). Endurance exercise performance in Masters athletes: Age-associated changes and underlying physiological mechanisms. *Journal of Physiology*, *586*, 55–63.

Trappe, S.W., Costill, D. L., Vukovich, M. D., Jones, J., & Melham, T. (1996). Aging among elite distance runners: A 22-yr longitudinal study. *Journal of Applied Physiology*, *80*, 285–290.

U.S. Preventive Services Task Force. (2009). Using nontraditional risk factors in coronary heart disease risk assessment: U. S. Preventive Services Task Force recommendation statement. *Annals of Internal Medicine*, *151*, 474–482.

Verghese, J., Lipton, R. B., Katze, M. J., Hall, C. B., Derby, C. A., Kuslansky, G., . . . Buschke, H. (2003). Leisure activities and risk of dementia in the elderly. *New England Journal of Medicine*, *348*, 2508–2516.

Weuve, J., Kang, J. H., Manson, J. E., Breteler, M. M. B., Ware, J. H., & Grodstein, F. (2004). Physical activity, including walking, and cognitive function in older women. *Journal of the American Medical Association*, *292*, 1454–1461.

Yataco, A. R., Busby-Whitehead, J., Drinkwater, D. T., & Katzel L. I. (1997). Relationship of body composition and cardiovascular fitness to lipoprotein lipid profiles in master athletes and sedentary men. *Aging, Clinical and Experimental Research*, *9*, 88–94.

6

Behavioral Stability and Change in Health Across the Adult Life Cycle

Ilene C. Siegler and Adam Davey

Knowledge of the behavioral factors that promote health and longer life and of the behavioral factors that lead to increases in disease and shorten life are central for the study of the aging process. In general, the behavioral risk factors that have been studied are called "risk factors" if they increase disease and "protective factors" if they decrease disease. The major risk factors that have been studied include smoking, obesity, and negative emotional states or personality traits such as hostility, pessimism, depression, and neuroticism. The major protective factors studied include exercise, social support, and positive emotions and traits such as conscientiousness and openness. Other behaviors such as alcohol use are seen as both risky (if practiced not enough or too much) and protective (if taken in modest amounts), as are other nutrients and components of the diet that have recommended levels for health, and following medical recommendations for treatments.

Theoretically, behavioral risk factors are important mechanisms whereby one can understand how internal psychological states such as personality are related to physical health outcomes such as heart disease, hypertension, and diabetes. One qualification to note is that the same risk factors may work differently for different diseases. For example, alcohol is risky for breast cancer and protective for heart disease.

The overarching question we will deal with in this chapter is to try to explain how these risk and protective factors change with age over the adult lifespan, how they are related to each other, how they are related to various diseases, and how they are related to longevity. The associations that stability or change in these factors have with morbidity (disease) and mortality (survival) during the adult years from age 18 to 60 are illustrated with findings from the University of North Carolina Alumni Heart Study (UNCAHS). A major focus of

The Wiley-Blackwell Handbook of Adulthood and Aging, First Edition. Edited by Susan Krauss Whitbourne and Martin J. Sliwinski. © 2012 Blackwell Publishing Ltd. Published 2012 by Blackwell Publishing Ltd.

that ongoing study has been to understand how developmental patterns of risky or protective behaviors are related to morbidity and mortality (Brummett, Helms, Dahlstrom, & Siegler, 2006; Siegler, 2007). Next, we use data we have analyzed from two nationally representative studies – the Health and Retirement Study (HRS; Juster & Suzman,1995) and the Georgia Centenarian Study (GCS; Davey et al., 2010; Poon & Perls, 2007) to estimate risk and aging associations from age 40 to age 100. These are cross-sectional data and give us a snapshot of middle-aged and older persons at one point in time.

Changes in risk factor behavior such as declines in smoking and increases in exercise are credited with reducing mortality from heart disease in the past 20 years (Ford et al., 2007) and thus it is assumed that if everyone followed recommendations for a healthier lifestyle we could increase longevity for the population as a whole (see Olshansky, Goldman, Zheng, & Rowe, 2009). Human behavior accounts for almost 40% of the risk associated with preventable premature deaths in the United States (National Institutes of Health, 2010).

Our approach in this chapter is to be very careful to document the study population and the characteristics of the research design that generated them. The devil is truly in the details. Broad generalizations that ignore whether the data are from cross-sectional or longitudinal study designs make findings hard to interpret; in addition, other design features of studies including the population studied, whether it is representative of the national population, and whether it is sampled from a particular single cohort, are also needed to have a full picture of what the findings mean. In other words, the details important to consider in studies of health and behavior pertain to both internal and external validity. In general, when the study samples the entire population, there are fewer problems with external validity and one can test whether models developed from such data apply fully to all individuals. However, this is generally at the cost of internal validity because larger studies tend to sacrifice measurement of the constructs of interest.

The NEO Personality Inventory (NEO-PI-R; Costa & McCrae, 1992; NEO-3; McCrae & Costa, 2010) is a good example of the problem of balancing internal and external validity. The full instrument has 240 items that measure the "Big Five" factors (Neuroticism, Extraversion, Openness, Agreeableness and Conscientiousness) – with 48 items per factor. Each factor has 6 facets with 8 items each. Large national data sets often estimate only the 5 factors and tend to use shortened scales with only 4 items per scale. Thus where the measure of Neuroticism or Conscientiousness comes from makes a difference in evaluating a study's findings on personality and health behavior, as it may or may not be the same measure. One needs to do analyses to see if the measures are comparable. Longitudinal studies, because they measure change over time, need to have more reliable scales so that change over time can be separated from unreliability of measurement.

At the risk of sounding pedantic, we will try to compare and contrast the findings from various types of studies to take advantage of the strength and weaknesses of each one because these details are so important to consider in evaluating a study's findings.

At present, current handbooks in behavioral medicine provide updated reviews by risk factor and by disease with a focus on interventions. They generally have one chapter on aging (see, e.g., Baum, Revenson, & Singer, 2001, in press; Siegler, Elias, & Bosworth, in press; Siegler, Hooker, Bosworth, Elias, & Spiro, 2010; Suls, Davidson, & Kaplan, 2010).

However, within the field of adult development and aging, coverage of health behaviors is expanding. For example, current undergraduate text books such as Hoyer and Roodin (2009) and Whitbourne and Whitbourne (2011) provide excellent discussions of physical health and aging. Books on healthy aging written for older persons to use to guide their own behavior (see Wei & Levkoff, 2000) also provide excellent guidelines for how older people should deal with exercise, smoking, nutrition, alcohol, safe sex, medications, immunizations, physical examinations, dentistry, and accident prevention as areas for risk factor modification.

In this chapter we are not dealing with psychiatric illness, cognitive decline, dementia, or the geriatric syndromes of frailty. Fried (2000) provides an excellent overview of the epidemiology of aging. The fields of geriatric medicine (Halter, Hazzard, Ouslander, Tinetti, & Studenski, 2009) and geriatric psychiatry (see Blazer & Steffens, 2009) are well established and deal with the explosion of research knowledge and clinical applications for the benefit of older persons and their families.

We will start with the UNCAHS, as it has detailed data from ages 18 to 60, with a gap from ages 19–39 when no data were collected. Next we will use data from the Health and Retirement Study as it covers age ranges from 50 to 100. We will compare it to data from the Georgia Centenarian Study, which has participants from ages 98 to 108. Thus using cross-sectional, longitudinal, and combined data analyses we can estimate the full adult life cycle.

The UNCAHS allows us to look in detail at the role of aging from 40–60 in a cohort of college-educated individuals (approximately 25% of the US population) with initial personality data collected 20 years earlier. The UNCAHS started in 1986–87 and enrolled persons who had attended the University of North Carolina 20 years earlier in the 1960s, at which time their personalities were measured (see Siegler, Peterson, Barefoot, & Williams, 1992). The study was designed to test the hypothesis that hostility is the toxic component of the Type A Behavior Pattern (see Barefoot, Dahlstrom, & Williams, 1983; Williams, 1994) in a cohort of baby boomers that included both men and women, from the theoretical perspective that personality would be related to risky or protective behaviors that would be related to health and disease in midlife.

Personality was measured in college with the MMPI, which has many clinical and research scales developed from its 544-item battery (Dahlstrom, Welsh, & Dahlstrom, 1972). The UNCAHS data were used to develop college student norms for the study. When the UNCAHS started enrolling subjects in 1987, approximately 20 years later, we only repeated 50 items to measure hostility and used the original version of the NEO Personality Inventory (NEO-PI) as we started data collection in 1988 and the inventory was not revised until 1992 (Costa & McCrae, 1992). The NEO-PI was given twice, approximately at age 42 and again at age 50. In order to keep a high response rate, we limited the information asked at any one wave; thus we do not have personality and risk measured at the same time as shown in the cross-sectional studies. We have shown that hostility in college predicts adult risk profiles at age 42 (Siegler, Peterson, Barefoot, & Williams, 1992) and furthermore that change in hostility of about 1 SD (7 points) predicts a full set of risk indicators during midlife (Siegler et al., 2003) with continuous and categorical measures of change. All of the measures of risk were collected from 21–32 years after the college measure of hostility and 1.3 to 8.9 years after the second

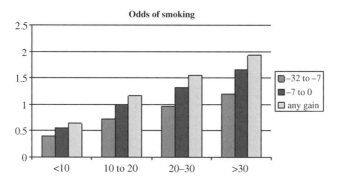

Figure 6.1   The odds of being a current smoker for 23-year change in hostility for each level of hostility in college. Created by Ilene Siegler

measure of hostility. Hostility change was measured 23 years later at approximately age 42 and risk indicators were from age 43–50. These risk indicators have all been implicated in increasing the probability of developing heart disease.

Risk was determined on the basis of setting the cut point in order to have a high risk category for each behavior studied: being a current smoker (12% of population, see Figure 6.1), being obese with a body mass index (BMI) > 30 (11.9%, see Figure 6.2), avoiding all exercise (3.9%, see Figure 6.3), drinking more than the recommended amount of alcohol (21%, see Figure 6.4), eating a high fat diet (21%), being socially isolated (6.3%), reporting inadequate social support (12.6%), having a reported income below the median for the level of education (5.5%), reporting less than expected in career achievement (25.2%), less than expected in personal relationships (30%), at high risk for depression with a CESD score > 16 (14%), and evaluating life as changing for the worse in terms of family life (13%), work life (19.8%), economic life (9.9%), and physical health (17.6%) in the past 7 years.

College hostility predicted high-risk behaviors for smoking, drinking, inadequate social support, achievements in career and personal relationships, risk for depression and reporting family life changing for the worse. Note the importance of this finding in that

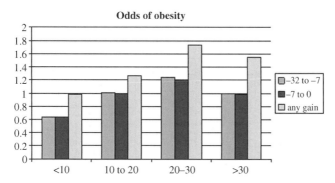

Figure 6.2   The odds of being obese for 23-year change in hostility for each level of hostility in college. Created by Ilene Siegler

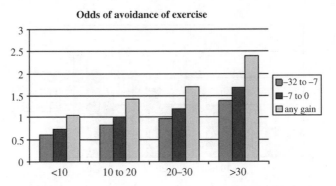

Figure 6.3   The odds of being sedentary for 23-year change in hostility for each level of hostility in college. Created by Ilene Siegler

a single measure taken at college entry predicted high-risk behaviors 21–32 years later. When using change in hostility to predict these same risk factors, smoking and alcohol were no longer significant. All of the rest of the risk indicators were predicted by changes in hostility. The results were the same for men and women in general but hostility change surprisingly predicted lower than average income for women but not for men.

The paper (Siegler et al., 2003) provides considerably more detail on the findings, but those reviewed here indicate that attention to the methodological differences are important as they suggest that the associations with risky behavior patterns during middle life are different according to how researchers treat a single measure of hostility (as a linear score vs. dividing into categories at one point in time) or as a change score. We will illustrate this with four of the risk behaviors that we use in the HRS and GCS (see Table 6.1). Figures 6.1 to 6.4 are graphs for four risk indicators that were not part of the original publication in 2003. The four sets of bars in each graph represent level of hostility in college. < 10 is very low, 10–20 is average for a college student, 20–30 is high and > 30 is very high. Each bar represents the amount of change in 23 years. In a residualized change analysis, those four sets of bars would be averaged over and controlled for. By displaying the data this way, it

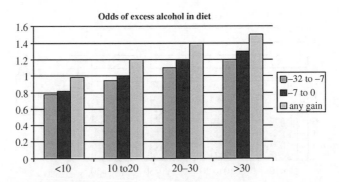

Figure 6.4   The odds of drinking too much alcohol for 23-year change in hostility for each level of hostility in college. Created by Ilene Siegler

shows how initial level in college and change over 23 years are related for each of the risk behaviors studied.

We have also studied change in personality during midlife in the UNCAHS. NEO-PI personality traits were measured twice approximately 7 years apart (early vs. late forties). Longitudinally, there was little change overall on the five personality factors; however, significant change was seen in subgroups with extreme life events during that interval (e.g., getting divorced vs. getting married, or getting fired vs. getting promoted). There were no differences when these extreme groups were compared to individuals who remained married or kept their jobs; see Costa, McCrae, Herbst, & Siegler, 2000).

We have also looked at changes in risk factors during midlife to see how these are related to personality. This research is illustrated by our work on changes in weight indexed by BMI (a ratio of weight to height) from ages 43–55. For example, while on average individuals in the sample gained weight over that time, individuals who were lower on Conscientiousness gained more weight than individuals who were high on Conscientiousness. The effects were similar for men and women. There were also important gender differences. When we compared average levels of weight using mixed models during midlife by levels of personality traits, we found no differences for men on Neuroticism, but did for women. Women high on Neuroticism were in the overweight range and women low in Neuroticism were in the normal range. For Extraversion, the association of weight and personality was not significant for women but extraverted men were heavier than introverted men. Conscientiousness (C) was important for both men and women, with low C persons heavier than high C persons; however, the relationship was stronger for women than for men (see Brummett et al., 2006). Additional information on the UNCAHS can be found in Hooker, Hoppmann, and Siegler (2010).

Thus data from the UNCAHS gives a detailed look at stability and change of risky behavior as well as personality over time during the middle years. These findings are critical as they point to the middle years as a time for intervention, depending on the risk factor of interest and the gender of the individual. In addition, it is important to know whether personality operates independently or through its association with risk factors. As we have shown above, personality is associated with health behaviors that are both risky (smoking) and protective (exercise and social support). An important question remains: Does personality predict disease after controlling for these associations? The answer appears to be complicated. It depends on the disease of interest and whether personality was measured in terms of the Big Five factors or the 30 related facets or traits.

We have just started to evaluate the role of average personality at age 45 on the development of disease in the next 15 years with controls for age, gender, education, BMI, smoking, exercise, drinking, social support, and income on the development of two psychological disorders – anxiety and depression – and four major chronic diseases: type 2 diabetes, hypertension, hyperlipidemia, and coronary heart disease that was reported between ages 45 and 60.

The data were analyzed with logistic regression which tested whether the person had the disease or not any time during 15 years between measurement points (i.e., ages 45 through 60). In terms of the Big Five factors, individuals who were higher on Neuroticism were more likely to develop depression and anxiety, individuals who were higher on Conscientiousness were less likely to develop depression, while individuals who were higher on Openness were less likely to develop coronary heart disease with all of the traditional risk indicators in the model. In the fully adjusted models, facets or individual traits were more likely to be significant than the major factors in predicting hypertension, diabetes, and high lipids (Siegler, Williams, et al., 2010).

We can consider these data to give one view of how risk factor behavior relates to the development of disease from ages 45–60. Individuals who developed disease before age 45 were not included in the analyses and thus some of the risk indicators that operated earlier in the life cycle are not part of this particular preliminary analysis of the study. The data on hypertension are particularly interesting and illustrate the role of behavioral risk factors including personality in a disease that is very common during middle age – 54% of the sample reported being hypertensive. Of these cases, 57% were reported after the age of 45 when NEO personality was measured. Thus analyses were conducted comparing 914 men and women who developed hypertension after age 45 to the 3,863 who did not. The results indicated that hypertension was more likely if the person was older (OR = 1.05) – a 5% increase per year of age, heavier (OR = 1.12) – a 12% increase for each point of BMI which is about 6 pounds, working full-time (OR 1.38) – a 38% increase over those not working. Hypertension was less likely in those who exercised (OR = .91) – about 9% less likely. The personality factors were entered in two different ways. We entered the 30 facets and found that 4 were significant predictors of hypertension. Two of the facets of Neuroticism (N1– Anxiety and N6 – Vulnerability) and one of Conscientiousness (C6 – Deliberation) each had an odds ratio of 1.22, such that for every 10-point increase in the trait, the individual was 22% more likely to be hypertensive. A facet of Openness (O2 – Openness to Aesthetics) was protective (OR = 0.90) or about 10% less likely. When we replaced the 30 facets with the 5 factors, none of the factors significantly predicted hypertension. The most important point of these findings is to illustrate that how you measure personality and what risk indicators are also included in the model, as well as when it is measured, all make a difference in understanding the findings.

What happens during the second half of the lifespan? We looked at associations among nine health risk behaviors: the Big Five personality factors, along with four behavioral risk indicators – smoking, alcohol use, being overweight, and vigorous exercise.

The Health and Retirement Study began in 1992 and now also includes the Asset and Health Dynamics Among the Oldest-Old (AHEAD) study, in order to represent the United States population over age 50. It has grown to include information from more than 30,000 individuals, with data collected biennially. Although the primary aim of the study is to provide current data on the antecedents and consequences of retirement, additional topics include constructs such as physical and cognitive functioning, family structure and transfers, demographic characteristics, and labor force participation. Additional linkages are possible between the survey data in the HRS and other data resources such as the National Death Index, Social Security Administration earnings and projected benefits data, and Medicare files.

Here, we focus on data from the 2006 wave of data collection, focusing our analyses on 7,107 individuals aged 40 or older (M_{age} = 67.5, 58.4% women, 12.5% Black, 2.6% other race, and 7.4% Hispanic) who participated in this wave of data collection and had complete data across all variables of interest. We have compared the associations between personality and risk from this data set with that of 244 older persons analyzed in similar fashion on the Georgia Centenarian Study population which has a larger group of

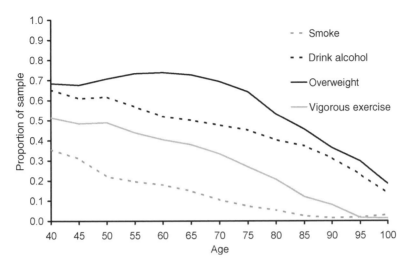

Figure 6.5 Proportions of each age group in the HRS who smoke, drink alcohol, are overweight, and engage in vigorous activity. Created by Adam Davey

centenarians. Because there is considerable data bearing on the question of stability and change in personality over the lifecycle, well represented by the findings of Terracciano, McCrae, Brant, and Costa (2005), there is no need to summarize here. Less is known about how risk behaviors are distributed. Data from HRS are shown in Figure 6.5

Very clear age differences are seen in the proportion of individuals engaging in risk behaviors, as shown in Figure 6.5. Between ages 40 and 80 years, a majority of individuals are classified as being overweight, with this proportion peaking between 55 and 70 years and declining after that, observations that might be attributable to survival effects or to loss of fat-free body mass. A majority of individuals also report drinking alcohol between the ages of 40 and 65, but a steady linear decline in the proportion drinking alcohol is seen at all ages beyond 40. Smoking shows an almost parallel trend, but with some 35% of the sample aged 40–44 reporting that they smoked. Age differences in the proportion of individuals engaging in vigorous physical exercise, a health behavior, unfortunately show similar trends to the health risk behaviors. Only at the youngest available age of 40 do a majority of individuals report engaging in vigorous physical exercise, with this health behavior showing a steady linear decline between younger and older ages.

From cross-sectional data such as these, it is impossible to distinguish between individuals changing their own health risk behaviors over time and those who are selected out of the population as a result of failing to change their health risk behaviors. In general, the role of mortality in affecting our conclusions about development is not well developed or fully integrated with theory and research. It is very likely, however, to affect conclusions that are reached from both cross-sectional and longitudinal data. For this reason, it requires considerably greater consideration in future research, particularly as longitudinal methods grow increasingly sophisticated and as nationally representative data are more widely used. Unfortunately, we do not have longitudinal data on personality and risk factors for individuals from age 40–100 to further elaborate the findings presented here.

Table 6.1   Personality factors as predictors of behavioral risks in the HRS and GCS (Odds ratios) Created by Adam Davey

Factor	Smoking		Alcohol		Overweight		Vigorous exercise	
	HRS	GCS	HRS	GCS	HRS	GCS	HRS	GCS
Neuroticism	1.15***	0.79	0.98	0.49*	0.95	0.74	0.92*	
Extroversion	0.95	1.60	0.99	0.78	0.95	1.21	1.31***	
Openness to Experience	1.10**	1.49	1.40***	1.24	0.99	1.02	1.15***	
Agreeableness	1.02	1.44	0.72**	0.99	1.03	0.89	0.71**	
Conscientiousness	0.88***	0.29*	1.18***	1.19	0.89***	0.68ˣ	1.28***	

$^x p < .10.$
$^* p < .05.$
$^{**} p < .01.$
$^{***} p < .001.$

Table 6.1 shows the associations between the Big Five personality factors and each of the risk behaviors using data from the HRS compared to the same analyses with data from the Georgia Centenarian study to see if these same relationships are seen at the very end of the life cycle. We have calculated the odds of having the risky behavior, given 1 standard deviation or a 10-point change in the NEO factor. Thus the table can be read as follows: Individuals who are 10 points higher on Neuroticism (this is a large change) are 2% more likely to be smokers in the HRS study; however, as we will discuss below, this association is not significant in the Georgia Centenarian study. The exact metrics are not as important as the significant associations and their direction. A number > 1.00 means the behavioral risk is higher and thus the personality factor is risky and a number < 1.00 means that the risky behavior is less likely and the personality factor is protective. As can be seen, HRS participants who score higher on Neuroticism and Openness to Experience and score lower on Conscientiousness are more likely to smoke. HRS participants who score higher on Openness to Experience and Conscientiousness, but lower on Agreeableness are more likely to drink alcohol. The probability of being overweight is higher only for individuals in the HRS who score lower on Conscientiousness. Finally, HRS participants who score higher on Extroversion, Openness to Experience, and Conscientiousness and score lower on Neuroticism and Agreeableness are more likely to report engaging in vigorous exercise.

Now we will turn to the Big Five factors as predictors of the same health behaviors among participants in the Georgia Centenarian Study by looking at the second column in Table 6.1 for each behavioral risk factor. As might be expected, smoking rates are very low in centenarians, and even those who smoke tend to smoke very little compared with younger smokers. However, even given this restricted range, high Conscientious scores are related to lower smoking rates among centenarians. Among these exceptional survivors, we also see that people high in Neuroticism are *less*, not more, likely to drink alcohol. Although relatively fewer centenarians are overweight, those who score higher on Conscientiousness are marginally less likely to be overweight than their less conscientious counterparts. Finally, none of the personality factors was associated with engagement in vigorous exercise for the simple reason that so very few centenarians (1.3%) exercise at all;

thus, odds ratios are not provided. In fact, with centenarians it is likely that being underweight is a risk factor for mortality (Poon et al., 2000) among this population where dietary insufficiencies are prevalent and ability to maintain adequate nutrition is the appropriate marker rather than overnutrition (Johnson et al., 2006, 2008, 2010).

It is also clear that the associations between personality factors and risk variables are complex. While each of the personality factors predicts at least one risk behavior, only conscientiousness is associated with all four risk behaviors. Even here, though, the direction of associations is not always the same across all behaviors. It is clear that if higher Neuroticism is protective of health it is not until the very end of the lifespan. Extroversion, on the other hand, is protective, but only for the likelihood of engagement in vigorous exercise. Openness to Experience is associated with higher probabilities of smoking and drinking alcohol, but also a higher probability of engaging in vigorous exercise. This perhaps counterintuitive finding that alcohol use is related to exercise frequency is found at earlier ages, and is consistent with ego depletion theory (Baumeister, Bratslavsky, Muraven, & Tice, 1998), suggesting that self-control is effortful, and that energy for this sort of self-control is finite. Agreeableness also cuts both ways, with higher levels predictive of lower likelihood of drinking alcohol, but also lower likelihood of engaging in vigorous exercise.

Among centenarians, higher Conscientiousness is perhaps the factor most closely aligned with health risk behaviors, being positively associated with all except for the probability of alcohol use. Although our sample represents nearly 20% of the population of centenarians from which it is drawn, the number of individuals represented is still small, suggesting that these findings may be difficult to generalize too broadly. These findings serve to underscore, however, the ways in which the same behavior or characteristic (i.e., personality factor) may serve both a risk and protective function, depending on (a) which health outcome and (b) which part of the lifespan is being considered.

Until now, it has been difficult to find good quality information on health and behaviors of the very oldest members of society. The U.S. Census, for example, only provides population estimates for individuals 85 + except in special reports (e.g., Krach & Velkoff, 1999). The most recent phase of the Georgia Centenarian Study, however, can provide at least preliminary data on the lives of society's oldest members. Participants were drawn from a population-based sample of 244 community-dwelling and institutionalized centenarians and near centenarians drawn from 44 counties in northeast Georgia. Few studies of centenarians have used a true population-based sample. Even large nationally representative samples of older adults tend to include very few centenarians. For example, of the 30,888 participants in the Health and Retirement Study (HRS), only 143 were aged 98 and older in their oldest interview. High mortality rates mean that the population aged 98 and older is not stable over the 2-year period required for data collection.

Normative data suggest differences in health behaviors within the centenarian population between men and women, Whites and African Americans, and centenarians living in facility versus community settings. We have provided detailed tables that should be of use to the research community (see Davey et al., 2010). Specifically, men are more likely than women to be current or former smokers and to be overweight or obese, and women are more likely to be underweight. African Americans are more likely than Whites to be current or former smokers, and to be overweight or obese. Interestingly, a higher proportion of facility residents are former smokers, but a higher proportion of community residents are current smokers. Differences in educational attainment generally account for the largest proportion of variance in cognitive functioning, and residential status generally accounts for the largest proportion of variance in physical performance measures.

In recognition that many centenarians survive with considerable burden of disease, Tom Perls, one of the early pioneers of centenarian research in the United States (see Evert, Lawler, Bogan, & Perls, 2003) has classified centenarians from the New England Centenarian Study into Survivors (centenarians with at least one chronic illness with onset before age 80, 43.0% of the GCS sample), Delayers (centenarians with at least one chronic illness with onset after age 80, 36.1% of the GCS sample), and Escapers (centenarians without chronic illness, 17.6% of the GCS sample), with another 3.3% that could not clearly be classified, such as those whose age at disease onset was unknown (Arnold et al., 2010). Among centenarians in the GCS sample, there are no associations between personality or health risk behaviors and membership in each of these classifications. Health behaviors may be more strongly associated with the development of disease earlier in the life cycle. At this point we do not know why this is true, as the balance of genetic, environmental, and behavioral factors can all change across the lifespan. The data to compare centenarians on the same measures as the general middle-aged and older samples have only just become available. Future work on the genetics of these individuals may help provide answers in the future.

Comparing individual cohort studies such as the UNCAHS with population-based studies such as HRS and the GCS is a useful exercise, as such comparisons point out some of the problems that have yet to be solved. It would be reasonable to have expected that what we see at one phase of the life cycle would be true at later phases. Our work on these studies challenges assumptions about the limits of lifespan developmental theory and data.

Findings from studies that have followed cohorts from birth to age 60, such as the National Survey of Health and Development (Wadsworth 1991; Kuh & Ben-Shlomo, 2007), can be pieced together with studies that go from age 60 to 100 to get an idea of the full lifespan from birth to 100 that may become possible in the future as study designs are harmonized and data are shared worldwide.

As our examples have shown, the conclusions are in the details. Small changes in how models are constructed, whether variables are continuous or categorical, and specific age ranges and nature of the samples, all make a difference in the conclusions about the role of behavioral factors in health and disease outcomes over the life cycle. Similarly, when in the life cycle we measure something and how long we measure it is also important. Finally, our experience in studying centenarians suggests that predictors at the very end of the life cycle are not well understood. It may be that survival at extremely old ages is beyond our ability to predict with the indicators we have access to today. Indeed, how far should we expect our data to predict? Now that we have data covering 40–50 years of the life cycle, maybe we should declare victory and look within large and overlapping chunks of the life cycle.

Acknowledgments

Dr. Siegler's work on this chapter has been supported by grants from the National Institute on Aging, R01 AG12458, Marchionne Foundation, The National Heart Lung and Blood

P01 HL55367, NHLBI with cofunding from NIA – R01 HL55356, the National Institute of Mental Health R01MH16607, and the Duke Behavioral Medicine Research Center.

Dr. Davey's work on this chapter has been supported by grants from the National Institute on Aging, P01 AG017533 and R01 AG13180. The HRS (Health and Retirement Study) is sponsored by the National Institute on Aging (grant number NIA U01AG009740) and is conducted by the University of Michigan.

References

Arnold, J., Dai, J., Nahapetyan, L., Arte, A., Johnson, M. A., Hausman, D. B.,. . . & Poon, L. W. (2010). Predicting successful aging in a population-based sample of Georgia centenarians. *Current Gerontology and Geriatrics Research*. doi: 10.1155/2010/989315

Barefoot, J. C., Dahlstrom, W. G., & Williams, R. B. (1983). Hostility, CHD incidence and total mortality: A 25-year follow-up study of 255 physicians. *Psychosomatic Medicine, 45,* 59–63.

Baum, A., Revenson T. A., & Singer, J. E. (Eds.). 2001. *Handbook of health psychology*. Mahwah, NJ: Erlbaum.

Baum, A., Revenson T. A., & Singer, J. E. (Eds.). (in press). *Handbook of health psychology* (2nd ed.). Mahwah, NJ: Erlbaum.

Baumeister, R. F., Bratslavsky, E., Muraven, M., & Tice, D. M. (1998). Ego depletion: Is the active self a limited resource? *Journal of Personality and Social Psychology, 74,* 1252–1265.

Blazer, D. G., & Steffens, D. C. (Eds.) (2009). *Textbook of geriatric psychiatry* (4th ed.). Washington D C: American Psychiatric Publishing.

Brummett, B. H., Babyak, M. A., Williams, R. B., Barefoot, J. C., Costa, P. T., & Siegler, I. C. (2006). NEO personality domains and gender predict levels and trends in body mass index over 14 years during midlife. *Journal of Research in Personality, 40,* 222–236.

Brummett, B. H., Helms, M. J., Dahlstrom, W. G., & Siegler, I. C. (2006). Prediction of all-cause mortality by the Minnesota Multiphasic Personality Inventory Optimism-Pessimism scale scores: Study of a college sample during a 40-year follow-up period. *Mayo Clinic Proceedings, 81,* 1541–1544.

Costa, Jr., P. T., Herbst, J. H., McCrae, R. R., & Siegler, I. C. (2000). Personality at midlife: Stability, intrinsic maturation, and response to life events. *Assessment, 7,* 365–378.

Costa P. T., & McCrae. R. R. (1992). *Revised NEO Personality Inventory (NEO-PI-R) and NEO Five Factor Inventory (FFI) professional manual*. Odessa, FL: Psychosocial Assessment Resources.

Dahlstrom, W. G., Welsh G. S., & Dahlstrom, L. E. (1972). *An MMPI handbook: Volume 1: Clinical interpretations* (revised ed.). Minneapolis, MN: University of Minnesota Press.

Davey, A., Elias, M. F. Siegler, I. C., Lele, U., Martin, P., Johnson M.A., . . . Poon, L. W. (2010). Cognitive function, physical performance, health, and disease: Norms from the Georgia Centenarian Study. *Experimental Aging Research, 34,* 394–425.

Evert, J., Lawler, E., Bogan, H., & Perls, T. (2003). Morbidity profiles of centenarians: Survivors, delayers, and escapers. *Journals of Gerontology: Biological Sciences, 58,* 232–237.

Fried, L. P. (2000). Epidemiology of aging. *Epidemiologic Reviews, 22,* 95–106.

Ford, E. S., Ajani, U. A., Croft, J. B., Critchley, J. A., Labarthe, D. R., Kottke, T. E., . . . Capwell, S. (2007). Explaining the decrease in US deaths from coronary disease 1980-2000. *New England Journal of Medicine, 356,* 2388–2398.

Halter, J. B., Hazzard, W. R., Ouslander, J. G., Tinetti, M., & Studenski, S. (2009). *Hazzard's geriatric medicine and gerontology*. New York: McGraw Hill Medical.

Hooker, K., Hoppmann, C., & Siegler, I. C. (2010). Personality: Lifespan compass for health. In K. E. Whitfield (Ed.), *Annual Review of Gerontology and Geriatrics: Vol. 30, Focus on Biobehavioral Perspectives in Later Life* (pp. 201–232). New York: Springer.

Hoyer W. J., & Roodin, P. A. (2009). *Adult development and aging* (6th ed.). New York: McGraw Hill.

Johnson, M. A., Davey, A., Hausman, D. B., Park, S., & Poon, L. W. (2006). Dietary differences between centenarians residing in communities and skilled nursing facilities: The Georgia Centenarian Study. *Age, 28,* 333–341.

Johnson, M. A., Davey, A., Park, S., Hausman, D. B., & Poon, L. W. (2008). Age, race and season predict vitamin D status in African American and White octogenarians and centenarians. *Journal of Nutrition, Health, and Aging, 12,* 690–695.

Johnson, M. A., Hausman, D. B., Davey, A., Poon, L. W., Allen, R. H., Stabler, S. P., and the Georgia Centenarian Study. (2010). Vitamin B12 deficiency in African American and white octogenarians and centenarians in Georgia. *Journal of Nutrition, Health, and Aging, 14,* 339–345.

Juster, F. T., & Suzman, R. (1995). An overview of the Health and Retirement Study. *Journal of Human Resources, 30,* S7–S56.

Krach, C. A., & Velkoff, V. A. (1999). *Centenarians in the United States* (Current Population Reports, Series P23-199RV). Washington, DC: U.S. Government Printing Office.

Kuh, D., & Ben-Shlomo, Y. (1997). *A life course approach to chronic disease epidemiology.* New York: Oxford University Press.

McCrae, R. R., & Costa, P. T. (2010). *NEO inventories for the NEO Personality Inventory-3, NEO Five Factor Inventory-3, NEO Personality Inventory-Revised professional manual.* Lutz, FL: Psychological Assessment Resources.

National Institutes of Health. (2010). Behavior change and maintenance. Retrieved from http://obssr.od.nih.gov/scientific_areas/health_behaviour/behaviour_changes/index.aspx

Olshansky S. J., Goldman, Y. Z., Zheng, Y., & Rowe, J. W. (2009). Aging in America in the 21st century: Demographic forecasts for the MacArthur Foundation Research Network on an Aging Society. *The Milbank Quarterly, 87,* 842–862.

Poon, L. W., Johnson, M. A., Davey, A., Dawson, D. V., Siegler, I. C., & Martin, P. (2000). Psychosocial predictors of survival among centenarians. In P. Martin, C. Rott, B. Hagberg, & K. Morgan (Eds.), *Autonomy versus dependence in the oldest old* (pp. 77–89). New York: Springer.

Poon, L. W., & Perls T. T. (2007). *Annual review of gerontology and geriatrics: Vol. 27. Biopsychosocial approaches to longevity.* New York: Springer.

Siegler, I. C. (2007, August). *Psychology of aging and the public health.* Developmental Health Award lecture presented at the meetings of the American Psychological Association, San Francisco.

Siegler, I. C., Costa, P. T., Brummett, B. H., Helms, M. J., Barefoot, J. C., Williams, R. B., . . . Rimer, B. K. (2003). Patterns of change in hostility from college to midlife in the UNC Alumni Heart Study predict high-risk status. *Psychosomatic Medicine, 65,* 738–745.

Siegler, I. C., Elias, M. F., & Bosworth, H. B. (in press). Aging and health. In A. Baum, T. A. Revenson, & J. E. Singer, J. E. (Eds.), *Handbook of health psychology* (2nd ed.). Mahwah, NJ: Erlbaum.

Siegler, I. C., Hooker, K., Bosworth, H. B., Elias, M. F., & Spiro, A. (2010). Adult development, aging and gerontology. In J. M. Suls, K. W. Davidson, & R. B. Kaplan (Eds.), *Handbook of health psychology and behavioral medicine* (pp. 147–162). New York: Guilford Press.

Siegler, I. C., Peterson, B. L., Barefoot, J. C., & Williams, R. B. (1992). Hostility during late adolescence predicts coronary risk factors at midlife. *American Journal of Epidemiology, 138,* 146–154.

Siegler, I. C., Williams, R. B., Rimer, B. K., Rubin, D. C., Brummett, B. H., Barefoot. J. C., & Costa, P. T. (2010). *When I'm 64: Findings from the UNC Alumni Heart Study*. Washington, DC: International Society of Behavioral Medicine.

Suls, J. M., Davidson, K. W, & Kaplan, R. B. (2010). *Handbook of health psychology and behavioral medicine*. New York: Guilford Press.

Terracciano, A., McCrae, R. R., Brant, L. J., & Costa, P. T., Jr. (2005). Hierarchical linear modeling analyses of the NEO-PI–R scales in the Baltimore Longitudinal Study of Aging. *Psychology and Aging, 20,* 493–506.

Wadsworth, M. E. J. (1991). *The imprint of time*. Oxford: Oxford University Press.

Wei, J., & Levkoff, S. (2000). *Aging well: The complete guide to physical and emotional health*. New York: Wiley.

Whitbourne, S. K., & Whitbourne, S. B. (2011). *Adult development and aging: Biopsychosocial perspectives*. New York: Wiley.

Williams, R. B. (1994). Neurobiology, cellular and molecular biology and psychosomatic medicine. *Psychosomatic Medicine, 56,* 308–315.

PART III

Cognition

7

Processing Speed

Judith Dirk and Florian Schmiedek

Introduction

One of the most solid findings in cognitive aging research is that older adults, on average, perform more slowly than younger adults on all kinds of tasks for which speed of responding can be measured in a meaningful way. This includes tasks as different as mental rotation, digit–symbol substitution, memory search, lexical decision, and speech discrimination. Evidence comes from cross-sectional as well as from longitudinal studies. Cross-sectional studies with continuous age indicate negative age differences starting in younger adulthood (e.g., Verhaeghen & Salthouse, 1997). Quasi-experimental studies comparing younger and older adults result in effect sizes of the age differences that are among the strongest observed effects in behavioral research (Meyer, Glass, Mueller, Seymour, & Kieras, 2001). Evidence from longitudinal studies confirms that these differences are not due to cohort effects and that declines are pretty linear across adulthood (Schaie, 1993).

Given the breadth and strength of the age-related changes in response speed and acknowledging that, even in older age, many cognitive activities in everyday life do require decision and action within limited time frames, it is clear that this is an important phenomenon to be explained. In this chapter we will present theoretical approaches that provide such explanations and will argue that such approaches work best if they treat response speed as one dependent variable characterizing cognitive performance among other aspects of performance, like accuracy and variability of reaction times (RT). To this end, we first selectively review findings that establish central aspects of cognitive slowing as a phenomenon. Before moving to attempts to explain this phenomenon, we present and discuss theoretical approaches that treat cognitive slowing itself as an explanatory construct

The Wiley-Blackwell Handbook of Adulthood and Aging, First Edition. Edited by Susan Krauss Whitbourne and Martin J. Sliwinski. © 2012 Blackwell Publishing Ltd. Published 2012 by Blackwell Publishing Ltd.

for age-related declines in other cognitive abilities, like fluid intelligence. These attempts will be criticized for three major reasons: (a) processing speed not being a unitary construct, (b) cognitive slowing not being a homogeneous phenomenon, and (c) methodological issues with statistical approaches to establish the causal role of processing speed for the aging of other cognitive abilities. We continue by introducing age differences in intraindividual variability in RTs, or more generally shapes of RT distributions, as additional aspects beyond mean RTs to be accounted for by theories of cognitive slowing, and show how an approach based on models from mathematical psychology, the diffusion model (Ratcliff, 1978), can be used to express individual and age differences in terms of meaningful processing parameters. We close with reviewing theoretical approaches to explain the neurobiological changes underlying cognitive slowing and attempts to improve processing speed with practice and training.

Age-Related Cognitive Slowing as a Phenomenon

For a long time, cognitive aging researchers have demonstrated that speed of processing decreases monotonically with age. In a meta-analysis of 91 studies with a continuous age distribution between 18 and 80 years, Verhaeghen and Salthouse (1997) reported a negative correlation between age and processing speed of -.52. Cerella and Hale (1994) showed that the average 70-year-old is comparable in speed of processing information to the average 8-year-old, indicating that the observed age differences across the lifespan are substantial. Research dating back to the 1960s established the age-related decline in processing speed as a ubiquitous phenomenon in aging (Birren, 1965; Welford, 1965). Birren (1965; see also Birren, Woods, & Williams, 1980) summarized studies demonstrating evidence for the slowing of behavior in healthy aging as well as in disease processes in all components of processing ranging from initial encoding to response execution. He concluded that age-related slowing was a general phenomenon apparent in any given task and could be considered a fundamental characteristic of the central nervous system (CNS). Although the neurophysiological evidence was rare at the time, Birren (1965) speculated that cell loss in the CNS might be one candidate mechanism contributing to the observed age-related slowing. In the search for a causal mechanism underlying age-related slowing, Welford (1965) proposed that processes in older adults' neural system take more time due to increased levels of "internal system noise" (i.e., irrelevant residual neural activity from previous processing, or increased spontaneous activity). This "neural noise hypothesis" continues to be an essential part of modern theories of age-related slowing and is supported by computational as well as empirical evidence (for a review, see Li, 2002; see also section on Explanatory Models of Cognitive Slowing below).

Following the hypotheses advanced in these early reviews, different models and theoretical accounts of age-related slowing have been proposed over the last 30 years. Prominent among them are Cerella's linear rate model (Cerella, 1985), Myerson and colleagues' information loss model (Myerson, Hale, Wagstaff, Poon, & Smith, 1990), and Salthouse's processing speed theory of cognitive aging (Salthouse, 1985, 1991, 1996). Cerella's linear rate model (1985) suggests that RTs of older adults are a linear function of

RTs of younger adults: Older adults' responses are slowed both by a constant term which is assumed to describe peripheral sensorimotor processes and by a multiplicative term describing central cognitive-computational processes. Contrary to Cerella's model, Myerson and colleagues' information loss model (1990) assumes that the RTs of older adults are best described by a positively accelerated power function of younger adults' responses. Behind this functional description lies the idea that total RT is the sum of RTs for discrete processing steps with longer step duration being related to greater information loss. Aging affects the amount of information that is lost at each step, in that the number of processing steps needed to successfully perform a task increases RTs more for older adults than for younger adults. Although the two theories differ in the shape of the function that describes age-related slowing, they agree in that performance of younger and older adults on all components of cognitive processing across a variety of tasks can be described on a single theoretical dimension, and that performance limits in old age are predominantly biologically based (cf. Cerella, 1990). Moreover, both theories assume that the age-related differences in performance between younger and older adults are exacerbated as the processing demands of a task increase (i.e., the "complexity hypothesis"; see also Cerella, Poon, & Williams, 1980).

In line with early reviews of age-related slowing, Salthouse's theory (1996) assumes that processing speed is a central construct influencing many behavioral outcomes. Somewhat different in scope from Cerella's (1985) and Myerson and colleagues' (1990) models, Salthouse's theory of processing speed aims at establishing to what degree common and task-specific influences play a role for age-related slowing across a variety of cognitive tasks. Thus the focus is not only on the relationship between RTs of younger and older adults but on the relationship between RTs and age in different tasks by applying different methodological approaches (i.e., hierarchical regression analysis and structural equation modeling), which is an important step to reach beyond the "issue isolationism" (Salthouse, 1985) of collecting evidence for age differences in all kinds of paradigms provided by general cognitive psychology without much effort to integrate findings that plague the field of cognitive aging research.

Common to the different theoretical accounts is the establishment of a general slowing factor describing older adults' performance as an approximately linear function of younger adults' performance. The best known illustration of this general slowing factor across a variety of tasks is the Brinley plot. In a typical Brinley plot, older adults' mean RTs in each task condition are plotted on the ordinate, as a function of the corresponding younger adults' mean RTs on the abscissa (see Figure 7.1; Brinley, 1965).

As demonstrated since the first meta-analyses using Brinley plots (see Cerella, 1985; Cerella et al., 1980), the Brinley function is approximately linear with a slope of around 1.5 and a negative intercept across a variety of tasks. This regularly observed pattern gave rise to the interpretation by cognitive aging researchers that a single general mechanism may account for age-related changes in information processing in various cognitive processes (i.e., the generalized slowing hypothesis). However, the interpretation of Brinley plots has been controversially discussed in the cognitive aging literature (e.g., Myerson, Adams, Hale, & Jenkins, 2003; Ratcliff, Spieler, & McKoon, 2000, 2004; Sliwinski & Hall, 1998; and the discussion regarding generalized slowing theories of aging in the *Journals of Gerontology*: Cerella, 1994; Fisk & Fisher, 1994; Myerson, Wagstaff, & Hale, 1994; Perfect, 1994).

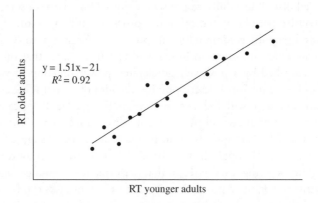

Figure 7.1   Brinley plot. Each data point represents the mean reaction time (RT) of older adults plotted as a function of the mean RT of younger adults for each of 17 task conditions (simulated data). This Brinley plot shows that older adults' RTs can approximately be described as a linear function of younger adults' RTs. Note that Brinley plots have been commonly applied in meta-analyses in which many more data points are available. Created by Judith Dirk and Florian Schmiedek

One position holds that across a variety of tasks the slope of the Brinley function can be interpreted as the factor by which older adults' responses are slowed relative to younger adults' responses (Myerson et al., 2003). Alternatively, Ratcliff and colleagues (Ratcliff, Spieler, & McKoon, 2000, 2004) argued that the Brinley plot can be mathematically described as quantile-quantile plots resulting from the distributions of younger and older adults' means across task conditions. According to Ratcliff, Spieler, and McKoon (2004), theoretical approaches can produce the typical Brinley plot and the meaning of the slope depends on the underlying theoretical model of the task. Thus the authors suggested that in order to constrain models, a comprehensive approach to RT data is needed which takes into account not only the correct RTs but also accuracy of responses, RTs of incorrect responses, and the shape of the corresponding RT distributions. We will report evidence for the utility of this view in accounting for individual and age differences in terms of meaningful processing parameters.

Age-Related Cognitive Slowing as an Explanatory Construct

Very much similar to approaches that try to explain individual differences in intelligence by processing speed on elementary cognitive tasks (e.g., Jensen, 1998; Vernon, 1987), the cognitive slowing hypothesis of age-related decreases in general cognitive abilities has been put forward by Salthouse (1996). In this account, the perspective is shifted from cognitive slowing as a phenomenon to be explained to a phenomenon that potentially might itself be a comprehensive explanation for cognitive aging. It is generally desirable to aim for integrative accounts of the multitude of age-related decreases in all sorts of tasks by putting forward parsimonious theories with wide scope. Moreover, a wealth of empirical studies, thought-provoking debates, and methodological developments has resulted from

Salthouse's account. In our view, however, the current evaluation of the cognitive slowing account has to be that it is overly reductionist and not well-supported empirically, for at least three reasons: processing speed not being a unitary construct, cognitive slowing not being a homogeneous phenomenon, and methodological problems associated with the data-analytical approaches employed to support the cognitive slowing account.

The psychometric perspective: Processing speed is not a unitary construct

In cognitive aging studies, speed is usually measured with a few established marker tasks from the psychometric literature, like digit–symbol substitution (Hoyer, Stawski, Wasylyshyn, & Verhaeghen, 2004) or letter comparison (Salthouse & Babcock, 1991). These tasks have in common that they could be solved with almost perfect accuracy if enough time was provided. Focusing on few or sometimes only single tasks, however, ignores that from the psychometric perspective, processing speed as a cognitive ability is not that homogeneous. Based on his literature review and reanalysis of several hundred factor-analytic studies, Carroll (1993) concluded that speed abilities can be separated from level abilities across the whole spectrum of cognitive abilities. That is, just as multiple narrow, broad, and general factors form the hierarchy of abilities with accuracy levels as dependent variables, one may build a similarly complex structure for speed abilities, provided that broad selections of speed tasks are investigated within the same study. The empirical basis for such a structure is relatively scarce, though, compared to the multitude of factor-analytic studies on the structure of level abilities. One notable exception is a study by Roberts and Stankov (1999), who investigated the structure of a set of marker tests of broad cognitive abilities, 12 measures of speed of test taking (of a subset of these marker tests), 4 tests of perceptual speed, and 11 elementary cognitive tasks (ECTs) taken from the experimental literature on processing speed. Besides a large number of narrow factors, three broad factors of general psychomotor speed, general decision speed, and general speed of test-taking on psychometric tasks could be identified. While those broad factors were positively correlated to a degree that justifies modeling a general factor on top of this structure, the general picture emerging was one of multidimensionality, indicating that treating mental speed as a unitary construct is an oversimplification. Similarly, Danthiir, Wilhelm, Schulze, and Roberts (2005) reported a differentiation of mental speed into separable factors for different paradigms often employed to measure speed (i.e., substitution coding, Odd Man Out, the Hick paradigm, and switching paradigms), each implemented with different task versions in their study. Again, these factors were positively correlated, but not so highly that one could subsume them under one unidimensional construct.

The picture is further complicated by the fact that performance on single speed tasks can be influenced by other abilities than those of mental speed. For example, performance as well as improvement over few trials of a digit–symbol substitution coding task are related to individual differences in memory (Piccinin & Rabbitt, 1999), apparently because learning the digit–symbol associations can strongly aid task performance. Similarly, the finding that lexical decision tasks show a different degree of slowing than nonlexical tasks can be explained by the involvement of the relatively well-preserved long-term memory for vocabulary in the former (Lima, Hale, & Myerson, 1991). In sum, the fact that tasks using speed of performance as the major outcome correlate highly with each other should not be overinterpreted as them being exchangeable because measuring the exact same underlying ability of mental speed. Rather, mental speed itself has a differentiated structure that deserves more attention than it has received so far. Performance on single "speed" tasks might be determined by different abilities within this as well as within the even broader structure of cognitive abilities in general. Whether this multidimensional nature of mental speed also turns the phenomenon to be explained into a set of phenomena that require not only one but a whole set of explanations, or whether cognitive slowing can be considered a unidimensional phenomenon, will be discussed next.

The experimental perspective: Cognitive slowing is not a homogeneous phenomenon

Including data from 1,354 participants in 190 studies, Verhaeghen and Cerella (2008) obtained a Brinley slope of 1.46 across a variety of tasks, but also found significant heterogeneity in slope values across tasks. This led them to classify the tasks based on previous theoretical considerations in simple decision tasks, lexical, spatial, and all other tasks, the last including executive control tasks like the Stroop, tasks including local and global switching costs, and dual tasks in which two tasks have to be performed concurrently. Analyzing the age-related differences with Brinley and state-trace plots, additive and multiplicative costs were determined, with additive costs prolonging responses by adding an extra processing step to the overall process and multiplicative costs prolonging each step in the processing relative to a baseline task. Whereas executive control and inhibition tasks like the Stroop showed multiplicative costs of similar size in younger and older adults, global switch and dual tasks demonstrated additive costs with older adults being slowed to a larger degree than younger adults in the complex task conditions relative to a baseline. In conclusion, Verhaeghen and Cerella's findings (2008) make a strong point for the importance of working memory load as present in complex global switch and dual tasks as a central mechanism underlying age-related slowing.

This conclusion fits well with empirical observations and theoretical interpretations by Mayr, Kliegl, and Krampe (1996) that tasks that differ by their *sequential complexity* (i.e., the number of processing steps that can be worked through in sequence) are slowed by a smaller factor than tasks of *coordinative complexity*, which put demands on working memory by requiring to keep several pieces of information active simultaneously. In several studies, the use of time-accuracy functions made it possible to identify different slowing constants for sequential versus coordinative complexity in tasks like mental arithmetic or figural search with or without storage and retrieval demands (e.g., Mayr et al., 1996; Verhaeghen, Kliegl, & Mayr, 1997). These studies also show that even if provided unlimited time, older adults are not able to perform tasks of some level of coordinative complexity at the same level of performance as younger adults.

The methods perspective: Deficiencies of methods used to support the generality and causal role of speed

The strong age-related effects on speed, together with the finding that individual differences in speed correlated substantially with individual differences in other general abilities, like fluid intelligence or episodic memory, has led researchers to propose that cognitive slowing is the cause, or at least one very important cause, of age-related losses in higher cognition in general (e.g., Verhaeghen & Salthouse, 1997). Salthouse (1996) has proposed two mechanisms for such a causal role of speed. First, the *limited time mechanism* affects task performance by prolonging each information-processing step that is involved by a certain amount, leading to slower overall performance. More importantly for tasks of higher cognition, the *simultaneity mechanism* affects performance on tasks that require keeping several elements of information active, like intermediate results in arithmetic tasks, or sets of inferred rules in inductive reasoning tasks, by requiring more time for information processing than decaying memory traces of these elements allow for. Thereby, necessary information is lost before it can be combined for solving a task.

Empirical evidence for the leading role of speed in the cognitive aging of general cognitive abilities largely comes from cross-sectional studies that employ mediation models, with speed being the purported mediator of age-related effects on the cognitive ability. Statistically, attempts have been made to test these mediation hypotheses with either hierarchical regression analyses, trying to identify the amount of age-related differences in the cognitive ability (i.e., the dependent variable) that is "shared" with age-related differences in speed, or equivalently with path analyses, testing how much direct effects of age on the dependent variable are reduced when controlling for indirect effects via speed. As shown by Lindenberger and Pötter (1998), these approaches share the problem that results are strongly dependent on the age-independent relation of speed and the dependent variable, which drastically reduces the interpretability of such analyses. Furthermore, Lindenberger, Oertzen, Ghisletta, and Hertzog (2011) have shown analytically that results generated this way, even if they suggest full mediation of age-related effects via speed, virtually do not constrain the possible underlying relations of changes in speed and changes in the dependent variable at all. Longitudinal analyses of the relation of speed and other broad cognitive abilities indicate that the correlations of individual differences in changes are considerably smaller than cross-sectional correlations of individual differences in level (e.g., Sliwinski & Buschke, 1999; Zimprich & Martin, 2002).

Multivariate extensions of such mediation models that attempt to explain the pattern of age relations of a number of different tasks with age relations of one or a few underlying latent factors (e.g., Salthouse & Czaja, 2000), denote a progress, as they put emphasis on first modeling the structure of tasks before investigating which factors of the structure mediate age differences. The way such models have been implemented as structural equation models, however, is often prone to bias findings toward general factor explanations (Schmiedek & Li, 2004). Also, such models do not overcome the general problem that cross-sectional age-heterogeneous data do not allow us to disentangle the causal chains that may exist between different cognitive variables. The most such models can provide are tests of whether age relations of a limited number of latent factors suffice to describe the multivariate pattern of age relations (as well as the interrelations) of a larger number of cognitive tasks (Schmiedek & Li, 2004). To this end, empirical findings indicate that one general factor alone is not sufficient to account for the age relations of broad selections of cognitive tasks, but that additional age relations of more specific factors, like reasoning, memory, fluency, and knowledge, need to be included (e.g., Salthouse, 2004; Schmiedek & Li, 2004). As a general conclusion, we want to note that cognitive slowing should be investigated in ways that take the structural relations of performance on different speed tasks into account, without oversimplifying this structure. In addition to the need to accommodate such a multivariate perspective on cognitive slowing, in the following, we would like to underscore the importance of also taking into account different aspects of performance, beyond mean RTs or number of items solved within a given time.

Intraindividual Variability

Intraindividual variability (IIV) has been acknowledged as an important measure of performance in psychology for over half a century. Early on, IIV was considered as a predictor of a variety of behaviors (Fiske & Rice, 1955). Among others, Jensen (1982, 1992) demonstrated that IIV expressed as the standard deviation (*SD*) across trials of a given RT task (i.e., RT variability) correlates negatively with psychometric intelligence in different tasks (e.g., Hick paradigm, Odd Man Out). He further reported evidence that RT variability shares variance with measures of intelligence independent of mean RT and is an even better predictor of performance than mean or median RT. Similarly, Rabbitt, Osman, Moore, and Stollery (2001) investigated RT variability in individuals 60 to 80 years old who performed a choice RT task and found greater IIV over shorter intervals (i.e., trial-to-trial) and longer intervals (i.e., weekly) to be related to poorer performance on the Cattell Culture Fair intelligence test. Moreover, across the adult lifespan, RT variability has been shown to increase across a variety of cognitive tasks and is negatively related to level of performance (see Hultsch, Strauss, Hunter, & MacDonald, 2008 for a review). The overall picture that emerges is that age differences in RT variability parallel those observed for RT means. Furthermore, IIV and level of performance expressed as the *SD* RT and the mean RT show a strong positive relationship across individuals (e.g., Jensen, 1992). This has led researchers to apply statistical control approaches to account for variance of mean RT in *SD* RT (see Dirk, Ghisletta, & de Ribaupierre, 2010, for a comparison of common statistical approaches to IIV). Among them are the coefficient of variation (Guilford, 1965) which is calculated by dividing *SD* RT by mean RT as well as regression approaches (e.g., Hultsch, MacDonald, & Dixon, 2002; Salthouse & Berish, 2005) in which the mean RT is residualized when considering the relationship of the *SD* RT to other variables. All these approaches implicitly assume that mean RT and *SD* RT are linearly related and that this relationship is invariant within and across individuals (Wagenmakers, Grasman, & Molenaar, 2005). However, Schmiedek, Lövdén, and Lindenberger (2009) have shown that the assumption of a linear relationship between the *SD* RT and mean RT does not necessary hold for all individuals and can also vary between groups (e.g., younger and older adults). Schmiedek and colleagues (2009) therefore suggested applying theoretical models of cognitive processes (e.g., the diffusion model, Ratcliff, 1978) that take the relationship between mean RT and *SD* RT into account in order to comprehensively study age-related and individual differences in different aspects of cognitive performance.

   Somewhat different in scope, another approach to studying RT variability and avoiding difficulties resulting from statistical dependencies between mean RT and *SD* RT consists in the decomposition of individual RT distributions. RT distribution decomposition approaches underscore the utility of taking into account aspects of performance beyond mean RT in the study of age-related differences in information processing. In particular, larger IIV in older adults indicates that above and beyond the general finding of older adults being slower than younger adults, their RT distributions are wider and potentially more skewed. This observation led researchers to ask whether more pronounced individual differences in certain parts of the RT distribution (i.e., slowest or fastest responses) may be the source of the observed age–speed relation (Salthouse, 1993, 1998). The hypothesis was that older adults' slower responding might be due to a small number of particularly slow responses which are in turn more strongly related to general ability level than fast responses (cf. the "worst performance rule" in individual differences research on intelligence; see Coyle, 2003, for a review). Whereas Salthouse (1993, 1998) did not find evidence for the particular importance of slowest responses for the prediction of age-related differences in cognitive performance, several studies in the cognitive aging literature have advanced the idea of lapses of attention resulting from a small number of particularly slow responses being responsible for age-related performance declines (West, Murphy, Armilio, Craik, & Stuss, 2002). In most of these studies the ex-Gaussian distribution, a combination of an exponential and a Gaussian function, was applied to investigate lapses of attention (e.g., Spieler, Balota, & Faust, 1996; West et al., 2002). This distribution is characterized by three parameters: *mu* (μ), *sigma* (σ), and *tau* (τ). *Mu* and *sigma* represent the mean and the standard deviation, respectively, of the Gaussian composite. *Tau* represents both the mean and the standard deviation of the exponential composite. Of particular interest has been the *tau* parameter. Across studies, large *tau* parameters have been associated with increased IIV and have been interpreted as reflecting lapses of attention and lack of inhibitory control (Spieler et al., 1996; West et al., 2002). However, this interpretation has been challenged. Schmiedek, Oberauer, Wilhelm, Süss, and Wittmann (2007) obtained measurement models of the ex-Gaussian distribution and parameters from eight different choice RT tasks. Applying latent regression analysis to determine the relationship between the latent factors (i.e., for ex-Gaussian parameters) and the general cognitive ability factors, they found that the *tau* parameter was among the strongest predictors of working memory, reasoning, and processing speed. Individuals with smaller *tau* parameter showed better cognitive performance. However, in a simulation including parameters of a cognitive process model (i.e., the diffusion model, see next section) the authors did not find evidence for the hypothesis that increased performance variability is a reflection of lapses of attention during task performance. In particular, attributing the relation of *tau* to cognitive ability factors solely to trial-to-trial variability in the efficiency of information accumulation (i.e., lapses of attention) did not allow accounting for the empirically observed relation. Contrarily, attributing the relation of *tau* to cognitive abilities to individual differences in the average efficiency of information accumulation was sufficient to account for the empirical correlations. Thus the authors concluded that there is no need to explain the relation between *tau* and working memory by trial-to-trial variability in information accumulation (i.e., lapses of attention). However, they did not exclude the possibility that attentional lapses contribute to the observed correlations between *tau* and working memory. Yet their results showed that a model that did not include the assumption of lapses of attention was more parsimonious.

Taken together, both statistical control approaches to RT variability, as well as the decomposition of individual RT distributions, are limited in scope. Statistical control approaches rely on very strong assumptions that do not necessarily hold in comparisons of individuals from different age groups. RT distribution decomposition considering quantiles or fitting particular distributions to empirical data allow for more fine-grained analyses of aspects of information processing (i.e., processing speed both in terms of mean RT as well as RT variability) yet they do not allow for direct theoretical conclusions and interpretations of the observed effects in terms of cognitive processes. In the following we will argue that the effects of age on processing speed in relatively simple two-choice tasks as well as the speed–cognition relationship can best be explained from a diffusion model perspective (Schmiedek et al., 2007; Ratcliff, Schmiedek, & McKoon, 2008).

The Diffusion Model

There has been a long debate as to whether Brinley plots are a good means of describing age-related differences in processing speed (Myerson et al., 2003; Ratcliff, Spieler, & McKoon, 2000, 2004). A major contribution to this discussion came from the introduction of the diffusion model to cognitive aging research (Ratcliff, Spieler, & McKoon, 2000). The diffusion model can make predictions about mean RT of correct and incorrect responses and the associated accuracy information. It describes how the information provided by a stimulus is accumulated over time in the cognitive system until it reaches one of two response boundaries. The diffusion model gives a comprehensive picture and a straightforward interpretation of the cognitive processes at work in two-choice response tasks. Compared to other approaches to demonstrate age-related differences in processing speed in its different aspects of performance (i.e., Brinley plots, different approaches to study the role of RT variability), the diffusion model has several advantages. The diffusion model takes several important aspects of performance into account (i.e., RT and accuracy of correct and incorrect responses, RT distribution shape) and thereby it provides a comprehensive picture of the processes at work in information processing. Further, the diffusion model puts strong constraints on theoretical explanations of age-related differences in information processing (Ratcliff et al., 2000). For example, the meaning of the slope of the Brinley plot is ultimately dependent upon the underlying theoretical model of a task, whereas the parameters of the diffusion model have a straightforward theoretical meaning. The parameter describing the average rate of accumulation of information over time is called drift rate. Larger drift rates indicate faster accumulation of information and thus higher efficiency in responding. Thus the drift rate describes the quality of accumulation of information. For example, in a choice RT task, easier choices would have a larger drift rate value than complex choices. Similarly, in a recognition memory task, well-remembered items would have larger drift rates than items that are not well-remembered. The boundary separation describes an individual's response conservativeness and is included in the model as the distance between the two response boundaries. Larger boundary separations reflect more conservative responding and indicate an individual's need for more information to generate a response. For example, it has been suggested that older adults prefer accuracy over speed of responding. By moving the boundary positions, the diffusion model can account for such speed–accuracy trade-offs. The farther away the boundaries from the starting point, the slower the responses, and the less likely are errors. The third central parameter is called nondecision time and reflects sensorimotor processes necessary for sensory encoding as well as motor response preparation and execution. Beyond these central parameters the model also includes parameters for across-trial and within-trial variability. Thereby it allows also for testing the assumption that RT variability reflects lapses of attention (cf. Schmiedek et al., 2007).

The diffusion model has proven to be a useful tool in the study of age-related slowing because it allows for a rigid test of the general slowing hypothesis according to which the rate of accumulation of information is at the core of age-related slowing. The quality of information uptake is reflected in the drift parameter of the diffusion model and the hypothesis of age-related decline in drift can be empirically tested. As opposed to Brinley plots, this analysis takes into account not only mean RTs but also RT distributions for correct and incorrect responses, and accuracy information. In a number of studies, Ratcliff and colleagues (e.g., Ratcliff, Gomez, & McKoon, 2004; Ratcliff, Thapar, & McKoon, 2001, 2003, 2004, 2006a, 2006b, 2007, 2010) and Spaniol, Madden, and Voss (2006) have tested the general slowing hypothesis in different tasks ranging from signal detection over numerosity discrimination and recognition memory to lexical decision. Across tasks, the most reliable pattern of findings was an increase in nondecision time and boundary separation, indicating that older adults' overall longer RTs are based upon longer response preparation and motor processes, and higher response conservatism leading to greater care not to make errors. Depending on the type of task, age-related differences in drift rate have been found. In particular, age-related differences in the accumulation of information have been observed in tasks for which the perceptual information is limited (e.g., a masked letter discrimination task). Moreover, comparing old-old adults (i.e., 75–90 yrs) with young-old adults (i.e., 60–75 yrs) and young adults, Ratcliff and colleagues (2007) have found that there is a tendency for variability across trials in drift rate, boundary, and nondecision time to increase with age. In sum, the overall pattern of results indicates that the effects of aging cannot be attributed to a single slowing factor but for most tasks, motor performance and response cautiousness contribute substantially to older adults' worse performance as compared to younger adults. Across a variety of tasks, older adults are slower than younger adults because they set more conservative response criteria.

It is important to acknowledge that other sequential sampling models (cf. Ratcliff & Smith, 2004) lead to similar conclusions concerning the processes underlying age-related slowing (Ratcliff, Thapar, Smith, & McKoon, 2005). Given the possible theoretically based predictions, the diffusion model is an attractive model for testing hypotheses about age-related slowing and speed–cognition relationships. However, it assumes a decision process with two response boundaries as typically presented in two-choice RT tasks. Thus it does not apply to tasks including more than two choices in responding or more than one decision process (e.g., the Stroop task). Another practical difficulty with the diffusion model is the fact that it requires a large amount of data for parameters to be fitted accurately (i.e., with 95% accuracy, about 200 trials are needed to obtain an estimate of the distribution). Despite these disadvantages, the diffusion model represents a valid alternative methodological approach to test hypotheses about age-related differences in information processing and their importance for cognitive functioning. Recent developments of the classical diffusion model include the EZ diffusion model (Wagenmakers, van der Maas, & Grasman, 2007) and hierarchical Bayesian approaches to estimate diffusion model parameters (Vandekerckhove, Tuerlinckx, & Lee, 2011; see Chicherio, Dirk, Vandekerckhove, Ghisletta, & de Ribaupierre, 2010, for an application to age-related differences across the lifespan). The EZ model does not include variability within and across trials for the different parameters. Although this seems a strong constraint, particularly for researchers interested in IIV, the EZ model has been successfully applied to the study of age and individual differences in cognitive performance (Schmiedek et al., 2009; Schmiedek et al., 2007). The Bayesian hierarchical modeling approach to the diffusion model (Vandekerckhove et al., 2011) includes random effects which can account for unexplained variation between participants or items and thus allows for a more flexible estimation of diffusion model parameters and individual differences therein.

Explanatory Models for Cognitive Slowing

While the diffusion model allows for important progress in disentangling different processing aspects in speed tasks, it stays at a more descriptive level regarding the underlying causes of age-related slowing, as it does not provide explanations for age differences in drift rates that have been observed at least for some tasks (e.g., masked letter discrimination). Accounts of cognitive slowing that have been advanced early on related cognitive slowing to deficits at the brain level (e.g., Birren, 1965; Welford, 1965). Probably the most influential account of cognitive slowing stems from Welford (1965). Welford had proposed the "neural noise hypothesis," stating that processes in older adults' neural system take more time due to increased levels of "internal system noise." He assumed that the signal-to-noise ratio in older adults' central nervous system is much smaller than in younger adults due to increased noise (i.e., irrelevant activity from residual neural activity from previous processing, or increased spontaneous activity), but potentially also due to weaker input signals, or a combination of both. Welford attributed age-related decrease in the signal-to-noise ratio among others to age-related changes in the sense organs, progressive loss of brain cells, and poorer cerebral blood flow. He argued that most phenomena observed in cognitive aging, particularly age-related slowing, can be attributed to the decrease in the signal-to-noise ratio in the brain. Welford's theory has been very important for cognitive aging research and continues to be an essential part of modern theories of age-related deficits in information processing (e.g., Li & Lindenberger, 1999; Li, Lindenberger, & Sikström, 2001).

Integrating these and other theoretical accounts and empirical findings from different disciplines Li and colleagues (1999, 2001) showed in simulation work that increased IIV at the behavioral level may reflect dysfunctions in catecholaminergic neurotransmission (e.g., serotonin, dopamine). The dopaminergic system in particular has gained much interest in the cognitive aging literature (for a review, see Bäckman, Lindenberger, Li, & Nyberg, 2010). Dopaminergic neuromodulation affects essentially prefrontal regions. Alterations in prefrontal brain regions have also been postulated to affect performance in many cognitive tasks (i.e., the frontal lobe hypothesis; West, 1996). The striatum, as one of the most important areas of dopaminergic neurotransmission, shows abundant reciprocal connections to the frontal cortex (e.g., Bäckman & Farde, 2005; Bäckman et al., 2006). Deficiencies in the dopamine receptor system (e.g., reported with increasing age) may thus lead to "poor" input to the frontal cortex, thereby reducing executive functioning capacity and related cognitive functions (e.g., working memory, inhibition; see Arnsten, 1998). Further, the concentration and the binding mechanisms of dopamine decline with age in various brain regions. For example, the number of D2 receptors in the nigrostriatal region declines from age 20 on at a rate of 10% per decade (Wong, Young, Wilson, Meltzer, & Gjedde, 1997). This development parallels decline in cognitive capacities such as working memory and processing speed. Further, many aging-related diseases such as dementia and Parkinson's disease (and also schizophrenia although not typically occurring in old age) are accompanied by changes in dopaminergic neurotransmission. Interestingly, patients suffering from these diseases also show increased behavioral variability. Moreover, deficient neuromodulation of dopamine has also been directly linked to cognitive decline: For example, Bäckman and colleagues (2000) studied the relationship between cognitive performance in perceptual speed and episodic memory tasks and D2 receptor binding in a small adult sample of individuals 21 to 68 years of age. D2 receptors are one of the five subtypes of dopamine receptors which exist in high concentrations in the striatum. D2 receptor binding describes the potential of D2 receptors at postsynaptic neurons to bind dopamine that has been released into the synaptic cleft. Higher binding potential is assumed to increase the signal-to-noise ratio, which in turn leads to more distinct cortical representations and increased cognitive performance (for a review of the role of dopamine for cognitive performance across the lifespan, see Li, Lindenberger, & Bäckman, 2010). Bäckman and colleagues (2000) found that attenuated D2 receptor binding is associated with age-related decreases in episodic memory and processing speed.

Linking dopamine neuromodulation and the neural noise hypothesis of cognitive aging, Li and colleagues (Li & Lindenberger 1999; Li et al., 2001) showed that alterations in dopamine neuromodulation result in increased neural noise and less distinct cortical representations, and thereby could cause decreases in cognitive performance. More precisely, the authors simulated age-related decline in dopamine systems by modulating the gain parameter in neural networks. In their computational model, the gain parameter G captures dopaminergic activity by changing the slope of a logistic activation function. In a neural network model, this function relates the strength of excitatory and inhibitory input signals to subsequent activation (i.e., a neuron's firing rate). Generally, higher levels of input lead to a higher probability of activation. The shape of this logistic function is sigmoidal (i.e., S-shaped). The steeper the slope of this function the higher the gain parameter G and the higher in turn the dopaminergic activity. The gain parameter G is assumed to be lower in older adults than in younger adults, reflecting a unit's reduced responsivity to incoming inhibitory and excitatory signals. Further, lower average gain parameters (i.e., from older networks) result in a unit's responses being more variable compared to those from higher average gain parameters (i.e., from younger networks) indicating decreased signal transmission fidelity and thus more neural noise in older networks. The authors further showed that this increased random variability in activation leads to less distinct cortical representations. The latter may reflect everyday examples of older adults' representations of events and contexts being less distinct. A variety of cognitive aging phenomena (i.e., increased variability in behavior, ability dedifferentiation, learning rate in paired associate learning, interference susceptibility) could be successfully simulated with Li and colleague's neurocomputational model (Li, 2002).

Taken together, neuromodulatory changes across adulthood, and particularly age-related changes in dopaminergic neuromodulation, might be an important agent of age-related slowing. Linking functional, anatomical, and neuromodulatory changes at the brain level to behavioral phenomena as described by cognitive process models might be a fruitful venue to advance explanations of age-related slowing. In that sense, the study of the association between genetic variation and cognition might also contribute to explanations about individual differences in cognitive aging (cf. McGue & Johnson, 2008). Last but not least, the role of contextual and environmental influences as well as experience and training should not be neglected in explanatory models for age-related slowing, leading to the question of experience-dependent changes and plasticity in processing speed.

Plasticity of Processing Speed

Practice on tasks of processing speed generally leads to decreases of RT and also reductions of RT variability (e.g., Ram, Rabbitt, Stollery, & Nesselroade, 2005). From a diffusion model perspective, these changes do not necessarily map onto a single parameter, but may be explained, for example, by practice-induced improvements in drift rates and nondecision times, as well as adaptations of boundary separation (e.g., Dutilh, Vandekerckhove, Tuerlinckx, & Wagenmakers, 2009; Ratcliff et al., 2006b). Therefore, even simple practice on processing speed tasks might involve a number of parameters which change in quite task-specific ways.

Training approaches to improve speed of processing in a more general manner include intensive practice on visual perception tasks in the ACTIVE Study (Ball et al., 2002), which led to strong improvements of performance on these tasks that were maintained over at least two years. There were no significant transfer effects, however, to either other cognitive abilities, or to processing speed tasks with everyday materials (like quickly looking up telephone numbers). Still, claims have been made that training of perceptual speed could lead to improvements that generalize to speed of everyday activities (Ball, Edwards, & Ross, 2007). Given that processing speed has to be conceptualized as a broad ability factor, convincing evidence for training-induced improvements of this broad ability would have to include transfer effects at the level of latent factors, which are defined by broad and heterogeneous selections of speed tasks (cf. Schmiedek, Lövdén, & Lindenberger, 2010). In the COGITO Study, 101 younger and 103 older participants practiced six perceptual speed tasks (choice reaction and stimulus comparison tasks with verbal, numerical, and figural-spatial content) over 100 training sessions. While performance improvements on all tasks were considerable, there was no generalized effect to perceptual speed as a latent ability construct defined by a set of nine psychometric transfer tasks of mental speed (Schmiedek et al., 2010). Skepticism seems therefore advised regarding whether processing speed in general can be improved by practicing on a limited set of speed tasks. Practice-induced improvements might be strongly tied to increases in task-specific processing aspects, which show little to no transfer (cf. Clancy & Hoyer, 1994), and even for relatively simple perceptual speed tasks, particular task-specific strategies may be employed and change the nature of tasks considerably (Piccinin & Rabbitt, 1999).

Concluding Remarks

While the progress denoted by employing a process model like the diffusion model to processing speed tasks is considerable, currently the successful application of such models in cognitive aging research is pretty much limited to simple two-choice tasks. We are convinced, however, that moving beyond the more descriptive approaches that have dominated research on cognitive slowing for a long time and developing process models for more and more complicated tasks will, in the long run, render processing speed one among other important aspects of performance to be explained. This development will also hand over the interpretative power to theoretically more meaningful parameters that describe individual and age differences in cognitive mechanisms, motivational and strategic influences, and their complex interplay. Ideally, similar developments of models for more complex tasks of, for example, working memory or episodic memory, will then make it possible to shed light on the patterns of interrelations and age relations among processing speed and other cognitive abilities.

References

Arnsten, A. F. T. (1998). Catecholamine modulation of prefrontal cortical cognitive function. *Trends in Cognitive Sciences, 2,* 436–447.

Bäckman, L., & Farde, L. (2005). The role of dopamine systems in cognitive aging. In R. Cabeza, L. Nyberg, & D. Park (Eds.), *Cognitive neuroscience of aging* (pp. 58–84). New York: Oxford University Press.

Bäckman, L., Ginovart, N., Dixon, R. A., Wahlin, T. B. R., Wahlin, Å, Halldin, C., & Farde, L. (2000). Age-related cognitive deficits mediated by changes in the striatal dopamine system. *American Journal of Psychiatry, 157,* 635–637.

Bäckman, L., Lindenberger, U., Li, S. C., & Nyberg, L. (2010). Linking cognitive aging to alterations in dopamine neurotransmitter functioning: Recent data and future avenues. *Neuroscience and Biobehavioral Reviews, 34,* 670–677.

Bäckman, L., Nyberg, L., Lindenberger, U., Li, S. C., & Farde, L. (2006). The correlative triad among aging, dopamine, and cognition: Current status and future prospects. *Neuroscience and Biobehavioral Reviews, 30,* 791–807.

Ball, K., Berch, D. B., Helmers, K. F., Jobe, J. B., Leveck, M. D., Marsiske, M. ... Willis, S. L. (2002). Effects of cognitive training interventions with older adults – a randomized controlled trial. *Journal of the American Medical Association, 288,* 2271–2281.

Ball, K., Edwards, J. D., & Ross, L. A. (2007). The impact of speed of processing training on cognitive and everyday functions. *Journals of Gerontology: Series B: Psychological Sciences and Social Sciences, 62,* P19–P31.

Birren, J. E. (1965). Age changes in speed of behavior: Its central nature and physiological correlates. In A. T. Welford, & J. E. Birren (Eds.), *Behavior, aging and the nervous system* (pp. 191–216). Springfield, IL: Charles C. Thomas.

Birren, J. E., Woods, A. E., & Williams, M. V. (1980). Behavioral slowing with age: Causes, organization, and consequences. In L. W. Poon (Ed.), *Aging in the 1980's* (pp. 293–308). Washington, DC: American Psychological Association.

Brinley, J. F. (1965). Cognitive sets, speed and accuracy of performance in the elderly. In A. T. Welford & J. E. Birren (Eds.), *Behavior, aging, and the nervous system* (pp. 114–149). Springfield, IL: Charles C. Thomas.

Carroll, J. B. (1993). *Human cognitive abilities.* Cambridge, UK: Cambridge University Press.

Cerella, J. (1985). Information-processing rates in the elderly. *Psychological Bulletin, 98,* 67–83.

Cerella, J. (1990). Aging and information-processing rate. In J. E. Birren & K. W. Schaie (Eds.), *Handbook of the psychology of aging* (3rd ed., pp. 201–221). San Diego, CA: Academic Press.

Cerella, J. (1994). Generalized slowing in Brinley plots. *Journals of Gerontology: Series B: Psychological Sciences and Social Sciences, 49,* P65–P71.

Cerella, J., & Hale, S. (1994). The rise and fall in information-processing rates over the life span. *Acta Psychologica, 86,* 109–197.

Cerella, J., Poon, L. W., & Williams, D. H. (1980). Age and the complexity hypothesis. In L. W. Poon (Ed.), *Aging in the 1980's* (pp. 332–340). Washington, DC: American Psychological Association.

Chicherio, C., Dirk, J., Vandekerckhove, J., Ghisletta, P., & de Ribaupierre, A. (2010, April). *Delineating inter- and intraindividual variability in speeded two-choice response times across the lifespan: A hierarchical Bayesian extension to diffusion modeling.* Poster presented at the 13th Cognitive Aging Conference 2010, Atlanta, GA.

Clancy, S. M., & Hoyer, W. J. (1994). Age and skill in visual search. *Developmental Psychology, 30,* 545–552.

Coyle, T. R. (2003). A review of the worst performance rule: Evidence, theory, and alternative hypotheses. *Intelligence, 31,* 567–587.

Danthiir, V., Wilhelm, O., Schulze, R., & Roberts, R. D. (2005). Factor structure and validity of paper-and-pencil measures of mental speed: Evidence for a higher-order model? *Intelligence, 33,* 491–514.

Dirk, J., Ghisletta, P., & de Ribaupierre, A. (2010). *Interindividual and intraindividual variability in cognitive performance across the lifespan: Evidence from the Geneva Variability Study.* Manuscript submitted for publication.

Dutilh, G., Vandekerckhove, J., Tuerlinckx, F., & Wagenmakers, E.-J. (2009). A diffusion model decomposition of the practice effect. *Psychonomic Bulletin & Review, 16,* 1026–1036.

Fisk, A. D., & Fisher, D. L. (1994). Brinley plots and theories of aging: The explicit, muddled, and implicit debates. *Journals of Gerontology: Series B: Psychological Sciences and Social Sciences, 49,* P81–P89.

Fiske, D. W., & Rice, L. (1955). Intra-individual response variability. *Psychological Bulletin, 52,* 217–250.

Guilford, J. P. (1965). *Fundamental statistics in psychology and education* (4th ed.). New York: McGraw-Hill.

Hoyer, W. J., Stawski, R. S., Wasylyshyn, C., & Verhaeghen, P. (2004). Adult age and digit symbol substitution performance: A meta-analysis. *Psychology and Aging, 19,* 211–214.

Hultsch, D. F., MacDonald, S. W. S., & Dixon, R. A. (2002). Variability in reaction time performance of younger and older adults. *Journals of Gerontology: Series B: Psychological Sciences and Social Sciences, 57,* P101–P115.

Hultsch, D. F., Strauss, E., Hunter, M. A., & MacDonald, S. W. S. (2008). Intraindividual variability, cognition, and aging. In F. I. M. Craik & T. A. Salthouse (Eds.), *The handbook of aging and cognition* (3rd ed., pp. 491–556). New York: Psychology Press.

Jensen, A. R. (1982). Reaction time and psychometric g. In H. J. Eysenck (Ed.), *A model for intelligence* (pp. 93–132). New York: Springer.

Jensen, A. R. (1992). The importance of intraindividual variation in reaction time. *Personality and Individual Differences, 13,* 869-881.

Jensen, A. R. (1998). *The g factor: The science of mental ability.* London: Prager.

Li, S.-C. (2002). Connecting the many levels and facets of cognitive aging. *Current Directions in Psychological Science, 11,* 38–43.

Li, S.-C., & Lindenberger, U. (1999). Cross-level unification: A computational exploration of the link between deterioration of neurotransmitter systems and dedifferentiation of cognitive abilities in old age. In L.-G. Nilsson & H. J. Markowitsch (Eds.), *Cognitive neuroscience of memory* (pp. 103–146). Lidingo, Sweden: Hogrefe & Huber.

Li, S.-C., Lindenberger, U., & Bäckman, L. (2010). Dopaminergic modulation of cognition across the life span. *Neuroscience & Biobehavioral Reviews, 34,* 625–630.

Li, S.-C., Lindenberger, U., & Sikström, S. (2001). Aging cognition: From neuromodulation to representation. *Trends in Cognitive Sciences, 5,* 479–486.

Lima, S. D., Hale, S., & Myerson, J. (1991). How general is general slowing? Evidence from the lexical domain. *Psychology & Aging, 6,* 416–425.

Lindenberger, U., & Pötter, U. (1998). The complex nature of unique and shared effects in hierarchical linear regression: Implications from developmental psychology. *Psychological Methods, 3,* 218–230.

Lindenberger, U., von Oertzen, T., Ghisletta, P., & Hertzog, C. (2011). Cross-sectional age variance extraction: What's change got to do with it? *Psychology and Aging, 26*(1), 34–47.

Mayr, U., Kliegl, R., & Krampe, R. T. (1996). Sequential and coordinative processing dynamics in figural transformations across the life span. *Cognition, 59,* 61–90.

McGue, M., & Johnson, W. (2008). Genetics of cognitive aging. In F. I. M. Craik & T. A. Salthouse (Eds.), *The handbook of aging and cognition* (3rd ed., pp. 55–96). New York: Psychology Press.

Meyer, D. E., Glass, J. M., Mueller, S. T., Seymour, T. L., & Kieras, D. E. (2001). Executive-process interactive control: A unified computational theory for answering twenty questions (and more) about cognitive aging. *European Journal of Cognitive Psychology, 13,* 123–164.

Myerson, J., Adams, D. R., Hale, S., & Jenkins, L. (2003). Analysis of group differences in processing speed: Brinley plots, Q-Q plots, and other conspiracies. *Psychonomic Bulletin & Review, 10,* 224–237.

Myerson, J., Hale, S., Wagstaff, D., Poon, L. W., & Smith, G. A. (1990). The information-loss model: A mathematical theory of age-related cognitive slowing. *Psychological Review, 97,* 475–487.

Myerson, J., Wagstaff, D., & Hale, S. (1994). Brinley plots, explained variance, and the analysis of age difference in age-related cognitive slowing. *Journals of Gerontology: Series B: Psychological Sciences and Social Sciences, 49,* P72–P80.

Perfect, T. J. (1994). What can Brinley plots tell us about cognitive aging? *Journals of Gerontology: Series B: Psychological Sciences and Social Sciences, 49,* P60–P64.

Piccinin, A. M., & Rabbitt, P. M. A. (1999). Contribution of cognitive abilities to performance and improvement on a substitution coding task. *Psychology and Aging, 14,* 539–551.

Rabbitt, P. M. A., Osman, P., Moore, B., & Stollery, B. (2001). There are stable individual differences in performance variability, both from moment to moment and from day to day. *Quarterly Journal of Experimental Psychology, 54A,* 981–1003.

Ram, N., Rabbitt, P. M. A., Stollery, B., & Nesselroade, J. R. (2005). Cognitive performance inconsistency: Intraindividual change and variability. *Psychology and Aging, 20,* 623–633.

Ratcliff, R. (1978). A theory of memory retrieval. *Psychological Review, 85,* 59–109.

Ratcliff, R., Gomez, P., & McKoon, G. (2004). A diffusion model account of the lexical decision task. *Psychological Review, 111,* 159–182.

Ratcliff, R., Schmiedek, F., & McKoon, G. (2008). A diffusion model explanation of the worst performance rule for reaction time and IQ. *Intelligence, 36,* 10–17.

Ratcliff, R., & Smith, P. L. (2004). A comparison of sequential sampling models for two-choice reaction time. *Psychological Review, 111,* 333–367.

Ratcliff, R., Spieler, D. H., & McKoon, G. (2000). Explicitly modeling the effects of aging on response time. *Psychonomic Bulletin & Review, 7,* 1–25.

Ratcliff, R., Spieler, D. H., & McKoon, G. (2004). Analysis of group differences in processing speed: Where are the models of processing? *Psychonomic Bulletin & Review, 11,* 755–769.

Ratcliff, R., Thapar, A., & McKoon, G. (2001). The effects of aging on reaction time in a signal detection task *Psychology and Aging, 16,* 323–341.

Ratcliff, R., Thapar, A., & McKoon, G. (2003). A diffusion model analysis of the effects of aging on brightness discrimination. *Perception & Psychophysics, 65,* 523–535.

Ratcliff, R., Thapar, A., & McKoon, G. (2004). A diffusion model analysis of the effects of aging on recognition memory. *Journal of Memory and Language, 50,* 408–424.

Ratcliff, R., Thapar, A., & McKoon, G. (2006a). Aging and individual differences in rapid two-choice decisions. *Psychonomic Bulletin & Review, 13,* 626–635.

Ratcliff, R., Thapar, A., & McKoon, G. (2006b). Aging, practice, and perceptual tasks: A diffusion model analysis. *Psychology and Aging, 21,* 353–371.

Ratcliff, R., Thapar, A., & McKoon, G. (2007). Application of the diffusion model to two-choice tasks for adults 75–90 years old. *Psychology and Aging, 22,* 56–66.

Ratcliff, R., Thapar, A., & McKoon, G. (2010). Individual differences, aging, and IQ in two-choice tasks. *Cognitive Psychology, 60,* 127–157.

Ratcliff, R., Thapar, A., Smith, P. L., & McKoon, G. (2005). Aging and response times: A comparison of sequential sampling models. In J. Duncan, P. McLeod, & L. Phillips (Eds.), *Measuring the mind: Speed, control, and age* (pp. 3–32). Oxford: Oxford University Press.

Roberts, R. D., & Stankov, L. (1999). Individual differences in speed of mental processing and human cognitive abilities: Toward a taxonomic model. *Learning and Individual Differences, 11,* 1–120.

Salthouse, T. A. (1985). *A theory of cognitive aging.* Amsterdam: North Holland.

Salthouse, T. A. (1991). *Theoretical perspectives on cognitive aging.* Hillsdale, NJ: Erlbaum.

Salthouse, T. A. (1993). Attentional blocks are not responsible for age-related slowing. *Journals of Gerontology: Series B: Psychological Sciences and Social Sciences, 48,* P263–P270.

Salthouse, T. A. (1996). The processing-speed theory of adult age differences in cognition. *Psychological Review, 103,* 403–437.

Salthouse, T. A. (1998). Relation of successive percentiles of reaction time distributions to cognitive variables and adult age. *Intelligence, 26,* 153–166.

Salthouse, T. A. (2004). What and when of cognitive aging. *Current Directions in Psychological Science, 13,* 140–144.

Salthouse, T. A., & Babcock, R. L. (1991). Decomposing adult age differences in working memory. *Developmental Psychology, 27,* 763–776.

Salthouse, T. A., & Berish, D.E. (2005). Correlates of within-person (across-occasion) variability in reaction time. *Neuropsychology, 19,* 77–87.

Salthouse, T. A., & Czaja, J. (2000). Structural constraints on process explanations in cognitive aging. *Psychology and Aging, 15,* 44–55.

Schaie, K. W. (1993). The Seattle Longitudinal Study of Adult Intelligence. *Current Directions in Psychological Science, 2,* 171–175.

Schmiedek, F., & Li, S.-C. (2004). Toward an alternative representation for disentangling age-associated differences in general and specific cognitive abilities. *Psychology and Aging, 19,* 40–56.

Schmiedek, F., Lövdén, M., & Lindenberger, U. (2009). On the relation of mean reaction time and intraindividual reaction time variability. *Psychology and Aging, 24,* 841–857.

Schmiedek, F., Lövdén, M., & Lindenberger, U. (2010). Hundred days of cognitive training enhance broad cognitive abilities in adulthood: Findings from the COGITO study. *Frontiers in Aging Neuroscience, 2,* 1–10.

Schmiedek, F., Oberauer, K., Wilhelm, O., Süss, H.-M., & Wittmann, W. M. (2007). Individual differences in components of reaction time distributions and their relations to working memory and intelligence. *Journal of Experimental Psychology: General, 136,* 414–429.

Sliwinski, M. J., & Buschke, H. (1999). Cross-sectional and longitudinal relationships among age, cognition, and processing speed. *Psychology and Aging, 14,* 18–33.

Sliwinski, M. J., & Hall, C. B. (1998). Constraints on general slowing: A meta-analysis using hierarchical linear models with random coefficients. *Psychology and Aging, 13,* 164–175.

Spaniol, J., Madden, D. J., & Voss, A. (2006). A diffusion model analysis of adult age differences in episodic and semantic long-term memory retrieval. *Journal of Experimental Psychology: Learning, Memory, and Cognition, 32,* 101–117.

Spieler, D. H., Balota, D. A., & Faust, M. E. (1996). Stroop performance in healthy younger and older adults and in individuals with dementia of the Alzheimer's type. *Journal of Experimental Psychology: Human Perception and Performance, 22,* 461–179.

Vandekerckhove, J., Tuerlinckx, F., & Lee, M. D. (2011). Hierarchical diffusion models for two-choice response times. *Psychological Methods, 16*(1), 44–62.

Verhaeghen, P., & Cerella, J. (2008). Everything we know about aging and response times. In S. M. Hofer, & D. F. Alwin (Eds.), *Handbook of cognitive aging: Interdisciplinary perspectives* (pp. 134–150). Thousand Oaks, CA: Sage.

Verhaeghen, P., Kliegl, R., & Mayr, U. (1997). Sequential and coordinative complexity in time-accuracy functions for mental arithmetic. *Psychology and Aging, 12,* 555–564.

Verhaeghen, P., & Salthouse, T. A. (1997). Meta-analyses of age-cognition relations in adulthood: Estimates of linear and nonlinear age effects and structural models. *Psychological Bulletin, 122,* 231–249.

Vernon, P. A. (1987). *Speed of information processing and intelligence.* Norwood, NJ: Ablex.

Wagenmakers, E.-J., Grasman, R. P. P. P., & Molenaar, P. C. M. (2005). On the relation between the mean and the variance of a diffusion model response time distribution. *Journal of Mathematical Psychology, 49,* 195–204.

Wagenmakers, E.-J., van der Maas, H. L. J., & Grasman, R. P. P. P. (2007). An EZ-diffusion model for response time and accuracy. *Psychonomic Bulletin & Review, 14,* 3–22.

Welford, A. T. (1965). Performance, biological mechanisms and age: A theoretical sketch. In A. T. Welford, & J. E. Birren (Eds.), *Behavior, aging, and the nervous system* (pp. 3–20). Springfield, IL: Thomas.

West, R. (1996). An application of prefrontal cortex function theory to cognitive aging. *Psychological Bulletin, 120,* 272–292.

West, R., Murphy, K. J., Armilio, M. L., Craik, F. I. M., & Stuss, D. T. (2002). Lapses of intention and performance variability reveal age-related increases in fluctuations of executive control. *Brain and Cognition, 49,* 402–419.

Wong, D. F., Young, D., Wilson, P. D., Meltzer, C. C., & Gjedde, A. (1997). Quantification of neuroreceptors in the living human brain. D-2-like dopamine receptors: Theory, validation, and changes during normal aging. *Journal of Cerebral Blood Flow and Metabolism, 17,* 316–330.

Zimprich, D., & Martin, M. (2002). Can longitudinal changes in processing speed explain longitudinal age changes in fluid intelligence? *Psychology and Aging, 17,* 690–695.

8

Working Memory

David P. McCabe and Vanessa M. Loaiza

A great deal of cognitive aging research has been concerned with identifying *cognitive primitives* that could potentially explain age-related declines in fluid cognitive abilities (e.g., long-term memory, reasoning). Cognitive primitives that have been proposed to account for age differences in cognition include working memory capacity (Hasher & Zacks, 1988; McCabe, Roediger, McDaniel, Balota, & Hambrick, 2010), processing speed (Salthouse, 1996); sensory functioning (Lindenberger & Baltes, 1994), and executive functioning (Glisky, 2002; McCabe et al., 2010; West, 1996), among others. The current chapter focuses on summarizing several theoretical perspectives on the cognitive aging of working memory, and includes a selective review of research findings associated with these perspectives. The chapter includes reviews of several theoretical approaches that have been investigated for decades, as well as some contemporary approaches to the study of working memory that have yet to be considered widely in the context of cognitive aging.

What is Working Memory?

Perhaps the most widely used definition of working memory (WM) is that it is a memory system responsible for the online maintenance and processing of information in service of task goals (Engle, 2002; Miyake & Shah, 1999). This definition has been particularly useful as a framework for the investigation of individual differences, including age differences, in WM abilities. This definition is also based on the first comprehensive model of WM (Baddeley & Hitch, 1974) – the multicomponent model – which suggests

The Wiley-Blackwell Handbook of Adulthood and Aging, First Edition. Edited by Susan Krauss Whitbourne and Martin J. Sliwinski. © 2012 Blackwell Publishing Ltd. Published 2012 by Blackwell Publishing Ltd.

that the WM system is composed of a central executive component, as well as modality-specific maintenance buffers. According to the multicomponent model, the central executive is responsible for the control of attention, whereas the modality-specific buffers maintain specific types of information (e.g., verbal, visuospatial) for brief periods of time. An alternative definition of WM that has been useful for investigating cognitive aging is that WM involves the capacity of immediate attention (e.g., Cowan et al., 2005; Oberauer, 2002). These models owe their heritage more to the notion of capacity limits on immediate attention (Broadbent, 1958; Miller, 1956), though these more recent models are certainly more dynamic and complex than early capacity models of attention. Regardless of its specific definition, researchers agree that WM provides the mental workplace for conscious cognitive function, making it central to theorizing about cognitive aging.

Issues to Consider in the Study of Aging and Working Memory

There are several fundamental issues to consider when attempting to gain a comprehensive understanding of the influence of adult aging on WM:

1. What is the most useful way to define WM? The conceptual definition of WM determines the way in which it is operationalized, so this issue is of critical importance.
2. To what extent is WM similar to, or distinct from, other similar constructs? For example, executive functioning, fluid intelligence, and processing speed bear considerable conceptual similarity to WM. Can these constructs be distinguished from one another empirically?
3. What are the best methods for investigating WM? In particular, both microanalytic (i.e., univariate experimental designs) and macroanalytic (i.e., multivariate factor analytic) methods have been employed to investigate WM (Hambrick, 2005). What are the strengths and weaknesses of these approaches?

One of the most typically employed approaches to studying age-related differences in WM has been to consider performance on simple and complex span tasks. Simple span tasks require that research participants hear or view a series of to-be-remembered items (e.g., digits or words), and report those items back immediately in serial order. Thus, there is no explicit processing component required during these tasks, and some have argued that these tasks solely measure the maintenance function of WM. In contrast to simple span tasks, complex span tasks require that a processing task (e.g., reading comprehension, math operations) be completed prior to the presentation of each to-be-remembered item, with encoding of the to-be-remembered items and presumably the retrieval requirement being the same as simple span tasks. Performance on complex span tasks is typically referred to as "WM capacity," which is believed to reflect the efficiency of the WM system. Thus, a comparison of simple and complex span tasks has been crucial to gaining a better understanding of the WM system. Of course the study of WM is not limited to the use of span tasks, and other tasks (e.g., n-back, running memory span; Cohen, Perlstein,

Braver, & Nystrom, 1997; Oberauer, Süss, Wilhelm, & Wittmann, 2003; Schmiedek, Hildebrandt, Lövdén, Wilhelm, & Lindenberger, 2009) have been useful for investigating WM as well, particularly more recently. Indeed, Oberauer and colleagues have specifically, and perhaps wisely, advocated using heterogeneous WM tasks in order to broadly define the WM construct in multivariate studies (Oberauer, Süss, Wilhelm, & Sander, 2007).

In terms of understanding the degree to which WM is similar to other fluid ability constructs, several studies have sought to determine the extent to which WM is similar or distinct from other ability constructs (e.g., executive function, fluid intelligence, etc.). Indeed, the utility of the WM framework in general is dependent on WM having some distinct characteristics that distinguish it from other ability constructs. Stated differently, if WM and other abilities (e.g., processing speed) were essentially identical constructs, or if all of the age-related variability in WM could be accounted for using a conceptually simpler construct, it would undermine the utility of WM as an explanatory construct for cognitive aging.

With respect to different methodological approaches to studying WM, univariate approaches, in which age effects on a single outcome measure are considered, are often useful when these studies are designed to isolate specific mechanisms that are affected by age. However, a notable disadvantage of univariate approaches is that no task is "process-pure" (Jacoby, 1991), and thus it is often difficult to determine the specific ability that is affected by aging for a single task. Moreover, univariate approaches make it difficult to determine if aging would affect WM if task parameters (e.g., timing, type of stimuli) change. Multivariate approaches to understanding WM involve measuring multiple tasks in order to isolate functions of the WM system at the latent variable level. This approach has the advantage of circumventing the process purity issue to a great extent, but often this approach provides little specificity regarding the WM mechanisms affected by aging. Thus, it is critical for both microanalytic and macroanalytic approaches to WM to inform one another in order to gain a comprehensive understanding of the influence of aging on WM.

Theoretical Frameworks of Working Memory

The multicomponent model first introduced by Baddeley and Hitch (1974) guided early research on the cognitive aging of WM (e.g., Salthouse & Babcock, 1991), but other approaches have been influential as well. WM frameworks that have been particularly useful for cognitive aging research include the processing speed theory (Salthouse, 1996), the inhibitory deficit framework (Hasher & Zacks, 1988; Lustig, May, & Hasher, 2001), the controlled attention framework (Engle & Kane, 2004; McCabe et al., 2010), and the embedded-processes model (Cowan, 1999; Oberauer, 2005). Although many of these approaches make different assumptions regarding the principles by which the WM system operates, each proposes some sort of central attentional resource, or executive attention component, responsible for directing attention during cognitive processing. Indeed, it is the central executive component of WM that appears to be most dramatically affected by aging (Park et al., 1996). Thus, of primary interest to most cognitive aging researchers has been the central executive, or attentional control component, of the WM system. Toward that end, more recent WM frameworks that include novel explanations of the functioning of the central executive will be considered, including the primary–secondary memory framework (Unsworth & Engle, 2007a) and the time-based resource-sharing model (Barrouillet, Bernardin, & Camos, 2004).

The multicomponent model

The *multicomponent model* suggests that processing and so-called storage operations are independent components of the WM model. As previously mentioned, attentional abilities are associated with the central executive component of the WM model, whereas storage of information is associated with passive buffers specialized for different types of information (i.e., verbal and visuospatial). Research motivated by the multicomponent model suggests that the central executive component of the WM system is more dramatically affected by age than the storage components (Park et al., 2002; see also Jenkins, Myerson, Joerding, & Hale, 2000). Support for univariate approaches to studying aging and WM include the finding that meta-analyses of age effects are larger for complex span tasks (measuring the executive component of WM) as compared to simple span tasks (measuring the storage component of WM; Bopp & Verhaeghen, 2005; Verhaeghen & Salthouse, 1997). However, as noted below, due to differences in the temporal constraints of simple and complex span tasks, it seems unlikely that these tasks reflect similar "storage" requirements, and only differ in the extent to which they tax the central executive. Instead, complex span tasks may be more similar to long-term, or episodic, memory tasks than simple span tasks because they require retrieval of information that has been displaced from consciousness (McCabe, 2008; Unsworth & Engle, 2006).

Although the aforementioned meta-analyses provide support for the multicomponent model to some extent, there are other data that are not entirely consistent with the multicomponent model. For example, age effects for some simple span tasks (e.g., word span) are reliably larger than for complex span tasks (e.g., reading span; Bopp & Verhaeghen, 2005) that require encoding and retrieval of the same types of information. These data are inconsistent with the idea that aging affects the central executive more than the modality-specific storage buffers. If the storage requirements were similar for both the word span and reading span tasks (i.e., recalling words), but reading span additionally taxed the central executive, there should have been larger age effects for reading span than word span. Other data that are inconsistent with the multicomponent model include findings that processing and storage rely on a single attentional resource in both younger and older adults (McCabe, 2010), calling into question the notion that processing and storage functions are independent.

Another issue that clouds interpretation of the multicomponent model is the finding that the rate of decline for visuospatial WM tasks is sharper than the rate of decline for verbal WM span tasks (Jenkins et al., 2000). This has led some to speculate that there are distinct WM resources (i.e., central executive mechanisms) specialized for distinct types of information, specifically, for verbal and visuospatial information. Research supporting the differentiation of verbal and visuospatial WM has been reported (Park et al., 2002;

Hale et al., 2011), although others have reported data consistent with a single central executive component (McCabe et al., 2010). It is not entirely clear whether distinct verbal and visuospatial WM systems can be distinguished, but research from younger adults from both univariate and multivariate approaches seem to strongly favor the interpretation of a single central executive, or attentional control, component that is not modality-specific (Kane et al., 2004; Vergauwe, Barrouillet, & Camos, 2010).

The processing speed model

Arguably, the most influential explanation of age-related slowing is the *processing speed model* proposed by Salthouse (1996). According to this model, age-related differences in WM performance result from slower processing limiting the amount of information that can be simultaneously activated in WM. Support for the model comes from data demonstrating that the relationship between WM and other cognitive measures (e.g., reasoning, intelligence, episodic memory) is attenuated by statistically controlling for performance on perceptual comparison tests believed to measure the speed with which simple discriminations can be made (Salthouse, 1996). These data support the idea that higher-order cognition is constrained by the fundamental ability to process information quickly.

The processing speed model of cognitive aging is arguably the most parsimonious explanation of age-related declines in WM capacity, though data have suggested that this explanation is limited as a complete explanation of age differences in WM. For example, Park et al. (1996) demonstrated that while processing speed accounts for age-related variance in episodic memory performance, WM capacity accounts for variance in episodic memory beyond processing speed. More recently, McCabe et al. (2010) found that although measures of processing speed were strongly related to WM capacity in a lifespan sample ($r = .77$), accounting for age differences in processing speed did not attenuate the relationship between WM capacity and episodic memory. Similarly, Chen and Li (2007) found that the relation between age and fluid intelligence was mediated by measures of WM capacity, rather than processing speed.

Although age-related declines in processing speed are well-documented, these declines depend on whether the tasks involve sequential or coordinative complexity (Oberauer, Demmrich, Mayr, & Kliegl, 2001; Oberauer, Wendland, & Kliegl, 2003; Verhaeghen, Kliegl, & Mayr, 1997). For example, Oberauer et al. (2003) developed a WM task in which the number of digits that required updating (memory load) varied, and either required switching between the digits to update, or updating the same digit (memory access). While there were no differences between older and younger adults in the rate of decline in memory accuracy for increasing memory demands, or in slowing in response to switch costs, older adults were selectively slower for nonswitch trials as the number of digits to update increased (Oberauer et al., 2003). Hence, the costs of slower processing speed in older adults are not similar across tasks, but rather are more evident when the coordinative conditions of the task increase. This presents a challenge to the processing speed hypothesis because the relation between age and working memory performance is not mediated in a similar fashion by processing speed for different types of tasks.

The inhibitory deficit framework

According to the *inhibitory deficit framework*, age differences in WM result from age-related declines in the ability to inhibit irrelevant information from gaining access to consciousness (Hasher & Zacks, 1988; Hasher, Zacks, & May, 1999). Specifically, older adults show deficits in WM capacity and other measures of fluid cognition because of a decreased efficiency in blocking or deleting unnecessary information from WM. These inhibitory deficits interfere with the ability to process relevant information in WM because WM is "cluttered" with irrelevant information. Hence, age-related declines in WM capacity do not result from declines in *capacity* per se, but rather from increases in *the amount of information* in WM. Furthermore, a central prediction of the inhibitory deficit framework is that increasing the necessity of inhibitory processes during a complex span task should also increase the correlation between measures of WM capacity and other measures of higher cognition.

Support for the inhibitory deficit framework has come primarily from a univariate, experimental approach. These studies involve examining the role of inhibitory functioning in attentional tasks such as negative priming (May, Kane, & Hasher, 1995) and saccadic eye movements (Campbell, Al-aidroos, Pratt, & Hasher, 2009), as well as higher-level cognitive tasks, such as the fan effect (Gerard, Zacks, Hasher, & Radvansky, 1991) and reading comprehension (Connelly, Hasher, & Zacks, 1991). For example, with respect to attention tasks, findings from the negative priming paradigm indicate that younger adults show a relatively greater deficit in performance (i.e., slower processing) for stimuli that had been suppressed as compared to older adults (see May et al., 1995 for a review). Thus, because older adults have declines in inhibitory functioning, their performance shows weaker deleterious effects of previously suppressed information. Also consistent with the inhibitory deficit account is the finding that older adults show priming for information that needed to be suppressed during reading comprehension, but younger adults do not (Hartman & Hasher, 1991). Hartman and Hasher (1991) reported that when "garden path" sentences ended with unexpected words (e.g., She ladled the soup in her *lap*) older adults showed priming for words that would have been expected to end the sentence (i.e., *bowl*). According to the inhibitory deficit framework, both younger and older adults implicitly generate "bowl" as the expected ending, but older adults are not able to suppress the expected, but irrelevant word, leading to an increased availability of the irrelevant information in memory on a later test. Although this inhibitory deficit can have negative consequences with respect to maintaining task goals, Hasher and colleagues have also noted that there are potential benefits as well. For example, the increased availability of irrelevant information for older adults can facilitate performance on other tasks (Healey, Campbell, & Hasher, 2008).

The role of inhibitory deficits in WM has also been examined by assessing its influence on complex span task performance. Specifically, several studies have indicated that proactive interference (interference caused by previously presented stimuli influencing later performance) limits complex span task performance, and this effect is greater for older adults than for younger adults (Lustig et al., 2001; May, Hasher, & Kane,1999; Rowe, Hasher, & Turcotte, 2008). The influence of proactive interference on complex span tasks has been investigated using several methods. For example, presenting complex span task trials using a procedure in which the length of the trials (i.e., number of to-be-remembered items per trial) increases (the ascending condition) is expected to cause greater proactive interference than a procedure in which the trial lengths decrease across the task (the descending condition). Proactive interference is high in the ascending condition because items that were processed earlier in the task can be inadvertently retrieved during trials of longer lengths, thereby decreasing estimates of maximum capacity. By contrast, in the descending presentation format, shorter trials are presented later, and it is easier to constrain WM retrieval to trials with only a few items, thus maximizing estimates of WM capacity.

Lustig et al. (2001) found that older adults' recall was greater for a reading span task administered using descending list lengths as compared to ascending list lengths, whereas the opposite was the case for younger adults. Moreover, older adults' performance for only the ascending condition, in which the proactive interference was greatest for longer list lengths, was correlated with prose recall. Performance for the descending condition was not related to prose recall. Lustig et al. concluded that what is common to the increasing list length complex span tasks and prose recall was not the capacity of WM, but the ability to resolve response competition. Results using visuospatial complex span tasks are also consistent with these findings, with older adults showing reduced span task performance in high-PI conditions as compared with low-PI conditions, whereas the opposite pattern was found for younger adults (Rowe, Hasher, & Turcotte, 2008, 2009). Support for the role of proactive interference on span tasks also comes from research demonstrating more intrusion errors for older adults as compared to younger adults during complex span recall (Borrella, Carretti, & Mammarella, 2006; Lustig et al., 2001). Intrusion errors presumably occur because participants cannot gate out previously presented but now irrelevant items on later trials.

While the findings reviewed thus far are consistent with the inhibitory deficit framework, alternative explanations for these findings have been proposed as well. For example, some have suggested that results consistent with the inhibitory deficit can be explained as source memory errors (Hedden & Park, 2003; Oberauer, 2005) or recollection failures (Hay & Jacoby, 1999; Jacoby, 1999). A study by Oberauer (2005) illustrates how alternative explanations can account for data consistent with an inhibitory deficit explanation. Specifically, slower reaction times to intrusion probes were still evident in a local recognition task that exclusively necessitated binding of the item to remember its location rather than inhibition of previously studied items (Oberauer, 2005). Structural equation models also demonstrated that performance on this task requiring explicit recollection was uniquely predictive of WM capacity. On the other hand, performance on the modified Sternberg task, in which participants could potentially inhibit irrelevant items, shared all of its variance with the task requiring explicit recollection (Oberauer, 2005). Thus, although inhibitory deficits are a potential explanation of age differences in working memory performance, other explanations that do not involve inhibition can explain these data as well.

Other studies have documented inconsistent findings concerning the predicted role of proactive interference build-up in the relationship between WM capacity and higher cognitive variables. For example, Salthouse and Pink (2008) administered randomly presented trial lengths of several complex span tasks, all of which were significantly related to measures of fluid intelligence. However, none of the list lengths beyond the shortest lengths (either 2 or 3 to-be-remembered items), nor the trials later in the task (regardless of list length), predicted unique variance in general fluid intelligence (Salthouse & Pink, 2008). These findings are inconsistent with the inhibitory deficit framework prediction that proactive interference building up across the task for longer list lengths drives the relationship between span task performance and fluid intelligence. Instead, what appears to influence the overlap between the two constructs is captured in the shortest trials, and early in the task (Salthouse & Pink, 2008).

The embedded processes model

The *embedded processes model* posits that age differences in WM arise due to problems with binding information within, and retrieving information into, an immediate focus of attention. Specifically, the model suggests that retrieval of information over short periods of time (i.e., WM) relies on the functioning of two distinct components: the focus of attention and activated long-term memory (Cowan, 1993, 1999). The focus of attention is a capacity-limited component that can be "zoomed in" to maintain a single item or goal, or "zoomed out" to maintain approximately four items (Cowan et al., 2005). If more than four items need to be maintained, items become displaced from the focus of attention into activated long-term memory. Activated long-term memory keeps information that is not currently in conscious awareness (i.e., the focus of attention) in a highly activated state, allowing it to be accessed during on-going processing. Thus, according to the embedded processes model, the efficiency of WM depends on the capacity of the focus of attention, and perhaps to the efficiency with which information in activated long-term memory can be accessed by the focus of attention, both of which have shown age-related declines.

Research on age differences in the embedded processes model has focused on binding information into chunks in the focus of attention, and how information is transferred between the focus of attention and activated long-term memory. This transfer of information has frequently been referred to as either "focus switching" (Garavan, 1998; Oberauer, 2002; Unsworth & Engle, 2008; Verhaeghen & Hoyer, 2007), "refreshing" (Camos, Lagner, & Barrouillet, 2009; Higgins & Johnson, 2009; Johnson, Reeder, Raye, & Mitchell, 2002), or "updating" (Kessler & Meiran, 2006; Schmiedek, Hildebrandt, Lövdén, Wilhelm, & Lindenberger, 2009). Although these terms are to some extent distinct, all of them are related to the retrieval of information into the focus of attention. For simplicity, we will refer to this mechanism as focus switching. Much of Cowan's research supporting the embedded processes model is based on WM differences in children and younger adults (e.g., Cowan et al., 2005), but recent studies have focused on adult aging, emphasizing the role of chunking in the focus of attention as a source of age differences in WM (Gilchrist, Cowan, & Naveh-Benjamin, 2009; Naveh-Benjamin, Cowan, Kilb, & Chen, 2007). Specifically, Cowan and colleagues have proposed a binding deficit hypothesis of age differences in chunking, such that older adults are less likely to use effective chunking, which in turn decreases the likelihood of accessing these associations in later recall from WM (Naveh-Benjamin et al., 2007). Naveh-Benjamin et al. (2007) found support for this binding deficit, reporting that reduced attentional resources may be responsible for age-related decreases in chunking efficiency. Specifically, a divided-attention younger adult group simulated a similar pattern of recall performance of chunked word pairs compared to older adults' performance, suggesting that attentional resources subserve the binding of information in the focus of attention and are deficient in older adults. Hence, there is evidence that age limits both forming and maintaining chunks in the focus of attention.

Oberauer and colleagues (Oberauer, 2002, 2005; Oberauer, Wendland, and Kliegl, 2003) have extensively explored the focus of attention and the focus switching mechanism in older adults. According to this *concentric model*, which can be considered a modified version of Cowan's embedded processes model, the focus of attention can only maintain a single item in a larger *direct access* region (Oberauer, 2002). Oberauer (2002) further suggested that actively processed information is maintained within the direct access region, which briefly resides there until one item is selected for processing by the focus of attention. Other less active information is more passively maintained within activated long-term memory (Oberauer, 2002). Support for this view is substantiated by dissociations between reaction times and accuracy in a modified Sternberg task, during which a row of one to three frames of digits are cued as "relevant" and require successive updating while another row is cued as "irrelevant" after a variable amount of time (cue stimulus interval or CSI). The results largely confirm the concentric model's predictions, such that response times show an effect of having switched the focus of attention between elements in the active "relevant" row, especially as the number of items that were required to update increases, whereas only passively maintaining the "irrelevant" information in activated long-term memory shows no effect of set size (Oberauer, 2002). Moreover, decreases in accuracy (Vaughan, Basak, Hartman, & Verhaeghen, 2008; Verhaeghen & Hoyer, 2007) have been shown for information that must be retrieved from activated long-term memory, thus supporting a role of focus switching during WM that declines with age.

The theoretical implications of separable processing and storage elements in WM, which can be dissociated with age, are in conflict with some resource-sharing perspectives (Barrouillet et al. 2004). Oberauer and colleagues (2001; Oberauer, Wendland, and Kliegl, 2003) have argued that more active information could be accessed and manipulated without being influenced by passively maintained information in activated long-term memory. Vaughan et al. (2008) have also supported this argument for the dissociation between intact accessibility, as evidenced by similar response time functions between age groups, and diminished availability, evident by more substantial decreases in performance as a result of focus switching.

The executive attention framework

Engle, Kane, and colleagues have proposed a two-factor theory of individual differences in WM capacity, focusing their investigations on younger adult samples (see Engle & Kane, 2004 for a review). According to this two-factor theory, individual differences in WM capacity are determined by (a) the ability to maintain task goals, and (b) the ability to resist interference by prepotent distracters. Support for this model comes from both large-scale factor-analytic studies, as well as extreme group designs, wherein individuals with high versus low WM capacity, as measured by complex span tasks, are compared. Findings from this program of research indicate that WM capacity is associated with controlled attention tasks (e.g., the antisaccade task), as well as more complex cognitive tasks (e.g., fluid intelligence). Although this model has not been applied to aging widely, there are data from cognitive aging studies that support the framework in principle, mirroring data from high-span and low-span younger adults.

For example, Kane, Bleckley, Conway, and Engle (2001) reported that high-span individuals make fewer errors on the antisaccade task, in which participants have to overcome a prepotent, or habitual, response, in order to look away from a cued location. By contrast, in a prosaccade condition, in which participants are to respond in a manner consistent with their prepotent response tendencies, performance does not differ as a function of WM capacity. These data support the notion that WM capacity is important under high-interference conditions that put a premium on maintenance of task goals (see also Kane & Engle, 2003). Similar research has been reported in comparisons of younger and older adults, indicating that older age is associated with more antisaccade errors and slower response times due to failures to maintain task goals (Nieuwenhuis, Ridderinkhof, de Jong, Kok, & van der Molen, 2000). Similar differences between high- and low-WM capacity younger adults, and younger and older adults, have been reported for Stroop tasks that place a premium on goal maintenance (Kane & Engle, 2003; West, 1999), as well as other tasks that require goal maintenance (Braver et al., 2001; Frank & O'Reilly, 2006).

The executive attention framework also suggests that it is the general efficiency of the central executive component of the WM system that drives relations between WM capacity tasks and measures of complex cognition (e.g., fluid intelligence, episodic memory). As mentioned previously in the discussion of the processing speed model, WM capacity mediates the age relations with episodic memory (McCabe et al., 2010; Park et al., 1996) and fluid intelligence (Chen & Li, 2007), providing support for this proposal. And there are data strongly supporting the notion that processing speed measures and WM capacity measures do, indeed, measure different constructs. However, another issue to consider in the context of the executive attention framework is to what extent executive attention is similar or distinct from other, similar constructs (e.g., fluid intelligence, executive function), which have often been argued to be essentially indistinguishable (Blair, 2006). The term *jingle fallacy* has been used when the same verbal label is applied to different psychological constructs (Thorndike, 1904), whereas the term *jangle fallacy* has been used when different verbal labels are applied to similar psychological constructs (Kelley, 1927).

It is well established that WM capacity is strongly related to, but distinct from, processing speed, in both young adult and lifespan samples (McCabe et al., 2010; Park et al., 1996). Some have argued that WM capacity and fluid intelligence (or reasoning) may reflect the same ability, which would be an instance of the jangle fallacy. In young adult samples using factor-analytic approaches, the relation between WM capacity and fluid intelligence appears to be ~.70 (Oberauer, Schulze, Wilhelm, & Süss, 2005), which is certainly strong, but still indicates that these are distinct constructs. Similar results have been found in studies employing lifespan samples (Chen & Li, 2007; Salthouse & Pink, 2008).

There is also some ambiguity regarding the distinction between WM capacity and executive function. Many early studies using a univariate approach indicate that relations between executive function and WM capacity tasks are substantially less than 1.0, but this tells us little about whether they represent distinct constructs. All individual tasks are less than perfectly reliable and include task-specific variance that constrains the strength of their correlations with other variables. A recent factor-analytic study directly addressed this issue by comparing a factor based on four WM capacity tasks and a factor based on four executive functioning tasks in a lifespan sample (McCabe et al., 2010). A battery of processing speed tasks was also administered to this sample. As shown in Figure 8.1, results indicated that the correlation between the WM capacity and executive function batteries was .97, indicating that a common underlying ability was responsible for performance on these tasks (i.e., these constructs shared nearly all of their variance at the latent variable level). Moreover, these tasks were strongly correlated with processing speed, but were clearly distinct from processing speed (each sharing less than two-thirds of their variance with processing speed).

Unlike the McCabe et al. study, which specifically examined a heterogeneous battery of executive function tasks, other recent studies have used the approach of administering several measures of each of several distinct executive functions. This approach was made popular by Miyake and colleagues (Friedman et al., 2006; Miyake et al., 2000), and allows a comparison of models in which distinct executive function factors (e.g., shifting, updating, inhibition) load on a single common executive function factor, or are distinct from one another. For example, Hull, Martin, Beier, Lane, and Hamilton (2008) used this approach in a sample of older adults and found that although distinct shifting and updating (i.e., WM) factors emerged, inhibition tasks did not load together. Moreover, only the updating factor was uniquely related to other tasks (e.g., the Wisconsin Card Sorting task). Vaughan and Giovanello (2010) used a similar approach and found that shifting, updating, and inhibition factors could be distinguished from one another, and that a three-factor model fit the data better than a single factor model. However, at least three of the nine executive

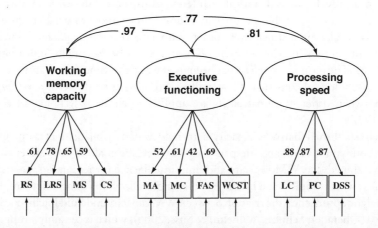

Figure 8.1 The relation between working memory capacity, executive function, and processing speed factors in an adult lifespan sample. *Source*: Adapted from McCabe et al. (2010).

function measures, including two of the updating (i.e., WM) measures, used in this study showed floor effects. This makes it difficult to assess the validity of the conclusions from this study. Thus, although it is still somewhat unclear whether using the terms executive functioning and WM capacity represent an instance of the jangle fallacy, this is clearly an issue that will require more attention in order to provide theoretical clarity for researchers interested in either or both of these constructs.

The time-based resource-sharing model

Another recent theoretical approach to WM that has highlighted the role of attentional control in WM is the *time-based resource-sharing model* (Barrouillet et al., 2004; Camos et al., 2009). According to this model, the processing component of a complex span task consumes attentional resources that might otherwise be devoted to maintenance of to-be-remembered items. Thus, unlike some other models that assume independence between processing and maintenance of information (Baddeley, 1996; Towse, Hitch, & Hutton, 1998), the time-based resource-sharing model proposes a direct relationship between processing and maintenance in WM (Barrouillet et al., 2004; Barrouillet, Bernardin, Portrat, Vergauwe, & Camos, 2007; Camos et al., 2009). A central assumption of the time-based resource-sharing model is that any time not consumed by the processing component of the task is used to rehearse or attentionally refresh to-be-remembered items. One notable advantage of the time-based resource-sharing model is that it provides a straightforward quantitative estimate of recall from WM, which makes the relationship between processing and maintenance explicit. According to the time-based resource-sharing model, recall from span tasks is determined by the cognitive load (CL) associated with the task, which can be considered a model of central executive functioning (Barrouillet et al., 2007; Camos et al., 2009): $CL = aN/T$. In this model N is the number of retrievals that must be completed, T is the amount of time available to complete those retrievals, and a is the difficulty of the processing operations (i.e., the amount of time an operation requires). Barrouillet and colleagues have provided considerable support for this model, demonstrating that this simple model of cognitive load predicts recall from complex span tasks with great precision.

To our knowledge the only study to examine this model in older adults is a study reported by McCabe (2010). McCabe administered a complex span task (Stroop task) to a lifespan sample of adults under one of two conditions. In the experimenter-paced condition, participants were told to complete the processing operations as quickly and accurately as possible, but they had some control over how long they took to complete the processing. This is the typical administration procedure used to administer these tasks, and is referred to as experimenter-paced because the experimenter exerts control through instructing and administering the task individually to the participant. The other condition, the fixed-pace condition, provided the same limited amount of time for all participants to complete the processing component of the task, which was controlled by the computer. Note that according to the time-based resource-sharing model formula, if participants in the experimenter-paced condition can slow down during the processing portion of the task they can reduce cognitive load (CL) by increasing the amount of time available for maintenance of to-be-remembered items (T). This should have the effect of not only improving recall by allowing attentional resources to be devoted to maintenance, but should also add noise to the measurement of WM capacity (due to increased strategy use; see Turley-Ames & Whitfield, 2003).

Results from McCabe (2010) supported the hypotheses of the time-based resource-sharing model. Both younger and older adults slowed their processing in the experimenter-paced task as trials got longer, suggesting a trade-off between processing and maintenance. This slower processing was directly related to increased recall on the experimenter-paced task compared to the fixed-pace task. Moreover, despite the fixed-pace task being more strongly related to measures of processing speed than the experimenter-paced task, the fixed pace task accounted for unique variance in episodic memory (i.e., free recall), executive function, and fluid intelligence factor scores, above and beyond that accounted for by processing speed. By contrast, the experimenter-paced task did not account for any unique variance in these outcome measures once individual differences in processing speed were accounted for. Thus, at least in terms of the predictive utility of the tasks, the fixed-pace task was a better measure of WM capacity. These results are consistent with the predictions of the time-based resource-sharing model. We should note, however, that the complex span task used in this study, Stroop task, included a very simple processing component (noting whether the font color and name of Stroop color words matched or not), and it is unclear whether these results would replicate with a more traditional complex span task (e.g., reading span; Daneman & Carpenter, 1980) that included a more difficult processing component.

The primary–secondary memory framework

Recently, Unsworth and Engle (2007a, 2007b) have explained individual differences in WM capacity as resulting from individual differences in the efficiency of retrieval from primary memory and secondary memory. According to this primary–secondary memory account of WM, primary memory (PM) can be conceived of as the information currently available to conscious awareness, and is essentially identical to the focus-of-attention component of Cowan's WM model (discussed previously). In other words, the capacity of PM is limited, such that it is believed to be capable of maintaining up to approximately four items (Cowan, 2001; Watkins, 1974). Importantly though, according to the primary–secondary memory framework, when the limited capacity of PM is exceeded, items become displaced from PM and must then be retrieved from secondary memory (SM) in order for them to be brought back into conscious awareness. Retrieval from SM is believed to involve an error-prone cue-dependent search for target items, which is affected by response competition (i.e., interference). Thus, the primary–secondary memory framework differs from Cowan's embedded-process model by suggesting that a central factor influencing the relationship between WM capacity and complex cognition is retrieval from SM.

To our knowledge there are few studies examining how aging is related to PM and SM. One approach that has been used to examine how age is related to PM and SM is to decompose immediate free recall performance into PM and SM components (Craik, 1968; Delbecq-Derouesné & Beauvois, 1989). The rationale underlying this procedure is that if an item was output early on an immediate free recall test it was likely in PM, whereas items output later must have been retrieved from SM. Estimates from the Craik and Delbecq-Derouesné and Beauvois studies were calculated using estimates based on the retrieval of recency items (the last few items in a list) from free recall tasks. Both the Craik and Delbecq-Derouesné and Beauvois studies indicated that the PM estimate was age-invariant, whereas there were age differences in SM estimates. However, when tasks such as running memory span, which are assumed to measure PM (i.e., focus of attention; Cowan et al., 2005), age-related deficits in primary memory have been found (e.g., Parkinson, 1980; Trick, Perl, & Sethi, 2005).

Another method of estimating PM and SM is to decompose performance on simple and complex span tasks (Unsworth & Engle, 2006). The rationale for this analysis is that shorter trials on simple span tasks, those up to length four or five, measure the capacity of PM, whereas longer simple span trials require SM retrieval because they exceed the capacity of PM. Complex span trials are believed to all measure SM, because the processing component displaces all of the to-be-remembered words. Unsworth and Engle (2006) provided data supporting this idea, showing that complex span task trials all loaded on a single factor, whereas short list length simple span task trials loaded on one factor, and longer list length trials loaded on a separate factor. Moreover, the longer trial simple span factor and complex span task factor both accounted for unique variance in fluid intelligence, whereas the shorter simple span trials did not. McCabe and Loaiza (2010) recently conducted a conceptual replication of the Unsworth and Engle (2006) study, decomposing simple and complex span task performance with an adult lifespan sample. McCabe and Loaiza (2010) found that age was moderately correlated with both PM, as estimated by short list-length simple span trials, and SM estimates, derived from long list-length simple span trials and complex span trials. PM and SM were also correlated with one another, but only SM predicted unique variance in fluid intelligence. However, when PM was estimated as the longest trial length at which participants could attain perfect recall (see Unsworth & Engle, 2006), PM and SM were nearly perfectly correlated. Thus, it is unclear whether different estimates of PM actually measure the same construct.

At this early stage of investigating the viability of the primary–secondary memory framework it appears that there are several questions that need to be answered in order to move forward. First, do different measures of PM and SM actually measure the same construct? Because age is related to some measures of PM, but not others, it seems plausible that these measures are not measuring the same construct. Given this possibility, what are the best measures of PM, or SM for that matter? As these questions receive answers the utility of the primary–secondary memory framework as an approach to individual differences in WM capacity will become clearer.

Summary

In this chapter we have tried to provide an overview of traditional and more recent theoretical approaches to understanding the relation between adult age and WM performance. Of course, a complete review of all of the important issues related to aging and WM capacity is beyond the scope of the chapter. For example, we did not review research on neuroanatomical correlates of aging and WM capacity, though there are recent reviews the reader can refer to for more information on this topic (Braver & West, 2008; Fernandes, 2010; Reuter-Lorenz & Sylvester, 2005). Another issue that is beginning to receive considerable attention, and likely will attract more in the near future, is training interventions aimed at improving or slowing the decline of WM capacity. Again, we point the reader to recent work on this emerging field (Basak, Boot, Voss, & Kramer, 2008; Lustig, Shah, Seidler, & Reuter-Lorenz, 2009). Certainly advances in understanding brain changes and the effects of interventions on aging and WM will inform our theoretical understanding of the relation between aging and WM, and vice versa. At this point, a considerable amount has been learned about the relation between age and WM. However, as with all scientific endeavors, interesting research findings generate more interesting questions to be addressed in the future. Thus, there is still considerable work to be done in terms of understanding the relation between age and WM.

References

Baddeley, A. (1996). Exploring the central executive. *Quarterly Journal of Experimental Psychology A: Human Experimental Psychology, 49,* 5–28.

Baddeley, A., & Hitch, G. (1974). Working memory. In G. Bower (Ed.), *The psychology of learning and motivation* (pp. 47–89). New York: Academic Press.

Barrouillet, P., Bernardin, S., & Camos, V. (2004). Time constraints and resource sharing in adults' working memory spans. *Journal of Experimental Psychology: General, 133,* 83–100.

Barrouillet, P., Bernardin, S., Portrat, S., Vergauwe, E., & Camos, V. (2007). Time and cognitive load in working memory. *Journal of Experimental Psychology: Learning, Memory, and Cognition, 33,* 570–585.

Basak, C., Boot, W., Voss, M., & Kramer, A. (2008). Can training in a real-time strategy video game attenuate cognitive decline in older adults? *Psychology and Aging, 23,* 765–777.

Blair, C. (2006). Toward a revised theory of general intelligence: Further examination of fluid cognitive abilities as unique aspects of human cognition. *Behavioral and Brain Sciences, 29,* 145–160.

Bopp, K., & Verhaeghen, P. (2005). Aging and verbal memory span: A meta-analysis. *Journals of Gerontology: Series B: Psychological Sciences and Social Sciences, 60,* 223–233.

Borrella, E., Carretti, B., & Mammarella, I. C. (2006). Do working memory and susceptibility to interference predict individual differences in fluid intelligence? *European Journal of Cognitive Psychology, 18,* 51–69.

Braver, T., & West, R. (2008). Working memory, executive control, and aging. In F. I. M. Craik and T. A. Salthouse (Eds.), *The handbook of aging and cognition* (3rd ed., pp. 311–372). New York: Psychology Press.

Braver, T., Barch, D., Keys, B., Carter, C., Cohen, J., Kaye, J. . . . Bruce, R. (2001). Context processing in older adults: Evidence for a theory relating cognitive control to neurobiology in healthy aging. *Journal of Experimental Psychology: General, 130,* 746–763.

Broadbent, D. (1958). *Perception and communication.* Elmsford, NY: Pergamon Press.

Camos, V., Lagner, P., & Barrouillet, P. (2009). Two maintenance mechanisms of verbal information in working memory. *Journal of Memory and Language, 61,* 457–469.

Campbell, K., Al-Aidroos, N., Pratt, J., & Hasher, L. (2009). Repelling the young and attracting the old: Examining age-related differences in saccade trajectory deviations. *Psychology and Aging, 24,* 163–168.

Connelly, S., Hasher, L., & Zacks, R. (1991). Age and reading: The impact of distraction. *Psychology and Aging, 6,* 533–541.

Chen, T., & Li, D. (2007). The roles of working memory updating and processing speed in mediating age-related differences in fluid intelligence. *Aging, Neuropsychology, and Cognition, 14,* 631–646.

Cohen, J., Perlstein, W., Braver, T., & Nystrom, L. (1997). Temporal dynamics of brain activation during a working memory task. *Nature, 386,* 604–608.

Cowan, N. (1993). Activation, attention, and short-term memory. *Memory and Cognition, 21,* 162–167.

Cowan, N. (1999). An embedded-processes model of working memory. In A. Miyake & P. Shah (Eds.), *Models of working memory: Mechanisms of active maintenance and executive control* (pp. 62–101). New York: Cambridge University Press.

Cowan, N. (2001). The magical number 4 in short-term memory: A reconsideration of mental storage capacity. *Behavioral and Brain Sciences, 24,* 87–185.

Cowan, N., Elliott, E., Saults, J., Morey, C., Mattox, S., & Hismjatullina, A. (2005). On the capacity of attention: Its estimation and its role in working memory and cognitive aptitudes. *Cognitive Psychology, 51,* 42–100.

Craik, F. (1968). Two components in free recall. *Journal of Verbal Learning & Verbal Behavior, 7,* 996–1004.

Daneman, M., & Carpenter, P. (1980). Individual differences in working memory and reading. *Journal of Verbal Learning & Verbal Behavior, 19,* 450–466.

Delbecq-Derouesné, J., & Beauvois, M. (1989). Memory processes and aging: A defect of automatic rather than controlled processes? *Archives of Gerontology and Geriatrics, Suppl. 1,*121–150.

Engle, R. W. (2002). Working memory capacity as executive attention. *Current Directions in Psychological Science, 11,* 19–23.

Engle, R. W., & Kane, M. J. (2004). Executive attention, working memory capacity, and a two-factor theory of cognitive control. In B. Ross (Ed.), *The psychology of learning and motivation* (Vol. 44, pp. 145–199). New York: Elsevier.

Fernandes, M. (2010). Functional neuroanatomy of aging and cognition. In H. J. Aizenstein, C. F. Reynolds, & M. Fernandes (Eds.), *Neuroimaging research in geriatric mental health* (pp. 125–148). New York: Springer.

Frank, M., & O'Reilly, R. (2006). A mechanistic account of striatal dopamine function in human cognition: Psychopharmacological studies with cabergoline and haloperidol. *Behavioral Neuroscience, 120*(3), 497–517.

Friedman, N., Miyake, A., Corley, R., Young, S., DeFries, J., & Hewitt, J. (2006). Not all executive functions are related to intelligence. *Psychological Science, 17,* 172–179.

Garavan, H. (1998). Serial attention within working memory. *Memory & Cognition, 26,* 263–276.

Gerard, L., Zacks, R., Hasher, L., & Radvansky, G. (1991). Age deficits in retrieval: The fan effect. *Journals of Gerontology, 46,* P131–P136.

Gilchrist, A., Cowan, N., & Naveh-Benjamin, M. (2009). Investigating the childhood development of working memory using sentences: New evidence for the growth of chunk capacity. *Journal of Experimental Child Psychology, 104,* 252–265.

Glisky, E. L. (2002). Source memory, aging, and the frontal lobes. In M. Naveh-Benjamin, M. Moscovitch, & H. L. Roediger III (Eds.), *Perspectives on human memory and cognitive aging: Essays in honour of Fergus Craik* (pp. 265–276). New York: Psychology Press.Hale, S., Rose, N. S.,

Myerson, J., Strube, M., Sommers, M., Tye-Murray, N., & Spehar, B. (2011). The structure of working memory abilities across the adult life span. *Psychology and Aging, 26*(1), 92–110.

Hambrick, D. (2005). The role of domain knowledge in higher-level cognition. In O. Wilhelm & R. W. Engle (Eds.), *Handbook of understanding and measuring intelligence* (pp. 361–372). Thousand Oaks, CA: Sage.

Hartman, M., & Hasher, L. (1991). Aging and suppression: Memory for previously relevant information. *Psychology and Aging, 6,* 587–594.

Hasher, L., & Zacks, R. (1988). Working memory, comprehension, and aging: A review and a new view. *The psychology of learning and motivation: Advances in research and theory* (Vol. 22, pp. 193–225). San Diego, CA: Academic Press.

Hasher, L., Zacks, R., & May, C. (1999). Inhibitory control, circadian arousal, and age. In D. Gopher & A. Koriat (Eds.), *Attention and performance, XVII: Cognitive regulation of performance: Interaction of theory and application* (pp. 653–675). Cambridge, MA: MIT Press.

Hay, J. F., & Jacoby, L. L. (1999). Separating habit and recollection in young and older adults: Effects of elaborative processing and distinctiveness. *Psychology and Aging,14,* 122–134.

Healey, M. K., Campbell, K. L., & Hasher, L. (2008). Cognitive aging and increased distractibility: Costs and potential benefits. In W. S. Sossin, J. C. Lacaille, V. F. Castellucci, & S. Belleville (Eds.), *Progress in brain research* (Vol. 169, pp. 353–363). Amsterdam: Elsevier.

Hedden, T., & Park, D. (2003). Contributions of source and inhibitory mechanisms to age-related retroactive interference in verbal working memory. *Journal of Experimental Psychology: General, 132,* 93–112.

Higgins, J., & Johnson, M. (2009). The consequence of refreshing for access to nonselected items in young and older adults. *Memory & Cognition, 37,* 164–174.

Hull, R., Martin, R., Beier, M., Lane, D., & Hamilton, A. (2008). Executive function in older adults: A structural equation modeling approach. *Neuropsychology, 22,* 508–522.

Jacoby, L. (1991). A process dissociation framework: Separating automatic from intentional uses of memory. *Journal of Memory and Language, 30,* 513–541.

Jacoby, L. L. (1999). Ironic effects of repetition: Measuring age-related differences in memory. *Journal of Experimental Psychology: Learning, Memory, and Cognition, 25,* 3–22.

Jenkins, L., Myerson, J., Joerding, J., & Hale, S. (2000). Converging evidence that visuospatial cognition is more age-sensitive than verbal cognition. *Psychology and Aging, 15,* 157–175.

Johnson, M. K., Reeder, J. A., Raye, C. L., & Michell, K. J. (2002). Second thoughts versus second looks: An age-related deficit in reflectively refreshing just-activated information. *Psychological Science, 13,* 64–67.

Kane, M., Bleckley, M., Conway, A., & Engle, R. (2001). A controlled-attention view of working-memory capacity. *Journal of Experimental Psychology: General, 130,* 169–183.

Kane, M., & Engle, R. (2003). Working-memory capacity and the control of attention: The contributions of goal neglect, response competition, and task set to Stroop interference. *Journal of Experimental Psychology: General, 132,* 47–70.

Kane, M. J., Hambrick, D. Z., Tuholski, S. W., Wilhelm, O., Payne, T. W., & Engle, R. W. (2004). The generality of working memory capacity: A latent variable approach to verbal and visuospatial memory span and reasoning. *Journal of Experimental Psychology: General, 133,* 189–217.

Kelley, E. L. (1927). *Interpretation of educational measurements.* Yonkers, NY: World.

Kessler, Y., & Meiran, N. (2006). All updateable objects in working memory are updated whenever any of them are modified: Evidence from the memory updating paradigm. *Journal of Experimental Psychology: Learning, Memory, and Cognition, 32,* 570–585.

Lindenberger, U., & Baltes, P. (1994). Sensory functioning and intelligence in old age: A strong connection. *Psychology and Aging, 9,* 339–355.

Lustig, C., May, C. P., & Hasher, L. (2001). Working memory span and the role of proactive interference. *Journal of Experimental Psychology: General, 130,* 199–207.

Lustig, C., Shah, P., Seidler, R., & Reuter-Lorenz, P. (2009). Aging, training, and the brain: A review and future directions. *Neuropsychology Review, 19,* 504–522.

May, C., Hasher, L., & Kane, M. (1999). The role of interference in memory span. *Memory & Cognition, 27,* 759–767.

May, C., Kane, M., & Hasher, L. (1995). Determinants of negative priming. *Psychological Bulletin, 118,* 35–54.

McCabe, D. P. (2008). The role of covert retrieval in working memory span tasks: Evidence from delayed recall tests. *Journal of Memory and Language, 58*(2), 480–494.

McCabe, D. P. (2010). The influence of complex working memory span task administration methods on prediction of higher level cognition and metacognitive control of response times. *Memory and Cognition, 38*(7), 868–882.

McCabe, D. P., & Loaiza, V. (2010, April). *Primary and secondary memory estimates derived from working memory span tasks: Relations with age and fluid intelligence.* Poster presented at the biennial Cognitive Aging Conference. Atlanta, GA.

McCabe, D. P., Roediger, H. L., McDaniel, M. A., Balota, D. A., & Hambrick, D. Z. (2010). The relationship between working memory capacity and executive functioning: Evidence for an executive attention construct. *Neuropsychology, 24*(2), 222–243.

Miller, G. (1956). The magical number seven, plus or minus two: Some limits on our capacity for processing information. *Psychological Review, 63,* 81–97.

Miyake, A., Friedman, N. P., Emerson, M. J., Witzki, A. H., Howerter, A., & Wager, T. (2000). The unity and diversity of executive functions and their contributions to complex "frontal lobe" tasks: A latent variable analysis. *Cognitive Psychology, 41,* 49–100.

Miyake, A., & Shah, P. (Eds.) (1999). *Models of working memory: Mechanisms of active maintenance and executive control.* New York: Cambridge University Press.

Naveh-Benjamin, M., Cowan, N., Kilb, A., & Chen, Z. (2007). Age-related differences in immediate serial recall: Dissociating chunk formation and capacity. *Memory & Cognition, 35,* 724–737.

Nieuwenhuis, S., Ridderinkhof, K., de Jong, R., Kok, A., & van der Molen, M. (2000). Inhibitory inefficiency and failures of intention activation: Age-related decline in the control of saccadic eye movements. *Psychology and Aging, 15,* 635–647.

Oberauer, K. (2002). Access to information in working memory: Exploring the focus of attention. *Journal of Experimental Psychology: Learning, Memory, and Cognition, 28,* 411–421.

Oberauer, K. (2005). The measurement of working memory capacity. In O. Wilhelm & R. W. Engle (Eds.), *Handbook of understanding and measuring intelligence* (pp. 393–407). Thousand Oaks, CA: Sage.

Oberauer, K., Demmrich, A., Mayr, U., & Kliegl, R. (2001). Dissociating retention and access in working memory: An age-comparative study of mental arithmetic. *Memory & Cognition, 29*(1), 18–33.

Oberauer, K., Schulze, R., Wilhelm, O., & Süss, H.-M. (2005). Working memory and intelligence – their correlation and their relation: A comment on Ackerman, Beier, and Boyle (2005). *Psychological Bulletin, 131,* 61–65.

Oberauer, K., Süss, H., Wilhelm, O., & Sander, N. (2007). Individual differences in working memory capacity and reasoning ability. In A. Conway, C. Jarrold, M. Kane, A. Miyake, & J. Towse (Eds.), *Variation in working memory* (pp. 49–75). New York: Oxford University Press.

Oberauer, K., Süss, H., Wilhelm, O., & Wittman, W. (2003). The multiple faces of working memory: Storage, processing, supervision, and coordination. *Intelligence, 31,* 167–193.

Oberauer, K., Wendland, M., & Kliegl, R. (2003). Age differences in working memory: The roles of storage and selective access. *Memory & Cognition, 31,* 563–569.

Park, D., Lautenschlager, G., Hedden, T., Davidson, N., Smith, A., & Smith, P. (2002). Models of visuospatial and verbal memory across the adult life span. *Psychology and Aging, 17,* 299–320.

Park, D., Smith, A., Lautenschlager, G., Earles, J., Frieske, D., Zwahr, M., & Gaines, C. L. (1996). Mediators of long-term memory performance across the life span. *Psychology and Aging, 11,* 621–637.

Parkinson, S. (1980). Aging and amnesia: A running span analysis. *Bulletin of the Psychonomic Society, 15,* 215–217.

Reuter-Lorenz, P., & Sylvester, C. (2005). The cognitive neuroscience of working memory and aging. In R. Cabeza, L. Nyberg, & D. Park (Eds.), *Cognitive neuroscience of aging: Linking cognitive and cerebral aging* (pp. 186–217). New York: Oxford University Press.

Rowe, G., Hasher, L., & Turcotte, J. (2008). Age differences in visuospatial working memory. *Psychology and Aging, 23,* 79–84.

Rowe, G., Hasher, L., & Turcotte, J. (2009). Age and synchrony effects in visuospatial working memory. *Quarterly Journal of Experimental Psychology, 62,* 1873–1880.

Salthouse, T. (1996). The processing-speed theory of adult age differences in cognition. *Psychological Review, 103,* 403–428.

Salthouse, T., & Babcock, R. (1991). Decomposing adult age differences in working memory. *Developmental Psychology, 27,* 763–776.

Salthouse, T., & Pink, J. (2008). Why is working memory related to fluid intelligence?. *Psychonomic Bulletin & Review, 15,* 364–371.

Schmiedek, F., Hildebrandt, A., Lövdén, M., Wilhelm, O., & Lindenberger, U. (2009). Complex span versus updating tasks of working memory: The gap is not that deep. *Journal of Experimental Psychology: Learning, Memory, and Cognition, 35,* 1089–1096.

Thorndike, E. L. (1904). *An introduction to the theory of mental and social measurements.* New York: Teachers College, Columbia University.

Towse, J., Hitch, G., & Hutton, U. (1998). A reevaluation of working memory capacity in children. *Journal of Memory and Language, 39,* 195–217.

Trick, L., Perl, T., & Sethi, N. (2005). Age-related differences in multiple-object tracking. *Journals of Gerontology: Series B: Psychological Sciences and Social Sciences, 60B,* 102–105.

Turley-Ames, K., & Whitfield, M. (2003). Strategy training and working memory task performance. *Journal of Memory and Language, 49,* 446–468.

Unsworth, N., & Engle, R. (2006). Simple and complex memory spans and their relation to fluid abilities: Evidence from list-length effects. *Journal of Memory and Language, 54,* 68–80.

Unsworth, N., & Engle, R. (2007a). The nature of individual differences in working memory capacity: Active maintenance in primary memory and controlled search from secondary memory. *Psychological Review, 114,* 104–132.

Unsworth, N., & Engle, R. (2007b). On the division of short-term and working memory: An examination of simple and complex span and their relation to higher order abilities. *Psychological Bulletin, 133,* 1038–1066.

Unsworth, N., & Engle, R. (2008). Speed and accuracy of accessing information in working memory: An individual differences investigation of focus switching. *Journal of Experimental Psychology: Learning, Memory, and Cognition, 34,* 616–630.

Vaughan, L., Basak, C., Hartman, M., & Verhaeghen, P. (2008). Aging and working memory inside and outside the focus of attention: Dissociations of availability and accessibility. *Aging, Neuropsychology, and Cognition, 15,* 703–724.

Vaughan, L., & Giovanello, K. (2010). Executive function in daily life: Age-related influences of executive processes on instrumental activities of daily living. *Psychology and Aging, 25,* 343–355.

Vergauwe, E., Barrouillet, P., & Camos, V. (2010). Do mental processes share a domain-general resource? *Psychological Science, 21,* 384–390.

Verhaeghen, P., & Hoyer, W. J. (2007). Aging, focus switching, and task switching in a continuous calculation task: Evidence toward a new working memory control process. *Aging, Neuropsychology, and Cognition, 14,* 22–39.

Verhaeghen, P., Kliegl, R., & Mayr, U. (1997). Sequential and coordinative complexity in time–accuracy functions for mental arithmetic. *Psychology and Aging, 12,* 555–564.

Verhaeghen, P., & Salthouse, T. (1997). Meta-analyses of age–cognition relations in adulthood: Estimates of linear and nonlinear age effects and structural models. *Psychological Bulletin, 122,* 231–249.

Watkins, M. (1974). Concept and measurement of primary memory. *Psychological Bulletin, 81,* 695–711.

West, R. L. (1996). An application of prefrontal cortex function theory to cognitive aging. *Psychological Bulletin, 120,* 272–292.

West, R. (1999). Age differences in lapses of intention in the Stroop task. *Journals of Gerontology: Series B: Psychological Sciences & Social Sciences, 54,* P34–P43

9

Memory and Aging

Brent J. Small, Kerri S. Rawson, Sarah Eisel, and Cathy L. McEvoy

A common concern among older adults is decline in cognitive performance, especially memory ability, and the existing literature suggests that some of these concerns are valid (see Craik & Salthouse, 2007; Hofer & Alwin, 2008, for reviews). In this chapter we review evidence regarding the nature of age-related declines in one cognitive domain – memory performance. We begin by articulating a common typology of memory performance and describe whether or not age-related deficits are a prominent feature of each memory component. Next, we focus on the presence of age-related differences and age-related changes in episodic memory, the most commonly studied domain of memory performance. Finally, we describe interventions that have been employed to lessen age-related changes in memory performance to determine whether typical declines can be modified.

Memory Systems and Age-Related Decrements

A commonly cited model of memory has been articulated by Tulving (1983, 1999). In this view, memory is classified into a number of systems that differ in terms of the nature and duration of the information that is stored, as well as the neural basis of behavior. Moreover, and of critical importance for the current chapter, the presence and magnitude of age-related deficits in performance also varies across the different memory systems. In this section, we describe several of the memory systems and whether or not age-related decrements in performance are a prominent feature.

The Wiley-Blackwell Handbook of Adulthood and Aging, First Edition. Edited by Susan Krauss Whitbourne and Martin J. Sliwinski. © 2012 Blackwell Publishing Ltd. Published 2012 by Blackwell Publishing Ltd.

Procedural memory

Procedural memory underlies the acquisition of skills and other aspects of knowledge that are not directly accessible to consciousness and whose presence can only be demonstrated indirectly by action (e.g., walking, skating). It involves the acquisition of motor, perceptual, and/or cognitive operations that occur gradually as a function of practice (Nyberg & Tulving, 1996). At an early point, the acquisition of any skill poses demands on other types of memory, but practice will transfer the performance of the skill to procedural memory (e.g., learning to drive, learning to type). Once a skill has become part of procedural memory it can be carried out relatively automatically, requiring fewer attentional resources (Shiffrin & Schneider, 1977). In contrast to other types of knowledge, procedural knowledge is little influenced by the passage of time, which is reflected by the fact that we can adequately perform skills that we may not have practiced for years.

It is commonly held that procedural memory is largely unaffected by age (e.g., Light & La Voie, 1993; Rieckmann & Bäckman, 2009). Evidence in favor of the robustness of skill acquisition in old age was reported by Schugens, Daum, Spindler, and Birbaumer (1997). In this study, skill learning within the context of a mirror reading task was unaffected by age, whereas explicit recall of verbal and visual materials declined steadily with increasing age. However, there is evidence that aging may affect procedural memory negatively and there are indications that age differences may vary as a function of the complexity of the task, as well as the stage of the memory assessment (acquisition stage, maintenance stage). For example, Ghisletta and colleagues (Ghisletta, Kennedy, Rodrigue, Lindenberger, & Raz, 2010) recently reported a trial-by-trial analysis of skill acquisition in a pursuit rotor task. Older age was negatively associated with the acquisition of this skill in early stages of the task, as well as negatively associated with final performance when late trials were considered. The authors concluded that older adults exhibited comparable performance to younger adults when both groups were novices, but that older adults were slower to acquire the skill originally, and repeated practice on the same task beyond the novice level resulted in greater gains for younger adults. Thus, among studies that examine procedural memory, there may be important differences during different phases of acquisition and test.

Priming

Repetition priming refers to the unconscious facilitation of performance following prior exposure to a target item or a related stimulus (Schacter, 1987). Similar to procedural memory tasks, priming tasks have been referred to as "implicit," because the test instructions do not inform the participants to actively think back to a previous study episode. For example, having been exposed to a word (e.g., *treat*) in a prior episode results in a greater likelihood of completing a word stem (e.g., *tre—*) with that word, as compared to other possible items (e.g., tree), even in the absence of remembering the word from the previous episode. Implicit retrieval is often contrasted with "explicit" retrieval, as measured by standard episodic memory tasks in which subjects are told to recollect information from the study session.

The initial work on the effects of aging in priming tasks revealed nonexistent differences between young and older adults (e.g., Light & Albertson, 1989). Although this pattern of results has been largely confirmed, some studies (Hultsch, Masson, & Small, 1991; Small, Hultsch, & Masson, 1995) and a comprehensive meta-analysis indicated a small overall priming advantage for young over older adults (La Voie & Light, 1994). Fleischman and colleagues reported that in contrast to longitudinal declines in tests of episodic memory, tests of implicit memory failed to exhibit significant declines over a 4-year follow-up period (Fleischman, Wilson, Gabrieli, Bienias, & Bennett, 2004). One issue among tests that assess priming is whether the age differences are more likely to occur for conceptual tests, which emphasize the meaning of the primed items, compared with perceptual tests, which depend upon the physical characteristics of the items (Maki, Zonderman, & Weingartner, 1999; Small et al., 1995). Although Fleischman and Gabrieli (1998) found no support for this distinction in their overview, they argued that the dominant pattern for both perceptual and conceptual priming tests is age equivalence. Finally, the presence of deficits in priming has been attributed by some authors (Fleischman, 2007) to underlying cognitive pathology, such as with Alzheimer's disease.

Semantic memory

Semantic memory deals with our general knowledge of the world, including meanings about words, concepts, and symbols, and their associations, as well as rules for manipulating these concepts and symbols (Tulving, 1983). The information in semantic memory is stored without reference to the temporal and spatial context present at the time of acquisition, and is built up over a lifetime of interacting with one's environment. Semantic memory can be assessed both implicitly and explicitly. Implicitly, associations among concepts may be assessed by measuring whether the processing of one concept (e.g., reading the word *doctor*) is facilitated by having just processed a related concept (e.g., *nurse*). Such implicit measures of semantic memory have consistently indicated either increases with age or age invariance (Laver & Burke, 1993). Explicitly, semantic memory is measured by asking individuals to report their knowledge of word meanings, facts, and so forth. In general, compared with episodic tests of memory, the negative impact of aging on semantic memory is observed later in life, especially when recognition measures are used, rather than recall measures (Bäckman & Nilsson, 1996; Christensen, 2001), Longitudinal tests of semantic memory suggest minimal loss up to the 7th or 8th decade of life, as described later in this chapter.

Episodic memory

Episodic memory deals with the acquisition and retrieval of information that is acquired in a particular place at a particular time. Tulving (1999) has described this memory as a sort of mental time travel, whereby one goes back to retrieve information regarding personally experienced events. There are a number of excellent reviews on the impact of older age on task performance of episodic memory (Bäckman, Small, & Wahlin, 2001; Dixon, Small,

MacDonald, & McArdle, in press; Old & Naveh-Benjamin, 2008a; Zacks, Hasher, & Li, 2000). On the basis of these reviews, as well as empirical evidence, three general themes emerge from the study of age-related deficits on episodic memory. First, the nature and the magnitude of age deficits varies greatly as a function of manipulations when the material is being learned (encoding), as well as when the material is being retrieved (retrieval). Second, one characteristic of to-be-remembered information that appears to be particularly sensitive in old age is the involvement of a binding process in which previously unassociated stimuli must become associated, such as learning the name of a newly made acquaintance (Old & Naveh-Benjamin, 2008b). Finally, disparities in the magnitude of deficits on tests of memory exist depending upon whether the evidence is derived from cross-sectional or longitudinal studies. We treat each of these issues below.

An important issue in research on aging and episodic memory has been whether the size of the age-related impairment varies systematically across different encoding and retrieval conditions. It was argued that differences in memory performance between young and older adults should be magnified when the task offers little cognitive support and attenuated when task conditions are more supportive (e.g., free vs. cued recall of words; word vs. object recognition). Although the observation that older adults exhibit worse performance on tests that are less supported (e.g., free recall), as compared to tests that are more supported (e.g., recognition; Craik & McDowd, 1987), numerous other studies have not supported this pattern of results (for a review see Craik & Jennings, 1992). Bäckman and Small (1998) reported that older adults were able to benefit from the provision of cognitive support at encoding (related vs. unrelated words), as well as at recall (cued vs. free recall), but that persons with Alzheimer's disease (AD) and those who would be diagnosed with AD after a 3-year follow-up period required the provision of support at both encoding and retrieval in order to exhibit a facilitation of performance.

A distinction can be made between memory for units of information and memory for associations among those units, and research suggests that aging has a much greater impact on associative memory as compared to item memory (Naveh-Benjamin, 2000). This general finding has been described as an associative deficit, and the deficit has been observed for a wide range of stimuli, including face–name learning and associating stimuli with their context (Old & Naveh-Benjamin, 2008b). For example, large age differences are found when people are asked to remember pairs of unrelated words (e.g., *lamp–tree*), whereas memory for pairs of related words (e.g., *flower–tree*) shows only small age differences (McEvoy, Nelson, Holley, & Stelnicki, 1992). When faced with remembering the arbitrary pairing the learner must develop a new binding that frequently is in conflict with well-established associations in semantic memory, a cognitive challenge that is not required with the related pairing. Associative deficits have also been implicated in age differences in memory for the source of information, such as whether a fact was read in a reliable source or a tabloid newspaper. In their meta-analysis of 46 studies, Spencer and Raz (1995) noted that memory for source was impaired more by aging than memory for content, suggesting that older adults are less effective in binding the source and content information. Age-related associative deficits have been linked to decreased functioning of the hippocampus and prefrontal cortex (Cabeza, 2006; Mitchell & Johnson, 2009).

Finally, a critical distinction among studies that have investigated adult differences in episodic memory performance is whether the evidence is derived from cross-sectional comparisons, whereby a group of younger adults are compared to a group of older adults, or longitudinal comparisons, whereby the same group of older adults is measured repeatedly. The majority of research that has examined episodic memory in old age has utilized cross-sectional comparisons between younger adults and older adults. These data have suggested that declines in episodic memory performance occur quite early in development. For example, Salthouse (2009) reported that peak word recall performance occurred among individuals 25 to 30 years of age, whereas persons who were 55 to 60 years of age performed almost 1 standard deviation (SD) lower (see Park et al., 1996, for similar results). Evidence from longitudinal studies of aging has suggested that the declines in memory performance that accompany old age occur much later in the lifespan. Indeed, a long-standing question in the field of cognitive aging concerns the extent and timing of cognitive decline with aging, and whether patterns may differ when followed longitudinally over longer bands of the older adult lifespan, as compared to comparing groups of individuals of different ages (Baltes & Nesselroade, 1979; Salthouse, 2009, 2010; Schaie, 2009).

The timing of declines in episodic memory performance on the basis of longitudinal data was recently examined using data from the Victoria Longitudinal Study (Small, Dixon, & McArdle, 2011). In this study, 988 adults initially 55 to 85 years of age (mean age = 68.8 years) were tested every 3 years for up to 12 years. At each testing occasion, participants were assessed using a comprehensive battery of cognitive, health, lifestyle, and psychosocial measures (see Hultsch, Hertzog, Dixon, & Small, 1998 for a detailed description). The measures of episodic memory included a word recall task, which was assessed by the free recall of 30 categorized words, and a story recall task, which was evaluated by the gist recall of two narrative stories. In addition, a measure of semantic memory was assessed, which comprised a fact recall task that was based upon the correct answers to 40 diverse questions that tested individuals' recall of world knowledge.

The results of piecewise random effects analysis (shown in Figure 9.1), that evaluated longitudinal changes prior to and including age 75, in contrast to changes in performance after age 75, revealed differences across the memory tasks, as well as within the domain of episodic memory. For word and fact recall, statistically significant declines in functioning were seen before age 75, corresponding to approximately .25 SD decline for every additional decade of age. However, the story recall task failed to exhibit statistically significant declines up until age 75. After age 75, performance on all three outcomes exhibited significant declines, but the magnitude varied across tests. For fact and story recall, the change was approximately half a standard deviation per decade. For word recall, the declines were almost one standard deviation per decade after age 75. The results indicate that significant change did not occur until well into the late-life years and stand in stark contrast to results from cross-sectional studies.

Understanding the differences between cross-sectional and longitudinal estimates of cognitive change is a very active area of debate (Salthouse, 2009, 2010; Schaie, 2009). On the one hand, cross-sectional estimates suffer from cohort effects, whereby the groups who differ in age also differ in terms of early- and late-life exposures to environments that may facilitate cognitive performance (Nilsson, Sternäng, Rönnlund, & Nyberg, 2009). On the other hand,

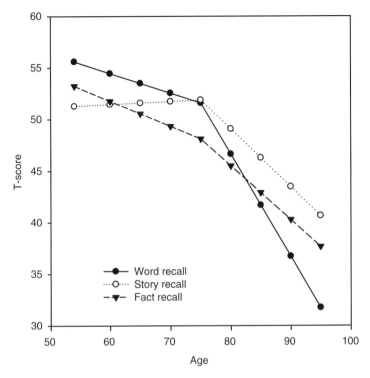

Figure 9.1   Estimated means for tests of word, story, and fact recall. Adapted from Small, B. J., Dixon, R. A., & McArdle, J. J. (2011). Tracking Cognition–Health Changes From 55 to 95 Years of Age. The Journals of Gerontology Series B: Psychological Sciences and Social Sciences.

one of the criticisms of longitudinal estimates of age-related changes in cognitive performance is that positive practice effects help to maintain cognitive performance across the lifespan. That is, in repeated testing session participants may remember specific materials that were presented during earlier testing occasions, or they may experience reduced anxiety or stress associated with the testing environment, with both factors potentially resulting in better cognitive performance and minimizing longitudinal changes in performance.

In the paper described above (Small, Dixon, & McArdle, 2011), the tests of cognitive performance were counterbalanced across occasions so that persons would not see the same materials for 9 years after exposure, which should have reduced the effect of test-specific practice (Dixon et al., in press), although participants may have experienced less test anxiety across the follow-up period. Despite this fact, the story recall task failed to exhibit statistically significant declines until after age 75, and is indicative of variability within the domain of episodic memory in terms of the timing of longitudinal declines in functioning. The research reviewed in this section indicates that it is important to consider characteristics of the memory tasks (e.g., free recall vs. recognition; associative vs. item), as well as the type of the research design (e.g., cross-sectional vs. longitudinal) when considering the nature of memory decline in late life.

Can Age-Related Declines in Memory Be Remediated?

In addition to describing age-related differences and changes in episodic memory performance, considerable attention has been directed at efforts to remediate age-related changes in memory performance (Raz, 2009; Shineman et al., 2010). In this section we distinguish between direct and indirect methods as they relate to the remediation of episodic memory performance. Direct methods are those that specifically target episodic memory performance and attempt to ameliorate functioning by teaching strategies, such as mnemonic techniques, to improve performance. In contrast, indirect techniques do not target episodic memory per se, but describe or intervene through methods that are more broadly based. Specifically, factors such as health, diet, as well as lifestyle characteristics such as participation in physical exercise and cognitively engaging behaviors, have been linked to performance on tests of episodic memory.

Direct methods of remediation

Over the past 25 years, many studies have demonstrated that among relatively healthy older adults without dementia, cognitive abilities can be enhanced through training (Elias & Wagster, 2007; Langbaum, Rebok, Bandeen-Roche, & Carlson, 2009; Rasmusson, Rebok, Bylsma, & Brandt, 1999). A variety of cognitive interventions have facilitated the cognitive performance of older adults, including word and number mnemonic strategies (Rebok, Carlson, & Langbaum, 2007), method of loci techniques (Baltes & Kliegl, 1992; Verhaegen & Marcoen, 1996), and practice-based skill acquisition (Nair, Czaja, & Sharit, 2007).

Recently, Smith and colleagues (Smith et al., 2009) reported on a large randomized trial designed to improve cognitive functioning through the use of a computer-based training program that is designed to "improve the function of the auditory system through intensive brain plasticity-based learning" (p. 595). In this trial, participants were randomized to the computer-based brain training program or an educational training active control condition. The results indicated that persons in the computer-based intervention condition exhibited significant gains over the 8-week period on multiple measures of memory, the trained ability, as well as nontrained abilities such as attention and processing speed. The control group did not exhibit comparable gains in performance. Thus the results indicated that memory performance can be improved through the use of a targeted intervention over a relatively short follow-up period.

Another study examined the neural basis for gains in memory performance through training (Dahlin, Stigsdotter Neely, Larsson, Backman, & Nyberg, 2008). In this study, 24 younger adults were randomized to an intervention or control condition. In the intervention group, participants were trained using updating tasks, which reflects the ability to simultaneously hold information in memory while incorporating new information. After the 5-week study period, the intervention group exhibited significantly greater letter memory performance, relative to the control group. Moreover, the intervention group exhibited a task-specific increase in brain activity in the striatal region which mirrors the gains shown from the outcome measures.

Indirect methods of remediation

Although the use of direct methods of cognitive intervention have shown great promise, a limitation of these studies is that the positive benefits of training are generally associated with the trained domain and do not transfer to untrained abilities (S. L. Willis et al., 2006). This implies that in order to realize improvements to multiple cognitive abilities, multiple training interventions may need to be implemented in order to observe gains in global cognitive health. In part, this has led to considerable attention being focused on the extent to which memory and cognitive performance is influenced by broad-based lifestyle and enrichment activities, including physical activity, cognitive activity, and dietary factors (Lövdén, Bäckman, Lindenberger, Schaefer, & Schmiedek, 2010; Salthouse, 2006; Small, Hughes, Hultsch, & Dixon, 2007; Tan, Xue, Li, Carlson, & Fried, 2006). For example, in their recent comprehensive review, Hertzog and colleagues (Hertzog, Kramer, Wilson, & Lindenberger, 2008) concluded that "engaging in intellectually and mentally stimulating activities (a) slow rates of cognitive aging and (b) enhance levels of cognitive functioning in late life" (p. 41).

There is considerable interest in the impact of physical exercise on the cognitive performance of older adults (Colcombe et al., 2004; Kramer et al., 1999). Voss and colleagues (2010) randomized older adults into an aerobic exercise or nonaerobic exercise intervention group, with brain function and cognitive performance as the primary outcomes. They reported that the group who participated in the aerobic activity, walking, exhibited increased functional plasticity on the basis of fMRI scans, as well as better short-term memory performance at the 12-month follow-up, as compared to the nonaerobic stretching and toning group. However, a recent Cochrane review on the impact of physical activity to improve cognitive functioning among older adults without known cognitive impairment concluded that the evidence is somewhat mixed concerning the potential beneficial effects of physical activity interventions on cognitive performance (Angevaren, Aufdemkampe, Verhaar, Aleman, & Vanhees, 2008). Specifically, they reported that 8 of 11 randomized controlled interventions showed increased cardiovascular fitness in the intervention group, but that the positive impact of exercise interventions on cognitive performance may be limited to select domains and is greatly impacted by variation in the nature of the study inclusion criteria and the specific exercise intervention, as well as the cognitive outcomes. They did report that exercise interventions were related to gains in motor speed, cognitive speed, visual attention, and auditory attention, but the positive effects on tests of episodic memory were not statistically significant.

Another indirect means of ameliorating cognitive decline among older adults has been to focus on cognitively engaging lifestyle activities (e.g., playing bridge, crossword puzzles) and relate the frequency of such activities to cross-sectional differences and longitudinal changes in functioning (e.g., Hultsch, Hertzog, Small, & Dixon, 1999; Wilson et al., 2005). Wilson and colleagues (2005) reported that cognitive activity was positively associated with performance on tests of semantic memory, as well as on tests of processing speed. Similarly, Richards and colleagues (Richards, Hardy, & Wadsworth, 2003) reported that "spare-time activity" was related to memory performance at age 43, but not to decline in memory functioning between ages 43 and 53.

Although evidence is generally in favor of a positive relationship between participation in cognitively engaging activities and memory performance, Hertzog and colleagues (2008) have also identified several limitations in the literature. These include (a) lack of breadth in the measurement of lifestyle activities as predictors, (b) restriction of domains of cognitive performance used as outcomes, and (c) limitations on the ability to infer the direction of these relationships with cross-sectional designs or correlational data. The latter point is critical, because it concerns the direction of the effects – whether persons who are experiencing cognitive declines give up enriching activities or whether giving up enriching activities leads to subsequent declines in cognitive performance.

Using Latent Change Score statistical models (LCS; Ferrer & McArdle, 2010; McArdle, 2009) researchers have been better able to investigate four competing hypotheses concerning the relationship between cognitive activities and cognitive performance: (a) there is no relationship between changes in activity lifestyle and changes in cognitive performance; (b) active lifestyles are a "leading indicator" in that they precede changes in cognitive functioning; (c) cognitive performance is the "leading indicator" of changes in activity participation; or (d) a form of "dynamic coupling" exists among both variables, whereby changes in both variables influence changes in the other, in relation to lifestyle activities and changes in cognitive performance. Lövdén and colleagues (Lövdén, Ghisletta, & Lindenberger, 2005) reported that changes in social participation were related to subsequent changes in perceptual speed, but that preceding changes in perceptual speed were not related to changes in social participation. Similarly, Ghisletta, Bickel, and Lövdén (2006) reported that changes in lifestyle activity, measured by frequency of media activities (e.g., reading a book) and leisure activity (e.g., playing a game) were related to subsequent changes in perceptual speed, but not to a measure of verbal fluency.

In a recent study using the LCS models (Small, Dixon, McArdle, & Grimm, 2011), changes in episodic memory performance were examined in relation to changes in the frequency of cognitive (e.g., playing bridge, using a computer), social (e.g., visiting with friends, attending a concert), and physical (e.g., gardening, jogging) lifestyle activities across a 12-year follow-up period. The results indicated a complex pattern of results. First, declines in cognitive lifestyle activities were related to subsequent declines in episodic memory performance, supporting the tenet that persons who are less engaged cognitively may be susceptible to declines in cognitive performance. The dynamic relationships between the paired variables are illustrated in Figure 9.2. Specifically, vector field plots (Boker & McArdle, 1995) were constructed to portray the dynamic relationship between the measures of cognitive lifestyle activities and measures of episodic memory performance. For cognitive activity/episodic memory pairs of scores, the arrow indicates the expected changes in both activity and cognition at the next measurement occasion. The direction of the arrows indicates whether future changes will be negative, positive, or neutral and the relative size of the arrow relates to the relative size of predicted changes. However, the results of this study also indicated that participation in social activities did not buffer subsequent changes in cognitive performance, but that declines in episodic memory functioning were related to subsequent declines in the frequency of social activities. Finally, for physical activities the dynamic coupling model provided the best fit to the data whereby declines in activity frequency were related to subsequent changes in episodic memory and declines in cognitive performance were related to subsequent changes in activity participation.

Finally, attention has been paid to the impact of dietary factors (Luchsinger & Mayeux, 2004; Shukitt-Hale, Lau, & Joseph, 2008) on the cognitive functioning of older adults. There is evidence for benefit of dietary supplementation in reducing age-related cognitive

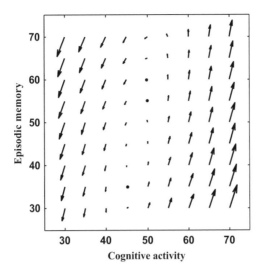

Figure 9.2   Vector field plots for cognitively engaging lifestyle activities and episodic memory. Adapted from Small, Dixon, McArdle, and Grimm (2011).

decline (Letenneur, Proust-Lima, Le Gouge, Dartigues, & Barberger-Gateau, 2007; Morris, Evans, Tangney, Bienias, & Wilson, 2006) and cognitive impairment syndromes such as AD (Luchsinger & Mayeux, 2004). Among humans, this research is in its infancy, but there are good reasons to believe from the animal literature (Joseph et al., 1999; L. M. Willis, Shukitt-Hale, Cheng, & Joseph, 2008) that certain dietary compounds, especially those that are rich in antioxidant polyphenols, are likely to convey benefits to memory and cognitive performance. A recent study reported that a high intake of fruit and vegetable juices reduces the risk of AD and substantial cognitive decline in a population-based prospective study of Japanese-Americans (Dai, Borenstein, Wu, Jackson, & Larson, 2006). Using episodic memory performance as an outcome, one recent report (Krikorian, Nash, Shidler, Shukitt-Hale, & Joseph, 2008) described a pilot randomized control trial whereby persons were assigned to consume 100% Concord grape juice or a placebo beverage for 12 weeks and their memory functioning was examined. The results from this small trial (12 adults per arm) indicated significant improvement in list learning, a measure of episodic memory, for the intervention group. Moreover, the reported effect size was medium to large, with partial eta-squared values between 29% and 40% of variance accounted for in memory performance.

Summary

The impact of aging on human memory is far from straightforward. Both aging and memory are complex, multidimensional processes. Normal aging is associated with declines in memory, but the extent of those declines varies widely across the domains of memory performance. Greater decline is observed on explicit episodic tests of memory, especially when new associations must be formed. Less decline is observed when implicit forms of memory are tested, such as procedural memory, priming, and semantic memory. However, within these broad generalizations the extent of observed age differences is influenced by the specific measures used to test memory. In addition, differing conclusions about the trajectory of age-related memory decline can be drawn depending on whether cross-sectional or longitudinal studies are used. Memory differences observed cross-sectionally tend to be larger than those observed longitudinally.

Despite the complexity of the role of aging in memory performance, there is great interest in developing interventions to improve memory. We discussed interventions that target memory performance directly, by teaching mnemonic skills or using computer-based memory practice. These interventions have proven successful, at least over the short term, although there is little evidence of generalizing beyond the trained tasks. More global interventions, targeting factors that correlate with cognitive change in aging, such as exercise and diet, are also being tested. Although the studies have been relatively small and the results have been restricted to only a few outcome measures, they nevertheless suggest that improved cardiovascular conditioning or a diet rich in antioxidants may contribute to improved memory performance. Another lifestyle factor, engagement in cognitively stimulating activities, shows promise from the correlational research but has not yet been widely studied as an experimental intervention. Further research is needed on all forms of interventions, including combinations of targeted and global interventions. Given the complexity of human memory, it is reasonable to expect that effective intervention strategies will also be complex.

Acknowledgments

Preparation of this chapter was supported by a National Institute of Aging (NIA) grant to the National Alzheimer's Coordinating Center (U01 AG016976; P.I., B. J. Small) and a University of South Florida Neuroscience Collaborative Grant to Brent Small.

References

Angevaren, M., Aufdemkampe, G., Verhaar, H. J. J., Aleman, A., & Vanhees, L. (2008). Physical activity and enhanced fitness to improve cognitive function in older people without known cognitive impairment. *Cochrane Database of Systematic Reviews, 3*. doi:10.1002/14651858. CD005381.pub3

Bäckman, L., & Nilsson, L.-G. (1996). Semantic memory functioning across the adult life span. *European Psychologist, 1,* 27–33.

Bäckman, L., & Small, B. J. (1998). Influences of cognitive support on episodic remembering: Tracing the process of loss from normal aging to Alzheimer's disease. *Psychology and Aging, 13*(2), 267–276.

Bäckman, L., Small, B. J., & Wahlin, Å. (2001). Aging and memory: Cognitive and biological perspectives. In J. E. Birren & K. W. Schaie (Eds.), *Handbook of the psychology of aging* (5th ed., pp. 349–377). San Diego, CA: Academic Press.

Baltes, P. B., & Kliegl, R. (1992). Further testing the limits of cognitive plasticity: Negative age differences in mnemonic skill are robust. *Developmental Psychology, 28,* 121–125.

Baltes, P. B., & Nesselroade, J. R. (1979). History and rationale of longitudinal research. In J. R. Nesselroade & P. B. Baltes (Eds.), *Longitudinal research in the study of behavior and development* (pp. 1–39). New York: Academic Press.

Boker, S. M., & McArdle, J. J. (1995). Statistical vector field analysis applied to mixed cross-sectional and longitudinal data. *Experimental Aging Research, 21,* 77–93.

Cabeza, R. (2006). Prefrontal and medial temporal lobe contributions to relational memory in young and older adults. In D. Zimmer, A. Mecklinger, & U. Lindenberger (Eds.), *Binding in human memory: A neurocognitive approach* (pp. 595–626). New York: Oxford University Press.

Christensen, H. (2001). What cognitive changes can be expected with normal ageing? *Australian and New Zealand Journal of Psychiatry, 35,* 768–775.

Colcombe, S. J., Kramer, A. F., Erickson, K. I., Scalf, P., McAuley, E., Cohen, N. J. . . . Elavsky, S. (2004). Cardiovascular fitness, cortical plasticity, and aging. *Proceedings of the National Academy of Sciences of the United States of America, 101*(9), 16–21.

Craik, F. I. M., & Jennings, J. M. (1992). Human memory. In F. I. M. Craik & T. A. Salthouse (Eds.), *Handbook of aging and cognition* (Vol. 1, pp. 51–110). Mahwah, NJ: Erlbaum.

Craik, F. I. M., & McDowd, J. M. (1987). Age differences in recall and recognition. *Journal of Experimental Psychology: Learning, Memory, and Cognition, 13,* 474–479.

Craik, F. I. M., & Salthouse, T. A. (Eds.). (2007). *The handbook of aging and cognition.* New York: Psychology Press.

Dahlin, E., Stigsdotter Neely, A., Larsson, A., Backman, L., & Nyberg, L. (2008). Transfer of learning after updating training mediated by the striatum. *Science, 320,* 1510–1512.

Dai, Q., Borenstein, A. R., Wu, Y., Jackson, J. C., & Larson, E. B. (2006). Fruit and vegetable juices and Alzheimer's disease: The KAME project. *American Journal of Medicine, 119,* 751–759.

Dixon, R. A., Small, B. J., MacDonald, S. W. S., & McArdle, J. J. (in press). Yes, memory declines with aging – but when, how, and why? In M. Naveh-Benjamin & N. Ohta (Eds.), *Memory and aging.* New York: Psychology Press.

Elias, J. W., & Wagster, M. V. (2007). Developing context and background underlying cognitive intervention/training studies in older populations. *Journal of Gerontology: Psychological Sciences, 62,* 5–10.

Ferrer, E., & McArdle, J. J. (2010). Longitudinal modeling of developmental changes in psychological research. *Current Directions in Psychological Science, 19*(3), 149–154. doi: 10.1177/0963721410370300

Fleischman, D. A. (2007). Repetition priming in aging and Alzheimer's disease: An integrative review and future directions. *Cortex, 43*(7), 889–897.

Fleischman, D. A., & Gabrieli, J. (1998). Repetition priming in normal aging and Alzheimer's disease: A review of findings and theories. *Psychology and Aging, 13*(1), 88–119.

Fleischman, D. A., Wilson, R. S., Gabrieli, J. D. E., Bienias, J. L., & Bennett, D. A. (2004). A longitudinal study of implicit and explicit memory in old persons. *Psychology and Aging, 19*(4), 617–625.

Ghisletta, P., Bickel, J.-F., & Lövdén, M. (2006). Does activity engagement protect against cognitive decline in old age? Methodological and analytical considerations. *Journal of Gerontology: Psychological Sciences, 61B,* P253–P261.

Ghisletta, P., Kennedy, K. M., Rodrigue, K. M., Lindenberger, U., & Raz, N. (2010). Adult age differences and the role of cognitive resources in perceptual-motor skill acquisition: Application of a multilevel negative exponential model. *Journals of Gerontology: Series B: Psychological Sciences and Social Sciences, 65B*(2), 163–173. doi: 10.1093/geronb/gbp126

Hertzog, C., Kramer, A. F., Wilson, R. S., & Lindenberger, U. (2008). Enrichment effects on adult cognitive development: Can the functional capacity of older adults be preserved and enhanced? *Psychological Science in the Public Interest, 9*(1), 1–65.

Hofer, S. M., & Alwin, D. F. (Eds.). (2008). *Handbook of cognitive aging: Interdisciplinary perspectives.* Los Angeles, CA: Sage.

Hultsch, D. F., Hertzog, C., Dixon, R. A., & Small, B. J. (1998). *Memory change in the aged.* New York: Cambridge University Press.

Hultsch, D. F., Hertzog, C., Small, B. J., & Dixon, R. A. (1999). Use it or lose it: Engaged lifestyle as a buffer of cognitive decline in aging? *Psychology and Aging, 14*(2), 245–263.

Hultsch, D. F., Masson, M. E., & Small, B. J. (1991). Adult age differences in direct and indirect tests of memory. *Journals of Gerontology: Series B: Psychological Sciences and Social Sciences, 46*(1), P22–P30.

Joseph, J. A., Shukitt-Hale, B., Denisova, N. A., Bielinski, D., Martin, A., McEwen, J. J., & Bickford, P. C. (1999). Reversals of age-related declines in neuronal signal transduction, cognitive, and motor behavioral deficits with blueberry, spinach, or strawberry dietary supplementation. *Journal of Neuroscience, 19*(18), 8114–8121.

Kramer, A. F., Hahn, S., Cohen, N. J., Banich, M. T., McAuley, E., Harrison, C. R., . . . Colcombe, A. (1999). Ageing, fitness and neurocognitive function. *Nature, 400*(6743), 418–419. doi: 10.1038/22682

Krikorian, R., Nash, T. A., Shidler, M. D., Shukitt-Hale, B., & Joseph, J. A. (2008, May-June). *Concord grape juice supplementation improves memory function in older adults.* Paper presented at the American Aging Association, Boulder, CO.

Langbaum, J. B. S., Rebok, G. W., Bandeen-Roche, K., & Carlson, M. C. (2009). Predicting memory training response patterns: Results from ACTIVE. *Journals of Gerontology: Series B: Psychological Sciences and Social Sciences, 64B*(1), 14–23. doi: 10.1093/geronb/gbn026

Laver, G. D., & Burke, D. M. (1993). Why do semantic priming effects increase in old age? A meta-analysis. *Psychology and Aging, 8,* 34–43.

La Voie, D., & Light, L. L. (1994). Adult age differences in repetition priming – a meta-analysis. *Psychology and Aging, 9*(4), 539–553.

Letenneur, L., Proust-Lima, C., Le Gouge, A., Dartigues, J. F., & Barberger-Gateau, P. (2007). Flavonoid intake and cognitive decline over a 10-year period. *American Journal of Epidemiology, 165,* 1364–1371.

Light, L. L., & Albertson, S. A. (1989). Direct and indirect tests of memory for category exemplars in young and older adults. *Psychology and Aging, 4*(4), 487–492.

Light, L. L., & La Voie, D. (1993). Direct and indirect measures of memory in old age. In P. Graf & M. E. J. Masson (Eds.), *Implicit memory: New directions in cognition, development, and neuropsychology* (pp. 207–230). Hillsdale, NJ: Erlbaum.

Lövdén, M., Bäckman, L., Lindenberger, U., Schaefer, S., & Schmiedek, F. (2010). A theoretical framework for the study of adult cognitive plasticity. *Psychological Bulletin, 136*(4), 659–676. doi: 1037/a0020080

Lövdén, M., Ghisletta, P., & Lindenberger, U. (2005). Social participation attenuates decline in perceptual speed in old and very old age. *Psychology and Aging, 20*(3), 423–434. doi: 1037/0882-7974.20.3.423

Luchsinger, J. A., & Mayeux, R. (2004). Dietary factors and Alzheimer's disease. *The Lancet Neurology, 3,* 579–587.

Maki, P. M., Zonderman, A. B., & Weingartner, H. (1999). Age differences in implicit memory: Fragmented object identification and category exemplar generation. *Psychology and Aging, 14*(2), 284–294.

McArdle, J. J. (2009). Latent variable modeling of differences and changes with longitudinal data. *Annual Review of Psychology, 60*(1), 577–605. doi: 10.1146/annurev.psych.60.110707.163612

McEvoy, C. L., Nelson, D. L., Holley, P. E., & Stelnicki, G. S. (1992). Implicit processing in the cued recall of young and old adults. *Psychology and Aging, 7,* 401–408.

Mitchell, K. J., & Johnson, M. K. (2009). Source monitoring 15 years later: What have we learned from fMRI about the neural mechanisms of source memory? *Psychological Bulletin, 135,* 683–677.

Morris, M. C., Evans, D. A., Tangney, C. C., Bienias, J. L., & Wilson, R. S. (2006). Associations of vegetable and fruit consumption with age-related cognitive change. *Neurology, 67*(8), 1370–1376. doi: 10.1212/01.wnl.0000240224.38978.d8

Nair, S. N., Czaja, S. J., & Sharit, J. (2007). A multilevel modeling approach to examining individual differences in skill acquisition for a computer-based task. *Journal of Gerontology: Psychological Sciences, 62,* 85–96.

Naveh-Benjamin, M. (2000). Adult age differences in memory performance: Tests of an associative deficit hypothesis. *Journal of Experimental Psychology: Learning, Memory, and Cognition, 26,* 1170–1187.

Nilsson, L.-G., Sternäng, O., Rönnlund, M., & Nyberg, L. (2009). Challenging the notion of an early-onset of cognitive decline. *Neurobiology of Aging, 30*(4), 521–524. doi: 10.1016/j.neurobiolaging.2008.11.013

Nyberg, L., & Tulving, E. (1996). Classifying human long-term memory: Evidence from converging dissociations. *European Journal of Cognitive Psychology, 8,* 163–183.

Old, S. R., & Naveh-Benjamin, M. (2008a). Age-related changes in memory: Experimental approaches. In D. F. Alwin & S. M. Hofer (Eds.), *Handbook of cognitive aging: Interdisciplinary perspectives* (pp. 151–167). Thousand Oaks, CA: Sage.

Old, S. R., & Naveh-Benjamin, M. (2008b). Differential effects of age on item and associative measures of memory: A meta-analysis. *Psychology and Aging, 23,* 104–118.

Park, D. C., Smith, A. D., Lautenschlager, G., Earles, J. L., Frieske, D., Zwahr, M., & Gaines, C. L. (1996). Mediators of long-term memory performance across the life span. *Psychology and Aging, 11*(4), 621–637.

Rasmusson, D. X., Rebok, G. W., Bylsma, F. W., & Brandt, J. (1999). Effects of three types of memory training in normal elderly. *Aging, Neuropsychology, and Cognition, 6,* 56–66.

Raz, N. (2009). Decline and compensation in aging brain and cognition: Promises and constraints. *Neuropsychology Review, 19*(4), 411–414. doi: 10.1007/s11065-009-9122-1

Rebok, G. W., Carlson, M. C., & Langbaum, J. B. S. (2007). Training and maintaining memory abilities in healthy older adults: Traditional and novel approaches. *Journal of Gerontology: Psychological Sciences, 62,* 53–61.

Richards, M., Hardy, R., & Wadsworth, M. E. J. (2003). Does active leisure protect cognition? Evidence from a national birth cohort. *Social Science & Medicine, 56*(4), 785–792.

Rieckmann, A., & Bäckman, L. (2009). Implicit learning in aging: Extant patterns and new directions. *Neuropsychology Review, 19*(4), 490–503. doi: 10.1007/s11065-009-9117-y

Salthouse, T. A. (2006). Mental exercise and mental aging: Evaluating the validity of the "use it or lose it" hypothesis. *Perspectives on Psychological Science, 1*(1), 68–87.

Salthouse, T. A. (2009). When does age-related cognitive decline begin? *Neurobiology of Aging, 30* (4), 507–514.

Salthouse, T. A. (2010). The paradox of cognitive aging. *Journal of Clinical and Experimental Neuropsychology, 32*(6), 622–629.

Schacter, D. L. (1987). Implicit memory: History and current status. *Journal of Experimental Psychology: Learning, Memory, and Cognition, 13,* 477–494.

Schaie, K. W. (2009). "When does age-related cognitive decline begin?" Salthouse again reifies the "cross-sectional fallacy." *Neurobiology of Aging, 30*(4), 528–529.

Schugens, M. M., Daum, I., Spindler, M., & Birbaumer, N. (1997). Differential effects of aging on explicit and implicit memory. *Aging, Neuropsychology, and Cognition, 4,* 33–44.

Shiffrin, R. M., & Schneider, W. (1977). Controlled and automatic human information processing: II. Perceptual learning, automatic attending, and a general theory. *Psychological Review, 84,* 127–190.

Shineman, D. W., Salthouse, T. A., Launer, L. J., Hof, P. R., Bartzokis, G., Kleiman, R., . . . Fillit, H. M. (2010). Therapeutics for cognitive aging. *Annals of the New York Academy of Sciences, 1191* (S1), 1–10.

Shukitt-Hale, B., Lau, F. C., & Joseph, J. A. (2008). Berry fruit supplementation and the aging brain. *Journal of Agricultural and Food Chemistry, 56*(3), 636–641.

Small, B. J., Dixon, R. A., & McArdle, J. J. (2011). Tracking cognition–health changes from 55 to 95 years of age. *The Journals of Gerontology Series B: Psychological Sciences and Social Sciences, 66B* (suppl 1), i153–i161.

Small, B. J., Dixon, R. A., McArdle, J. J., & Grimm, K. J. (2011). *Do changes in lifestyle engagement moderate cognitive decline in normal aging? Evidence from the Victoria Longitudinal Study.* Manuscript submitted for publication.

Small, B. J., Hughes, T. F., Hultsch, D. F., & Dixon, R. A. (2007). Lifestyle activities and late-life changes in cognitive performance. In Y. Stern (Ed.), *Cognitive reserve* (pp. 173–186). New York: Taylor and Francis Group.

Small, B. J., Hultsch, D. F., & Masson, M. E. J. (1995). Adult age differences in perceptually based, but not conceptually based implicit tests of memory. *Journal of Gerontology: Psychological Sciences, 50,* 162–170.

Smith, G. E., Housen, P., Yaffee, K., Ruff, R., Kennison, R. F., Mahncke, H. W., & Zelinski, E. M. (2009). A cognitive training program based on principles of brain plasticity: Results from the Improvement in Memory with Plasticity-based Adaptive Cognitive Training (IMPACT) study. *Journal of the American Geriatrics Society, 57*(4), 594–603.

Spencer, W. D., & Raz, N. (1995). Differential effects of aging on memory for content and context: A meta-analysis. *Psychology and Aging, 10*(4), 527–539.

Tan, E. J., Xue, Q.-L., Li, T., Carlson, M. C., & Fried, L. P. (2006). Volunteering: A physical activity intervention for older adults – The Experience Corps program in Baltimore. *Journal of Urban Health, 83,* 954–969.

Tulving, E. (1983). *Elements of episodic memory.* Oxford: Oxford University Press.

Tulving, E. (1999). On the uniqueness of episodic memory. In L.-G. Nilsson & H. Markowitsch (Eds.), *Cognitive neuroscience of memory* (pp. 11–42). Göttingen, Germany: Hogrefe & Huber.

Verhaegen, P., & Marcoen, A. (1996). On the mechanisms of plasticity in young and older adults after instruction in the method of loci: Evidence for an amplification model. *Psychology and Aging, 11,* 164–178.

Voss, M. W., Prakash, R. S., Erickson, K. I., Basak, C., Chaddock, L., Kim, J. S., . . . Kramer, A. F. (2010). Plasticity of brain networks in a randomized intervention trial of exercise training in older adults. *Frontiers in Aging Neuroscience, 2,* 32. doi: 10.3389/fnagi.2010.00032

Willis, L. M., Shukitt-Hale, B., Cheng, V., & Joseph, J. A. (2008). Dose-dependent effects of walnuts on motor and cognitive function in aged rats. *British Journal of Nutrition, 9,* 1–5.

Willis, S. L., Tennstedt, S. L., Marsiske, M., Ball, K., Elias, J., Koepke, K. M., . . . Wright, E. (2006). Long-term effects of cognitive training on everyday functional outcomes in older adults. *Journal of the American Medical Association, 296,* 2805–2814.

Wilson, R. S., Barnes, L. L., Krueger, K. R., Hoganson, G., Bienias, J. L., & Bennett, D. A. (2005). Early and late life cognitive activity and cognitive systems in old age. *Journal of the International Neuropsychological Society, 11*(4), 400–407.

Zacks, R. T., Hasher, L., & Li, K. Z. H. (2000). Human memory. In F. I. M. Craik & T. A. Salthouse (Eds.), *The handbook of aging and cognition* (pp. 293–358). Mahwah, NJ: Erlbaum.

10

Everyday Cognition

Jason C. Allaire

Introduction

Over the past 30 years, there has been a growing interest in assessing older adults' cognitive competency using assessments other than traditional psychometric or neuropsychological measures of cognition. Many researchers have argued that it is important to assess the real-world manifestation of cognitive functioning or "cognition in context" by testing older adults' ability to solve cognitively complex everyday problems (e.g., Allaire & Marsiske, 2002; Berg & Klaczynski, 1996; Blanchard-Fields, Chen, & Norris, 1997; Denney, 1990, 1989; Sternberg & Wagner, 1986; Willis, 1991) instead of performance on acontextual measures of cognition. This interest has resulted in a field of study broadly referred to as everyday problem solving.

Within the literature on everyday problem solving there are two branches or sub-domains: socioemotional problem solving and everyday cognition. Socioemotional problem solving includes social/affective everyday problems (Berg & Klaczynski, 1996; Blanchard-Fields, 2009). Everyday cognition involves the application of basic cognitive abilities (e.g., memory, processing speed, inductive reasoning) and domain-specific knowledge to solving problems that are integrated within instrumental domains of functioning (Allaire & Marsiske, 1999; Willis, 1996). Specifically, these problems are drawn from the instrumental activities of daily living (IADL), domains in which older adults frequently engage in their daily lives (M. M. Baltes, Wahl, & Schmid-Furtoss, 1990; Horgas, Wilms, & M. M. Baltes, 1998; Rogers, Meyer, Walker, & Fisk, 1998).

As initially outlined by Allaire & Marsiske (1999) and more clearly articulated by Berg (2008), the two domains of everyday problem solving differ other than content domain in two important ways. First, in everyday cognition the real-world problems tend to be

The Wiley-Blackwell Handbook of Adulthood and Aging, First Edition. Edited by Susan Krauss Whitbourne and Martin J. Sliwinski. © 2012 Blackwell Publishing Ltd. Published 2012 by Blackwell Publishing Ltd.

well-defined ones, where the initial problem and desired goal is clear, whereas in the socioemotional domain the problems are typically less defined, particularly with respect to the end state or goal associated with the problem. That is, there is no real "answer" to the problem. For instance, a problem such as "Your teenage granddaughter just confided in you that she is pregnant. What do you do?" does not lend itself to a "correct answer." Second, everyday cognition performance is assessed by some metric of solution efficacy such as correct versus incorrect or the number of safe and effective solutions generated. Given that the end goal of the problem is relatively undefined, such as with the pregnancy example, socioemotional problem solving focuses less on performance and more on assessing the problem-solving or coping styles older adults use when faced with such problems.

While socioemotional problem solving is an important and growing area of research, this chapter provides an overview of the current everyday cognition research. Specifically, focus is on the predictors of, and outcomes associated with, individual differences in older adults' everyday cognitive functioning. As will be discussed in more detail below, everyday cognition is particularly important because it is concerned with instrumental real-world problems. On an intuitive level, the ability to successfully solve instrumental real-world problems is directly associated with older adults' ability to remain independent. For outstanding reviews of the socioemotional problem solving literature the interested reader should consider a chapter by Berg (2008) and review article by Blanchard-Fields (2009).

In order to better understand the current research, it is important to briefly review the development of everyday cognition as an area of research. Next, the focus of the chapter will turn to discussing the major predictors of, and outcomes associated with, everyday cognitive functioning in older adults. The chapter concludes with a look at the future of research on older adults' everyday cognitive functioning.

Theoretical and Historical Underpinnings of Everyday Cognition

Cognitive functioning has arguably received the most research attention of any other construct in the field of the psychology of aging. As noted elsewhere in this book, decades of research have generally supported the fluid–crystallized distinction of cognitive functioning, as initially outlined by Horn (Horn & Cattell, 1966; Horn & Hofer, 1992) and elaborated upon by P. B. Baltes (1987, 1997). Abilities in the broad fluid domain such as memory, reasoning, and processing speed are vulnerable to age-related declines, while abilities associated with the crystallized domain include domain-general and domain-specific knowledge structures that tend to increase and remain stable well into advanced old age (Lindenberger & Baltes, 1997; Schaie, 1993, 1996).

As this distinction began to gain traction in the literature, some researchers began to question whether or not the psychometric tests used to assess fluid abilities were appropriate assessments of older adults' cognitive functioning. Three observations or arguments supported this line of thinking. First, cognition is considered a fundamental tool serving adaptive functions to promote the survival of individuals (e.g., Berg & Klaczynski, 1996; Blanchard-Fields & Chen, 1996; Dixon & Baltes, 1986; Sternberg, 1997), and despite significant, normative age-related declines in many cognitive abilities most older adults retained their ability to effectively function in their daily lives. Second, most psychometric tests were designed for and validated in samples of children and young adults within an academic setting. Therefore, if psychometric tests were primarily designed for academic settings emphasizing academic skills, they may have little to say about the functioning and competence of individuals who have been removed from school environments for many decades (e.g., Demming & Pressey, 1957; Denney, 1989; Schaie, 1978; Sinnott, 1989; Sternberg, 1997; Willis & Schaie, 1986). Third, in order to reduce cultural bias, psychometric measures of cognition are designed to be context-free, which eliminates the possibility that older adults call upon a lifetime of accumulated knowledge to solve the problem. That is, in the real world, individuals can draw upon domain-relevant experiences and naturalistic motivations to enhance their cognitive performance (e.g., Ceci & Bronfenbrenner, 1991; Neisser, 1978, 1991; Weisz, 1978), and so relatively "acontextual" laboratory-based assessments of cognition may produce an underestimation of true performance competencies (Bronfenbrenner, 1979; Conway, 1991; Wagner, 1986). Taken together, these observations can be summarized as concerns about the external or ecological validity of psychometric measures of cognitive functioning (Schaie, 1978). These concerns led some to propose that real-world measures assessing cognitive competency within everyday domains might be a more accurate way to assess older adults' cognitive competency.

Early research on everyday problem solving focused on identifying and cataloging the specific everyday problems older adults faced (e.g., Marsiske & Margrett, 2006). What quickly became apparent from the results of these studies was that the everyday problems older adults faced could be classified into one of two overarching groups: socioemotional or instrumental in nature. Early studies assessing individual differences in performance included both problem types, such as the seminal work by Denney (Denney, 1989; Denney & Palmer, 1981; Denney & Pearce, 1989) as well as Cornelius and Caspi (1987). However, what quickly began to emerge was a focus on examining performance specifically within only one of the two domains. Generally, researchers with a background in cognitive aging that was focused on examining problem solving within instrumental domains of functioning began to focus on understanding performance to solve problems within a single instrumental functioning (Hartley, 1989; Willis & Schaie, 1986; Willis, Jay, Diehl, & Marsiske, 1992) or socioemotional problems (Blanchard-Fields, Chen, & Norris, 1997; Blanchard-Fields, Jahnke, & Camp, 1995; Strough, Berg, & Sansone, 1996) at the expense of the other.

Assessment of Everyday Cognition

Another activity that dominated much of the early literature, and continues to be a focus of some current work, is the development of measures of everyday cognition. Assessments of everyday cognition tend to have at least three things in common. First, they generally focus on instrumental tasks of daily living which older adults must be able to solve effectively in order to function independently. Second, the problem state is typically clearly defined, such that the participants know exactly what they are supposed to solve, for instance, "You woke up this morning and your refrigerator is not working." Third, the desired goal or end state is also apparent from the problems (e.g., you want your refrigerator to work).

Though they are similar in many ways, there are a few key differences between measures of everyday cognition. First, measures usually differ with respect to how they assess performance on any single item. One approach includes items that clearly have one correct answer (e.g., Allaire & Marsiske, 1999, 2002; Burton, Strauss, Bunce, Hultsch, & Hunter, 2009; Marsiske & Willis, 2006). For instance, participants may be shown different nutrition labels for different cereals and asked to pick the brand that contains the most fiber and lowest sodium. Another approach includes everyday problems that might be solved through a number of different means and the participant is asked to generate as many safe and effective solutions as possible (Artistico, Orom, Cervone, Krauss, & Houston, 2010; Berg, Meegan, & Klaczynski, 1999; Denney & Palmer, 1981; Margrett & Marsiske, 2002; Strough, McFall, Flinn, & Schuller, 2008). These two scoring approaches are often referred to as accuracy versus fluency (e.g., Margrett, Allaire, Neely, Daugherty, & Weatherbee, 2009) and each has its own strengths and weaknesses. The closed-ended measures provide scores that are intuitively easy to understand, focusing on accuracy (e.g., either the answer is right or wrong), and are similar in style to the items of many psychometric measures of cognition. However, in their specificity they may fail to capture the numerous different problem-solving approaches many older adults have developed through their unique life experiences. While open-ended questions allow older adults to tackle a problem from their own unique perspective, they are more difficult to score due to the fact that higher scores are based on the number and efficacy of the solutions generated. Consequently, older adults who generate one correct answer because they know it solves the problem would get a lower score than those who generated multiple mediocre but acceptable answers (e.g., Berg et al., 1999; Blanchard-Fields, Mienaltowski, & Seay, 2007).

Second, measures can differ with respect to problem presentation. One approach is to use a vignette-like structure where the problem is described, such as the refrigerator example above. A second approach is to use real-world stimuli and ask questions based on these stimuli. Within this second approach measures either use real-world printed stimuli such as nutrition or medication labels or use actual real-world objects such as products with nutrition labels or bottles of medicine. The Everyday Problems Test (EPT; Marsiske & Willis, 1995) presents participants with printed stimuli from each of the IADL domains such as a telephone bill or a recipe, and participants are instructed to solve problems using the information found in the stimuli.

Based on the EPT, the Everyday Cognition Battery (ECB; Allaire & Marsiske, 1999, 2002) also uses real-world stimuli but differs from the EPT as it focuses on only the three instrumental domains: medication use, financial management, and food preparation/nutrition. It also differs from the EPT in that it consists of three separate tests, each designed to assess the real-world manifestation of either memory, inductive reasoning, or knowledge. For instance, a traditional memory test might present a list of words and the participant is asked to study the list and recall as many of the words as possible after the list is removed. The analogous ECB test (the ECB Memory test) asks participants to study real-world printed material such as a nutrition label and then answer questions about the information included in the stimulus once it is removed. In this way, the ECB tests were designed to be real-world analogs for the basic ability tests.

The Observed Tasks of Daily Living (OTDL) developed by Diehl and colleagues (Diehl et al, 2005; Diehl, Willis, and Schaie, 1995) presents participants with actual real-world objects or "props" such as medication bottles. Participants are then presented with a daily problem that an older adult might face, and they must use the props to correctly answer the question. The OTDL also awards participants partial credit on the everyday problems and participants are also provided prompts if they seem to be having difficulty with any one particular item.

The vignette approach allows for the broader assessment of everyday problems since many problems, such as nonfunctioning refrigerators, do not lend themselves to real-world stimuli. It also allows the researcher to ascertain exactly how the participants would or would not solve the problem instead of limiting their solutions a priori. However, the second approach provides a deeper level of ecological validity since participants are actually faced with everyday problems and the real-world materials/stimuli from which those problems emerge. In addition, it also provides an interpretable objective assessment of performance that can easily be examined alongside other variables.

Individual Differences in Everyday Cognition

With the development of these everyday cognition assessments, researchers have been primarily interested in identifying the sources of individual differences in performance. Most of this work has centered on the mapping of age differences in everyday cognitive performance as well as understanding the underlying role basic cognitive abilities play in everyday cognitive performance.

Age differences

As previously mentioned, the study of everyday problem solving in general and everyday cognition in particular was, in part, predicated on the idea that psychometric measures of cognition might underestimate older adults' true cognitive competency. Consequently, a number of studies have focused on whether or not there are age differences in everyday cognition performance, guided by the assumption that age differences should be minimized given older adults' familiarity with the real-world domains and tasks within those domains (e.g., Marsiske & Margrett, 2006).

Unfortunately, there has been very little evidence to support this assumption. In a meta-analysis of over 33 age-comparative studies, Thornton and Dumke (2005) reported that older adults performed significantly worse than both middle-age and younger adults (Cohen's $d = .48$) on measures of everyday problem solving. In fact, these age differences were exacerbated when examining performance on measures of everyday cognition where the focus was on everyday problems drawn from instrumental domains of daily living. Interestingly, age differences were attenuated when examining performance on measures that included content primarily drawn from the social-emotional and interpersonal domains. Studies examining age differences within samples of exclusively older adults have also found evidence of significant and negative age differences in performance (Allaire & Marsiske, 1999; Allaire & Whitfield, 2004; Burton, Strauss, Hultsch, & Hunter, 2009; Diehl et al., 1999; Diehl et al., 2005; Marsiske & Willis, 1995; Whitfield, Baker-Thomas, Heyward, Gatto, & Williams, 1999). On average, these studies have found within samples of older adults that up to 50% of the variance in performance is accounted for by chronological age (e.g., Marsiske & Margrett, 2006).

However, it is important to note that not all studies have found negative age-related differences in everyday problem solving. For instance, Cornelius and Caspi (1987) reported that older adults performed better on their Everyday Problem Solving Inventory (EPSI) than younger adults. Similar results were also found for the Practical Problems test (PPT; Denney & Pearce, 1989). In fact, in a single study no relationship between age and the EPSI or PPT was found, while no significant age differences for the EPT were observed (Marsiske & Willis, 1995). More recently, Artistico and colleagues (2010) assessed everyday cognitive performance using vignette-style problems within instrumental domains. The authors reported that older adults performed better than younger age groups on everyday problems set within "older adult contexts." Presumably, older adults benefited from their familiarity with the context and their domain-specific knowledge of the problem. Unfortunately, the authors did not assess domain-specific knowledge. However, Thornton, Paterson, Yeung, and Kubik (in press) failed to find an age-related benefit for age-matched everyday problems, calling into question the earlier work by Artistico and colleagues.

Taken together, these findings suggest that older adults' ability to solve cognitively complex everyday problems is, in general, compromised with age. However, it is possible that in some situations, perhaps where tacit knowledge for the problem or context is strongly age-related, differences may be minimized. However, it is important to keep in mind that while identifying the pattern of age differences in everyday cognition is an important first step, it is very important to move beyond age differences and identify proximal predictors that might explain these age differences.

Basic cognitive abilities

Most theoretical perspectives consider everyday cognition as a kind of "compiled" cognition (Salthouse, 1990), which is superordinate to and comprises a set of underlying basic abilities (Berry & Irvine, 1986; Marsiske & Willis, 1998; Willis & Marsiske, 1991; Willis & Schaie, 1986, 1993). That is, an amalgam of basic abilities is responsible for cognitive performance within everyday contexts. Therefore, weaknesses in basic abilities should predict weaknesses in resulting everyday cognitive performance. For example, older adults with losses in memory functioning would be expected to have losses in everyday cognitive tasks that depend upon memory, if other abilities cannot compensate.

The great majority of the research has found strong associations between basic cognitive abilities (e.g., inductive reasoning, memory, and verbal ability) and various measures of everyday cognitive performance (Allaire & Marsiske, 1999; Bertrand & Willis, 1999; Burton, Strauss, Hultsch, & Hunter, 2009; Diehl et al., 2005; Diehl et al., 1999). Across studies, lower performance on basic ability tests is associated with lower everyday cognitive functioning. For instance, Allaire and Marsiske (1999) reported that as much as 80% of the variance in their Everyday Cognition Battery was accounted for by basic cognitive abilities, particularly memory and inductive reasoning ability. It is not surprising that the ECB is strongly related to basic cognitive functioning, given that it was specifically designed to serve as a real-world analog to basic cognitive ability tests. However, even measures designed to assess both instrumental and socioemotional problem solving such as the EPSI have been found to be strongly related to both fluid and crystallized cognitive abilities (Cornelius & Caspi, 1987).

In the cognitive aging literature there has been a growing interest in understanding short-term fluctuations or intraindividual variability in cognitive performance (Ram, Rabbitt, Stollery, & Nesselroade, 2005). Previous studies have, in general, reported that greater inconsistency is related to poorer level of cognitive performance (e.g., Hultsch et al., 2008), which may be indicative of compromised neurobiological functioning (Li & Lindenberger, 1999; MacDonald, Hultsch, & Dixon, 2003). In a recent study, Burton and colleagues (Burton, Strauss, Hultsch, & Hunter, 2009) examined the relationship between intraindividual variability in reaction time and older adults' performance on the EPT. The authors reported that slower reaction time and greater variability in reaction time was significantly related to poorer everyday cognitive performance. That is, individuals whose reaction times were characterized by greater fluctuations performed worse on the EPT. In addition, the relationship between intraindividual variability in reaction time and EPT performance remained significant even after controlling for overall level of reaction time, age, and education, suggesting that perhaps variability in basic cognitive ability has a unique effect on older adults' everyday cognitive competency.

Additional support for the centrality of cognitive functioning comes from research examining brain functioning and everyday cognitive performance. In a study by Channon and Crawford (1999), participants with frontal lobe lesions performed significantly worse on a measure of everyday cognition than participants with lesions in areas other than the frontal lobe and control participants with no lesions. In particular, they exhibited reduced fluency in generating alternative solutions, poor quality of solutions selected, and worse selection of solutions, even presented in rank order.

Knowledge

Taken together, the extant research clearly suggests that older adults' ability to solve cognitively complex real-world problems is closely tied to their basic cognitive competency. However, this should not be very surprising given that most of the instrumental problems included in these measures are cognitively complex. However, it is somewhat surprising that studies have not examined the extent to which knowledge within a domain may serve to buffer the impact of declining mental abilities on everyday cognitive performance. Because these instrumental tasks used in measures of everyday cognition have been described elsewhere as universal, basic, and mandatory (see M. M. Baltes, Mayr, Borchelt, Maas, & Wilms, 1993), an underlying assumption is that most older adults will have substantial experience in, and acquired knowledge about, these domains. This specialized knowledge, in turn, would decrease the reliance on other basic mental abilities (e.g., inductive reasoning, working memory, speed) for everyday task performance within those domains (P. B. Baltes, 1997; Berg & Sternberg, 1985; Denney, 1990; Rybash & Hoyer, 1994; Salthouse, 1991). Older adults, as noted above, perform worse than middle-age and younger adults despite their greater experience within these instrumental domains. However, to date, studies of everyday cognition have not explicitly tested whether there are age differences in everyday knowledge and whether the actual amount of knowledge for a domain serves to "buffer against," or compensate for, age-related decline of fluid abilities or other sources of individual differences.

Other potential sources of individual differences

Little is known about what other individual-differences factors have significant impact in everyday cognition. There have been very few studies that have moved beyond age and basic cognitive abilities by attempting to identify other sources of individual differences in older adults' everyday cognitive competency (e.g., Marsiske & Margrett, 2006). Given the importance of underlying basic cognitive abilities, it can be argued that constructs related to basic cognitive performance may also explain individual differences in everyday cognition. Specifically, research has found that cognition is uniquely related to health (Gamaldo, Weatherbee, & Allaire, 2008; Garrett et al., 2004), stress (Neupert, Almeida, Mroczek, & Spiro, 2006; Sliwinski, Smyth, Hofer, & Stawski, 2006), and affect (Butters, et al., 2004; Carstensen, Mikels, & Mather, 2006; Chow, Hamagami, & Nesselroade, 2007). In one study, Neupert and colleagues (2008) found that higher levels of daily stress are related to poor real-world memory though the assessment of memory was actually self-reported real-world memory failures rather than everyday cognitive performance. None-theless, this study of older adults' ability to remember within a real-world context is impacted by stressors that arise in their daily lives.

A few studies have found a modest association between health and everyday cognitive performance where poor subjective health is associated with worse everyday cognition (Diehl et al., 2005; Thornton, Deria, Gelb, Shapiro, & Hill et al., 2007; Whitfield, Allaire, & Wiggins, 2004). For instance, Whitfield and colleagues (2004) found that the number of chronic conditions and older adults' perceived change in health relative to 5 years prior were significant predictors of performance on the EPT even after controlling for demographic characteristics. It is likely, however, that the relationship between health and everyday cognition is more complicated than what can typically be captured by cross-sectional and even longitudinal designs. Given the instrumental nature of everyday cognition tasks it is likely that health declines impact basic cognitive functioning, which in turn decreases everyday cognitive performance. Decline in the ability to solve problems associated with medication use and food preparation/nutrition likely exacerbate health conditions and the cycle starts all over again. Examining this dynamic interplay between health, basic abilities, and everyday cognition is an important next step in the study of predictors and outcomes of everyday cognition.

Most of the previous research on everyday cognition has focused on developing measures and examining age differences in performance. Research has also tended to focus on identifying the underlying basic cognitive abilities that are related to performance on measures of everyday cognition. Very few studies have moved beyond basic cognitive abilities by attempting to identify other sources of individual differences in everyday cognition (e.g., Marsiske & Margrett, 2006). This has led to a serious gap in our understanding as to why some older adults might maintain adequate levels of real-world cognitive competency while others do not.

Outcomes Associated with Everyday Cognition

The gap in our understanding of everyday cognition is even bigger when one considers that little is known about what outcomes are associated with preserved or impaired everyday cognitive functioning. Given that everyday cognition is thought to be the "real-world manifestation" of cognitive functioning, it is surprising that few studies have explicitly examined the connection between everyday cognition and actual real-world outcomes. If measures of everyday cognition are not uniquely related to important real-world outcomes then the usefulness of including them in studies of aging is not obvious.

Few studies have attempted to identify outcomes that are significantly and uniquely related to everyday cognitive competency. However, this task is of central importance because if everyday cognition is thought to assess cognition in the real world it should be strongly related to real-world outcomes (e.g., Berg, 2008; Marsiske & Margrett, 2005). Moreover, everyday cognition was, in part, originally designed as an "alternative" to traditional measures of intelligence or cognitive functioning. Therefore, if it does not provide added value beyond basic cognitive abilities then there may be no need to include assessments of everyday cognition in addition to basic cognitive ability tests. This argument is made even more pressing by the fact that performance on basic ability tests and performance on measures of everyday cognition are so similar. If they are so similar, then it might appear that including only the standard measures of cognition would be more advisable. Luckily, there is a growing body of researchers that recognizes the importance of establishing the predictive validity of everyday cognition. They have begun examining the extent to which everyday cognitive competency is related to clinically important outcomes such as instrumental functioning, mortality, and mild cognitive impairment (MCI).

Instrumental functioning

Given that instrumental domains are typically included in measures of everyday cognition, it is not surprising that some studies have examined whether individual differences in everyday cognition predict actual functional competency. In one early study, Allaire and Marsiske (2002) found that performance on the ECB serves as a unique predictor of older adults' instrumental functioning in an ethnically heterogeneous sample of older adults. The ECB not only accounted for all of the individual differences in subjective instrumental functioning associated with basic abilities, but also added unique explanatory power. More recently, Gelb and colleagues (Gelb, Shapiro, & Thornton, 2010) examined the relationship between medication adherence and everyday cognitive functioning in a sample of middle-aged adults who had recently undergone a kidney transplant. The authors reported that poorer performance on their vignette-style everyday cognition measure was significantly related to worse self-reported medication adherence. While both of these studies provide some support for the efficacy of everyday cognition relative to basic abilities, instrumental functioning was assessed using a subjective measure of performance rather than an objective assessment.

Mortality

It is well known in the cognitive aging literature that there exists a link between cognition and mortality (Maier & Smith, 1999; Small & Bäckman, 1997; Swan, Carmelli, & LaRue, 1995). That is, older adults who died subsequent to completing a battery of cognitive measures tended to have performed worse than surviving participants (Bosworth, Schaie, & Willis, 1999; Johansson, Hofer, & Allaire, 2004; Small & Bäckman, 1997). In addition, individual differences in cognitive performance are associated with death, such that poorer performance is uniquely associated with the increased risk of dying (Bassuk, Wypij, & Berkman, 2000; Maier & Smith, 1999; Small & Bäckman, 1997; Smits, Deeg, & Kriegsman). Given that everyday cognition is strongly tied to basic abilities (Allaire & Marsiske, 1999; Willis, 1996), it is logical to expect a similar relationship between mortality and everyday cognition.

Weatherbee and Allaire (2008) followed 171 older adults originally included in an earlier study examining the psychometric properties of the ECB (Allaire & Marsiske, 1999). The authors found that the sample of subsequently deceased participants performed significantly worse on the ECB reasoning, memory, and knowledge test compared to surviving older adults. In addition, performance on everyday knowledge was a significant and unique predictor of death even after controlling for a number of basic cognitive abilities (Weatherbee & Allaire, 2008). The authors concluded that deficiencies in everyday knowledge could actually be associated with real-world behaviors that compromise competency and put older adults at risk for serious adverse outcomes such as death (e.g., Maier & Smith, 1999). Similar results were also reported by Allaire & Willis (2006) where prior performance on the EPT was significantly worse in subsequently deceased participants relative to nondeceased. Moreover, EPT performance was a significant and unique predictor of nearness to death.

Mild cognitive impairment

One outcome of growing interest is mild cognitive impairment (MCI), which is considered the transitional period between normal cognition and dementia (Albert, 2008; Petersen et al., 1999). Though rates of conversion to dementia vary, previous research has clearly shown that older adults with MCI are at a greater risk of developing dementia (Morris et al., 2001; Petersen et al., 2001). Research suggests that older adults with MCI are significantly less competent in performing instrumental tasks of daily living than older adults without MCI and show a greater rate of decline in everyday competency over a 3-year period (Pereira et al., 2010; Perneczky, Pohl, Sorg, Hartmann, Komossa et al., 2006; Perneczky, Pohl, Sorg, Hartmann, Tosic et al., 2006; Wadley et al. 2007). A few studies have also reported that older adults with MCI score lower on informant- and self-reported subjective assessments of everyday cognition (Aretouli & Brandt, 2010; Farias et al., 2008).

Most of these studies assessed instrumental competency using self-report or proxy (e.g., relative, friend, or caregiver) assessments. While subjective evaluations are important, they do not assess actual ability nor do they assess older adults' ability to perform various tasks within a single domain. Therefore, a few researchers have attempted to examine performance differences between MCI and noncognitively impaired older adults using objective measures of everyday cognition. For instance, performance on the Everyday Problems for Cognitively Challenged Elderly (EPCCE; Bertrand & Willis, 1999), a version of the EPT designed for lower functioning older adults, was significantly associated with clinical dementia ratings (CDR) and change in CDR after controlling for general cognitive status (Allaire & Willis, 2006). More recently, Burton and colleagues (Burton, Strauss, Hultsch, &, Hunter, 2009) found that older adults with multiple domain MCI (amnestic and nonamnestic) performed significantly worse than nonimpaired older adults on the EPT; furthermore, the EPT was a unique and significant predictor of MCI status. Allaire and colleagues (Allaire, Gamaldo, Ayotte, Sims, & Whitfield, 2009) reported that older adults with MCI performed significantly worse on the three instrumental sub-domains of the ECB Memory test and that performance on the Financial Management subdomain was a significant and unique predictor of MCI status even after controlling for a number of basic cognitive abilities. Other studies have also reported that differences between MCI and non-MCI older adults are particularly salient when the everyday task is memory laden (Farias et al., 2006) and/or focused on financial abilities (Giovannetti et al., 2008; Griffith et al., 2003; Okonkwo, Wadley, Griffith, Ball, & Marson, 2006).

Future Directions

The study of everyday cognition has generated a considerable amount of research, but the work can still be considered in its infancy. Far too much time has been spent on creating measures of everyday cognition and arguing about the appropriate content domain for everyday problem solving and cognition. Though a good start has been made, considerably more scholarship is needed to establish the validity of everyday cognition as a construct that is related to, but uniquely different from, basic cognitive abilities. One potential avenue of research is to examine older adults' cognitive performance on a day-to-day basis rather than using static assessments of performance. As already mentioned, there is considerable research examining short-term variability in cognitive functioning and it is reasonable to assume that, given its association with basic abilities, everyday cognition might also be characterized by significant within-person variability. Moreover, on an intuitive level it makes sense that an older adult's ability to solve medication problems might vary day-to-day depending on his or her environment and personal attributes.

Another area of future research is to develop interventions explicitly designed to improve older adults' cognitive functioning. With a few exceptions (e.g., Edwards et al., 2005) there has been little research supporting the notion that the effects of cognitive interventions actually transfer to real-world measures of cognition (Ball et al., 2002). Consequently, it may be that nontraditional approaches to improving older adults' cognitive abilities and ultimately their everyday cognition (e.g., Berch & Wagster, 2004) or perhaps interventions directly targeted at performance within everyday domains is needed. Finally, research should consider beginning to reduce the barriers between socioemotional and instrumental problem solving. Having two separate lines of research that ultimately have the same goal, determining how older adults function in the real world, hampers the progress of scientific discovery.

References

Albert, M. S. (2008). The neuropsychology of the development of Alzheimer's disease. In F. I. M. Craik & S. Salthouse (Eds.), *The handbook of aging and cognition* (3rd ed., pp. 97–132). New York: Psychology Press.

Allaire, J. C., Gamaldo, A., Ayotte, B. J., Sims, R., & Whitfield, K. (2009). Mild cognitive impairment and objective instrumental everyday functioning: The Everyday Cognition Battery Memory test. *Journal of the American Geriatric Society, 57,* 120–125.

Allaire, J. C., & Marsiske, M. (1999). Everyday cognition: Age and intellectual ability correlates. *Psychology and Aging, 14,* 627–644.

Allaire, J. C., & Marsiske, M. (2002). Well- and ill-defined measures of everyday cognition: Relationship to elders' intellectual ability and functional status. *Psychology and Aging, 17,* 101–115.

Allaire, J. C., & Whitfield, K. E. (2004). Relationships among education, age, and cognitive functioning in older African Americans: The impact of desegregation. *Aging, Neuropsychology, and Cognition, 11,* 443–449.

Allaire, J. C., & Willis, S. L. (2006). Competence in everyday activities as a predictor of cognitive risk and mortality. *Aging, Neuropsychology, and Cognition, 2,* 227–224.

Aretouli, E., & Brandt, J. (2010). Everyday functioning in mild cognitive impairment and its relationship with executive cognition. *International Journal of Geriatric Psychiatry, 25*(3), 224–233.

Artistico, D., Orom, H., Cervone, D., Krauss, S., & Houston, E. (2010). Everyday challenges in context: The influence of contextual factors on everyday problem solving among young, middle-aged, and older adults. *Experimental Aging Research, 36,* 230–247.

Ball, K., Berch, D. B., Helmers, K. F., Jobe, J. B., Leveck, M. D., Marsiske, M., . . . Willis, S. L. (2002). Effects of cognitive training interventions with older adults: A randomized controlled trial. *Journal of the American Medical Association, 288*(18), 2271–2281.

Baltes, P. B. (1987). Theoretical propositions of life-span developmental psychology: On the dynamics between growth and decline. *Developmental Psychology, 23,* 611–626.

Baltes, P. B. (1997). On the incomplete architecture of human ontogeny: Selection, optimization, and compensation as foundation of developmental theory. *American Psychologist, 52,* 366–380.

Baltes, M. M., Mayr, U., Borchelt, M., Maas, I., & Wilms, H.-U. (1993). Everyday competence in old and very old age: An inter-disciplinary perspective. *Ageing and Society, 13,* 657–680.

Baltes, M. M., Wahl, H. W., & Schmid-Furtoss, U. (1990). The daily life of elderly Germans: Activity patterns, personal control, and functional health. *Journal of Gerontology, 45,* 173–179.

Bassuk, S. S., Wypij, D., & Berkman, L. F. (2000). Cognitive impairment and mortality in the community-dwelling elderly. *American Journal of Epidemiology, 151,* 676–688.

Berch, D. B., & Wagster, M. V. (2004). Future directions in cognitive aging: Perspectives from the National Institute on Aging. In R. Dixon, L. Backman, & L. Nilsson (Eds.), *New frontiers in cognitive aging* (pp. 333–335). Oxford: Oxford University Press.

Berg, C. A. (2008). Everyday problem solving in context. In S. Hofer & D. Alwin (Eds.), *Handbook of cognitive aging: Interdisciplinary perspectives* (pp. 207–223). Thousand Oaks, CA: Sage.

Berg, C. A., & Klaczynski, P. (1996) Practical intelligence and problem solving. In F. Blanchard-Fields & T. M. Hess (Eds.), *Perspectives on cognitive change in adulthood and aging* (pp. 323–357). New York: McGraw-Hill.

Berg, C. A., Meegan, S. P., & Klaczynski, P. (1999). Age and experiential differences in strategy generation and information requests for solving everyday problems. *International Journal of Behavioral Development, 23,* 615–639.

Berg, C. A., & Sternberg, R.J. (1985). A triarchic theory of intellectual development during adulthood. *Developmental Review, 5,* 334–370.

Berry, J., & Irvine, S. (1986). Bricolage: Savages do it daily. In R. J. Sternberg & R. Wagner (Eds.), *Practical intelligence* (pp. 236–270). New York: Cambridge University Press.

Bertrand, R. M., & Willis, S. L. (1999). Everyday problem solving in Alzheimer's patients: A comparison of subjective and objective assessments. *Aging and Mental Health, 3,* 281–293.

Blanchard-Fields, F. (2009). Flexible and adaptive socio-emotional problem solving in adult development and aging. *Restorative Neurology and Neuroscience, 27,* 1–12.

Blanchard-Fields, F., Jahnke, H. C., & Camp, C. (1995). Age differences in problem-solving style: The role of emotional salience. *Psychology and Aging, 10,* 173–180.

Blanchard-Fields, F., & Chen Y. (1996). Adaptive cognition and aging. *American Behavioral Scientist, 39,* 231–248.

Blanchard-Fields, F., Chen, Y., & Norris, L. (1997). Everyday problem solving across the adult life span: Influence of domain specificity and cognitive appraisal. *Psychology and Aging, 12,* 684–693.

Blanchard-Fields, F., Mienaltowski, A., & Seay, R. B. (2007). Age differences in everyday problem solving effectiveness: Older adults select more effective strategies for interpersonal problems. *Journal of Gerontology: Psychological Science, 62B,* P61–P64.

Bosworth, H. B., Schaie, K. W., & Willis, S. L. (1999). Cognitive and sociodemographic risk factors for mortality in the Seattle longitudinal study. *Journal of Gerontology: Psychological Sciences and Social Sciences, 54B,* P273–P283.

Bronfenbrenner, U. (1979). *The ecology of human development: Experiments by nature and design.* Cambridge, MA: Harvard University Press.

Burton, C. L., Strauss, E. H., Bunce, D., Hunter, M. A., & Hultsch, D. F. (2009). Functional abilities in older adults with mild cognitive impairment. *Gerontology, 55,* 570–581.

Burton, C. L., Strauss, E., Hultsch, D. F., & Hunter, M. A. (2009). The relationship between everyday problem solving and inconsistency in reaction time in older adults. *Aging, Neuropsychology, and Cognition, 16,* 607–632.

Butters, M. A., Whyte, E. M., Nebes, R. D., Begley, A. E., Dew, M. A., Mulsant, B. H., . . . Becker, J. T. (2004). The nature and determinants of neuropsychological functioning in late-life depression. *Archives of General Psychiatry, 61*(6), 587–595.

Carstensen, L. L., Mikels, J. A., & Mather, M. (2006). Aging and the intersection of cognition, motivation, and emotion. In J. E. Birren & K.W. Schaie (Eds.), *Handbook of the psychology of aging* (6th ed., pp. 315–342). Boston, MA: Academic Press.

Ceci, S. J., & Bronfenbrenner, U. (1991). On the demise of everyday memory: "The rumors of my death are much exaggerated." *American Psychologist, 46,* 27–31.

Channon, S., Crawford, S. (1999). Problem-solving in real-life-type situations: The effects of anterior and posterior lesions on performance. *Neuropsychologia* (37), 757–770.

Chow, S., Hamagami, F., & Nesselroade, J.R. (2007). Age differences in dynamical emotion-cognition linkages. *Psychology and Aging, 22,* 765–780.

Conway, M. A. (1991). In defense of everyday memory. *American Psychologist, 46,* 19–26.

Cornelius, S. W., & Caspi, A. (1987). Everyday problem solving in adulthood and old age. *Psychology and Aging, 2,* 144–153.

Demming, J. A., & Pressey, S. L. (1957). Tests "indigenous" to the adult and older years. *Journal of Counseling Psychology, 4,* 144–148.

Denney, N. W. (1989). Everyday problem solving: Methodological issues, research findings, and a model. In L. W. Poon, D. C. Rubin, & B. A. Wilson (Eds.), *Everyday cognition in adulthood and late life* (pp. 330–351). New York: Cambridge University Press.

Denney, N. W. (1990). Adult age differences in traditional and practical problem solving. In E. A. Lovelace (Ed.), *Aging and cognition: Mental processes, self-awareness, and interventions* (pp. 329–349). Amsterdam: Elsevier.

Denney, N. W., & Palmer A. M. (1981). Adult age differences on traditional and practical problem solving measures. *Journal of Gerontology, 36,* 323–328.

Denney, N. W., & Pearce, K. A. (1989). A developmental study of practical problem solving in adults. *Psychology and Aging, 4,* 438–442.

Diehl, M., Marsiske, M., Horgas, A. L., Rosenberg, A., Saczynski, J. S., & Willis, S. L. (2005). The revised Observed Tasks of Daily Living: A performance-based assessment of everyday problem solving in older adults. *Journal of Applied Gerontology, 24,* 211–230.

Diehl, M., Willis, S. L., & Schaie, K. W. (1995). Everyday problem solving in older adults: Observational assessment and cognitive correlates. *Psychology and Aging, 10,* 478–491.

Dixon, R. A., & Baltes, P. B. (1986). Toward life-span research on the functions and pragmatics of intelligence. In R J. Sternberg & R. K. Wagner (Eds.), *Practical intelligence: Nature and origins of competence in the everyday world* (pp. 203–235). New York: Cambridge University Press.

Edwards, J. D., Wadley, V. G., Vance, D. E., Wood, K., Roenker, D. L., & Ball, K. K. (2005). The impact of speed of processing training on cognitive and everyday performance. *Aging and Mental Health, 9*(3), 262–271.

Farias, S. T., Mungas, D., Reed, B. R., Bruce, R., Cahn-Weiner, D., Jagust, W., . . . DeCarli, C. (2008). The measurement of everyday cognition (ECog): Scale development and psychometric properties. *Neuropsychology, 22*(4), 531–544.

Farias, S. T., Mungas, D., Reed, B. R., Harvey, D., Cahn-Weiner, D., & DeCarli, C. (2006). MCI is associated with deficits in everyday functioning. *Alzheimer Disease and Associated Disorders, 20,* 217–223.

Garrett, K. D., Browndyke, J. N., Whelihan, W., Paul, R. H., DiCarlo, M., Moser, D. J., . . . Ott, B. R. (2004). The neuropsychological profile of vascular cognitive impairment – no dementia: Comparisons to patients at risk for cerebrovascular disease and vascular dementia. *Archives of Clinical Neuropsychology, 19*(6), 745–757.

Gamaldo, A., Weatherbee, S. R., Allaire, J. C. (2008). Exploring the within-person coupling of blood pressure and cognition in the elderly. *Journal of Gerontology: Psychological Science, 63,* 386–389.

Gelb, S. R., Shapiro, R. J., & Thornton, W. J. L. (2010). Predicting medication adherence and employment status following kidney transplant: The relative utility of traditional and everyday cognitive approaches. *Neuropsychology, 24*(4), 517–526.

Giovannetti, T., Bettcher, M. B., Brennan, L., Libon, D. J., Burke, M., Duey, K., . . . Wambach, D. (2008). Characterization of everyday functioning in mild cognitive impairment: A direct assessment approach. *Dementia and Geriatric Cognitive Disorders, 25,* 359–365.

Griffith, H.R, Belue, K., Sicola., A., Krzywanski, S., Zamrini, E. Y., Harrell, L. E., & Marson, D. C. (2003). Impaired financial abilities in mild cognitive impairment: A direct assessment approach. *Neurology, 60*(3), 449–457.

Hartley, A. A. (1989). The cognitive ecology of problem solving. In L.W. Poon, D. C. Rubin, & B. A. Wilson (Eds.), *Everyday cognition in adulthood and late life* (pp. 300–329). New York: Cambridge University Press.

Horgas, A. L., Wilms, H. U., & Baltes, M. M. (1998). Daily life in very old age: Everyday activities as an expression of successful living. *Gerontologist, 38*, 556–568.

Horn, J. L., & Cattell, R. B. (1966). Refinement and test of the theory of fluid and crystallized general intelligences. *Journal of Educational Psychology, 57*, 253–270.

Horn, K. L., & Hofer, S. M. (1992). Major abilities and development in the adult period. In R. J. Sternberg & C. A. Berg (Eds.), *Intellectual development* (pp. 444–449). New York: Cambridge University Press.

Hultsch, D. F., Strauss, E., Hunter, M., & MacDonald, S. W. S. (2008). Intraindividual variability, cognition, and aging. In: F. I. M. Craik & T. A. Salthouse (Eds.), *The handbook of aging and cognition* (3rd ed., pp. 491–556). New York: Psychology Press.

Johansson, B., Hofer, S. M., & Allaire, J. C. (2004). Change in cognition capabilities in the oldest old: The effects of proximity to death in genetically related individuals over a 6-year period. *Psychology and Aging, 19*(1), 145–156.

Li, S. C., & Lindenberger, U. (1999). Cross-level unification: A computational exploration of the link between deterioration of neurotransmitter systems and dedifferentiation of cognitive abilities in old age. In L.-G. Nilsson & H. J. Markowitsch (Eds.), *Cognitive neuroscience of memory* (pp. 103–146). Kirkland, WA: Hogrefe & Huber.

Lindenberger, U., & Baltes, P. B. (1997). Intellectual functioning in old and very old age: Cross-sectional results from the Berlin aging study. *Psychology and Aging, 12*, 410–432.

MacDonald, S. W. S., Hultsch, D. F., & Dixon, R. A. (2003). Performance variability is related to change in cognition: Evidence from the Victoria Longitudinal Study. *Psychology and Aging, 18*, 510–523.

Maier, H., & Smith, J. (1999). Psychological predictors of mortality in old age. *Journal of Gerontology: Psychological Sciences, 54B*, P44–P54.

Margrett, J. A., Allaire, J. C., Neely, T. L., Daugherty, K., & Weatherbee, S. R. (2009). Everyday problem solving. In J. C. Cavanaugh & C. K. Cavanaugh (Eds.) *Aging in America* (pp. 80–101). Westport, CT: Praeger.

Margrett, J. A., & Marsiske, M. (2002). Gender differences in older adults' everyday cognitive collaboration. Collaboration in later life. *International Journal of Behavior Development, 26*, 45–59.

Marsiske, M. & Margrett, J. A. (2006). Everyday problem solving and decision making. In J. E. Birren & K. W. Schaie (Eds.), *Handbook of the psychology of aging* (6th ed., pp. 315–342). Boston, MA: Academic Press.

Marsiske, M., & Willis, S. L. (1995). Dimensionality of everyday problem solving in older adults. *Psychology and Aging, 10*, 269–283.

Marsiske, M., & Willis, S. L. (1998). Practical creativity in older adults' everyday problem solving: Lifespan perspectives. In C. E. Adams-Price (Ed.), *Creativity and aging: Theoretical and empirical approaches* (pp. 73–113). New York: Springer.

Morris, J. C., Storandt, M., Miller, J. P., McKeel, D. W., Price, J. L. Rubin, E. H., & Berg, L. (2001). Mild cognitive impairment represents early-stage Alzheimer disease. *Archives of Neurology, 58*(3), 397–405.

Neisser, U. (1978). Memory: What are the important questions? In M. M. Gruneberg, P. E. Morris, & R. N. Sykes (Eds.), *Practical aspects of memory* (pp. 3–24). London: Academic Press.

Neisser, U. (1991). A case of misplaced nostalgia. *American Psychologist, 46,* 34–36.

Neupert, S. D., Mroczek, D. K., & Spiro, A. III (2008). Neuroticism moderates the daily relation between stressors and memory failures. *Psychology and Aging, 23*(2), 287–296.

Neupert, S. D., Almeida, D. M., Mroczek, D. K., & Spiro, A. III. (2006). Daily stressors and memory failures in a naturalistic setting: Findings from the VA Normative Aging Study. *Psychology and Aging, 21,* 424–429.

Okonkwo, O. C., Wadley, V. G., Griffith, H. R., Ball, K., & Marson, D. C. (2006). Cognitive correlates of financial abilities in mild cognitive impairment. *Journal of the American Geriatric Society, 54,* 1745–1750.

Pereira, F. S., Yassuda, M. S., Oliveira, A. M., Diniz, B. S., Radonovic, M., Talib, L. L., . . . Forlenza, O.V. (2010). Profiles of functional deficits in mild cognitive impairment and dementia: Benefits from objective measurement. *Journal of the International Neuropsychological Society, 16* (2), 297–305.

Perneczky, R., Pohl, C., Sorg, C., Hartmann, J., Komossa, K., Alexopoulos, A., . . . Kurz, A. (2006). Complex activities of daily living in mild cognitive impairment: Conceptual and diagnostic issues. *Age and Ageing, 35,* 240–245.

Perneczky, R., Pohl, C., Sorg, C., Hartmann, J., Tosic, N., Grimmer, T., . . . Kurz, A. (2006). Impairment of activities of daily living requiring memory or complex reasoning as part of the MCI syndrome. *International Journal of Geriatric Psychiatry, 21*(2), 158–162.

Petersen, R. C., Smith, G. E., Waring, S. C., Ivnik, R. J., Tangalos, E. G., & Kokmen, E. (1999) Mild cognitive impairment: Clinical characterization and outcome. *Archives of Neurology, 56*(3), 303–308.

Petersen, R. C., Stevens, J. C., Ganguli, M., Tangalos, E. G., Cummings, J. L., & DeKosky S. T. (2001). Practice parameter: Early detection of dementia. Mild cognitive impairment (an evidence-based review). Report of the Quality Standards Subcommittee of the American Academy of Neurology. *Neurology, 56,* 1133–1142.

Ram, N., Rabbitt, P., Stollery, B., & Nesselroade, J. R. (2005). Cognitive performance inconsistency: Intraindividual change and variability. *Psychology and Aging, 20,* 623–633.

Rogers, W. A., Meyer, B., Walker, N., & Fisk, A. D. (1998). Functional limitations to daily living tasks in the aged: A focus group analysis. *Human Factors, 40,* 111–125.

Rybash, W. J. & Hoyer, J. M. (1994). Characterizing adult cognitive development. *Journal of Adult Development, 1,* 7–12.

Salthouse, T. A. (1990). Cognitive competence and expertise in aging. In J. E. Birren & K. W. Schaie (Eds.), *Handbook of the psychology of aging* (pp. 310–319). New York: Academic Press.

Salthouse, T. A. (1991). Expertise as the circumvention of human processing limitations. In K. A. Ericsson & J. Smith (Eds.), *Toward a general theory of expertise* (pp. 286–300). New York: Cambridge University Press.

Schaie, K. W. (1978). External validity in the assessment of intellectual development in adulthood. *Journal of Gerontology, 33,* 695–701.

Schaie, K. W. (1993). The course of adult intellectual development. *American Psychologist, 49,* 304–313.

Schaie, K. W. (1996). *Intellectual development in adulthood: The Seattle longitudinal study.* New York: Cambridge University Press.

Sinnot, J. D. (Ed.) (1989). *Everyday problem solving: Theory and application.* Westport, CT: Greenwood Press.

Sliwinski, M. J., Smyth, J. M., Hofer, S. M., & Stawski, R. S. (2006). Intraindividual coupling of daily stress and cognition. *Psychology and Aging, 21,* 545–557.

Small, B. J., & Bäckman, L. (1997). Cognitive correlates of mortality: Evidence from a population-based sample of very old adults. *Psychology and Aging, 12,* 309–313.

Smits, C. H., Deeg, D. J., Kriegsman, D. M., & Schmand, B. (1999). Cognitive functioning and health as determinants of mortality in an older population. *American Journal of Epidemiology 150* (9): 978–986.

Sternberg, R. J. (1997). The concept of intelligence and its role in lifelong learning and success. *American Psychologist, 52,* 1030–1037.

Sternberg, R. J., & Wagner, R.K. (1986). *Practical intelligence: Nature and origins of competence in the everyday world.* New York: Cambridge University Press.

Strough, J., Berg, C. A., & Sansone, C. (1996). Goals for solving everyday problems across the life span: Age and gender differences in the salience of interpersonal concerns. *Developmental Psychology, 32,* 1106–1115.

Strough, J., McFall, J. P., Flinn, J. A., & Schuller, K. L. (2008). Collaborative everyday problem solving among same-gender friends in early and later adulthood. *Psychology and Aging, 23*(3), 517–530.

Swan, G. E., Carmelli, D., & LaRue, A. (1995). Performance on the digit symbol substitution task and 5-year mortality on the Western Collaborative Group Study. *American Journal of Epidemiology, 141,* 32–40.

Thornton, W. J. L., Deria, S., Gelb, S., Shapiro, R. J., & Hill, A. (2007). Neuropsychological mediators of the links between age, chronic illness, and everyday problem solving. *Psychology and Aging, 22*(3) 470–481.

Thornton, W. J. L. & Dumke, H. A. (2005). Age differences in everyday problem-solving and decision-making effectiveness: A meta-analytic review. *Psychology and Aging, 20,* 85–99.

Thornton, W. J. L., Paterson, T., Yeung, S., & Kubik, J. (in press). Age differences in everyday problem solving: The roles of problem context and self-efficacy. *Journal of Gerontology, Psychological Sciences.*

Wadley, V. G., Crowe, M., Marsiske, M., Cook, S. E., Unverzagt, F. W., Rosenberg, A. L., & Rexroth, D. (2007). Changes in everyday functioning among individuals with psychometrically defined mild cognitive impairment in the ACTIVE Study. *Journal of the American Geriatric Society, 55,* 1192–1198.

Wagner, R. K. (1986). The search for interterrestrial intelligence. In R. J. Sternberg & R. K. Wagner (Eds.), Practical intelligence: Nature and origins of competence in the everyday world (pp. 361–378). New York: Cambridge University Press.

Weatherbee, S. R., & Allaire, J. C. (2008). Everyday cognition and mortality: Performance differences and predictive utility of the Everyday Cognition Battery. *Psychology and Aging, 23,* 216–221.

Weisz, J. (1978). Transcontextual validity in developmental research. *Child Development, 49,* 1–12.

Whitfield, K. E, Allaire, J. C., & Wiggins, S. A. (2004). Relationships between health factors and everyday problem solving in African Americans. *Health Psychology, 23,* 641–644.

Whitfield, K. E., Baker-Thomas, T., Heyward, K., Gatto, M., & Williams, Y. (1999). Evaluating a measure of everyday problem solving for use in African Americans. *Experimental Aging Research, 25*(3), 209–221.

Willis, S. L. (1991). Cognition and everyday competence. In K. W. Schaie (Ed.), *Annual Review of Gerontology and Geriatrics* (Vol. 11, pp. 80–109). New York: Springer.

Willis, S. L. (1996). Everyday cognitive competence in elderly persons: Conceptual issues and empirical findings. *Gerontologist, 51,* 11–17.

Willis, S. L., Jay, G. M., Diehl, M., & Marsiske, M. (1992). Longitudinal change and the prediction of everyday task competence in the elderly. *Research on Aging, 14,* 68–91.

Willis, S. L., & Marsiske, M. (1991). Life span perspective on practical intelligence. In T. E. Tupper & K. D. Cicerone (Eds.), *The neuropsychology of everyday life: Issues in development and rehabilitation* (pp. 183–197). Boston: Kluwer.

Willis, S. L., & Schaie, K. W. (1986). Practical intelligence in later adulthood. In R. J. Sternberg & R. K. Wagner (Eds.), *Practical intelligence: Nature and origins of competence in the everyday world* (pp. 236–268). New York: Cambridge University Press.

Willis, S. L., & Schaie, K.W. (1993). Everyday cognition: Taxonomic and methodological considerations. In J. M. Puckett & H. W. Reese (Eds.), *Mechanisms of everyday cognition* (pp. 33–54). Hillsdale, NJ: Erlbaum.

PART IV

Personality

11

Personality Development in Adulthood

Nicky J. Newton and Abigail J. Stewart

In the first half of the 20th century adulthood was viewed as a period in which personality was stable. Psychologists and lay people alike believed that during adulthood individuals simply enacted the personality temperament and traits that resulted from inborn endowment and early experience. Experiences in childhood and adolescence (e.g., parenting style and approach, birth order, family habits and patterns) were widely viewed as consequential for the rest of an individual's life. At mid-century Erik Erikson, among others, intervened in this perspective. He challenged two main notions (Erikson, 1950, 1963; see also Erikson, 1982): that adulthood is a flat and stable landscape with respect to personality, and that the impact of life experience on personality change stops when an individual reaches majority.

Erikson offered a broad view of personality across the lifespan, suggesting in his epigenetic theory that individuals negotiate eight stages of personality development, each prompted by other developments (e.g., cognitive ones) and social demands from the environment. Each stage involves a central dilemma of human existence that recurs many times throughout life, but is center-stage for a time. During that period the individual is faced with a psychosocial demand to adopt a stance toward an important aspect of life, and each of us achieves some balance or resolution of the dilemma. The overall stance adopted as a result of each stage in turn influences the stance toward the next one, and at the same time the next psychosocial encounter may stimulate new development of the issue addressed in a previous stage. Although Erikson viewed development as proceeding along a sequence of stages, he built in a notion that previous dilemmas linger and are sometimes revisited in substantial ways.

Erikson was not particularly interested in specifying the ages at which an individual would be preoccupied with a particular dilemma, but he did view the first four stages as

The Wiley-Blackwell Handbook of Adulthood and Aging, First Edition. Edited by Susan Krauss Whitbourne and Martin J. Sliwinski. © 2012 Blackwell Publishing Ltd. Published 2012 by Blackwell Publishing Ltd.

marking "childhood" (the period before adolescence); the fifth begins in the period of adolescence and the transition to adulthood. This leaves three more to fill the remaining adult years. The childhood stages begin with the dilemma of trust versus mistrust, and a favorable resolution of this issue results in the development of a hopeful or optimistic stance toward life. The second tension is between autonomy and shame or doubt about the capacity to take actions; here the child struggles to develop a positive capacity to express his or her will. In the third stage, children struggle with the development of greater scope in time and space for their initiative versus an increasing capacity to feel guilt about those actions. Ideally, the child develops a sense of purpose, and capacity to initiate projects and plans. That development in turn enables children to make efforts to learn many things and accomplish valued goals, while also increasing their sense of other people's accomplishments. During this fourth stage, the child struggles to develop a sense of competence out of the dilemma between working hard and failing at many efforts at which others succeed (industriousness versus inferiority).

These childhood stages give way in adolescence, under social pressure for young people to find their place in the larger society, to a struggle to accomplish a sense of stable and reliable selfhood or "fidelity" to an identity that incorporates a sense of the past and enables movement into the future. This accomplishment of identity includes a notion of a vocation for oneself, and personal ideological commitments to stable values, politics, and religious beliefs. This sense of identity does not, however, end personality development, but enables the individual to take on the project of committing that stable self to an intimate relationship with another person (intimacy versus isolation), to productivity and reproduction (generativity versus stagnation), and to leaving a legacy that includes a wider community of human beings (integrity versus despair). The accomplishments of these stages (fidelity, love, care, and wisdom) are the personality developmental achievements of adulthood, according to Erikson.

During the second half of the 20th century, Erikson's theory of adult development stimulated considerable empirical research, and the notion that personality develops and changes throughout the period is now widely accepted by psychologists and in lay writing. Psychological research has assessed both the relevance of the dilemmas and issues Erikson mapped out, and the role of social experiences in adulthood in provoking personality change. After reviewing what we know about these two primary issues, we will conclude with a consideration of how, in the 21st century, we can both build on what has been well established in this literature, and stake out new territory that has not yet been explored.

Personality Development in Adulthood

Identity

There have been two major measurement foci in research on identity: (a) assessments of preoccupations with identity issues, often in the context of assessing other psychosocial issues in an omnibus or more narrowly targeted measure (Constantinople, 1969; Ochse &

Plug, 1986; Stewart, Franz, & Layton, 1988; Whitbourne & Waterman, 1979); and (b) assessment of the overall resolution of the identity dilemma at a particular point in time (Marcia, 1966; Sneed & Whitbourne, 2001). Each of these foci has been addressed using multiple kinds of methods (e.g., closed-ended items; open-ended items that are content-coded; analysis of personal documents, narratives, and interviews). These different methods of assessment can make it difficult to reconcile conflicting results, but it has allowed for a rich picture of the issue of identity development. Moreover, it sometimes has permitted us to see that across different kinds of assessments similar results are obtained. Finally, a number of case studies have been conducted – using both quantitative and qualitative approaches (Espin, Stewart, & Gomez,1990; Franz, 1994, 1995; Kroger, 1993; Stewart, Franz, & Layton, 1988). This is consistent with the complexity of Erikson's theory and his own example (in *Childhood and Society*, 1950, 1963, and his studies of Luther, 1962, and Gandhi, 1969). In case studies it is, perhaps, easiest to see the ways in which social provocations and personality developments are connected and have mutual influences.

One important strand of empirical research has focused on whether adolescents' struggle to develop relatively broadly integrative and stable identities characterizes the period of the transition to young adulthood in a central way; Greenberger, 1984; Whitbourne, Sneed & Sayer, 2009). Marcia (1966) formulated four identity statuses based on the dimensions of commitment and exploration: achieved identity, identity moratorium, identity foreclosure, and identity diffusion. In this research the focus was mainly on documenting the range of different kinds of identity resolutions among adolescents and young adults (see, e.g., Rowe & Marcia, 1980; Waterman, 1982), and on identifying precursors to and consequences of different resolutions (Fitch & Adams, 1983; Grotevant & Cooper, 1985). Marcia and colleagues (Stephen, Fraser, & Marcia, 1992) later revised this measure to include a more dynamic process of oscillation between moratorium and achievement statuses (MAMA cycles) that continue throughout adulthood. This emphasis on the persistent importance of identity issues in later stages of adulthood has also been recognized by other researchers (Helson & Soto, 2005; Helson, Stewart, & Ostrove, 1995; Josselson, 2003; Kroger, 1997; Stewart, Ostrove, & Helson, 2001; Whitbourne & Skultety, 2006; Zucker, Ostrove, & Stewart, 2002).

On the one hand, Josselson (2003) observed that midlife is a time when it is almost impossible to disentangle identity development from the other Eriksonian stages of intimacy and generativity, and perhaps all three together are paramount in adulthood, especially for women. On the other hand, researchers have also recognized that increasing age does not preclude continuing identity development. Zucker et al. (2002) found that identity increased into the sixties for three cohorts of women. Kroger (2002), in researching identity in the younger old (65 to 75) and very old (75 +), observed similarities between adolescence and late adulthood as transitional times in the lifespan, commenting: "For those in early late adulthood, identity reintegration and reevaluation were the most common exploration processes, whereas identity refinement and readjustment predominated in the older late-adulthood group" (p. 95). Consistent with Kroger's observations regarding the dynamic nature of identity across the lifespan, Whitbourne et al. (2009) observed a curvilinear growth pattern for identity across adulthood, although the rate of growth decreased between early adulthood and midlife.

One of the more controversial areas of Erikson's theorizing about identity focuses on his comments about gender. He suggested (Erikson, 1968) that women's identities are necessarily provisional until they make an intimate life commitment, usually with a man; thus he implied that the sequence of personality development for women might involve intimacy before identity (Franz & White, 1985, provide an excellent critique on this subject). There is little evidence to support this expectation, perhaps because of the dramatic social changes in the last half of the 20th century in American women's social status. However, there is evidence that the process of identity revision changes with age somewhat differently for men and women. Skultety and Whitbourne (2004; see also Whitbourne & Skultety, 2006) examined gender differences in identity assimilation (or maintaining identity as we age), identity accommodation (changing identity with age), and a balance of the two. In seeking to answer the question of how women's self-esteem is maintained in the face of age-related changes and society's response to those changes, the authors proposed that identity assimilation, which involves ignoring or minimizing an aging-related experience, is a mechanism that allows women to maintain a stable sense of self over time while at the same time maintaining their self-esteem. Optimally, achieving a balance between identity assimilation and identity accommodation encourages the maintenance of self-esteem. In this study, however, women were more likely than men to engage in identity accommodation, which was negatively related to self-esteem. In further exploration of women's use of identity accommodation versus assimilation, Skultety and Whitbourne (2004) found that identity assimilation was more often used by women than men to maintain a sense of self, whereas the demands of new roles or situations across the lifespan (such as widowhood, retirement, or empty nest) required the use of identity accommodation.

As we noted, Erikson argued that the social context elicited personality development, and we focus on social roles later in the chapter; however, it is worth reviewing here some of the research pertaining to the domains in which people invest their identities, which can vary by gender, cohort, or social context. In a study of New Zealanders between the ages of 40 and 63, Kroger (1997) found that, in defining themselves, both women and men used relationships as frameworks in which they formed their identities. A study by Helson et al. (1995) looked at the similarities and differences in personality for three cohorts of women, assessed in their early forties; that is, data were collected in 1969 from the Berkeley Guidance Study (young adults in the 1950s), in 1981 from the Mills Longitudinal study (young adults in the early 1960s), and in 1986 from the Radcliffe Class of 1964; (young adults in the late 1960s). The authors found that identity was related to work and family outcomes only in the younger, less socially restricted cohorts, whereas identity was less related to life pattern for the older cohort: those who followed a more nontraditional path in that cohort (e.g., by working outside the home), often did so as a result of a partner's death or financial need – that is, external pressures. Similarly, Van Manen & Whitbourne (1997), in another longitudinal study, found that women who had come of age in the early 1960s had a strong sense of identity that was related to greater progress in their careers; however, women of this cohort were more likely to express their identity through their roles as homemakers. These latter two studies highlight the influence of the larger context in which many of these women lived: for women born in the early period of the baby boom, social expectations were fairly constraining, but they changed dramatically in the course of their early adult lives. Pals (1999) also underscored the importance of cohort influences in her study of Mills College women's identity consolidation as it relates to ego-resiliency and identity in marriage among women of the pre-baby boom generation. She identified four prototypes of identity in marriage: anchored (equal partner with husband; other identities as well as "wife"); defined (primarily wife); restricted (constrained by identity-limiting situation); and confused (unsupportive marriage, low self-esteem as a result). Positive subjective outcomes were associated with anchored and defined identities; negative outcomes with restricted and confused identities in marriage.

Change of social role and cultural or ethnic differences can also affect the development of identity for both men and women. In a study of the transition from being solely a career professional to adding the role of parent, Lee, Dohring, MacDermid, and Kossek (2005) explored more fully the idea that identity is socially constructed and involves interactions among personality traits, social roles, and group memberships. They identified five types of preparenthood identity (career-defined; career-defined with family acquisition plans; career and family – a joint venture; alternating career and family; and career pursued in context) and compared these with postparenthood identities. Inevitably, because the authors chose a sample of men and women who were part-time employees due to family or lifestyle choices, 95% were women. However, there was still variability in how participants transitioned: although 40% of respondents were identified as interweaving career and family, and mostly had career-defined or joint venture identities preparenthood, 28% also identified family as a priority around which career was organized.

The relationship between ego identity and other social identities is also important. St. Louis and Liem (2005) found that students aged 17–26 who had achieved ego identity had a more positive sense of an ethnic identity than those with diffuse identities, although this was moderated by race: stronger ethnic identity was associated with more positive psychosocial outcomes among minority students, but not White students. Konik and Stewart (2004) similarly found that sexual minority students were more likely to have achieved identities than heterosexual students; they argue that carrying a sexual minority identity encourages earlier exploration and commitment to identity than a more comfortable majority identity. In the context of South African apartheid, Ochse and Plug (1986) considered the impact of both race and gender, finding that White women resolved identity crises earlier than White men did, whereas Black men resolved identity crises as late as age 40, rather than in early adulthood. At midlife, Black women experienced a lack of self-definition or identity formation, and consequently a lack of well-being.

Thus the empirical literature on identity in adulthood began with a focus on the age-related preoccupation, and confirmed Erikson's core expectation that adolescence is marked by this dilemma. At the same time, theory and research has generated little support for his expectation of a gender-differentiated developmental course in adolescence. Subsequent developments have focused on the continuing importance of identity, including revisions and changes in it, throughout the adult period, perhaps particularly for women. Finally, the role of contextual influences – both external social structures and pressures, and particular social identities – is well documented.

Intimacy

In comparison with the large volume of research on identity, there is comparatively little research on intimacy. Much of the research either supports or questions Erikson's ideas concerning intimacy's place in the progression of stages, and/or the gender differences in transitioning from identity to intimacy. Perhaps this area is underdeveloped because the central issue of adult relationships has been so thoroughly studied under two alternative rubrics: attachment (Edelstein & Gillath, 2008; Fraley & Shaver, 2000; Hazan & Shaver, 1987, 1994; Mikulincer & Shaver, 2005; Schachner, Shaver, & Gillath, 2008) and personal relationships (Botwin, Buss, & Shackelford, 1997; Hatton et al., 2008; Holland and Roisman, 2008; Sturaro, Denissen, Aken, & Asendorpf, 2008; Watson, Hubbard, & Wiese, 2000).

Consistent with Erikson's theorizing, Ochse and Plug (1986) found general intimacy themes to be predominant between the ages of 20 to 25 years. Other research has also found support for Erikson's predicted progression from identity to intimacy (Franz, 1995; Orlofsky, Marcia, & Lesser, 1973; Tesch & Whitbourne, 1982). Stein and Newcombe (1999) found that "Healthy identity formation in early adulthood facilitated the development of greater intimacy in young adulthood" (p. 39). Achieving intimacy may even promote the development of empathy, as suggested by Gold and Rogers (1995) in their work with entry-level counseling students aged 22–53. Although a few studies have supported Erikson's ideas concerning women's delayed or reversed progression from identity to intimacy, the evidence is thin and inconsistent. In a study of 40 male and 40 female college students aged 18–24, Schiedel and Marcia (1985) found that, as Erikson theorized, women had higher levels of intimacy than men, and there were more women than men with a low-identity/high intimacy profile. In contrast, and using a different research design, Zimmer-Gembeck and Petherick (2006) found no gender differences in intimacy dating goals or identity formation for students in a similar age group.

Erikson's expectations about the progression through identity to intimacy have been critiqued by many researchers as underscoring a masculine bias that values separateness from, rather than connection to, others. Barnett and Baruch (1978) noted that the proposed gender differences in identity resolution reflect the influences of the era in which Erikson wrote and that "the centrality of women's reproductive role is assumed and the importance of their work pattern is ignored" (p. 187). They also commented that this approach fails to account for the fact that different women adopt and shed different roles at different ages; thus there is no universal pattern of role sequencing among women. Horst (1995) recommends greater differentiation of identity and intimacy concepts, and notes that when male and female adolescents work through relational issues, they are often working on their own self-definitions. Thus she suggests that identity may be at stake in the context of intimate relationships for both male and female young adults. As with identity, intimacy is also closely linked to changes in the roles people undertake. Espin, Stewart, and Gomez (1990) analyzed letters from a Latin American emigrée to her teacher, finding that she had already resolved intimacy issues at the age of 22, by which time she was married and had her first child. In this and another study of a young woman's personal documents (diaries and letters; see Stewart, Franz, & Layton, 1988), adoption of adult social roles was associated with changes in expression of intimacy themes. Similarly, Pals (1999) – in a study of how different experiences of "identity within marriage" in early adulthood affected their subsequent development – found that women with "restricted and confused" identities in marriage (in contrast with women with "anchored and defined" identities in marriage) were less likely to have "consolidated identities." Van Manen and Whitbourne (1997) also found that college intimacy levels predicted the number of years in a stable committed relationship for men and women in their early thirties, whether married or not. Finally, in a more specific analysis of identity as a precursor of progression to intimacy using a group of unmarried Australian university students, Zimmer-Gembeck and Petherick (2006) found that younger adults with more well-formed vocational identities and less-formed sex role identities showed a stronger association between intimacy dating goals and relationship satisfaction.

If the body of research dealing with intimacy seems small, research concerning the relationship between age and intimacy is even scarcer, perhaps because it is assumed that intimacy is a concern only in young adulthood. Mirroring identity development, intimacy does indeed remain an issue well into later adulthood, as Gramling (2007) articulates:

> Midlife women continue concerns of intimacy into mid-adulthood. Primary relationships have endured over time, have been reconfigured to meet the women's needs, or have been abandoned. Unsupportive intimate relationships are rarely tolerated. Relationships with parents and children have evolved and most midlife women have extensive and supportive relationships with women. (p. 103)

This finding is supported by Whitbourne et al. (2009), who found a curvilinear relationship for intimacy development over a period of 40 years (ages 17 to 57). Those participants who were not in a committed relationship in early adulthood exhibited comparatively higher levels of intimacy in later life than those who had been in a committed relationship in early adulthood. In contrast, Newton and Stewart (2010) observed consistently low levels of intimacy in women aged 43 to 62 when compared to levels of identity and generativity over the same period. There are many possible reasons for these slightly different findings, not least of which is the use of different measures of intimacy. Perhaps, with increased awareness of the importance of intimate relationships across adulthood, more consistent, standardized measures will become available, or researchers will accumulate a sense of the distinctive meanings associated with each type of measure.

Generativity

Like identity, and in contrast to intimacy, many researchers have studied and elaborated Erikson's notion of generativity, or "the establishment, the guidance, and the enrichment of the living generation and the world it inherits" (Erikson, 1974, p.123). In this section we examine different approaches to measuring generativity, theoretical and empirical work considering its timing and course, and empirical studies of the relationship of generativity to parenting and career.

Researchers agree that generativity is multifaceted (see, e.g., Kotre, 1984; McAdams & de St. Aubin, 1992), and this agreement is reflected in the different ways in which it is measured. Arguably the most widely used tool is the Loyola Generativity Scale (LGS;

McAdams & de St. Aubin, 1992), a 20-item self-report scale developed to measure individual differences in generative concern. In developing this scale, the authors found significant convergent validity with measures of both generative behavior and narratives. Darling-Fischer and Leidy (1988) developed a generativity subscale to add to Rosenthal, Gurney, and Moore's (1981) Erikson Psychosocial Stage Inventory, or EPSI, calling it the modified EPSI (or MEPSI). They used key words or attributions taken from Erikson's writings, resulting in 10 items, 5 positive (generativity) and 5 negative (stagnation). In a similar manner, Whitbourne and Waterman (1979) added a generativity subscale to the extant Inventory of Psychosocial Development (IPD; Constantinople, 1969).

Other researchers have devised coding systems for open-ended survey or interview, as well as personal documents, such as diaries or letters. Stewart et al. (1988) developed a coding scheme for generativity (as well as identity and intimacy) based on Erikson's (1950, 1959, 1968, 1982) writings, which was later revised by Stewart, Franz, Paul, and Peterson (1991). This coding system identifies themes reflecting the three stages in terms of the definitions and examples contained in Erikson's accounts (see, e.g., Espin et al., 1990; Newton & Stewart, 2010; Peterson and Stewart, 1990; Stewart et al., 1988).

Both the California Q-sort (CAQ; Block, 1961, 1971) and the Thematic Apperception Test (TAT; Morgan & Murray, 1935) have also provided foundations for measures of generativity. Peterson and Klohnen (1995) created a measure of generative realization using the 13 top-rated CAQ items in a "single generativity index that contains elements of agency, communion, and insightfulness" (p. 24). This measure was related to reported health concerns for spouses and children as well as political activism in two longitudinal samples of women. In order to measure people's intrinsic motivations to act in generative ways, Peterson and Stewart (1996) developed a TAT measure that showed convergent validity with both the Q-sort measure and Stewart et al.'s (1988, 1991) coding system mentioned above.

A semistructured interview to assess different styles of resolving generativity issues was developed by Bradley and Marcia (1998). They used the dimensions of involvement (or active concern) and inclusivity (or care-giving concern) within the domains of self and other to create five prototypic categories: generative (high on both involvement and inclusivity for both self and other); agentic (high on involvement and inclusivity for self but low on both for other); communal (low on involvement for self and other, but high on inclusivity for self and other); conventional (high on involvement for self and other, low on inclusivity for self and other); and stagnant (low on both dimensions for self and other). This method of measuring generativity is positively correlated with McAdams and de St. Aubin's LGS (1992).

Of course, researchers have tried to assess whether generativity is a particular focus of concern specific to midlife, as Erikson suggested. There is mixed evidence about when generativity first emerges (McAdams, 2001; Peterson & Stewart, 1993) and when it peaks (Stewart et al., 2001; Peterson & Stewart, 1993; Zucker et al., 2002). Peterson and Stewart (1993) found that generativity was expressed as a concern by adults as early as their late twenties. McAdams, de St. Aubin, and Logan (1993) conducted a study of four out of seven components in their model of generativity (generative concern, commitment, action, and narration (leaving out generative demand, desire, and belief) using three cohorts aged 22–27 (young), 37–42 (middle), and 67–72 (old) and found an increase in generativity between young adulthood and midlife, with no clear evidence of any decrease after midlife. Other researchers have also found an increase in women's generativity levels through late middle age (Miner-Rubino, Winter, & Stewart, 2004; Newton & Stewart, 2010; Peterson and Stewart, 1990; Stewart et al., 2001; Zucker et al., 2002).

In an effort to reconcile these results, Stewart and Vandewater (1998) proposed that different aspects of generativity may peak at different ages. Thus they suggested that perhaps the desire for generativity emerges first, the capacity increases over adulthood, and a sense of accomplishment is achieved only relatively late in life. Erikson's suggestion that parenthood is central to generativity, and his closely related assumption that parenting is more important for women than for men, has been examined in several studies. One such study was conducted by McAdams and de St. Aubin (1992), who found that, although adult women had the highest levels of generativity when compared to adult men and college-age women and men, having children was more strongly linked with generativity for men than it was for women: Fathers scored higher on generativity than men without children, whereas there was no significant difference between women with and without children. Alternatively, in a later study of the consequences of generativity for well-being, Rothrauff and Cooney (2008) found that there were no differences in the association between generativity and well-being for women with children and those without, or between men with children and those without.

In a study of men's patterns of coping with infertility and their parenting outcomes, Snarey, Son, Kuehne, Hauser, and Vaillant (1987) found that earlier parenting predicted achievement of midlife generativity among men. They also found a link between intimacy and generativity that Erikson did not suggest: Those who were infertile and divorced were lower in generativity than those who were infertile yet happy in their marriage. Thus the meaning and consequences of infertility for men (and possibly women) depends substantially on the relational context.

The work place also provides an environment in which generativity can flourish, although it has not been studied as extensively as the family environment. In seeking to answer questions about the prevalence of generativity for men in midcareer, as well as which of McAdams et al.'s (1993) types of generativity (concern, commitment, or action) relate to career well-being, Clark and Arnold (2008) found work to be a distinct area of generative expression, although ranked behind family in importance for these men. They also found that men were more likely to find work satisfying and to feel successful when they promoted the growth of others or the common good, rather than when they pursued their own productivity or leadership (more self-focused goals). For women, Peterson and Stewart (1996) demonstrated that generativity can be achieved through occupational mastery and helping others.

Generativity is sometimes expressed in terms of concern not only for the next generation, but also for other members of one's family, especially ill and/or aging parents. Peterson (2002), in a study of intergenerational roles, found that women who provided care for a parent, particularly fathers, expressed higher levels of generativity than those who did not. Pratt, Norris, Gressman, Lawford, and Hebblethwaite (2008) built on these findings to suggest that adults who are more generative will be more concerned with caregiving and support for both children and older adult generations. They studied Canadian mothers and fathers who described a child-rearing problem with a grandparent when their children were 8 years old. Four basic problem types were identified, and one of them was associated with lower generativity in the parent: lack of grandparent investment and care for grandchild.

In sum, generativity is a multifaceted concept, involving parental and mentoring roles and also work, extended family, and – as life expectancy increases – different expectations for creating legacies that outlive the self (Kotre, 1984). These may even include more global goals, such as creating a more sustainable planet for future generations.

Ego integrity

Ego integrity has received the least attention of all of Erikson's stages. This may change with increasing demand for more research into the aging population, especially as the large population bulge of baby boomers progresses into old age. However, there is already some interest in differentiating old age periods (Baltes & Smith, 1999). Kroger (2002) found that older adults felt the need to "tie up the life package" (p. 92), although she also found that they were sometimes dealing with different packages. Specifically, women in their advanced years wanted more vocational activity, such as volunteer work, whereas men were facing the need to adjust to the relatively limited power they could exert given the loss of an occupational role.

Both Erikson (Erikson, Erikson, & Kivnick, 1986) and Butler (1974) argued that the last stage of life was characterized by a life review during which people integrate the positive and negative elements of the life they have lived, often in response to acknowledgment of approaching mortality. Butler further commented that older individuals are "searching for purpose, reconciliation of relationships, and resolution of conflicts and regrets" (p. 533) and that "only in old age can we experience a personal sense of the entire life cycle" (p. 534). Erikson et al. also linked the life review and the process of developing ego integrity to a reconciliation of sorts, or a "coming to terms with the life one has lived thus far" (p. 70), which often involves acknowledging and resolving one's regrets.

Torges, Stewart, & Duncan (2008) investigated the relationship between regret resolution and levels of ego integrity, finding that high levels of regret resolution were not only related to concurrent levels of ego integrity at age 62, but that regret resolution measured a decade earlier was also related to ego integrity at age 62. It should be noted, however, that a life review and its attendant regret may occur at any point in life, as Stewart and Ostrove (1998) observed, but serve a different purpose. For example, Stewart and Vandewater (1999) found that women at the beginning of middle age who took action after acknowledging traditional regrets had higher later well-being than those who did not take action. Thus regret resolution in early life stages may require action, while in later life stages it may be a more exclusively internal process. Changes in how goals are managed may be closely linked to the association between ego integrity and regret resolution in old age. Wrosch, Bauer, and Scheier (2005) found that older adults perceived fewer opportunities to redress their regrets; the intensity of their regret also predicted reduced quality of life. However, they also found that being able to disengage from the process of redressing regrets, as well as holding many future goals, diminished the intensity of older adults' regrets and thereby contributed to a better quality of life.

Sehnsucht, or "life longings" (Mayser, Scheibe, & Riediger, 2008; Scheibe, Freund, & Baltes, 2007) may be related to goals and regrets, as well as ego integrity. Scheibe et al. define *Sehnsucht* as "a high degree of intense, (recurring), and often painful desire for something, particularly if there is no hope to attain the desired, or when its attainment is uncertain, still far away" (p. 778). It can be either debilitating or motivating: As with many correlates of aging, a moderate amount of *Sehnsucht* is assumed to be an integral part of successful development. In Scheibe et al.'s research, *Sehnsucht* served as a regulatory mechanism for loss and nonrealization of life goals for older adults; life longings were also reported to be in the foreground when adults review, manage, plan, and reconstruct their lives (p. 790). However, higher levels of life longings were associated with lower well-being. Mayser et al. also differentiated life longings from goals, which were perceived by participants in their study (aged 20–69) to be more associated with everyday actions and to be more controllable, attainable, and concrete than life longings, which in turn were seen to be more emotionally ambivalent and more long-term-oriented. Future research will help refine the concept of *Sehnsucht,* as well as more fully describe its possible role in regret resolution and, by extension, ego integrity.

Ego integrity has been measured using Ryff & Heincke's (1983) 16-item instrument in much of the empirical work to date (e.g., James & Zarett, 2006; Torges et al., 2008). Consistent with Erikson's ideas, Ryff and Heincke found that older people rated themselves higher on ego integrity than they had been in the past, whereas young and middle-aged people anticipated being higher than they currently were. When Whitbourne and Waterman (1979) added their generativity subscale to the IPD (Constantinople, 1969), they also added a subscale for ego integrity that consisted of five positive items and five negative items rated on a 7-point Likert scale. Walaskay, Whitbourne, and Nehrke (1983–84) also developed a semistructured interview that reliably identified four integrity statuses, similar to Marcia's (1966) identity statuses: integrity-achieving, dissonant, foreclosed, and despairing. Most recently, Torges, Stewart, and Duncan (2009) developed a measure of narrative ego integrity that the authors feel provides a more nuanced assessment of ego integrity due to participants' expressions of their lives in their own words. This measure demonstrated convergent validity with Ryff and Heincke's measure of ego integrity, while at the same time providing a depth of response not tapped by a closed-ended measure.

As this last stage of Erikson's theory may become the longest developmental stage in the lifespan, given increases in life expectancy, it clearly would benefit from more scrutiny. From our review here, it is also evident that it is a time of fluctuation and stock-taking, and therefore no less dynamic or complex a stage than any of the previous ones.

Expansion of Erikson's theory

As we have noted, the sequence of Erikson's stages is a topic that has garnered much attention from personality development researchers, with mixed results. Often, the successful resolution of stages is targeted, as in Stein and Newcombe's (1999) study, which found that successful resolution of the identity crisis leads to greater intimacy in early adulthood and subsequent positive developmental outcomes in later adulthood.

On the other hand, many personality development researchers have also explored Erikson's belief that women and men experience particular and different sequences of development. Barnett and Baruch (1978) were among the first researchers to suggest that Erikson's model reflected male experience, especially when attempting to understand the experiences of middle-aged women. They observed that both the family life cycle stage and work status are also influences on development, especially for women who have children. Similarly, in more recent research, Kroger (1993, 1997) found inconsistent evidence of gender differences in identity development or in the domain ranked most important for self-definition; she suggested that the context of identity resolution is important for both genders. Miner-Rubino, Winter, and Stewart (2004) found no gender differences in relative preoccupation with identity certainty and generativity, whether assessed concurrently for men and women (in their sixties) or retrospectively (about past ages). Finally, in their study of Black and White South African men and women, Ochse and Plug (1986) suggest that men may also develop their identities through the experience of intimacy, much as Erikson suggested women do.

Though there is little research testing Erikson's epigenetic model, there is some evidence that childhood stages influence adulthood, much as Erikson suggested. In a sequential-design study of psychosocial development in two cohorts of participants in the Rochester Adult Longitudinal Study, Van Manen and Whitbourne (1997) found that levels of industry in college predicted both men's and women's education attainment. However, they also found gender differences concerning the timing of successful stage resolution in relation to predicting future development. For the older cohort (aged 42 in 1988), college psychosocial development scores predicted later life experiences for women, whereas life experiences in the early thirties predicted later psychosocial development scores for men; in fact, those men who had lower status occupations in their thirties were more likely to have higher levels of industry in midlife. The authors suggested that this finding is due to the numbers of men in this cohort who were working on advanced degrees, thus delaying the developmental increase of industry.

Franz and White (1985) suggested revisions to Erikson's theory, noting that his theory emphasizes themes of individuation and deemphasizes the area of attachment or relationships; they proposed, instead, that every stage includes elements of attachment and individuation. Thus, for example, identity is discussed in Erikson's theory entirely in terms of individuation, whereas Franz and White argued that becoming an individual who is both defined and connected to other people (family of origin, teachers, friends, intimates) is the real task, requiring attention to both individuation and attachment. Equally, the task of intimacy is how to retain selfhood in the context of a committed close relationship, a task that requires new capacities for both individuation and attachment.

Some have suggested that Erikson's set of stages is not complete. For example, Vaillant and Koury (1993) proposed two additional stages on either side of generativity. "Career consolidation," situated between the stages of intimacy and generativity, involves the "gathering of technical skills, role definitions, awards, achievements, and work-centered relationships" (p. 3). The authors also commented that in more recent times finding one's occupational niche can often occur later than Erikson proposed (p. 4). The "keeper of the meaning" stage, situated between generativity and ego integrity, involves wisdom and the preservation of culture; unlike the directly generative process of parenting or mentoring, it is a process in which groups or organizations are guided towards preservation of culture or traditions. The concept of extending the generative stage is approached in a similar manner by MacDermid, Franz, and DeReus (1998), who suggested that generativity is taken up in two quite different ways: initially in terms of proximal family issues, and later in terms of other distal social roles. The idea of having concerns that relate to one's close circle versus those relating to a wider circle is also captured by Bradley and Marcia's (1998) measurement of generativity, mentioned above. This involves combinations of the dimensions of involvement and inclusivity for both self and others, resulting in five categories: generative, agentic, communal, conventional, and stagnant.

The most recent addition to Erikson's stage theory to generate interest amongst researchers is Arnett's (2000) concept of emerging adulthood. Arnett conceived of this extra stage as being contiguous with – while also being separate from – identity and intimacy, and occurring between ages 18 and 25 in individuals in industrialized societies. He theorized that the concept has developed in response to large demographic shifts in marriage and work roles in the last 50 years or so (Douglass, 2007), with long-term adult roles being undertaken later in the lifespan. The period of emerging adulthood is distinct in five ways: It is an age of increased identity explorations and instability, self-focus, of feeling in-between, and of increased possibilities. Arnett believes that it is "the most heterogeneous period of the life course" (2007, p. 69). Adulthood is thus "emerging" due to the period's dynamic nature, although as Schwartz, Côté, and Arnett (2005) comment, emerging adults are diverse in their characteristics, with some being well prepared to enter adult roles and responsibilities, whereas others may require external help to do so. Researchers have criticized many of the theory's facets, pointing out that development is not linear, and that the process of identity formation and consolidation is a lifelong task (Hendry & Kloep, 2007). In fact, these researchers go further, criticizing stage theories in general as being only concerned with certain Western cultures, and failing to address gender and class issues. Other specific criticisms of emerging adulthood include that the particular stage is not a universal phenomenon, especially for those who do not attend college (Eccles, Templeton, Barber, & Stone, 2003; Hendry & Kloep, 2007), or do not have the financial means or opportunities that allow for a more leisurely completion of the tasks associated with adulthood (Douglass, 2007). The debate concerning emerging adulthood's usefulness and contribution will no doubt continue.

In research connecting Erikson's theory to life history theory, Dunkel and Sefcek (2009) examined the different ways in which people invest resources (money, time, energy, cognitive resources) in intimate relationships and reproduction. Using identity formation as an example, the authors found that role confusion was associated with low parental investment, early sexual promiscuity, short-term mating strategies, and unstable shallow pair bonds.

An alternative and radical departure from Erikson is the possibility that adult development should be conceived as made up of elements with different developmental trajectories rather than as occurring in discrete stages (McAdams & de St. Aubin, 1998; Stewart & Vandewater, 1998; Zucker, Ostrove & Stewart, 2002). Even researchers who believe that Erikson catalogued important themes and dilemmas in personality development sometimes express doubt about the notion that these themes and dilemmas occur in distinct stages. In her discussion of women's personality development, Josselson (2003) commented that disentangling midlife women's concerns in terms of identity, intimacy, and generativity is extremely difficult (p. 432), further stating "I don't believe there are definable 'stages.' Each woman fits these pieces in place in a sequence and pattern different from those of another" (p. 433).

Social Roles and Personality Development

The notion of a relationship between adult personality development and social roles has been explored in many studies (Barnett & Baruch, 1978; Duncan & Agronick, 1995; Helson, Mitchell, & Moane, 1984; Helson, Pals, & Solomon, 1997; Lodi-Smith & Roberts, 2007; Roberts, Helson, & Klohnen, 2002; Roberts, Walton, Bogg, & Caspi, 2006; Roberts, Wood, & Smith, 2005; Stewart & Vandewater, 1993; Vandewater & Stewart, 1998). In this section we review how facets of psychosocial personality development relate to the social roles people undertake and their investment in these roles, how personality development can influence relationship satisfaction, and how role addition and loss (such as becoming a grandparent or the death of a spouse) can affect personality development. We consider evidence not only about the personality developmental themes proposed by Erikson, but also ones that have been documented in the empirical literature as showing consistent increases or decreases across the lifespan, related to changes in social roles. Thus we are considering Erikson's broader notion of psychosocial origins of personality development in this section, rather than his specific stage-related themes (though we include attention to those when they have been studied in relation to changes in social roles).

In describing the connection between social pressures and personality development, Neugarten proposed that the "social clock," or the normative timing for undertaking social roles such as wife and mother, may provoke adult personality development (Neugarten, Moore, & Lowe, 1996). Neugarten and her colleagues pointed out that there are widely shared beliefs and conventions about the usual and ideal flow of life events, or certain age-appropriate life changes, such as getting married, having children, and retiring. Building on this work, Helson et al. (1984) studied individual differences in patterns of social clock adherence. They highlighted the variability in commitment to "on time" social clock projects in a group of women who graduated from Mills College in 1958 and 1960, and found that these women's midlife personalities had been influenced by their earlier choice of social clock projects. Stewart and Vandewater (1993) further refined this focus with their finding that women's postcollege commitment to different social roles affected their levels of identity and generativity in midlife: Women who committed to a family but not a career at age 28 were more concerned with generativity at age 43, whereas those committed to a career but not a family at age 28 had little focus on generativity at age 43. Similarly, Vandewater and Stewart (1998) found relationships between work and family commitments and personality factors, such as instrumentality, interpersonal orientation, and valuation of social norms. For example, women continuously committed to careers showed high levels of instrumentality and assertiveness, whereas women who had never committed to careers showed relatively low levels of instrumentality, high dependence, low ambition, and low self-reliance. Interestingly, the study highlighted the wisdom of studying women's patterns of commitments over time, given that personality profiles assessed at one time in relation to social roles may be misleading: Women continuously committed to traditional family roles (always married) and those who kept trying such roles (divorced and/or remarried) were most similar to each other regarding positive feelings about social norms.

More recently, research by Newton and Stewart (2010) also found that women committed solely to family in early midlife (their forties) expressed higher levels of generativity in late midlife (their sixties), whereas women committed solely to careers in early midlife expressed higher levels of generativity in late midlife.

However, generative expression has also been found in social roles other than the family. MacDermid, Heilbrun, and DeHaan (1997) explored levels of generativity in employed, married mothers, finding that all three roles (wife, mother, worker) provided areas in which women expressed generativity, although levels of generativity in the parenting role were higher compared to those of wife or worker, and generativity was also higher in the wife rather than worker role. The authors not only highlighted the importance of examining the context of generative expression, but also commented that patterns of work and family have changed for men and women in recent times: There are more women in full-time positions, men are no longer staying in one job throughout their entire career, and couples are having fewer children.

Being psychologically invested in a social role is also an element in the social role–personality development association. Roberts and colleagues found that investment in age-graded social roles such as work and relationships influenced personality development (Roberts, Wood, & Smith, 2005), and that people of all ages held expectations for the behavior associated with the role (Wood & Roberts, 2006). For example, parents were expected to possess relatively high levels of agreeableness and conscientiousness; this also held true for grandparents, although they were also expected to exhibit low levels of extraversion. Those who were employed in the labor force were expected to be closer to the positive end of all Big Five traits. Moreover, actual patterns of personality change over time generally fit these expectations. Conversely, being psychologically deinvested in one's occupation can also affect personality development. In a longitudinal study of 18–26-year-olds, Roberts et al. (2006) found that counterproductive workplace behaviors, such as being late for work or engaging in conflicts with co-workers, was negatively related to social closeness (a blend of sociability and agreeableness). This pattern contradicted normative developmental trends in these traits for this age group.

The people to whom one commits can also influence the quality of the role and one's personality, and vice versa. Engaging in romantic relationships – whether dating, newly wed, or long-term married – has proven to be a rich context in which to study personality development, especially how partners' personalities affect and are affected by relationship satisfaction. However, results are not consistent, possibly due to the wide variety of personality factors studied. For example, Botwin et al. (1997) found that having an agreeable partner was a strong predictor of relationship satisfaction for both men and women in either dating or newly wed relationships; conversely, Holland and Roisman (2008) found that conscientiousness was the most consistent predictor of relationship quality for dating and engaged couples. However, in a similar study of heterosexual dating and married couples, Watson et al. (2000) found differences in the personality factors associated with relationship satisfaction. Specifically, conscientiousness and agreeableness were associated with relationship satisfaction for dating couples, but for married couples, extraversion was associated with relationship satisfaction. This study differs from the previous study in that the married couples had been married (on average) for 17 years; another difference is that both positive and negative affect were associated with relationship satisfaction, as judged by "target" and partner.

Some researchers have also recognized the importance of the broader context in which relationship satisfaction may occur. Gorchoff, John, and Helson (2008) used data collected from women who participated in the Mills College Longitudinal Study at three waves to investigate the relationship between marital satisfaction and presence of children (rather than personality). They found that marital satisfaction increased over middle age, and was linked to the time when children left home. Finally, in research that highlights the interaction of gender, personality, and social role, Roberts, Smith, Jackson, and Edmonds (2009) investigated "compensatory conscientiousness" in married couples, finding that husbands' conscientiousness was associated with better subjective health and fewer physical limitations for their wives, and vice versa. The authors speculate that having a conscientious partner translates to more reliable support, and more constructive advice and feedback concerning issues related to health (p. 556).

The dissolution of a traditional social role can also be related to psychosocial personality development. Social expectations about the type of personality exhibited by people who get divorced may best be summed up as the reverse of expectations for married people in a study conducted by Wood and Roberts (2006): They found that people who were married were expected to be more extraverted, agreeable, conscientious, and more emotionally stable than those who were not. Fahs (2007), in a study of middle-aged female University of Michigan graduates, explored the actual differences between divorced women and married women, finding divorced women to be more liberal and to have an active commitment to feminist identity. The negative aspects of getting a divorce are acknowledged by Roberts et al. (2002), who speculate that the lower rate of increase in Dominance for divorced Mills College women between the ages of 27 and 43 is associated with the disruptive nature of divorce.

More nuanced approaches to the study of divorce uncover differences in the way in which individuals cope with divorce and how these reflect existing and potentially emerging personality factors. Both men and women who achieved the best postdivorce adjustment showed significantly higher levels of traits such as dominance, assertiveness, self-assurance, intelligence, and self-sufficiency in a study by Thomas (1982). Similarly, in a longitudinal study of women in the early stages of separation and divorce, Bursik (1991) found that women who, in response to their changed circumstance, progressed from a low initial level of adjustment to a subsequently high level of adjustment also exhibited increases in levels of ego development. For women (and possibly men) divorce can also lead to "increased freedom from gender-role constraints" (Stewart, Copeland, Chester, Malley, & Barenbaum, 1997, p. 3). Other factors, such as who initiates the divorce, may also be key. Sakraida (2005) found that the transition to divorce differed among women who self-classified as the initiator, the noninitiator, or a mutual decider; initiators spoke of growth and optimism, whereas noninitiators felt abandoned and engaged in rumination.

Interestingly, no distinct personality profile emerged for the mutual deciders. Young, Stewart, and Miner-Rubino (2001) found that women's accounts of their divorces contained developmental themes that were most relevant at the timing of the divorce: Women in their twenties conceived of their divorce mainly in identity terms, women in their thirties in intimacy terms, and those in their forties in terms of the need for new outlets for generative goals.

Though several researchers have focused on issues of identity revision or generativity in midlife as a result of social role change, little has been written regarding potential revision of intimacy issues in midlife. One exception is a longitudinal case study by Mitchell (2007) in which one woman revisits issues of intimacy throughout adulthood. When her marriage of 23 years ended, she was able to view her divorce in retrospect as enabling her to "overhaul" her professional identity and to initiate a new intimate relationship with a woman. Thus in late middle age this individual achieved the kind of intimacy Erikson defined as arising in early adulthood. Case studies such as this one cannot provide a basis for generalization about common patterns for life courses, but they can provide critical insight into the ways common patterns may crucially vary for individuals.

Other life transitions have also received attention from researchers. One such transition is the "empty nest," especially as it relates to women. Although this experience is often couched in negative terms, Barnett and Baruch (1978) provide evidence of increased well-being and decreased depression among women whose children have left home. Perhaps, as they suggest, the negative psychological outcomes of the empty nest may be more prevalent in women whose identity is primarily focused on child-rearing. Gorchoff et al. (2008) found that "transition to an empty nest increases marital satisfaction via an increase in women's enjoyment of time with their partners" (p. 1194).

Another life transition, and one of the few new roles available to older individuals, is becoming a grandparent. Not only is there a set of societal expectations for the type of people grandparents are, but these expectations are borne out in actual development in research by Wood and Roberts (2006). As judged by individuals in all age groups, grandparents were both expected to have – and actually did exhibit – high levels of agreeableness and emotional stability while also being low on extraversion and intellect. Issues such as whether the transition to grandparenthood occurs on- or off-time or investment in the role are also important for subjective aging (Kaufman & Elder, 2003; Thiele & Whelan, 2006). Becoming a grandparent when one is young may accelerate one's subjective aging, although interacting positively with grandchildren may "keep one younger." Grandparenting is often seen as the beginning of old age, or the next (and last) stage of development in the life course, occurring in the context of other changes in social roles such as career progression or retirement, health status, or marital situation. This contextual complexity of role losses and gains prompted Thiele and Whelan to call for the inclusion of grandparenting in future identity research.

Finally, the death of a spouse entails both the loss of a loved one and the loss of a long-held role, and is often associated with change in personality. Mroczek and Spiro (2003), in a sample of 1,663 men aged 43–91 who were surveyed six times over 12 years, found that the death of a spouse was initially associated with an increase in neuroticism but that its subsequent decline was faster for widowers than for those not widowed. They speculate that resiliency may be a possible cohort effect for men who came of age and survived adversity during the Great Depression and World War II (as these did).

As we have seen, there is considerable research concerning adult roles and psychosocial personality development, as well as an expanding body of research concerning how personality and social roles both change in adulthood as a result of the end of a marriage, children leaving home, becoming a grandparent, and dealing with bereavement. Clearly Erikson's emphasis on the dynamic interplay of changing social roles and personality development across the life span is supported by this research.

Conclusion

We have seen that the second half of the 20th century has confirmed the insight that personality develops and changes throughout adulthood. To some extent there is a pattern and regularity to the ways it changes, but there is also considerable variation across individuals in timing, sequence, and emphasis of different preoccupations. That said, issues of identity, intimacy, generativity, and integrity do seem to preoccupy many adults at broadly consistent times in adulthood. Equally importantly, research has confirmed the expected close links among life experiences, important changes in social roles, and personality development. What, then, remains for us to consider in the 21st century?

One important focus for future research is a much more extensive exploration of the roles of culture, race, ethnicity, and sexual orientation in providing a context for personality development, and indeed in shaping its very nature. We have pointed to a few empirical studies in different cultures (e.g., Ochse and Plug, 1986) and a few concepts that may reflect cultural differences (e.g., *Sehnsucht*; see Scheibe et al., 2007). We need much more research that focuses on articulating how personality development may be different – even in subtle ways – both across cultures and in particular diverse groups within a large and heterogeneous culture.

Equally, we know relatively little about how social structure provides a context for personality development in adulthood. In this chapter we have seen evidence of the important role of gender in theory and in some studies. Some studies have assumed its importance in research on women (e.g., Pals, 1999; Stewart et al., 2001; Whitbourne & Skultety, 2006) or men (Snarey et al., 1987). Miner-Rubino et al. (2004) examined the roles of both gender and social class. We know that social structure shapes opportunities and life experiences, including social roles. Nevertheless, we have very few studies that address directly the impact of gender, class, and race as social structures in shaping personality development in adulthood and its relationship to social role transitions or other aspects of social experience.

We have noted instances where researchers have pointed to the importance of historical events and periods as context for personality development. Several longitudinal researchers have particularly emphasized the importance of generations or cohort-linked experiences in their research on personality development (Duncan & Agronick, 1995; Helson et al., 1995; Whitbourne & Willis, 2006). These studies focus on the power of particular events to shape generational identities, as well as subsequent adult experiences (see also Stewart & Healy, 1989).

In short, the next task for scholars of adulthood development is to articulate in theoretical terms how these different aspects of the social context – culture, structure, and significant events – may be expected to influence both social roles and experiences in adulthood and personality development. (Of course the fields of sociology and history have resources for us here.) It is equally important for us to develop research methods that allow us to investigate directly how these macrosocial contexts matter for individuals' experience of their own lives.

References

Arnett, J. J. (2000). Emerging adulthood. *American Psychologist, 55*(5), 469–480.

Arnett, J. J. (2007). Emerging adulthood: What is it, and what is it good for? *Child Development Perspectives Special Issue: Emerging Adulthood Around the World, 1*(2), 68–73.

Baltes, P. B., & Smith, J. (1999). Multilevel and systematic analyses of old age: Theoretical and empirical evidence for a fourth age. In V. L. Bengtson & K. W. Schaie (Eds.), *Handbook of theories of aging* (pp. 153–173). New York: Springer.

Barnett, R. C., & Baruch, G. K. (1978). Women in the middle years: A critique of research and theory. *Psychology of Women Quarterly, 3,* 187–197.

Block, J. (1961). *The Q-sort method in personality assessment and psychiatric research*. Oxford: Charles C. Thomas.

Block, J. (1971). *Lives through time.* Berkeley, CA: Bancroft Books.

Botwin, M. D., Buss, D. M., & Shackelford, T. K. (1997). Personality and mate preferences: Five factors in mate selection and marital satisfaction. *Journal of Personality, 65*(1), 107–136.

Bradley, C. L., & Marcia, J. E. (1998). Generativity-stagnation: A five-category model. *Journal of Personality, 66*(1), 40–64.

Bursik, K. (1991). Adaptation to divorce and ego development in adult women. *Journal of Personality and Social Psychology, 60*(2), 300–326.

Butler, R. (1974). Successful aging and the role of life review. *Journal of the American Geriatrics Society, 22,* 529–535.

Clark, M., & Arnold, J. (2008). The nature, prevalence, and correlates of generativity among men in middle career. *Journal of Vocational Behavior, 73,* 473–484.

Constantinople, A. (1969). An Eriksonian measure of personality development in college students. *Developmental Psychology, 1,* 357–372.

Darling-Fischer, C. S., & Leidy, N. K. (1988). Measuring Eriksonian development in the adult: The modified Erikson Psychosocial Stage Inventory. *Psychological Reports, 62,* 747–754.

Douglass, C. B. (2007). From duty to desire: Emerging adulthood in Europe and its consequences. *Child Development Perspectives Special Issue: Emerging Adulthood Around the World, 1*(2), 101–108.

Duncan, L. E., & Agronick, G. S. (1995). The intersection of life stage and social events: Personality and life outcomes. *Journal of Personality and Social Psychology, 69,* 558–568.

Dunkel, C. S., & Sefcek, J. A. (2009). Eriksonian lifespan theory and life history theory: An integration using the example of identity formation. *Review of General Psychology, 13*(1), 13–23.

Eccles, J., Templeton, J., Barber, B., & Stone, M. (2003). Adolescence and emerging adulthood: The critical passage ways to adulthood. In M. Bornstein, L. Davidson, C. L. Keyes, & K. A. Moore (Eds.), *Well-being: Positive development across the life course* (pp. 383–406). Mahwah, NJ: Erlbaum.

Edelstein, R. S., & Gillath, O. (2008). Avoiding interference: Adult attachment and emotional processing biases. *Personality and Social Psychology Bulletin, 34*(2), 171–181.

Erikson, E. H. (1950). *Childhood and society*. New York: Norton.

Erikson, E. H. (1959). Identity and the life cycle: Selected papers. *Psychological Issues, 1,* 1–171.

Erikson, E. H. (1962). *Young man Luther: A study in psychoanalysis and history*. New York: Norton.

Erikson, E. H. (1963). *Childhood and society* (Rev. ed.) New York: Norton.

Erikson, E. H. (1968). *Identity: Youth and crisis*. New York: Norton.

Erikson, E. H. (1969). *Gandhi's truth*. New York: Norton.

Erikson, E. H. (1974). *Dimensions of a new identity: The 1973 Jefferson Lectures in the Humanities*. Oxford: Norton.

Erikson, E. H. (1982). *The life cycle completed*. New York: Norton.

Erikson, E. H., Erikson, J. M. & Kivnick, H. Q. (1986). *Vital involvement in old age*. New York: Norton.

Espin, O., Stewart, A. J., & Gomez, C. A. (1990). Letters from V: Adolescent personality development in sociohistorical context. *Journal of Personality, 58*(2), 347–363.

Fahs, B. (2007). Second shifts and political awakenings: Divorce and the political socialization of middle-aged women. *Journal of Divorce and Remarriage, 47*(3/4), 43–66.

Fitch, S. A., & Adams, G. R. (1983). Ego identity and intimacy status: Replication and extension. *Developmental Psychology, 19*(6), 839–845.

Fraley, R. C., & Shaver, P. R. (2000). Adult romantic attachment: Theoretical developments, emerging controversies, and unanswered questions. *Review of General Psychology, 4*(2), 132–154.

Franz, C. E. (1994). Reconstituting the self: The role of history, personality and loss in one woman's life. In C. E. Franz and A. J. Stewart (Eds.), *Women creating lives: Identities, resilience, & resistance* (pp. 213–226). Boulder, CO: Westview.

Franz, C. E. (1995). A quantitative case study of longitudinal changes in identity, intimacy, and generativity. *Journal of Personality, 63*(1), 27–46.

Franz, C. E., & White, K. M. (1985). Individuation and attachment in personality development: Extending Erikson's theory. *Journal of Personality, 53*(2), 224–256.

Gold, J. M., & Rogers, J. D. (1995). Intimacy and isolation: A validation study of Erikson's theory. *Journal of Humanistic Psychology, 35,* 78–86.

Gorchoff, S. M., John, O. P., & Helson, R. (2008). Contextualizing change in marital satisfaction during middle age: An 18-year longitudinal study. *Psychological Science, 19*(11), 1194–2000.

Gramling, L. F. (2007). Women in young and mid-adulthood: Theory advancement and retroduction. *Advances in Nursing, 30*(2), 95–107.

Greenberger, E. (1984). Defining psychosocial maturity in adolescence. *Advances in Child Behavioral Analysis & Therapy, 3,* 1–37.

Grotevant, H. D., & Cooper, C. R. (1985). Patterns of interaction in family relationships and the development of identity exploration in adolescence. *Child development, 56*(2), 415–428.

Hatton, H., Donnellan, M. B., Maysn, K., Feldman, B. J., Larsen-Rife, D., & Conger, R. D. (2008). Family and individual difference predictors of trait aspects of negative interpersonal behaviors during emerging adulthood. *Journal of Family Psychology, 22*(3), 448–455.

Hazan, C, & Shaver, P. (1987). Conceptualizing romantic love as an attachment process. *Journal of Personality and Social Psychology, 52,* 511–524.

Hazan, C, & Shaver, P. R. (1994). Attachment as an organizationalframework for research on close relationships. *Psychological Inquiry,5,* 1–22.

Helson, R., Mitchell, V., & Moane, G. (1984). Personality and patterns of adherence and nonadherence to the social clock. *Journal of Personality and Social Psychology,46*(5), 1079–1096.

Helson, R., Pals, J., & Solomon, M. (1997). Is there adult development distinctive to women? In R. Hogan, J. Johnson, & S. Briggs (Eds.), *Handbook of personality psychology* (pp. 291–314). San Diego, CA: Academic Press.

Helson, R., & Soto, C. J. (2005). Up and down in middle age: Monotonic and nonmonotonic changes in roles, status, and personality. *Journal of Personality and Social Psychology, 89*(2), 194–204.

Helson, R., Stewart, A. J., & Ostrove, J. (1995). Identity in three cohorts of midlife women. *Journal of Personality and Social Psychology, 69*(3), 544–557.

Hendry, L. B., & Kloep, M. (2007). Conceptualizing emerging adulthood: Inspecting the emperor's new clothes? *Child Development Perspectives Special Issue: Emerging Adulthood Around the World, 1*(2), 74–79.

Holland, A. S., & Roisman, G. I. (2008). Big Five personality traits and relationship quality: Self-reported, observational, and physiological evidence. *Journal of Social and Personal Relationships, 25*(5), 811–829.

Horst, G. A. (1995). Reexamining gender issues in Erikson's stages of identity and intimacy. *Journal of Counseling and Development, 73*(3), 271–278.

James, J. B., & Zarett, N. (2006). Ego integrity in the lives of older women. *Journal of Adult Development, 12*(4), 61–75.

Josselson, R. (2003). Revisions: Processes in development in midlife women. In J. Demick & C. Andreotti (Eds.), *Handbook of adult development* (pp. 431–441). New York: Kluwer.

Kaufman, G., & Elder, G. H. Jr. (2003). Grandparenting and age identity. *Journal of Aging Studies, 17,* 269–282.

Konik, J., & Stewart, A. J. (2004). Sexual identity development in the context of compulsory heterosexuality. *Journal of Personality, 72,* 815–844.

Kotre, J. (1984). *Outliving the self.* Baltimore: Johns Hopkins University Press.

Kroger, J. (1993). Identity and context: How the identity statuses choose their match. In R. Josselson & A. Lieblich (Eds.), *The narrative study of lives* (Vol. 1, pp. 130–162). Newbury Park, CA: Sage.

Kroger, J. (1997). Gender and identity: The intersection of structure, content, and context. *Sex Roles, 36*(11/12), 747–770.

Kroger, J. (2002). Identity processes and contents through the years of late adulthood. *Identity, 2*(1), 81–99.

Lee, M. D., Dohring, P. L., MacDermid, S. M., & Kossek, E. E. (2005). Professionals becoming parents: Socialization, adaptation, and identity transformation. In E. E. Kossek & S. J. Lambert (Eds.), *Work and life integration: Organizational, cultural, and individual perspectives* (pp. 287–317). Mahwah, NJ: Erlbaum.

Lodi-Smith, J., & Roberts, B. W. (2007). Social investment and personality: A meta-analysis of the relationship of personality traits to investment in work, family, religion, and volunteerism. *Personality and Social Psychology Review, 11,* 68–86.

MacDermid, S., Franz, C. E., & De Reus, L. A. (1998). Generativity at the crossroads of social roles and personality. In D. P. McAdams and E. de St. Aubin (Eds.), *Generativity and adult development* (pp. 181–226). Washington, DC: American Psychological Association.

MacDermid, S. M., Heilbrun, G., & DeHaan, L. G. (1997). The generativity of employed mothers in multiple roles: 1979 and 1991. In M. E. Lachman & J. B. James (Eds.), *Multiple paths to midlife development* (pp. 207–240). Chicago: University of Chicago Press.

Marcia, J. E. (1966). Development and validation of ego identity status. *Journal of Personality and Social Psychology, 5,* 551–558.

Mayser, S., Scheibe, S., & Riediger, M. (2008). (Un)reachable? An empirical differentiation of goals and life longings. *European Psychologist, 13*(2), 126–140.

McAdams, D. P. (2001). Generativity in midlife. In M. E. Lachman (Ed.), *Handbook of midlife development* (pp. 395–443). Hoboken, NJ: Wiley.

McAdams, D. P., & de St. Aubin, E. (1992). A theory of generativity and its assessment through self-report, behavioral acts, and narrative themes in autobiography. *Journal of Personality and Social Psychology, 62,* 1003–1015.

McAdams, D. P., & de St. Aubin, E. (1998). *Generativity and adult development: How and why we care for the next generation.* Washington, DC: American Psychological Association.

McAdams, D. P., de St. Aubin, E., & Logan, R. L. (1993). Generativity among young, midlife, and older adults. *Psychology and Aging, 8*(22), 221–230.

Mikulincer, M., & Shaver, P. R. (2005). Attachment theory and emotions in close relationships: Exploring the attachment-related dynamics of emotional reactions to relational events. *Personal Relationships, 12,* 149–168.

Miner-Rubino, K., Winter, D. G., & Stewart, A. J. (2004). Gender, social class, and the subjective experience of aging: Self-perceived personality change from early adulthood to late midlife. *Personality and Social Psychology Bulletin, 30*(12),1599–1610.

Mitchell, V. (2007). Earning a secure attachment style: A narrative of personality change in adulthood. In R. Josselson, A. Lieblich, & D. P. McAdams (Eds.), *The meaning of others: Narrative studies of relationships* (pp. 93–116). Washington, DC: American Psychological Association.

Morgan, C. D., & Murray, H. H. (1935). A method for investigating fantasies: The Thematic Apperception Test. *Archives of Neurology and Psychiatry (Chicago), 34,* 289–306.

Mroczek, D. K., & Spiro, A. (2003). Modeling intraindividual change in personality traits: Findings from the normative aging study. *Journal of Gerontology: Psychological Sciences 58B(3),* 153–165.

Neugarten, B., Moore, J. W., & Lowe, J. C. (1996). Age norms, age constraints, and adult socializations. In D. A. Neugarten (Ed.), *The meanings of age: Selected papers of Bernice L. Neugarten* (pp. 24–33). Chicago: University of Chicago Press.

Newton, N. J., & Stewart, A. J. (2010). The middle ages: Change in women's personalities and social roles. *Psychology of Women Quarterly, 34,* 39–48.

Ochse, R., & Plug, C. (1986). Cross-cultural investigation of the validity of Erikson's theory of personality development. *Journal of Personality and Social Psychology, 50*(6), 1240–1252.

Orlofsky, J. L., Marcia, J. E., & Lesser, I. M. (1973). Ego identity status and the intimacy versus isolation crisis of young adulthood. *Journal of Personality and Social Psychology, 27*(2), 211–219.

Pals, J. (1999). Identity consolidation in early adulthood: Relations with ego-resiliency, the context of marriage, and personality change. *Journal of Personality, 67,* 295–329.

Peterson, B. E. (2002). Longitudinal analysis of midlife generativity, intergenerational roles, and caregiving. *Psychology and Aging, 17*(1), 161–168.

Peterson, B. E., & Klohnen, E. C. (1995). Realization of generativity in two samples of women at midlife. *Psychology and Aging, 10*(1), 20–29.

Peterson, B. E., & Stewart, A. J. (1990). Using personal and fictional documents to assess psychosocial development: A case study of Vera Brittain's generativity. *Psychology and Aging, 5*(3), 400–411.

Peterson, B. E., & Stewart, A. J. (1993). Generativity and social motives in young adults. *Journal of Personality and Social Psychology, 65*(1), 186–198.

Peterson, B. E., & Stewart, A. J. (1996). Antecedents and context of generativity motivation at midlife. *Psychology and Aging, 11*(1), 21–33.

Pratt, M. W., Norris, J. E., Gressman, K., Lawford, H., & Hebblethwaite, S. (2008). Parents' stories of grandparenting concerns in the three-generational family: Generativity, optimism, and forgiveness. *Journal of Personality, 76*(3), 581–604.

Roberts, B. W., Helson, R., & Klohnen, E. C. (2002). Personality development and growth in women across 30 years: Three perspectives. *Journal of Personality, 70*(1), 79–102.

Roberts, B. W., Smith, J., Jackson, J. J., & Edmonds, G. (2009). Compensatory conscientiousness and health in older couples. *Psychological Science 20*(5), 553–559.

Roberts, B. W., Walton, K., Bogg, T., & Caspi, A. (2006). De-investment in work and non-normative personality trait change in young adulthood. *European Journal of Personality, 20*, 461–474.

Roberts, B. W., Wood, D., & Smith, J. L. (2005). Evaluating Five Factor Theory and social investment perspectives on personality development. *Journal of Research in Personality 39*, 166–184.

Rosenthal, D. A., Gurney, R. M., & Moore, S. M. (1981). From trust to intimacy: A new inventory for examining Erikson's stages of psychosocial development. *Journal of Youth and Adolescence, 10*(6), 525–537.

Rothrauff, T., & Cooney, T. M. (2008). The role of generativity in psychological well-being: Does it differ for childless adults and parents? *Journal of Adult Development, 15*, 148–159.

Rowe, I., & Marcia, J. E. (1980). Ego identity status, formal operations, and moral development. *Journal of Youth and Adolescence, 9*(2), 87–99.

Ryff, C. D., & Heincke, S. G. (1983). Subjective organization of personality in adulthood and aging. *Journal of Personality and Social Psychology, 44*(4), 807–816.

Sakraida, T. J. (2005). Divorce transition differences of midlife women. *Issues in Mental Health Nursing, 26*, 225–249.

Schachner, D. A., Shaver, P. R., & Gillath, O. (2008). Attachment style and long-term singlehood. *Personal Relationships, 15*, 479–491.

Scheibe, S., Freund, A. M., & Baltes, P. B. (2007). Toward a developmental psychology of *Sehnsucht* (life longings): The optimal (utopian) life. *Developmental Psychology 43*(3), 778–795.

Schiedel, D. G., & Marcia, J. E. (1985). Ego identity, intimacy, sex role orientation, and gender. *Developmental Psychology, 21*(1), 149–150.

Schwartz, S. J., Côté, J. E., & Arnett, J. J. (2005). Identity and agency in emerging adulthood: Two developmental routes in the individualization process. *Youth & Society, 37*(2), 201–229.

Skultety, K. M., & Whitbourne, S. K. (2004). Gender differences in identity processes and self-esteem in middle and later adulthood. *Journal of Women & Aging, 16*, 175–188.

Snarey, J., Son, L., Kuehne, V. S., Hauser, S., & Vaillant, G. (1987). The role of parenting in men's psychosocial development: A longitudinal study of early adulthood infertility and midlife generativity. *Developmental Psychology, 23*, 593–603.

Sneed, J. R., & Whitbourne, S. K. (2001). Identity processing styles and the need for self-esteem in middle-aged and older adults. *International Journal of Aging & Human Development, 52*(4), 311–321.

Stephen, J., Fraser, E., & Marcia, J. E. (1992). Moratorium-achievement (Mama) cycles in lifespan identity development: Value orientations and reasoning system correlates. *Journal of Adolescence, 15*, 283–300.

St. Louis, G. R., & Liem, J. H. (2005). Ego identity, ethnic identity, and the psychosocial well-being of ethnic minority and majority of college students. *Identity: An International Journal of Theory and Research, 5*(3), 227–246.

Stein, J. A., & Newcombe, M. D. (1999). Adult outcomes of adolescent conventional and agentic orientations: A 20-year longitudinal study. *The Journal of Early Adolescence, 19*, 39–65.

Stewart, A. J., Copeland, A. P., Chester, N. L., Malley, J. E., & Barenbaum, N. B. (1997). *Separating together*. New York: Guilford Press.

Stewart, A. J., Franz, C. E., & Layton, L. B. (1988). The changing self: Using personal documents to study lives. *Journal of Personality, 56*(1), 41–74.

Stewart, A. J., Franz, C. E., Paul, E. P., & Peterson, B. E. (1991). *Revised coding manual for three aspects of adult personality development: Identity, intimacy, and generativity.* Unpublished coding manual, Department of Psychology, University of Michigan.

Stewart, A. J., & Healy, J.M., Jr. (1989). Linking individual development and social changes. *American Psychologist, 44*(1), 30–42.

Stewart, A. J., & Ostrove, J. M. (1998). Women's personality in middle age: Gender, history, and midcourse corrections. *American Psychologist, 53*(11), 1185–1194.

Stewart, A. J., Ostrove, J. M., & Helson, R. (2001). Middle aging in women: Patterns of personality change from the 30s to the 50s. *Journal of Adult Development, 8*(1), 23–37.

Stewart, A. J., & Vandewater, E. A. (1993). The Radcliffe class of 1964: Career and social clock projects in a transitional cohort. In K. D. Hulbert & D. T. Schuster (Eds.), *Women's lives through time: Educated American women of the twentieth century* (pp. 235–258). San Francisco, CA: Jossey-Bass Inc.

Stewart, A. J., & Vandewater, E. A. (1998). The course of generativity. In D. P. McAdams & E. de St. Aubin (Eds.), *Generativity and adult development* (pp. 75–100). Washington, DC: American Psychological Association.

Stewart, A. J., & Vandewater, E. A. (1999). "If I had it to do over again. . .": Midlife review, midcourse corrections, and women's well-being in midlife. *Journal of Personality and Social Psychology, 76,* 270–283.

Sturaro, C., Denissen, J. J. A., van Aken, M. A. G., & Asendorpf, J. B. (2008). Person-environment transactions during emerging adulthood: The interplay between personality characteristics and social relationships. *European Psychologist, 13*(1), 1–11.

Tesch, S. A., & Whitbourne, S. K. (1982). Intimacy and identity status in young adults. *Journal of Personality and Social Psychology, 43*(5), 1041–1051.

Thiele, D. M., & Whelan, T. A. (2006). The nature and dimensions of the grandparent role. *Marriage & Family Review, 40*(1), 93–108.

Thomas, S. P. (1982). After divorce: Personality factors related to the process of adjustment. *Journal of Divorce, 5*(3), 19–36.

Torges, C. M., Stewart, A. J., & Duncan, L. E. (2008). Achieving ego integrity: Personality development in late midlife. *Journal of Research in Personality, 42,* 1004–1019.

Torges, C. M., Stewart, A. J., & Duncan, L. E. (2009). Appreciating life's complexities: Assessing narrative ego integrity in late midlife. *Journal of Research in Personality, 43,* 66–74.

Vaillant, G. E., & Koury, S. H. (1993). Late midlife development. In G. H. Pollock & S. I. Greenspan (Eds.), *The course of life, Vol. 6: Late adulthood* (pp. 1–22). Madison, CT: International Universities Press.

Van Manen, K.-J., & Whitbourne, S. K. (1997). Psychological development and life experiences in adulthood: A 22-year sequential study. *Psychology and Aging, 12*(2), 239–246.

Vandewater, E. A., & Stewart, A. J. (1998). Making commitments, creating lives: Linking women's roles and personality at midlife. *Psychology of Women Quarterly, 22,* 717–738.

Walaskay, M., Whitbourne, S. K., & Nehrke, M. F. (1983–84). Construction and validation of an ego integrity status interview. *International Journal of Aging and Human Development, 18*(1), 61–72.

Waterman, A. (1982). Identity development from adolescence to adulthood: An extension of theory and a review of research. *Developmental Psychology, 18*(3), 341–358.

Watson, D., Hubbard, B., & Wiese, D. (2000). General traits of personality and affectivity as predictors of satisfaction in intimate relationships: Evidence from self- and partner-ratings. *Journal of Personality, 68*(3), 413–449.

Whitbourne, S. K., & Skultety, K. M. (2006). Aging and identity: How women face later life transitions. In J. Worell & C. D. Goodheart (Eds.), *Handbook of girls' and women's psychological health* (pp. 370–378). New York: Oxford University Press.

Whitbourne, S. K., Sneed, J. R., & Sayer, A. (2009). Psychosocial development from college through midlife: A 34-year sequential study. *Developmental Psychology 45*(5), 1328–1340.

Whitbourne, S. K., & Waterman, A. S. (1979). Psychosocial development in young adulthood: Age and cohort comparisons. *Developmental Psychology, 15,* 373–378.

Whitbourne, S. K., & Willis, S.L. (2006). *The baby boomers grow up: Contemporary perspectives on midlife*. Mahwah, NJ: Erlbaum.

Wood, D., & Roberts, B. W. (2006). The effect of age and role information on expectations for big five personality traits. *Personality and Social Psychology Bulletin, 32*(11), 1482–1496.

Wrosch, C., Bauer, I., & Scheier, M. F. (2005). Regret and quality of life across the adult lifespan: The influence of disengagement and available future goals. *Psychology and Aging, 20*(4), 657–670.

Young, A. M., Stewart, A. J., & Miner-Rubino, K. (2001). Women's understandings of their own divorces: A developmental perspective. In D. P. McAdams, R. Josselson, & A. Lieblich (Eds.), *Turns in the road: Narrative stories of lives in transition* (pp. 203–226). Washington, DC: American Psychological Association.

Zimmer-Gembeck, M. J., & Petherick, J. (2006). Intimacy dating goals and relationship satisfaction during adolescence and emerging adulthood: Identity formation, age, and sex as moderators. *International Journal of behavioral Development, 30*(2), 167–177.

Zucker, A. N., Ostrove, J. M., & Stewart, A. J. (2002). College-educated women's personality development in adulthood: Perceptions and age differences. *Psychology and Aging, 17*(2), 236–244.

12

Socioemotional Perspectives on Adult Development

Jennifer Tehan Stanley and Derek M. Isaacowitz

Despite stereotypical thinking about aging that focuses on the losses that occur in late adulthood (such as memory problems and general "slowing down"), psychological research often suggests a more textured story, and research on socioemotional aging is no exception. Like cognition, there are aspects of socioemotional aging that show decline, similar to aspects of fluid intelligence such as episodic memory (Bäckman, Small, & Wahlin, 2001) and processing speed (Salthouse, 1996), but there also some that show stability or improvement with age, similar to crystallized intelligence (i.e., knowledge; Schaie, 1996). While overall cognition declines with age, it is not as bad as people think: Many aspects of cognition decline, some remain stable, and still others improve with age. Socioemotional aging is nearly the flipside of this; many aspects of socioemotional functioning show improvement with age, some exhibit stability, and others decline with age. Thus socioemotional aging is good, and perhaps better than people think. None-theless, as indicated from the empirical evidence reviewed below, the pattern of socio-emotional aging *is* positive, but not wholly positive.

Our consideration of the generally, but not entirely, positive story of emotion and aging is based on two fundamental assumptions. First we approach the literature from a lifespan developmental perspective (Baltes, 1987), emphasizing growth and loss throughout development. Within this framework, it makes sense to ask about positive as well as negative trajectories. Secondly, because many aspects of socioemotional functioning do not depend on an ability to quickly process information or recall information from short-term memory (Consedine, 2010; Shiota & Levenson, 2009) – functions that show age-

The Wiley-Blackwell Handbook of Adulthood and Aging, First Edition. Edited by Susan Krauss Whitbourne and Martin J. Sliwinski. © 2012 Blackwell Publishing Ltd. Published 2012 by Blackwell Publishing Ltd.

related declines (Bäckman et al., 2001) – this is an arena where age-related gains in *experience* carry some cachet and warrant serious consideration (Williams et al., 2006).

Socioemotional functioning is a conceptual class of skills and abilities that relate to how individuals navigate through the social and emotional events of their daily lives. Socioemotional functioning in the context of aging subsumes questions such as: How do people feel on a daily basis as they grow older? Are people more or less satisfied with life in late adulthood compared to young adulthood? Socioemotional functioning also refers to how individuals handle interpersonal conflict and whether they are able to understand the emotional cues of social partners, such as facial expressions. Thus this chapter on socioemotional functioning in adulthood examines how these social and emotional abilities change (or do not change) as people grow older.

In this review, we focus on normative healthy aging, so we will not be addressing age differences in socioemotional functioning among individuals with pathology such as Alzheimer's disease. The chapter begins with the main descriptive findings of socioemotional aging organized by methodology – self-report data and experimental – and concludes by describing the theories most frequently used to explain these findings, and a consideration of what we believe to be the critical questions to be answered in the coming years. Researchers in this area face the challenge of understanding and explaining the mechanisms responsible for producing this textured pattern of socioemotional aging. The field is at a theoretical crossroads where emerging evidence has revealed a more complicated picture than current theories may parsimoniously explain. It is both an exciting and challenging time, as researchers attempt to describe the origins of the mostly positive – but not all positive – profile of socioemotional functioning in late adulthood.

The main research findings on socioemotional aging can be categorized by topic and methodology. We consider empirical findings on topics ranging from emotional experience, emotion regulation, social networks, and emotion recognition. The methods used to investigate how these processes do and do not change with age can be categorized broadly as either self-report questionnaire or experimental evidence.

Self-Report Questionnaire Data

A major method of research in socioemotional aging is to simply use a questionnaire to ask people of different ages how they feel. This method has high face validity, and it is fairly inexpensive so large sample sizes can be obtained. However, critics of self-report data worry that individuals may not have direct access to their feelings (Nisbett & Wilson, 1977). A host of other issues with self-report, such as socially desirable responding, question order effects, and other context effects must be taken into consideration when interpreting such findings (see Schwarz & Strack, 1999, for a review), especially given evidence that these context effects manifest differentially in young and older adults (Schwarz, Park, Knäuper, & Sudman, 1999).

In addition, many affect questionnaires require participants to reflect back over a week or a day to how often and intensely they felt certain emotions. However, it is difficult for people to accurately recall the intensity and frequency of their feelings (Thomas & Diener,

1990). Given the challenges older adults face with episodic memory (Bäckman et al., 2001), questionnaires that require such recall of past feelings pose special concern for researchers. One recent innovative way to avoid this *retrospective bias* is to use an experience-sampling methodology where participants are signaled throughout the day to record their current feelings on cell phones or personal digital assistants (Csikszentmihalyi & Larson, 1992). Although self-report data may not be 100% accurate, such information does provide a pulse of overall age differences in how people report feeling. Thus self-report data can certainly be an informative *relative* measure of affect, comparing individuals' responses across the lifespan, as long as response biases do not systematically differ with age.

In self-report data, positive and negative affect exhibit interesting trends in later adulthood. Although positive and negative affect may seem like two sides of the same coin, research shows that these two concepts are actually distinct dimensions with distinct trajectories across the lifespan (Lawton, Kleban, Dean, Rajagopal, & Parmelee, 1992).

Emotional experience

How do people feel as they get older? Are they depressed and downtrodden by the myriad losses in physical prowess and cognitive sharpness (Bäckman et al., 2001; Salthouse, 1996; Shephard, 1999)? Evidence from cross-sectional and longitudinal studies suggests quite the contrary. Both young and older adults share a common misconception that happiness declines with age (Lacey, Smith, & Ubel, 2006), but older adults actually report feeling just as positive, if not more so, as their younger counterparts.

Maintenance of positive affect with age.   Turning to age-related differences and changes in reported positive emotional experience, research suggests either maintenance or even small increases in positive affect with increasing age. Specifically, most of the findings from cross-sectional studies suggest that older adults are no different from young adults in reported frequency and intensity of positive emotions (e.g., joy, enthusiasm, interest; Barrick, Hutchinson, & Deckers, 1989; Carstensen, Pasupathi, Mayr, & Nesselroade, 2000; Charles et al., 2010; Chipperfield, Perry, & Weiner, 2003). Some studies even find that older adults report experiencing more positive affect than their younger counterparts (E.-M. Kessler & Staudinger, 2009; Kunzmann, Little, & Smith, 2000; Mroczek & Kolarz, 1998; cf. Costa, Zonderman, McCrae, & Cornoni-Huntley, 1987; Diener & Suh, 1998; Stacey & Gatz, 1991). Evidence from longitudinal studies is more mixed: Some studies find no age changes in positive affect (i.e., positive affect remains stable across the lifespan; Costa et al., 1987); while other studies have found a small decrease in positive affect over time (Charles, Reynolds, & Gatz, 2001; Stacey & Gatz, 1991).

What can account for this discrepancy in findings? One possibility is that some studies included participants who could be considered among the oldest-old age group (from late eighties; Isaacowitz & Smith, 2003), while other studies focus more on the young-old (people in their 6th and 7th decades). The increased likelihood of physical, cognitive, and health constraints among the oldest-old compared to the young-old (Bäckman, Small, Wahlin, & Larsson, 2000; Zhao et al., 2010) may contribute to a downward trend in emotional well-being in very late life. Indeed, in one cross-sectional study of age differences in affect (Kunzmann et al., 2000), the initial finding was that older adults had *lower* positive affect than young adults. However, after statistically controlling for functional health constraints, the relationship was reversed such that older adults exhibited *higher* positive affect than young adults. Another possible source for studies finding different patterns lies in the types of emotion adjectives rated. Older adults tend to endorse feeling low-arousal positive emotions (e.g., serene, relaxed) more than young adults but do not differ from young adults in feelings of self-reported high-arousal positive emotions (e.g., elated, excited; E.-M. Kessler & Staudinger, 2009). Thus some of the discrepant findings in the literature could be due to across-study differences in the arousal levels of the affective words rated. Although somewhat mixed, taken together these findings suggest overall maintenance of positive affect in later adulthood.

Decreased negative affect with age.   The research on negative affect (e.g., depressed, unhappy, lonely) and aging is less mixed than that on positive affect. The majority of cross-sectional and longitudinal studies suggest that the frequency of reporting negative affect is lower at older ages (Barrick et al., 1989; Carstensen et al., 2000; Charles et al., 2010; Charles et al., 2001; Costa et al., 1987; Gross et al., 1997; E.-M. Kessler & Staudinger, 2009; R. C. Kessler, Foster, Webster, & House, 1992; Kunzmann et al., 2000; Mroczek & Kolarz, 1998; Stacey & Gatz, 1991). This age-related decrease was found to be true for both high-arousal negative emotions (e.g., anxious, annoyed) and low-arousal negative emotions (e.g., sluggish, dull) (E.-M. Kessler & Staudinger, 2009). Some studies, both cross-sectional and longitudinal, have found that negative affect remains stable with age, rather than decreasing (Costa et al., 1987; Diener & Suh, 1998; Kunzmann et al., 2000). Overall, however, the majority of research finds small decreases in negative affect with age.

Related to experienced negative affect is the occurrence of depressive symptoms. Initially, people assume that older adults are more likely to be depressed than young because of all of the negative changes in social, physical, and cognitive domains that occur with age. Actually, data from two large national surveys suggest a curvilinear relationship of depressive symptoms with age such that self-reported depressive symptoms decline from young adulthood to middle age, with their lowest point around ages 50 and 60 (R. C. Kessler et al., 1992). Depressive symptoms then increase again into advanced old age. Thus older adults *do not* appear to experience more depressive symptoms than young adults, at least in cross-sectional data.

Findings from experience-sampling research generally converge with the survey data. For example, experience-sampling studies have shown that daily negative affect decreases with age until about age 60 and then levels off (Carstensen et al., 2000); older adults are less likely than young adults to report experiencing anger when recalling interpersonal tensions (Birditt & Fingerman, 2003); and report fewer interpersonal tensions and experience less stress, even when age differences in exposure to problems were controlled (Birditt, Fingerman, & Almeida, 2005). A recent study found that among an older sample of women age differences in the occurrence of daily stressors accounted for less frequent negative affect (Charles et al., 2010). Similarly, in an age-comparison study, older adults reported less daily negative affect than young adults, but also reported reduced exposure to stressors compared to young adults (Stawski, Sliwinski, Almeida, & Smyth, 2008). Thus, while research on self-reported negative affect consistently finds small age-related decreases in experienced negative affect, the mechanisms underlying these differences are less clear.

Age differences in emotional stability.   Recent work has started to investigate whether there are age differences in the degree of fluctuation of negative and positive affect on a daily basis. Consistent with a preservation of the emotional system with age, intraindividual variability in affect does not seem to increase with age. In a daily diary study spanning nine weeks, older adults actually had less variability in reported positive and (to some degree) negative affect than young adults (Röcke, Li, & Smith, 2009).

Subjective well-being

Research on life satisfaction (e.g., responses to the question *How satisfied are you currently with your life, all things considered?*) finds that levels of well-being remain relatively stable with age (Diener, Suh, Lucas, & Smith, 1999; Diener & Suh, 1998) until about 4 years prior to death, at which point there is a tripling in the rate of decline of life satisfaction (Gerstorf et al., 2008; Gerstorf et al., 2010). This decline in life satisfaction parallels a terminal drop, or precipitous decline, in cognitive functioning in the few years most proximal to death (Reimanis & Green, 1971; Riegel & Riegel, 1972; Siegler, 1975). Thus, at least until the last few years before death, the subjective well-being literature suggests stability with age.

Emotion regulation

Emotion regulation occurs any time individuals influence which emotion they experience, when it is experienced, and how it is experienced and expressed (Gross, 1998). James Gross (1998) has proposed a *process model of emotion regulation*, which emphasizes the temporal nature of emotion regulation: An emotion can be regulated at different points in the unfolding process. It is assumed that regulatory strategies that come later in the emotion response process use more cognitive resources because once the emotion response is fully activated, the response must be continually and effortfully controlled. This difference in the cognitive resources required for different strategies may be an important factor in determining the types of strategies older adults prefer or are most effective at executing.

Indeed, age differences in self-reported emotion regulation skills and styles have been found. For example, young women report ruminating more than older women (Thomsen, Mehlsen, Viidik, Sommerlund, & Zachariae, 2005). In addition, older adults report higher emotional control (Gross et al., 1997; Lawton, Kleban, Rajagopal, & Dean, 1992), better perceived affect regulation (E.-M. Kessler & Staudinger, 2009; Orgeta, 2009), and mood stability (Lawton, Kleban, Rajagopal et al., 1992; Orgeta, 2009; Williams et al., 2006) than their younger counterparts, suggesting age-related enhancement in emotion regulation skills.

Social networks

Age differences have been found for both the types and number of social partners that younger and older adults report having (Carstensen, 2006). These smaller, "pruned down" networks minimize peripheral partners but still include emotionally close social partners, which is important for mental health (Fung, Carstensen, & Lang, 2001; Lang & Carstensen, 1994). Social networks can serve as protective factors for both mental and physical well-being. Indeed, support from social networks may protect against cognitive decline such as dementia (Fratiglioni, Wang, Ericsson, Maytan, & Winbald, 2000) and a lack of social support is related to health risks. In the first weeks and year after a spouse's death there are increased rates of mortality for the surviving spouse (Buckley, Mckinley, Tofler, & Bartrop, 2010; Martikainen & Valkonen, 1996) and married individuals have better immune functioning than single people (Graham, Christian, & Kiecolt-Glaser, 2006). Individuals with strong social networks seem to be at a lower risk for morbidity and mortality (Berkman, 2000) as well. Thus it may be that older adults' enhanced focus on the closer relationships (family and close friends) rather than peripheral acquaintances is adaptive in a time when social support can ameliorate some of the losses in other domains.

Along with the positive health benefits of supportive social networks, they also bring the potential for conflict. Across age groups, interpersonal tensions are the most commonly reported daily stressors (Almeida, 2005). Research suggests that older adults tend to endorse passive emotion regulation strategies more than young adults (Coats & Blanchard-Fields, 2008) and are more effective at solving interpersonal problems than young adults (Blanchard-Fields, Mienaltowski, & Seay, 2007), perhaps because they are more flexible in tailoring their problem-solving strategy to the situation than their younger counterparts (Blanchard-Fields, 2007). For example, older adults are more likely than young adults to use a combination of strategies to effectively solve interpersonal problems (Watson & Blanchard-Fields, 1998) and older adults are better at avoiding interpersonal conflict than young adults (Birditt et al., 2005).

Despite the methodological concerns with self-report data described earlier, research suggests that positive profiles of self-reported affect are associated with a number of important health outcomes (Salovey, Rothman, Detweiler, & Steward, 2000). For example, better anger regulation is related to better mental health (Phillips, Henry, Hosie, & Milne, 2006) and the self-reported experience of positive affect is related to less reactivity and faster recovery from stressful events (Ong, Bergeman, Bisconti, & Wallace, 2006; Ong, Edwards, & Bergeman, 2006). For example, the experience of positive emotions actually reduces the amount of cardiovascular reactivity in response to negative emotions and is related to faster cardiac recovery following a negative emotional experience (Ong & Allaire, 2005). Indeed, it is thought that positive affect may help buffer an older adults' more vulnerable system (Blanchard-Fields, 2007; Consedine, Magai, & Bonanno, 2002).

Thus self-report data on emotional experience, subjective well-being, emotion regulation, and social networks paint a fairly positive picture of the affective and social lives of older adults. But a nagging question emerges from this self-report literature: Are older adults avoiding their way into positivity by not being in situations that would create negativity? One way to study this question is to force older adults to face negative emotions or stressors in an experimental paradigm and see if they are still able to maintain positive moods.

Experimental Data

Experimental research investigating online emotion regulation further informs our understanding of the emotional lives of older adults. Although these studies typically rely on self-reported affect, they differ from the questionnaire data in that self-reported affect is measured within an experimental context where stimuli or instructions are manipulated.

Online emotion regulation

Based on the self-report data above, and given that older adults have had more life experience than young adults, researchers began to wonder if older adults might be better at regulating their emotions than young adults. Experimental data is critical in determining whether older adults are just more likely to say they feel good than young adults. Another possibility is that older adults do not face as many negative situations as young adults because they are retired from work and finished with raising children, two areas of life that bring conflict. If older adults are good at regulating their emotions when faced with negative stimuli, the case is stronger that older adults are better emotion regulators, not just reporting better affective lives.

Research from experimental paradigms suggests that older adults might be better emotion regulators than young adults, at least in some scenarios. In a dual-task paradigm following a disgust-inducing film clip, young and older adults were instructed to down-regulate their feelings of disgust while concurrently performing a working memory task (Scheibe & Blanchard-Fields, 2009). Older adults did not show a decline in working memory performance when concurrently successfully down-regulating their emotions (compared to older adults not down-regulating their mood), but young adults did show a decrement in performance, suggesting that emotion regulation may be less costly for older adults than young adults. Another study had young and older adults listen to conversations where people were making disparaging remarks about them. Older adults reported feeling more anger but equal levels of sadness as young adults, and made fewer negative comments about the speakers than young adults (Charles & Carstensen, 2008). The authors interpreted this as older adults being more adept at disengaging from negative situations because they are less likely to encode and ruminate on negative information.

Older adults may be most adept at the least resource-taxing emotion regulatory strategies because older age is associated with a reduction in available cognitive resources (Salthouse, 1996). Indeed, older adults were better able to regulate their emotions than young and middle-aged adults when following instructions to positively reappraise a negative film clip, but were less successful at regulating their emotions in a detached reappraisal condition (Shiota & Levenson, 2009). The authors suggest that these differential age effects are driven by the reliance of successful detached reappraisal (but not positive reappraisal) on executive functioning, which declines with age. Also consistent with an age-related advantage for early types of emotion regulatory strategies, older adults were more successful at positively refocusing their attention to regulate their moods than young adults, but no age differences were found for successfully suppressing emotional expressions (Phillips, Henry, Hosie, & Milne, 2008).

Attentional and memorial preferences.   Preferences in information processing may also support older adults' attempts at emotion regulation. It does appear that the negativity bias to attend more to and better remember negative information that is dominant in young adults (Rozin & Royzman, 2001) may not persist into old age. Instead, a number of lab-based studies have found that older adults preferentially attend to and remember positive stimuli over negative stimuli in their information processing. These patterns are termed *positivity effects* (Carstensen & Mikels, 2005). For example, older adults, but not young adults, responded to a dot probe faster if it was behind a neutral face compared to a negative face (Experiment 2, Mather & Carstensen, 2003). In the same study, older adults remembered positive faces better than negative faces. A number of other studies have found that older adults, compared to young adults, show a preference for remembering positive pictures over negative pictures (Charles, Mather, & Carstensen, 2003), or a lack of a negativity bias as when older adults remember both positive and negative information equally whereas young adults remember negative information better (Kensinger, Garoff-Eaton, & Schacter, 2007).

In terms of attentional preferences, several eye-tracking studies have found that older adults, but not young, tend to fixate on positive images more than negative images (Isaacowitz, Allard, Murphy, & Schlangel, 2009; Isaacowitz, Toner, Goren, & Wilson, 2008; Isaacowitz, Toner, & Neupert, 2009; Isaacowitz, Wadlinger, Goren, & Wilson, 2006a, 2006b). Although not present in every paradigm (see also Murphy & Isaacowitz, 2008), there do appear to be age-related differences in how some types of emotional material is remembered and processed. The majority of the evidence suggests that the negativity bias that young adults have is not found in older adults; however, strong links to emotion regulation outcomes have yet to be shown.

Individual differences in emotion regulation

Attentional functioning.   In addition to age, individual differences in attentional functioning also play a role in emotion regulation. For example, older adults with better executive functioning are able to resist mood declines by employing positive gaze preferences (Isaacowitz, Toner, et al., 2009). It seems that gaze preferences as an emotion regulation strategy may not require extensive cognitive effort (Allard, Wadlinger, & Isaacowitz, 2010), so this may be a relatively "cheap" emotion regulation strategy for older adults with fewer available cognitive resources. Indeed, older adults' tendency to avoid negative stimuli was reversed in a divided attention condition (Knight et al., 2007), suggesting that when cognitive control resources are usurped by a concurrent secondary task, older adults are no longer able to display positivity effects.

Personality.   Personality traits may be yet another key influence on age differences in emotional experience. Personality traits do seem to moderate the relationship between age and (a) emotion regulation, and (b) attentional preferences. For example, in one study, older adults who rapidly regulated out of a negative mood were lower in trait anxiety and depressive symptoms, and had higher levels of optimism, compared to older adults who did not rapidly regulate their moods (Larcom & Isaacowitz, 2009). Similarly, agreeableness, but not age, was found to be related to levels of sadness such that individuals who were more agreeable were more sad than those low in agreeableness when they viewed sad pictures (Pearman, Andreoletti, & Isaacowitz, 2010). Furthermore, age was related to emotional recovery such that older adults reported lower levels of sadness at posttest than young adults.

In an experimental study that investigated both cognitive and personality influences on mood change in young and older adults, four different subgroups of individuals were identified based on distinct mood-change trajectories (Stanley & Isaacowitz, 2011). The most positive and the most negative subgroups included more older adults than young adults, and the most negative group had slower processing speed, more state anxiety and neuroticism, and looked less at happy faces than other groups, suggesting that both cognitive and personality factors are important for determining emotion regulatory success, especially among older adults.

Personality differences may also moderate age differences in attentional preferences. In a dot-probe task presenting negative-neutral pairs of facial expressions and words, low anxiety older adults avoided sad faces, whereas high anxiety older adults did not show this pattern (Lee & Knight, 2009). In addition, older adults with high anxiety levels initially avoided negative words, but later dwelled on them. Thus it seems that personality factors are important for determining when age effects in emotion regulation and attentional preferences are likely to emerge.

Emotion recognition

Another experimental literature exposes participants to stimuli varying in emotional valence, but rather than measuring their response to it, the focus of this work is on their ability to categorize the stimuli. Older adults are less accurate than young adults at recognizing angry, sad, and fearful faces (Ruffman, Henry, Livingstone, & Phillips, 2008). The evidence suggests age-related difficulty in recognizing facial expressions in photos of strangers, especially for these certain discrete emotions. Currently, it is not clear why older adults have trouble recognizing these types of facial expressions or whether these deficits found in the lab translate to consequences in everyday communication. Older adults are also less accurate than young adults at recognizing emotion in sentences (Isaacowitz et al., 2007), voices, and bodies (Ruffman et al., 2008), but the emotions older adults have the most trouble identifying varies by modality.

Putting the Evidence Together: The Paradox of Well-Being Reconsidered

The overall picture of emotional experience in older adulthood is surprisingly positive. Although not all aspects of emotional life improve with age (e.g., emotion recognition), overall there is more maintenance and improvement than might be expected given the losses in social, physical, and cognitive domains: This maintenance has sometimes been referred to as the "paradox of well-being" (Mroczek & Kolarz, 1998).

It may not really be a paradox. We may assume that because older adults as a group have more loss and have positive affective lives, that this represents a paradox. First of all, the *set point perspective* suggests that personality traits (such as extraversion) may be more influential in determining well-being than current life circumstances (Mroczek & Kolarz, 1998). Secondly, we should also examine individual differences to see if those older adults who are experiencing the most loss are the same older adults reporting positive well-being (or not). As described above, individual differences play an important role in moderating age effects in emotional experience and processing. There may be less of a paradox between losses and emotional well-being on an individual level than we see on the group level. That is, an older individual who has experienced several physical and social losses such as the loss of mobility and the loss of a spouse may not self-report more positive affect and less negative affect than when they were younger before experiencing such loss. Another possibility is that identity assimilation plays a role such that individuals adjust to age-related changes in order to maintain consistent identities (Sneed & Whitbourne, 2003), thus self-reporting positive well-being throughout their lifespan.

Another possible confound in the literature is selection bias. Perhaps older adults with the least loss live the longest and make up more of the sample population of older adults in these studies (selective mortality), or perhaps older adults with the most positive lives to begin with are the ones who are the most likely to participate in our laboratory studies. In other words, those who suffer the most are dead or are not participating in studies. Indeed, nonmortality attrition from longitudinal studies is often associated with low cognitive performance, everyday activity, and education level (Aartsen, Smits, van Tilburg, Knipscheer, & Deeg, 2002).

Moreover, every aspect of emotional life does not improve with age. Maybe what has been presented as a paradox of well-being is now better interpreted as a fairly positive yet complicated picture of socioemotional growth, maintenance, and loss in late adulthood. Indeed, the literature on emotion recognition suggests an area of emotional processing that declines with age. And although the research on emotion regulation suggests some healthy adaptations in late adulthood, these may be constrained by cognitive resources. Perhaps a revised "paradox of aging" is the challenge of understanding how the positive aspects, such as interpersonal relationships, fit with the negative aspects, such as emotion recognition.

Current Theories of Socioemotional Aging

Selective optimization with compensation

One framework that attempts to guide theories trying to reconcile the dynamic interplay between gains and losses in older adulthood is the principle of selective optimization with compensation (Baltes & Baltes, 1990). The selection aspect refers to choosing goals that can be met with your current abilities. The optimization components are the actions taken to meet those goals (such as practicing a new skill). And the compensation component refers to any action taken to counteract loss or decline in goal-relevant means (such as increasing time allocation). Many of the developmental theories described below fit within this metatheory framework, with some theories focusing more on selection and optimization and others focusing on compensation aspects as well.

Socioemotional selectivity theory

A motivational account of age differences in the processing of emotional information is provided by socioemotional selectivity theory (SST; Carstensen, 1995; Carstensen, Isaacowitz, & Charles, 1999). As adults perceive their time as more limited (e.g., with increasing age), they are motivated to prioritize close social partners and emotionally gratifying experiences (Carstensen & Mikels, 2005). Importantly, other endings besides age-related endings also lead to this shift in prioritizing emotionally relevant goals (Carstensen & Fredrickson, 1998). For example, one year prior to the 1997 handover of Hong Kong to the People's Republic of China, older adults showed a preference for familiar partners, but young adults did not. Two months prior to the handover, with an ending looming, both young and older adults preferred to spend time with familiar social partners (Fung, Carstensen, & Lutz, 1999).

SST is consistent with much of the data on attentional and memorial preferences in older adulthood reported above. The positivity effects which emerge in many studies (though not all) suggest that there *is* something related to future time perspective that catalyzes a change in how individuals process emotional information. In addition, the pruning of social networks to include close others but exclude peripheral partners, and evidence that emotion regulation abilities improve with age, are also consistent with SST.

Less easily explained by SST is why older adults would be poorer at recognizing facial expressions of emotion than young adults. There is not a clear positivity bias in the emotion recognition and aging literature. Older adults are less accurate than young adults at recognizing both positive and negative stimuli, whether they are faces or voices (Ruffman et al., 2008). Moreover, in order to avoid negative information in the environment, as SST posits, older adults would first need to be able to recognize the information as negative in order to know what to avoid. It is of course possible that this recognition happens on an automatic, subconscious level (see Mather & Knight, 2006), but even if this is the case, the lack of evidence for older adults exhibiting better recognition of positive versus negative emotions indicates that a preference for positive material over negative may not be at play here. Instead, theorists suggest that these age differences may be more determined by age-related changes in the function and structure of emotion-processing centers in the brain (e.g., amygdala, orbitofrontal cortex) or that the artificiality of the lab task disadvantages older adults who may not be motivated to perform well in a task that seems to have no meaning or consequences (see Hess, Follett, & McGee, 1998).

Evidence that individual differences in personality and cognitive resources moderate age differences in emotion regulation success and attentional preferences further elucidate boundary conditions of SST. This creates a fuller picture of when motivational shifts related to future time perspective will and will not explain age differences in emotional processing. Future research should also pinpoint the nature of this motivational shift toward prioritizing emotional goals. For example, is the shift gradual or more steplike? And when in the lifespan does it occur – late middle-age or older adulthood? Do all individuals experience this shift?

Furthermore, emotion theorists have made a case for the utility of negative emotions, suggesting there are some situations in which negative emotions are functional, such as when they serve long-term goals or provide learning experiences (Tamir, 2009). What are the consequences of avoiding negative emotions? Are older adults' goals of maintaining a positive mood state inhibiting growth or are these goals a good fit for this stage of life? Is the age-related reduction in negative emotional experiences a side effect of age-related changes in the environment (Folkman, Lazarus, Pimley, & Novacek, 1987), such that reduced occurrence of daily stressors renders fewer negative events for older adults to need to regulate? A proposed theory of strength and vulnerability integration (SAVI; Charles & Piazza, 2009) recognizes the need to integrate the context of the daily lives of older adults with their emotional outcomes.

Affect optimization and cognitive-affective complexity

Labouvie-Vief proposes two criteria for successful self-regulation: affect optimization and cognitive-affective complexity. Affect optimization is the maximizing of positive affect and the dampening of negative affect. Cognitive-affective complexity is the ability to coordinate positive and negative emotions. In her work Labouvie-Vief has found that participants' descriptions of their emotions increase in cognitive-affective complexity with age until middle adulthood and decrease thereafter (Labouvie-Vief, Diehl, Jain, & Zhang, 2007). Furthermore, it is posited that age-related increases in affect optimization are used to compensate for decreases in cognitive-affective complexity.

The notion that affect optimization increases with age is consistent with the positivity effects in the literature reviewed above where older adults attend to and remember more positive material and less negative material than their younger counterparts. The idea that cognitive-affective complexity declines with age is more difficult to evaluate due to differences in the definition of emotional complexity. In contrast with the Labouvie-Vief model, several developmental theories of emotion predict more complex emotional experience with advancing age, which is attributed to increased life experience (Carstensen et al., 2000; Izard, Ackerman, Schoff, & Fine, 1999; Magai, 2001; Ong & Bergeman, 2004).

Conclusions

The theories described above are not mutually exclusive, nor are they exhaustive (see, e.g., Consedine, 2010). Instead, they are a selection of current theories that tend to be called upon to explain some of the findings on socioemotional aging we have reviewed. The success of these and any future socioemotional theories of aging will be determined by whether they can explain not just some of the above findings, but many or all of the textured research findings reviewed in this chapter and from future studies. It may be the case that one theory can truly subsume the majority of these textured findings; alternately, there may not be a grand theory of socioemotional functioning and aging in its entirety, but rather two or three theories that are each best suited to deal with particular trajectories (e.g., emotion regulation vs. emotion recognition). Current theories seem best able to explain the positivity observed throughout the study of socioemotional aging; the challenge for the future is to integrate, both conceptually and empirically, the nuances and texture that seem to characterize the mostly positive picture of socioemotional functioning in old age. Given the variability in both the emotional experiences of older adults and the outcomes of emotion regulation strategies, future research should focus on adaptive matches between individual differences strategies and outcomes. Indeed, individual differences should be considered to best understand the configuration(s) of individual differences and strategies that lead to adaptive functioning. Although not all paths and mechanisms lead to positive affective lives, the current question put to researchers is to identify the various paths: those that lead to positive socioemotional outcomes for older adults, and those that do not.

References

Aartsen, M. J., Smits, C. H. M., van Tilburg, T., Knipscheer, K. C. P. M., & Deeg, D. J. H. (2002). Activity in older adults: Cause of consequence of cognitive functioning? A longitudinal study on everyday activities and cognitive performance in older adults. *Journals of Gerontology, 57B*, 153–162.

Allard, E. S., Wadlinger, H. A., & Isaacowitz, D. M. (2010). Positive gaze preferences in older adults: Assessing the role of cognitive effort with pupil dilation. *Aging, Neuropsychology, & Cognition, 17,* 296–311.

Almeida, D. M. (2005). Resilience and vulnerability to daily stressors assessed via diary methods. *Current Directions in Psychological Science, 14,* 64–68.

Bäckman, L., Small, B. J., & Wahlin, Å. (2001). Aging and memory: Cognitive and biological perspectives. In J. E. Birren & K. W. Schaie (Eds.), *Handbook of the psychology of aging* (5th ed., pp. 349–377). San Diego, CA: Academic Press.

Bäckman, L., Small, B. J., Wahlin, Å., & Larsson, M. (2000). Cognitive functioning in very old age. In F. I. M. Craik & T. A. Salthouse (Eds.), *The handbook of aging and cognition* (2nd ed., pp. 499–558). Mahwah, NJ: Erlbaum.

Baltes, P. B. (1987). Theoretical propositions of life-span developmental psychology: On the dynamics between growth and decline. *Developmental Psychology, 23,* 611–626.

Baltes, P. B., & Baltes, M. M. (1990). Psychological perspectives on successful aging: The model of selective optimization with compensation. In P. B. Baltes & M. M. Baltes (Eds.), *Successful aging: Perspectives from the behavioral sciences* (pp. 1–34). New York: Cambridge University Press.

Barrick, A. L., Hutchinson, R. L., & Deckers, L. H. (1989). Age effects on positive and negative emotions. *Journal of Social Behavior & Personality, 4,* 421–429.

Berkman, L. (2000). Social support, social networks, social cohesion and health. *Social Work in Health Care, 31,* 3–14.

Birditt, K. S., & Fingerman, K. L. (2003). Age and gender differences in adults' descriptions of emotional reactions to interpersonal problems. *Journal of Gerontology, 58B,* 237–245.

Birditt, K. S., Fingerman, K. L., & Almeida, D. M. (2005). Age differences in exposure and reactions to interpersonal tensions: A daily diary study. *Psychology and Aging, 20,* 330–340.

Blanchard-Fields, F. (2007). Everyday problem solving and emotion: An adult developmental perspective. *Current Directions in Psychological Science, 16,* 26–31.

Blanchard-Fields, F., Mienaltowski, A., & Seay, R. B. (2007). Age differences in everyday problem-solving effectiveness: Older adults select more effective strategies for interpersonal problems. *Journal of Gerontology, 62B,* 61–64.

Buckley, T., Mckinley, S., Tofler, G., & Bartrop, R. (2010). Cardiovascular risk in early bereavement: A literature review and proposed mechanisms. *International Journal of Nursing Studies, 47,* 229–238.

Carstensen, L. L. (1995). Evidence for a life-span theory of socioemotional selectivity. *Current Directions in Psychological Science, 4,* 151–156.

Carstensen, L. L. (2006). The influence of a sense of time on human development. *Science, 312,* 1913–1915.

Carstensen, L. L., & Fredrickson, B. L. (1998). Influence of HIV status and age on cognitive representations of others. *Health Psychology, 17,* 494–503.

Carstensen, L. L., Isaacowitz, D. M., & Charles, S. T. (1999). Taking time seriously: A theory of socioemotional selectivity. *American Psychologist, 54,* 165–181.

Carstensen, L. L., & Mikels, J. A. (2005). At the intersection of emotion and cognition: Aging and the positivity effect. *Current Directions in Psychological Science, 14,* 117–121.

Carstensen, L. L., Pasupathi, M., Mayr, U., & Nesselroade, J. R. (2000). Emotional experience in everyday life across the adult life span. *Journal of Personality and Social Psychology, 79,* 644–655.

Charles, S. T., & Carstensen, L. L. (2008). Unpleasant situations elicit different emotional responses in younger and older adults. *Psychology and Aging, 23,* 495–504.

Charles, S. T., Luong, G., Almeida, D. M., Ryff, C., Sturm, M., & Love, G. (2010). Fewer ups and downs: Daily stressors mediate age differences in negative affect. *Journal of Gerontology: Psychological Sciences, 65B,* 279–286.

Charles, S. T., Mather, M., & Carstensen, L. L. (2003). Aging and emotional memory: The forgettable nature of negative images for older adults. *Journal of Experimental Psychology: General, 132,* 310–324.

Charles, S. T., & Piazza, J. R. (2009). Age differences in affective well-being: Context matters. *Social and Personality Psychology Compass, 3,* 1–14.

Charles, S. T., Reynolds, C. A., & Gatz, M. (2001). Age-related differences and change in positive and negative affect over 23 years. *Journal of Personality and Social Psychology, 80,* 136–151.

Chipperfield, J. G., Perry, R. P., & Weiner, B. (2003). Discrete emotions in later life. *Journal of Gerontology, 58B,* 23–34.

Coats, A. H., & Blanchard-Fields, F. (2008). Emotion regulation in interpersonal problems: The role of cognitive-emotional complexity, emotion regulation goals, and expressivity. *Psychology and Aging, 23,* 39–51.

Consedine, N. S. (2010). Capacities, targets, and tactics: Lifespan emotion regulation viewed from developmental functionalism. In I. Nyclicek & A. Vingerhoets (Eds.), *Emotion regulation and wellbeing* (pp. 1–40). Dordrecht, Netherlands: Springer.

Consedine, N. S., Magai, C., & Bonanno, G. A. (2002). Moderators of the emotion inhibition-health relationship: A review and research agenda. *Review of General Psychology, 6,* 204–228.

Costa, P. T., Zonderman, A. B., McCrae, R. R., & Cornoni-Huntley, J. (1987). Longitudinal analyses of psychological well-being in a national sample: Stability of mean levels. *Journal of Gerontology, 42,* 50–55.

Csikszentmihalyi, M., & Larson, R. (1992). Validity and reliability of experiencing sampling method. In M. W. deVries (Ed.), *The experience of psychopathology: Investigating mental disorders in their natural settings* (pp. 43–57). New York: Cambridge University Press.

Diener, E., Suh, E. M., Lucas, R. E., & Smith, H. L. (1999). Subjective well-being: Three decades of progress. *Psychological Bulletin, 125,* 276–302.

Diener, E., & Suh, M. E. (1998). Subjective well-being and age: An international analysis. In K. W. Schaie & M. P. Lawton (Eds.), *Annual review of gerontology and geriatrics: Focus on emotion and adult development* (Vol. 17, pp. 304–324). New York: Springer.

Folkman, S., Lazarus, R. S., Pimley, S., & Novacek, J. (1987). Age differences in stress and coping processes. *Psychology and Aging, 2,* 171–184.

Fratiglioni, L., Wang, H.-X., Ericsson, K., Maytan, M., & Winbald, B. (2000). Influence of social network on occurrence of dementia: A community-based longitudinal study. *Lancet, 355,* 1315–1319.

Fung, H. H., Carstensen, L. L., & Lang, F. R. (2001). Age-related patterns in social networks among European Americans and African Americans: Implications for socioemotional selectivity across the life span. *International Journal of Aging and Human Development, 52,* 185–206.

Fung, H. H., Carstensen, L. L., & Lutz, A. M. (1999). Influence of time on social preferences: Implications for life-span development. *Psychology and Aging, 14,* 595–604.

Gerstorf, D., Ram, N., Estabrook, R., Schupp, J., Wagner, G. G., & Lindenberger, U. (2008). Life satisfaction shows terminal decline in old age: Longitudinal evidence from the German Socio-Economic Panel Study (SOEP). *Developmental Psychology, 44,* 1148–1159.

Gerstorf, D., Ram, N., Mayraz, G., Hidajat, M., Lindenberger, U., Wagner, G. G., & Schupp, J. (2010). Late-life decline in well-being across adulthood in Germany, the United Kingdom, and the United States: Something is seriously wrong at the end of life. *Psychology and Aging, 24,* 296–309.

Graham, J. E., Christian, L. M., & Kiecolt-Glaser, J. K. (2006). Marriage, health, and immune function. In S. R. Beach, M. Z. Wamboldt, N. J. Kaslow, R. E. Heyman, M. B. First, L. G. Underwood, & D. Reiss (Eds.), *Relational processes and DSM-V: Neuroscience, assessment, prevention, and treatment* (pp. 61–76). Washington, D C: American Psychiatric Association.

Gross, J. J. (1998). The emerging field of emotion regulation: An integrative review. *Review of General Psychology, 2,* 271–299.

Gross, J. J., Carstensen, L. L., Pasupathi, M., Tsai, J., Götestam Skorpen, C., & Hsu, A. Y. C. (1997). Emotion and aging: Experience, expression, and control. *Psychology and Aging, 12,* 590–599.

Hess, T. M., Follett, K. J., & McGee, K. A. (1998). Aging and impression formation: The impact of processing skills and goals. *Journal of Gerontology: Psychological Sciences, 53B,* 175–187.

Isaacowitz, D. M., Allard, E. S., Murphy, F. C., & Schlangel, M. (2009). The time course of age-related preferences toward positive and negative stimuli. *Journal of Gerontology: Psychological Sciences, 64B,* 188–192.

Isaacowitz, D. M., Loeckenhoff, C., Lane, R., Wright, R., Sechrest, L., Riedel, R., & Costa, P. T. (2007). Age differences in recognition of emotion in lexical stimuli and facial expressions. *Psychology and Aging, 22,* 147–259.

Isaacowitz, D. M., & Smith, J. (2003). Positive and negative affect in very old age. *Journal of Gerontology, 58B,* 143–152.

Isaacowitz, D. M., Toner, K., Goren, D., & Wilson, H. (2008). Looking while unhappy: Mood congruent gaze in young adults, positive gaze in older adults. *Psychological Science, 19,* 848–853.

Isaacowitz, D. M., Toner, K., & Neupert, S. D. (2009). Use of gaze for real-time mood regulation: Effects of age and attentional functioning. *Psychology and Aging, 24,* 989–994.

Isaacowitz, D. M., Wadlinger, H. A., Goren, D., & Wilson, H. R. (2006a). Is there an age-related positivity effect in visual attention? A comparison of two methodologies. *Emotion, 6,* 511–516.

Isaacowitz, D. M., Wadlinger, H. A., Goren, D., & Wilson, H. R. (2006b). Selective preference in visual fixation away from negative images in old age? An eye-tracking study. *Psychology and Aging, 21,* 40–48.

Izard, C. E., Ackerman, B. P., Schoff, K. M., & Fine, S. E. (1999). Self-organization of discrete emotions, emotion patterns, and emotion–cognition relations. In M. D. Lewis & I. Granic (Eds.), *Emotion, development, and self-organization: Dynamic systems approaches to emotional development* (pp. 12–36). New York: Cambridge University Press.

Kensinger, E. A., Garoff-Eaton, R., & Schacter, D. L. (2007). Effects of emotion on memory specificity in young and older adults. *Journal of Gerontology: Psychological Sciences, 62B,* P208–P215.

Kessler, E.-M., & Staudinger, U. M. (2009). Affective experience in adulthood and old age: The role of affective arousal and perceived affect regulation. *Psychology and Aging, 24,* 349–362.

Kessler, R. C., Foster, C., Webster, P. S., & House, J. S. (1992). The relationship between age and depressive symptoms in two national surveys. *Psychology and Aging, 7,* 119–126.

Knight, M., Seymour, T. L., Gaunt, J. T., Baker, C., Nesmith, K., & Mather, M. (2007). Aging and goal-directed emotional attention: Distraction reverses emotional biases. *Emotion, 7,* 705–714.

Kunzmann, U., Little, T. D., & Smith, J. (2000). Is age-related stability of subjective well-being a paradox? Cross-sectional and longitudinal evidence from the Berlin Aging Study. *Psychology and Aging, 15,* 511–526.

Labouvie-Vief, G., Diehl, M., Jain, E., & Zhang, F. (2007). Six-year change in affect optimization and affect complexity across the adult life span: A further examination. *Psychology and Aging, 22,* 738–751.

Lacey, H. P., Smith, D. M., & Ubel, P. A. (2006). Hope I die before I get old: Mispredicting happiness across the adult lifespan. *Journal of Happiness Studies, 7,* 167–182.

Lang, F. R., & Carstensen, L. L. (1994). Close emotional relationships in late life: Further support for proactive aging in the social domain. *Psychology and Aging, 9,* 315–324.

Larcom, M. J., & Isaacowitz, D. M. (2009). Rapid emotion regulation after mood induction: Age and individual differences. *Journal of Gerontology: Psychological Sciences, 64B,* 733–741.

Lawton, M. P., Kleban, M. H., Dean, J., Rajagopal, D., & Parmelee, P. A. (1992). The factorial generality of brief positive and negative affect measures. *Journal of Gerontology, 47,* P228–P237.

Lawton, M. P., Kleban, M. H., Rajagopal, D., & Dean, J. (1992). Dimensions of affective experience in three age groups. *Psychology and Aging, 7,* 171–184.

Lee, L. O., & Knight, B. G. (2009). Attentional bias for threat in older adults: Moderation of the positivity bias by trait anxiety and stimulus modality. *Psychology and Aging, 24,* 741–747.

Magai, C. (2001). Emotions over the life span. In J. E. Birren & K. W. Schaie (Eds.), *Handbook of the psychology of aging* (5th ed., pp. 399–426). San Diego, CA: Academic Press.

Martikainen, P., & Valkonen, T. (1996). Mortality after the death of a spouse: Rates and causes of death in a large Finnish cohort. *American Journal of Public Health, 86,* 1087–1093.

Mather, M., & Carstensen, L. L. (2003). Aging and attentional biases for emotional faces. *Psychological Science, 14,* 409–415.

Mather, M., & Knight, M. R. (2006). Angry faces get noticed quickly: Threat detection is not impaired among older adults. *Journal of Gerontology, 61,* 54–57.

Mroczek, D. K., & Kolarz, C. M. (1998). The effect of age on positive and negative affect: A developmental perspective on happiness. *Journal of Personality and Social Psychology, 75,* 1333–1349.

Murphy, N. A., & Isaacowitz, D. M. (2008). Preferences for emotional information in older and younger adults: A meta-analysis of memory and attention tasks. *Psychology and Aging, 23,* 263–286.

Nisbett, R. E., & Wilson, T. D. (1977). Telling more than we can know: Verbal reports on mental processes. *Psychological Review, 84,* 231–259.

Ong, A. D., & Allaire, J. C. (2005). Cardiovascular intraindividual variability in later life: The influence of social connectedness and positive emotions. *Psychology and Aging, 20,* 476–485.

Ong, A. D., & Bergeman, C. S. (2004). The complexity of emotions in later life. *Journal of Gerontology: Psychological Sciences, 59B,* P117–P112.

Ong, A. D., Bergeman, C. S., Bisconti, T. L., & Wallace, K. A. (2006). Psychological resilience, positive emotions, and successful adaptation to stress in later life. *Journal of Personality and Social Psychology, 91,* 730–749.

Ong, A. D., Edwards, L. M., & Bergeman, C. S. (2006). Hope as a source of resilience in later adulthood. *Personality and Individual Differences, 41,* 1263–1273.

Orgeta, V. (2009). Specificity of age differences in emotion regulation. *Aging & Mental Health, 13,* 818–826.

Pearman, A., Andreoletti, C., & Isaacowitz, D. M. (2010). Sadness prediction and response: Effects of age and agreeableness. *Aging & Mental Health, 14,* 355–363.

Phillips, L. H., Henry, J. D., Hosie, J. A., & Milne, A. B. (2006). Age, anger regulation and well-being. *Aging & Mental Health, 10,* 250–256.

Phillips, L. H., Henry, J. D., Hosie, J. A., & Milne, A. B. (2008). Effective regulation of the experience and expression of negative affect in old age. *Journal of Gerontology: Psychological Sciences, 63B,* 138–145.

Reimanis, G., & Green, R. F. (1971). Imminence of death and intellectual decrement in the aging. *Developmental Psychology, 5,* 270–272.

Riegel, K. F., & Riegel, R. M. (1972). Development, drop, and death. *Developmental Psychology, 6,* 306–319.

Röcke, C., Li, S.-C., & Smith, J. (2009). Intraindividual variability in positive and negative affect over 45 days: Do older adults fluctuate less than young adults? *Psychology and Aging, 24,* 863–878.

Rozin, P., & Royzman, E. B. (2001). Negativity bias, negativity dominance, and contagion. *Personality and Social Psychology Review, 5,* 296–320.

Ruffman, T., Henry, J. D., Livingstone, V., & Phillips, L. H. (2008). A meta-analytic review of emotion recognition and aging: Implications for neuropsychological models of aging. *Neuroscience & Biobehavioral Reviews, 32,* 863–881.

Salovey, P., Rothman, A. J., Detweiler, J. B., & Steward, W. T. (2000). Emotional states and physical health. *American Psychologist, 55,* 110–121.

Salthouse, T. A. (1996). The processing-speed theory of adult age differences in cognition. *Psychological Review, 103,* 403–428.

Schaie, K. W. (1996). Intellectual development in adulthood. In J. E. Birren & K. W. Schaie (Eds.), *Handbook of the psychology of aging* (4th ed., pp. 266–286). San Diego, CA: Academic Press.

Scheibe, S., & Blanchard-Fields, F. (2009). Effects of regulating emotions on cognitive performance: What is costly for young adults is not so costly for older adults. *Psychology and Aging, 24,* 217–223.

Schwarz, N., Park, D. C., Knäuper, B., & Sudman, S. (1999). *Cognition, aging, and self-reports.* Philadelphia, PA: Psychology Press.

Schwarz, N., & Strack, F. (1999). Reports of subjective well-being: Judgmental processes and their methodological implications. In D. Kahneman, E. Diener, & N. Schwarz (Eds.), *Well-being: The foundations of hedonic psychology* (pp. 61–84). New York: Russell Sage Foundation.

Shephard, R. J. (1999). Age and physical work capacity. *Experimental Aging Research, 25,* 331–343.

Shiota, M. N., & Levenson, R. W. (2009). Effects of aging on experimentally instructed detached reappraisal, positive reappraisal, and emotional behavior suppression. *Psychology and Aging, 24,* 890–900.

Siegler, I. C. (1975). The terminal drop hypothesis: Fact or artifact? *Experimental Aging Research, 1,* 169–185.

Sneed, J. R., & Whitbourne, S. K. (2003). Identity processing and self-consciousness in middle and later adulthood. *Journals of Gerontology: Psychological Sciences, 58B,* 313–319.

Stacey, C. A., & Gatz, M. (1991). Cross-sectional age differences and longitudinal change on the Bradburn Affect Balance Scale. *Journal of Gerontology, 46,* P76–P78.

Stanley, J. T., & Isaacowitz, D. M. (2011). Age-related differences in profiles of mood-change trajectories. *Developmental Psychology, 47,* 318–330.

Stawski, R. S., Sliwinski, M., Almeida, D. M., & Smyth, J. M. (2008). Reported exposure and emotional reactivity to daily stressors: The roles of adult age and global perceived stress. *Psychology and Aging, 23,* 52–61.

Tamir, M. (2009). What do people want to feel and why? Pleasure and utility in emotion regulation. *Current Directions in Psychological Science, 18,* 101–105.

Thomas, D. L., & Diener, E. (1990). Memory accuracy in the recall of emotions. *Journal of Personality and Social Psychology, 59,* 291–297.

Thomsen, D. K., Mehlsen, M. Y., Viidik, A., Sommerlund, B., & Zachariae, R. (2005). Age and gender differences in negative affect – Is there a role for emotion regulation? *Personality & Individual Differences, 38,* 1935–1946.

Watson, T. L., & Blanchard-Fields, F. (1998). Thinking with your head and your heart: Age differences in everyday problem-solving strategy preferences. *Aging, Neuropsychology, & Cognition, 5,* 225–240.

Williams, L. M., Brown, K. J., Palmer, D., Liddell, B. J., Kemp, A. H., Olivieri, G., . . . Gordon, E. (2006). The mellow years?: Neural basis of improving emotional stability over age. *Journal of Neuroscience, 26,* 6422–6430.

Zhao, J., Barclay, S., Farquhar, M., Kinmonth, A. L., Brayne, C., & Fleming, J. (2010). The oldest old in the last year of life: Population-based findings from the Cambridge City over 75s Cohort Study participants aged 85 and older at death. *Journal of the American Geriatric Society, 58,* 1–11.

13

Personality and Aging

Cognitive Perspectives and Processes

Eileen Kranz Graham and Margie E. Lachman

Introduction and Overview

Personality is a core factor in defining a person. Much of the emphasis on personality and aging has focused on the stability of individual differences. Yet there is some evidence for personality change in adulthood and old age. Many studies focus on the Big Five personality traits, but there are other conceptions and dimensions of personality that are relevant for aging. In this chapter we focus on personality, broadly defined, in relation to aging-related changes in key domains, with an emphasis on relationships to cognitive processes. It is of interest whether personality can serve a protective role or serve as a resource, in that some characteristics may enable resilience or attenuate aging-related changes. We also consider the personal action constructs (PACs; Hooker & McAdams, 2003) and cognitive processes as possible mechanisms that underlie these relationships. Understanding the dynamics of these linkages may be helpful for developing strategies to optimize aging. Even if personality itself is difficult to modify, it is possible to consider individual differences in personality when developing interventions, and to tailor programs to allow for person-by-treatment variations. In this chapter, we discuss personality traits, cognitive aspects of personality, and their relation to cognitive abilities and performance across adulthood.

The Wiley-Blackwell Handbook of Adulthood and Aging, First Edition. Edited by Susan Krauss Whitbourne and Martin J. Sliwinski. © 2012 Blackwell Publishing Ltd. Published 2012 by Blackwell Publishing Ltd.

Interaction of Personality Traits and Cognitive Functioning

There is a wide range of research examining the relationship of personality traits to several domains of cognitive functioning known to show age differences and age-related declines. Neuroticism is negatively correlated with several domains of performance for all age groups (Ackerman & Heggestad, 1997), including information processing, manual dexterity, pattern analysis, working memory, and long-term memory (Costa, Fozard, McCrae, & Bosse, 1976; McCrae, 1987; Willis & Boron, 2008).

Extraversion is related to faster response speed (Schaie, Willis, & Caskie, 2004), verbal performance, and higher long-term recall, but lower performance on tests of general knowledge (Baker & Bichsel, 2006; Chamorro-Premuzic, Furnham, & Ackerman, 2006), reasoning, and verbal ability (Ackerman & Heggestad, 1997; McCrae, 1987; Moutafi, Furnham, & Crump, 2003; Moutafi, Furnham, & Paltiel, 2005; Willis & Boron, 2008). One possible explanation for the direction of these findings is that less extraverted individuals are more invested in intellectual activities because introverts prefer studying more than socializing, or that intelligent individuals are likely to form good study habits early on and develop less extraverted characteristics (Chamorro-Premuzic & Furnham, 2005). Furthermore, it appears that introverts consistently perform better on problem-solving tasks, where extraverts tend to perform better on measures of reaction time or speed of processing, but more poorly on accuracy-based tasks (see also Chamorro-Premuzic & Furnham, 2004; Matthews, 1997).

Openness to experience as a trait is related to higher scores on measures of divergent thinking (McCrae, 1987), verbal ability, crystallized intelligence (Ackerman & Heggestad, 1997), verbal memory (Baker & Bichsel, 2006), spatial orientation, and reasoning, in addition to knowledge of humanities and civics in adulthood (Ackerman & Rolfhus, 1999; Costa et al., 1976; Schaie et al., 2004; Willis & Boron, 2008). On the facet level, Moutafi, Furnham, and Crump (2006) have found that openness to actions and ideas are the two facets of openness that are most closely associated with intelligence (Holland, Dollinger, Holland & MacDonald, 1995; Moutafi, Furnham, & Crump, 2003).

Conscientiousness has also had some inconsistent findings in the literature, with both positive and negative associations to reasoning, speed, and general cognition (Ackerman & Heggestad, 1997), but lower intelligence (Moutafi, Furnham & Crump, 2003), verbal ability (Schaie et al., 2004), and abstract/verbal/numerical reasoning (Moutafi, Furnham, & Paltiel, 2005; Willis & Boron, 2008). Order, discipline, and deliberation are the facets of conscientiousness that have been linked to higher performance on intelligence tests, which indicates that individuals with low intelligence test scores may become more organized, self-disciplined, cautious, and deliberate in order to compensate for lower ability levels (Moutafi, Furnham & Crump, 2006).

Finally, agreeableness, which historically is not associated with cognitive ability, is negatively associated with scores on tests of inductive reasoning, spatial orientation, and general cognition (Schaie et al., 2004; Willis & Boron, 2008).

The model proposed by Chamorro-Premuzic and Furnham (2004) very elegantly describes one possible pathway to explaining how personality and cognitive performance are related. Their main argument is that all personality traits are related to self-assessed intelligence (SAI, or intellectual self-efficacy), and that for neuroticism and extraversion this relation in turn affects an individual's test performance. Conscientiousness and openness are typically related to higher SAI, and, according to their model, are thereby associated with high scores on tests of crystallized and fluid intelligence. Applying a model like this to aging would be useful in determining how personality traits can influence the cognitive aging process. Specifically, this type of model helps elucidate the processes involved in linking personality with cognitive ability across the adult lifespan.

Many of the existing studies in the literature do not take age into consideration or are conducted only on young adult samples. Nevertheless, it is useful to consider these findings on the nature of the relationship between personality and cognitive ability across adulthood as an important first step. It is possible, for example, that personality serves as a resource that can protect against cognitive declines. The model proposed by Chamorro-Premuzic and Furnham (2004), for example, uses self-efficacy, a component of sense of control, as a key mechanism related to performance.

It is important to consider how the relations between personality and ability vary across the lifespan in the context of changes in both personality and cognitive abilities. Middle age, for example, is a time of transition and responsibility, one during which individuals may be pulled in multiple directions, therefore requiring peak performance in order to achieve optimal functioning. Many middle-aged adults describe themselves as being responsible, hardworking, caring, friendly, helpful, sympathetic, warm, and softhearted, all of which are necessary characteristics for adaptive functioning (i.e., more conscientious or agreeable) (Lachman & Bertrand, 2001). Being conscientious would thereby be expected to serve as a helpful characteristic for middle-aged adults to have in order to perform at high cognitive levels, or to protect against the impending age-related declines in cognition. While many argue that conscientiousness on average does not increase in midlife, others have found that this trait continues to develop as individuals approach and proceed through midlife (e.g., Costa, Herbst, McCrae, & Siegler, 2000; Roberts, Walton, & Bogg, 2005). A recent study on the development of facet-level conscientiousness found that older adults continue to increase in impulse control, reliability, and conventionality (Jackson et al., 2009). Further, studies have also shown that conscientiousness is associated with adaptive health behaviors, which may contribute to greater physical and cognitive health in later life (Roberts et al., 2005).

While personality is clearly a well-established predictor of cognitive performance, it is also important to consider personality more broadly as it relates to aging. It is possible that personality plays a role in regulating change, and that those with certain characteristics (e.g., high in conscientiousness, low in neuroticism) fare better in aging. Some person-alities may be more or less vulnerable to cognitive declines. If so, personality could be used as a warning sign or indicator of high risk for declines. Not all individuals show cognitive decline nor do declines occur in all domains of cognitive functioning. It is of interest which aspects of personality and cognition are related, and whether personality traits can serve to buffer age-related changes in cognition.

As early as the 1970s, researchers examined personality traits in relation to cognitive functioning in later life. Costa and colleagues found that openness was positively related to information processing ability and pattern analysis, introversion was positively related to pattern analysis, and anxiety was negatively related to all components of the general aptitude test. They did not, however, find that personality mediated the relation between age and cognition (Costa et al., 1976). This is not entirely surprising however, since a significant mediation would suggest that personality fully explains the relation between age and cognition. The decline of cognition across the lifespan is generally robust enough that full mediation is unlikely; however, it is possible that certain personality traits are related to age-related cognitive declines. For example, research has found that poor memory performance and memory self-efficacy (to be discussed in greater detail in a later section) is associated with high extraversion and high neuroticism among older adults (Arbuckle, Gold & Andres, 1986; Perrig-Chiello, Perrig, & Staehelin, 2000). Dixon and de Frias (2004) found that neuroticism and extraversion were both negative predictors of memory, while education and intellectual engagement were the strongest positive predictors. Furthermore, they suggest that older introverts may perform better due to slower nervous system inhibition, and not because of greater intellectual engagement.

Baker and Bichsel (2006) examined how personality's influence on cognition differed in various age groups, including a group which they referred to as "cognitively superior" older adults. They found that for young adults, openness is a positive predictor of crystallized intelligence and short-term memory, while extraversion is positively related to speed but negatively related to crystallized intelligence. The "cognitively comparable old" had similar results, with positive links between extraversion and long-term retrieval, as well as openness and auditory processing. Finally, the cognitive superior old not only had a similar relationship between openness and visual spatial ability, but in this group high conscientiousness was also associated with auditory and short-term memory while low agreeableness was linked to better crystallized intelligence (Baker & Bichsel, 2006). While these results cover the spectrum of cognitive abilities, there are a number of interesting interpretations that can be derived from them. First, as explored above, extraversion has seemingly inconsistent associations with cognition, which is apparent when different measurements of cognition are used. However, it is expected that introverts have greater ability to study hard and remain focused, so their overall achievement or knowledge acquisition would be better than that of extraverts (see also Moutafi et al., 2003). In addition, these findings are consistent with the reports that extraverts typically do better on processing speed tasks, mainly because of the necessary short-term arousal needed to perform a task as quickly as possible, though such speed may come at the expense of poorer accuracy. Furthermore, Baker and colleagues (Baker & Bichsel, 2006) examined cognitively superior older adults, a group which has not been widely explored. In this unique population, those who were high in conscientiousness and low in agreeableness performed the best. It appears that in order to maximize cognitive ability later in life, being socially outgoing and cooperative, more critical (disagreeable), while being highly motivated, organized, and attentive (conscientious) appear to be key factors. Being conscientious is also related to increased memory compensation in later adulthood (Dixon & de Frias, 2004) because individuals high in conscientiousness will be better equipped to cope and compensate for memory declines. This not only supports prior work examining the main effects of personality on cognitive abilities but it also addresses how these effects vary across the lifespan and, more importantly, what aspects of personality are associated with optimized abilities in later adulthood (Baker & Bichsel, 2006).

In a similar vein, Willis and Boron (2008) addressed the ways in which the direct relations between personality and cognition vary within age groups and genders, particularly in middle and old age, in addition to how personality is associated with risk of cognitive impairment. Although there is evidence for a positive relation between conscientiousness and some performance in some cognitive domains, this relationship is negative in midlife. Extraversion in late midlife is positively related to cognition for women, but negatively related for men (Willis & Boron, 2008). Additionally, high arousal is associated with greater cognitive impairment (H. J. Eysenck, 1967), and high neuroticism and low extraversion are also associated with greater cognitive impairment, greater risk of Alzheimer's disease, and higher mortality (Crowe, Andel, Pedersen, Fratiglioni, & Gatz, 2006; Duchek, Balota, Storandt, & Larsen, 2007; Wilson et al., 2006; Wilson et al., 2005). There is also evidence that high neuroticism is associated with higher distress, which has been linked to greater risk of cognitive impairment and mortality (Willis & Boron, 2008; Wilson, Krueger, et al., 2005). In a sample of older adults, it was found that low neuroticism and high extraversion are separately related to better episodic memory (Meier, Perrig-Chiello & Perrig, 2002). This study also found that the correlation between neuroticism and episodic memory decreases with age (Meier et al., 2002), which is also supported by Jelicic and colleagues (2003), who found that neuroticism is not related to cognitive impairment in old age. This suggests that after a certain point in life, cognitive abilities will decline regardless of personality traits. Although these findings may also be due to cohort effects of selective survival, it still may be possible to preserve cognition throughout the earlier period of later adulthood.

As traits operate interactively, another approach to examining the effects of personality and cognition across the lifespan looked at the interactions between traits as predictors of cognitive impairment over a 25-year period (Crowe et al., 2006). It was found that those with both high neuroticism and low extraversion in combination were at greatest risk for cognitive impairment, perhaps because they have high levels of anxiety and greater stress reactivity, which may impede cognitive performance and accelerate declines. Additionally, Gold et al. (1995) found that neuroticism is, as expected, negatively related to verbal/nonverbal ability; however, they found that this link is indirect. Their model suggests that high neuroticism is more closely associated with low mastery and self-efficacy, which affects life choices in younger adulthood, such as educational achievement, thus impacting cognition in later adulthood. As will be discussed later, self-efficacy and sense of control are strong predictors of cognitive ability and performance, and can influence the trajectory of cognitive aging. In congruence with these findings, Gow, Whiteman, Pattie, and Deary (2005) found that within the Five-Factor model (openness, neuroticism, conscientiousness, agreeableness, and extraversion), neuroticism and openness were related to intelligence at both Time 1 (age 11) and Time 2 (age 79). They found that neuroticism was associated with cognitive change, such that those with higher neuroticism had greater decline relative to baseline intelligence.

All told, these studies suggest that not only does personality have a significant influence on cognitive performance, but that this relation varies across the lifespan and has the potential to serve as a buffer against decline in old age. A number of these studies posit explanations for why this may be the case, for example that self-efficacy and education in young adults with high neuroticism influences cognition in later adulthood (Gold et al.,

1995), or that arousal and anxiety associated with extraversion and neuroticism may also influence the cognitive aging process (e.g., Crowe et al., 2006; Duchek et al., 2007). These findings suggest that specific characteristics of personality may partially explain these relationships.

Other Approaches to Personality: Personal Action Constructs

A second class of personality characteristics, known as personal action constructs (PACs; Hooker & McAdams, 2003) are also related to cognition. PACs are distinctive from traits in that they are more malleable and show greater change across situations and time. Thus they may play an important role in explaining how cognitive performance is tied to individual differences. Not only are PACS directly related, but they also may play a role as mediators of the relationship between personality traits and cognitive functioning. Although it is clear that personality is related to cognitive functioning, little is known about how and why this is the case. The following sections explore a number of possible factors that could help to elucidate these links.

Included in the study of PACs is the notion of control beliefs. According to this view, the amount of control one feels over one's environment and over the ability to affect outcomes in life (based effort), has an actual impact on later life outcomes. Having a high sense of mastery (also the ability to cope with stressful situations) and low perceived constraints (the extent to which factors interfere with your desired outcomes), are related to higher cognitive performance. This is particularly salient in middle and later adulthood, which indicates that having a sense of control may help buffer against the effects of age on cognition (Miller & Lachman, 2000). Furthermore, having attentional control and using compensatory techniques such as inhibiting attention away from distractions and processing resources may buffer against the effects of anxiety on performance, and also may moderate age differences in cognition (M. W. Eysenck, Derakshan, Santos, & Calvo, 2007).

Achievement motivation

Another example of PACs in relation to cognition is achievement motivation. Motivation represents a person's interest and engagement in projects and tasks and their level of commitment to handling issues that arise in their life (Little, 1999). Individuals who are motivated to work hard may do well despite possible intellectual disadvantages (Chamarro-Premuzic & Furnham, 2005). High motivation is highly adaptive because it promotes "a process of selective optimization in the chosen domain of functioning," such as cognitive performance (Maciel, Heckhausen, & Baltes, 1994, p. 81).

Major, Turner, and Fletcher (2006) recently studied personality and motivation to learn in workplace environments. Factor and facet levels of the Five-Factor model were examined, in addition to what they called the "proactive personality," which is based on the facet levels of assertiveness and activity (extraversion), actions, ideas, and values (openness), altruism (agreeableness), dutifulness, and achievement striving (conscientiousness). Extraversion, openness, and conscientiousness (most strongly) were related to high motivation to learn (Major, Turner, & Fletcher, 2006).

Thus there is evidence suggesting that motivation may be a key individual difference factor in predicting cognitive performance. The adaptive nature of motivation and control is largely dependent upon individuals' realistic evaluation of their own abilities. Thus, as adults age, their expectations about performance capacities will continually need adjustment in order to account for the declines taking place (Maciel et al., 1994). Part of this adjustment process involves removing false belief that an individual is helpless in the face of decline.

Sense of control

Control beliefs, defined as individuals' belief in their ability to influence their performance outcomes, are essential to the study of personality and cognition across the lifespan (Maciel, Heckhausen, & Baltes, 1994). Low control and self-efficacy can impede performance irrespective of how capable an individual actually is. A high sense of control is valuable to healthy aging (Lachman & Prenda-Firth, 2004; Miller & Lachman, 2000). Self-estimated intelligence, or self-assessed intelligence (SAI) is also related such that people who believe that they have high levels of ability would more likely also have a high sense of control over their ability to do well. Chamorro-Premuzic and colleagues (Chamorro-Premuzic & Furnham, 2004; Chamorro-Premuzic et al., 2006) found that SAI mediates the relation between openness and psychometric intelligence. Therefore, it may not be trait-level openness that is directly associated with higher performance, but beliefs in the abilities to do well may be an intervening variable (Chamorro-Premuzic & Furnham, 2004; Chamorro-Premuzic et al., 2006).

Another study linked situational constraints, personality, performance, and self-efficacy in a sample of young adults (Gerhardt, Rode, & Peterson, 2007). Conscientiousness and neuroticism were expected to be related to both self-management and perceived constraints, which should influence self-efficacy and thereby affect performance. The results supported their hypothesis such that individuals high in conscientiousness had higher self-efficacy. However, it appears that the high control/self-efficacy relationship partially mediates the link between conscientiousness and both academic performance and general cognitive ability. For neuroticism, they found a negative link to self-efficacy, which was associated with performance, suggesting that individuals higher in neuroticism have lower self-efficacy, which partially mediates its relation to performance (Gerhardt et al., 2007). In later life, those who are high in neuroticism may be more vulnerable to declining cognitive abilities because of their lower self-efficacy.

In an attempt to explore variables involved in linking personality to various cognitive outcomes, Lee and colleagues used goal patterns, goal levels, mental focus, autonomy, and control as predictors of performance in young adults. They found that high control orientations are related to performance-approach related goals, which increases mental focus, thereby positively impacting performance (Lee, Sheldon, & Turban, 2003). This supports other findings (e.g., Gerdhardt et al., 2007; Lachman et al., 2004) that high control and mental engagement are related to better performance.

In the memory domain, Lachman and Andreoletti (2006) investigated mechanisms linking control beliefs to memory in a study of 335 adults aged 21 to 83, by asking participants to recall a list of categorizable words such as types of fruits and flowers. They found that control beliefs were positively related to effective strategy use and to recall performance for middle-aged and older adults, but not for young adults. Moreover, the relationship between control beliefs and recall was mediated by strategy use for the middle-aged and partially mediated for older adults. Those who had a higher sense of control were more likely to use an effective strategy, in this case categorizing the words, and they in turn had better recall. Although the directional relationship cannot be confirmed, given the correlational design, they tested alternative directional models and this mediational model provided the best fit. Other studies have also found that control beliefs are related to strategic behavior including compensatory strategy use (Hertzog, McGuire, & Lineweaver, 1998; Riggs, Lachman, & Wingfield, 1997) and effective goal setting (West & Yassuda, 2004). Moreover, Amrhein, Bond, and Hamilton (1999) found that older adults with a lower sense of internal control had lower episodic memory recall and less categorical clustering, whereas the younger adults did not show any relations of control beliefs on either clustering or recall performance.

There are also empirical arguments supporting the role of stress level or stress reactivity as mediator between control beliefs and memory performance. First, control beliefs play a key role in the stress response (Müller, Günther, Habel, & Rockstroh, 1998). Experiencing high personal control in a challenging situation has been shown to reduce stress-related neuroendocrine response such as the hypothalamic-pituitary-adrenal (HPA) axis response (Kirschbaum et al., 1995; Seeman & Robbins, 1994). Other results reveal that stressors can activate responses in the HPA and autonomic nervous system (e.g., slowing or increasing in heart rate), especially if the stimulus is appraised as being out of personal control (Kemeny, 2003). Moreover, when stressors are seen as uncontrollable and the goal is important or desirable, the reactivity level is higher (Dickerson & Kemeny, 2004). Second, high levels of stress have been shown to affect memory performance among younger (Kirschbaum, Wolf, May, Wippich, & Hellhammer, 1996) as well as older adults (Lupien et al., 1997). The evidence suggests that acute stress affects memory performance by causing hippocampal damage (Kirschbaum et al., 1996; Lupien et al., 1997). Similarly, prolonged exposure to stress has also been associated with a loss of hippocampal neurons (McEwen, 2001).

Memory self-efficacy (MSE) is defined as individuals' beliefs about their own memory function, and their confidence in the effectiveness of their ability in a given situation (Valentijn et al., 2006). Studies indicate that memory self-efficacy is associated with better memory performance in later adulthood (Valentijn et al., 2006), and that self-efficacy and control are strong indicators of better outcomes across the lifespan (Agrigoroaei & Lachman, 2010; Lachman, Neupert, & Agrigoroaei, 2011).

Concerning MSE beliefs, a low level may result in a reduction in memory performance, for example, by increasing the level of anxiety and arousal (Bandura, Cioffi, Taylor, & Brouillard, 1988) or by creating an expectation of failure (Desrichard & Köpetz, 2005) that may lead individuals to make less effort and be less persistent (Berry & West, 1993; Cavanaugh & Green, 1990) in memory situations. In the literature, effort is usually operationalized as strategy use and persistence as allocated time or number of attempted items. Although Hertzog, Hultsch, and Dixon (1989) reported a consistent small negative correlation between an individual's MSE and that person's scores on the mnemonics usage scales, several studies have shown that MSE is not significantly linked to the tendency to use such strategies (Jonker, Smits, & Deeg, 1997; McDonald-Miszczak, Gould, & Tychynski, 1999; McDougall, 1995; Troyer & Rich, 2002). Furthermore, in a recent study, Wells and Esopenko (2008) did not find a relationship between MSE and the amount of time participants spent on a free-recall task. MSE, however, has been shown to impact the person's goal system and the choice of activities (Berry & West, 1993; West, Dark-Freudeman, & Bagwell, 2009). For instance, Elliott and Lachman (1989) suggested that persons with a lower MSE level tend to avoid challenging memory situations. According to the results obtained by Bagwell and West (2008), MSE also tends to predict individual investment in memory intervention programs.

Studies have shown that control beliefs and self-efficacy in older adults can be modified using cognitive behavioral techniques such as cognitive restructuring or performance feedback (Elliott & Lachman, 1989; Lachman, 2006). Moreover, when individuals are encouraged or trained to use specific strategies, not only do they have better performance overall, but older adults in these conditions report higher self-efficacy as well (Lachman, Andreoletti, & Pearman, 2006; West, Bagwell, & Dark-Freudeman, 2007). This indicates that performance expectancies are amenable to change in response to performance feedback even in later life.

Activity and engagement

One of the key characteristics of openness to experience is curiosity, which can be operationally defined in a number of ways, including cognitive involvement, intellectual engagement, and creativity. Some studies claim that individuals with intellectually and socially engaged lifestyles have slower rates of cognitive decline with age, and that the complexity of one's environment has an effect on intellectual functioning (Ashton, Lee, Vernon, & Jang, 2000; Bates & Shieles, 2003; Schooler & Mulatu, 2001; Schooler, Mulatu, & Oates, 1999).

Recently, Ashton and colleagues looked specifically at how the openness/intellect factor was related to fluid and crystallized intelligence domains and found that openness was related to both. They also examined individual markers of openness, (a) understanding/intellectual curiosity, (b) sentience/aesthetic sensitivity, (c) change/variety seeking, and (d) autonomy/independence, and found that understanding (intellectual curiosity) was most strongly related to both fluid and crystallized intelligence, which is consistent with the notion that engagement is one underlying factor that may be mediating the link between openness and cognition, particularly across the lifespan (Ashton et al., 2000).

Bates and Shieles (2003) computed a series of structural equation models, which linked general intelligence, measured by Raven's Advanced Progressive Matrices and crystallized intelligence, measured by vocabulary, with openness and processing speed (inspection time of a computerized stimulus task) on a sample of 64 young adults. The model that best fit their data indicated that openness is independent of information processing speed, but related to crystallized knowledge and general ability. This suggests that openness's predictive power of intelligence is driven by creativity, interest, curiosity, and crystallized knowledge (Bates & Shieles, 2003). Turning to older adults, Schooler and colleagues have conducted a number of longitudinal studies examining the effects of substantively complex work environments and leisure activities on cognitive functioning and found that engagement in more cognitively complex work or leisure activities was associated over time with increased cognitive functioning (Schooler et al., 1999; Schooler & Mulatu, 2001).

Health, lifestyle, and socioeconomic status (SES) may also play a role in the relationship between personality and abilities. Gold and colleagues (1995) proposed a structural equation model which links lifestyle, age, education, SES, health, and personality to verbal and nonverbal ability in older men, based on the hypothesis that individual differences in cognitive aging result from early life characteristics that are related to more favorable cognitive outcomes across the lifespan. Their model suggests that there is a greater likelihood in having an engaged lifestyle (which helps retain cognition in later life) among the highly educated (high SES) and intellectually oriented. Their findings indicate that high SES and having higher intelligence as a young adult also leads to a high sense of mastery and control over one's environment, thus making it more likely for these individuals to achieve more as they age (Gold et al., 1995).

In summary, it appears that the openness trait is significantly related to cognitive performance in part due to the tendency of the highly open to be more intellectually engaged, imaginative, and creative. While openness and engagement are not completely equivalent, some evidence suggests that engagement may be an important mechanism, and that continued engagement in one's environment may be a protective factor against cognitive decline. Control beliefs and engagement are related, such that individuals with a high sense of control are more apt to engage in activities that benefit their cognitive health as they age. The possibility exists for these underlying components of openness to be enhanced in individuals, with a goal of maximizing performance of older adults as they age.

Anxiety and its relationship to cognition

Anxiety is studied in many different ways, including self-reports of general trait anxiety, state anxiety, and domain-specific aspects of anxiety, such as test anxiety (Spielberger & Vagg, 1995). It is widely documented that test anxiety has a significant impact on processing (M. W. Eysenck et al., 2007) and performance (Booth, Schinka, Brown, Mortimer, & Borenstein, 2006; Chamorro-Premuzic & Furnham, 2005; Dobson, 2000; M. W. Eysenck & Calvo, 1992; Hagtvet & Renmin, 1996; Humphreys & Revelle, 1984; Moutafi, Furnham, & Tsaousis, 2006). State anxiety reflects the tension, stress, and autonomic arousal associated with a specific situation in the here-and-now, while trait-anxiety reflects a stable characteristic or anxiety proneness. One model linking both types of anxiety is illustrated with stress and trait anxiety being directly related to state anxiety, and indirectly related to cognitive processing and test performance via state anxiety (Dobson, 2000). In addition, neuroticism is associated with higher perceived stress (Hooker, Monahan, Shifren, & Hutchinson, 1992), and greater reactivity to stress

(Mroczek & Almeida, 2004), which may explain why stress and neuroticism are closely linked in predicting cognitive performance.

According to the state-trait model of anxiety, "the effects of neuroticism on anxiety will be most evident under stress" (Bolger & Schilling, 1991, p. 357). Evidence suggests that the link between neuroticism and distress is explained more by stress reactivity than stress exposure. Bolger and colleagues have looked at this phenomenon in more detail, by examining how personality influences exposure and reactivity to stress and how this in turn impacts health and psychological outcomes. They found that not only is high neuroticism associated with greater stress reactivity (measured by change in anger and depression in conflict vs. nonconflict conditions), but there is also a differential coping pattern between people high and low in neuroticism (Bolger & Zuckerman, 1995). The high neuroticism group exhibited significantly higher rates of problem solving, self-controlling, support seeking, and escape avoidance behaviors (Bolger & Zuckerman, 1995). H. J. Eysenck (1967) argues that introverts have high baseline cortical arousal, which results in lower performance under stress, whereas extraverts have lower levels of cortical arousal, which may result in higher performance under stress. This explanation may be useful in understanding the seemingly inconsistent findings with regard to extraversion. Some theories suggest that anxiety cannot be simply termed as a source or cause of cognitive distraction, but rather that moderate levels of anxiety can facilitate cognitive performance (Luu, Tucker, & Derryberry, 1998). According to achievement motivation theory, if outcome uncertainty is maximized, the motivation to avoid failure and approach success is subsequently maximally aroused. Others have also found that individuals high in neuroticism tend to utilize coping strategies such as avoidance and self-blame which can be counterproductive when attempting to relieve stress and anxiety (Costa, Somerfield, & McCrae, 1996; Kokkonen & Pulkinen, 2001; Robinson, Wilkowsky, Kirkeby, & Meier, 2006).

In addition to self reports of anxiety, others have considered physiological indicators such as heart rate and stress hormones (e.g., cortisol) (Kirschbaum et al., 1996). Vedhara and colleagues collected salivary cortisol from undergraduate samples during nonexam and exam periods. They found that self-reported stress was significantly higher during exam periods and that cortisol was significantly lower. Although this was unexpected, they did find that this reduction in cortisol was associated with better short-term memory performance, indicating that cognitive performance is more directly related to physiological measures of stress than self-reported stress (Vedhara, Hyde, Gilchrist, Tytherleigh, & Plummer, 2000). Other reports suggest that increased cortisol activity is related to declines with age in memory performance and, conversely, that declines in cortisol are associated with improved memory performance (Kirschbaum et al., 1996; Wright, Kunz-Ebrecht, Iliffe, Foese, & Steptoe, 2005).

To summarize, anxiety has a major influence on performance, and may partially explain the relations of neuroticism and extraversion with cognitive performance. Evidence suggests that moderate levels of arousal are necessary to motivate performance, but that greater reactivity to stress is detrimental to performance. Anxiety in anticipation of a cognitive task is associated with lower memory performance in middle and later adulthood, which further indicates that anxiety's effect on cognition is a particularly salient issue to address in cognitive aging research (Andreoletti, Veratti, & Lachman, 2006).

Personality and Coping with Cognitive Losses

Across the lifespan and throughout the aging process, most individuals are forced to face some inevitable declines and losses. Although this is, to some extent, unavoidable, there is still the possibility of maintaining a high sense of well-being and psychological health despite losses. Coping is one such process that allows individuals to maintain well-being as they age, and a number of studies have examined the ways in which personality facilitates and/or inhibits coping behavior. For example, the Victoria Longitudinal Study (Dixon & de Frias, 2004) has examined memory compensation as one such problem-focused coping strategy by examining ways in which personality traits are related to cognitive change and memory compensation over time. Their analyses are based on a number of subscales of the Memory Compensation Questionnaire (MCQ): Effort, Success, Change, External, and Internal. One of their key findings was that personality traits were significantly related to change in memory compensation (coping) over time. Specifically, high neuroticism was associated with greater decline in memory compensation effort, while individuals high in conscientious and agreeableness continued to use memory compensation techniques over a 6-year period. Finally, high extraversion was associated with increased MCQ success. These findings indicate that personality traits not only are associated with cognition itself, but also with using strategies and coping skills that help optimize age-related cognitive change (Dixon & de Frias, 2004).

Since coping is a process that takes place in response to problems and stress exposure, individual personality traits are expected to be associated with coping, in part, because of their differential relations to ways of handling stress, specifically in terms of emotion-focused coping and problem-focused coping. For instance, conscientiousness is linked to lower exposure to stressors, while extraversion is linked to lower reactivity and positive coping resources (Gunthert, Cohen, & Armeli, 1999; Penley & Tomaka, 2002; Suls & Martin, 2005; Vollrath, 2001). Neuroticism in particular has been associated with negative outcomes and maladaptive strategies geared towards these outcomes, such as disengagement, lack of problem solving, emotion regulation, wishful thinking, withdrawal, and emotion-focused coping (Conner-Smith & Flachsbart, 2007). There is a strong association between daily stress and negative affect among individuals high in neuroticism, and this association is particularly strong in adulthood (Mroczek & Almeida, 2004), which suggests that older adults with high neuroticism may have more difficulty coping with daily stress. Furthermore, agreeableness, extraversion, openness, and conscientiousness all tend to predict more positive coping strategies (such as primary control, problem solving, and social support) (Conner-Smith & Flachsbart, 2007). There is also evidence that the use of maladaptive defensive mechanisms such as denial and projection predicts increased neuroticism and decreased extraversion and agreeableness, a relation which appears to grow stronger with age (Cramer, 2003).

Brandstädter and colleagues have developed a model that relates two types of coping strategies to goal achievement (Brandtstädter, 1989; Brandtstädter & Rothermund, 2002; Rothermund & Brandtstädter, 2003). This dual-process model describes the interaction between active coping mechanisms, or assimilation (via instrumental, self-corrective, and compensatory means, changing the environment to meet goals), and of accommodation, that is, adjusting one's personal goals to changing abilities or resources (e.g., via devaluation, disengagement, lowering of standards). Their recent work suggest that individuals who maintain an assimilative approach when goals are unattainable, and engage in compensatory efforts in the face of change, are better off taking more accommodative actions. In this way, individuals adjust their goals (accommodation) in order to maintain a positive outlook of themselves and their lives (Rothermund & Brandtstädter, 2003).

This has also been identified via Whitbourne's identity process theory which postulates a relatively similar model, such that individuals process age-related changes via assimilation, accommodation, and identity balance. Whitbourne's model is distinctly different than Brandtstädter's, such that Whitbourne defines identity assimilation as the change in an individual's goals (not of the self), which is more consistent with the Piagetian line of reasoning. When individuals are in a state of identity balance, they are better equipped to deal with changes when faced with challenges while at the same time maintaining a "consistent sense of self" (Sneed & Whitbourne, 2005, p. 384).

Similarly, Heckhausen and colleagues have developed the Lifespan Theory of Control to describe coping in terms of primary and secondary control (Heckhausen & Schulz, 1995; Heckhausen, Wrosch, & Schulz, 2010). Primary control refers to the active expansion of goals, while secondary control comes into play as an individual's goals become no longer attainable (Haynes, Heckhausen, Chipperfield, Perry, & Newall, 2009). These studies inform us as to the ways in which the aging population differentially copes or manages challenges associated with changes and declines.

Summary and Conclusions

Personality is a resource that can influence the way one is able to negotiate the terrain of aging. There is clear evidence that personality changes for some of the people some of the time (Cramer, 2003; Helson & Kwan, 2000; Roberts, Walton, & Viechtbauer, 2006; Schaie et al., 2004). It is of interest what personality can do for human beings in terms of optimal aging. In the face of aging-related changes, personality may serve as an adaptive resource that can promote resilience, such that the combination of personality traits and the underlying characteristics (anxiety, stress, coping, etc.) result in optimal cognitive functioning. Although personality may protect against cognitive decline, further work is needed to examine whether changes in cognitive functioning, such as severe cognitive impairment, lead to changes in personality, or whether those with adaptive personalities engage in behaviors and select situations that help to minimize declines. Personality is related to cognitive functioning and health in adulthood and old age, but we do not have a clear understanding of the mechanisms that underlie these links. Further investigation is needed to consider the best targets for interventions, including the more malleable personality mechanisms such as PACs and coping beliefs. Moreover, future intervention studies are needed, which are focused on mechanisms such as self-efficacy and coping (Lachman et al., 2006; West et al., 2007), which may also have a positive influence on their cognitive outcomes. Interventions can be tailored to match personalities to specific programs designed to optimize functioning in later adulthood.

Acknowledgments

We appreciate the multiple sources of support that facilitated preparation of this chapter, including NIA grants RO1 AG17920, PO1 AG20166, and T32 AG00204. The chapter was written while the second author was a fellow at the Center for Advanced Study in the Behavioral Sciences and a member of the working group sponsored by the Stanford Center on Longevity.

References

Ackerman, P. L., & Heggestad, E. D. (1997). Intelligence, personality and interests: Evidence for overlapping traits. *Psychological Bulletin, 121*, 219–245.

Ackerman, P. L., & Rolfhus, E. L. (1999). The locus of adult intelligence: Knowledge, abilities, and nonability traits. *Psychology and Aging, 14*, 314–330.

Agrigoroaei, S., & Lachman, M.E. (2010). Personal control and aging: How beliefs and expectation matter. In J. C. Cavanaugh & C. K. Cavanaugh (Eds.), *Aging in America. Vol. 1: Psychological aspects* (pp. 177–201). Santa Barbara, CA: Praeger.

Amrhein, P. C., Bond, J. K., & Hamilton, D. A. (1999). Locus of control and the age difference in free recall from episodic memory. *Journal of General Psychology, 126*, 149–164.

Andreoletti, C., Veratti, B. W., & Lachman, M. E. (2006). Age differences in the relationship between anxiety and recall. *Aging and Mental Health, 10*, 265–271.

Arbuckle, T. Y., Gold, D., & Andres, D. (1986). Cognitive functioning of older people in relation to social and personality variables. *Journal of Psychology and Aging, 1*, 55–62.

Ashton, M. C., Lee, K., Vernon, P. A., & Jang, K. L. (2000). Fluid intelligence, crystallized intelligence, and the openness/intellect factor. *Journal of Research in Personality, 34*, 198–207.

Bagwell, D. K., & West, R. L. (2008). Assessing compliance: Active versus inactive trainees in a memory intervention. *Clinical Interventions in Aging, 3*, 371–382.

Baker, T. J., & Bichsel, J. (2006). Personality predictors of intelligence: Differences between young and cognitively health older adults. *Personality and Individual Differences, 41*, 861–871.

Bandura, A., Cioffi, D., Taylor, C. B., & Brouillard, M. E. (1988). Perceived self-efficacy in coping with cognitive stressors and opioid activation. *Journal of Personality and Social Psychology, 55*, 479–488.

Bates, T. C., & Shieles, A. (2003). Crystallized intelligence as a product of speed and drive for experience: The relationship of inspection time and openness to g and gc. *Intelligence, 31*, 275–287.

Berry, J. M., & West, R. L. (1993). Cognitive self-efficacy in relation to personal mastery and goal setting across the life span. *International Journal of Behavioral Development, 16*, 351–379.

Bolger, N., & Schilling, E. A. (1991). Personality and the problems of everyday life: The role of neuroticism in exposure and reactivity to daily stressors. *Journal of Personality, 59*, 355–386.

Bolger, N., & Zuckerman, A. (1995). A framework for studying personality in the stress process. *Personality Processes and Individual Differences, 69*, 890–902.

Booth, J. E., Schinka, J. A., Brown, L. M., Mortimer, J. A., & Borenstein, A. R. (2006). Five-factor personality dimensions, mood states, and cognitive performance in older adults. *Journal of Clinical and Experimental Neuropsychology, 28,* 676–683.

Brandtstädter, J. (1989). Personal self-regulation of development: Cross-sequential analyses of development-related control beliefs and emotions. *Developmental Psychology, 25,* 96–108.

Brandtstädter, J., & Rothermund, K. (2002). The life-course dynamics of goal pursuit and goal adjustment: A two-process framework. *Developmental Review, 22,* 117–150.

Cavanaugh, J. C., & Green, E. E. (1990). I believe, therefore I can: Self-efficacy beliefs in memory aging. In E. A. Lovelace (Ed.), *Aging and cognition: Mental processes, self-awareness, and interventions* (pp. 189–230). Amsterdam: Elsevier.

Chamorro-Premuzic, T., & Furnham, A. (2004). A possible model for understanding the personality-intelligence interface. *British Journal of Psychology, 95,* 249–264.

Chamorro-Premuzic, T., & Furnham, A. (2005). *Personality and intellectual competence.* Mahwah: NJ: Erlbaum.

Chamorro-Premuzic, T., Furnham, A., & Ackerman, P.L. (2006). Ability and personality correlates of general knowledge. *Personality and Individual Differences, 41,* 419–429.

Conner-Smith, J. K., & Flachsbart, C. (2007). Relations between personality and coping: A meta-analysis. *Journal of Personality and Social Psychology, 93,* 1080–1107.

Costa, P. T., Fozard, J. L., McCrae, R. R., & Bosse, R. (1976). Relations of age and personality dimensions to cognitive ability factors. *Journal of Gerontology, 31,* 663– 669.

Costa, P. T., Herbst, J. H., McCrae, R. R., & Siegler, I. C. (2000). Personality at midlife: Stability, intrinsic maturation, and response to life events. *Assessment: Special issue: Innovations in assessment using the Revised NEO Personality Inventory, 74,* 365–378.

Costa, P. T., & McCrae, R. R. (2000). Neo personality inventory. In A. E. Kazdin (Ed.), *Encyclopedia of psychology* (Vol. 5, pp. 407–409). Washington, DC: American Psychological Association.

Costa, P. T., Somerfield, M. R., & McCrae, R. R. (1996). Personality and coping: A reconceptualization. In M. Zeidner & N. S. Endler (Eds.), *Handbook of coping: Theory, research, applications* (pp. 44–61). New York: Wiley.

Cramer, P. (2003). Personality change in later adulthood is predicted by defense mechanism use in early adulthood. *Journal of Research in Personality, 27,* 76–104.

Crowe, M., Andel, R., Pedersen, N. L., Fratiglioni, L., & Gatz, M. (2006). Personality and risk of cognitive impairment 25 years later. *Psychology and Aging, 21,* 573–580.

Desrichard, O., & Köpetz, C. (2005). A threat in the elder: The impact of task-instructions, self-efficacy and performance expectations on memory performance in the elderly. *European Journal of Social Psychology, 35,* 537–552.

Dickerson, S. S., & Kemeny, M. E. (2004). Acute stressors and cortisol responses: A theoretical integration and synthesis of laboratory research. *Psychological Bulletin, 130,* 355–391.

Dixon, R. A., & de Frias, C. M. (2004). The Victoria Longitudinal Study: From characterizing cognitive aging to illustrating changes in memory compensation. *Aging Neuropsychology and Cognition, 11,* 346–376.

Dobson, P. (2000). An investigation into the relationship between neuroticism, extraversion and cognitive test performance in selection. *International Journal of Selection and Assessment, 8,* 99–110.

Duchek, J. M., Balota, D. A., Storandt, M., & Larsen, R. (2007). The power of personality in discriminating between health aging and early-stage Alzheimer's disease. *Journal of Gerontology: Psychological Sciences, 62B,* P353–P361.

Elliot, E., & Lachman, M. E. (1989). Enhancing memory by modifying control beliefs, attributions and performance goals in the elderly. In P. S. Fry (Ed.), *Advances in psychology: Psychological perspectives of helplessness and control in the elderly* (pp. 339–368). Amsterdam: Elsevier.

Eysenck, H. J. (1967). *The biological basis of personality.* Springfield, IL: Thomas.

Eysenck, M. W., & Calvo, M. G. (1992). Anxiety and performance: The processing efficiency theory. *Cognition and Emotion, 6,* 409–434.

Eysenck, M. W., Derakshan, N., Santos, R., & Calvo, M. G. (2007). Anxiety and cognitive performance: Attentional control theory. *Emotion, 7,* 336–353.

Gerhardt, M. W., Rode, J. C., & Peterson, S. J. (2007). Exploring mechanism in the personality-performance relationship: Mediating roles of self-management and situational constraints. *Personality and Individual Differences, 43,* 1344–1355.

Gold, D. P., Andres, D., Etezadi, J., Arbuckle, T., Schwartzman A., & Chaikelson, J. (1995). Structural equation model of intellectual change and continuity and predictors of intelligence in older men. *Psychology and Aging, 10,* 294–303.

Gow, A. J., Whiteman, M. C., Pattie, A. & Deary, I.J. (2005). The personality-intelligence interface: Insights from an ageing cohort. *Personality and Individual Differences, 29,* 751–761.

Gunthert, K. C., Cohen, L. H., & Armeli, S. (1999). The role of neuroticism in daily stress and coping. *Journal of Personality and Social Psychology, 77,* 1087–1100.

Hagtvet, K. A., & Renmin, Y. (1996). Anxiety and stress in a time-based performance process. *Anxiety, Stress, and Coping, 9,* 33–51.

Haynes, T. L., Heckhausen, J., Chipperfield, J. G., Perry, R. P., & Newall, N. E. (2009). Primary and secondary control strategies: Implications for health and well-being among older adults. *Journal of Social and Clinical Psychology, 28,* 165–197.

Heckhausen, J., & Schulz, R. (1995). A life-span theory of control. *Psychological Review, 102,* 284–304.

Heckhausen, J., Wrosch, C., & Schulz, W. C. (2010). A motivational theory of life-span development. *Psychological Review, 117,* 32–60.

Helson, R., & Kwan, V. S. Y. (2000). Personality development in adulthood: The broad picture and processes in one longitudinal study. In S. Hampson (Ed.), *Advances in personality psychology* (Vol. 1, pp. 77–106). Hove, UK: Psychology Press.

Hertzog, C., Hultsch, D. F., & Dixon, R. A. (1989). Evidence for the convergent validity of two self-report metamemory questionnaires. *Developmental Psychology, 25,* 687–700.

Hertzog, C., McGuire, C. L., & Lineweaver, T. T. (1998). Aging, attributions, perceived control, and strategy use in a free recall task. *Aging, Neuropsychology, and Cognition, 5,* 85–106.

Holland, D. C., Dollinger, S. J., Holland, C. J., & MacDonald, D. A. (1995). The relationship between psychometric intelligence and the five-factor model of personality in a rehabilitation sample. *Journal of Clinical Psychology, 51,* 79–90.

Hooker, K., & McAdams, D. P. (2003). Personality reconsidered: A new agenda for aging research. *Journal of Gerontology: Psychological Sciences, 58,* 296–304.

Hooker, K., Monahan, D., Shifren, K., & Hutchinson, C. (1992). Mental and physical health of spouse caregivers: The role of personality. *Psychology and Aging, 7,* 367–375.

Humphreys, M. S., & Revelle, W. (1984). Personality, motivation, and performance: A theory of the relationship between individual differences and information processing. *Psychological Review, 91,* 153–185.

Jackson, J. J., Bogg, T., Walton, K. E., Wood, D., Harms, P. D., Lodi-Smith, J., . . . Roberts, B. W. (2009). Not all conscientiousness scales change alike: A multimethod, multisample study of age differences in the facets of conscientiousness. *Journal of Personality and Social Psychology, 96,* 446–459.

Jelicic, M., Bosma, H., Ponds, R. W. H. M., Van Boxtel, M. P. J., Houx, P. J., & Jolles, J. (2003). Neuroticism does not affect cognitive functioning in later life. *Experimental Aging Research, 29,* 73–78.

Jonker, C., Smits, C. M., & Deeg, D. J. H. (1997). Affect-related metamemory and memory performance in a population-based sample of older adults. *Educational Gerontology, 23,* 115–128.

Kemeny, M.E. (2003). The psychobiology of stress. *Current Directions in Psychological Science, 12,* 124–129.

Kirschbaum, C., Prussner, J. C., Stone, A. A., Federenko, I., Gaab, J., Lintz, D. . . . Hellhammer, D. H. (1995). Persistent high cortisol responses to repeated psychological stress in a subpopulation of healthy men. *Psychosomatic Medicine, 57,* 468–474.

Kirschbaum, C., Wolf, O. T., May, M., Wippich, W., & Hellhammer, D. H. (1996). Stress- and treatment-induced elevations of cortisol levels associated with impaired declarative memory in health adults. *Life Sciences, 58,* 1475–1483.

Kokkonen, M., & Pulkkinen, L. (2001). Extraversion and neuroticism as antecedents of emotion regulation and dysregulation in adulthood. *European Journal of Personality, 15,* 407–424.

Lachman, M. E. (2006). Perceived control over aging-related declines: Adaptive beliefs and behaviors. *Current Directions in Psychological Science, 15,* 282–288.

Lachman, M. E. & Andreoletti, C. (2006). Strategy use mediates the relationship between control beliefs and memory performance for middle-aged and older adults. *Journals of Gerontology: Psychological Sciences, 61B,* P88–P94.

Lachman, M. E., Andreoletti, C., & Pearman, A. (2006). Memory control beliefs: How are they related to age, strategy use and memory improvement? *Social Cognition, 24,* 359–385.

Lachman, M. E., & Bertrand, R. M. (2001). Personality and the self in midlife. In M. E. Lachman (Ed.), *Handbook of midlife development* (pp. 279–309). New York: Wiley.

Lachman, M. E., Neupert, S. D., & Agrigoroaei, S. (2011). The relevance of control beliefs for health and aging. In K. W. Schaie & S. L. Willis (Eds.), *Handbook of the psychology of aging* (7th ed., pp. 175–190). New York: Elsevier.

Lachman, M. E., & Prenda-Firth, K. M. F. (2004). The adaptive value of feeling in control during midlife. In O. G. Brim, C. D. Ryff, & R. C. Kessler (Eds.), *How healthy are we? A national study of well-being at midlife* (pp. 320–349). Chicago: University of Chicago Press.

Lee, F. K., Sheldon, K. M., & Turban, D. B. (2003). Personality and the goal-striving process: The influence of achievement goal patterns, goal level, and mental focus on performance and enjoyment. *Journal of Applied Psychology, 88,* 256–265.

Little, B. R. (1999). Personality and motivation: Personality action and the conative evolution. In L. A. Pervin & O. P. John (Eds.), *Handbook of personality: Theory and research* (2nd ed., pp. 501–524). New York: Guilford Press.

Lupien, S. J., Gaudreau, S., Tchiteya, B. M., Maheu, F., Sharma, S., Nair, N. P. V., . . . Meaney, M. J. (1997). Stress-induced declarative memory impairment in healthy elderly subjects: Relationship to cortisol reactivity. *Journal of Clinical Endocrinology and Metabolism, 82,* 2070–2075.

Luu, P., Tucker, D. M., & Derryberry, D. (1998) Anxiety and the motivational basis of working memory. *Cognitive Therapy and Research, 22,* 577–594.

Maciel, A. G., Heckhausen, J., & Baltes, P. B. (1994). A lifespan perspective on the interface between personality and intelligence. In R. J. Sternberg & P. Ruzgis (Eds.), *Personality and intelligence* (pp. 61–103). New York: Cambridge University Press.

Major, D. A., Turner, J. E., & Fletcher, T. D. (2006). Linking proactive personality and the big five to motivation to learn and developmental activity. *Journal of Applied Psychology, 91,* 927–935.

Matthews, G. (1997). Intelligence, personality and information-processing: An adaptive perspective. *Advances in Cognition and Educational Practice, 4,* 175–200.

McCrae, R. R. (1987). Creativity, divergent thinking and openness to experience. *Journal of Personality and Social Psychology, 52,* 1258–1265.

McCrae, R. R., Costa, P. T., Ostendorf, F., Angleitner, A., Hřebíčková, M., Avia, M. D., . . . Smith, P. B. (2000). Nature over nurture: Temperament, personality and life span development. *Journal of Personality and Social Psychology, 78,* 173–186.

McDonald-Miszczak, L., Gould, O. N., & Tychynski, D. (1999). Metamemory predictors of prospective and retrospective memory performance. *Journal of General Psychology, 126,* 37–52.

McDougall, G. J. (1995). Memory self-efficacy and strategy use in successful elders. *Educational Gerontology, 21,* 357–373.

McEwen, B. S. (2001). Plasticity of the hippocampus: Adaptation to chronic stress and allostatic load. In B. A. Sorg & I. R. Bell (Eds.), *The role of neural plasticity in chemical intolerance* (pp. 265–277). New York: New York Academy of Sciences.

Meier, B., Perrig-Chiello, P., & Perrig, W. (2002). Personality and memory in old age. *Aging Neuropsychology and Cognition, 9,* 135–144.

Miller, L. M., & Lachman, M. E. (2000). Cognitive performance and the role of control beliefs in midlife. *Aging Neuropsychology and Cognition, 7,* 69–85.

Moutafi, J., Furnham, A., & Crump, J. (2003). Demographic and personality predictors of intelligence: A study using the NEO personality inventory and the Myers-Briggs type indicator. *European Journal of Personality, 17,* 79–94.

Moutafi, J., Furnham, A., & Crump, J. (2006). What facets of openness and conscientiousness predict fluid intelligence score? *Learning and Individual Differences, 16,* 31–41.

Moutafi, J., Furnham, A., & Paltiel, L. (2005). Can personality factors predict intelligence? *Personality and Individual Differences, 38,* 1021–1033.

Moutafi, J., Furnham, A., & Tsaousis, I. (2006). Is the relationship between intelligence and trait neuroticism mediated by test anxiety? *Personality and Individual Differences, 40,* 587–597.

Mroczek, D. K., & Almeida, D. M (2004). The effect of daily stress, personality, and age on daily negative affect. *Journal of Personality, 72,* 355–380.

Müller, M. M., Günther, A., Habel, I., & Rockstroh, B. (1998). Active coping and internal locus of control produces prolonged cardiovascular reactivity in young men. *Journal of Psychophysiology, 12,* 29–39.

Penley, J. A., & Tomaka, J. (2002). Associations among the Big Five, emotional responses and coping with acute stress. *Personality and Individual Differences, 32,* 1215–1128.

Perrig-Chiello, P., Perrig, W. J., & Stahelin, H. B. (2000). Differential aspects of memory self-evaluation in old and very old people. *Aging & Mental Health, 4,* 130–135.

Riggs, K. M., Lachman, M. E., & Wingfield, A. (1997). Taking charge of remembering: Locus of control and older adults' memory for speech. *Experimental Aging Research, 23,* 237–256.

Roberts, B. W., Walton, K. E., & Bogg, T. (2005). Conscientiousness and health across the life course. *Review of General Psychology: Special Issue: Positive Psychology, 9,* 156–168.

Roberts, B. W., Walton, K. E., & Viechtbauer, W. (2006). Patterns of mean-level change in personality traits across the life course: A meta-analysis of longitudinal studies. *Psychological Bulletin, 132,* 1–25.

Robinson, M. D., Wilkowski, B. M., Kirkeby, B. S., & Meier, B. P. (2006). Stuck in a rut: Perseverative response tendencies and the neuroticism-distress relationship. *Journal of Experimental Psychology: General, 135,* 78–91.

Rothermund, K., & Brandtstädter, J. (2003). Coping with deficits and losses in later life: From compensatory action to accommodation. *Psychology and Aging, 18,* 896–905.

Schaie, K. W., Willis, S. L., & Caskie, G. I. L. (2004). The Seattle Longitudinal Study: Relationship between personality and cognition. *Aging Neuropsychology and Cognition, 11,* 304–324.

Schooler, C., & Mulatu, M. S. (2001). The reciprocal effects of leisure time activities and intellectual functioning in older people: A longitudinal analysis. *Psychology and Aging, 16,* 466–482.

Schooler, C., Mulatu, M. S., & Oates, G. (1999). The continuing effects of substantively complex work on the intellectual functioning of older workers. *Psychology and Aging, 14,* 483–906.

Seeman, T. E., & Robbins, R. J. (1994). Aging and hypothalamic-pituitary-adrenal response to challenge in humans. *Endocrine Reviews, 15,* 233–260.

Sneed, J. R., & Whitbourne, S. K. (2005). Models of the aging self. *Journal of Social Issues, 61,* 375–388.

Spielberger, C. D., & Vagg, P. R. (1995). Test anxiety: A transactional process model. In C. D. Spielberger & P. R. Vagg (Eds.), *Test anxiety: Theory, assessment, and treatment* (pp. 3–14). Washington, DC: Taylor & Francis.

Suls, J., & Martin, R. (2005). The daily life of the garden-variety neurotic: Reactivity, stressor exposure, mood spillover, and maladaptive coping. *Journal of Personality: Special Issues: Advances in Personality and Daily Experience, 73,* 1485–1510.

Troyer, A. K., & Rich, J. B. (2002). Psychometric properties of a new metamemory questionnaire for older adults. *Journals of Gerontology: Psychological Sciences, 57B,* P19–P27.

Valentijn, S. A. M., Hill, R. D., van Hooren, S., Bosma, H., van Boxtel, M. P. J., Jolles, J. and Ponds, W. H. M. (2006). Memory self-efficacy predicts memory performance: Results from a 6-year follow-up study. *Psychology and Aging, 21*(1), 165–172.

Vedhara, K., Hyde, J., Gilchrist, I. D., Tytherleigh, M., & Plummer, S. (2000). Acute stress, memory, attention and cortisol. *Psychoneuroendocrinology, 25,* 535–549.

Vollrath, M. (2001). Personality and stress. *Scandinavian Journal of Psychology, 42,* 335–347.

Wells, G. D., & Esopenko, C. (2008). Memory self-efficacy, aging, and memory performance: The roles of effort and persistence. *Educational Gerontology, 34,* 520–530.

West, R. L. Bagwell, D. K., & Dark-Freudeman, A. (2007). Self-efficacy and memory aging: The impact of a memory intervention based on self-efficacy. *Aging, Neuropsychology, and Cognition, 15,* 302–329.

West, R. L., Dark-Freudeman, A., & Bagwell, D. K. (2009). Goals-feedback conditions and episodic memory: Mechanisms for memory gains in older and younger adults. *Memory, 17,* 233–244.

West, R. L., & Yassuda, M. S. (2004). Aging and memory control beliefs: Performance in relation to goal setting and memory self-evaluation. *Journals of Gerontology: Psychological Sciences, 59B,* P56–P65.

Willis, S. L., & Boron, J. B. (2008). Midlife cognition: The association of personality with cognition and risk of cognitive impairment. In S. M. Hofer & D. F. Alwin (Eds.), *Handbook of cognitive aging: Interdisciplinary perspectives* (pp. 647–660). Thousand Oaks, CA: Sage.

Wilson, R. S., Arnold, S. E., Schneider, J. A., Kelly, J. F., Tang, Y., & Bennett, D. A. (2006). Chronic psychological distress and risk of Alzheimer's disease in old age. *Neuroepidemiology, 27,* 143–153.

Wilson, R. S., Krueger, K. R., Gu, L., Bienias, J. L., Mendes de Leon, C. F., & Evans, D. A. (2005). Neuroticism, extraversion, and mortality in a defined population of older persons, *Psychosomatic Medicine, 67,* 841–845.

Wright, C. E., Kunz-Ebrecht, S. R., Iliffe, S., Foese, O. & Steptoe, A. (2005). Physiological correlates of cognitive functioning in an elderly population. *Psychoneuroendocrinology, 30,* 826–838.

PART V

Abnormal Aging

14

Affective Disorders and Age

The View Through a Developmental Lens

Jennifer R. Piazza and Susan Turk Charles

The growing interest in positive psychology and successful aging in recent years has led to a paradigm shift in the way people view later adulthood. This period was once considered a time of universal loss, but researchers have since discovered that emotional well-being and mental health actually improves with age (e.g., Charles, Reynolds, & Gatz, 2001; Stone, Schwartz, Broderick, & Deaton, 2010). With the exception of the dementias, prevalence rates of mental disorders – including depression and anxiety – are lower among older adults compared to their younger and middle-aged counterparts (Kessler et al., 2005). These age differences are substantial, with some researchers estimating that rates of affective disorders are as much as 50% lower among older primary care patients compared to younger and middle-aged patients (e.g., Brenes et al., 2008).

Despite the decreased rates of mental disorders among older adults, depression and anxiety are still prevalent in this population. These disorders are costly – to the individuals afflicted, to their families, and to society. They are associated with decreased quality of life (Brenes et al., 2005; Porter, 2009), greater utilization of medical services (Cole & Dendukuri, 2003), and – in the case of depression – less adherence to medical regimens (DiMatteo, Lepper, & Croghan, 2000). The ramifications of affective disorders on general functioning surpass those from any other chronic illness; for example, depression alone is the most common reason for disability among adults in the United States, ranking higher than cardiovascular disease, hearing or vision loss (World Health Organization, 2008). Over time, these disorders lead to an increased risk of both physical morbidity and mortality (Bryant, Jackson, & Ames, 2008; Charney et al., 2003).

The Wiley-Blackwell Handbook of Adulthood and Aging, First Edition. Edited by Susan Krauss Whitbourne and Martin J. Sliwinski. © 2012 Blackwell Publishing Ltd. Published 2012 by Blackwell Publishing Ltd.

Researchers estimate that by 2050 the number of people in the United States who will be diagnosed with a depressive disorder will increase by 35%, and this increase is expected to disproportionately affect older adults (Heo, Murphy, Fontaine, Bruce, & Alexopoulos, 2008). Whereas depressive disorders are expected to increase by 25% among adults younger than age 65, they are expected to increase by 117% among adults over the age of 65 (Heo et al., 2008). Given that symptoms of anxiety are reported more frequently than symptoms of depression (Bryant et al., 2008), similar age-related trends may also occur for anxiety disorders. Researchers have referred to this expected increase in affective disorders as an impending crisis in geriatric psychiatry (Jeste et al., 1999).

A number of factors may account for the projected increase in rates of affective disorders among future cohorts of older adults. Most notably, the older adult population has significantly increased in recent years, and is expected to double by the year 2050 (U.S. Census Bureau, 2008). As the number of older adults increases, so too will the segment of older adults with depression and anxiety. In addition, younger cohorts are more likely to report symptoms of psychological distress than are older cohorts (Kessler et al., 2010). As these younger cohorts enter into later adulthood, their willingness to disclose symptoms of mental illness will likely continue, leading to increases in late life depression and anxiety diagnoses. Another potential reason for the projected age-related upswing in rates of affective disorders is that medical advances have enabled people with chronic physical health conditions to live longer (K. Christensen, Doblhammer, Rau, & Vaupel, 2009). Given that chronic physical health conditions often place people at risk for depression and anxiety-related disorders (Schnittker, 2005), an increase in the number of people with complicated physical health problems may contribute to the expected rise in affective disorders among older adults.

Depression and Anxiety: Definition and Age Differences

The affective disorders reviewed in this chapter are those that affect the largest number of people: For depression, we discuss major depressive disorder (MDD) and for anxiety, we discuss generalized anxiety disorder (GAD). We also review literature on depression and anxiety symptoms, as they increase the risk for diagnosable disorders (Blazer, 2003), and because subclinical symptoms interfere with daily life even if they do not meet thresholds for diagnosis (Blazer & Hybels, 2005). Criteria for MDD and GAD may change with the upcoming 5th edition of the *Diagnostic and Statistical Manual for Mental Disorders* (*DSM*); however, all research reviewed in this chapter is based on the diagnostic criteria set forth by the current manual (American Psychiatric Association, 2000). According to the current criteria, a single episode of MDD refers to the presence of one major depressive episode, whereas recurrent MDD refers to the presence of two or more major depressive episodes. Depressive episodes are defined as either a depressed mood or loss of interest/pleasure over a 2-week period, accompanied by at least five additional symptoms (e.g., diminished interest in most activities, loss of energy or fatigue, significant weight loss) that represent a change from previous levels of functioning.

Generalized anxiety disorder (GAD) is characterized by uncontrollable and excessive worry and anxiety that lasts for at least 6 months and that includes the occurrence of at least three symptoms on most days (e.g., problems concentrating, feeling wound-up or tense, experiencing significant muscle tension). For both depression and anxiety disorders, symptoms must cause significant distress and must not be explained by a medical illness or another mental disorder (American Psychiatric Association, 2000).

Age differences in symptom presentation

Diagnostic criteria for depression and anxiety-related disorders are the same for people of all ages. However, specific symptom constellations are more common in some age groups than others. For example, compared to older adults, younger adults with depression are more likely to present with dysphoric mood (Balsis & Cully, 2008) and decreases in positive affect (Wetherell, Gatz, & Pedersen, 2001). Older adults, in contrast, are more likely to report a greater number of unexplained somatic or cognitive complaints (Balsis & Cully, 2008; Gonclaves, Albuquerque, Byrne, & Pachana, 2009), such as sleep disturbance, fatigue, memory complaints, and poor concentration (H. Christensen et al., 1999). Older adults with depression are also more likely to withdraw socially, lack motivation, and lose interest in personal care than are younger adults (Gallo & Rabins, 1999).

Fewer age differences emerge for symptoms of anxiety disorders (Fuentes & Cox, 2000; Nuevo et al., 2008). Among adults of all ages, symptoms of anxiety include muscle tension, fatigue, inability to control worry, and sleep disturbance (American Psychiatric Association, 2000). However, the physical symptoms associated with anxiety are not always indicative of an anxiety disorder; instead, they may reflect physiological changes associated with medical conditions, side effects of medications, or both (e.g., Lenze et al., 2001; Wijeratne & Hickie, 2001). If endorsed symptoms are due to coexisting medical problems, the somatic items on questionnaires assessing anxiety may be particularly problematic for older adults, who have higher rates of chronic physical health conditions than do younger adults (Kogan, Edelstein, & McKee, 2000).

Diagnosing depression and anxiety in later adulthood

Additional issues may also complicate depression and anxiety diagnoses in later adulthood. For example, older adults experiencing symptoms of depression or anxiety are more likely to seek the care of a primary care physician (PCP) instead of a mental health specialist (Alexopoulos et al., 2002). This is problematic because PCPs do not always adequately evaluate their patients' mental health status, due, in part, to competing demands during appointments, a lack of knowledge regarding symptom manifestation during later adulthood, and a general reluctance to discuss mental health issues (Delano-Wood & Abeles, 2005). Misconceptions of aging by both patients and physicians may also lead them to erroneously attribute symptoms of depression and anxiety to normal aging (Delano-Wood & Abeles, 2005; Kim, Braun, & Kunik, 2001). In addition, both physicians and patients may inaccurately label the physical symptoms of depression and anxiety as symptoms of medical conditions (Delano-Wood & Abeles, 2005). This lack of recognition by patients and physicians may partially explain why up to 65% of older adults with MDD are not accurately diagnosed (Conwell & Duberstein, 2001) and why only a small percentage of older adults needing treatment for a mental disorder actually receive it (Comer, 2004).

Depression, delirium, and dementia.   An additional complicating factor involved in diagnosing depression in older adults is that the disorder shares symptoms with dementia and delirium, both of which increase in prevalence with age (Gagliardi, 2008). All three disorders are associated with cognitive changes (Insel & Badger, 2002). Yet careful neuropsychological testing often enables practitioners to accurately differentiate among these disorders (Milisen, Braes, Fick, & Foreman, 2006). For example, both depression and dementia are associated with decrements in memory, verbal fluency, processing speed, and executive functioning. These impairments, however, are much more severe in patients with dementia (Wright & Persad, 2007). The reason for impairments in these cognitive domains also differs between people with dementia and people with depression. Whereas individuals with depression tend to score poorly on cognitive tasks due to an apparent lack of effort and motivation, individuals with dementia show all-round ability-based deficits (Wright & Persad, 2007). In addition, people with depression generally have no impairment in language, visuospatial tasks, and visuoconstriction areas, which are often impaired among people with common types of dementia (Twamley & Bondi, 2004). Symptoms of delirium and depression also overlap, with both conditions associated with hypoactivity and psychomotor retardation (Manepalli, Gebretsadik, Hook, & Grossberg, 2007). Other common symptoms of delirium, however, such as its rapid onset, perceptual abnormalities, and fluctuating course, help professionals distinguish this condition from depression (Manepalli et al., 2007). The comorbidity of these disorders not only complicates the diagnosis of depression, but also increases the likelihood of adverse outcomes, such as functional declines and nursing home placement (Givens, Sanft, & Marcantonio, 2008).

Comorbidity of depression and anxiety.   A further challenge when diagnosing and treating depression and anxiety in adults of all ages is that these disorders frequently co-occur (Hirschfield, 2001). The genetic risk factors for MDD and GAD are strongly correlated (Kendler, Gardner, Gatz, & Pedersen, 2007), and it is estimated that nearly half of all adults diagnosed with depression also meet the criteria for an anxiety disorder (Kessler et al., 2005). Some researchers, however, posit that pure GAD is actually fairly common (Schoevers, Beekman, Deeg, Jonker, & van Tilburg, 2003), but that people are less likely to seek treatment when GAD symptoms occur in isolation. Instead, they are more likely to seek treatment for comorbid anxiety and depression symptoms (Lenze et al., 2000). The danger in not seeking treatment for individual disorders, however, is that one disorder often leads to or exacerbates the other (e.g., Wetherell, Gatz, & Pederson, 2001), which results in more severe pathology, a more challenging illness course, and a delayed treatment response (Lenze et al., 2001). Increasing our understanding of how mental disorders change across the lifespan will enable health professionals to provide earlier and more accurate diagnoses and treatment plans.

Moreover, as clinicians and physicians become more adept at diagnosing depression and anxiety in older adults, rates of these disorders may more accurately reflect baseline levels of distress in the older adult population.

Using the Biopsychosocial Model to Understand Age Differences in Risk Factors of Depression and Anxiety

Depression and anxiety do not have simple etiologies; nor do they follow the same course in all people. Instead, they result from a number of factors, the relative influence of which may vary across people, time, and age groups. The biopsychosocial model provides a way to capture the multiple influences contributing to these complex diseases. According to this model, a disorder develops from the interplay among biological, psychological, and social factors. For example, an individual may have a genetic vulnerability that increases his or her risk of developing depression or anxiety, but the disorder may not manifest unless he or she also encounters significant psychological or social risk factors. Similarly, an accumulation of psychological and social risk factors may increase an individual's susceptibility for depression, but unless a biological vulnerability also exists, the disorder may not develop. This model also allows for an examination of how these risk factors change as a function of age. For example, certain biological risk factors, such as genetic vulnerabilities, are usually expressed earlier in life, whereas certain social factors, such as bereavement, are more likely to occur later in life (Blazer & Hybels, 2005). In this section, we use the biopsychosocial model as a framework for describing the factors that contribute to depression and anxiety, and discuss how these factors change across the lifespan.

Genetic influences on depression and anxiety

Genes and depression. Both depression and anxiety-related disorders are genetically influenced (Blazer & Hybels, 2005). For example, the likelihood of having MDD increases considerably if a first degree relative also has the disorder (Janzing et al., 2009), and the effect is much stronger if the relative is a parent (Lieb, Isensee, Hofler, Pfister, & Wittchen, 2002). Although certain genetic polymorphisms may increase the risk for depression at all ages, their influence varies according to age of initial depression onset. In one study, for example, the earlier the age of onset for MDD, the greater the chances of one's co-twin also being diagnosed with MDD. This association was no longer significant when the unaffected twin reached age 35 (Kendler, Gatz, Gardner, & Petersen, 2005). A later study by the same researchers again showed that early onset age predicted MDD in the unaffected co-twin. However, when an individual had a later age of onset, his or her co-twin had an increased likelihood of being diagnosed with vascular depression, a type of depression that primarily occurs in later adulthood (Kendler, Fiske, Gardner, & Gatz, 2009).

Genes and anxiety.   The risk of developing an anxiety disorder is also significantly higher if a first-degree relative has an anxiety disorder (Li, Sundquist, & Sundquist, 2008; Smoller, Block, & Young, 2009). Twin studies that focus on GAD are limited in number; the few that have been conducted estimate a moderate heritability of the disorder (Hettema, Neale, & Kendler, 2001), although a large portion of this heritability is thought to be the result of environmental factors (e.g., Mackintosh, Gatz, Wetherell, & Pedersen, 2006). The genetic susceptibility for anxiety disorders appears to present itself earlier, rather than later in life, with the majority of genetic and environmental determinants of anxiety disorders apparent by age 20 (Gillespie et al., 2004).

Age-related changes in physical functioning

A number of normative age-related physical changes occur that may place older adults at greater risk for depression and anxiety. For example, age is associated with decreases in serotonin (Benek-Higgens, McReynolds, Hogan, & Savickas, 2008) and serotonin receptors (Blazer & Hybels, 2005), both of which have been implicated in the etiology of affective disorders (aan het Rot, Mathew, & Charney, 2009). Hormones and neurotransmitters related to the sympathetic nervous system (SNS) and the hypothalamic-pituitary-adrenal (HPA) axis are also elevated in older adults. Higher levels of these substances, in turn, are associated with affective disorders (e.g., McKay & Zakzanis, 2009; Otte et al., 2005; Veen et al., 2009).

For adults of all ages, temporary elevations in certain hormones and neurotransmitters occur when they encounter a stressor. These changes are adaptive, but can be damaging if elicited too frequently or without reprieve (McEwen, 1998). For example, cortisol is vital for the maintenance of several organ systems, including the immune system, the central nervous system, and the metabolic system (G. E. Miller, Chen, & Zhou, 2007). In excess, however, it is associated with damage to the hippocampus, decreases in innate and adaptive immunity (Lovallo & Thomas, 2000), and increases in depression (McKay & Zakzanis, 2009). Moreover, chronically high levels of cortisol are hypothesized to lead to greater reactivity to future stressors (Sapolsky, 2000). This vicious cycle, whereby heightened reactivity to stressors leads to excess cortisol, which, in turn, leads to heightened reactivity to stressors, is not age-dependent. However, as a result of stressor exposure across a greater number of years, older adults are more likely to show the effects of continual cortisol exposure than are younger adults (Sapolsky, Krey, & McEwen, 1985). These physiological changes may have adverse consequences. For example, among older adults with mood disorders, those who show evidence of a dysregulated HPA axis are more likely to commit suicide than are those who do not show HPA axis dysregulation (Jokinen & Nordstrom, 2008). The authors of this study conclude that neuroendocrine testing may potentially be used as a complementary tool in assessing suicidal risk among older adults (Jokinen & Nordstrom, 2008).

HPA-axis dysregulation may also occur in GAD. In one study, for example, diurnal cortisol was estimated to be 40–50% higher among older adults with GAD compared to nonanxious older adults. Older adults with GAD also showed higher levels of baseline and peak cortisol compared with older adults who did not have GAD (Mantella et al., 2008).

These associations may be magnified on days older adults encounter stressors. In one study, cortisol levels of anxious versus nonanxious older adults did not differ on nonstressor days. When a stressor was encountered, however, people with anxiety disorders had a prolonged recovery period compared with their nonanxious counterparts (Chaudieu et al., 2008). HPA axis hyperactivity in older adults with GAD appears to be modifiable, however, with successful antidepressant treatment leading to decreases in cortisol (Lenze et al., 2011).

Inflammatory processes and depression.   The immune system also undergoes age-related changes that are implicated in the etiology of depression. Specifically, aging is associated with increases in proinflammatory cytokines, which mediate the inflammatory response. Aging is also associated with a greater incidence of inflammatory diseases such as cardiovascular disease (CVD), autoimmune disease, and cancer (Piazza et al., 2007). Chronic inflammation, in turn, is associated with adverse health outcomes, including higher rates of depression and depressive symptoms (e.g., Dowlati et al., 2010; Howren, Lamkin, & Suls, 2009). Since inflammation is associated with depression, and older adults have higher incidence rates of inflammatory diseases, as well as increased levels of proinflammatory cytokines, their risk for inflammation-associated depression may be elevated.

The link between depression and inflammation has been illustrated in a number of studies (e.g., Maes, 2011; A. H. Miller, Maletic, & Raison, 2009; Raison, Capuron, & Miller, 2006). For example, in a prospective study of individuals 85 years and older with no history of affective disorders, the advent of depression was preceded by elevated inflammatory biomarkers (van den Biggelaar et al., 2007). Similarly, when healthy volunteers were injected with a substance that elicited an inflammatory response, symptoms of depression and anxiety increased (Reichenberg et al., 2001). People undergoing immunotherapy, which stimulates the immune system so that it can fend off diseased cells, have also reported an increase in depressive symptoms following treatment (Musselman et al., 2001; Prather, Rabinovitz, Pollock, & Lotrich, 2009). When the treatments were interrupted, these symptoms significantly decreased (Musselman et al., 2001). Moreover, antidepressants in conjunction with substances that inhibit inflammation appear to be more effective at treating depression than antidepressants alone (Mendlewicz et al., 2006). Conversely, interventions aimed at treating depression appear to reduce inflammation (Thornton, Andersen, Schuler, & Carson, 2009), indicating that the link between depression and inflammation may be bidirectional and in need of further study.

Vascular depression.   Cerebrovascular disease is an inflammatory disease that increases with age and is associated with depression. According to the vascular depression hypothesis, proposed by Alexopoulos and colleagues (Alexopoulos et al., 1997), cerebrovascular disease is associated with an increased number of white matter lesions (WMLs). These lesions affect neuroanatomical structures implicated in depression, such as the prefrontal cortex, which is critical for mood regulation (Alexopoulos et al., 1997). This theory is supported by both cross-sectional and longitudinal studies, which indicate that an increased number of WMLs are associated with an increased likelihood of developing depression (e.g., Firbank et al., 2005; Godin et al., 2008), particularly when these lesions occur in regions associated with emotional and cognitive control (Dalby et al., 2010). Symptoms of vascular and nonvascular depression are similar, but cognitive impairment and disability are more common in vascular depression (Alexopoulos, 2005). Vascular depression can occur at any age, but it is more likely to occur in later life because of the increased likelihood of being diagnosed with cerebrovascular disease (e.g., Sneed, Rindskopf, Steffens, Krishan, & Roose, 2008).

Medication and substance use

Symptoms of depression and anxiety may also result from medication use and substance abuse. Depression in conjunction with alcohol or illicit drug use occurs more often in younger adults compared to older adults. Conversely, depression is more often a side effect of medication use among older adults, particularly among those taking multiple medications (Alexopolous, 2005). Drugs most frequently associated with depression are those prescribed for the most common age-related chronic illnesses, including antihypertensives, beta-blockers, and steroids. In addition, anxiety-related symptoms are often the result of medication that causes sympathetic nervous system disruption. These symptoms, which include shakiness, increased heart rate, and muscle tension, can all be attributed to anxiety (Kogan et al., 2000). Older adults with chronic health conditions are therefore not only at risk because of the biological and psychosocial ramifications of their illnesses, but also because these conditions require the use of medications for which depression and anxiety are frequent side effects.

Psychosocial factors

Despite the physical vulnerabilities that increase their susceptibility to depression and anxiety, older adults still report lower rates of affective disorders than do their younger counterparts (Kessler et al., 2005). These lower rates may be due to inaccuracies when assessing depression in later adulthood (Bryant et al., 2008) or to reluctance on the part of older adults to reveal symptoms of psychological distress (Kogan, et al., 2000). Another possibility, however, is that older adults may have a greater psychosocial reserve than their younger counterparts, which protects them in the face of biological risk factors. For example, compared to their younger counterparts, older adults report greater contentment with their social networks (Carstensen, 1992), fewer life regrets (Riediger & Freund, 2008), and higher concordance between their ideal and actual selves (Ryff, 1991), all of which may partially explain why older adults report levels of emotional well-being and life satisfaction that are similar – if not more positive – than those reported by younger adults (e.g., Mroczek & Kolarz, 1998).

Yet not all older adults score highly on these measures, and although some psychosocial risk factors decrease across adulthood, others sharply increase. These risk factors may make a subset of older adults with recurring anxiety or depression more likely to relapse, and may cause some individuals to experience these disorders for the first time in late life. Below we discuss three psychosocial risk factors that are associated with depression and anxiety and are more common in later adulthood than at any other point across the lifespan: chronic health conditions, spousal bereavement, and caregiving for a spouse with dementia.

Chronic physical health conditions.   Chronic physical health conditions are associated with increased rates of depression and anxiety (e.g., McWilliams, Cox, & Enns, 2003). For example, MDD affects approximately 6% of people nationwide (National Institute of Mental Health, 2006), but approximately 30% of people with diabetes (Egede, 2005) and approximately 40% of people with chronic obstructive pulmonary disease (Yohannes, Baldwin, & Connolly, 2000). A similar pattern occurs for depressive symptoms (Ranga et al., 2002; Schnittker, 2005) and anxiety disorders (McWilliams et al., 2003). Moreover, these effects are compounded among people who have more than one chronic health condition (Cooke et al., 2007).

Just as there are biological reasons why chronic health conditions are associated with affective disorders, there are psychological reasons, as well. In the face of chronic illness, goals may need to be shifted, ambitions put aside, and activities limited, as self-care monopolizes an individual's time, and pain and fatigue dictate daily activities (Larsen, 2006). Chronic conditions also create a number of stressors, including financial strains due to medical costs, a decreased sense of autonomy, and the stigma of being ill (Larsen, 2006; Mann & Stuenkel, 2006), all of which may increase the likelihood of experiencing depression and anxiety-related symptoms.

Chronic health conditions may also infringe upon an individual's ability to engage in pleasurable activities. According to the integrative model of depression articulated by Lewinsohn and his colleagues (Lewinsohn, Hoberman, Teri, & Hautzinger, 1985), depression in the context of chronic health conditions is more likely to occur when these conditions lead to a disruption of pleasant activities, but is unlikely to occur if a health condition does not disrupt engagement in pleasant activities. Because many of the conditions diagnosed in later adulthood lead to functional impairment, they more often lead to an impaired quality of life. For example, CVD often limits daily activities, macular degeneration may result in an inability to drive, and arthritis may result in difficulty pursuing activities requiring both fine and gross motor skills. Indeed, a cross-national European study of nine countries indicates that although chronic health conditions and functional disabilities are independently associated with incremental increases in depression, this relationship is stronger among people with functional disabilities (Braam et al., 2005).

Social losses and bereavement.   Social loss is another risk factor that disproportionately affects older adults. Humans have an inherent need to belong, and research attests to the importance of social integration for health and well-being (e.g., Cohen & Wills, 1985). People achieve a sense of social belonging through the relationships they cultivate with family members, friends, and community groups. Loss of these social ties may result in a lack of social belonging. Lack of social belonging, in turn, is associated with depression (Cacioppo, Hughes, Waite, Hawkley, & Thisted, 2006), adverse physiological changes (Hawkley, Masi, Berry, & Cacioppo, 2006), and increased mortality (Holt-Lunstad, Smith, & Layton, 2010). This is true for people of all ages, but the probability of experiencing social losses significantly increases with age, thereby increasing older adults' risk for depression and anxiety.

One relationship that quite often fulfills the need for social belonging more than any other is marriage. Married adults report higher levels of well-being (Diener, Gohm, Suh, & Oishi, 2000) and – with the notable exception of those who report high marital discord (Whisman & Ueblacker, 2009) – have a lower risk of most mental disorders than their nonmarried counterparts (Scott et al., 2010). When the loss of the marital union occurs through bereavement, the likelihood of experiencing depression or anxiety increases (Onrust & Cuijipers, 2006), particularly among men (Waddell & Jacobs-Lawson, 2010). One speculated reason for this gender difference is that men have most of their social needs fulfilled in the marital relationship, whereas women have strong social networks outside of the marriage (e.g., Cheng & Chan, 2006). Consistent with this premise, women have larger social networks than do men (McLaughlin, Vagenas, Pachana, Begum, & Dobson, 2010) and feel a stronger sense of belonging from these networks (Martire, Schulz, Mittelmark, & Newsom, 1999). Gender differences in social integration may also explain why unmarried older men have higher rates of suicide than unmarried older women. Indeed, in a study conducted to examine the potential reasons why older men are more likely to commit suicide, lack of social integration best explained the association, underscoring the importance of social integration for overall mental well-being (Cutright, Stack, & Fernquist, 2006).

Caregiving.　Negative life events, such as living in poverty or being exposed to domestic violence, often result in ongoing, chronic stressors that affect quality of life (Moos, Brennan, Schutte, & Moose, 2006). Of all the difficult situations that occur more often in late life, one of the most researched in psychology is caregiving for a spouse with dementia. Dementia is a debilitating and progressive disease that affects both individuals in a relationship. The cognitively intact person often becomes the primary caregiver, a role requiring both physical and emotional stamina that takes its toll on both of these domains (Schulz & Beach, 1999). The strain of caregiving manifests itself through increased rates of depression (Sorensen, Duberstein, Gill, & Pinquart, 2006), cognitive deficits (Vitaliano et al., 2005) morbidity (Vitaliano, Zhang, & Scanlan, 2003), and mortality (Schulz & Beach, 1999). Recent research also suggests that being married to an individual with dementia increases one's own risk of dementia, which may be due to the ongoing stressors associated with spousal caregiving (Norton et al., 2010).

Being a spousal caregiver also presents a double jeopardy for older adults: Not only is it a chronic, unremitting stressor, but it is also a situation in which the caregiver slowly loses an individual who provided him or her with a sense of social belonging. The caregiver witnesses his or her spouse slowly deteriorating, until he or she has lost all memories of their married life together. Perhaps this is one reason why even after the caregiving responsibilities cease, the negative effects of having been a caregiver remain. For example, levels of depression among strained caregivers often remain unchanged after spousal bereavement (Schulz et al., 2001), and sometimes continue for years after bereavement (Robinson-Whelen, Tada, MacCallum, McGuire, & Kiecolt-Glaser, 2001). Recent research, however, indicates that interventions focused on providing support and counseling to the caregiver may ameliorate depression in this population up to one year postbereavement (Haley et al., 2008), illustrating the need for psychosocial interventions for both current and former caregivers.

Suicide

Negative life events, such as physical health problems, bereavement, and caregiving lead to decreases in well-being that can last several years or more, with some people never returning to levels of satisfaction they felt prior to the event (Lucas, 2007). Life events related to loss significantly increase with age. Researchers argue that older adults are more resilient in the face of these losses and are better able to adjust to these negative events because they are more predictable, or "on-time," for older adults compared to younger adults (Blazer & Hybels, 2005). Although this may be the case for some older adults, these situations may be too much to bear for others. Not only do these situations place older adults at a greater risk for depression and anxiety; they are also associated with elevated suicide risk (Garand, Mitchell, Dietrick, Hijjawi, & Pan, 2006).

Suicide is a complex phenomenon that results from a series of risk factors, and no two people present with the same scenario (Conwell, 2001). Yet some commonalities exist that health care professionals can use to guide risk assessment. For example, younger adults are more likely to commit suicide if they have a substance abuse problem, but major depression is a stronger precipitating factor in older adults' suicides. Older adults who commit suicide are also more likely to have been bereaved, socially isolated, and exposed to stressful events such as an ongoing physical illness (Garand et al., 2006).

Summary and Conclusions

Stressful life events in late life increase the likelihood that an individual will experience an affective disorder, but not all people exposed to stressful life events will develop these disorders. An individual born into a family with a history of GAD is not destined to receive the same diagnosis, and having a chronic health condition does not inevitably lead to an affective disorder. A multitude of factors contribute to the etiology of MDD and GAD, and it is the combination of these factors that places one at risk for an affective disorder. This is true for people of all ages, and a clinician must be aware of the circumstances leading up to the onset of symptoms. When assessing risk in older adults, they must also consider potential age differences not only in factors contributing to MDD and GAD, but also how affective disorders present themselves in later adulthood. This chapter addressed some of these issues, but many questions remain unanswered. For example, is our current understanding of symptom presentation accurate or does it need refinement? What are the gene and environment interactions that increase one's susceptibility to affective disorders across the lifespan? Could a prospective look at the physiological correlates of stressor exposure lead to a greater understanding of why some, but not all, older adults faced with adverse scenarios develop depression or anxiety? Could interventions aimed at social isolation decrease the rates of suicide among older Caucasian men?

Knowledge and understanding of depression and anxiety in later adulthood has grown considerably in recent years. Researchers have refined these constructs, and clinicians are better able to diagnose mental illness among older adults. Laypersons and medical professionals are more knowledgeable about normative age-related changes that are not the result of depression and anxiety. As researchers continue to investigate the association between physiological processes and emotional experience, the ties between health problems and emotional distress are becoming more clearly articulated. Still, there is more to discover, and the study of mental disorders in later adulthood continues to be a demanding and necessary area of inquiry for both practical and theoretical reasons.

References

aan het Rot, M., Mathew, S. J., & Charney, D. S. (2009). Neurobiological mechanisms in major depressive disorder. *Canadian Medical Association Journal, 180,* 305–313.

Alexopoulos, G. S. (2005). Depression in the elderly. *Lancet, 365,* 1961–1970.

Alexopoulos, G. S., Borsen, S., Cuthbert, B. N., Devanand, D. P., Mulsant, B. H., Olin, J. T., & Oslin, D. (2002). Assessment of late life depression. *Biological Psychiatry, 52,* 164–174.

Alexopoulous, G. S., Meyers, B. S., Yong, R. C., Kakuma, T., Silbersweig, D., & Charlson, M. (1997). Clinically defined vascular depression. *American Journal of Psychiatry, 154,* 562–565.

American Psychiatric Association (APA). (2000). *Diagnostic and statistical manual of mental disorders* (4th ed., Text Revision). Washington, DC: Author.

Balsis, S., & Cully, J. A. (2008). Comparing depression diagnostic symptoms across younger and older adults. *Aging & Mental Health, 12,* 800–806.

Benek-Higgins, M., McReynolds, C. J., Hogan, E., & Savickas, S. (2008). Depression and the elder person: The enigma of misconceptions, stigma, and treatment. *Journal of Mental Health Counseling, 30,* 283–296.

Blazer D. G. (2003). Depression in late life: Review and commentary. *Journal of Gerontology: Series A: Biological and Medical Sciences, 58,* 249–265.

Blazer, D. G., & Hybels, C. F. (2005). Origins of depression in later life. *Psychological Medicine, 35,* 1241–1252.

Braam, A. W., Prince, M. J., Beekman, A. T. F., Delespaul, P., Dewey, M. E., Geerlings, S. W., . . . Copelan, J. R. (2005). Physical health and depressive symptoms in older Europeans. *British Journal of Psychiatry, 187,* 35–42.

Brenes, G., Guralnik, J., Williamson, J., Fried, L., Simpson, C., Simonsick, E., & Penninx, B. W. (2005). The influence of anxiety on the progression of disability. *Journal of the American Geriatrics Society, 53,* 34–39.

Brenes, G., Penninx, B., Judd, P., Rockwell, E., Sewell, D., & Wetherell, J. (2008). Anxiety, depression and disability across the lifespan. *Aging & Mental Health, 12,* 158–163.

Bryant, C., Jackson, H., & Ames, D. (2008). The prevalence of anxiety in older adults: Methodological issues and a review of the literature. *Journal of Affective Disorders, 109,* 233–250.

Cacioppo, J. T., Hughes, M. E., Waite, L. J., Hawkley, L. C., & Thisted, R. A. (2006). Loneliness as a specific risk factor for depressive symptoms: Cross-sectional and longitudinal analyses. *Psychology and Aging, 21,* 140–151.

Carstensen, L. L. (1992). Social and emotional patterns in adulthood: Support for socioemotional selectivity theory. *Psychology and Aging, 7,* 331–338.

Charles, S. T., Reynolds, C. A., & Gatz, M. (2001). Age-related differences and change in positive and negative affect over 23 years. *Journal of Personality and Social Psychology, 80,* 136–151.

Charney, D., Reynolds, C., Lewis, L., Lebowitz, B., Sunderland, T., Alexopoulos, G., . . . Young, R. C. (2003). Depression and Bipolar Support Alliance consensus statement on the unmet needs in diagnosis and treatment of mood disorders in late life. *Archives of General Psychiatry, 60,* 664–672.

Chaudieu, I., Beluche, I., Norton, J., Boulenger, J., Ritchie, K., & Ancelin, M. L. (2008). Abnormal reactions to environmental stress in elderly persons with anxiety disorders: Evidence from a population study of diurnal cortisol. *Journal of Affective Disorders, 106,* 307–313.

Cheng, S., & Chan, A. C. M. (2006). Relationship with others and life satisfaction in later life: Do gender and widowhood make a difference? *Journal of Gerontology: Psychological Sciences, 61,* 46–53.

Christensen, H., Jorm, A. F., Mackinnon, A. J., Korton, A. E., Jacomb, P. A., Henderson, A. S., & Rodgers, B. (1999). Age differences in depression and anxiety symptoms: A structural equation modeling analysis of data from a general population sample. *Psychological Medicine, 29,* 325–339.

Christensen, K., Doblhammer, G., Rau, R., & Vaupel, J. W. (2009). Ageing populations: The challenges ahead. *Lancet, 374,* 1196–1208.

Cohen, S., & Wills, T. (1985). Stress, social support, and the buffering hypothesis. *Psychological Bulletin, 98,* 310–357.

Cole, M. G., & Dendukuri, N. (2003). Risk factors for depression among elderly community subject: A systemic review and meta-analysis. *American Journal of Psychiatry, 160,* 1147–1156.

Comer, E. (2004). Integrating the health and mental health needs of the chronically ill: A group for individuals with depression and sickle cell disease. *Social Work in Health Care, 38,* 57–76.

Conwell, Y. (2001). Suicide in later life: A review and recommendations for prevention. *Suicide and Life-Threatening Behavior, 31,* 32–47.

Conwell, Y., & Duberstein, P. (2001). Suicide in elders. In H. Hendin & J. J. Mann (Eds.), *The clinical science of suicide prevention* (pp. 132–150). New York: New York Academy of Sciences.

Cooke, D., Newman, S., Sacker, A., DeVellis, B., Bebbington, P., & Meltzer, H. (2007). The impact of physical illnesses on non-psychotic psychiatric morbidity: Data from the household survey of psychiatric morbidity in Great Britain. *British Journal of Health Psychology, 12,* 463–471.

Cutright, P., Stack, S., & Fernquist, R. (2007). Marital status integration, suicide disapproval, and societal integration as explanations of marital status differences in female age-specific suicide rates. *Suicide & Life Threatening Behavior, 37,* 715–724.

Dalby, R. B., Chakravarty, M. M., Ahdidan, J., Sørensen, L., Frandsen, J., Jonsdottir, K. Y., . . . Videbech, P. (2010). Localization of white-matter lesions and effect of vascular risk factors in late-onset major depression. *Psychological Medicine: A Journal of Research in Psychiatry and the Allied Sciences, 40,* 1389–1399.

Delano-Wood, L., & Abeles, N. (2005). Late-life depression: Detection, risk reduction, and somatic intervention. *Clinical Psychology: Science and Practice, 12,* 207–217.

Diener, E., Gohm, C. L., Suh, E., & Oishi, S. (2000). Similarity of the relations between marital status and subjective well-being across cultures. *Journal of Cross-Cultural Psychology, 31,* 419–436.

DiMatteo, M. R., Lepper, H. S., & Croghan, T. W. (2000): Depression is a risk factor for non-compliance with medical treatment. Metaanalysis of the effects of anxiety and depression on patient adherence. *Archives of Internal Medicine, 160,* 2101–2107.

Dowlati, Y., Herrmann, N., Swardfager, W., Liu, H., Sham, L., Reim, E. K., & Lanctôt, K. L. (2010). A meta-analysis of cytokines in major depression. *Biological Psychiatry, 67,* 446–457.

Egede, L. (2005). Effect of comorbid chronic diseases on prevalence and odds of depression in adults with diabetes. *Psychosomatic Medicine, 67,* 46–51.

Firbank, M. J., O'Brien, J. T., Pakrasi, S., Pantoni, L., Simoni, M., Erkinijuntti, T., . . . Inzitari, D. (2005). White matter hyperintensities and depression–preliminary results from the LADIS study. *International Journal of Geriatric Psychiatry, 20,* 674–679.

Fuentes, K., & Cox, B. (2000). Assessment of anxiety in older adults: A community-based survey and comparison with younger adults. *Behaviour Research and Therapy, 38,* 297–309.

Gagliardi, J. P. (2008). Differentiating among depression, delirium, and dementia in elderly patients. *American Medical Association Journal of Ethics, 10,* 383–388.

Gallo, J. J., & Rabins, P. V. (1999). Depression without sadness: Alternative presentations of depression in late life. *American Family Physician, 60,* 820–826.

Garand, L., Mitchell, A., Dietrick, A., Hijjawi, S., & Pan, D. (2006). Suicide in older adults: Nursing assessment of suicide risk. *Issues in Mental Health Nursing, 27,* 355–370.

Gillespie, N., Kirk, K. M., Evans, D. M., Heath, A. C., Hickie, I. B., & Martin, N. G. (2004). Do the genetic or environmental determinants of anxiety and depression change with age? A longitudinal study of Australian twins. *Twin Research, 7,* 39–53.

Givens, J. L., Sanft, T., & Marcantonio, E. R. (2008). Functional recovery after hip fracture: The combined effects of depressive symptoms, cognitive impairment and delirium. *Journal of the American Geriatrics Society, 56,* 1075–1079.

Godin, O., Dufoil, C., Maillard, P., Delcroix, N., Mazover, B., Crivello, F.. . . . Tzourio, C. (2008). White matter lesions as a predictor of depression in the elderly: The 3C-Dijon study. *Biological Psychiatry, 63,* 663–669.

Gonclaves, D. C., Albuquerque, P. B., Byrne, G. J., & Pachana, N. A. (2009). Assessment of depression in aging contexts: General considerations when working with older adults. *Professional Psychology: Research and Practice, 40,* 609–616.

Haley, W. E., Bergman, E. J., Roth, D. L., McVie, T., Gaugler, J. E., & Mittelman, M. S. (2008). Long-term effects of bereavement and caregiver intervention on dementia caregiver depressive symptoms. *The Gerontologist, 48,* 732–740.

Hawkley, L. C., Masi, C. M., Berry, J. D., & Cacioppo, J. T. (2006). Loneliness is a unique predictor of age-related differences in systolic blood pressure. *Psychology and Aging, 21,* 152–64.

Heo, M., Murphy, C., Fontaine, K., Bruce, M., & Alexopoulos, G. (2008). Population projection of US adults with lifetime experience of depressive disorder by age and sex from year 2005 to 2050. *International Journal of Geriatric Psychiatry, 23,* 1266–1270.

Hettema, J. M., Neale, M. C., & Kendler, K. S. (2001). A review and meta-analysis of the genetic epidemiology of anxiety disorders. *American Journal of Psychiatry, 158,* 1568–1578.

Hirschfield, R. M. A. (2001). The comorbidity of major depression and anxiety disorders: Recognition and management in primary care. *Primary Care Companion to Journal of Clinical Psychiatry, 3,* 244–254.

Holt-Lunstad, J., Smith, T. B., & Layton, J. B. (2010). Social relationships and mortality risk: A meta-analytic review. *Social Relationships and Mortality, 7,* 1–20.

Howren, M. B., Lamkin, D. M., & Suls, J. (2009). Associations of depression with c-reactive protein, IL-1, and IL-6: A meta-analysis. *Psychosomatic Medicine, 71,* 171–186.

Insel, K. C., & Badger, T. A. (2002). Deciphering the 4 D's: Cognitive decline, delirium, depression and dementia–A review. *Journal of Advanced Nursing, 38,* 360–368.

Janzing, J. G. E., de Graaf, R., ten Have, M., Vollerbergh, W. A., Verhagen, M., & Buitelaar, J. K. (2009). Familiality of depression in the community: Associations with gender and phenotype of major depressive disorder. *Social Psychiatry and Psychiatric Epidemiology, 44,* 1067–1074.

Jeste, D., Alexopoulos, G. S., Bartels, S. J., Cummings, J. L., Gallo, J., Gottlieb, G. L., . . . Lebowitz, D. B. (1999). Consensus statement on the upcoming crisis in geriatric mental health: Research agenda for the next 2 decades. *Archives of General Psychiatry, 56,* 848–853.

Jokinen, J., & Nordstrom, P. (2008). HPA axis hyperactivity as suicide predictor in elderly mood disorder inpatients. *Psychoneuroendocrinology, 33,* 1387–1393.

Kendler, K. S., Fiske, A., Gardner, C. O., & Gatz, M. (2009). Delineation of two genetic pathways to major depression. *Biological Psychiatry, 65,* 808–811.

Kendler, K. S., Gardner, C. O., Gatz, M., & Pedersen, N. L. (2007). The sources of co-morbidity between major depression and generalized anxiety disorder in a Swedish national twin sample. *Psychological Medicine: A Journal of Research in Psychiatry and the Allied Sciences, 37,* 453–462.

Kendler, K. S. Gatz, M., Gardner, C. O., & Petersen, N. L. (2005). Age at onset and familial risk for major depression in a Swedish national twin sample. *Psychological Medicine, 35,* 1573–1579.

Kessler, R. C., Berglund, P., Demler, O., Jin, R., Merikangas, K. R., & Walters, E. E. (2005). Lifetime prevalence and age-of-onset distributions of DSM-IV disorders in the National Comorbidity Survey Replication. *Archives of General Psychiatry, 62,* 593–602.

Kessler, R. C., Birnbaum, H. G., Shahly, V., Bromet, E., Hwang, I., McLaughlin, K. A., . . . Stein, D. J. (2010). Age differences in the prevalence and co-morbidity of DSM-IV Major Depressive Episodes: Results from the WHO World Mental Health Survey Initiative. *Depression and Anxiety, 27,* 351–364.

Kim, H. F. S., Braun, U., & Kunik, M. E. (2001). Anxiety and depression in medically ill older adults. *Journal of Clinical Geropsychology. Special Issue: Mental Health Issues for Older Adults in Medical Settings, 7,* 117–130.

Kogan, J. N., Edelstein, B. A., & McKee, D. R. (2000). Assessment of anxiety in older adults: Current status. *Journal of Anxiety Disorders, 14,* 109–132.

Larsen, P. D. (2006). Chronicity. In I. M. Lubkin & P. D. Larsen (Eds.), *Chronic illness: Impact and interventions* (6th ed., pp. 3–22). Sudbury, MA: Jones and Bartlett.

Lenze, E. J., Mantella, R. C., Shi, P., Goate, A. M., Nowotny, P., Butters, M. A., Rollman, B. L. (2011). Elevated cortisol in older adults with generalized anxiety disorder is reduced by treatment: A placebo-controlled evaluation of Escitalopram. *American Journal of Geriatric Psychiatry, 19,* 402–90.

Lenze, E. J., Miller, M., Dew, M., Martire, L., Mulsant, B., Begley, A., . . . Reynolds, C. F. (2001). Subjective health measures and acute treatment outcomes in geriatric depression. *International Journal of Geriatric Psychiatry, 16,* 1149–1155.

Lenze, E. J., Mulsant, B. H., Shear, M. K., Schulberg, H. C., Dewe, M. A., Begley, A. E., . . . Renolds, C. F. (2000). Comorbid anxiety disorders in depressed elderly patients. *American Journal of Psychiatry, 157,* 722–728.

Lewinsohn, P. M., Hoberman, H., Teri, L., & Hautzinger, M. (1985). An integrative theory of depression. In S. Reiss & R. Bootzin (Eds.), *Theoretical issues in behavior therapy* (pp. 331–359). New York: Academic Press.

Li, X., Sundquist, J., & Sundquist, K. (2008). Age-specific familial risks of anxiety. *European Archives of Psychiatry and Clinical Neuroscience, 258,* 441–445.

Lieb, R., Isensee, B., Hofler, M., Pfister, H., & Wittchen, H. U. (2002). Parental major depression and the risk of depression and other mental disorders in offspring: A prospective-longitudinal community study. *Archives of General Psychiatry, 59,* 365–374.

Lovallo, W. R., & Thomas, T. L. (2000). Stress hormones in psychophysiological research: Emotional, behavioral, and cognitive implications. In J. Cacioppo, L. Tassinary, & G. Bentson (Eds.), *The handbook of psychophysiology* (pp. 342–376). Cambridge, UK: Cambridge University Press.

Lucas, R. E. (2007). Adaptation and the set-point model of subjective well-being: Does happiness change after major life events? *Current Directions in Psychological Science, 16,* 75–79.

Mackintosh, M. A., Gatz, M., Wetherell, J. L., & Pedersen, N. L. (2006). A twin study of lifetime generalized anxiety disorder (GAD) in older adults: Genetic and environmental influences shared by neuroticism and GAD. *Twin Research and Human Genetics, 9,* 30–37.

Maes, M. (2011). Depression is an inflammatory disease, but cell-mediated immune activation is the key component of depression. *Progress in Neuropsychopharmacoly and Biological Psychiatry, 35,* 664–675.

Manepalli, J. N., Gebretsadik, M., Hook, J., & Grossberg, G. T. (2007). Differential diagnosis of the older patient with psychotic symptoms. *Primary Psychiatry, 14,* 55–62.

Mann, R. J., & Stuenkel, D. (2006). Stigma. In I. M. Lubkin & P. D. Larsen (Eds.), *Chronic illness: Impact and interventions* (6th ed., pp. 45–65). Sudbury, MA: Jones and Bartlett.

Mantella, R. C., Butters, M. A., Amico, J. A., Mazumdar, S., Rollman, B. L., Begley, A. E., . . . Lenze, E. J. (2008). Salivary cortisol is associated with diagnosis and severity of late-life generalized anxiety disorder. *Psychoneuroendocrinology, 33,* 773–781.

Martire, L. M., Schulz, R., Mittelmark, M. B., & Newsom, J. T. (1999). Stability and change in older adults' social contact and social support: The Cardiovascular Health Study. *Journals of Gerontology: Series B: Psychological Sciences and Social Sciences, 54,* 302–311.

McEwen, B. S. (1998). Stress, adaptation, and disease: Allostasis and allostatic load. *Annals of the New York Academy of Sciences, 840,* 33–44.

McKay, M. S., & Zakzanis, K. K. (2009). The impact of treatment on HPA axis activity in unipolar major depression. *Journal of Psychiatric Research, 44,* 183–192.

McLaughlin, D., Vagenas, D., Pachana, N. A., Begum, N., & Dobson, A. (2010). Gender differences in social network size and satisfaction in adults in their 70s. *Journal of Health Psychology, 15,* 671–679.

McWilliams, L. A., Cox, B. J., & Enns, M. W. (2003). Mood and anxiety disorders associated with chronic pain: An examination in a nationally representative sample. *Pain, 106,* 127–133.

Mendlewicz, J., Kriwin, P., Oswald, P., Souery, D., Aboni, S., & Brunello, N. (2006). Shortened onset of action of antidepressants in major depression using acetylsalicylic acid augmentation: A pilot open-label study. *International Clinical Psychopharmacology, 21,* 227–231.

Milisen, K., Braes, T., Fick, D. M., & Foreman, M. D. (2006). Cognitive assessment and differentiating the 3 Ds (dementia, depression, delirium). *Nursing Clinics of North America, 41,* 1–22.

Miller, A. H., Maletic, V., & Raison, C. L. (2009). Inflammation and its discontents: The role of cytokines in the pathophysiology of major depression. *Biological Psychiatry, 65,* 732–741.

Miller, G. E., Chen, E., & Zhou, E. S. (2007). If it goes up, must it come down? Chronic stress and the hypothalamic-pituitary-adrenocorticol axis in humans. *Psychological Bulletin, 133,* 25–45.

Moos, R. H., Brennan, P. L., Schutte, K. K., & Moose, B. S. (2006). Older adults' coping with negative life events: Common processes of managing health, interpersonal, and financial/work stressors. *International Journal of Aging and Human Development, 62,* 39–59.

Mroczek, D. K., & Kolarz, C. M. (1998). The effect of age on positive and negative affect: A developmental perspective on happiness. *Journal of Personality & Social Psychology, 75,* 1333–1349.

Musselman, D. L., Miller, A. H., Porter, M. R., Manatunga, A., Gao, F., Feng, G., . . . Nemeroff, C. B. (2001). Higher than normal plasma interleukin-6 concentrations in cancer patients with depression: Preliminary findings. *American Journal of Psychiatry, 158,* 1252–1257.

National Institute of Mental Health (2006). *The number count: Mental disorders in America.* Retrieved from http://www.nimh.nih.gov/health/publications/the-numbers-count-mental-disorders-in-america/index.shtml

Norton, M. C., Smith, K. R., Østbye, T., Tschanz, J. T., Corcoran, C., Schwartz, S., . . . Welsh-Bohmer, K. A. (2010). Greater risk of dementia when spouse has dementia? The Cache County Study. *Journal of the American Geriatric Society, 58,* 895–900.

Nuevo, R., Ruiz, M., Izal, M., Montorio, I., Losada, A., & Márquez-González, M. (2008). A comparison of the factorial structure of DSM-IV criteria for generalized anxiety disorder between younger and older adults. *Journal of Psychopathology and Behavioral Assessment, 30,* 252–260.

Onrust, S. A., & Cuijpers, P. (2006). Mood and anxiety disorders in widowhood: A systematic review. *Aging and Mental Health, 10,* 327–334.

Otte, C., Hart, S., Neylan, T. C., Marmar, C. R., Yaffe, K., & Mohr, D. C. (2005). A meta-analysis of cortisol response to challenge in human aging: Importance of gender. *Psychoneuroendocrinology, 30,* 80–91.

Piazza, J. R., Charles, S. T., & Almeida, D. M. (2007). Living with chronic health conditions: Age differences in affective well-being. *Journals of Gerontology, 62,* 313–321.

Porter, M. E. (2009). Nature of generalized anxiety disorder. In M. E. Porter (Ed.), *Generalized anxiety disorder across the lifespan* (pp. 1–15). New York: Springer.

Prather, A. A., Rabinovitz, M., Pollock, B. G., & Lotrich, F. E. (2009). Cytokine-induced depression during IFN-α treatment: The role of IL-6 and sleep quality. *Brain, Behavior, and Immunity, 23,* 1109–1116.

Raison, C. L., Capuron, C., & Miller, A. H. (2006). Cytokines sing the blues: Inflammation and the pathogenesis of depression. *Trends in Immunology, 227,* 24–31.

Ranga, K., Krishnan, R., Delong, M., Kraemer, H., Carney, R., Spiegel, D., . . . Wainscott, C. (2002). Comorbidity of depression with other medical diseases in the elderly. *Biological Psychiatry, 52,* 559–588.

Reichenberg, A., Yirmiya, R., Schuld, A., Kraus, T., Haack, M., Morag, A., & Pollmächer, T. (2001). Cytokine-associated emotional and cognitive disturbances in humans. *Archives of General Psychiatry, 58,* 445–452.

Riediger, M., & Freund, A. M. (2008). Me against myself: Motivational conflict and emotional development in adulthood. *Psychology and Aging, 23,* 479–494.

Robinson-Whelen, S., Tada, Y., MacCallum, R. C., McGuire, L., & Kiecolt-Glaser, J. K. (2001). Long-term caregiving: What happens when it ends? *Journal of Abnormal Psychology, 110,* 573–584.

Ryff, C. D. (1991). Possible selves in adulthood and old age: A tale of shifting horizons. *Psychology and Aging, 6,* 286–295.

Sapolsky, R. M. (2000). Glucocorticoids and hippocampal atrophy in neuropsychiatric disorders. *Archives of General Psychiatry, 57,* 925–935.

Sapolsky, R. M., Krey, L. C., & McEwen, B. S. (1985). Prolonged glucocorticoid exposure reduces hippocampal neuron number: Implications for aging. *Journal of Neuroscience, 5,* 1222–1227.

Schnittker, J. (2005). When mental health becomes health: Age and the shifting meaning of self-evaluations of general health. *Milbank Quarterly, 83,* 397–423.

Schoevers, R., Beekman, A., Deeg, D., Jonker, C., & van Tilburg, W. (2003). Comorbidity and risk-patterns of depression, generalised anxiety disorder and mixed anxiety-depression in later life: Results from the AMSTEL study. *International Journal of Geriatric Psychiatry, 18*(11), 994–1001.

Schulz, R., & Beach, S.R. (1999). Caregiving as a risk factor for mortality: The Caregiver Health Effects Study. *Journal of the American Medical Association, 282,* 2215–2219.

Schulz, R., Beach, S. R., Lind, B., Martire, L. M., Zdaniuk, B., & Hirsch, C., . . . Burton, L. (2001). Involvement in caregiving and adjustment to death of a spouse: Findings from the caregiver health effects study. *Journal of the American Medical Association, 285,* 3123–3129.

Scott, K. M., Wells, J. E., Angermeyer, M., Brugha, T. S., Bromet, E., Demyttenaere, K., . . . Kessler, R. C. (2010). Gender and the relationship between marital status and first onset of mood, anxiety, and substance use disorders. *Psychological Medicine, 40,* 1495–1505.

Smoller, J. W., Block, S. R., & Young, M. M. (2009). Genetics of anxiety disorders: The complex road from DSM to DNA. *Depression and Anxiety, 26,* 965–975.

Sneed, J. R., Rindskopf, D., Steffens, D. C., Krishnan, R. R., & Roose, S. P. (2008). The vascular depression subtype: Evidence of internal validity. *Biological Psychiatry, 64,* 491–497.

Sorensen, S., Duberstein, P., Gill, D., & Pinquart, M. (2006). Dementia care: Mental health effects, intervention strategies, and clinical implications. *Lancet Neurology, 5,* 961–973.

Stone, A., Schwartz, J., Broderick, J., & Deaton, A. (2010). A snapshot of the age distribution of psychological well-being in the United States Proceedings of the National Academy of Sciences, 107, 9985–9990.

Thornton, L. M., Andersen, B. L., Schuler, T. A., & Carson, W. E. (2009). A psychological intervention reduces inflammatory markers by alleviating depressive symptoms: Secondary analysis of a randomized controlled trial. *Psychosomatic Medicine, 71,* 715–724.

Twamley, E. W., & Bondi, M. W. (2004). The differential diagnosis of dementia. In J. H. Ricker (Ed.), *Differential diagnosis in adult neuropsychological assessment* (pp. 276–326). New York: Springer.

U.S. Census Bureau (2008). *2008 National population projections.* Retrieved from http://www.census.gov/population/www/projections/2008projections.html

van den Biggelaar, A. H., Gussekloo, J., de Craen, A. J., Frolich, M., Stek, M. L., van der Mast, R. C., & Westendorp, R. G. J. (2007). Inflammation and interleukin-1 signaling network contribute to depressive symptoms but not cognitive decline in old age. *Experimental Gerontology, 42,* 693–701.

Veen, G., Giltay, E. J., DeRijk, R. H., van Vliet, I. M., van Pelt, J., & Zitman, F. G. (2009). Salivary cortisol, serum lipids, and adiposity in patients with depressive and anxiety disorders. *Metabolism Clinical and Experimental, 58,* 821–827.

Vitaliano, P. P., Echeverria, D., Yi, J., Phillips, P. E. M., Young, H., & Siegler, I. C. (2005). Psychophysiological mediators of caregiver stress and differential cognitive decline. *Psychology & Aging, 20,* 402–411.

Vitaliano, P. P., Zhang, J., & Scanlan, J. M. (2003). Is caregiving hazardous to one's physical health? A meta-analysis. *Psychological Bulletin, 129,* 946–972.

Waddell, E. L. & Jacobs-Lawson, J. M. (2010). Predicting positive well-being in older men and women. *International Journal of Aging and Human Development, 70,* 181–197.

Wetherell, J., Gatz, M., & Pedersen, N. (2001). A longitudinal analysis of anxiety and depressive symptoms. *Psychology and Aging, 16,* 187–195.

Whisman, M. A., & Ueblacker, L. A. (2009). Prospective associations between marital discord and depressive symptoms in middle-aged and older adults. *Psychology & Aging, 24,* 184–189.

Wijeratne, C., & Hickie, I. (2001). Somatic distress syndromes in later life: The need for paradigm change. *Psychological Medicine: A Journal of Research in Psychiatry and the Allied Sciences, 31,* 571–576.

World Health Organization (2008). The burden of disease: 2004 update. Geneva, Switzerland. Retrieved from www.who.int/healthinfo/bodestimates/

Wright, S. L., & Persad, C. (2007). Distinguishing between depression and dementia in older persons: Neuropsychological and neuropathological correlates. *Journal of Geriatric Psychiatry and Neurology, 20,* 189–198.

Yohannes, A. M., Baldwin, R. C., & Connolly, M. J. (2000). Mood disorders in elderly patients with chronic obstructive pulmonary disease. *Review in Clinical Gerontology, 10,* 193–202.

15

Alzheimer's Disease and Other Dementias

Joshua R. Steinerman and Richard B. Lipton

Introduction

The syndrome of dementia is diagnosed in patients with acquired impairments of cognition of sufficient severity so as to interfere with everyday function. By convention, at least two domains of cognition must be impaired. This syndrome has many potential causes and can occur at any age, though it is most common in late life. Jack and coworkers have conceptualized dementia as "the clinically observable result of the cumulative burden of multiple pathological insults in the brain" (Jack et al., 2010, p. 119). Many distinct etiologic processes can contribute to the biological and clinical manifestations of the dementias.

In older adults, Alzheimer's disease (AD) is the most common and important cause of dementia. Clinically, AD is characterized by progressive cognitive decline, usually beginning in the domain of episodic memory. Prominent memory loss reflects the selective vulnerability and early involvement of medial temporal lobe brain structures, including the hippocampus and entorhinnal cortex (Squire, 2009). As illness unfolds, other cognitive domains, including frontal-executive function, language, and visuospatial abilities are compromised (Grober et al., 2008; Hall et al., 2001). These behavioral changes are thought to reflect accumulating pathology and neuronal loss in the brain regions that mediate these functions (Querfurth & LaFerla, 2010). Ultimately, persons with AD may become severely amnestic and progressively unable to function (Querfurth & LaFerla, 2010).

The clinical course of AD is attributed to a process of neurodegeneration. Particular neuronal populations are lost at an accelerated rate as AD unfolds. In addition to neuronal

The Wiley-Blackwell Handbook of Adulthood and Aging, First Edition. Edited by Susan Krauss Whitbourne
and Martin J. Sliwinski. © 2012 Blackwell Publishing Ltd. Published 2012 by Blackwell Publishing Ltd.

loss, AD is characterized by the accumulation of β-amyloid plaques and neurofibrillary tangles (Querfurth & LaFerla, 2010). Plaques and tangles are thought to result from abnormal protein processing giving rise to the formation of protein aggregates. These processes are thought to contribute to both the loss of neurons and synapses, because the protein aggregates themselves, or the processes that lead to their formation, are toxic to nerve cells (Jack et al., 2010; Querfurth & LaFerla, 2010).

While AD is the major cause of neurocognitive decline in late life, expression of AD pathology is highly variable; a multiplicity of factors may modify cognitive and functional status. In about one fifth of older adults with the syndrome of dementia, there is no evidence of AD pathology (Crystal et al., 2000; Querfurth & LaFerla, 2010). Other neurodegenerative disorders may cause the dementia syndrome, including Lewy body dementia and frontotemporal dementias, among others. Vascular disease can cause several forms of dementia. Many toxic-metabolic disorders including hypothyroidism and vitamin B12 deficiency may give rise to the dementia syndrome. Infectious diseases and structural brain disease may also give rise to the dementia syndrome in the absence of AD. In addition to causing dementia on their own, all of these conditions may occur with AD and alter the clinical expression of the disorder.

Additional complexity arises from the multiplicity of mechanisms that contribute to cognitive status. These include cognitive reserve (Hall et al., 2007; Hall et al., 2009; Stern, 2009), life experience (Scarmeas et al., 2011; Verghese, Lipton, Katz, et al., 2003), as well as concomitant medical disorders (Helzner et al., 2009; Verghese, Lipton, Hall, Kuslansky, & Katz, 2003) and neuropsychiatric disorders (Bierman, Comijs, Jonker, Scheltens, & Beekman, 2009). Though AD is presented herein as a singular nosologic entity, the reality is far more complex; simplifications are made for the sake of communication and clarity.

In the traditional clinical approach to AD, the first step was to diagnose dementia. Once that syndromic diagnosis was established, the next step was to determine the specific type or types of dementia that accounted for the syndrome. In this context, AD was sometimes conceptualized as a clinical diagnosis of exclusion. Diagnostic tests were used to exclude alternative structural, infectious, metabolic, and vascular causes. In a patient with a typical course, probable AD was diagnosed. The term "probable" was meant to imply that definitive diagnosis required a brain autopsy to look for pathologic evidence of AD. Since 1993, there have been treatments for AD directed to the underlying biochemical deficiency of acetylcholine. This cholinergic deficiency is treated with drugs that raise brain levels of acetylcholine by blocking the major enzyme involved in its degradation – acetylcholinesterase.

This conceptualization of AD has been transformed in recent years by several factors; here we emphasize two of these factors. First, results of treating AD with cholinergic drugs have been disappointing. Treatment improved cognitive function and maintained it above a pretreatment baseline for about a year. And second, there has been an increasing recognition that AD, as a pathologic entity, begins well before dementia becomes diagnosable (Jack et al., 2010). An increased understanding of the molecular and neurobiological mechanisms of AD has supported the development of biomarkers that improve diagnostic accuracy and create opportunities to predict cognitive trajectories. Thus AD is no longer primarily a diagnosis of exclusion. It is now increasingly viewed as a disorder that arises from specific biological substrates that can be reliably detected using distinctive behavioral symptoms coupled with laboratory studies and neuroimaging measures (Dubois et al., 2010). The diagnostic tests no longer seek to exclude other disorders; they instead help establish the presence of a specific patho-biological entity.

If AD can be diagnosed based on biological measurement before dementia develops, that raises the possibility that the onset of the dementia syndrome might be prevented (Dubois et al., 2010; Jack et al., 2010; Thal, 2006). Thus much of the therapeutic development for AD has shifted from managing symptoms (improving memory) towards disease-modifying and preventive interventions that delay the onset of clinical disease in persons at risk or slow the rate of progression of the brain disease (Thal, 2006). The concomitant diseases that modify the clinical expression of AD also become potential targets for intervention. Perhaps the onset of AD dementia can be delayed by addressing mood disorders, vascular risk factors, and metabolic derangements, for example (Jack et al., 2010; Thal, 2006). Given the wide range of attitudes and beliefs regarding brain aging and AD, and recognizing the diversity of symptoms and clinical concerns, person-centered care is essential.

In this chapter, we begin by presenting a model for staging AD. Next we consider the public health impact of AD. We then present an approach to clinical evaluation, diagnosis, and therapeutics. Additional details regarding pathobiology, neurocognitive aspects, psychosocial dimensions, and emerging therapies can be gleaned from the recommended references and other chapters in this volume.

A Staging Approach to Alzheimer's Disease

Several lines of AD research have been summarized and integrated in the form of staging models. These models inevitably divide a process of continuous change into discrete and therefore somewhat artificial units. Nonetheless, these stages provide a useful heuristic and generate hypotheses amenable to testing. In Table 15.1 and Figure 15.1 we present a four-stage model which considers cognitive status and functional status, as well as biochemical and anatomic biomarkers. We define these stages as Stage 1: no cognitive impairment–no evidence of AD; Stage 2: no cognitive impairment–biological AD; Stage 3: mild cognitive impairment (MCI) due to AD; and Stage 4: AD dementia (Jack et al., 2010).

Most adults attain stable levels of cognitive performance and everyday functioning before midlife. In this first stage, individuals are considered to be unaffected by AD; cognitive and everyday function are preserved, especially when compared to their personal baseline. This is shown in Figure 15.1 by the period of stable memory performance in Stage 1. The available biochemical and anatomic markers of AD, detailed below, are absent. At some future date, markers of risk that are present early in life may be discovered; if AD is a lifespan neurodevelopmental disorder we would predict that such markers exist. At present, there are genetic and environmental risk factors in Stage 1 that are associated with an increased risk of developing symptoms; these include risk factors such as the ApOE4 genotype and vascular risk factors, for example (Querfurth & LaFerla, 2010). During Stage 2 (no cognitive impairment–biological AD), cognitive and everyday

Table 15.1 Four-Stage Model for AD

Domains of observation	Presymptomatic stages		Symptomatic stages	
	1. No Cognitive impairment- No evidence of AD	2. No cognitive impairment- biological evidence of AD	3. MCI due to AD	4. AD dementia
Cognition abilities	Normal	Within expected range (may have subtle subjective complaint or intraindividual cognitive change on detailed objective testing)	Impaired (in one or more cognitive domains to a greater degree than expected for age and education; subjective concern by patient, informant, or clinician)	Progressive impairment (in at least two cognitive domains)
Functional status	Normal	Normal (any functional impairments are not attributable to cognitive factors)	Preserved independence (may have mild difficulties with complex everyday tasks)	Impaired functional status or decline in ADL (typically requiring increasing assistance and supervision)
Biochemical biomarkers	Absent	Present (Initially decreasing CSF Aβ and increasing PET amyloid; subsequently, increasing CSF tau)	Present (amyloid markers abnormal; CSF tau continues to rise)	Present (amyloid markers persistently abnormal; CSF tau ultimately plateaus)
Anatomic and metabolic biomarkers	Absent	Emerging	Present	Progressive

ADL = Activities of daily living; CSF Aβ = Cerebrospinal fluid concentration of the Aβ peptide; PET amyloid = Positron Emission Tomography neuroimaging of cerebral amyloid; CSF tau = Cerebrospinal fluid concentration of tau peptide

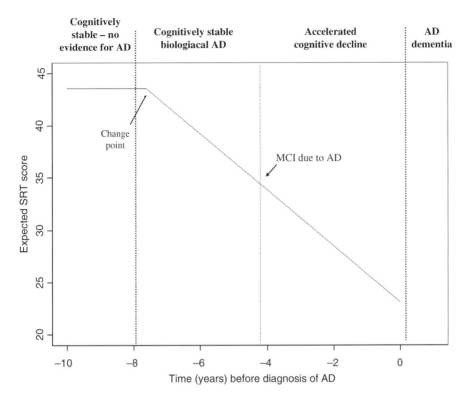

Figure 15.1   Course of Cognitive Decline Across the Stages of AD. Data from the Bronx Aging Study courtesy of Richard B. Lipton

function are preserved. There may be some cognitive decline but it does not cross the threshold for impairment (Figure 15.1). There is evidence that within-person variability in cognitive tests may precede the development of cognitive decline (Holtzer et al., 2008). This stage is distinguished by observable biological evidence of AD, which could include markers of toxic proteins of early pathology, such as amyloid or tau, as well as downstream consequences such as synaptic dysfunction, and/or neuronal loss. Evidence for the role of these biochemical and anatomic markers has been reviewed in more detail elsewhere (Jack et al., 2010; Trojanowski et al., 2010).

Biological markers for AD have been an area of intense research for many years (Jack et al., 2010; Trojanowski et al., 2010). Some of the better validated markers are summarized in Table 15.2. We divide these markers into three broad groups: biochemical markers, anatomic markers, and brain-metabolic markers. The biochemical markers reflect alterations in the synthesis, degradation, and accumulation of toxic proteins involved in AD. The anatomic markers characterize the structural changes in specific brain regions that are thought to reflect the downstream consequences of the biochemical changes. The brain-metabolic markers identify areas of reduced brain metabolism which may reflect biochemical changes.

Table 15.2   Selected Biochemical and Anatomic Markers for AD

Type of marker	Marker	Measurement strategy	Comment
Biochemical-amyloid	$A\beta_{42}$ and $A\beta_{40}$	CSF	Validated marker with complex time course
		Blood	Emerging marker
Biochemical-Neurofibrillary	Tau; P-tau	CSF	Promising marker of neurofibrillary degeneration
Biochemical-imaging amyloid	Amyloid	PET	High sensitivity; false-positive rate uncertain
Anatomic	Hippocampal or entorhinnal cortex volume	MRI	Good discriminative validity
Metabolic	Temporoparietal hypometabolism	FDG-PET; SPECT	Medicare-approved to distinguish FTD from AD
	Hippocampal NAA (neuronal metabolism)	MRS	Promising

$A\beta_{42} = 42$-amino acid $A\beta$ peptide generated via selective beta- and gamma-secretase cleavage; P-tau $=$ phosphorylated tau; MRI $=$ Magnetic resonance imaging; FDG-PET $=$ 18F-fluro-deoxy-glucose positron emission tomography; MRS $=$ Magnetic resonance spectroscopy; SPECT $=$ Single-photon emission computed tomography.

The most robust biochemical markers to date are associated with the amyloid cascade hypothesis of AD. This hypothesis states that during the earliest stages of AD, abnormalities in the synthesis, processing, and degradation of amyloid is a major causal factor in the unfolding of AD. Amyloid markers include spinal fluid levels of $A\beta_{40}$ and $A\beta_{42}$ and perhaps measures of these species in blood. In addition, amyloid deposition in the brain can be measured using positron emission tomography (PET) scans. Neurofibrillary degeneration can be detected by examining spinal fluid levels of tau or phosphotau; neuroimaging methods are in development.

"Anatomic" biomarkers are assessed using a number of imaging modalities. Markers include hippocampal or medial temporal lobe atrophy on MRI. In addition, temporoparietal hypometabolism or hypoperfusion on PET or single photon emission computed tomography (SPECT) has been used. Emerging evidence suggests a role for magnetic resonance spectroscopy (MRS) as a technique for imaging neuronal metabolism (Zimmerman et al., 2008).

We predict that biochemical and anatomic biomarkers will be used to stage AD and that stage -specific treatment may emerge. In general, treating cognitively stable patients with no evidence of AD represents primary prevention (Table 15.3), that is, the treatment of asymptomatic individuals to prevent disease. Treatment of cognitively stable patients with biological AD represents a form of secondary prevention for AD (Table 15.3). In secondary prevention, asymptomatic but high risk individuals are treated. Treating

Table 15.3 Stages of AD, Level of Prevention and Treatment Goals

Stage of AD	Levels of prevention and goal of treatment
Stage 1 – No cognitive impairment No evidence of AD	Primary prevention. Prevent Stages 2,3 and 4 in individuals free of clinical manifestations or biomarkers
Stage 2 – No cognitive impairment, "biological" AD	Secondary prevention. Prevent Stages 3 and 4
Stage 3 – MCI due to AD	Secondary prevention of Stage 4 (prevent progression from MCI to AD)
	Tertiary prevention of Stage 3 (Prevent MCI from leading to functional decline
Stage 4 – AD dementia	Tertiary prevention of AD dementia
	Slow progression
	Maintain function

persons with MCI to prevent AD is also a form of secondary prevention. But the goal is to prevent progression of MCI, that is, tertiary prevention of MCI. Treating persons with AD dementia is a form of tertiary prevention, directed towards slowing progression and retaining function.

Evolution of stage-specific therapy requires progress in the area of rational therapeutic design. Ideally, reliable information on the proteins associated with impending and evolving brain dysfunction and where the effects are manifested could help inform stage- and mechanisms-specific treatment. If other mechanisms, such as oxidative stress or inflammation, are shown to be etiologically important they become targets for treatment.

Stage 3, or MCI due to AD, describes a state of symptomatic cognitive impairment in a person free of dementia (Petersen et al., 2009). In practice, cognitive impairment is often assessed in relation to an age- and education-matched normative sample. The usual operational definition of MCI requires that a person fall 1.5 standard deviations below the mean for their age and education mates. One difficulty with this definition is that a person with a superior memory may experience substantial decline without meeting the definition and so may be misclassified as normal. A person with lifelong poor memory may have little or no memory loss and meet the definition. Thus an approach which considers within-person change relative to an observed or estimated baseline may improve diagnostic accuracy.

MCI is usually attributable to an underlying disorder, most often AD. MCI may also arise from other neurodegenerative disorders, cerebrovascular disease, or the full range of disorders that cause dementia. Because the MCI syndrome is neuropsychologically and etiologically heterogeneous, biomarkers can increase certainty that the cognitive impairment is due to AD. Memory is frequently but not invariably affected in MCI due to AD. By definition, functional independence is preserved. Memory impairment has been shown to predict the onset of AD in older adults (Grober et al., 2008; Grober, Lipton, Hall, & Crystal, 2000; Petersen et al., 2009).

The stage of AD dementia is defined by cognitive impairment in memory and at least one other cognitive domain of sufficient severity to interfere with social or occupational functioning. Functional decline is determined, in part, by the individual's level of premorbid function. The math professor may become unable to prove new theorems, with cognitive abilities that are still well above average. A resident of an assisted living facility may experience severe loss before functional decline occurs. Thus the onset of Stage 4 is determined by factors that have as much to do with environmental conditions and circumstances as they do with neurobiology.

While Table 15.1 and Figure 15.1 suggest that the stages are clearly delineated and operationally defined, aging is far less orderly. Some individuals will conform to the temporal progression of clinical and biological change specified in this model while others do not. The model provides a useful framework for classifying individuals at cross-section or when limited longitudinal data is available. Follow-up is an invaluable tool; patients progress or fail to progress in a way that clarifies their diagnosis. For purposes of observational research and in some clinical settings, one can more reliably classify older adults retrospectively based on their longitudinal course over many years (Steinerman, Hall, Sliwinski, & Lipton, 2010).

Risk Factors and Public Health Perspectives

The single most important risk factor associated with the development of AD is advancing age. AD is an extremely common disorder whose prevalence is increasing as the population ages. In the United States, more than 5 million individuals over the age of 65 (approximately 1 in 8 older adults) have the disease, and 17 million worldwide have the disorder (Ferri et al., 2005). AD is a major cause of both disability and death' accounting for healthcare expenditures which exceed $150 billion. Although the disease is less common at younger ages, an estimated 200,000 Americans under 65 also have AD.

As the population ages, the public health impact of AD is projected to increase, absent a meaningful change in its treatment or prevention. By 2025, the prevalence of AD is projected to increase by 50%. At that point, Medicare spending for AD will approach 300 billion dollars annually. By 2050, there will be 14 million Americans with AD with proportionate increases in medical costs. In addition to these direct costs, indirect costs attributable to lost workplace productivity and the unpaid caregiver burden are substantial. There are nearly 11 million unpaid caregivers for individuals with AD. Against this backdrop, a hypothetical intervention that delayed the onset of AD by 5 years would result in more than a 50% reduction in the number of AD patients, and reduce AD-associated Medicare costs from $627 to $344 billion dollars.

Alzheimer's disease is both a national and a global public health threat of enormous importance. The best hope for stemming the tide requires the early development of preventive interventions and early treatment. Approaches to prevention are sometimes divided into primary, secondary, and tertiary preventive interventions, as discussed above (Table 15.3).

Early recognition of persons with AD, perhaps before symptoms develop, is likely a vital step towards effective preventive interventions. It should be increasingly possible to identify healthy (presymptomatic) individuals who are at increased risk of developing

AD symptoms, based on known medical or environmental risk factors, measuring relevant biomarkers, or both.

The relationship between AD and "normal" aging is complex and incompletely understood (Steinerman et al., 2010). AD is not an inevitable consequence of aging and should not be considered normative. Race and ethnicity have a role (Weiner, 2008). The higher incidence and prevalence of AD in older African American and Latino populations is incompletely understood. It may be explained, at least in part, by the higher rates of hypertension, diabetes, and other vascular risk factors among these populations. Some have speculated that poor treatment of these disorders in underserved communities may contribute. In addition to age and race, a number of other putative risk and protective factors have been reported.

According to a recent state-of-the-science consensus report, the best demonstrated factors associated with an increased risk of AD include diabetes, the epsilon 4 allele of the apolipoprotein E gene (APOE e4), smoking, and depression. Factors consistently associated with a decreased risk of AD and cognitive decline included high levels of education, cognitive engagement, and physical activity (Hall et al., 2007; Hall et al., 2009; Scarmeas et al., 2011; Stern, 2009). Dietary and nutritional factors also appear to play a role in determining AD risk. While there is inconsistent evidence associated with specific foods or nutrients, there is increasing evidence that certain dietary patterns (e.g., a Mediterranean diet consisting of high intake of fruits and vegetables; high intake of unsaturated fatty acids and low saturated fatty acids; moderately high intake of fish; a low-to-moderate intake of dairy products; a low intake of meat and poultry; and a regular but moderate amount of alcohol, primarily in the form of wine) confers protection against the development of AD (Feart et al., 2009; Scarmeas, Stern, Tang, Mayeux, & Luchsinger, 2006). In addition, certain genetic variants, associated with exceptional longevity, are thought to protect against the onset of AD and dementia (Lipton et al., 2010; Sanders et al., 2010).

Despite its burden, the diagnosis of the dementia syndrome as well as the diagnosis of AD are often delayed, particularly in very early stages (Grober et al., 2000, Grober et al., 2008; Querfurth & LaFerla, 2010; Steinerman et al., 2010). Several factors may contribute to diagnostic delay and to missed diagnostic opportunities. First, cognitive decline may be attributed to problems of normal aging and may fail to be brought to medical attention. Even if it is brought to medical attention, primary care doctors may not screen for cognitive impairment, in line with several major public health recommendations. This may be due to a variety of factors including lack of time or knowledge of screening tools and the modest psychometric properties of commonly used instruments (Buschke et al., 1999; Grober, Sanders, Hall, & Lipton, 2010; Iliffe et al., 2009; Lipton et al., 2003). In addition, there is a perception that available treatments are not sufficiently effective to justify early detection. Some advocacy groups argue for routine and wide-scale screening, and many individuals are motivated to check their current brain performance and institute multimodal lifestyle interventions intended to mitigate risk of brain failure. Indeed, self-administered cognitive screening and even genetic tests are currently offered directly to consumers.

There are two general points of agreement. First, screening, risk assessment, and presymptomatic diagnosis will become more important as disease-modifying therapeutics become available. Second, these approaches are essential to the early detection of disease so that preventive interventions can be studied.

Clinical Assessment

The clinical interview should include both the patient and, whenever possible, a knowledgeable informant. The interview should focus on current aspects of the patient's cognitive, behavioral, and motor experiences. Earlier life experiences are also important, including educational and occupational attainment. A knowledgeable informant who has regular contact with the patient is extremely helpful, if not essential. When the concern originates from a family member or friend, or is corroborated by such an informant, the likelihood of objective impairment on cognitive testing is higher. It is often observed that individuals with AD may remain unaware of their deficits, or deny them, although this is frequently not the case.

Cognitive features

The clinical history can be used to assess a broad range of cognitive function. The episodic memory dysfunction typical of AD presents with a variety of helpful historical features. The patient may have a history of repeating questions or statements, forgetting recent events or conversations, frequently losing objects, increasingly relying on written notes or lists. While all of these occur intermittently throughout the lifespan, when they occur consistently and increase with age, AD is more likely. Sometimes forgotten episodes or information comes back reliably when the individual is given cues, prompts, or reminders; this so-called "retrieval deficit" is less characteristic of AD, in which memories remain irretrievable despite assistance or clues. Also, the very common cognitive complaints of briefly forgetting names, specific words, or the reason an individual entered a room are not necessarily ominous, as they occur frequently with normative aging. In general, the amnestic syndrome of AD is especially pronounced for recent memories; remote and autobiographical memories are often spared until late stages of the disease.

The clinician should also probe for evidence of temporal or spatial disorientation. For example, individuals with AD may misreport the day of the week, or even the year. There may be difficulty finding destinations, even in familiar environments. Executive dysfunction can accompany a wide range of neuropsychiatric disorders, including AD. Examples from everyday life might include difficulty maintaining finances, keeping appointments, attending to household chores, or multitasking. Attention and concentration may be reduced, and increased distractibility may result in numerous unfinished conversations, tasks, and projects. Language can similarly be affected in AD, though it is typically not a primary symptom or complaint; examples might include problems finding the right words to use in conversation or understanding spoken instructions. Spontaneous verbal output may decrease overall with a preference for words of unspecified reference ("thing," "that"), resulting in empty speech. Circumlocution and confabulation are also commonly observed.

Behavioral features

Behavioral manifestations of underlying AD pathology are extremely common (Cummings, 2005). In many cases, behavioral and psychological disturbances exert the biggest effect on quality of life and present the greatest challenge to caregivers and clinicians. Apathy is among the most frequently observed behavioral symptoms, characterized by reduced interest in life activities and loss of emotional engagement. Although apathy is often not recognized as a clinical problem or targeted for therapeutic intervention, it can be considered a silent enemy in AD; the insidious loss of motivation and purposeful action is tantamount to a diminished self. To those close to the apathetic individual, he or she may be ruefully viewed as "withdrawn" or simply "slipped away." Apathy is sometimes accompanied by aberrant motor activity such as pacing or rummaging, and may also coexist with depression, another frequent behavioral manifestation of AD. The depression of AD may be characterized by typical symptoms of sadness, hopelessness, and loss of pleasure. However, subtler depressive symptoms may be evident, such as disturbed sleep, diminished appetite, irritability, or fatigue. Anxiety is not uncommon, occasionally with situationally triggered panic.

Among psychotic symptoms, delusions are most characteristic of AD. In particular, delusions of theft or spousal infidelity are so typical that their presence may assist in diagnosing AD. Other delusions are seen, including believing people are not who they claim to be, prescribed medications are poisonous or harmful, and the house in which the patient lives in is not his or her true home. Certain psychotic symptoms, such as recurrent auditory or visual hallucinations, are less common in AD and should raise the possibility of an alternate diagnosis (McKeith, 2006). Because AD psychosis is associated with aggression, caregiver burden, and institutionalization, and because the drugs most likely to reduce psychotic symptoms carry significant risk of serious adverse effects, careful attention should be given to identifying delusions at their earliest manifestation and implementing preventative or low-risk strategies to mitigate their damage.

Motor features

Especially at early stages, AD should not affect gross motor or sensory function. However, subtle changes in locomotion may precede diagnosis by several years, and with disease progression gait impairment may become obvious (Verghese et al., 2002; Verghese, Wang, Katz, Sanders, & Lipton, 2009). At advanced stages, individuals with AD may be bedbound and exhibit myoclonus (involuntary muscle twitching). Apraxia, an inability to carry out learned motor programs such as those necessary for using tools and devices, is a sign of higher cortical dysfunction which can be seen in AD. Other movement disorders, such as prominent tremor or Parkinsonism, should raise the possibility of other causes. In addition, since AD is primarily a disorder of aging, other common diseases of aging, including rheumatologic, orthopedic, and vascular disorders, may lead to impaired movement and locomotion in AD patients. As with all evaluations of an older adult, attention should be paid to identifying and reducing the risk of falls.

Office-based cognitive testing

Although a careful clinical interview for subjective impressions of cognitive symptoms is essential, obtaining objective data on cognitive performance greatly assists diagnostic ability. Although time constraints are imposed on clinical workflow in most settings, brief standardized instruments should be utilized when a cognitive disorder such as AD is suspected. Cognitive status can be assessed using (a) tests of global cognition; (b) tests designed to gauge one or more specific cognitive domain (e.g., verbal memory, attention); or (c) experimental cognitive procedures. Global measures of cognitive function, such as the Mini-Mental State Examination (MMSE; Folstein, Robins, & Helzer, 1983), can be administered by trained professionals from various disciplines in approximately 10 minutes. The advantages of familiarity and ease of use are offset by some disadvantages. Although multiple domains, including orientation, memory, language, and visual construction, are assessed, global tests of mental status do not separately identify impairments by domain and specificity is limited, especially for differential diagnosis. In the particular case of the MMSE, executive functions are not assessed in detail, although the 5 items assessing temporal orientation may be independently helpful for diagnosing AD and predicting future cognitive decline. Other tests of global cognition include the Blessed Information-Memory-Concentration test (BIMC; Blessed, Tomlinson, & Roth, 1968) and the Montreal Cognitive Assessment (MoCA; Nasreddine et al., 2005) for cases of milder impairment.

When memory is the cognitive domain of greatest interest, for example in diagnosing AD, a clinician would do well to focus on assessing this cognitive domain. A number of brief memory tests are available, typically involving word list learning and subsequent recall following a delay. Among these, instruments which feature encoding specificity are best suited to detect the genuine amnesia typical of AD and are able to control for the potentially confounding effects of poor attention and effort. An example is the Memory Impairment Screen (MIS) which is also available in a validated telephone revision (MIS-T; Buschke et al., 1999; Lipton et al., 2003). Other instruments which are applicable to office administration and assess cognition with some domain specificity include clock drawing (visuospatial and executive functions) and category fluency (language and executive functions). Multistage screening strategies may prove useful in primary care settings (Grober et al., 2010).

More recently, a number of computer-based cognitive assessments have been developed with varying degrees of validation in clinical populations of interest. In general, these can yield significant advantages in standardization of administration and scoring. These often require less extensive rater training and involvement. Some batteries make use of the computer's capacity in ways that human administration does not allow, for example with enhanced temporal resolution to assess processing speed and certain aspects of attention and executive functions, as well as for algorithmic administration of task stimuli to adapt to user performance in real time.

Formal neuropsychological evaluation

When available, referral to a neuropsychologist for extended assessment can serve the purpose of ascertaining quantitative information regarding the patient's abilities in specified cognitive domains using population-based norms. A neuropsychologist can also often make productive use of qualitative factors and observable cognitive styles for ascertaining the presence and nature of brain dysfunction. In some cases, these can form the basis of therapeutic recommendations in the form of rehabilitation programs or adaptive strategies. In our experience, clinical neuropsychological testing in elders is most helpful for detecting mild impairments, especially in individuals with high premorbid intellectual abilities, as well as for differentiating neurocognitive disorders from symptoms largely attributable to psychological causes. Norms for neuropsychological tests are often developed in samples that include individuals with preclinical dementia. Excluding these individuals from normative samples improves diagnostic accuracy (Holtzer et al., 2008; Sliwinski et al., 1996).

Laboratory studies

Standard office practice typically includes blood tests to detect treatable systemic factors, such as vitamin B12 deficiency or hypothyroidism, which may explain the perceived cognitive symptoms in part. Other metabolic factors, such as diabetes and hyperlipidemia, should be assessed as they can have an effect on the clinical course of AD, and also can contribute to cerebrovascular injury as a concurrent mechanism. When the clinical syndrome is atypical or uncertain, a broader range of neurodegenerative, infectious, and inflammatory disorders should be screened for using blood tests and/or spinal fluid analysis. In particular, low levels of the Aβ peptide and elevated tau protein in the spinal fluid can increase confidence that the pathologic cascade of AD has taken hold.

Neuroimaging

Several professional organizations have issued guidelines endorsing structural radiographic imaging, either via computed tomography (CT) or magnetic resonance imaging (MRI), in cases of suspected acquired cognitive impairment. This can serve the purpose of excluding brain injuries such as subdural hematoma or neoplasm. Increasingly, structural neuroimaging (especially MRI) is also used for the positive identification of medial temporal lobe atrophy or other patterns of atrophy consistent with AD. Neuroimaging is also extremely helpful in determining the extent and clinical relevance of cerebrovascular injuries. Regional brain metabolism and cerebral blood flow can also be assessed using nuclear medicine procedures such as positron emission tomography (PET) and single photon emission computed tomography (SPECT); the pattern of bilateral parietal and temporal lobe dysfunction suggests AD and can increase confidence in the diagnosis.

Diagnosis

Constructs and criteria

There is a substantial gap between research diagnostic capabilities to detect AD at mild or presymptomatic stages and customary clinical practice. Important differences have also repeatedly been found between systematically recruited population-based samples and samples drawn from individuals seeking clinical attention for cognitive symptoms. For example, it has become customary to classify dementia-free individuals who perform poorly on objective neuropsychological tests as MCI; in clinic-based samples and population studies, such individuals are at substantially increased risk of developing dementia, at a rate of approximately 12–15% per year.

Differential diagnosis

Whenever an older adult presents for evaluation of perceived cognitive change, AD is a likely culprit, and the clinician should attempt to confirm the expected syndromic and biomarker features, as detailed above. However, when there are unexpected features or additional clinical factors, a more expansive differential diagnosis should be considered. Often, the goal is not to establish an *alternate* diagnosis, but to identify *concurrent* diagnoses which contribute to symptomatology, especially remediable conditions.

In particular, alternative etiologies are far more prevalent in individuals under age 65. Early or prominent motor symptoms, such as Parkinsonism, as well as visual hallucinations, prominent fluctuations, or REM sleep parasomnias raise the suspicion of Lewy Body disease. Pronounced behavioral or language dysfunction can suggest frontotemporal lobar degeneration (Rabinovici & Miller, 2010). Clinical progression over days to months should trigger concern for prion disease, neoplasm, infection, or any number of neuropsychiatric or systemic disorders.

The most common concurrent etiology which modulates the clinical expression of AD is cerebrovascular disease, which should be considered in individuals with multiple vascular risk factors, supportive structural neuroimaging, or appropriate clinical features. Other systemic and homeostatic conditions which can influence symptoms include medication side effects (especially anticholinergic agents), polypharmacy, alcohol intake, poor nutrition, mood dysregulation, sleep disturbance, and pain.

Atypical AD syndromes

It should be emphasized that there is no simple match between observed clinical syndromes and causative etiologies. For example, AD does not always selectively target the medial temporal lobe and produce amnesia. The "posterior variant" of AD can produce visuospatial impairment, agnosia, apraxia, and other symptoms which implicate posterior cortical regions. Conversely, the syndrome of "progressive posterior cortical dysfunction" is etiologically heterogeneous, and can be caused by AD, tauopathies, Lewy Body disease, and prion disorders, among other mechanisms (Renner et al., 2004). Similarly, frontotemporal dementia syndromes are also produced by a range of pathologies, including AD in up to one-third of cases. The key conceptual point is that biomarkers are critically positioned toward clarifying what are ultimately the most important diagnostic questions: *What* has gone awry and *where* are the effects manifest? Once satisfactory answers to such questions are proposed, the clinician, patient, and caregivers can engage in formulating a rational therapeutic strategy.

Therapeutic Approaches

Pharmacologic therapies

Currently, two classes of medications are FDA-approved for use in AD. The cholinesterase-inhibitors donepezil, rivastigmine, and galantamine act by increasing levels of the neurotransmitter acetylcholine, which is known to be deficient in AD. Among the three, there are some distinctions in pharmacologic properties and available routes of administration, though as a class all have similar efficacy as demonstrated though large clinical trials (Birks, 2006). Although the effect sizes are modest, the cholinesterase inhibitors consistently show better cognition and certain aspects of everyday function compared to placebos. The most common adverse effects, especially gastrointestinal symptoms and diminished appetite, which are observed on one of the medications, may be less prominent if another cholinesterase inhibitor is tried. Memantine represents a second mechanism of action, in that it modulates the effects of the neurotransmitter glutamate and has demonstrated modest cognitive benefits in controlled clinical trials (Reisberg et al., 2003).

On the other hand, there is no firm evidence or consensus that available medications fundamentally alter the progressive brain pathologies associated with AD. Such disease-modifying therapies would be of tremendous value and are the goal of intensive drug development efforts (Salloway, Mintzer, Weiner, & Cummings, 2008). At this point, medications used in AD are purely *symptomatic* and should target the areas which would most improve quality of life. In this context, individuals with AD, caregivers, and healthcare professionals may consider judicious use of antidepressants, antipsychotics, or other CNS medications; such off-label use must be accompanied by an open discussion of the potential risks, benefits, and goals of therapy (Mittal, Kurup, Williamson, Muralee, & Tampi, 2011).

Nonpharmacologic and preventative interventions

It is commonly and erroneously perceived that there is "nothing one can do" if AD is diagnosed or destined. Such therapeutic nihilism may be understood in light of the great unmet need for breakthrough biomedical therapeutic advances, but such an attitude is ultimately unjustified and unnecessary. In fact, the strategic vision to implement trans-formative treatments and delay or prevent the onset of symptomatic AD is manifest in a coordinated research infrastructure and United States law.

For many individuals and families, there is already "much to be done" if Alzheimer's is on the agenda. Since lifestyle factors, including physical activity, balanced diet, and cognitive enrichment, are consistently associated with reduced AD risk, *brain fitness* has emerged as a proactive behavioral approach to promote cognitive health at all ages, even in the face of brain failure. Increasingly, we anticipate that such nonpharmacologic inter-ventions will be coupled with emerging biomedical therapeutics to prevent or delay the onset of MCI and brain failure (Fernandez, 2009).

In addition to clinical guidance, anticipatory legal and financial planning is frequently beneficial, and should not be deferred. Thoughtful consideration of these practical matters, as well as of advanced healthcare directives, should be given at the very earliest point in time, ideally during presymptomatic stages. Caregiver burden is also a critical determinant of quality of life, especially in later symptomatic stages, and is an effective therapeutic target which is successfully addressed via community and peer organizations.

Conclusion

As a complex and wide-ranging phenomenon, Alzheimer's insinuates into the essence of an individual's consciousness and self, while posing an unrelenting public health challenge for our aging society. In this chapter, we have distilled current clinical and research knowledge into a simplified but applicable heuristic model of AD. It is our hope that this presentation will prove useful to readers who attend to the Alzheimer's challenge in their professional and personal pursuits.

References

Bierman, E. J., Comijs, H. C., Jonker, C., Scheltens, P., & Beekman, A. T. (2009). The effect of anxiety and depression on decline of memory function in Alzheimer's disease. *International Psychogeriatrics, 21,* 1142–1147.

Birks, J. (2006). Cholinesterase inhibitors for Alzheimer's disease. *Cochrane Database of Systematic Reviews, 1,* CD005593.

Blessed, G., Tomlinson, B. E., & Roth, M. (1968). The association between quantitative measures of dementia and of senile change in the cerebral grey matter of elderly subjects. *British Journal of Psychiatry, 114,* 797–811.

Buschke, H., Kuslansky, G., Katz, M., Stewart, W. F., Sliwinski, M. J., Eckholdt, H. M., & Lipton, R. B. (1999). Screening for dementia with the memory impairment screen. *Neurology, 52,* 231–238.

Crystal, H. A., Dickson, D., Davies, P., Masur, D., Grober, E., & Lipton, R. B. (2000). The relative frequency of "dementia of unknown etiology" increases with age and is nearly 50% in nonagenarians. *Archives of Neurology, 57,* 713–719.

Cummings, J. L. (2005). Behavioral and neuropsychiatric outcomes in Alzheimer's disease. *CNS Spectrums, 10,* 22–25.

Dubois, B., Feldman, H. H., Jacova, C., Cummings, J. L., Dekosky, S. T., Barberger-Gateau, P. . . . Scheltens, P. (2010) Revising the definition of Alzheimer's disease: A new lexicon. *Lancet Neurology, 9,* 1118–1127.

Feart, C., Samieri, C., Rondeau, V., Amieva, H., Portet, F., Dartigues, J.-F., . . . Barberger-Gateau, P. (2009). Adherence to a Mediterranean diet, cognitive decline, and risk of dementia. *Journal of the American Medical Association, 302,* 638–648.

Fernandez, A. (2009). Preparing society for the cognitive age. *Frontiers in Neuroscience, 3,* 128–129.

Ferri, C. P., Prince, M., Brayne, C., Brodaty, H., Fratiglioni, L., Ganguli, M. . . . Scazufca, M. (2005). Global prevalence of dementia: A Delphi consensus study. *Lancet, 366,* 2112–2117.

Folstein, M. F., Robins, L. N., & Helzer, J. E. (1983). The Mini-Mental State Examination. *Archives of General Psychiatry, 40,* 812.

Grober, E., Hall, C., Lipton, R. B., Zonderman, A. B., Resnick, S. M., & Kawas, C. (2008). Memory impairment, executive dysfunction, and intellectual decline in preclinical Alzheimer's disease. *Journal of the International Neuropsychological Society, 14*(2), 266–278.

Grober, E., Lipton, R. B., Hall, C., & Crystal, H. (2000). Memory impairment on free and cued selective reminding predicts dementia. *Neurology, 54,* 827–832.

Grober, E., Sanders, A. E., Hall, C., & Lipton, R. B. (2010). Free and cued selective reminding identifies very mild dementia in primary care. *Alzheimer Disease and Associated Disorders, 3*(24), 284–290.

Hall, C. B., Derby, C. A., LeValley, A. J., Katz, M. J., Verghese, J., & Lipton, R. B. (2007). Education delays accelerated decline in memory in persons who develop dementia. *Neurology, 69*(17), 1657–1664.

Hall, C. B., Lipton, R. B., Sliwinski, M., Katz, M. J., Derby, C. A, & Verghese, J. (2009). Cognitive activities delay onset of memory decline in persons who develop dementia. *Neurology, 73,* 356–361.

Hall, C. B., Ying, J., Kuo, L, Sliwinski, M., Buschke, H., Katz, M. J., & Lipton, R. B. (2001). Estimation of bivariate measurements having different change points, with application to cognitive ageing. *Statistics in Medicine, 20,* 3695–3714.

Helzner, E. P., Luchsinger, J. A., Scarmeas, N., Cosentino, S., Brickman, A. M., Glymour, M. M., & Stern, Y. (2009). Contribution of vascular risk factors to the progression in Alzheimer disease. *Archives of Neurology, 66,* 343–348.

Holtzer, R., Goldin, Y., Zimmerman, M., Katz, M., Buschke, H., & Lipton, R. B. (2008). Robust norms for selected neuropsychological tests in older adults. *Archives of Clinical Neuropsychology, 23*(5), 531–541.

Iliffe, S., Robinson, L., Brayne, C., Goodman, C., Rait, G., Manthorpe, J., & Ashley, P. (2009). Primary care and dementia: 1. Diagnosis, screening and disclosure. *International Journal of Geriatric Psychiatry, 24,* 895–901.

Jack, C. R., Jr., Knopman, D. S., Jagust, W. J., Shaw, L. M., Aisen, P. S., Weiner MW, . . . Trojanowski, J. Q. (2010). Hypothetical model of dynamic biomarkers of the Alzheimer's pathological cascade. *Lancet Neurology, 9,* 119–128.

Lipton, R. B., Hirsch, J., Katz, M. J., Wang, C., Sanders, A. E., Verghese, J., . . . Derby, C. (2010). Exceptional parental longevity: Reduced risk of Alzheimer's disease and memory decline. *Journal of the American Geriatrics Society, 58*(6), 1043–1049.

Lipton, R. B., Katz, M. J., Kuslansky, G., Sliwinski, M. J., Stewart, W. F., Verghese, J., . . . Buschke, H. (2003). Screening for dementia by telephone with the memory impairment screen. *Journal of the American Geriatrics Society, 51,* 1382–1390.

McKeith, I. G. (2006). Consensus guidelines for the clinical and pathologic diagnosis of dementia with Lewy bodies (DLB): Report of the Consortium on DLB International Workshop. *Journal of Alzheimer's Disease, 9,* 417–423.

Mittal, V., Kurup, L., Williamson, D., Muralee, S., Tampi, R. R. (2011). Review: Risk of cerebrovascular adverse events and death in elderly patients with dementia when treated with antipsychotic medications: A literature review of evidence. *American Journal of Alzheimer's Disease & Other Dementias, 26,* 10–28.

Nasreddine, Z. S., Phillips, N. A., Bédirian, V., Charbonneau, S., Whitehead, V., Collin, I., . . . Chertkow, H. (2005). The Montreal Cognitive Assessment, MoCA: A brief screening tool for mild cognitive impairment. *Journal of the American Geriatrics Society, 53,* 695–699.

Petersen, R. C., Roberts, R. O., Knopman, D. S., Boeve, B. F, Geda, Y. E., Ivnik, R. J . . . Jack, C. R. (2009). Mild cognitive impairment: Ten years later. *Archives of Neurology, 66,* 1447–1455.

Querfurth, H. W., & LaFerla, F. M. (2010). Alzheimer's disease. *New England Journal of Medicine, 362,* 329–344.

Rabinovici, G. D., & Miller, B. L. (2010) Frontotemporal lobar degeneration: Epidemiology, pathophysiology, diagnosis and management. *CNS Drugs, 24,* 375–398.

Reisberg, B., Doody, R., Stoffler, A., Schmitt, F., Ferris, S., & Mobius, H. J. (2003). Memantine in moderate-to-severe Alzheimer's disease. *New England Journal of Medicine, 348,* 1333–1341.

Renner, J. A., Burns, J. M., Hou, C. E., McKeel, D. W., Jr., Storandt, M., & Morris, J. C. (2004). Progressive posterior cortical dysfunction: A clinicopathologic series. *Neurology, 63,* 1175–1180.

Salloway, S., Mintzer, J., Weiner, M. F., & Cummings, J. L. (2008). Disease-modifying therapies in Alzheimer's disease. *Alzheimer's and Dementia, 4,* 65–79.

Sanders, A. E., Wang, C., Katz, M., Derby, C. A, Barzilai, N., Ozelius, L., & Lipton, R. B (2010). Association of a functional polymorphism in the cholesteryl ester transfer protein (*CETP*) gene with memory decline and incidence of dementia. *Journal of the American Medical Association, 303*(2), 150–158.

Scarmeas, N., Luchsinger, J. A., Brickman, A. M., Cosentino, S., Schupf, N., Xin-Tang, M., . . . Stern Y. (2011). Physical activity and Alzheimer disease course. *American Journal of Geriatric Psychiatry, 19*(5), 471–481.

Scarmeas, N., Stern, Y., Tang, M. X., Mayeux, R., & Luchsinger, J. A. (2006). Mediterranean diet and risk for Alzheimer's disease. *Annals of Neurology, 59,* 912–921.

Squire, L. R. (2009). Memory and brain systems: 1969–2009 (2009). *Journal of Neuroscience, 29,* 12711–12716.

Sliwinski, M., Lipton, R. B., Buschke, H., & Stewart, W. F. (1996). The effects of preclinical dementia on estimates of normal cognitive function in aging. *Journal of Gerontology: Psychological Sciences, 51B,* 217–225.

Steinerman, J. R., Hall, C. B., Sliwinski, M., & Lipton, R. B. (2010). Modeling cognitive trajectories within longitudinal studies: A focus on older adults. *Journal of the American Geriatrics Society, 58*(Suppl. 2), S313-S318.

Stern, Y. (2009). Cognitive reserve. *Neuropsychologia, 47,* 2015–2028.

Thal, L. J. (2006). Prevention of Alzheimer disease. *Alzheimer Disease & Associated Disorders, 20,* S97–S99.

Trojanowski, J. Q., Vandeerstichele, H., Korecka, M., Clark, C. M, Aisen, P. S, Petersen, R. C. . . . Shaw, L. M. (2010).Update on the biomarker core of the Alzheimer's Disease Neuroimaging Initiative subjects. *Alzheimer's and Dementia, 6,* 230–238.

Verghese, J, Lipton, R. B., Hall, C. B., Kuslansky, G., & Katz, M. J. (2003). Low blood pressure and the risk of dementia in very old individuals. *Neurology, 61,* 1667–1672.

Verghese, J., Lipton, R. B., Hall, C. B., Kuslansky G, Katz, M. J., & Buschke, H. (2002). Abnormality of gait as a predictor of non-Alzheimer's dementia. *New England Journal of Medicine, 347,* 1760–1767.

Verghese, J., Lipton, R. B., Katz, M. J., Hall, C. B., Derby CA, Kuslansky, G., . . . Buschke H (2003). Leisure activities and the risk of dementia in the elderly. *New England Journal of Medicine, 348,* 2508–2516.

Verghese, J., Wang, C, Katz, M. J., Sanders, A., & Lipton, R. B. (2009). Leisure activities and risk of vascular cognitive impairment in older adults. *Journal of Geriatric Psychiatry and Neurology, 22*(2), 110–118.

Weiner, M. F. (2008). Perspective on race and ethnicity in Alzheimer's disease research. *Alzheimer's and Dementia, 4,* 233–238.

Zimmerman, M. E., Pan, J. W., Hetherington, H. P., Katz, M. J., Verghese, J., Buschke, H., . . . Lipton, R. B. (2008). Hippocampal neurochemistry, neuromorphometry and verbal memory in nondemented older adults. *Neurology, 70,* 1594–1600.

16

Personality Disorders in Later Life

Daniel L. Segal, Richard Zweig, and Victor Molinari

Personality disorders (PDs) are an interesting and provocative form of psychopathology known to exert a deleterious impact across the adult lifespan. This chapter provides a discussion of measurement and diagnostic issues, epidemiology, assessment instruments, and theoretical controversies regarding PDs in later life. We begin with some definitions and a description of the relationship between PDs and personality.

PDs and Personality

Personality may simply be defined as one's typical and habitual way of responding to environmental circumstances. When one's responses are lifelong, extreme, inflexible, impede relationships, and are maladaptive across a variety of situations, we label an individual with a PD. Current diagnostic standards, represented by the *DSM-IV-TR*, formally define a PD as "an enduring pattern of inner experience and behavior that deviates markedly from an individual's culture" (American Psychiatric Association, 2000, p. 685) that is stable and of long duration, maladaptive (associated with significant distress or impaired functioning), inflexible and pervasive across a range of contexts, and not accounted for by any other physical or psychiatric disorder.

The *DSM-IV-TR* describes 10 prototypical and categorically defined individual PDs fitting into three broad categories: Cluster A is the odd or eccentric type, which includes paranoid, schizoid, and schizotypal PDs; Cluster B is the impulsive and erratic type, which includes antisocial, borderline, histrionic, and narcissistic PDs; and Cluster C is the anxious type, which includes avoidant, dependent, and obsessive-compulsive PDs. In fact, most individuals with PDs do not fit neatly into one of these categories. Indeed, one of the most common PD types is PD Not Otherwise Specified (Johnson et al., 2005), which includes characteristics of different individual PDs and often clusters of PDs.

The Wiley-Blackwell Handbook of Adulthood and Aging, First Edition. Edited by Susan Krauss Whitbourne and Martin J. Sliwinski. © 2012 Blackwell Publishing Ltd. Published 2012 by Blackwell Publishing Ltd.

Research on personality characteristics across the lifespan has a long history, and there are well-validated tests for a whole host of personality characteristics. Attempting to make sense of this literature, researchers have tried to pare down the list and identify core salient personality characteristics. Early on, Hans Eysenck used his Personality Inventory (Eysenck & Eysenck, 1964) to quantify personality across two broad dimensions: introversion–extraversion and neuroticism–psychoticism. Costa and McCrae (2002) built upon his scheme via factor analytic studies and identified five robust lexically based factors: neuroticism, extraversion, openness to experience, agreeableness, and conscientiousness. Using the NEO-PI to test the Five-Factor model (FFM) in longitudinal and cross-sectional research, a series of studies found that in general these five broad personality factors remain *relatively* constant (but not immutable) throughout life (Costa & McCrae, 2002), although some evidence points to perhaps more substantial FFM changes, especially in the facets (i.e., subscales) of the major dimensions (Roberts, Walton, & Viechtbauer, 2006b; Terracciano, McCrae, Brant, & Costa, 2005). Related evidence suggests that some people can show marked changes in personality features particularly due to variations in social support over the years (Roberts et al., 2006b; Vaillant, 2002) or to other specific life experiences (e.g., divorce, remarriage, trauma, loss, disability, career problems or success) that pertain to a person's stage of life (Roberts & Mroczek, 2008).

Unfortunately, there is little interface between the literature on personality and research on PD. The PD literature evolved from two sources. The first source was the case-oriented writings of Freud and colleagues who built an overarching clinical framework and a supporting diagnostic classification system based on psychoanalytic theories that attempt to modify underlying personality dynamics. The early versions of *DSM*, particularly *DSM-II* (American Psychiatric Association, 1968) were based on a psychoanalytic schema. The second source was empirical research. Starting with *DSM-III* (American Psychiatric Association, 1980), the evolving psychiatric classification system has relied more on studies relating to categorical diagnoses based on meeting evidence-based clinical criteria rather than measures of dimensional personality traits. A number of scales were subsequently developed that link formal *DSM* criteria to specific PD scores (several are described later in this chapter). It is expected that the mapping of the empirically based FFM both onto clinical theory and the *DSM-IV-TR* (American Psychiatric Association, 2000) and ultimately *DSM-5* categories will yield dividends in terms both of our evidential understanding of the link between personality and PDs, as well as pointing in the direction of clinical applications for all age groups.

Measurement Issues and Diagnostic Challenges

The accurate measurement and diagnosis of personality pathology have been ongoing struggles for investigators and clinicians since the dawn of the field, and these issues are magnified when the task turns to measuring PDs in older adults (Abrams & Bromberg, 2006; Agronin & Maletta, 2000; Balsis, Woods, Gleason, & Oltmanns, 2007; Segal, Coolidge, & Rosowsky, 2006; Zweig & Hillman, 1999). One source of the difficulty, as mentioned above, has been the separate evolution of the study of personality and PD, which has led to the development of different methods for investigating personality but has impeded the development of a comprehensive theoretical model (Widiger & Trull, 2007).

Those who have investigated normal personality have tended to favor dimensional trait models, such as the FFM, and have traditionally employed multifactor self-report inventories as a "gold standard." They have viewed personality pathology as traits that deviate from normative levels and are associated with impaired psychosocial functioning. In contrast, those who have investigated personality pathology directly have tended to favor a categorical (or prototypal) model of personality such as that depicted in the *DSM-IV-TR* and have traditionally employed structured interview techniques as a "gold standard." Over the course of the past three decades, the strengths and weaknesses of each approach have led to further refinements of methods and measures. Below we review some of the common challenges, faced by researchers and clinicians alike, in measuring and diagnosing personality pathology and in applying these tools in the older adult population.

Measurement issues

Reporting bias and avoidance of disclosure. Assessments of personality pathology in clinical populations are typically affected by reporting biases. Such reporting biases are not unexpected, as distorted perceptions regarding attributes of self and others are one of the hallmarks of PDs, and these may become even more pronounced in later life due to disordered individuals having a longer history of the disorder (Segal et al., 2006). For example, individuals with antisocial PD may minimize or not recognize their abrasive personality styles and may consequently underreport symptoms; in contrast, those with avoidant PD may overendorse symptoms. Although the effects of response bias are reduced by the inclusion of validity scales into modern self-report personality inventories (e.g., MMPI-2; MCMI-III), they are not entirely eliminated, and trait measures developed for use in nonclinical populations (e.g., NEO-PI) do not include such scales. For the researcher, such response biases represent sources of extraneous variance which may add to the difficulty of studying traits prevalent in clinical populations. For the clinician, such response biases may yield diagnostic confusion, blurring the differentiation between Axis I and Axis II symptomatology.

Rater bias. Since deficits in interpersonal functioning are another hallmark of PD, the objectivity of raters (particularly those with insufficient training) may be readily compromised by the strong feelings these individuals engender in others, leading to a negative bias effect. Less discussed, but relevant to the measurement of personality pathology in older adults, is the possibility that raters may exhibit overly positive biases due to concerns regarding stigmatizing older adults, hold mistaken beliefs that PD is rare, or use a lower reference point for normal personality functioning in older persons (Zweig, 2008). One might imagine that structured interview-based measures of PD would be less prone to such biases. Yet even these ratings, subject as they are to item-by-item judgments by raters as to the categorical presence or absence of a pathological symptom, are not immune to raters' context-dependent (e.g., situational) and context-independent (e.g., attitudinal) biases to some degree, and thus issues of diagnostic accuracy (for the clinician) and error variance (for the researcher) remain. Further, rater bias may unwittingly be introduced when the same interviewer collects data from both the patient and an informant, as this has been demonstrated to artificially inflate concordance of ratings of late life PD. The use of dimensional rather than categorical ratings as well as the use of a multimethod approach, which incorporates interview ratings, self-ratings, and informant/other ratings of personality pathology may reduce the magnitude and influence of rater bias (Molinari, Kunik, Mulsant, & Rifai, 1998).

Instrumentation.   Another source of barriers pertains to the properties of currently available assessment tools. For example, no broad self-report and interview-based measures were developed to detect personality pathology in older adults. Although some have been initially validated in research with older adults, the research base regarding the psychometric properties of many such tools in older populations is thin, and there are few guidelines regarding the practical application of existing measures to older adults (Balsis, Segal, & Donahue, 2009; Zweig, 2008). It is unclear, for example, how any interview-based assessment of PD in an older adult could satisfy the time course criterion that a maladaptive trait be present for a long duration, as reporting over decades-long intervals is undoubtedly subject to error (Abrams & Bromberg, 2006; Agronin & Maletta, 2000). Segal, Hersen, Van Hasselt, Silberman, and Roth (1996) have noted that it is unclear how raters assess functional impairment due to personality pathology among older adults. Certainly, normative developmental changes in social and occupational functioning may require raters to recalibrate such judgments for an older population. From a practical standpoint, as interview-based measures of PD tend to be lengthy, especially for those with a long history of the disorder, the motivational and energy levels of older participants may also affect findings.

DSM Theoretical model and PD Criteria.   All of the prominent interview-based measures and broad self-report measures of personality pathology (described later in this chapter) are based upon the *DSM* theoretical model of PD that is flawed in several respects, including arbitrary diagnostic thresholds with limited empirical support, high co-occurrence of PD typologies, and inadequate coverage of diverse presentations of PD (Coolidge & Segal, 1998; Widiger & Trull, 2007). The last point may have particular relevance for manifestations of PD in late life, as some have noted that "as changes that accompany old age begin to impinge, the individual's behavioral responses become less reliable measures of personality (i.e., internal) processes or disorder" (Sadavoy & Fogel, 1992, p. 434). Others have noted that clinicians treating older adults with PD tend to use vague, general descriptors (e.g., "PD Not Otherwise Specified") and have questioned whether PD criteria sets are sufficiently universal as to capture the behavioral variants of PD in late life, or may themselves be subject to age bias (Abrams & Bromberg, 2006; Agronin & Maletta 2000; Balsis et al., 2009; Segal et al., 1996).

In a large cross-sectional epidemiologic survey which compared younger and older adults with equivalent levels of self-reported PD pathology, an item analysis found evidence for age bias in 29% of PD criteria (Balsis, Gleason, Woods, & Oltmanns, 2007). Whether such findings are due to items that are overly broad or narrow, or the effects of age or cohort on the expression of PD, awaits further investigation. However, such findings suggest that current tools and some PD criteria may operate differently in younger and older populations. In a speculative approach to the possible manifestations of particular geriatric variants PDs, Segal et al. (2006) provided a theorized pattern for each of the PDs, although empirical validation of the patterns is sorely needed.

Diagnostic issues

Just as researchers face measurement issues that pose threats to validity, so do clinicians face diagnostic challenges that threaten accuracy. As mentioned above, the *DSM-IV-TR* conception of PD requires that personality pathology not be attributable to a psychiatric syndrome such as a mood disorder, a cultural role or a given context, or a physical illness or substance. Since older adults with PD often have concurrent psychiatric syndromes and medical problems, frequently report stressors which may include changes in their psychosocial environment, and represent a population which is becoming increasingly culturally and ethnically diverse, disentangling PD from these issues represents a formidable diagnostic challenge for clinicians.

Trait versus state measures.   Self-reports of personality are known to be state-dependent. Indeed, mood states markedly influence how one selects, recalls, and forms judgments about inner experiences and behaviors that inform self-appraisals of one's personality traits. It is for this reason that a diagnosis of PD cannot be based on experiences or behaviors which may be attributable to a mood state or psychiatric syndrome. In one study, for example, older adults' appraisals of pathological personality characteristics varied depending upon whether they were describing their "usual self" or themselves in the midst of a depressive episode (Thompson, Gallagher, & Czirr, 1988). Moreover, some mood symptoms (e.g., irritability, helplessness) may mimic features of personality pathology, particularly when these symptoms are long-standing or have resisted treatment efforts. Although many popular self-report measures designed for clinical populations include scales that control for current mood symptoms, the potentially confounding effect of mood state on self-reported traits or behaviors cannot be entirely eliminated. One might imagine that structured interview measures which are objectively rated by trained clinicians would be less prone to state effects, and some (e.g., International Personality Disorder Examination; Loranger, 1999) have demonstrated this in rigorous validation studies. In practice settings, clinicians are often advised to consider the effect of concurrent syndromes on reporting of personality pathology, to seek corroborating data regarding long-standing traits from informants, and to consider confirming a diagnosis of PD only after concurrent syndromes have been maximally treated (Segal et al., 2006; Zweig & Agronin, 2006).

Trait versus context-dependent behavior or role.   Some older adults experience difficulties in adapting to situational stressors (e.g., acute physical illness, interpersonal loss) or in coping with new life contexts or environments (e.g., hospital, retirement community) which may be associated with transient maladaptive inner experiences or behaviors that may mimic features of PD. Others from diverse cultures may exhibit role-related behaviors (e.g., in traditional Asian cultures: deference to authority, emotional restraint) that could be mistaken for personality pathology. Assessment methods and measures that are sensitive to cultural nuances, that examine whether maladaptive traits are long-standing and pervasive, and that corroborate findings with an informant, may help differentiate culturally normative behavior or an episode of poor adaptation (e.g., an adjustment disorder) from personality pathology. However, differentiating pathological traits from context-dependent behaviors may be more difficult when a stressor is chronic or a change in life contexts persists.

Person–environment interactions can mold personality processes to some degree, and growing evidence supports the notion that significant life events (e.g., divorce, retirement, disability) may be among the change mechanisms that affect the trajectory of personality across the lifespan (Hooker & McAdams, 2003). Such interactive effects are consistent with the clinical observation that for some older adults, the experience of a major life event coupled with a falling away of supportive "buffers" appears associated with a late-life exacerbation of PD features (Sadavoy & Fogel, 1992; Segal et al., 2006). Further, personality may moderate person–environment interactions, as research indicates that individuals with high neuroticism (which is associated with PD) tend to experience different stressors, evaluate them differently, and cope with them less well than others; in effect, such individuals may live their lives in a manner that increases the likelihood of negative life events (Lahey, 2009). In sum, although situational maladjustment must be differentiated from personality pathology, there is likely a bidirectional relationship between some personality processes and person–context interactions over long periods.

Trait versus medical condition.   Some medical conditions and neurological problems that are relatively prevalent in late life (such as Parkinson's disease, Alzheimer's disease, and other forms of dementia) are commonly associated with behavioral or personality changes. For example, recent evidence suggests that changes in personality such as increased egocentricity, emotional lability, rigidity, or apathy may represent early manifestations of dementia (Balsis, Carpenter, & Storandt, 2005). When personality changes are prominent or seem to magnify preexisting traits, and deficits in cognition or functioning are subtle, these symptoms may be mistaken for PD. Another common scenario is that individuals show evidence of both PD and concurrent neurological problems. In such cases it may be difficult to know to which disorder deviant behavior should be attributed. Although methods and measures for evaluating PD which require longitudinal evidence of maladaptive traits and behaviors may lend clarity to such complex diagnostic issues, clinicians (or researchers) may require the combined efforts of an interdisciplinary team (or sophisticated statistical models) to sort out symptoms that should be ascribed to PD traits rather than a medical condition.

Epidemiology

Reflecting some of these measurement problems, research on the prevalence of PD in older adults is fraught with methodological and conceptual limitations. Perhaps first and foremost, the overall term "PD" encompasses 10 specific types of extreme variants in personality traits. Although the overall prevalence of PD in older adults per se may have some important academic meaning, for practical purposes one would like to know which specific PDs increase, decrease, or remain the same with age. Unfortunately, a count of each individual PD would require prohibitively large sample sizes to make an adequate determination of true differences in prevalence rates between one PD and the other. As detailed below, these sampling problems are compounded by the fact that the sparse extant empirical literature includes community, medical, psychiatric inpatient, and psychiatric outpatient samples, all of which cover very different pools of older adults.

Adding to the problems is the fact that these studies use different criteria for defining older adults in terms of age (e.g., 55, 60, 65). They also vary in the assessment measures used to identify PD including clinical diagnoses extracted from charts, self-report, consensus case conference, and structured/unstructured PD instruments yoked to diverse PD diagnostic criteria. Therefore, it is no wonder that the total rates are imprecise. Indeed, concerns over insensitive *DSM* criteria and the need for a new geriatric nosology have been voiced for a long time (Rosowsky & Gurian, 1992; Segal et al., 1996), with recent data empirically confirming significant age bias in many PD diagnostic criteria (Balsis, Gleason, et al., 2007). Balsis et al. analyzed data from a public data set in which large groups of younger adults and older adults were interviewed about PD symptoms for seven specific PDs. Working within an item response theory framework, they found that whereas the latent variable structure for each PD was quite similar across younger and older age groups, many individual PD criteria were differentially endorsed by younger and older adults with equivalent PD pathology, thus indicating a measurement bias for these particular criteria.

The above notwithstanding, attempts have been made over the years to provide estimates of rates of overall and specific PDs in older adults. At first it was believed that the higher energy Cluster B PDs tended to attenuate with age, whereas the low energy Cluster C PDs increased as age-related stressors overwhelmed brittle anxiety-ridden defense structures (Sadavoy & Fogel, 1992; Tyrer & Seivewright, 2000). However, early empirical studies did not necessarily validate these formulations, finding wide variability in PD prevalence rates even within the same settings. PD rates varied from 6% to 63% in community-dwelling older adults (Ames & Molinari, 1994; Cohen et al., 1994; Coolidge, Burns, Nathan & Mull, 1992; Segal et al., 1998; Segal, Hook, & Coolidge, 2001); 12%–15% in nursing home settings (Margo, Robinson, & Corea, 1980; Teeter, Garetz, Miller, & Heiland, 1976); 7%–58% for geropsychiatric inpatients (Coolidge et al., 2000; Kenan et al., 2000; Kunik et al., 1994; Molinari, Ames, & Essa, 1994; Molinari, Kunik, Snow-Turek, Deleon, & Williams, 1999); 58% for geropsychiatric outpatients (Molinari & Marmion, 1993); and 24%–63% in depressed patients (Kunik et al., 1993; Molinari & Marmion, 1995). The only obvious clear conclusion is that PDs do not necessarily "burn out" with age.

In their seminal meta-analyses of PD prevalence rates, Abrams and Horowitz (1996, 1999), conducted reviews of the most sophisticated PD prevalence studies up until 1994 and then again until 1997. Both studies yielded similar gross fluctuations. Their first meta-analysis established an overall PD rate of 10% for those over the age of 50, with study findings varying from 6% to 33%. In their second meta-analysis, they detected an overall PD prevalence rate of 20%, with paranoid, self-defeating, and schizoid PDs the most common for older adults compared to paranoid and narcissistic PDs in younger adults.

They also discovered, somewhat surprisingly, that older adults living in the community or treated in psychiatric clinics showed higher levels of PD compared with psychiatric inpatients. This counterintuitive finding could be accounted for by the fact that PD diagnosis is de-emphasized in inpatient settings where the focus is on treating the more acute Axis I symptomatology.

Since the last meta-analysis, few PD prevalence studies have been conducted with older adults. In one community-based study, Segal et al. (2001) explored PD, coping strategies, and clinical symptoms in younger and older adults, finding that older adults scored higher on obsessive-compulsive and schizoid PD scales, but lower on the antisocial, borderline, histrionic, narcissistic, and paranoid scales. These results provide some validation for the aforementioned early clinical formulations, but obviously need to be replicated. Perhaps more importantly, this study suggests a direction that PD research should be taking: that is, less of a focus on exact prevalence rates, and more of an emphasis on the linkage over time among personality traits, coping mechanisms, and symptomatology. Such an approach may allow applied researchers to plot the varied trajectories of diverse PDs that occur during the life course and thereby perhaps help to chart therapeutic strategies based on a more in-depth understanding and integration of developmental theory, personality research, psychopathology, and PD dynamics.

Assessment Instruments

Two problems common to all of the broad PD assessment instruments are that they were developed for adult populations (and not older adults) and they are based on *DSM-IV* diagnostic criteria which, as described earlier, fail both to capture the unique presentation of some PDs in later life and to consider the unique context of later life. These facts are cause for some caution regarding use of these instruments for the assessment of PDs in later life, although at present no better alternatives exist. A typical use of the self-report inventories is to screen for the presence of PDs or PD features, whereas semistructured interviews are often used to diagnose formal PDs. Self-report inventories and structured interview methods designed to measure personality pathology tend to be only weakly correlated (Perry, 1992), leading some to suggest that each method may uniquely explain variance in personality pathology.

Objective multiscale self-report instruments

The Coolidge Axis II Inventory (CATI; Coolidge, 2000) assesses the 10 standard *DSM-IV* PDs, as well as passive-aggressive, depressive, sadistic, and self-defeating PDs, and several Axis I clinical disorders such as generalized anxiety disorder, posttraumatic stress disorder, social phobia, schizophrenia, and major depressive disorder. It also includes three scales that may be particularly relevant to older adults: (a) a Personality Change Due to a General Medical Condition scale; (b) a Neuropsychological Dysfunction scale, with 3 subscales (language and speech dysfunction, memory and concentration problems, neurosomatic complaints related to brain dysfunction), and (c) an Executive Functions of the Frontal Lobe scale with 3 subscales (poor planning, decision-making difficulty, task incompletion).

The Millon Clinical Multiaxial Inventory-III (MCMI-III; Millon, Davis, & Millon, 1997) includes 14 PD scales that are based on Millon's comprehensive theory of personality. It also includes 10 Axis I clinical syndromes scales. Age appears to minimally impact MCMI-III scale scores, with a slight tendency for scores to decrease with age for all scales except for the Histrionic, Narcissistic, and Compulsive PD scales on which scores tend to increase slightly (Haddy, Strack, & Choca, 2005).

The Personality Diagnostic Questionnaire-4+ (PDQ-4+; Hyler, 1994) assesses the 10 standard *DSM-IV* PDs as well as passive-aggressive and depressive PDs. Because scores are not normed or transformed in any way, but rather reflect a simple count of diagnostic criteria endorsed by the respondent, there is a significant concern about a high false-positive rate. As such, we do not advise using this measure with older adults, except perhaps to rule out PDs since it has a low false-negative rate.

The Schedule for Nonadaptive and Adaptive Personality (SNAP-2; Clark, Simms, Wu, & Casillas, in press) is not a direct measure of PDs per se. Rather, it evaluates trait dimensions relevant to the understanding of personality pathology. It includes 12 primary trait scales which are subsumed into 3 broad temperament dimensions. The Negative Temperament dimension includes 6 scales: mistrust, manipulativeness, aggression, self-harm, eccentric perceptions, and dependency. The Positive Temperament dimension includes 3 scales: exhibitionism, entitlement, and detachment; and the Disinhibition Temperament dimension includes 3 scales: impulsivity, propriety, and workaholism. Among adults, the SNAP-2 yields predictable and meaningful relations with dimensional ratings of PDs (Clark et al., in press) although validity studies with older adults are presently lacking.

The Wisconsin Personality Disorders Inventory (WISPI-IV; Smith, Klein, & Benjamin, 2003) measures the 10 standard *DSM-IV* PDs, as well as passive-aggressive PD, and includes a social desirability score. A unique feature is that is it based on an interpersonal theory and approach to the PDs. Scoring options include dimensional scores for each of the 11 PD scales as well as a categorical diagnosis. Whereas the WISPI-IV has solid psychometric properties among adult respondents (Smith et al., 2003), studies targeting older adults are needed.

Semistructured interviews

The most prominent semistructured interviews for PDs are the Diagnostic Interview for *DSM-IV* Personality Disorders (DIPD-IV; Zanarini, Frankenburg, Sickel, & Yong, 1996); the International Personality Disorder Examination (IPDE; Loranger, 1999); the Personality Disorder Interview-IV (PDI-IV; Widiger, Mangine, Corbitt, Ellis, & Thomas, 1995); the Structured Clinical Interview for *DSM-IV* Axis II Personality Disorders (SCID-II; First, Gibbon, Spitzer, Williams, & Benjamin, 1997); and the Structured Interview for *DSM-IV* Personality (SIDP-IV; Pfohl, Blum, & Zimmerman, 1997). These measures are similar in that they measure the 10 standard PDs in *DSM-IV-TR* and possess solid evidence for reliability and validity among diverse adult respondents. Most of these measures have been used in research studies with older adults, providing some preliminary support for their utility. Because these measures are comprehensive, and therefore lengthy to administer, their use with some older adults may be perceived as burdensome.

A specialized measure: the Gerontological Personality Disorders Scale

To aid in the screening of PD pathology in later life, Van Alphen, Engelen, Kuin, Hoijtink, and Derksen (2006) have developed the Gerontological Personality Disorders Scale (GPS) which is a brief self-report measure. The items on the GPS are all based on the *DSM-IV-TR* General Diagnostic Criteria for PDs, and as a consequence the measure does not assess specific PDs. The GPS includes 2 subscales (habitual behavior and biographical information). In the validation study, the sensitivity and specificity of the GPS as compared to a clinical diagnosis were both 69%, which suggests the measure has moderate diagnostic accuracy. Although this research measure is promising, it does not fill the important need for a broad screening measure. Clearly, an elder-specific measure of individual PDs that takes into account the unique manifestations of PD pathology in the context of later life is needed. This effort will be hampered to the extent that future editions of the *DSM* fail to address the later life context (Balsis et al., 2009).

Theoretical Issues

What is the trajectory of PD over the lifespan? What mechanisms might explain constancy or change in PD over time? Although there are limited data to answer these questions, theoretical models and indirect evidence drawn from aging-related research in personality and developmental psychology may hold clues. Some basic premises of personality and lifespan developmental psychology are helpful in organizing theories and data from disparate fields. First, there is increasing evidence that lifespan development is characterized by dialectical processes of both constancy and change, which act to foster overall adaptation (Baltes, 1997). Second, this dialectic may be an inherent feature of personality, as structural aspects of personality (e.g., traits, motivations) tend to be more stable, whereas process aspects (e.g., characteristic mood states, self-regulation) tend to fluctuate over the life course (Hooker & McAdams, 2003). Third, current *DSM-IV-TR* models of PD emphasize not only the structural aspects (i.e., culturally nonnormative traits) but also the process elements (e.g., coping behaviors, perceived self-efficacy) of these disorders that manifest across domains of cognitive, affective, and interpersonal functioning as well as impulse control in ways that are both maladaptive and inflexible (i.e., show adaptive failure in the face of person–environment interactions). In keeping with premises of developmental psychology, recent integrative models of PD (Livesley, 2003) tend to view PDs as comprised of both stable and mercurial elements, as characterized by an enduring failure to adapt to the environment, and as indicative of a derailment of normative development.

Extant data support two leading theories regarding constancy and change in personality which are relevant to understanding the trajectory of personality disorder across the lifespan. One approach, represented by proponents of the trait model of personality development (e.g., Costa & McCrae, 1994) hold that basic personality traits described by the FFM (including those associated with PDs) are universal, have a prominent genetic basis, are relatively impervious to environmental influences, and display remarkable constancy over the lifespan. According to this model, when changes in traits occur over the course of life they tend to be selective, relatively modest in scope, and are likely driven by intrinsic (biological or genetic) maturational processes.

Extending this model to personality disorder, Tyrer and Seivewright (2000) proposed that maturational processes may differentially affect selected PD types over the lifespan; "immature" types (i.e., borderline, narcissistic, and histrionic PD) were hypothesized to diminish in intensity with age, whereas mature types (i.e., obsessive-compulsive, schizoid, schizotypal, and paranoid PD) were hypothesized to remain stable. In general, trait models would predict relative stability of PD throughout the life course, although allowing for predictable, minor mean-level changes due to maturation.

Some, but not all, studies of structural aspects of personality tend to provide indirect support for the maturational model as a means to explain the lifespan trajectory of PD. In longitudinal studies, FFM personality traits show substantial rank-order stability over extended periods (Costa & McCrae, 1988, 1994). Substantive mean-level changes tend to occur in the first third of the lifespan and are selective (e.g., decreases in neuroticism, increases in conscientiousness), suggesting a preprogrammed maturational process as a driving force. By extension, one might expect structural aspects of PD to be relatively invariant over time, except perhaps in young adulthood. However, recent longitudinal studies which followed participants from late adolescence through young adulthood found a reduction in manifestations of PD, and much less stability in PD-related traits than predicted (Clark, 2005). Similarly, cross-sectional studies of the epidemiology of antisocial PD find that rates decline dramatically with age, and decline most in early adulthood (Robins & Regier, 1991). Thus, although research findings regarding FFM traits and PDs converge as to evidence of a positive maturation effect early in the life course, they differ regarding the magnitude and selectivity of this effect. These effects may be accounted for by the disappearance from the population of individuals with antisocial PD due to incarceration or premature demise.

Studies of process aspects of personality, such as cross-sectional studies that compare emotion regulation in younger and older samples, also provide indirect support for the maturational model and suggest possible maturational change mechanisms. For example, when faced with emotion-laden dilemmas older adults show greater cognitive complexity, self-regulation of affect, and more flexible reasoning than younger adults (Isaacowitz, Charles, & Carstensen, 2000; Labouvie-Vief, DeVoe, & Bulka, 1989). Other cross-sectional studies find that compared with younger adults, older adults "show greater affective control, greater avoidance of stressors, engage in less negative start-up with partners, and de-emphasize the negative in interpersonal relations" (Magai & Passman, 1997, pp. 128–129). Since inflexible reasoning, affective dyscontrol, and interpersonal difficulties are hallmarks of PD, one might imagine that normative developmental processes that ameliorate these problems would benefit those with PD. Were such findings replicated in longitudinal studies of mixed-age individuals with and without PD, they might suggest that maturation is akin to a "rising tide that raises all boats," dampening affective dysregulation and improving coping in individuals with PD as they age. However, as current findings derive from cross-sectional studies, cohort or survivor effects could also explain age differences.

Lifespan developmental theory, and in particular developmental systems theory, provides an alternate approach to understanding constancy and change in personality and personality disorder. While acknowledging the role of genetically based temperaments, this approach highlights person–context interactions as the driving forces that shape aspects of personality (Hooker & McAdams, 2003). From this perspective, "personality development occurs largely as a consequence of the expectations and experiences that come with age-graded roles" (Roberts, Walton, & Viechtbauer, 2006a, p. 19), such as being a child, friend, student, worker, marital partner, parent, retired person, or grandparent. Since individuals differ in their temperaments, environmental contexts and roles, and active efforts to modify their own behaviors, variability in trajectories of personality development are to be expected (Mroczek, Spiro, & Griffin, 2006). In older adults with PD, through a process known as "heterotypic continuity," such variability may find expression in changes in the behaviors that typify PDs in late life, while underlying core psychological dispositions remain constant (Mroczek, Hurt, & Berman, 1999). These important changes in the behavioral expressions of many PD features in later life highlight the need for revisions of the diagnostic criteria to more fully consider the late life context (Balsis et al., 2009).

Might person–context interactions result in structural changes in personality across the lifespan? Support for this view derives from a meta-analysis of 92 longitudinal studies (Roberts et al., 2006a) which examined patterns of mean-level changes in FFM personality traits across the lifespan. Changes of significant magnitude were not only noted in early adulthood (increases in social dominance, emotional stability and conscientiousness), but continued into midlife and old age (increases in agreeableness and conscientiousness, decreases in social vitality and openness). Moreover, the authors noted that the patterns of change, which were often nonlinear and were linked to cohort, suggested that age-graded social role experiences, rather than chronological age, were the mechanisms of change. Although this meta-analysis was designed to determine normative trends in personality development rather than the path followed by those with PD, the authors note that

> there remains a sizable minority that does not follow the normative trend and demonstrates, for example, a decrease in conscientiousness. Moreover, these non-normative patterns of change can be predicted from life experiences, such as having an unstable marriage or participating in unconventional activities ... (Roberts et al., 2006a, p. 20)

Whether this sizable minority typifies individuals with the defining features of PD remains an area for future research.

Longitudinal studies of PD, which typically follow individuals into early adulthood or midlife, suggest that different domains of personality functioning may undergo varied rates of change, possibly accounting for changes in the behaviors that typify PD in middle and older adults. For example, a longitudinal study of psychiatric inpatients who were followed up after an average of 15 years discovered that those who had been diagnosed with borderline PD (at one time considered to be one of the most intransigent of PDs) improved more than those with unipolar depression or schizophrenia on measures of instrumental and global functioning, but still evidenced problematic interpersonal functioning (McGlashan, 1986). A similar 16–45-year follow-up of male inpatients diagnosed with antisocial PD found that most had improved significantly, but continued to experience problematic occupational or interpersonal functioning (Black, Baumgard, & Bell, 1995). Adding to these unexpected findings, a 10-year follow-up of inpatients with borderline PD found that 88% achieved "remission" (often within two years), particularly in symptoms of impulsivity, but that problems in interpersonal functioning remained (Zanarini et al., 2006; Zanarini et al., 2007). Although the implications for studies of late life PD are not entirely clear, such findings suggest that PD may exhibit substantially more plasticity than originally believed, and that patterns of change may be nonlinear or uneven across structural and process dimensions.

Selection, Optimization, and Compensation (SOC) Theory and PDs

As noted earlier in this chapter, the field of PD research needs to be better integrated with basic psychological and gerontological research exploring normal human development. As detailed by Hyer and Intrieri (2006), Baltes' Selection-Optimization-Compensation (SOC; Baltes & Baltes, 1990) model is of strong heuristic value in understanding the aging challenges of older adults, particularly those who are frail and in need of support (Molinari, Kier, & Rosowsky, 2006). In brief, SOC posits that over time older adults tend to be more selective in the activities that they engage in (particularly those involving personal relationships), optimizing their strengths (e.g., perhaps focusing on intellectual or creative activities over athletic ones) and in the process compensating for their weaknesses (e.g., if they have had a stroke rendering them unable to drive but leaving higher cognition relatively intact, leaning how to use the public transportation system to attend art openings).

The SOC model is useful in understanding how an individual with PD may react to age-related changes. For example, it is axiomatic that older adults who are more flexible in terms of their adjustment to life's challenges will most probably fare better psychologically because they have a greater repertoire of adequate coping responses to choose from when faced with barriers to achieving their needs. Unfortunately, by definition, those with PDs engage in repetitive behaviors reflective of a rigid, constricted way of perceiving the world and of managing stressors. A loss of even one skill may be especially difficult for a "one-key typewriter" approach to managing life's affairs, particularly when individuals are unable to be selective in their personal lives because of few stable relationships and limited compensatory strategies from which to draw. When faced with an age-related normative event such as impaired functional abilities due to medical problems or general frailty, those with PD therefore may be unable to make an easy adjustment. Indeed, their maladaptive behaviors and coping strategies may escalate as a defense against the self-deflating blow of such a medical event happening to them. This may be especially true if due to such limitations they must rely on others for help. Because one of the hallmarks of individuals with PD is that their behavior often grates on others, such forced interaction with paid formal caregivers in a hospital or residential placement, or intensified interaction with informal family caregivers in a community setting, sets the stage for chronic interpersonal distress.

For example, individuals with a narcissistic PD may expect that their every need should be attended to by family caregivers whom the narcissistic person with PD self-centeredly believes owes them a great debt, or attended to by paid caregivers whom they claim are overpaid because they do not immediately fulfill their every whim. When the caregiver inevitably fails to meet the incessant demands, the family member may withdraw his or her tenuous support, or the paid caregiver may quit or provide even more perfunctory care leading to an ever-spiraling cycle of recrimination and counterrecrimination. Even those individuals with the more prosocial PDs, such as those with dependent PD, may have a difficult time because their genuine need for others becomes so exaggerated that they tax even the most robust support system.

The SOC model not only provides a framework for understanding this unfortunate behavior but yields hints about how to manage it. For example, given their inordinate need to be showered with attention, individuals with narcissistic PD will have a limited repertoire of more psychologically healthy activities from which to choose if their narrow special talents are no longer viewed with admiration by others. It may mean that health professionals in their immediate environment need to devise a plan to provide the attention they crave. If an older man considered himself to be a master mechanic, then perhaps it could be arranged that he give a lecture to schoolchildren or at a local YMCA so that once again he could be the center of attention.

For the person with a dependent PD residing in a long-term care setting, a recommendation derived from the SOC model might be to encourage the person to select a few controlling, dominant residents with whom to associate, join a peer support group, and assign one caregiver to provide counsel at specific intervals. This might optimize the strengths of a person who likes to be socially engaged, while also compensating for anxiety over lack of independent decision-making skills by eliciting support from others in the immediate environment. The SOC model appears to be underutilized in the understanding of and planning for deviant behaviors of old age, particularly for those who have had long-standing chronic interpersonal issues which are exacerbated by the aging process and brought to the attention of the geriatric mental health professional. There appears to be a need for the continued development of gerontological models of intervention to guide treatment strategies and to bridge the gap between lifespan research and clinical practice.

Conclusions and Future Directions

In this chapter, we attempted to summarize, synthesize, and perhaps nudge forward the major conceptual and methodological challenges in the area of later life PDs. PD in older adults is certainly a difficult area of practice and research. With the anticipated publication of *DSM-5* (slated for May, 2013 at the time of this writing; see www. dsm5.org), significant changes to the PD diagnostic category are likely, especially a move toward some combination of dimensional and categorical ratings. Whereas some move toward dimensional ratings will likely improve the general validity of the PD diagnoses (since the underlying constructs of PDs are believed to be dimensional in nature), failure of the *DSM* to fully take into account the context of later life and the possible geriatric variants of PDs will remain problematic whether diagnosis reflects a dimensional or categorical model (Balsis et al., 2009).

In addition to the problem of the lack of diagnostic validity for PD among older adults, other important issues remain. For example, the true impact of aging on personality pathology is still poorly understood. Although development of a unifying theory of PDs across the adult lifespan is a lofty goal (e.g., Tackett, Balsis, Oltmanns, & Krueger, 2009), empirical validation of any such theory is far from a reality. The relationships between PDs and Axis I clinical disorders among older adults is yet another important area with a limited research base, possibly with the exception of the PD and depression literature. To what extent do PDs cause, exacerbate, or limit effectiveness of treatment for anxiety disorders, psychotic disorders, substance abuse disorders, eating disorders, somatoform disorders, and sexual disorders among older adults? Whether the looming changes to the PD category in the *DSM-5* turn out to be a conceptual leap forward or a move backwards will not be decided for many years, but one certainty is that research on PDs across the adult lifespan will continue to be an important but challenging field of inquiry.

References

Abrams, R. C., & Bromberg, C. E. (2006). Personality disorders in the elderly: A flagging field of inquiry. *International Journal of Geriatric Psychiatry, 21,* 1013–1017.

Abrams, R. C., & Horowitz, S. V. (1996). Personality disorders after age 50: A meta analysis. *Journal of Personality Disorders, 10,* 271–281.

Abrams, R. C., & Horowitz, S. V. (1999). Personality disorders after age 50: A meta-analytic review of the literature. In E. Rosowsky, R. C. Abrams, & R. A. Zweig (Eds.), *Personality disorders in older adults: Emerging issues in diagnosis and treatment* (pp. 55–68). Mahwah, NJ: Erlbaum.

Agronin, M., & Maletta, G. (2000). Personality disorders in late life: Understanding and overcoming the gap in research. *American Journal of Geriatric Psychiatry, 8,* 4–18.

American Psychiatric Association, (1968). *Diagnostic and statistical manual of mental disorders* (2nd ed.). Washington, DC: Author.

American Psychiatric Association, (1980). *Diagnostic and statistical manual of mental disorders* (3rd ed.). Washington, DC: Author.

American Psychiatric Association, (2000). *Diagnostic and statistical manual of mental disorders* (4th edition, text revision.). Washington, DC: Author.

Ames, A., & Molinari, V. (1994). Prevalence of personality disorders in community-living elderly. *Journal of Geriatric Psychiatry and Neurology, 7,* 189–194.

Balsis, S., Carpenter, B., & Storandt, M. (2005). Personality change precedes clinical diagnosis of dementia of the Alzheimer type. *Journals of Gerontology: Psychological Sciences, 60B,* P98–P101.

Balsis, S., Gleason, M. E. J., Woods, C. M., & Oltmanns, T. F. (2007). An item response theory analysis of DSM-IV personality disorder criteria across younger and older age groups. *Psychology and Aging, 22,* 171–185.

Balsis, S., Segal, D. L., & Donahue, C. (2009). Revising the personality disorder diagnostic criteria for the *Diagnostic and Statistical Manual of Mental Disorders-Fifth Edition* (*DSM-V*): Consider the later life context. *American Journal of Orthopsychiatry, 79,* 452–460.

Balsis, S., Woods, C. M., Gleason, M. E. J., & Oltmanns, T. F. (2007). Overdiagnosis and underdiagnosis of personality disorders in older adults. *American Journal of Geriatric Psychiatry*, *15*, 742–753.

Baltes, P. B. (1997). On the incomplete architecture of human ontogeny: Selection, optimization, and compensation as foundation for developmental theory. *American Psychologist*, *52*, 366–380.

Baltes, P. B., & Baltes, M. M. (1990). Psychological perspectives on successful aging: The model of selective optimization with compensation. In P. B. Baltes & M. M. Baltes (Eds.), *Successful aging: Perspectives from the behavioral sciences* (pp. 1–34). Cambridge, UK: Cambridge University Press.

Black, D. W., Baumgard, C. H., & Bell, S. E. (1995). A 16- to 45-year follow-up of 71 men with antisocial personality disorder. *Comprehensive Psychiatry*, *36*, 130–140.

Clark, L. A. (2005). Stability and change in personality pathology: Revelations of three longitudinal studies. *Journal of Personality Disorders*, *19*, 524–532.

Clark, L. A., Simms, L. J., Wu, K. D., & Casillas, A.(in press). *Schedule for Nonadaptive and Adaptive Personality (SNAP-2). Manual for administration, scoring, and interpretation.* Minneapolis: University of Minnesota Press.

Cohen, B. J., Nestadt, G., Samuels, J. F., Romanoski, A. J., McHugh, P. R., & Rabins, P. V. (1994). Personality disorder in later life: A community study. *British Journal of Psychiatry*, *165*, 493–499.

Coolidge, F. L. (2000). *Coolidge Axis II Inventory: Manual.* Colorado Springs, CO: Author.

Coolidge, F. L., Burns, E. M., Nathan, J. H., & Mull C. E. (1992). Personality disorders in the elderly. *Clinical Gerontologist*, *12*, 41–55.

Coolidge, F. L. & Segal, D. L. (1998). Evolution of the personality disorder diagnosis in the *Diagnostic and statistical manual of mental disorders. Clinical Psychology Review*, *18*, 585–599.

Coolidge, F. L., Segal, D. L., Pointer, J. C., Knaus, E. A., Yamazaki, T. G., & Silberman, C. S. (2000). Personality disorders in older adult inpatients with chronic mental illness. *Journal of Clinical Geropsychology*, *6*, 63–72.

Costa, P. T., & McCrae, R. R. (1988). Personality in adulthood: A six-year longitudinal study of self-reports and spouse ratings on the NEO Personality Inventory. *Journal of Personality and Social Psychology*, *54*, 853–863.

Costa P. T., & McCrae, R. R. (1994). Set like plaster? Evidence for the stability of adult personality. In T. F. Heatherton & J. L. Weinberger (Eds.), *Can personality change?* (pp. 21–40). Washington, DC: American Psychological Association.

Costa, P. T., Jr., & McCrae, R. R. (2002). Looking backward: Changes in the mean levels of personality traits from 80 to 12. In D. Cervone & W. Mischel (Eds.), *Advances in personality science* (pp. 219–237). New York: Guilford Press.

Eysenck, H. J., & Eysenck S. B. G. (1964). *Manual of the Eysenck Personality Inventory.* London: University of London Press.

First, M. B., Gibbon, M., Spitzer, R. L., Williams, J. B. W., & Benjamin, L. S. (1997). *Structured Clinical Interview for DSM-IV Axis II Personality Disorders (SCID-II).* Washington, DC: American Psychiatric Press.

Haddy, C., Strack, S., & Choca, J. P. (2005). Linking personality disorders and clinical syndromes on the MCMI-III. *Journal of Personality Assessment*, *84*, 193–204.

Hooker, K., & McAdams, D. P. (2003) Personality reconsidered: A new agenda for aging research. *Journal of Gerontology: Psychological Sciences*, *58B*, 296–304.

Hyer, L., & Intrieri, R. C. (2006). Introduction. In L. Hyer& R. C. Intrieri (Eds.), *Geropsychological interventions in long-term care* (pp. xix–xxv). New York: Springer.

Hyler, S. E. (1994). *Personality Diagnostic Questionnaire, 4th edition*, PDQ-4 + . New York: New York State Psychiatric Institute.

Isaacowitz, D. M., Charles, S. T., & Carstensen, L. L. (2000). Emotion and cognition. In F. Craik & T. A. Salthouse (Eds.), *Handbook of aging and cognition* (2nd ed., pp. 593–631). Mahwah, NJ: Erlbaum.

Johnson, J. G., First, M. B., Cohen, P., Skodol, A. E., Kasen, S., & Brook, J. S. (2005). Adverse outcomes associated with personality disorder not otherwise specified in a community sample. *American Journal of Psychiatry, 162,* 1926–1932.

Kenan, M. M., Kendjelic, E. M., Molinari, V. A., Williams, W., Norris, M., & Kunik, M. E. (2000). Age-related differences in the frequency of personality disorders among inpatient veterans. *International Journal of Geriatric Psychiatry, 15,* 831–837.

Kunik, M. E., Mulsant, B. H., Rifai, A. H., Sweet, R. A., Pasternak, R., Rosen, J., & Zubenko, G. S. (1993). Personality disorders in elderly inpatients with major depression. *American Journal of Geriatric Psychiatry, 1,* 38–45.

Kunik, M. E., Mulsant, B. H., Rifai, A. H., Sweet, R. A., Pasternak, R. & Zubenko, G. S. (1994). Diagnostic rate of comorbid personality disorder in elderly psychiatric inpatients. *American Journal of Psychiatry, 151,* 603–605.

Labouvie-Vief, G., DeVoe, M., & Bulka, D. (1989). Speaking about feelings: Conceptions of emotion across the life span. *Psychology and Aging, 4,* 425–437.

Lahey, B. B. (2009). Public health significance of neuroticism. *American Psychologist, 64,* 241–256.

Livesley, W. J. (2003). *Practical management of personality disorder.* New York: Guilford Press.

Loranger, A. W. (1999). *International Personality Disorder Examination. DSM-IV and ICD-10 Interviews.* Odessa, FL: Psychological Assessment Resources.

Magai, C., & Passman, V. (1997). The interpersonal basis of emotional behavior and emotion regulation in adulthood. *Annual Review of Geriatrics and Gerontology, 17,* 104–137.

Margo, J. L., Robinson, J. R., & Corea, S. (1980). Referrals to a psychiatric service from old people's homes. *British Journal of Psychiatry, 136,* 396–401.

McGlashan, T. H. (1986). The Chestnut Lodge follow-up study III: Long-term outcome of borderline personalities. *Archives of General Psychiatry, 43,* 20–30.

Millon, T., Davis, R., & Millon, C. (1997). *MCMI-III manual* (2nd ed.). Minneapolis, MN: National Computer Systems.

Molinari, V., Ames, A., & Essa, M. (1994). Prevalence of personality disorders in two geropsychiatric inpatient units. *Journal of Geriatric Psychiatry and Neurology, 7,* 209–215.

Molinari, V., Kier, F. J., & Rosowsky, E. (2006). SOC, personality, and long term care. In L. Hyer & R. C. Intrieri (Eds.), *Geropsychological interventions in long-term care* (pp. 139–155). New York: Springer.

Molinari, V, Kunik, M. E., Mulsant, B., & Rifai, A. H. (1998). The relationship between patient, informant, social worker, and consensus diagnoses of personality disorder in elderly depressed inpatients. *American Journal of Geriatric Psychiatry, 6,* 136–144.

Molinari, V., Kunik, M. E., Snow-Turek, A. L., Deleon, H., & Williams, W. (1999). Age-related personality differences in inpatients with personality disorder: A cross-sectional study. *Journal of Clinical Geropsychology, 5,* 191–202.

Molinari, V., & Marmion, J. (1993). Personality disorders in geropsychiatric outpatients. *Psychological Reports, 73,* 256–258.

Molinari, V., & Marmion, J. (1995). Relationship between affective disorders and Axis II diagnoses in geropsychiatric patients. *Journal of Geriatric Psychiatry and Neurology, 8,* 61–64.

Mroczek, D. K., Hurt, S. W., & Berman, W. H. (1999). Conceptual and methodological issues in the assessment of personality disorders in older adults. In E. Rosowsky, R. C. Abrams, & R. A. Zweig (Eds.), *Personality disorders in older adults: Emerging issues in diagnosis and treatment* (pp. 135–150). Mahwah, NJ: Erlbaum.

Mroczek, D. K., Spiro, A., & Griffin, P. W. (2006). Personality and aging. In J. E. Birren, & K. W. Schaie (Eds.), *Handbook of the psychology of aging* (6th ed., pp. 363–377). San Diego, CA: Academic Press.

Perry, J. C. (1992). Problems and considerations in the valid assessment of personality disorders. *American Journal of Psychiatry, 149*, 1645–1653.

Pfohl, B., Blum, N., & Zimmerman, M. (1997). *Structured Interview for DSM-IV Personality (SIDP-IV)*. Arlington, VA: American Psychiatric Publishing.

Roberts, B. W., & Mroczek, D. (2008). Personality trait change in adulthood. *Current Directions in Psychological Science, 17*, 31–35.

Roberts, B. W., Walton, K. E., & Viechtbauer, W. (2006a). Patterns in mean-level change in personality traits across the life course: A meta-analysis of longitudinal studies. *Psychological Bulletin, 132*, 1–25.

Roberts, B. W., Walton, K. E., & Viechtbauer, W. (2006b). Personality traits change in adulthood: Reply to Costa and McCrae (2006). *Psychological Bulletin, 132*, 29–32.

Robins, L., & Regier, D. (1991). *Psychiatric disorders in America: The epidemiologic catchment area study*. New York: Free Press.

Rosowsky, E., & Gurian, B. (1992). Impact of borderline personality disorder in late life on systems of care. *Hospital and Community Psychiatry, 43*, 386–389.

Sadavoy, J., & Fogel, B. (1992). Personality disorders in old age. In J. E. Birren, R. B. Sloane, & G. D. Cohen (Eds.), *Handbook of mental health and aging* (2nd ed., pp. 433–462). San Diego, CA: Academic Press.

Segal, D. L., Coolidge, F. L., & Rosowsky, E. (2006). *Personality disorders and older adults: Diagnosis, assessment, and treatment*. Hoboken, NJ: Wiley.

Segal, D. L., Hersen, M., Kabacoff, R. I., Falk, S. B., Van Hasselt, V. B., & Dorfman, K. (1998). Personality disorders and depression in community-dwelling older adults. *Journal of Mental Health and Aging, 4*, 171–182.

Segal, D. L., Hersen, M., Van Hasselt, V. B., Silberman, C. S., & Roth, L. (1996). Diagnosis and assessment of personality disorders in older adults: A critical review. *Journal of Personality Disorders, 10*, 384–399.

Segal, D. L., Hook, J. N., & Coolidge, F. L. (2001). Personality dysfunction, coping styles, and clinical symptoms in younger and older adults. *Journal of Clinical Geropsychology, 7*, 201–212.

Smith, T. L., Klein, M. H., & Benjamin, L. S. (2003). Validation of the Wisconsin Personality Disorders Inventory IV with the SCID II. *Journal of Personality Disorders, 17*, 173–187.

Tackett, J. L., Balsis, S., Oltmanns, T. F., & Krueger, R. F. (2009). A unifying perspective on personality pathology across the lifespan: Developmental considerations for the fifth edition of the *Diagnostic and Statistical Manual of Mental Disorders. Development and Psychopathology, 21*, 687–713.

Teeter, R. B., Garetz, F. K., Miller, W. R., & Heiland, W. F. (1976). Psychiatric disturbances of aged patients in skilled nursing homes. *American Journal of Psychiatry, 133*, 1430–1434.

Terracciano, A., McCrae, R. R., Brant, L. J., & Costa, P. T. J. (2005). Hierarchical linear modeling analyses of the NEO-PI-R Scales in the Baltimore Longitudinal Study of Aging. *Psychology and Aging, 20*, 493–506.

Thompson, L. W., Gallagher, D., & Czirr, R. (1988). Personality disorder and outcome in the treatment of late-life depression. *Journal of Geriatric Psychiatry, 21*, 133–146.

Tyrer, P., & Seivewright, H. (2000). Studies of outcome. In P. Tyrer (Ed.), *Personality disorders: Diagnosis, management, and course* (2nd ed., pp. 119–136). Oxford: Butterworth Heinemann.

Vaillant, G. E. (2002). *Aging well*. Boston: Little, Brown.

Van Alphen, S. P. J., Engelen, G. J. J. A., Kuin, Y., Hoijtink, H. J. A., & Derksen, J. J. L. (2006). A preliminary study of the diagnostic accuracy of the Gerontological Personality disorders Scale (GPS). *International Journal of Geriatric Psychiatry, 21*, 862–868.

Widiger, T. A., Mangine, S., Corbitt, E. M., Ellis, C. G., & Thomas, G. V. (1995). *Personality Disorder Interview-IV. A semistructured interview for the assessment of personality disorders. Professional manual.* Odessa, FL: Psychological Assessment Resources.

Widiger, T. A., & Trull, T. J. (2007). Plate tectonics in the classification of personality disorder: Shifting to a dimensional model. *American Psychologist, 62*, 71–83.

Zanarini, M. C., Frankenburg, F. R., Hennen, J., Reich, D. B., & Silk, K. R. (2006). Prediction of the 10-year course of borderline personality disorder. *American Journal of Psychiatry, 163*, 827–832.

Zanarini, M. C., Frankenburg, F. R., Reich, D. B., Silk, K. R., Hudson, J. I., & McSweeney, L. B. (2007). The subsyndromal phenomenology of borderline personality disorder: A 10-year follow-up study. *American Journal of Psychiatry, 164*, 929–935.

Zanarini, M. C., Frankenburg, F. R., Sickel, A. E., & Yong, L. (1996). *The Diagnostic Interview for DSM-IV Personality Disorders (DIPD-IV).* Belmont, MA: McLean Hospital.

Zweig, R. A. (2008). Personality disorder in older adults: Assessment challenges and strategies. *Professional Psychology: Research and Practice, 39*, 298–305.

Zweig, R. A., & Agronin, M. E. (2006). Personality disorders in late life. In M. E. Agronin & G. J. Maletta (Eds.), *Principles and practice of geriatric psychiatry* (pp. 449–469). Philadelphia: Lippincott, Williams, & Wilkins.

Zweig, R. A., & Hillman J. (1999). Personality disorders in adults: A review. In E. Rosowsky, R. C. Abrams, & R. A. Zweig, (Eds.), *Personality disorders in older adults: Emerging issues in diagnosis and treatment* (pp. 31–53). Mahwah, NJ: Erlbaum.

17

Assessment of Older Adults

Christine E. Gould, Barry A. Edelstein, and Lindsay A. Gerolimatos

The assessment of older adults can be a challenging task. Older adults present with psychological symptoms that can arise from multiple contributing factors (e.g., medical disorders, medications, personal losses), which complicate the task of assessment. In the following sections, we first discuss the goals of assessment of older adults. The assessment of multiple dimensions of functioning is then reviewed. This is followed by consideration of multiple methods of assessment, which collectively enable the clinician to avoid the shortcomings of any single method. To draw upon all the information in this chapter, a sample assessment case is presented, in which the assessment process is described in detail.

Goals of Assessment

The potential goals of assessment are considerable in number and variety, although most can be incorporated into the following categories: (a) screening for psychiatric disorders or cognitive impairment, (b) determination of psychiatric diagnosis (e.g., Generalized Anxiety Disorder), (c) determination of decision-making capacity (e.g., capacity to consent to medical treatment), (d) prediction of adjustment to particular environments (e.g., assisted living facility), (e) determination of functional living skill strengths and deficits, (f) identification and measurement of problem behaviors, and (g) monitoring of behaviors or disorders over time (e.g., following treatment). For the purpose of brevity, we will discuss the two most common of these goals, screening and diagnosis.

The Wiley-Blackwell Handbook of Adulthood and Aging, First Edition. Edited by Susan Krauss Whitbourne and Martin J. Sliwinski. © 2012 Blackwell Publishing Ltd. Published 2012 by Blackwell Publishing Ltd.

Screening

Screening involves the administration of an assessment instrument that is sensitive to symptoms or behaviors associated with various psychiatric disorders or cognitive deficits. Such instruments are typically administered easily and quickly, and often involve a trade-off between the breadth of coverage (i.e., bandwidth; Cronbach, 1960) and depth of coverage (i.e., fidelity; Cronbach, 1960). For example, the popular Mini Mental State Examination (MMSE; Folstein, Folstein, & McHugh, 1975) that is used to screen for cognitive impairment has 30 items and requires only about 10 minutes to administer. Several domains of cognitive functioning (e.g., short-term memory) are covered by the instrument, although each domain is assessed with very few items. Although the MMSE is not a thorough measure of memory, it may be used as a screening instrument for identifying individuals who may have recent or short-term memory problems. The assumption behind such screening is that if the total score on the instrument is below a previously established cut-off score, further in-depth assessment may be needed. Thus one might then administer an assessment instrument designed specifically to measure memory (e.g., Hopkins Verbal Learning Test–Revised; Benedict, Schretlen, Groninger, & Brandt, 1998). Similarly, if one earns a score that exceeds the clinical cut-off score for the Geriatric Depression Scale (Yesavage et al., 1993), then further assessment for depression is warranted.

Diagnosis of psychopathology

Another potential goal of assessment is to determine whether an individual meets the diagnostic criteria for a psychiatric disorder listed in the fourth edition of the *Diagnostic and Statistical Manual of Mental Disorders* (*DSM-IV-TR*; American Psychiatric Association, 2000). The *DSM-IV-TR* utilizes a syndromal approach to classification, which involves the identification of signs and symptoms that characterize particular disorders and that distinguish one disorder from others. The information upon which a diagnosis is based can be obtained through the administration of tests that are sensitive to the diagnostic criteria for one or more disorders, through unstructured, semistructured, and structured diagnostic interviews, and through the administration of a mental status examination (e.g., Strub & Black, 2000). The current diagnostic system has been criticized over the past several decades for a variety of reasons, a discussion of which is beyond the scope of this chapter. However, concern has been expressed about the adequacy of the *DSM-IV* criteria when applied to older adults (e.g., Jeste, Blazer, & First, 2005). More specifically, it appears that older adults may experience or present a different constellation of symptoms than young adults for certain disorders (e.g., anxiety, depression).

For example, depressed older adults are more likely than younger adults to report hopelessness and helplessness (Christensen et al., 1999), somatic symptoms (Gallo, Anthony, & Muthén, 1994), psychomotor retardation (Gallo et al., 1994), weight loss (Blazer, Bachar, & Hughes, 1987), and loss of appetite (Blazer et al., 1987). Depressed older adults are less likely than younger adults to report suicidal ideation (Blazer, Bachar, & Hughes, 1987), guilt (Gallo, Rabins, & Anthony, 1999; Musetti et al., 1989; Wallace & Pfohl, 1995), and dysphoria (Gallo et al., 1994; Gallo et al., 1999). Another concern with the current *DSM-IV* diagnostic criteria is that older adults may experience disabling symptoms of anxiety or depression, yet not meet the diagnostic criteria for any of the disorders. These symptom clusters are often termed subsyndromal anxiety or depression.

Some authors (e.g., Brown & Barlow, 2009; Nease, Volk, & Cass, 1999; Shankman & Kline, 2002) have argued for dimensional approaches to diagnosis. For example, Nease et al. (1999) have argued for a severity dimension to be incorporated into the current diagnostic system. This dimension would be consistent with the proposed *DSM-V*, which may permit inclusion of dimensional quantification of symptoms that cut across diagnostic syndromes (e.g., anxiety, depression) and possibly subsyndromal disorders. Nease et al. (1999) have identified clusters of symptom severity (e.g., low severity, high severity) and established relations between these clusters and other outcome variables (e.g., health-related quality of life). Such an approach could be beneficial for older adults whose symptoms do not currently meet diagnostic criteria for a disorder (e.g., subsyndromal depression), but whose quality of life suffers as a function of these symptoms.

Multidimensional Assessment

Assessment of older adults necessitates consideration of multiple aspects of health and functioning. It is widely understood that the aging adult experiences notable physical, mental, and social changes, and these changes interact with one another and influence diagnosis, prognosis, and treatment of disorders (Wieland & Hirth, 2003). Because of these late life changes, assessment of older adults often requires the input of a team of healthcare workers, including physicians, psychologists, nurses, and physical therapists; this integrated team provides comprehensive care for the older patient (Wieland & Hirth, 2003). It is important that psychologists consider the assessment of physical, cognitive, psychological, adaptive, social, and capacity statuses of older adults (e.g., Edelstein, Martin, & McKee, 2000).

Physical health

By the time an individual is 65 years of age, several age-related changes have occurred, including changes in sensory systems, muscle strength, and bone density, and the presence of chronic disease (Whitbourne, 2002). These particular changes are relevant to the psychological assessment of older adults. Age-related deficits in the visual and auditory systems are of greatest relevance to the psychological assessment of older adults, as both are involved in the processing of information presented in the form of instructions or test items. Presbyopia is the most common age-related change in the visual system (Jackson & Owsley, 2003), which results in difficulty viewing close objects (e.g., reading materials). Such visual deficits can influence test performance when acute vision is required. In addition, age-related changes in the visual system can contribute to falls resulting from slowed dark adaptation and depth perception, automobile accidents due to headlight glare and rapid changes in light intensity, and even changes in social behavior due to failure to recognize friends and acquaintances (Edelstein, Drozdick, & Kogan, 1998).

Approximately one in three adults over the age of 60 suffers from hearing loss (National Institute on Deafness and Other Communication Disorders, 2009). Especially common are presbycusis (hearing loss for high-pitched sounds) and tinnitus (persistent ringing, clicking, or hissing sound), both of which become ever more present in older adults. Hearing aids can be used to compensate for hearing loss; however, only about one in five persons who need a hearing aid actually uses one (NIDCD, 2009). Accordingly auditory deficits can significantly impact other areas of the patient's life, including social interactions and participation in a number of activities (Dalton et al., 2003; Resnick, Fries, & Verbrugge, 1997). Thus it is essential to assess the extent of sensory deficits.

Age-related changes in muscle strength and bone density also have implications for the psychological assessment of older adults. For example, changes in musculature and bone density contribute to limitations in mobility (Whitbourne, 2002). The changes can contribute to difficulties in fine motor movement, such as writing (Whitbourne, 2002). In fact, musculoskeletal change is the leading cause of limitations in daily functioning in adults over the age of 65 (Center for Disease Control and Prevention, 2009). As a result, older adults must adapt to their physical limitations and come to terms with the implications of these changes (e.g., no longer being able to engage in favorite activities). Thus it is important for psychologists to assess the impact of physical and sensory changes on the patient's quality of life, and determine the extent to which deficits in these domains may influence the assessment process and outcome.

The likelihood of developing a chronic disease increases with age. Most older adults suffer from at least one chronic disease, with the most common being hypertension (41%), arthritis (49%), heart disease (39%), and cancer (22%) (Administration on Aging, 2010). The increase in number of chronic diseases is accompanied by an increase in the number of medications taken by older adults. Older adults represent approximately 15% of the US population, but use one third of all prescription drugs and 40% of all nonprescription drugs (Maiese, 2002). Hajjar, Cafiero, and Hanlon (2007) found that community-based older adults take two to nine prescription drugs per day. Moreover, there is a greater chance that older adults will be taking more medications than are necessary (Hajjar & Hanlon, 2006). In light of the potential number of medications taken by older adults, the clinician must determine to what extent presenting problems are possibly due to the potential adverse side effects of these medications (e.g., sedation, cognitive impairment, anxiety, depression).

Finally, the presentation of some disorders (e.g., hypothyroidism) may look remarkably similar to other psychological disorders (e.g., depression), thus further complicating the assessment of older patients (Edelstein et al., 2000). Therefore it is important to first rule out medical conditions as the cause of the psychological symptoms. Assessment in this domain is accomplished with a physical examination by a physician and any necessary laboratory testing. The results of the findings can then inform the psychologist's conceptualization of the older adult's presenting problems.

Cognitive functioning

Cognitive functioning involves multiple skills that are important for social relations, day-to-day living, and psychological functioning (e.g., Farias et al., 2009; Yaffe et al., 1999).

Across the lifespan, some normative age-related declines occur in processing speed (Salthouse, 1994), working memory, episodic memory, and prospective memory (Luo & Craik, 2008), whereas other cognitive abilities are maintained into late life (e.g., recognition memory, procedural memory, semantic memory; Luo & Craik, 2008). The assessment of cognitive functioning may be complicated by the age-related changes in cognitive functioning. One must attempt to discriminate between age-related and nonnormative cognitive deficits. A common assessment referral question is whether an individual is cognitively impaired. Another common referral question is whether a person is cognitively impaired, depressed, or both. In addition to these specific referral questions, screening of cognitive functioning is essential during assessment of older adults. To address this question, a mental health professional often begins with the use of a cognitive screening instrument. If the instrument suggests the presence of cognitive deficits, thorough neuropsychological assessment can be conducted.

The most widely used cognitive screening instrument is the MMSE (Folstein et al., 1975). The MMSE takes about 10 minutes to administer and captures several facets of cognitive functioning (e.g., orientation, working memory, immediate and delayed recall). In a recent meta-analysis, Mitchell (2008) found that the MMSE has adequate sensitivity and specificity in distinguishing between those with and without cognitive impairment. However, the MMSE has several limitations. Individuals with lower levels of education, and ethnic minorities, tend to perform poorer on the MMSE. Consequently, when interpreting scores, it is important to use age and education norms (Kiddoe, Whitfield, Andel, & Edwards, 2008). Additionally, the MMSE is not a sensitive tool for the detection of mild cognitive impairment (Tombaugh & McIntyre, 1992).

Recently, newer cognitive screening instruments have been developed that have been found to be more sensitive in the detection of mild cognitive impairment compared to the MMSE, for example, the Montreal Cognitive Assessment (MoCA; Nasreddine et al., 2005) and the Saint Louis University Mental Status Examination (SLUMS; Tariq, Tumosa, Chibnall, Perry, & Morley, 2006). The MoCA is easy to administer and takes about 10 minutes to complete. The MoCA is an improvement on the MMSE in that it also includes measures of executive functioning, verbal fluency, and response speed which are useful in detecting dementia. The measure demonstrates good sensitivity and specificity for the detection of dementia and mild cognitive impairment (Nasreddine et al., 2005). Differences in performance due to education level are also accounted for in the scoring of the MoCA. The SLUMS is easy to administer and includes several tasks that are not include on the MMSE, specifically, animal naming, digit span, clock drawing, figure recognition/size differentiation, and story recall (Tariq et al., 2006). The SLUMS demonstrates good sensitivity and specificity for the detection of dementia and mild cognitive impairment (Tariq et al., 2006).

Psychological functioning

Approximately 1 to 5% of older adults suffer from depression (Beekman, Copeland, & Prince, 1999) and 1.2 to 15% of community-dwelling older adults suffer from an anxiety disorder (Bryant, Jackson, & Ames, 2008). Almost 15 to 20% of older adults have significant depressive symptoms (Gallo & Lebowitz, 1999) and 15 to 52.3% have anxiety symptoms (Bryant et al., 2008). A few measures have been developed that assess depression and anxiety in older adults specifically. For example, the Geriatric Anxiety Inventory (GAI; Pachana et al., 2007) has good preliminary support for its validity and reliability, and demonstrated good sensitivity and specificity for detecting generalized anxiety disorder and the presence of any anxiety disorders in older samples (Pachana et al., 2007). The Geriatric Depression Scale (GDS; Yesavage et al., 1983), a measure of depression tailored to older populations, is widely used and has good support for its reliability and validity (for a review, see Montorio & Izal, 1996). Additionally, the GDS differs from other measures of depression in that it eliminates somatic items, which older adults may endorse due to the natural aging process. The elimination of somatic items is somewhat controversial and may be a potential weakness of the GDS (Edelstein et al., 2008; Norris, Snow-Turek, & Blankenship, 1995). More commonly, the Beck Anxiety Inventory (Beck & Steer, 1990) and the Beck Depression Inventory-II (Beck, Steer, & Brown, 1996) have been used to assess anxiety and depression in older adults, respectively. Both of these measures have good preliminary support for their validity and reliability with community-dwelling older adults and older adults in residential facilities (e.g., Morin et al., 1999; Segal, Coolidge, Cahill, & O'Riley, 2008).

Older adults are also at the greatest risk of suicide compared to all other age groups. Specifically, males over the age of 65 years have the highest rates of suicide, with suicide completion becoming even more prevalent in adults over 85 years old (U.S. Census Bureau, 2009). Notably, completed suicides are rare, even in the oldest adults (in 2006, the rate of completed suicides was 15.9 per 100,000 individuals ages 85 and older; U.S. Census Bureau, 2009). However, suicidal ideation and behavior is not normative, and therefore warrants clinical attention. Furthermore, older adults in long-term care facilities are at a higher risk for depression and suicidal ideation compared to community-dwelling age-mates (Reiss & Tishler, 2008). Consequently, assessment of suicidality in older populations is important, particularly among the oldest adults and those in nursing homes. Guides, such as the Suicide Older Adults Protocol (Fremouw, McKoy, Tyner, & Musick, 2009), can aid clinicians in the evaluation of an older adult's suicide risk. A self-report measure, the Geriatric Suicide Ideation Scale (GSIS) was developed to identify and measure the severity of suicidal ideation among older adults (Heisel & Flett, 2006). Additionally, assessment of protective factors is also important. The Reasons for Living–Older Adults Scale (Edelstein, Heisel, McKee, Martin, Koven, Duberstein, et al., 2009) can be a useful tool for this purpose. This measure examines factors such as religious and moral beliefs and family connectedness as potential protective factors. The scale demonstrates good psychometric properties although it has yet to be tested on more diverse populations and settings. Overall, evaluation of both risk and protective factors for suicide during the assessment of older adults' psychological well-being is essential.

Adaptive functioning

Adaptive functioning refers to the ability of the older adult to carry out activities of daily living (ADL; e.g., walking, bathing, eating) and instrumental activities of daily living (IADL; e.g., using the telephone, managing money). As suggested earlier in this chapter and elsewhere, age-related changes in physical and cognitive functioning can interfere with these activities (Whitbourne, 2002). For example, due to changes in muscle strength, some older adults may have difficulty transferring from bed to a chair, or engaging in physically demanding tasks, such as housework. Similarly, inability to perform these tasks can have implications for other aspects of functioning, such as health and social interactions (Everard, Lach, Fisher, & Baum, 2000).

The best-known assessment instruments that are used to evaluate an individual's ability to carry out daily tasks are the Katz Activities of Daily Living Scale (Katz, Downs, Cash, & Gratz, 1970) and the Lawton Instrumental Activities of Daily Living Scale (Lawton & Brody, 1969). The Katz ADL Scale measures six areas of functioning: bathing, toileting, transferring (e.g., from bed to chair), eating, continence, and dressing. The Lawton IADL assesses eight areas of instrumental functioning and the extent to which a person can adequately perform that function (e.g., does own laundry completely, does small amounts of laundry, or has laundry completed by someone else). These scales are easy to use and provide useful information about a person's level of functioning. The most recently published measure of living skills is the Texas Functional Living Scales (Cullum et al., 2001) which measures four domains: time, money and calculation, communication, and memory (e.g., remembering to take medications). Recently, researchers have suggested that measuring ADLs and IADLs may not be the best assessment of adaptive functioning of older adults (e.g., Albert, Bear-Lehman, & Burkhardt, 2009). Criticisms of ADL and IADL measures focus on the limited number of activities assessed. Additionally, ADL and IADL measures do not adjust for life experiences. For instance, if a person was never responsible for managing money earlier in adulthood, he or she would not endorse an item about money management on the IADL measure.

Recent performance-based measures have been developed that examine older adults from a variety of populations (e.g., those with dementia, healthy older adults). The interested reader is referred to Moore, Palmer, Patterson, and Jeste (2007) for a more complete review of these measures. These authors recommend the Direct Assessment of Functional Status (DAFS; Loewenstein et al., 1989) and the Structured Assessment of Independent Living Skills (SAILS; Mahurin, DeBettignies, & Pirozzolo, 1991) for individuals with dementia, and the Independent Living Scales (ILS; Loeb, 1996) and the Observed Tasks of Daily Living (OTDL; Diehl, Willis, & Schaie, 1995) for healthy older adults. These measures assess a wide range of functional domains, including telephone and communication skills, medication management, financial skills, and meal preparation. Overall, it appears that the best assessment of an older adult's adaptive functioning should cover a broad range of diverse skills.

Social functioning

Social relationships continue to be an important part of the older adult's overall well-being. Research has illustrated the many benefits of social relationships, such as buffering against stress (e.g., Krause, 1986) and physical and mental illness (e.g., Everard et al., 2000). Assessment of social functioning evaluates the extent of an older adult's social isolation and can provide a baseline level of functioning against which to evaluate the effectiveness of a psychological intervention (Levin, 2000). In light of the potential consequences of social interactions, both positive and negative, it behooves the clinician to assess social functioning. Social functioning comprises several domains, including social networks, social support, social resources, social roles, role functioning, and engagement in activities (Levin, 2000). Each of these domains needs to be assessed in order to fully understand the extent of the older patient's social functioning. There are a number of measures available for assessment of social functioning but many of these measures fail to capture all the dimensions of social functioning (e.g., assessing only positive interactions, while neglecting negative interactions). Therefore it may be necessary to include several measures to assess social functioning, which will be discussed below.

Social networks.   Like many other domains, social networks change over the later parts of life. Older adults tend to have fewer social ties compared to younger cohorts, resulting in smaller social networks for older adults (Antonucci & Akiyama, 1987; Fung, Carstensen, & Lang, 2001). Some research suggests that older adults may be at greater risk for social isolation, which can have adverse effects on health and well-being (e.g., Cornwell & Waite, 2009a). Although the older client's social network may be smaller than in previous years, these connections continue to meet a variety of needs for those within it, such as emotional support, social interactions, and financial help. When assessing social networks, it is important to consider both quantitative (e.g., frequency of interactions, number of members in social support network) and qualitative (e.g., negative or positive interactions, satisfaction) characteristics of the network. Further, it is also important to consider actual social connectedness and perceived social connectedness, as perceived social connectedness also predicts indicators of physical and mental health (Cornwell & Waite, 2009a).

One of the most widely utilized measures of social networks is the Social Convoy Questionnaire (Kahn & Antonucci, 1980), which is useful for determining the size and quality of social networks. Likewise, the Lubben's Social Network Scale (LSNS; Lubben and Gironda, 2000) gathers similar information, but also asks about frequency of contact with different types of individuals (e.g., friends, relatives, and neighbors) and reliance on these relationships for advice and assistance in activities. Further, this version of the LSNS assesses for perceived and received social support. The LSNS contains 18 items, and has adequate internal consistency (Cronbach's αs range from .747 to .821 in a sample of community-dwelling older adults; Choi & McDougall, 2007), suggesting its usefulness in clinical settings. Recently, Cornwell and Waite (2009a) developed two separate scales for assessing social disconnectedness and perceived isolation based on data collected from a large national study on older adults. The social disconnectedness scale assesses for the size and quality of social ties as well as participation in social activities using eight items (Cronbach's $\alpha = .73$). The social isolation scale contains nine items, and assesses both perceived social support (e.g., supportiveness, closeness) and loneliness (Cronbach's $\alpha = .70$). Interestingly, actual disconnectedness and perceived loneliness are positively but weakly associated ($r = .25$). As connectedness and perceived loneliness are related to health status, it is essential to assess for both when evaluating a client's social network (Cornwell & Waite, 2009a). One limitation of these new measures is the absence of sufficient psychometric evaluation; therefore, use of these scales in both clinical and research settings should be done with caution. However, the perceived loneliness scale provides useful information not covered by the Social Convoy Questionnaire.

Social support. Social networks also provide the people within them with various types of social support, such as instrumental support (e.g., loaning money or helping with housework), emotional support, and informational support (e.g., giving advice; Vaux, Riedel, & Stewart, 1987; Wills & Shinar, 2000). Notably, perceived social support has been shown to better predict mortality (Lyyra & Heikkinen, 2006) and physical and mental health outcomes in comparison to the predictive power of received social support (Cadzow & Servoss, 2009; McDowell & Serovich, 2007). In other words, individuals who perceive themselves as having adequate support may report higher subjective well-being than individuals who do not perceive themselves to have sufficient social support, even if these individuals may actually receive *more* social support than others. Thus it is important to assess for perceived social support in addition to actual social support received.

Social support is one area of social functioning in which numerous assessment measures exist. Further, many assessments tap into both perceived and received social support. The Social Support Questionnaire (SSQ) is a self-report measure that assesses actual support received, as well as the individual's satisfaction with the received support (Sarason, Levine, Basham, & Sarason, 1983). Four-week test–retest reliability is high ($r = .90$) with an internal consistency of $\alpha = .97$ (Levin, 2000). Similarly, the Interview Schedule for Social Interaction (ISSI), a semistructured interview, measures the actual availability of support in addition to the individual's perceived satisfaction with the social relationship (Henderson, Duncan-Jones, Byrne, & Scott, 1980). Internal consistency for each of the subscales range from .67 to .79 (Levin, 2000; Wills & Shinar, 2000), and 18-day test–retest reliability ranges from .71 to .76 in a sample of older adults (Henderson et al., 1980). Additional measures include the Inventory for Socially Supportive Behaviors (ISSB; Barrera, Sandler, & Ramsay, 1981), the Interpersonal Support Evaluation List (ISEL; Cohen & Hoberman, 1983), and the Social Provisions Scale (SPS; Cutrona & Russell, 1987). The interested reader is referred to Wills & Shinar (2000) and Levin (2000) for an in-depth discussion of these and additional measures.

More recently, research on social functioning has considered the assessment of negative social interactions in addition to positive exchanges (e.g., Newsom, Rook, Nishishiba, Sorkin, & Mahan, 2005). To assess for both these constructs, Newsom and colleagues (2005) developed a measure of positive and negative social exchanges for older adults known as the PANSE. This measure consists of two subscales which assess for positive aspects of relationships (e.g., emotional and instrumental support) and negative aspects of social interactions (e.g., unwanted advice or neglect). Cronbach's α for both subscales is high, at .90 for each. Because this is a new measure, further evaluation of its psychometric properties are needed. However, it appears to be a promising measure of social functioning.

Social resources. Social resources may include finances, healthcare, housing, or community resources available to the older client. For example, enrollment in Medicare is considered a social resource, as well as local community organizations, such as senior centers and meal distribution programs, which provide tangible, instrumental support for the older client (Levin, 2000). Knowledge of whether an older adult receives these resources is important in order to determine which other resources are needed. The Older Americans Resources and Services (OARS) Multidimensional Functional Assessment Questionnaire is an interview that can be used to asses for resources and services available to the patient (Pfeiffer, 1975); this scale has demonstrated adequate psychometric properties (see Levin, 2000).

Social roles and role functioning.   Social roles, or an individual's position and relation to others within a network (Atchley, 2000) and subsequent behaviors associated with that position, are an essential part of evaluation of social functioning in the older patient. Role functioning is the ability to successfully meet the demands of these roles (Levin, 2000). Roles change over the lifespan (James, Witte, & Galbraith, 2006), such as when a parent becomes a grandparent, and the importance of each role may change as well, such as greater emphasis on family roles as opposed to maintaining acquaintances (Anatchkova & Bjorner, 2010; Fung, Carstensen, & Lang, 2001). Further, one's ability to function within these roles may also change. For example, financial limitations associated with retirement may interfere with the older adult's ability to provide financial support to children and grandchildren. Thus it is important to assess the number of roles an older individual currently maintains and how effective he or she is in meeting the demands of this role. Notably, few measures currently exist for the evaluation of social roles. The best-known measure is the Role Count Index (Cumming & Henry, 1961), which provides information regarding the number of roles one currently fills. However, the reliability and validity of this measure have not been evaluated (Levin, 2000). Although measures of role functioning do not presently exist, one potential measure is currently in development by Anatchkova and Bjorner (2010). This measure intends to assess for a person's actual ability to fulfill social, occupational, and family roles. Although formal evaluations of roles and role functioning are scarce, it is important to ask questions about these domains during a clinical interview.

Social activities.   Social activities include an individual's occupation, leisure activities, volunteer work, engagement in social clubs, and other entertaining activities a person may enjoy (Levin, 2000). It is important to assess for both current level of engagement in social activities as well as previous engagement. Doing so will allow the clinician or researcher to determine if the client is receiving the needed level of social stimulation. Further, this information can be used as a marker of improvement during treatment (Levin, 2000). Although assessment of engagement in social activities overlaps with assessments of adaptive functioning (see above), there are additional areas that may not be captured by the adaptive functioning measures (e.g., having conversations with friends, playing sports, etc). Clinicians may simply ask clients to describe the activities they enjoy and which ones they actually participate in. By assessing each of these domains described above, the mental health professional can garner a more complete picture of the older client's social functioning.

Capacity assessment

Requests for the assessment of capacity are increasing with the increasing number of older adults who are living longer, the transfer of wealth from the "baby boomer" generation, and the increasing number of contested wills. When we use the word "capacity," we are referring to the ability to make an informed decision, which is determined by a clinician (American Bar Association Commission on Law and Aging & American Psychological Association, 2008). In the legal domain, the term "competency" is used, but this term refers to a judicial determination of capacity (Moye, Gurrera, Karel, Edelstein, & O'Connell, 2006). The current trend in many states is to focus on individual capacities (e.g., ability to consent to medical treatment, drive, enter into a contract, and even consent to sexual activity), rather than an overall evaluation of the individual (i.e., competent versus incompetent). Most often, issues of capacity center on medical consent and financial affairs; however, as noted above, capacity can also extend to a wide variety of domains, each of which may require distinctly different sets of skills (Moberg & Rick, 2008). Consequently, an individual may have capacity in one of these domains, but not necessarily the others. According to Grisso and Appelbaum (1998), capacity is generally characterized by the ability to: (a) understand the information required to make the decision, (b) appreciate how the information relates to one's own life and circumstance, (c) reason about the information, and (d) express a choice. An adequate assessment of capacity should evaluate these four domains, which are common legal standards across states.

Several aids have been developed that may assist a clinician in determining capacity (Moye et al., 2006). *The Handbook on the Assessment of Older Adults with Diminished Capacity* (American Bar Association Commission on Law and Aging & American Psychological Association, 2008) contains invaluable information and a worksheet that can guide a psychologist through the process of evaluating and deciding on an individual's capacity. Psychometrically evaluated measures of capacity are available, although these are often restricted to medical consent and financial capacity. The Aid to Capacity Evaluation (Etchells et al., 1999) assesses understanding, appreciation, and reasoning in a semistructured interview. The Capacity Assessment Tool (Carney, Neugroschl, Morrison, Marin, & Siu, 2001) is a structured interview which assesses understanding, reasoning, and communicating a choice in a medical context. Some assessments employ the use of hypothetical vignettes, such as the Capacity to Consent to Treatment Instrument (Marson, Ingram, Cody, & Harrell, 1995). All of these measures demonstrate good to excellent interrater reliability. However, these measures should be supplemented with a clinical interview, and functional and cognitive assessment before determining a patient's capacity. Cognitive impairment is not a sufficient criterion for establishing incapacity. For example, an individual may have impaired memory, but may still be able to identify the risks and benefits associated with the taking of a medication, apply this information to his or her own situation, rationally weigh the risks and benefits in light of his or her own values, and express a choice. Hence, acquiring information from multiple sources and methods (see below) is essential for clinical decision making, especially in regards to patient capacity.

Multimethod Assessment

Older adults often present to psychologists with multiple medical problems, varied symptoms, and complex social histories. Furthermore, older adults may be living independently, with a spouse or adult child, or in a long-term care setting. At the present time, psychologists do not have a gold-standard method of assessing older adults. As reviewed earlier, it is important to assess multiple domains of functioning to obtain a complete picture. In order to assess multiple domains in a valid manner, psychologists employ multiple methods (e.g., self-report, direct observation, report by others) of assessment to avoid the weaknesses of any one method. For example, a psychologist may review medical records, interview the older adult, obtain reports by others (e.g., spouse), use a mental status assessment, administer self-report inventories, and directly observe the older adult's behavior. The remainder of this section will describe various methods of assessment.

Self-report

A considerable amount of information is gathered through self-report measures in psychology (Schwartz, 1999). In particular, there are two types of self-report instruments that are used for assessment purposes: interview and pencil-and-paper questionnaires or inventories. While self-reports of behaviors, thoughts, and emotions are central to most assessments of adults, self-report data have problems. An individual's self-report is influenced by the phrasing of the question asked, the format of the answer (e.g., open-ended or closed-format responses), the context of the questions (e.g., in the context of a paper-and-pencil questionnaire versus a conversation; Schwartz, 1999), and individual characteristics of the older adult (e.g., presence of cognitive impairment). Additionally, Schwartz (1999) suggests that individuals may often edit their covert thoughts before responding, due to social desirability and self-preservation. When individuals are more concerned with social desirability, they may underreport symptoms of psychopathology or stress. Krause (1986) found that older adults who scored higher on a measure of social desirability reported fewer stressful life events and fewer depressive symptoms compared to older adults with lower needs for social desirability. Moreover, older adults score higher than younger adults on measures of social desirability (Fraboni & Cooper, 1989; Ray, 1988; Stöber, 2001).

Consequently, it may be beneficial to administer a measure of social desirability if this is a possible concern. The Marlowe–Crowne Social Desirability Scale (Crowne & Marlow, 1960) is a frequently used measure of social desirability with established validity and internal consistency in older adults samples (e.g., Stöber, 2001). To date, there is little research on how cognitive impairment and social desirability may interact. However, older adults often report being a burden as one of their most frequent fears (Kogan & Edelstein, 2004), which suggests that self-preservation may be important to assess and include in case conceptualization.

General strategies for interviewing older adults are similar to those used in interviewing younger adults. As with younger adults, establishing rapport and active listening are essential aspects of the clinical interview. The accuracy of information obtained in the interview is affected by wording of questions, understanding of questions, and the cognitive skills and individual characteristics of the older adult. For example, the older adult's level of education, health literacy, hearing, and cognitive abilities can influence the understanding of the questions. Additionally, the use of open-ended versus close-ended questions may influence the information obtained during an interview. When older adults are asked about their pain, they report significantly more pain information when asked with open-ended questions (e.g., "Tell me about your pain, aches, soreness or discomfort") compared to close-ended questions (e.g., "What would you rate your pain ... with 0, no pain, and 10 the worst pain possible?"; McDonald, Shea, Rose, & Fedo, 2009, p. 1053). In sum, a flexible interviewing style and varied approaches may facilitate gathering detailed information gathering from older adult clients.

Interviews vary in length, structure, and format. Unstructured clinical interviews allow for rephrasing of questions, clarification of responses, and exploration of issues that may not be covered in a structured interview. Strengths of unstructured interviews include the flexible format and ease of establishing rapport. Unfortunately, it is difficult to ensure reliability among interviewers, and important information may be missed when using an unstructured interview format. Various structured and semistructured interviews have established validity for use with older adults (e.g., Structured Clinical Interview for the DSM-IV; First, Spitzer, Gibbon, & Williams, 1996; NIMH Diagnostic Interview Schedule; Robins, Helzer, Croughan, & Radcliff, 1981). For example, in an examination of the SCID when used with older adults, the overall percentage agreement on current diagnoses was 91% for masters-level clinician interviewers administering the SCID-I (Segal, Hersen, Van Hasselt, Kabacoff, & Roth, 1993). The strengths of structured and semistructured interviews lie in the interrater reliability of the diagnoses. However, more research is needed to examine the validity of diagnoses identified using structured interviews (for a discussion, see Segal, Hersen, & Van Hasselt, 1993). Weaknesses include the duration of the interview administration, lengthy training of the interviewer, and reduced flexibility in questioning (Edelstein et al., 2000).

Paper-and-pencil questionnaires are often used with older adults. A recent review (Edelstein et al., 2008) identified multiple questionnaires that are valid for use with older adults. As reviewed earlier, measures of anxiety and depression such as the Geriatric Anxiety Inventory (Pachana et al., 2007) and the Geriatric Depression Scale (GDS; Yesavage et al., 1983) have been developed for use specifically with older adults. The validity and reliability of assessment instruments developed for young adults (e.g., Beck Anxiety Inventory, Beck Depression Index) have been established using older adult samples. Additionally, assessment instruments that were created for young adults have been modified to ensure that the content of the questions are applicable and valid for older adults (e.g., Fear Survey Schedule-II for Older Adults; Kogan & Edelstein, 2004). Paper-and-pencil questionnaires are often included in assessments because of the ease in administration, reliability, broad review of symptoms, and access to an individual's privately held thoughts and beliefs (Edelstein et al., 2000). Additionally, paper-and-pencil questionnaires require little time on the part of the psychologist for administration and scoring. One caveat when considering the use of self-report instruments with older adults is that there is evidence that older adults may underreport symptoms (e.g., with depression; Gallo, Anthony, & Muthén, 1994).

Report by others

Obtaining reports from others (e.g., spouse, adult child, caregiver) about an older adult client can provide invaluable information about the older adult's physical and mental health history, course and onset of present symptoms, and day-to-day functioning. Both day and nighttime behaviors are important to assess. In institutional or long-term care settings, report by staff members, primarily nursing staff, can provide detailed information that clients may not be capable of providing themselves. Using a sample of nonimpaired older adults residing in long-term care facilities, Davison, McCabe, and Mellor (2009) administered the GDS and SCID to older adults without dementia and administered the SCID to the older adults' care providers. Interestingly, 22% of older adults met criteria for a diagnosis of major depressive disorder using the informant SCID interviews, compared to only 16% of older adults when using the individual SCID interviews. It appears that obtaining information from informants may help identify psychological distress. Moreover, report by others is particularly important with older adults whose cognitive functioning may compromise the reliability or accuracy of information provided.

Advantages and disadvantages of report by others are similar to those influencing the accuracy of self-reports. Additionally, the relationship between the reporter and the older adult can influence the information provided (Edelstein et al., 2000). While the accuracy of a caregiver's report may be influenced by the presence of depression and burden in the caregiver, it is still important to obtain reports from informants as a caregiver's stress could affect the care recipient's well-being and behavior. A number of studies have shown that depression and caregiver burden is associated with caregiver's underestimation of ADL functioning of a care recipient with dementia compared to direct measures of ADLs (Mangone et al., 1993; Zanetti, Geroldi, Frisoni, Bianchetti, & Trabucchi, 1999). Although there are disadvantages to obtaining reports from other informants, this method of assessment provides alternative perspectives and rich information about behavior and symptoms that may not have otherwise been identified.

Direct observation

Direct observation can provide detailed and accurate information about an individual. Observation can take place during the clinical interview, mental status testing, or any other portion of the assessment process. For individuals who may not be cooperative with assessment, direct observation can provide important information about their behavior (Edelstein et al., 2000). For example, if older adults ask to complete self-report inventories at home, this request may raise questions about their reading level, cognitive functioning, or health literacy (Safeer & Keenan, 2005). Direct observation can be used to assess effort and distress during testing, motor abilities, and gait. Additionally, observations of the older adult's appearance can inform other assessments of ADL functioning. Although direct observation is valuable, it is not without limitations. Conducting observations can be time-consuming and may involve staff time. To conduct behavior observations effectively, a mental health professional should provide staff with clear definitions of the target behaviors. If, for instance, the referral question is to identify why an older adult is behaving aggressively during care, specific examples of aggressive behavior should be defined for the coders. These behaviors could include hitting, kicking, spitting, scratching, cursing, or yelling. When possible, it is important to limit the number of behaviors being observed to avoid complicated coding schemes that can be a burden on staff.

The employment of multiple methods of assessment can result in a more complete and less biased picture of the client compared to reliance on only one method of assessment.

The Assessment Process

To address the goals of assessment, various assessment strategies can be employed as discussed earlier. In the following section, the assessment of multiple domains using multiple methods of assessment will be integrated in a discussion of the following case example.

Mr. Toefert is a 76-year-old nursing home resident who was referred for psychological evaluation by the director of nursing. He is a retired university professor who was admitted two weeks ago with a broken hip that apparently resulted from a fall at his home, where he resided alone. Since his admission to the nursing home, he frequently has refused to leave his room, has missed several meals, and has lost weight. Staff members have observed Mr. Toefert sobbing for periods of time in the mornings, but he has refused their attempts to console him. Staff members have also attempted to coax Mr. Toefert out of his room to attend various activities and to interact with other residents. He has consistently refused, stating, "I don't want to leave my valuables unattended any longer than necessary. You know what's going on around here. I don't feel like doing anything anyway." The director of nursing is concerned that Mr. Toefert is having difficulty adjusting to the nursing home, that he might be depressed, and that the depression is compromising his health status (Edelstein et al., 2000, p. 61).[1]

The goal of this assessment case is first to determine whether or not Mr. Toefert may be experiencing depression, as suggested by the director of nursing's referral question. In addressing this goal, it will be necessary to screen for other mental and physical disorders in order to perform a differential diagnosis. During the assessment process, it would be beneficial to interview multiple staff members in the nursing home setting and perhaps one of Mr. Toefert's family members to construct a complete picture of Mr. Toefert's presenting problem.

Review of medical history

As previously noted, most older adults have at least one chronic medical problem (Administration on Aging, 2010), which may have psychological symptoms that contribute to the overall presentation of psychological symptoms. Thus a psychologist must first rule out possible medical causes of psychological symptoms. To accomplish this, the psychologist would review Mr. Toefert's medical chart, laboratory tests (e.g., blood tests, urinalysis), results of neuroimaging, and nursing notes. In the case of Mr. Toefert, it would be important to rule out thyroid dysfunction, which could mimic symptoms of depression (hypothyroidism) or anxiety (hyperthyroidism) by checking the results of thyroid function tests. The results of a recent urinalysis should be examined, as urinary tract infections can result in behaviors that are atypical for the individual being assessed (Young & Inoyue, 2007). The etiology of dementia or cognitive disorders may be identified by reviewing a radiologist's interpreted report of neuroimaging and abnormal findings. Abnormal sleep patterns, weight loss, or agitation may be documented in nursing notes. These symptoms may represent depressive symptoms that an older adult may not verbally report during an interview or on paper-and-pencil assessment measures. Although a review of Mr. Toefert's medical history may help rule out or substantiate hypotheses, other methods of assessment are needed.

Clinical interview

The clinical interview with Mr. Toefert will enable the psychologist to assess his present psychological symptoms. Blazer (2004) recommends that the interviewer review important psychological symptoms in a structured manner in order to prevent biases in the older adult's reports. Reviewing emotional symptoms (e.g., depressed mood or the blues), cognitive symptoms (e.g., difficulty concentrating, memory problems), and physical symptoms or behaviors (e.g., sleep problems, loss of appetite, lethargy) is essential to the clinical interview. Some critical symptoms to review include suicidal ideation, loss of interest in formerly pleasurable activities (anhedonia), confusion, delusions, and hallucinations (Blazer, 2004). These symptoms could be indicative of depression or suicidality. Assessing the onset of the symptoms (e.g., Were the symptoms present before Mr. Toefert's fall?), duration, severity, and course (e.g., Do the symptoms change over the course of the day?) provides important information about the symptom presentation. Additionally, it is important to determine any change in Mr. Toefert's functioning in order to determine the extent and duration of his symptoms of dysphoria.

To supplement the information obtained from Mr. Toefert, a psychologist could interview one of Mr. Toefert's nurses or a family member. During this interview with other reporters, the psychologist could attempt to gather information about Mr. Toefert's mood, eating and sleeping habits, functioning, and any recent changes in cognitive status. Additionally, a nurse or family member could complete the Adult Functional Adaptive Behavior Scale (AFABS; Spirrison & Pierce, 1992) to assess Mr. Toefert's ADL and IADL functioning.

Screening assessment

Pencil-and-paper self-report symptom inventories can be administered to Mr. Toefert to assess for the presence of symptoms of depression and anxiety. The Geriatric Depression Scale and Geriatric Anxiety Inventory would be reasonable choices in this case. Often following falls, older adults experience anxiety and fear, which could result in subsequent avoidance behaviors (for a review, see Rubenstein, 2006).

Cognitive assessment

A brief cognitive screening instrument, such as the Montreal Cognitive Assessment could be administered to Mr. Toefert to detect the presence of mild cognitive impairment or symptoms of dementia. This instrument was selected because it includes executive functioning tasks, which may be impaired in late-onset depression (for a review, see Schweitzer, Tuckwell, O'Brien, & Ames, 2002). If Mr. Toefert's performance on the MoCA was below the cut-off for dementia (cut-off = 26), then formal cognitive testing should be conducted in order to determine whether he has a cognitive disorder.

Direct observation

Direct observation of Mr. Toefert's behavior, gait, appearance, and effort during cognitive testing provides additional information. In particular, does Mr. Toefert's affect match his self-report? Is his speech fluent, halting, or labored? Is Mr. Toefert dressed appropriately for the situation and the weather? With careful observation, much detailed information can be gathered during the assessment process. This information can be helpful in substantiating clinical hypotheses and in making a differential diagnosis.

In summary, using self-report, direct observation, report by others, and review of medical records, a psychologist could gather much information to supplement Mr. Toefert's presenting problem. This information can be used to assess multiple domains of functioning in order to differentiate among possible depressive disorders, anxiety disorders, adjustment disorders, underlying medical problems, and cognitive disorders. Additionally, it is common for a mood disorder to be comorbid with dementia.

Practical or General Considerations

During the assessment of older adults, some practical considerations can be taken into account in order to facilitate the assessment process. As age-related hearing loss is a common occurrence, so efforts to reduce environmental noise are important. Additionally, the interview should speak clearly and slowly. Printed materials should be in at least a 14-point font and printed on nonglossy paper to reduce glare. Similarly, it is important to determine whether older adults have any assistive devices that they need for the testing (e.g., spectacles, hearing aid).

Examination of medical records can be very important in light of the increased likelihood of more complicated medical histories among older adults. If applicable, one can obtain written authorization from the older adult to obtain medical records. Because older adults also often take multiple medications on a daily basis, a psychologist may ask the older adult to bring to the appointment a list of current medications, doses, and time of administration, or perhaps bring the bottles themselves. With the advent of computerized records, it is very simple to obtain information about an older adult's medical history at a particular facility. In addition to identifying past and current problems, a clinician can examine an older adult's pattern of health care utilization (e.g., Does the patient miss appointments? Does the patient visit his or her primary care doctor frequently? What about the use of specialists and diagnostic tests?). Within some larger organizations, such as the Veteran's Affairs Health Care system, a clinician can review a patient's medical history at VA hospitals across the United States, which can enhance psychological assessments.

Using multiple methods of assessment to obtain information about biological, social, and psychological functioning is central to the assessment of older adults. Whenever possible, the psychologist is encouraged to use assessment instruments that have established reliability and validity among older adults. As the *DSM-IV* classification system may not be adequate when applied to older adults (e.g., Jeste et al., 2005), it is important to assess the extent to which symptoms may interfere in the lives of older adults.

Summary

Assessment is performed to achieve a wide range of goals, ranging from screening to the evaluation of treatment process and outcome. Regardless of the goal, as the clinician moves from screening to a more comprehensive assessment, the assessment becomes multidimensional and ideally employs multiple methods that can often address the limitations of any one assessment method. The complexity of assessment with older adults demands a broad knowledge of the potential influence of age-related changes in biological and cognitive processes, and the ability to integrate information from multiple methods across multiple assessment dimensions. At the present time many of the psychologists and other clinicians conducting psychological assessments of older adults were not formally trained with older adult clients, and many of the assessment instruments employed in assessment were created with and for younger adults. As the field of clinical geropsychology continues to develop, we can hope that more psychologists will received specialized assessment training with older adults, and the development of assessment instruments designed specifically for older adults will yield more psychometrically sound measures that should enhance the quality and utility of assessment.

The adequacy of assessment of older adults also has important treatment implications for researchers and other mental health professionals. Evidence-based treatments rely entirely on the outcome of psychological assessment for the determination of the effectiveness and efficacy of these interventions. Moreover, assessment is used to evaluate the treatment process and to guide changes when necessary to obtain optimal outcomes. Thus assessment resides at the heart of our clinical interventions and its concomitant accountability

Note

1. This case study was originally published in Edelstein, Martin, & McKee (2000). The description of the case remains the same, but the discussion of the assessment process has been adapted and updated.

References

Administration on Aging (2010). Profile of Older Americans: 2009. Retrieved from http://www.aoa.gov/AoARoot/Aging_Statistics/Profile/2009/14.aspx

Albert, S. M., Bear-Lehman, J., & Burkhardt, A. (2009). Lifestyle-adjusted function: Variation beyond BADL and IADL competencies. *The Gerontologist, 49*(6), 767–77.

American Bar Association Commission on Law and Aging & American Psychological Association. (2008). *Assessment of older adults with diminished capacity: A handbook for psychologists.* Retrieved from http://www.apa.org/pi/aging/programs/assessment/capacity-psychologist-handbook.pdf

American Psychiatric Association. (2000). *Diagnostic and statistical manual of mental disorders, DSM-IV-TR* (4th ed.). Washington, DC: American Psychiatric Association.

Anatchkova, M. D., & Bjorner, J. B. (2010). Health and role functioning: The use of focus groups in the development of an item bank. *Quality of Life Research: An International Journal of Quality of Life Aspects of Treatment, Care, and Rehabilitation, 19*, 111–123.

Antonucci, T. C., & Akiyama, H. (1987). Social networks in adult life and a preliminary examination of the convoy model. *Journal of Gerontology, 42*(5), 519–527.

Atchley, R. C. (2000). Retirement as a social role. In J. F. Gubrium& J. A. Holstein (Eds.), *Aging and everyday life* (pp. 115–124). Malden, MA: Blackwell.

Barrera, M., Sandler, I. N., & Ramsay, T. B. (1981). Preliminary development of a scale of social support: Studies on college students. *American Journal of Community Psychology, 9*, 435–447.

Beck, A.T., & Steer, R.A. (1990). *Manual for the Beck Anxiety Inventory.* San Antonio, TX: Psychological Corporation.

Beck, A. T., Steer, R. A., & Brown, G. K. (1996). *Manual for the Beck Depression Inventory–II.* San Antonio, TX: Psychological Corporation.

Beekman, A. T., Copeland, J. R., & Prince, M. J. (1999). Review of community prevalence of depression in later life. *British Journal of Psychiatry, 174*, 307–311.

Benedict, R. H. B., Schretlen, D., Groninger, L., & Brandt, J. (1998). Hopkins Verbal Learning Test-Revised: Normative data and analysis of inter-form and test-retest reliability. *The Clinical Neuropsychologist, 12*(1), 43–55.

Blazer, D. (2004). The psychiatric interview of older adults. In D. G. Blazer& D. C. Steffens (Eds.), *Textbook of geriatric psychiatry* (4th. ed., pp. 224–235). Washington, DC: American Psychiatric Publishing.

Blazer, D., Bachar, J. R., & Hughes, D. C. (1987). Major depression with melancholia: A comparison of middle-aged and elderly adults. *Journal of the American Geriatrics Society, 35*(10) 927–932.

Brown, T., & Barlow, D. (2009). A proposal for a dimensional classification system based on the shared features of the DSM-IV anxiety and mood disorders: Implications for assessment and treatment. *Psychological Assessment, 21*(3), 256–271.

Bryant, C., Jackson, H., & Ames, D. (2008). The prevalence of anxiety in older adults: Methodological issues and a review of the literature. *Journal of Affective Disorders, 109*(3), 233–250.

Cadzow, R. B., & Servoss, T. J. (2009). The association between perceived social support and health among patients at a free urban clinic. *Journal of the National Medical Association, 101*, 243–250.

Carney, M. T., Neugroschl, J., Morrison, R. S., Marin, D., & Siu, A. L. (2001). The development and piloting of a capacity assessment tool. *The Journal of Clinical Ethics, 12*(1), 17–23.

Carstensen, L. L. (1991). Socioemotional selectivity theory: social activity in life-span context. *Annual Review of Gerontology and Geriatrics. 17*, 195–217.

Center for Disease Control and Prevention (2009). Limitation of activity caused by selected chronic health conditions among older adults, by age: United States, 2005-2006. Retrieved from http://www.cdc.gov/nchs/hus/older.htm.

Choi, N. G., & McDougall, G. J. (2007). Comparison of depressive symptoms between homebound older adults and ambulatory older adults. *Aging and Mental Health, 11*, 310–322.

Christensen, H., Jorm, A. F., Mackinnon, A. J., Korten, A. E., Jacomb, P. A., Henderson, A. S., & Rodgers, B. (1999). Age differences in depression and anxiety symptoms: A structural equation modeling of data from a community population sample. *Psychological Medicine*, *29*(2), 325–339.

Cohen, S., & Hoberman, H. M. (1983). Positive events and social supports as buffers of life change stress. *Journal of Applied Social Psychology*, *13*, 99–125.

Cornwell, E. Y., & Waite, L. J. (2009a). Measuring social isolation among older adults using multiple indicators from the NSHAP study. *Journals of Gerontology: Series B: Psychological Sciences and Social Sciences*, *64B*, i38–i46.

Cornwell, E. Y., & Waite, L. J. (2009b). Social disconnectedness, perceived isolation, and health among older adults. *Journal of Health and Social Behavior*, *50*, 31–48.

Cronbach, L. J. (1960). *Essentials of psychological testing*. New York: Harper-Collins.

Crowne, D. P., & Marlowe, D. (1960). A new scale of social desirability independent of psychopathology. *Journal of Consulting Psychology*, *24*, 349–354.

Cullum, C. M., Saine, K., Chan, L., Martin-Cook, K., Gray, K. F., & Weiner, M. F. (2001). Performance-based instrument to assess functional capacity in dementia: The Texas Functional Living Scale. *Neuropsychiatry, Neuropsychology & Behavioral Neurology*, *14*(2), 103–108.

Cumming, E.& Henry, W. E. (1961). *Growing old: The process of disengagement*. New York: Basic Books.

Cutrona, C. E., & Russell, D. W. (1987). The provisions of social relationships and adaptation to stress. In W. H. Jones& D. Perlman (Eds.), *Advances in personal relationships* (Vol. *1*, pp. 37–67). Greenwich, CT: JAI Press.

Dalton, D. S., Cruickshanks, K. J., Klein, B. E. K., Klein, R., Wiley, T. L., & Nondahl, D. M. (2003). The impact of hearing loss on quality of life in older adults. *The Gerontologist*, *43*(5), 661–668.

Davison, T. E., McCabe, M. P., & Mellor, D. (2009). An examination of the "gold standard" diagnosis of major depression in aged-care settings. *American Journal of Geriatric Psychiatry*, *17*, 359–367.

Diehl, M., Willis, S. L., Schaie K. W. (1995). Everyday problem solving in older adults: Observational assessment and cognitive correlates. *Psychology and Aging*, *10*(3), 478–491.

Edelstein, B. A., Drozdick, L. W., Kogan, J. N. (1998). Assessment of older adults. In A.S. Bellack& M. Hersen (Eds.), *Behavioral assessment: A practical handbook* (4th ed., pp. 179–209). Needham Heights, MA: Allyn & Bacon.

Edelstein, B. A., Heisel, M. J., McKee, D. R., Martin, R. R., Koven, L. P., Duberstein, P. R., & Britton, P. C. (2009). Development and psychometric evaluation of the Reasons for Living–Older Adults Scale: A suicide risk assessment inventory. *The Gerontologist*, *49*(6), 736–745.

Edelstein, B. A., Martin, R. R., & McKee, D.R. (2000). Assessment of older adult psychopathology. In S. K. Whitbourne (Ed.), *Psychopathology in later adulthood* (pp. 61–87). New York: Wiley.

Edelstein, B. A., Woodhead, E., Segal, D., Heisel, M., Bower, E., Lowery, A., & Stoner, S. (2008). Older adult psychological assessment: Current instrument status and related considerations. *Clinical Gerontologist*, *31*(3), 1–35.

Etchells, E., Darzins, P., Silberfeld, M., Singer, P. A., McKenny, J., Naglie, G., … Strang, D. (1999). Assessment of patient capacity to consent to treatment. *Journal of Internal Medicine*, *14*(1), 27–34.

Everard, K. M, Lach, H. W., Fisher, E. B., & Baum, M. C. (2000). Relationship of activity and social support to the functional health of older adults. *Journals of Gerontology: Series B: Psychological Sciences and Social Sciences*, *55B*(4), S208–S212.

Farias, S. T., Cahn-Weiner, D. A., Harvey, D. J., Reed, B. R., Mungas, D., Kramer, J. H., & Chui, H. (2009). Longitudinal changes in memory and executive functioning are associated with longitudinal change instrumental activities of daily living in older adults. *Clinical Neuropsychologist, 23*, 446–461.

First, M. B., Spitzer, R. L., Gibbon, M., & Williams, J. B. (1996). *Structured Clinical Interview for DSM-IV Axis I Disorders*. Washington, DC: American Psychiatric Press.

Folstein, M., Folstein, S. E., & McHugh, P. R. (1975). Mini-Mental State: A practical method for grading the cognitive state of patients for the clinician. *Journal of Psychiatric Research, 12*(3), 189–198.

Fraboni, M., & Cooper, D. (1989). Further validation of three short forms of the Marlowe Crowne Scale of Social Desirability. *Psychological Reports, 65*, 595–600.

Fremouw, W. J., McCoy, K., Tyner, E. A., & Musick, R. (2009). Suicidal older adults protocol –SOAP. In J. B. Allen, E. M. Wolf, & L. VandeCreek (Eds.), *Innovations in clinical practice: A 21st century sourcebook* (pp. 203–212). Sarasota, FL: Professional Resources Press.

Fung, H. H., Carstensen, L. L., & Lang, F. R. (2001). Age-related patterns in social networks among European Americans and African Americans: Implications for socioemotional selectivity theory across the lifespan. *International Journal of Aging and Human Development, 52*(3), 185–206.

Gallo, J. J., Anthony, J. C.& Muthén, B. O. (1994). Age differences in the symptoms of depression: A latent trait analysis. *Journal of Gerontology: Psychological Sciences, 49*(6), P251–P264.

Gallo, J. J., & Lebowitz, B. D. (1999). The epidemiology of common late-life mental disorders in the community: Themes for the new century. *Psychiatric Services, 50*(9), 1158–1166.

Gallo, J. J., Rabins, P. V., & Anthony, J. C. (1999). Sadness in older persons: 13-year follow-up of a community sample in Baltimore, Maryland. *Psychological Medicine, 29*(2), 341–350.

Grisso, T., & Appelbaum, P. S. (1998). *Assessing competence to consent to treatment*. New York: Oxford University Press.

Hajjar, E. R., Cafiero, A. C., & Hanlon, J. T. (2007). Polypharmacy in elderly patients. *American Journal of Geriatric Pharmacology, 5*(4), 345–356.

Hajjar, E. R., & Hanlon, J. T. (2006). Polypharmacy in the elderly. In K. Calhoun& D. E. Eibling (Eds.), *Geriatric otolaryngology* (pp. 667–673). New York: Taylor & Francis.

Heisel, M. J., & Flett, G. L. (2006). The development and initial validation of the Geriatric Suicide Ideation Scale. *American Journal of Geriatric Psychiatry, 14*(9), 742–751.

Henderson, S. Duncan-Jones, P., Byrne, D. G., & Scott, R. (1980). Measuring social relationships: The interview schedule for social interaction. *Psychological Medicine, 10*, 723–734.

Jackson, G. R.& Owsley, C. (2003). Visual dysfunction, neurodegenerative diseases, and aging. *Neurologic Clinics of North America, 21*, 709–728.

James, W. B., Witte, J. E., & Galbraith, M. W. (2006). Havighurst's social roles revisited. *Journal of Adult Development, 13*, 52–60.

Jeste, D. V., Blazer, D. G., & First, M. (2005). Aging-related diagnostic variations: Need for diagnostic criteria appropriate for elderly psychiatric patients. *Biological Psychiatry, 58*(4), 265–271.

Kahn, R. L., & Antonucci, T. C. (1980). Convoys over the life course: Attachment, roles, and social support. In P. B. Baltes& O. G. Brim (Eds.), *Life-span development and behavior* (pp. 254–283). San Diego, CA: Academic Press.

Katz, S., Downs, T. D., Cash, H. R., & Gratz, R. C. (1970). Progress in the development of the index of ADL. *The Gerontologist, 10*(1), 20–30.

Kiddoe, J. M., Whitfield, K. E., Andel, R., & Edwards, C. L. (2008). Evaluating brief cognitive impairment screening instruments among African Americans. *Aging and Mental Health, 12*(4), 488–493.

Kogan, J. N., & Edelstein, B. A. (2004). Modification and psychometric examination of a self-report measure of fear in older adults. *Journal of Anxiety Disorders, 18*(3), 397–409.

Krause, N. (1986). Social support, stress, and well-being among older adults. *Journal of Gerontology, 41*(4), 512–519.

Lawton, M. P., & Brody, E. M. (1969). Assessment of older people: Self-maintaining and instrumental activities of daily living. *The Gerontologist, 9*, 179–186.

Levin, C. (2000). Social functioning. In R. L. Kane and R. A. Kane (Eds.). *Assessing older persons* (pp. 170–199). New York: Oxford University Press.

Loeb, P. A. (1996). *Independent Living Scales (ILS)*. San Antonio, TX: The Psychological Corporation.

Loewenstein, D. A., Amigo, E., Duara, R., Guterman, A., Hurwitz, D., Berkowitz, N., . . . Gittelman, B. (1989). A new scale for the assessment of functional status in Alzheimer's disease and related disorders. *Journals of Gerontology, 44*(4), 114–121.

Lubben, J. E.& Gironda, M. W. (2000). Social support networks. In D. Osterweil, K. Brummel-Smith, & J. C. Beck (Eds.), *Comprehensive geriatric assessment* (pp. 127–137). New York: McGraw-Hill.

Luo, L., & Craik, F. I. M. (2008). Aging and memory: A cognitive approach. *Canadian Journal of Psychiatry, 53*(6), 346–353.

Lyyra, T., & Heikkinen, R. (2006). Perceived social support and mortality in older people. *Journals of Gerontology: Series B: Psychological Sciences and Social Sciences, 61*, S147–S152.

Mahurin, R. K., DeBettignies, B. H., & Pirozzolo, F. J. (1991). Structured assessment of independent living skills: Preliminary report of a performance measure of functional abilities in dementia. *Journals of Gerontology, 46*(2), 58–66.

Maiese, D. R. (2002). Healthy people 2010: Leading health indicators for women. *Women's Health Issues, 12*(4), 155–164.

Mangone, C. A., Sanguinetti, R. M., Baumann, P. D., Gonzalez, R. C., Pereyra, S., Bozzola, F. G., . . . Sica, R. E. (1993). Influence of feelings of burden on the caregiver's perception of the patient's functional status. *Dementia and Geriatric Cognitive Disorders, 4*(5), 287–293.

Marson, D. C., Ingram, K., Cody, H. A., & Harrell, L. E. (1995). Assessing the competency of patients with Alzheimer's disease under different legal standards. *Archives of Neurology, 52*(10), 949–954.

McDonald, D. D., Shea, M., Rose, L., & Fedo, J. (2009). The effect of pain question phrasing on older adult pain information. *Journal of Pain and Symptom Management, 37*(6), 1050–1061.

McDowell, T. L., & Serovich, J. M. (2007). The effect of perceived and actual support on the mental health of HIV-positive persons. *AIDS Care, 19*, 1223–1229.

Mitchell, A. J. (2008). A meta-analysis of the accuracy of the mini-mental state examination in the detection of dementia and mild cognitive impairment. *Journal of Psychiatric Research, 43*(4), 411–431.

Moberg, P. J., & Rick, J. H. (2008). Decision-making capacity and competency in the elderly: A clinical and neuropsychological perspective. *NeuroRehabilitation, 23*(5), 403–413.

Montorio, I., & Izal, M. (1996). The Geriatric Depression Scale: A review of its development and utility. *International Psychogeriatrics, 8*(1), 103–112.

Moore, D. J., Palmer, B. W., Patterson, T. L., & Jeste, D. V. (2007). A review of performance-based measures of functional living skills. *Journal of Psychiatric Research, 41*(1–2), 97–118.

Morin, C. M., Landreville, P., Colecchi, C., McDonald, K., Stone, J., & Ling, W. (1999). The Beck Anxiety Inventory: Psychometric properties with older adults. *Journal of Clinical Geropsychology, 5*(1), 19–29.

Moye, J., Gurrera, R. J., Karel, M. J., Edelstein, B., & O'Connell, C. (2006). Empirical advances in the assessment of the capacity to consent to medical treatment: Clinical implications and research needs. *Clinical Psychology Review*, 26(8), 1054–1077.

Musetti, L., Perugi, G., Soriani, A., Rossi, V. M., Cassano, G.B., & Akiskal, H. S. (1989). Depression before and after age 65. A reexamination. *British Journal of Psychiatry*, 155, 330–336.

Nasreddine, Z. S., Phillips, N. A., Bédirian, V., Charbonneau, S., Whitehead, V., Collin, I.,... Chertkow, H. (2005). The Montreal Cognitive Assessment, MoCA: A brief screening tool for mild cognitive impairment. *Journal of the American Geriatrics Society*, 53(4), 695–699.

National Institute on Deafness and Other Communication Disorders (2009). Hearing loss and older adults. Retrieved from http://www.nidcd.nih.gov/health/hearing/older.htm

Nease, D. E., Volk, R. J., & Cass, A. R. (1999). Investigation of a severity-based classification of mood and anxiety symptoms in primary care patients. *Journal of the American Board of Family Practice*, 12(1), 21–31.

Newsom, J. T., Rook, K. S., Nishishiba, M., Sorkin, D. H., & Mahan, T. L. (2005). Understanding the relative importance of positive and negative social exchanges: Examining specific domains and appraisals. *Journal of Gerontology: Psychological Sciences*, 60B, P304–P312.

Norris, M. P., Snow-Turek, A. L., & Blankenship, L. (1995). Somatic depressive symptoms in the elderly: Contribution or confound? *Journal of Clinical Geropsychology*, 1(1), 5–17.

Pachana, N. A., Byrne, G. J., Siddle, H., Koloski, N., Harley, E., & Arnold, E. (2007). Development and validation of the Geriatric Anxiety Inventory. *International Psychogeriatrics*, 19(1), 103–114.

Pfeiffer, E. (Ed.). (1975). *Multidimensional functional assessment: The OARS methodology*. Durham, NC: Center for the Study of Aging and Human Development.

Ray, J. J. (1988). Lie scales and the elderly. *Personality and Individual Differences*, 9, 417–418.

Reiss, N. S., & Tishler, C. L. (2008). Suicidality in nursing home residents: Part I prevalence, risk factors, methods, assessment, and management. *Professional Psychology: Research and Practice*, 39 (3), 264–270.

Resnick, H. E., Fries, B. E., & Verbrugge, L.M. (1997). Windows to their world: The effect of sensory impairments on social engagement and activity time in nursing home residents. *Journal of Gerontology: Social Science*, 52B, S135–S144.

Robins, L. N., Helzer, J. E., Croughan, J., & Radcliff, K. S. (1981). National Institute of Mental Health Diagnostic Interview Schedule: Its history, characteristics, and validity. *Archives of General Psychiatry*, 38(4), 381–389.

Rubenstein, L. Z. (2006) Falls in older people: Epidemiology, risk factors, and strategies for prevention. *Age and Ageing*, 35 (S2), ii37–ii41.

Safeer, R. S., & Keenan, J. (2005). Health literacy: The gap between physicians and patients. *American Family Physician*, 72(10), 463–468.

Salthouse, T. A. (1994). The nature of the influence of speed on adult age differences in cognition. *Developmental Psychology*, 30, 763–776.

Sarason, I. G., Levine, H. M., Basham, R. B., & Sarason, B. R. (1983). Assessing social support: The social support questionnaire. *Journal of Personality and Social Psychology*, 44, 127–139.

Schwartz, N. (1999). How the questions shape the answers. *American Psychologist*, 54(2), 93–105.

Schweitzer, I., Tuckwell, V., O'Brien, J., & Ames, D. (2002). Is late onset depression a prodrome to dementia? *International Journal of Geriatric Psychiatry*, 17(11), 997–1005.

Segal, D. L., Coolidge, F. L., Cahill, B. S., & O'Riley, A. A. (2008). Psychometric properties of the Beck Depression Inventory-II (BDI-II) among community-dwelling older adults. *Behavior Modification*, 32(1), 3–20.

Segal, D. L., Hersen, M., & Van Hasselt, V. B. (1993). Reliability of the structured clinical interview for DSM-III-R: An evaluative review. *Comprehensive Psychiatry, 35*(4), 316–327.

Segal, D. L., Hersen, M., Van Hasselt, V. B., Kabacoff, R. I., & Roth, L. (1993). Reliability of diagnosis in older psychiatric patients using the structured clinical interview for DSM-III R. *Journal of Psychopathology and Behavioral Assessment, 15*(4), 347–356.

Shankman, S., & Klein, D. (2002). Dimensional diagnosis of depression: Adding the dimension of course to severity and comparison to the DSM. *Comprehensive Psychiatry, 43*(6), 420–426.

Spirrison, C. L., & Pierce, P. S. (1992). Psychometric characteristics of the Adult Functional Adaptive Behavior Scale (AFABS). *The Gerontologist, 32*(2), 234–239.

Stöber, J. (2001). The Social Desirability Scale-17 (SDS-17): Convergent validity, discriminant validity, and relationship with age. *European Journal of Psychological Assessment, 17*, 222–232.

Strub, R. L., & Black, F. W. (2000). *The mental status examination in neurology.* Philadelphia: F. A. Davis.

Tariq, S. H., Tumosa, N., Chibnall, J. T., Perry, M. H., & Morley, J.E. (2006). Comparison of the Saint Louis University Mental Status Examination and the Mini-Mental State Examination for detecting dementia and mild neurocognitive disorder: A pilot study. *American Journal of Geriatric Psychiatry, 14*(11), 900–910.

Tombaugh, T. N., & McIntyre, N. J. (1992). The Mini-Mental State Examination: A comprehensive review. *Journal of the American Geriatrics Society, 40*(9), 922–935.

U.S. Census Bureau (2009). Death rates from suicide by selected characteristics. Retrieved from www.census.gov/compendia/statab/tables/09s0120.xls.

Vaux, A., Riedel, S., & Stewart, D. (1987). Modes of social support: The social support behaviors (SS-B) scale. *American Journal of Community Psychology, 15*, 1573–2770.

Wallace, J., & Pfohl, B. (1995). Age-related differences in the symptomatic expression of major depression. *Journal of Nervous and Mental Disease, 183*(2), 99–102.

Whitbourne, S.K. (2002). *The aging individual: Physical and psychological perspectives* (2nd ed.). New York: Springer.

Wieland, D, & Hirth, V. (2003). Comprehensive geriatric assessment. *Cancer Control, 10*(6), 454–462.

Wills, T. A., & Shinar, O. (2000). Measuring perceived and received social support. In S. Cohen, L. G. Underwood, & B. H. Gottlieb (Eds.), *Social support measurement and intervention: A guide for health and social scientists* (pp. 86–135). New York: Oxford University Press.

Yaffe, K., Blackwell, T., Gore, R., Sands, L., Reus, V., & Browner, W. S. (1999). Depressive symptoms and cognitive decline in nondemented elderly women: A prospective study. *Archives of General Psychiatry, 56*(5), 425–430.

Yesavage, J. A., Brink, T. L., Rose, T. L., Lum, O., Huang, V., Adey, M., & Leirer, V. O. (1983). Development and validation of a geriatric depression screening scale: A preliminary report. *Journal of Psychiatric Research, 17*(1), 37–49.

Young, J., & Inoyue, S. K. (2007). Delirium in older people. *British Medical Journal, 334*, 842–846.

Zanetti, O., Geroldi, C., Frisoni, G.B., Bianchetti, A., & Trabucchi, M. (1999). Contrasting results between caregiver's report and direct assessment of activities of daily living in patients affected by mild and very mild dementia: The contribution of the caregiver's personal characteristics. *Journal of the American Geriatrics Society, 47*(2), 196–202.

PART VI

Social Processes

18

Self-Regulation and Social Cognition in Adulthood

The Gyroscope of Personality

Cory Bolkan and Karen Hooker

Introduction

The uniquely human ability to imagine oneself in the future and ponder such questions as "Who am I?" and "What do I find to be meaningful?" provides the foundation for goal-setting, motivation, and personal direction. The ability to "stay the course" with one's goals, or to re-align them in the face of challenges, depends on our self-regulatory processes. Self-regulation skills are like an internal gyroscope – an apparatus that can turn freely in all directions, and is capable of maintaining the same absolute direction in space in spite of movements of the surrounding parts. Just as a gyroscope is used to maintain equilibrium and to provide guidance and control for mechanical systems, we see self-regulatory processes enacted in service of one's goals as the gyroscope of our personality system.

Ultimately, people become who they are via the ongoing activities, projects, or goals in which they engage over the course of their lives. The way individuals think about their social world and the people with whom they interact significantly shapes the choice of these activities and goals. Family members and friends can provide ongoing support or hindrance in an individual's goal pursuits. This chapter highlights how internal processes of self-regulation, along with social cognitive processes shaped by external influences, play a key role in understanding how individuals adapt, change, and grow over the lifespan.

The Wiley-Blackwell Handbook of Adulthood and Aging, First Edition. Edited by Susan Krauss Whitbourne and Martin J. Sliwinski. © 2012 Blackwell Publishing Ltd. Published 2012 by Blackwell Publishing Ltd.

Development can be understood as multidirectional processes including both growth and decline, from infancy to late life. Adaptive or positive development across the lifespan includes growth, maintenance of functional levels, and regulation of loss (Baltes, Lindenberger, & Staudinger, 2006). The ratio of gains to losses changes in later life as individuals are likely to face the onset of multiple losses associated with aging (e.g., physical functioning, social network size). As will be discussed later in this chapter, all forms of media tend to emphasize these losses, which may perpetuate negative aging stereotypes and downplay the potential for positive aspects of aging. Although older adults do experience losses, they may also simultaneously experience accumulated gains in certain personal resources (e.g., knowledge, wisdom, finances, emotion regulation). Consequently, their ability to self-regulate or manage goals may become increasingly important with age. We end the chapter by addressing external influences as the "push and pull" of development, noting how social cognition (or thoughts about others and thoughts about the self in relation to others) can influence the way people perceive the aging process in themselves and others. In order to further research on self-regulation, it is important to understand its links with the personality. Increasingly, theory and research is being targeted to the intersection between personality and self-regulation (e.g., Hoyle, 2010; McCrae & Löckenhoff, 2010; Morf & Horvath, 2010). Just as a gyroscope relies on three rings, or gimbals, that rotate with freedom in all three axes to maintain orientation and balance, self-regulation and social cognition may be best understood when all aspects of personality are also considered.

The Six-Foci Model of Personality

The current goals of lifespan personality psychologists are to identify fundamental and enduring human qualities, as well as to understand how these qualities develop, change, or are maintained across the lifespan. Advances in methodology and theory, a focus on intraindividual change over time, and studying behaviors within context have resulted in new evidence regarding personality development in adulthood (e.g., Hooker, Hoppmann, & Siegler, 2010; Noftle & Fleeson, 2010; Ram & Gerstof, 2009). The six-foci model of personality (Hooker & McAdams, 2003) is one example of a framework that integrates personality structures (traits, personal action constructs, and life stories) along with parallel personality processes (states, self-regulation, and self-narration) across three distinct levels in order to provide a richer understanding of people and what they are trying to accomplish.

Level I: Personality traits and states

Personality traits consist of the broad and universal descriptions of a person that are generally stable across time (e.g., Big Five traits), whereas states are ephemeral changes a person experiences: joy, anxiety, fatigue, hunger. Both of these foci have received increased attention with methodological advances in analyzing large and complex data sets in which people are examined multiple times over varying time frames (e.g., Ram & Gerstof, 2009). The examination of both interindividual differences in intraindividual variability is a new opportunity for researchers to address the complexity of personality stability and change.

Personality trait research is arguably one of the most influential contributions from psychological research. Personality traits are linked with a number of physical and mental health outcomes (Crowe, Andel, Pedersen, Fratiglioni, & Gatz, 2006; Siegler, 1994; Wilson, Schneider, Arnold, Bienias, & Bennett, 2007; see also Chapter 6, this volume). Although traits are often described as biologically based, with experience and learning playing little part in changing them (see McCrae & Costa, 2008), others have posited that social roles and environmental influences interact with biological influences in shaping personality traits (Mischel, 2004). For example, several studies have demonstrated high intraindividual variability in trait behaviors as people adapt their behavior to the varying characteristics of their current life circumstances (Almeida, 2005; Fleeson, 2004; Roberts, Walton, & Viechtbauer, 2006). In addition, Srivastava (2010) has argued for the importance of social perception in understanding personality trait models. In other words, traits may be reality-based perceptions of what people want to know about others (Srivastava, Guglielmo, & Beer, 2010). These findings suggest that triangulation (e.g., reliance on both self-report and other-report) may be the best approach for personality assessment.

Level II: Personal action constructs (PACs) and self-regulatory processes

The second level of the six-foci model is most closely tied to the focus of this chapter on developmental self-regulation and social cognitive processes. PACs are cognitive structures influenced by social context that emphasize the motivational aspects, or goal directedness, of human behavior. Self-regulatory processes, over time, enable one to meet goals. Researchers rely on many distinct constructs to measure PACs from slightly different levels of abstraction or temporal frames. Examples of these goal constructs include current concerns (Klinger, 1975), personal projects (Little, 1983), life tasks (Cantor & Kihlstrom, 1987), personal strivings (Emmons, 1986), identity goals (Gollwitzer & Wicklund, 1985) and possible selves (Markus & Nurius, 1986). All PACs are malleable and exist in an organized, hierarchical system of motivational structures (see Figure 18.1, further described later in the chapter).

PACs are also reflective of the developmental tasks, sociohistorical constraints, and opportunities of each age period (Hooker, 1999). Several studies have documented that the domains of goals in which individuals are invested across the lifespan vary by age (e.g., Hoppmann, Gerstorf, Smith, & Klumb, 2007; Nurmi, 1991; Smith & Freund, 2002). For example, younger adults tend to construct goals related to friends and careers, middle-aged adults tend to construct family- and health-related goals, and older adults tend to construct goals related to health or leisure (Cross & Markus, 1991; Hooker, 1992; 1999; Staudinger, 1996).

At the core of self-regulation are a person's attempts to monitor or modify inner states or responses (i.e., thoughts, emotions, behaviors) in order to avoid discrepancies between the current self and future, desired self (Carver & Scheier, 1991, 1998). More recently each

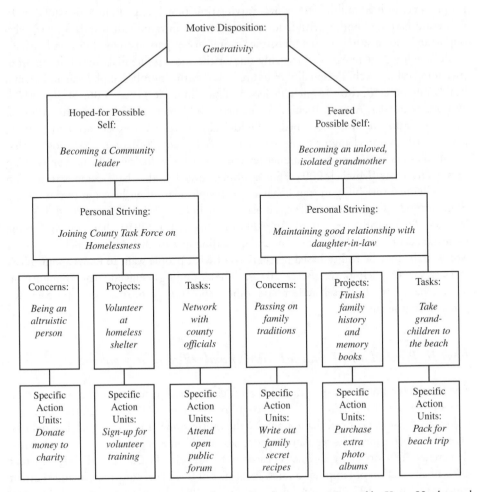

Figure 18.1   A hierarchical representation of motivational constructs. Created by Karen Hooker and Cory Bolkan

aspect of self-regulation across the lifespan and in various life domains has been elaborated upon by researchers (e.g., Baumeister & Vohs, 2004; de Ridder & de Wit, 2006; Lord, Diefendorff, Schmidt, & Hall, 2010; McClelland, Ponitz, Messersmith, & Tominey, 2010). Self-regulation, broadly defined, refers to goal-directed behaviors or the processes involved with one's exercise of control to attain or maintain desired outcomes. In this sense, self-regulatory processes refers to an individual's efforts to select and set goals, evaluate his or her progress toward meeting those goals, and adjust behaviors or cognitions if the current self does not align with the desired goal outcomes (Karoly, 1999; Vancouver & Day, 2005).

Self-efficacy is one example of a self-regulatory process that is crucial to the successful pursuit of PACs. The ability to feel competent and in control of one's goals is an important pathway to well-being (McGregor & Little, 1998). A person with high self-efficacy, for instance, may feel more successful in meeting goals and thus take on increasingly challenging goals. Furthermore, the pursuit and successful achievement of goals that are closely tied to one's self-esteem may increase motivation to achieve those goals. In a study on self-esteem and academics among college students, Crocker, Sommers, and Luhtanen (2002) found that the more participants reported that their self-esteem relied on academic performance, the more their self-esteem increased when they experienced academic success. Conversely, when participants whose self-esteem relied on academic performance experienced academic failure, the more their self-esteem decreased. Crocker, Moeller, & Burson (2010) also note that the simultaneous regulation of self-esteem balanced with concern regarding the impression others may form of them can also hinder the pursuit of important long-term goals. This finding highlights the complex interaction between self-regulation and social cognition in the pursuit of goals.

Self-regulatory processes also relate to the ability to feel in control. Psychological control has been a particularly important area of research because of the way in which it guides behavior and relates to well-being (Bandura, 1997; Heckhausen & Schulz, 1995; Lachman, 2006; Rook & Ituarte, 1999). Maintaining a sense of control throughout adulthood is associated with better health, cognitive functioning, and quality of social relationships (Lachman, Rosnick, & Röcke, 2009). Consequently, control beliefs (Lachman, Neupert, & Agrigoroaei, 2011), along with self-regulatory processes, can facilitate or inhibit motivation and goal setting which elucidates the importance of these processes in conjunction with PACs. We focus more on PACs and self-regulatory processes below, but this level of the personality system is "where the action is" in terms of adapting to change and managing losses. In concert with traits and momentary state influences, our goals, over time, provide the scaffolding on which our life stories are built.

Level III: Life stories and self-narration

People create internalized, evolving stories of their past in order to provide their lives with a sense of meaning, unity, and purpose that continues to develop over the life course as relationships and situations change. The life story also provides us with the richest and deepest sense of knowing a person (McAdams, 1995; Whitbourne, 1986, 1987). By the time one reaches later adulthood, the unique themes and patterns of one's life story come into focus. Self-narration processes necessary to construct the structure of life stories include social cognitive activities such as remembering, reminiscing, and storytelling. These activities influence how and what is revealed in one's life story. Because later life may be a unique time period in which the self is fully developed, new evidence indicates there are meaningful age differences in the narration of life events (Rice & Pasupathi, 2010). For example, older adults may be less engaged in the self-construction of narrating self-discrepant events than younger adults, which may signify that after the self is fully established, people may not as frequently use the narration of personal experiences for the purposes of self-concept development (Rice & Pasupathi, 2010).

Summary of the six-foci model

This framework for conceptualizing personality was presented because it is particularly useful in understanding how and why individuals select and pursue certain goals. For example, a person may be genetically constrained by a predisposition toward certain traits (e.g., high neuroticism), which influence one's actions or sense of comfort in various settings. This model, however, goes beyond the trait model of personality by acknowledging the importance to the personality system of the lifelong development of identity and life stories. The reflection on a life story may also influence action by serving as a reminder that time is finite, subsequently triggering individuals to select and pursue goals that are consistent with how they want their stories "written." When we account for all of the elements of personality, in concert with self-regulation as the guiding mechanism, we have a better understanding of how individuals pursue goals.

More on the Gyroscope of Personality

Goals and self-regulatory processes

Personal goals (what a person is trying to do) and self-regulation (how a person sets, achieves, maintains or avoids goals) are central to the "self." Many researchers also argue that the best way to understand the self over the lifespan is to study both personal goals and self-regulation, which occur in context with age-related changes in both internal and external resources (Brandtstädter; 1999; Freund & Ebner, 2005; Hooker, 1999). The systematic self-regulation of selection, optimization, and compensation helps to explain how people become active agents in guiding their own development via the goals they select, pursue, or abandon.

Selective optimization with compensation (SOC)

The selective optimization with compensation (SOC) model (Baltes & Baltes, 1990; Freund & Baltes, 2000) provides a structure for understanding how self-regulatory mechanisms guide the investment of resources across the lifespan. It is also useful to help explain how older adults can sustain well-being despite potentially contending with multiple losses in later life. The universal adaptive processes of SOC include selecting goals or outcomes, optimizing the means to achieving these outcomes, and compensating for loss in order to obtain successful outcomes (Baltes & Baltes, 1990).

The processes associated with selection refer to how individuals strategically distribute their efforts and resources to specific goals. Selection of specific goals also provides people with a specific direction in which to invest their energy and behavior. Goal selection may be driven by personal preference (e.g., to learn to knit versus to learn to play piano) or by loss of a resource (e.g., time, finances, physical abilities). With age, people are increasingly faced with selecting goals to maintain functioning and offset resource loss. For example, a 70-year-old woman may choose to forego driving based on her deteriorating vision, but she decides to invest in learning how to navigate public transportation. The second process of optimization encompasses one's ability to acquire, practice, or develop resources to achieve the selected goal. In the previous examples, this would refer to the investment of time to learn and practice new skills to knit, play piano, or learn how to interpret bus timetables and routes. The final process, compensation, refers to the development or use of alternative means in order to achieve one's desired level of functioning despite potential decreases in resources. For instance, this may mean compensating for arthritic fingers that may make knitting a difficult goal, by relying on larger, wooden, square-shaft knitting needles. The use of these three universal SOC processes can help individuals increase personal resources, maintain levels of functioning, and regulate losses, which becomes particularly important with age (Baltes & Baltes, 1990; Freund & Baltes, 2000).

Although the selection and pursuit of goals as outlined in the SOC framework may provide a road map to guide individuals in proactively managing their own lives and adapting to life transitions, an empirical question remains: What is it that actually drives our thoughts and behaviors? We argue that internal factors, such as personality, are what drive our motivation to pursue goals. Personality can be understood as the global executive function that regulates other systems, such as emotion, cognition, and motivation (Baltes et al., 2006). Personality, for instance, serves as the foundation for channeling motivation, which leads to behaviors that further reinforce aspects of the self (Staudinger & Bowen, 2010). If a person finds it easy to cultivate friendships, this likely results in motivation and behaviors that lead to building more social contacts (e.g., introduce oneself to a stranger at a party), whereas someone who finds it challenging to interact with others may be less likely to proactively build social networks. Consequently, personality and self play a key role in the self-regulation of goals, human behavior, and emotions.

As individuals face transitions over the lifespan, it is the role of personality to react to and manage developmental changes in psychological subsystems such as emotion, cognition, and motivation (Staudinger & Bowen, 2010). Transitions are a particularly important context for understanding human development because they test the adaptive abilities of an individual. Life often presents individuals with unique or stressful situations, which will require self-regulatory strategies in order to maintain a positive trajectory or to manage potential losses. Transition points can also serve as powerful learning experiences for mastering change in one's life and renegotiating current and future goals.

Models of Self-Regulation

Although it is beyond the scope of this chapter to present a detailed review of all models and theories of self-regulation across the lifespan (e.g., Hoyle, 2010; McClelland et al., 2010) we instead focus on general theories of self-regulation that emphasize how information about the self is processed and how this information affects motivation and behavior in the pursuit of multiple goals. As people set goals and compare their progress against their goals, they make adjustments to their behaviors (i.e., increasing or decreasing effort) or cognitions (i.e., modifying their expectations) if a discrepancy exists between their current self-representation and their future, desired goal outcomes (Carver & Scheier, 1998; Gollwitzer & Bargh, 1996; Higgins, 1987; Karoly, 1999; Pyszczynski & Greenberg, 1987).

An influential framework is Carver and Scheier's (1981, 1998) control-process model of self-regulation. This model emphasizes behavioral standards and the process by which discrepancy between standards and current self are managed. More specifically, individuals first have a sense of how well they are currently performing in line with their goals, but also hold images of desired states or goals that are actively maintained by the self-regulatory system. In this manner, individuals compare the current self-representation to their standard to determine if a discrepancy exists between the two images. If a discrepancy exists, then individuals will make behavioral or cognitive modifications in order to bring the two images closer to alignment.

A similar process is described in self-discrepancy theory (Higgins, 1997, 1998), although in this model, the behavioral standards are identified as either "ideal" or "ought" self-representations. Ideal self-guides are the internal images of desired end states, hopes, accomplishments, or aspiration, whereas ought self-guides serve as internal representations of desired end states related to safety, duties, or responsibilities. Self-discrepancy theory also emphasizes the emotions that result when discrepancies occur between the two self-images and assumes that self-regulation operates differently when serving these two different motivational strategies. More specifically, following an ideal self-guide will orient a person toward the presence or absence of possible outcomes and lead to heightened sensitivity toward opportunities for goal attainment (also known as a promotion focus). Following ought self-guides will orient a person toward presence or absence of negative outcomes, which may heighten sensitivity to goal impediments (also known as a prevention focus).

Both models offer comprehensive descriptions of what people are trying to do and what they are feeling when in the process of self-regulating goals. One limitation to these models, however, is the assumption that self-regulation is always a conscious and effortful process. Although people intentionally set goals and consciously focus on pursuing them, a growing line of evidence is demonstrating that unconscious processes also influence goal-directed behavior (Bargh & Williams, 2006; Johnson, Turner, & Iwata, 2003; Locke & Latham, 2006). Personal goals and self-regulation can be automatically activated by environmental or social cues. Even though personal goals may represent one's innermost thoughts and desires, there is a strong social component to them because they are influenced by one's interaction with others. It is the feedback individuals receive (or perceive) from others which encourages them to proceed with or disengage from certain goals that promote the self. This ongoing feedback serves to continually reconfirm sense of self. For example, Shah (2003a) found that significant others can unconsciously activate goals that the other person has for the self. When he subliminally primed participants with a significant other (e.g., "dad" or "father"), participants increased their goal commitment and task performance (Shah, 2003a). In addition to goal activation,

Shah has also demonstrated that the priming of significant others may also influence an individual's goal expectations, perceived value of goals, and regulatory focus (Shah, 2003b). Both conscious and nonconscious goal setting and goal appraisal may effectively motivate behavior, but it is unclear whether the process is similar in both effortful and automatic pursuits. Nonetheless, at least some of the time, self-regulation requires neither consciousness nor effort.

Possible selves: future-oriented goals

Complementary to self-regulation theories (Carver & Scheier, 1998, 2002; Higgins, 1997), possible selves represent individuals' ideas of what they would like to become (hoped-for selves) and what they are afraid of becoming (feared selves) (see Markus & Nurius, 1986). For example, a student who fears failing at school may have a strong, internal feared self of being unemployed or homeless in the future. Conversely, a struggling writer who hopes for success may have a hoped-for possible self as a recognized and respected author. As demonstrated in these examples, the potential selves of the future (i.e., becoming homeless or becoming recognized) motivate each individual from two distinct self-mechanisms. One individual will likely strive to avoid the feared self, whereas the other will strive to attain the hoped-for self. Possible selves are also resources used to help motivate and defend an individual's sense of self because they incorporate individuals' competence beliefs and values, as well as motivate behavior that propels individuals toward their goals. In other words, possible selves serve as the bridge between one's current state and one's desired hoped-for state (Markus & Ruvolo, 1989). What one expects about the future is dependent on what one is in the present. Possible selves are much more than simple "hopes" or "fears" for the future:

> Possible selves are conceptions of our selves in the future, including, at least to some degree, an experience of being an agent in a future situation. Possible selves get vital parts of their meaning in interplay with the self-concept, which they in turn moderate, as well as from their social and cultural context. (Erikson, 2007, p. 356)

By this definition – a clearer understanding of how possible selves can be seen in relation to meaning and meaning-making in everyday life – we can gain a better understanding of both the functioning and construction of possible selves. One way of creating meaning and coping with life transitions such as parenting, aging, or caregiving, is through goal construction (Nurmi & Salmela-Aro, 2002; Riediger, Freund, & Baltes, 2005), which may include the construction of possible selves (Frazier & Hooker, 2006).

Possible selves and self-regulatory processes

Parallel to self-discrepancy theory (Higgins, 1987) in which goals can be framed as promotion- or prevention-focused, the distinction between goals that are oriented toward gains or growth can also be understood as "approach" goals, and goals that are oriented toward the maintenance of functioning in the face of loss can be described as "avoidance" goals (Emmons, 1991). Similarly, possible selves represent two distinct regulatory mechanisms. Striving for hoped-for possible selves can be understood as a promotion or approach strategy to achieving a desired hoped-for outcome, whereas working to avoid a feared possible self is an example of a prevention or avoidance strategy. The framing of possible selves (i.e., approach versus avoidance) is an interesting area of research as positive and negative self-images (even within the same domain) can relate differentially to life outcomes (Hooker, 1992).

Behavioral inhibition and approach systems (BIS/BAS).   Hoped-for selves (an approach goal) and feared selves (an avoidance goal) relate to research on two general motivational systems that theoretically regulate behavior: behavioral inhibition systems (BIS) and behavioral approach systems (BAS) (Carver & White, 1994). Eysenck (1967) and Gray (1972) were among the first to be interested in physiological models of personality. They each proposed theories based on how individual differences in personality traits may reflect sensitivity of two physiological self-regulatory systems (approach versus avoidance). BIS and BAS systems represent different nervous system structures. The BIS is an aversive motivational system that relates to the experience of anxiety and negative feelings. It is also sensitive to signals of punishment, nonreward, and novelty. The BAS is a behavioral approach or activation system that is sensitive to reward and is associated with more positive feelings, which results in movement toward goals. The preliminary work on BIS/BAS neural motivational theories was based primarily on animal behavior and the effects of pharmacological interventions (Gray, 1972); however, more recent work has been devoted to development of valid and reliable BIS/BAS self-report measures (Carver & White, 1994; Erdle & Rushton, 2010; Gray & McNaughton, 2000; Jackson, 2009) and to the reported imbalance of BIS/BAS levels related to various forms of psychopathology (Biuckians, Miklowitz, & Kim, 2007; Johnson et al., 2003; Scholten, van Honk, Aleman, & Kahn, 2006).

The research on BIS/BAS systems alludes to the importance of individual differences with regard to sensitivities to distinct motivational strategies. Studies on regulatory fit between hoped-for and feared possible selves may also be useful in understanding outcomes such as health promotion or prevention in later life. For example, people who identify with a promotion-focused motivation strategy (approach) tend to be sensitive to positive outcomes, whereas people who identify with a prevention-focused strategy (avoidance) are sensitive to negative outcomes. Koo and Fishbach (2010) have also explored these dynamics of self-regulation and noted the importance of knowledge of the basis for motivation (either goal commitment or lack of goal progress). Finally, a growing awareness of age-related losses (e.g., vulnerability to health problems) may lead older adults to expend greater focus on prevention goals rather than promotion goals. Ultimately, this may result in a tendency for stronger prevention orientations in older adults, particularly in the realm of health, in order to evade threatening health outcomes. Across three separate studies, Lockwood and colleagues examined whether exposure to either excellent or poor physical health exemplars would influence participants' motivation to change health behaviors. Participants were universally motivated by positive exemplars; however, individuals unhappy with their current body shape, as well as older participants, were also motivated by negative exemplars (Lockwood, Chasteen, & Wong, 2005). This finding may signify that participants who experienced resource loss (i.e., poor current body shape) were working to regulate loss via a prevention-orientation goal.

Goal management

General self-regulation models are based on a hierarchical structure of goals where low-level goals serve as the means to attaining higher level goals (Little, 1989; Lord et al., 2010; Lord & Levy, 1994). In order to better understand how goal processes are tied to volition, we have provided a hierarchical representation of motivational constructs in Figure 18.1. When individuals pursue a specific goal, smaller action units are developed in support of the overarching goals. This provides the specific guide or map, which serves to direct and motivate people from smaller daily goals that build toward larger future pursuits. For the purposes of this illustration, we have used the general motive disposition of generativity as the main goal for guiding an individual's behavior. As demonstrated in Figure 18.1, an example of both a generative hoped-for and feared possible self is identified: "To become a community leader" (hoped-for self) and "To avoid becoming an unloved grandmother" (feared self). Both of these future images support the overall goal of being generative, just from differing motivational strategies. Beneath the future-oriented goals fall more present-oriented and ongoing strivings, tasks, projects, and concerns that are also in support of the main motive disposition (i.e., "Volunteer at homeless shelter," "Pass on family traditions"). Finally, these goals translate to very specific day-to-day action units of behavior (i.e., "Attend public forum," "Pack for trip"). The success or failure in one's ability to adapt to life situations may influence how one reconstructs or strives for goals in future situations, which directly impacts developmental trajectories (Brandtstädter, 1999; Brandtstädter & Renner, 1990; Heckhausen & Schulz, 1995). In this manner, individuals exhibit agency in constructing their own lives by selecting their developmental environments (Carver & Scheier, 1991; Freund & Ebner, 2005; Gollwitzer & Bargh, 1996). As highlighted in a lifespan perspective, these actions are representative of the multidirectionality of human development and illustrate how individuals can maximize or maintain resource gains, and regulate resource losses.

In general, human behavior can be understood as inherently goal-directed and driven by both internal and external factors (Bargh & Ferguson, 2000; Brandtstädter, 1999). The planning, evaluating, and modifying of goals (as described in Figure 18.1) is representative of internal cognitive factors that motivate behavior. As mentioned earlier, social interactions and social judgment are examples of external factors that also heavily influence human behavior. Additionally, cognition and emotion are fundamentally integrated in the self-regulation of goals. The emotional or affective system plays an important role in allowing people to balance their current goal-related activities, with the receipt of ongoing information about their goals and how they feel about them. Individual goal standards play an important role for the regulation of well-being (Brandtstädter & Greve, 1994) because the achievement of goals results in positive emotions, whereas the failure to attain goals has been linked to negative emotions. In recent years, the field of neuroscience has provided insights into this process, demonstrating that dopamine (an affect-related neurotransmitter) modulates the maintenance of goals in the prefrontal cortex (see Diefendorff & Lord, 2008), underscoring the significant link between affect and cognition in the pursuit of goals.

The example in Figure 18.1 is a simplified illustration because, in reality, people are constantly pursuing multiple goals at once. As longevity increases, late life will offer unique opportunities for goal selection and the creation of new developmental norms for later adulthood. Goals and strategies to achieve them are an important aspect of managing life transitions to promote optimal outcomes. This means that the adjustment of goal standards may be a protective factor for older adults, who are facing more resource losses in later life (Brandtstädter & Rothermund, 1994).

Older adults appear to manage their goals differently than do younger adults. For example, older adults are more likely than younger adults to express goals as aspirations to grow personally (Bauer & McAdams, 2004), are more engaged in their goal pursuits, and experience more facilitation among their goals (Riediger et al., 2005). Older adults are also more likely to pursue goals that are self-concordant (Sheldon, 2008) and prioritize maintenance by striving to regulate age-related loss rather than seeking new gains (Ebner, Freund, & Baltes, 2006). More specifically, older adults are less likely to pursue growth (or promotion) goals, but may pursue more prevention-focused goals than younger and middle-aged adults. When older adults do report pursuing growth or promotion-focused goals, they are also less strongly related to their subjective well-being (Ebner at al., 2006). Although it can be difficult to disengage from goals that are related to self-esteem, successful self-regulation requires a prudent evaluation of when to disengage from unattainable goals because repeated failure can lead to negative mental and physical health outcomes (Carver & Scheier, 1998; Crocker et al., 2010; Miller & Wrosch, 2007; Wrosch, Miller, Scheier, & Brun de Pontet, 2007).

Older adults may also be more likely to react to resource losses by modifying their goal hierarchies and emphasizing goals that are not affected by the loss of resources, whereas younger adults are more likely to persist in efforts to maintain performance when facing a loss (Freund & Ebner, 2005). This difference is reflective of the motivational orientation across adulthood from a focus toward gains or growth to goals oriented at maintaining performance and functioning in the face of loss and decline and is an appropriate adaptation of self-regulatory strategies within this life context (Ebner et al., 2006; Freund & Baltes, 2000; Freund & Ebner, 2005; Ogilvie, Rose, & Heppen, 2001).

Social Cognition and Goal Processes

Thus far, we have primarily focused on how internal factors (the self, personal goals) can drive human behavior. Although we have noted the importance of social forces on self-regulation, we now turn to focus more on how external factors (social interaction and social judgment) are also influential on goal-directed behaviors across the lifespan. We will also address how aging stereotypes in Western society influence how people interact with elders, as well as how age stereotypes affect one's own aging process.

Aging and age stereotypes

Age is one of the first features that we observe about other people and this information is used to guide how we behave and interact with them (Cuddy & Fiske, 2002; Fiske, 1998; Hummert, 2011). We also tend to form immediate impressions of people based on additional attributes (e.g., age, sex, race, physical characteristics), which shape our attitudes toward other people. Biases against older adults are particularly unique considering most individuals will eventually become part of an aging population. Unfortunately, despite the potential for positive or successful aging, most people tend to face the concept of their own aging with apprehension. People generally view late life negatively as it is often portrayed in the media as a period of decline and disengagement rather than a period of creativity and contribution (e.g., Dahmen & Cozma, 2009).

Most of the research on aging stereotypes has been conducted in the United States, but newer cross-cultural research indicates that while culture may influence the content or structure of age stereotypes, the general nature of age stereotypes still exist (Boduroglu, Yoon, Luo, & Park, 2006; Yun & Lachman, 2006). A recent study in which questionnaires were administered to over 3,000 college students from 26 cultures on six continents yielded a general consensus regarding an expected decline in some areas (e.g., ability to learn, perform everyday tasks, maintain physical attractiveness) but a perceived increase in domains such as wisdom or knowledge, indicating that basic patterns of perceptions about aging may be culturally shared (Löckenhoff et al, 2009). These findings are also in line with other empirical studies based on the stereotype content model in which older people are evaluated ambivalently, or as high on warmth but low on competence (Cuddy, Fiske, & Glick, 2008; Fiske, Cuddy, & Glick, 2007), a combination referred to as "dear, but doddering" (Cuddy & Fiske, 2002).

The aging self

The negative effects of aging stereotypes have implications for the personal awareness of one's own aging. How is it that the majority of older adults maintain a positive sense of self when contending with age-related declines and discrimination? Although theories that emphasize adaptation by the regulation of losses (e.g., the SOC model) have been useful to explain this phenomenon, other frameworks that focus on self and identity can highlight the plasticity and resilience of older adults (Sneed & Whitbourne, 2005). The ways in which individuals negotiate changes and challenges in life are central to the self. For example, based on identity process theory (Whitbourne, 1996), age-related changes in adulthood are a result of negotiating equilibrium between identity and experience. Over time, the ability to integrate age-related changes into one's identity and still maintain a positive view of oneself is an important element of successful aging and mental health (Sneed & Whitbourne, 2003).

According to identity process theory (Whitbourne, 1996), an adaptive approach to aging is the ability to maintain equilibrium in the processes of identity assimilation (evaluating identity-salient experiences and incorporating them into sense of self to maintain a sense of self-consistency) and identity accommodation (modifying identity to adjust to new discrepant experiences). People who maintain this balance in identity may be more likely to make positive changes in their self-concept to maintain a coherent sense of self; this also enables people to evaluate themselves realistically over time (Sneed & Whitbourne, 2005). For example, with age, people may face more identity-discrepant experiences (e.g., decline in physical abilities) and need to modify their sense of self in order to maintain a coherent identity (e.g., acknowledge physical limitations and adjust expectations).

Similarly, the concept of awareness of age-related change (AARC) (Diehl and Wahl, 2010) refers to an individual's sense that something in his or her life has changed due to aging. AARC has implications for which goals individuals may select or pursue. Chronological age is an important societal indicator by which we evaluate whether or not people are developing as social norms dictate; however, on an individual level, as people age they also begin to become more aware of their own life course. More specifically, people have a tendency to reevaluate their own lives from time-since-birth to time-left-to-live (Neugarten, 1968, 1979) and the subjective sense of remaining lifetime has significant effects on motivational, emotional, and cognitive processes (Carstensen, 2006).

The self-awareness of aging is relevant for setting or changing goals that guide our behavior and may also be linked to self-efficacy and outcome expectancy for those goals. For example, the first observation of one's own gray hair, wrinkles, and perceived changes in physical stamina can trigger self-regulatory processes with the intention to preserve one's self-identity and may result in health behavior changes (Diehl & Wahl, 2010; Sneed & Whitbourne, 2003). Awareness of age-related changes may elicit a diverse array of reactions as individuals find meaning in their own lives. Diehl and Wahl (2010) postulate that it may trigger temporal or social comparison processes (e.g., comparing one's current performance to one's past performance versus comparing one's own performance to others' performance) or a recalibration of personal goals as a mechanism for self-regulating these changes. The construction of possible selves is useful to this process, as the conceptions of future selves have an impact on current self-functioning (Packer & Chasteen, 2006).

Age stereotype process

Discrimination and the expression of prejudice toward social groups can be the result of multiple social psychological processes (e.g., attitudes, social norms, social identity concerns). Historically, social psychologists have examined age stereotypes as cognitive schemas in which people store overgeneralized beliefs and expectations about the traits and behaviors of another person or group. People may apply this mental representation – whether accurate or not – in social settings and use stereotypes to guide their social behavior as well as guide which additional information they select, process, and remember (Cuddy & Fiske, 2002; Fiske, 1998).

Two models (the prototype and the exemplar) have been established to help explain how one determines how well others fit into certain categories. The prototype refers to how people subjectively categorize others based on how well they perceive them to resemble the average category member. A prototype does not need to be an actual person, but rather an imagined individual who embodies the central tendencies of a group's key attributes. For example, the prototype for "elderly person" may be portrayed by such qualities as being slow and confused. Prototypes are simple abstractions, derived from one's life experiences. Exemplars, on the other hand, are memories of actual people or events. People tend to have multiple exemplars for multiple groups; for example, exemplars of "elderly people" may include: (a) the vivacious 89-year old Betty White, (b) a frail 90-year-old neighbor, or (c) a loving but demanding great-grandparent. The content of aging stereotypes generally consists of abstract knowledge from prototypes as well as information derived from exemplars in one's own life. These various mental representations provide the foundation for how people try to make sense of and organize their internal representations of others (Cuddy & Fiske, 2002).

Activation of age stereotypes

The information in aging stereotypes guides individuals' interactions with others, as well as influences their interpretation of social cues, and can change their behaviors in social settings. This ultimately leads people to behave in ways that continue to confirm the age stereotype. Infantilizing or patronizing speech when interacting with older adults is just one example of how this overaccomodation behavior activation (Giles & Gasiorek, 2011) results in undesirable outcomes for older adults. Overaccomodation can undermine older adults' ability to function effectively (e.g., Levy, 2003; Ryan, Kennaley, Pratt, & Shumovich, 2000; Ryan, Anas, & Gruneir, 2006).

The activation of age stereotyping can also affect one's social behavior subconsciously. In a classic study, after having been subliminally primed on a scrambled sentence task with words associated with stereotypes of older people, participants actually walked slower when leaving the experiment than did control group participants who had seen age-neutral words (Bargh, Chen, & Burrows, 1996). This finding suggested that people use stereotypic information not only to direct their behavior at others, but toward their own behavior in social interactions. In fact, it has been demonstrated in several studies that older adults often internalize societal aging stereotypes that can have negative consequences (Hess, 2006; Levy, 1996, 2003; Levy, Slade, Kunkel & Kasl, 2002). For example, Levy (1996) found that older adults who engaged in negative age-related self-stereotyping performed significantly worse on a memory task than those who engaged in positive self-stereotyping. Furthermore, Levy and her colleagues also discovered that individuals with positive self-perceptions lived approximately 7.5 years longer than those with less positive self-perceptions (Levy et al., 2002).

More recently, researchers have focused on the harmful effects of negative aging stereotypes on memory performance in older adults (Andreoletti & Lachman, 2004;

Chasteen, Bhattacharyya, Horhota, Tam, & Hasher, 2005; Hess, Auman, Colcombe, & Rahhal, 2003; Hess, Hinson, & Statham, 2004; Levy & Leifheit-Limson, 2009; Lineweaver, Berger, & Hertzog, 2009). Hess and colleagues (2004) conducted two experiments involving young and older participants in which both groups were implicitly primed with age stereotypes. The memory recall of the older participants, but not the younger participants, was adversely affected by the negative age stereotypes. Levy and Leifheit-Limson (2009) also found that subliminally inducing physical negative aging stereotypes had a harmful effect on the balance performance of older adults. In yet another study, Lineweaver and colleagues (2009) presented participants with targets of all ages, who were described with either positive or negative age stereotype traits. The participants were then asked to evaluate the memory for each target. Although participants reported a similar pattern of memory decline as each target increased in age, they also predicted the most drastic memory decline for targets who were both older and described with negative age stereotype traits.

While these studies indicate that age stereotypes may lead to negative attitudes and behavior toward older people, in contrast, it is also important to consider the potential benefits of positive age stereotypes. For example, in the Hess et al. (2004) study the implicit positive priming resulted in significantly better memory recall in older adults when compared to participants who were implicitly primed with negative age stereotypes. Similarly, when Levy and Leifheit-Limson (2009) presented older adults with positive physical aging stereotypes, they found better balance performance in their participants. Finally, Lineweaver et al. (2009) also noted that when participants evaluated targets who fit positive stereotypes of aging (e.g., fun, social, independent), then they expected memory to be better overall and to decline less with age when compared to targets who fit negative stereotypes of aging (e.g., afraid, miserly, wary). These findings indicate that positive age stereotypes may be useful in maintaining health and positive outcomes.

Conclusions

The research presented throughout this chapter illustrates the complexity of self-regulation and social cognition in adult development. We see personality, broadly defined, as the global function that manages emotions, cognitions, and behaviors. We also described self-regulation as the internal gyroscope, providing direction and equilibrium in service of one's goal pursuits. Over time, as people experience increases or decreases in personal resources, effective self-regulation is necessary in order to adapt to change. In addition to internal psychological processes, external factors, such as social context, play an important role in goals that people select, pursue, or abandon. Future researchers should continue explorations into the intersection between personality and self-regulatory and social cognitive processes. Although there are many avenues of research that will expand our understanding in this area, we will provide a few specific examples.

First, although goal pursuit is generally considered a conscious task, more research exploring nonconscious goal-oriented behaviors and the process by which significant others may automatically activate goal processes would be useful. The awareness and interpretation of a goal may have implications for motivation and affect (Oettingen, Grant, Smith, Skinner, & Gollwitzer, 2006). For example, how might nonconscious goal pursuits be primed by omnipresent age stereotypes projected by others and how would it influence behavior and well-being? Secondly, it is important to take into account individual personality differences in the self-regulation of goals. To achieve this aim, researchers should continue to build on daily life time-sampling methods and incorporate them into long-term longitudinal studies. A richer understanding of individual differences in lifespan trajectories can be attained as researchers explore how daily, weekly, and monthly life processes are tied to emotional, cognitive, and motivational systems (Hoppmann & Riediger, 2009; Nesselroade & Ghisletta, 2003). Finally, building on neural models of behavioral inhibition and approach (BIS/BAS) would also provide more detailed information regarding individual sensitivity to specific motivational strategies (i.e., an approach or avoidance focus to goal pursuits).

The examination of individual personality differences would also help to clarify the process by which age stereotypes and self-perceptions may shape age identities over time. Levy (2009) recently introduced a theory of stereotype embodiment to clarify the pathways in which aging stereotypes become increasingly self-relevant and ultimately affect physical and mental functioning. Stereotype embodiment is a lifelong process that begins in early childhood and is shaped by culture. By exploring the self in a social context, we can begin to identify both individual and situational characteristics that may make some people more susceptible or more resilient to the influence of age stereotypes (Hummert, 2011).

In summary, across the lifespan, well into later life, we are continually refining ourselves through our goal pursuits and the feedback we receive from others. How we see ourselves and how others see us are important influences on the activities we pursue in life.

References

Almeida, D. (2005). Resilience and vulnerability to daily stressors assessed via diary methods. *Current Directions in Psychological Science, 14,* 64–68.

Andreoletti, C., & Lachman, M. E. (2004). Susceptibility and resilience to memory aging stereotypes: Education matters more than age. *Experimental Aging Research, 30,* 129–148.

Baltes, P. B., & Baltes, M. M. (1990). Psychological perspectives on successful aging: The model of selective optimization with compensation. In P. B. Baltes & M. M. Baltes (Eds.), *Successful aging: Perspectives from the behavioral sciences* (pp. 1 – 34). New York: Cambridge University Press.

Baltes, P. B., Lindenberger, U., & Staudinger, U. M. (2006). Life span theory in developmental psychology. In W. Damon & R. M. Lerner (Eds.), *Handbook of child psychology: Vol. 1. Theoretical models of human development* (6th ed., pp. 569–664). New York: Wiley.

Bandura, A. (1997). *Self-efficacy: The exercise of control.* New York: Freeman.

Bargh, J. A., Chen, M., & Burrows, L. (1996). Automaticity of social behavior: Direct effects of trait construct and stereotype activation on action. *Journal of Personality and Social Psychology, 71,* 230–44.

Bargh, J. A., & Ferguson, M. J. (2000). Beyond behaviorism: On the automaticity of higher mental processes. *Psychological Bulletin, 126*(6), 925–945.

Bargh, J. A., & Williams, E. L. (2006). The automaticity of social life. *Current Directions in Psychological Science, 15,* 1–4.

Bauer, J. J., & McAdams, D. P. (2004). Growth goals, maturity, and well-being. *Developmental Psychology, 40,* 114–127.

Baumeister, R. F., & Vohs, K. D. (2004). *Handbook of self-regulation: Research, theory, and applications.* New York: Guilford Press.

Biuckians, A., Miklowitz, D. J., & Kim, E. Y. (2007). Behavioral activation, inhibition, and mood symptoms in early-onset bipolar disorder. *Journal of Affective Disorders, 97*(1–3), 71–76.

Boduroglu, A., Yoon, C., Luo T., & Park, C.D (2006). Stereotypes about young and old adults: A comparison of Chinese and American cultures. *Gerontology, 52*(5), 324–333.

Brandtstädter, J. (1999). The self in action and development: Cultural, biosocial, and ontogenetic bases of intentional self-development. In J. Brandtstädter & R. M. Lerner (Eds.), *Action and self-development: Theory and research through the life span* (pp. 37–66). Thousand Oaks, CA: Sage.

Brandtstädter, J., & Greve, W. (1994). The aging self: Stabilizing and protective processes. *Developmental Review, 14,* 52–80.

Brandtstädter, J., & Renner, G. (1990). Tenacious goal pursuit and flexible goal adjustment: Explication and age-related analysis of assimilative and accommodative strategies of coping. *Psychology and Aging, 5,* 58–67.

Brandtstädter, J., & Rothermund, K. (1994). Self-percepts of control in middle and later adulthood: Buffering losses by rescaling goals. *Psychology and Aging, 9,* 265–273.

Cantor, N., & Kihlstrom, J. F. (1987). *Personality and social intelligence.* Englewood Cliffs, NJ: Prentice-Hall. Carstensen, L. L. (2006). The influence of a sense of time on human development. *Science, 312*(5782), 1913–1915.

Carver, C. S., & Scheier, M. F. (1981). *Attention and self-regulation: A control theory approach to human behavior.* New York: Springer.

Carver, C. S., & Scheier, M. F. (1991). Self-regulation and the self. In J. Strauss & G. R. Goethals (Eds.), *The self: Interdisciplinary approaches* (pp. 168–207). New York: Springer.

Carver, C. S., & Scheier, M. F. (1998). *On the self-regulation of behavior.* New York: Cambridge University Press.

Carver, C. S., & Scheier, M. F. (2002). Control processes and self-organization as complementary principles underlying behavior. *Personality and Social Psychology Review, 6,* 304–315.

Carver, C. S., & White, T. L. (1994). Behavioral inhibition, behavioral activation, and affective responses to impending reward and punishment: The BIS/BAS scales. *Journal of Personality and Social Psychology, 67,* 319–333.

Chasteen, A. L., Bhattacharyya, S., Horhota, M., Tam, R., & Hasher, L. (2005). How feelings of stereotype threat influence older adults' memory performance. *Experimental Aging Research, 31,* 235–260.

Crocker, J., Sommers, S., & Luhtanen, R. (2002). Hopes dashed and dreams fulfilled: Contingencies of self-worth in the graduate school admissions process. *Personality and Social Psychology Bulletin, 28,* 1275–1286.

Crocker, J., Moeller, S., & Burson, A. (2010). The costly pursuit of self-esteem: Implications for self-regulation. In R. Hoyle (Ed.), *Handbook of personality and self-regulation* (pp. 403–429). Oxford: Wiley-Blackwell.

Cross, S., & Markus, H. (1991). Possible selves across the life span. *Human Development, 34,* 230–255.

Crowe, M., Andel, R., Pedersen, N. L., Fratiglioni, L., & Gatz, M. (2006). Personality and risk of cognitive impairment 25 years later. *Psychology and Aging, 21,* 573–580.

Cuddy, A. J. C., & Fiske, S. T. (2002). Doddering but dear: Process, content and function in stereotyping of older persons. In T. D. Nelson (Ed.), *Ageism: Stereotyping and prejudice against older adults* (pp. 3–26). Cambridge, MA: MIT Press.

Cuddy, A. J. C., Fiske, S. T., & Glick, P. (2008). Warmth and competence as universal dimensions of social perception: The Stereotype Content Model and the BIAS Map. In M. P. Zanna (Ed.), *Advances in experimental social psychology* (vol. 40, pp. 61–149). New York: Academic Press.

Dahmen, N. S., & Cozma, R. (Eds.). (2009). *Media takes: On aging.* Sacramento, CA: International Longevity Center–USA and Aging Services of California.

de Ridder, D. T. D., & de Wit, J. B. F. (Eds.). (2006). *Self-regulation in health behavior* Chichester, UK: Wiley.

Diehl, M., & Wahl, H.W. (2010). Awareness of age-related change: Examination of a (mostly) unexplored concept. *Journal of Gerontology: Social Sciences, 65B*(3), 340–350.

Diefendorff, J. M., & Lord, R. G. (2008). Self-regulation and goal striving processes. In R. Kanfer, G. Chen, & R. D. Pritchard (Eds.), *Work motivation: Past, present, and future* (pp. 151–196). San Francisco, CA: Jossey-Bass.

Ebner, N. C., Freund, A. M., & Baltes, P. (2006). Developmental changes in goal orientation from youth to late adulthood: From striving for gains to maintenance and prevention of losses. *Psychology and Aging, 21,* 664–678.

Emmons, R. A. (1986). Personal strivings: An approach to personality and subjective well-being. *Journal of Personality and Social Psychology, 51,* 1058–1068.

Emmons, R. A. (1991). Personal strivings, daily life events and psychological and physical well-being. *Journal of Personality, 59,* 455–472.

Erdle, S., & Rushton, J. P. (2010). The General Factor of Personality, BIS-BAS, expectancies of reward and punishment, self-esteem, and positive and negative affect. *Personality and Individual Differences, 48,* 762–766.

Erikson, M. G. (2007). The meaning of the future: Toward a more specific definition of possible selves, *Review of General Psychology 11*(4), 348–358.

Eysenck, H. J. (1967). *The biological basis of personality.* Springfield, IL: Charles C. Thomas.

Fiske, S. T. (1998). Stereotyping, prejudice, and discrimination. In D. T. Gilbert, S. T. Fiske, & C. Lindzey (Eds.), *The handbook of social psychology* (4th ed.). New York: McGraw–Hill.

Fiske, S. T., Cuddy, A. J. C., & Glick, P. (2007). Universal dimensions of social cognition: Warmth, then competence. *Trends in Cognitive Sciences, 11,* 77–83.

Fleeson, W. (2004). Moving personality beyond the person-situation debate. *Current Directions in Psychological Science, 13,* 83–87.

Frazier, L. D., & Hooker, K. (2006). Possible selves in adult development: Linking theory and research. In C. Dunkel & J. Kerpelman (Eds.), *Possible selves: Theory, research, and application* (pp. 41–59). Huntington, NY: Nova Science.

Freund, A. M., & Baltes, P. B. (2000). The orchestration of selection, optimization and compensation: An action-theoretical conceptualization of a theory of developmental regulation. In W. J. Perrig & A. Grob (Eds.), *Control of human behavior, mental processes, and consciousness: Essays in honor of the 60th birthday of August Flammer* (pp. 35–58). Mahwah, NJ: Erlbaum.

Freund, A. M., & Ebner, N. C. (2005). The aging self: Shifting from promoting gains to balancing losses. In W. Greve, K. Rothermund, & D. Wentura (Eds.), *The adaptive self: Personal continuity and intentional self-development* (pp. 185–202). Ashland, OH: Hogrefe & Huber.

Giles, H., & Gasiorek, J. (2011). Intergenerational communication practices. In K. W. Schaie & S. L. Willis (Eds.), *Handbook of the psychology of aging* (7th ed., pp. 233–247). London: Elsevier.

Gollwitzer, P. M., & Bargh, J. A. (Eds.) (1996). *The psychology of action: Linking cognition and motivation to behavior.* New York: Guilford Press.

Gollwitzer, P. M., & Wicklund, R. A. (1985). The pursuit of self-defining goals. In J. Kuhl & J. Beckmann (Eds.), *Action control: From cognition to behavior* (pp. 61–88). Berlin: Springer.

Gray, J. A. (1972). The psychophysiological basis of introversion–extraversion: A modification of Eysenck's theory. In V. D. Nebylitsyn & J. A. Gray (Eds.), *The biological bases of individual behavior* (pp. 182–205). New York: Academic Press.

Gray, J. A., & McNaughton, N. (2000). *The neuropsychology of anxiety: An enquiry into the functions of the septo-hippocampal system.* Oxford: Oxford University Press.

Heckhausen, J., & Schulz, R. (1995). A life-span theory of control. *Psychological Review, 102,* 284–304.

Hess, T. M. (2006). Attitudes toward aging and their effects on behavior. In J. E. Birren & K.W. Schaie (Eds.), *Handbook of the psychology of aging* (6th ed., pp. 379–406). San Diego, CA: Academic Press.

Hess, T. M., Auman, C., Colcombe, S. J., & Rahhal, T.A. (2003). The impact of stereotype threat on age differences in memory performance. *Journal of Gerontology: Psychological Sciences, 58B,* P3–P11.

Hess, T. M., Hinson, J. T., & Statham, J.A. (2004). Explicit and implicit stereotype activation effects on memory: Do age and awareness moderate the impact of priming? *Psychology and Aging, 19,* 495–505.

Higgins, E. T. (1987). Self-discrepancy: A theory relating self and affect. *Psychological Review, 94*(3), 319–340.

Higgins, E. T. (1997). Beyond pleasure and pain. *American Psychologist, 52,* 1280–1300.

Higgins, E. T. (1998). Promotion and prevention: Regulatory focus as a motivational principle. In M. Zanna (Ed.), *Advances in experimental social psychology* (vol. 30, pp. 1–46). San Diego, CA: Academic Press.

Hooker, K. (1992). Possible selves and perceived health in older adults and college students. *Journal of Gerontology: Psychological Sciences, 47,* 85–95.

Hooker, K. (1999). Possible selves in adulthood: Incorporating teleonomic relevance into studies of the self. In F. Blanchard-Fields & T. Hess (Eds.) *Social cognition and aging* (pp. 97–122). New York: Academic Press.

Hooker, K., Frazier, L., & Bolkan, C. (2003, August). *Possible selves: Selection mechanism of the distributed self in action.* Paper presented at the 111th Annual Convention of the American Psychological Association, Toronto, Canada.

Hooker, K., Hoppmann, C., & Siegler, I. C. (2010). Personality: Life span compass for health. In K. E. Whitfield (Ed.) *Annual review of gerontology and geriatrics* (vol. 30, pp. 199–230). New York: Springer.

Hooker, K. & McAdams, D. P. (2003). Personality reconsidered: A new agenda for aging research. *Journal of Gerontology: Psychological Sciences, 58*(6), P296–P304.

Hoppmann, C. A., Gerstorf, D., Smith, J., & Klumb, P. L. (2007). Linking possible selves and behavior: Do domain-specific hopes and fears translate into daily activities in very old age? *Journal of Gerontology: Psychological Sciences, 62B*(2), 104–111.

Hoppmann, C. A., & Riediger, M. (2009). Ambulatory assessment in lifespan psychology: An overview of current status and new trends. *European Psychologist, 14,* 98–108.

Hoyle, R. H. (2010). Personality and self-regulation. In R. H. Hoyle (Ed.), *Handbook of personality and self-regulation* (pp. 1–18). Malden, MA: Wiley-Blackwell.

Hummert, M. L. (2011). Age stereotypes and aging. In K. W. Schaie & S. L. Willis (Eds.), Handbook of the psychology of aging (7th ed., pp. 249–262). London: Elsevier.

Jackson, C. J. (2009). Jackson-5 scales of revised Reinforcement Sensitivity Theory (r- RST) and their application to dysfunctional real world outcomes. *Journal of Research in Personality, 43,* 556–569.

Johnson, S. L., Turner, R. J., & Iwata, N. (2003). BIS/BAS levels and psychiatric disorder: An epidemiological study. *Journal of Psychopathology and Behavioral Assessment, 25,* 25–36.

Karoly, P. (1999). A goal systems–self-regulatory perspective on personality, psychopathology, and change. *Review of General Psychology, 3*(4), 264–291.

Klinger, E. (1975). Consequences of commitment to and disengagement from incentives. *Psychological Review, 82,* 1–25.

Koo, M., & Fishbach, A. (2010). Climbing the goal ladder: How upcoming actions increase level of aspiration. *Journal of Personality and Social Psychology, 99*(1), 1–13.

Lachman, M. E. (2006). Perceived control over aging-related declines: Adaptive beliefs and behaviors. *Current Directions in Psychological Science, 15,* 282–286.

Lachman, L., Neupert, S. D., & Agrigoroaei, S. (2011). The relevance of control beliefs for health and aging. In K.W. Schaie & S. L. Willis (Eds.), *Handbook of the psychology of aging* (7th ed., pp. 175–190). London: Elsevier.

Lachman, M.E., Rosnick, C., & Röcke, C. (2009). The rise and fall of control beliefs in adulthood: Cognitive and biopsychosocial antecedents and consequences of stability and change over nine years. In H. Bosworth and C. Hertzog (Eds.), *Aging and cognition: Research methodologies and empirical advances* (pp. 143–160). Washington, DC: American Psychological Association

Levy, B. (1996). Improving memory in old age by implicit self-stereotyping. *Journal of Personality and Social Psychology, 71,* 1092–1107.

Levy, B. (2003). Mind matters: Cognitive and physical effects of aging self-stereotypes. *Journal of Gerontology, 58B*(4), 203–211.

Levy, B. R. (2009). Stereotype embodiment: A psychosocial approach to aging. *Current Directions in Psychological Science, 18,* 332–336.

Levy, B. R., & Leifheit-Limson, E. (2009), The stereotype-matching effect: Greater influence on functioning when age stereotypes correspond to outcomes. *Psychology and Aging, 24,* 230–233.

Levy, B. R., Slade, M., Kunkel, S., & Kasl, S. (2002). Longitudinal benefit of positive self-perceptions of aging on functioning health. *Journal of Gerontology: Psychological Sciences, 57B,* 409–417.

Lineweaver, T. T., Berger, A. K., & Hertzog, C. (2009). Expectations about memory change are impacted by aging stereotypes. *Psychology and Aging, 24,* 169–176.

Little, B. R. (1983). Personal projects: A rationale and method for investigation. *Environment and Behavior,15*(3), 273–309.

Little, B. R. (1989). Personal projects analysis: Trivial pursuits, magnificent obsessions, and the search for coherence. In D. M. Buss & N. Cantor (Eds.), *Personality psychology: Recent trends and emerging directions* (pp. 15–31), New York: Springer.

Locke, E. A., Latham, G. P. (2006). New directions in goal-setting theory. *Current Directions in Psychological Science, 15,* 265–268.

Löckenhoff, C. E., De Fruyt, F., Terracciano, A., McCrae, R. R., De Bolle, M., Costa, P.T. Jr. . . . Yik, M. (2009). Perceptions of aging across 26 cultures and their culture-level associates. *Psychology and Aging, 24,* 941–954.

Lockwood, P., Chasteen, A. L., & Wong, C. (2005). Age and regulatory focus determine preferences for health-related role models. *Psychology & Aging, 20,* 376–389.

Lord, R. G., Diefendorff, J. M., Schmidt, A. M., & Hall, R. J. (2010). Self-regulation at work. *Annual Review of Psychology, 61,* 543–568.

Lord, R. G., & Levy, P. E. (1994). Moving from cognition to action: A control-theory perspective. *Applied Psychology—An International Review, 43,* 335–398.

Markus, H. R., & Nurius P. (1986). Possible selves. *American Psychologist, 41,* 954–969.

Markus, H., & Ruvolo, A. (1989). Possible selves: Personalized representations of goals. In L. A. Pervin (Ed.), *Goal concepts in personality and social psychology* (pp. 211–241). Hillsdale, NJ: Erlbaum.

McAdams, D. P. (1995). What do we know when we know a person? *Journal of* Personality, *63*(3), 365–396.

McClelland, M. M., Ponitz, C. C., Messersmith, E., & Tominey, S. (2010). Self-regulation: The integration of cognition and emotion. In R. Lerner (Ed.), *Handbook of life-span human development. Vol. 1: Cognition, biology and methods* (pp. 509–553). Hoboken, NJ: Wiley.

McCrae, R., & Costa (2008). *The five-factor theory of personality.* In O. P. John, R. W. Robins, & L. A. Pervin (Eds.), *Handbook of personality* (pp. 159–181). New York: Guilford Press.

McCrae, R. R., & Löckenhoff, C. E. (2010). Self-regulation and the five factor model of personality traits. In R. Hoyle (Ed.), *Handbook of personality and self-regulation* (pp. 145–168). Oxford: Wiley-Blackwell.

McGregor, I., & Little, B. R. (1998). Personal projects, happiness and meaning: On doing well and being yourself. *Journal of Personality and Social Psychology, 74,* 494–512.

Morf, C. C., & Horvath, S. (2010). Self-regulation processes and their signatures: Dynamics of the self-system. In R. H. Hoyle (Ed.), *Handbook of personality and self-regulation* (pp. 117–144). Malden, MA: Wiley-Blackwell.

Miller, G. E., & Wrosch, C. (2007). You've gotta know when to fold 'em: Goal disengagement and systematic inflammation in adolescence. *Psychological Science, 18,* 773–777.

Mischel, W. (2004). Toward an integrative science of the person. In S. T. Fiske, D. L. Schacter, & C. Zahn-Waxler (Eds.), *Annual review of psychology* (vol. 55, pp. 1–19). Palo Alto, CA: Annual Reviews.

Nesselroade, J. R., & Ghisletta, P. (2003). Structuring and measuring change over the life span. In U. M. Staudinger & U. Lindenberger (Eds.), *Understanding human development: Dialogues with lifespan psychology* (pp. 317–337). Dordrecht, Netherlands: Kluwer.

Neugarten, B. L. (1979). Time, age, and the life cycle. *American Journal of Psychiatry, 136,* 887–894.

Neugarten, B. L. (1968). *Middle age and aging: A reader in social psychology.* Chicago: University of Chicago Press.

Noftle, E. E., & Fleeson, W. (2010). Age differences in Big Five behavior averages and variabilities across the adult life span: Moving beyond retrospective, global summary accounts of personality. *Psychology and Aging, 25,* 95–107.

Nurmi, J-E. (1991). How do adolescents see their future? A review of the development of future orientation and planning. *Developmental Review, 11,* 1–59.

Nurmi, J., & Salmela-Aro (2002). Goal construction, reconstruction and depressive symptoms in a life-span context: The transition from school to work. *Journal of Personality, 70*(3), 385–420.

Packer, D. J., & Chasteen, A. (2006). Looking to the future: How possible aged selves influence prejudice toward older adults. *Social Cognition, 24*(3), 218–247.

Pyszczynski, T., & Greenberg, J. (1987). Self-regulatory perseveration and the depressive self-focusing style: A self-awareness theory of the development and maintenance of reactive depression. *Psychological Bulletin, 102,* 122–138

Oettingen, G., Grant, H., Smith, P., Skinner, M., & Gollwitzer, P. (2006). Nonconscious goal pursuit: Acting in an explanatory vacuum. *Journal of Experimental Psychology, 42,* 668–675.

Ogilvie, D. M., Rose, K. M, & Heppen, J. B. (2001). A comparison of personal project motives in three age groups. *Journal of Basic and Applied Psychology, 63,* 207–215.

Ram, N., & Gerstorf, D. (2009). Time-structured and net intraindividual variability: Tools for examining the development of dynamic characteristics and processes. *Psychology and Aging, 24,* 778–791.

Rice C, & Pasupathi M, (2010). Reflecting on self-relevant experiences: Adult age differences. *Developmental Psychology, 46*(2), 479–490.

Riediger, M., Freund, A. M., & Baltes, P. B. (2005). Managing life through personal goals: Intergoal facilitation and intensity of goal pursuit in younger and older adulthood. *Journal of Gerontology: Psychological Sciences, 60B,* P84–P91.

Roberts, B. W., Walton, K. E., & Viechtbauer, W. (2006) Patterns of mean-level change in personality traits across the life course: A meta-analysis of longitudinal studies. *Psychological Bulletin, 132,* 3–27.

Rook, K. S., & Ituarte, P. H. G. (1999). Social control, social support, and companionship in older adults' family relationships and friendships. *Personal Relationships, 6,* 199–211.

Ryan, E. B., Anas, A. P., & Gruneir, A. J. S. (2006). Evaluations of overhelping and underhelping communication: Do old age and physical disability matter? *Journal of Language and Social Psychology, 25*(1), 97–107.

Ryan, E. B., Kennaley, D. E., Pratt, M. W., & Shumovich, M. A. (2000). Evaluations by staff, residents, and community seniors of patronizing speech: Impact of passive, assertive, or humorous responses. *Psychology and Aging, 15,* 272–285.

Scholten, M. R., van Honk, J., Aleman, A., & Kahn, R. S. *(2006).* Behavioral inhibition system (BIS), behavioral activation system (BAS) and schizophrenia: Relationship with psychopathology and physiology. *Journal of Psychiatric Research, 40,* 638–645.

Siegler, I. C. (1994). Hostility and risk: Demographic and lifestyle variables. In A. W. Siegman & T. W. Smith (Eds.), *Anger hostility and the heart* (pp. 199–214). Hillsdale, NJ: Erlbaum.

Shah, J. Y. (2003a). Automatic for the people: How representations of significant others implicitly affect goal pursuit. *Journal of Personality and Social Psychology, 84,* 661–681.

Shah, J. Y. (2003b). The motivational looking glass: How significant others implicitly affect goal appraisals. *Journal of Personality and Social Psychology, 85,* 424–439.

Sheldon, K. M. (2008). Changes in goal-striving across the life span: Do people learn to select more self-concordant goals as they age? In M. C. Smith & T. G. Reio, Jr. (Eds.), *Handbook of adult development and learning* (pp. 551–567). Mahwah, NJ: Erlbaum.

Smith, J., & Freund, A. M. (2002). The dynamics of possible selves in old age. *Journal of Gerontology: Psychological Sciences, 57*(6), 492–500.

Sneed, J. R., & Whitbourne, S. K. (2003). Identity processing and self-consciousness in middle and later adulthood. *Journal of Gerontology: Psychological Sciences and Social Sciences, 58,* 313–319.

Sneed, J. R., & Whitbourne, S. K. (2005). Models of the aging self. *Journal of Social Issues, 61,* 375–388.

Srivastava, S. (2010). The five-factor model describes the structure of social perceptions. *Psychological Inquiry, 21* (1), 69–75.

Srivastava, S., Guglielmo, S., & Beer, J. S. (2010). Perceiving others' personalities: Examining the dimensionality, assumed similarity to the self, and stability of perceiver effects. *Journal of Personality and Social Psychology, 98,* 520–534.

Staudinger, U. M. (1996). Wisdom and the social-interactive foundation of the mind. In P. B. Baltes & U. M. Staudinger (Eds.), *Interactive minds: Life-span perspectives on the social foundation of cognition* (pp. 276–315). Cambridge, UK: Cambridge University Press.

Staudinger, U. M., & Bowen, C. E. (2010). Lifespan perspectives on positive personality development in adulthood and old age. In A. Freund and M. Lamb (Eds.), *Handbook of lifespan psychology. Vol. 2: Social and emotional development* (pp. 254–297). Hoboken, NJ: Wiley.

Vancouver, J. B., & Day, D. V. (2005). Industrial and organisation research on self-regulation: From constructs to application. *Applied Psychology: An International Review, 54,* 155–185.

Whitbourne, S. K. (1986). *The me I know: A study of adult identity.* New York: Springer.

Whitbourne, S. K. (1987). Personality development in adulthood and old age: Relationships among identity style, health, and well-being. In K. W. Schaie (Ed.), *Annual review of gerontology and geriatrics* (vol. 7, pp. 189–216). New York: Springer.

Whitbourne, S. K. (1996). *The aging individual: Physical and psychological perspectives.* New York: Springer.

Wilson, R. S., Schneider, J. A., Arnold, S. E., Bienias, J. L., & Bennett, D. A. (2007). Conscientiousness and the incidence of Alzheimer's disease and mild cognitive impairment. *Archives of General Psychiatry, 64,* 1204–1212.

Wrosch, C., Miller, G. E., Scheier, M.F., & Brun de Pontet, S. (2007). Giving up on unattainable goals: Benefits for health? *Personality and Social Psychology Bulletin, 33,* 251–265

Yun, R. J., & Lachman, M. E. (2006). Perceptions of aging in two cultures: Korean and American views on old age. *Journal of Cross-Cultural Gerontology, 21,* 55–70.

19

Partners and Friends in Adulthood

Rosemary Blieszner and Karen A. Roberto

Two ubiquitous relationships throughout adulthood are romantic partnerships and friendship ties. Adults spend the majority of nonwork time interacting with partners and friends, from whom they typically gain social, emotional, and instrumental support. For some individuals, these relationships converge, as when romantic partners are best of friends or friends become romantic partners. Research has explored the benefits for health and well-being when these relationships are successful and, to a lesser extent, the effects that result when they go awry. In this chapter, we provide an overview of current understanding about interactions that take place within marital or marital-like relationships and within friendships, the difficulties that can occur within these relationships, how they aid individuals in coping with other life stressors, and the impact of these close bonds on health and well-being.

Given that adulthood covers some 75 or more years of life, it is important to take a developmental perspective when assessing the characteristics and effects of relationships over such a lengthy span of experience. Developmentalists certainly recognize that influential physical, cognitive, emotional, and social changes occur within persons through the course of life, but may be less sensitive to considering the effects of developmental changes within close relationships. Thus we begin with an overview of a lifespan development view of dyadic relationships. We then proceed with examination of romantic partnerships and friendships across the adult years. Our conclusion points to new approaches for research on these close relationships.

The Wiley-Blackwell Handbook of Adulthood and Aging, First Edition. Edited by Susan Krauss Whitbourne and Martin J. Sliwinski. © 2012 Blackwell Publishing Ltd. Published 2012 by Blackwell Publishing Ltd.

A Lifespan Development Perspective on Dyadic Relationships

Lifespan development theory embraces principles addressing the potential for change throughout life, the multidirectionality of developmental change, the joint occurrence of both developmental gains and developmental losses throughout life, the diversity and modifiability of developmental processes, the influence of sociohistorical and cultural contexts on development, and the multidimensionality of influences on development (Baltes, 1987; Baltes, Lindenberger, & Staudinger, 2006). Most lifespan development research has examined changing attributes and influences on those changes in terms of personal development. Yet this perspective can be applied usefully to study of personal relationships as well.

On the one hand, close relationships provide contexts in which many personal skills and competencies develop (Collins & Laursen, 2000). Significant others serve as cognitive, social, and affective resources that promote and challenge an individual's development throughout life (Lang, 2001). For example, Heyl and Schmitt (2007) examined the effects of both personality traits and remembered aspects of childhood relationships with parents on friendship in middle and old age. On the other hand, just as intersecting influences of biological, psychological, and social forces shape personal development, they also determine who people meet to establish romantic relationships and friendships. These same forces influence progression of relationships from acquaintance to casual interactions to increasing closeness and intimacy, the extent of stability of established relationships, and declines in closeness and intimacy. Thus developmental trajectories of relationships are influenced by the personal developmental trajectories of the partners. This means that relationships in late life have both similarities to and differences from relationships earlier in life, based on the life experiences of the partners (Blieszner & Roberto, 2004).

Further, acknowledging the reciprocal effects of personal development on relationships and of relationships on personal development and well-being provides a powerful theoretical lens for analyzing the literature on adult relationships. It challenges researchers to focus on the effects of personal characteristics such as age and gender, rather than assuming a unitary set of experiences and outcomes for all persons. Such an approach also calls attention to the prospect of relationship change over time and attendant effects on partners. Our review of romantic and friendship relationships in the following sections highlights these intersecting and reciprocal aspects of personal and relational development and their effects on health and psychological well-being in adulthood.

Contributions of Close Relationships to Health and Well-Being in Adulthood

Marriage and marital-like relationships

Prevalence.   In 2009, 60.8 million opposite-sex couples were married (U.S. Census Bureau, 2009). Among Americans 18 and older, 55% of men and 50% of women are married (Cohn, 2009). By the time men and women reach the age of 65, 95% have been married at some stage of their life. Similar information on couples in marital-like relationships is more difficult to ascertain. While Census information is available on cohabiting couples of the opposite sex (6.7 million in 2009; U.S. Census Bureau, 2009), the 2008 American Community Survey included the first official estimates for the number of same-sex couples who called one partner a "husband" or "wife" (Gates, 2009). Of the nearly 565,000 same-sex couples identified, 150,000 designated themselves as spouses. This number far exceeds the number of legally married same-sex couples in the United States – approximately 32,000 by the end of 2008. Fifty-six percent of same-sex spouses were female while unmarried same-sex partners were evenly split between the sexes.

Marriage and marital-like relationships influence the context of individual development. Within these partnerships, individuals reap many rewards and experience many challenges throughout their lives together. We focus our discussion on interactions in and the functions and quality of these intimate relationships, especially as related to personal development in the later years.

Marital interactions.   Reflecting both personal and relational developmental trajectories as well as the influence of social context, the ways in which couples interact vary at different points in their relationships and lives. Although most newly partnered couples begin with positive expectations, as spouses and partners become more comfortable with one another during the early years of their relationship they express increasingly negative affect and conflict (Lindahl, Clements, & Markman, 1998). Conversely, older adults tend to emphasize positive aspects of their interactions and reduce negative aspects, including those in marriage (Carstensen, Isaacowitz, & Charles, 1999). Positive features of intimate relationships associated with marital satisfaction include warmth and support (Snyder, Heyman, & Haynes, 2005). Negative behaviors, which include complaints, criticism, hostility, withdrawal, and defensiveness, are associated with deterioration in marital satisfaction over time (Karney & Bradbury, 1997) and across life stage (Bookwala & Jacobs, 2004).

Observations of interactions of middle-aged and older couples reveal that perceptions of negative behavior are more closely associated with marital satisfaction for older spouses (across genders) than for middle-aged spouses (Henry, Berg, Smith, & Florsheim, 2007). In addition, the relationship between positive partner behavior and spouse marital satisfaction is stronger in older couples, as is the relationship between negative partner behavior and marital satisfaction. These findings counter the assertion that older adults are biased toward maximizing positive experience within close relationships and ignore negative interactions (Carstensen et al., 1999). Henry et al. (2007) speculated that unlike with other social relationships, in which older adults might move away from hostile or unsatisfying social partners to optimize positive experiences, they are less likely to leave their long-term marital partners. In that case, their inability to regulate negative emotions is counter to theorized goals (e.g., to seek and sustain positive interactions) and contributes to less satisfaction with the marriage.

Gender also shapes marital interactions (Acitelli & Antonucci, 1994; Schmitt, Kliegel, & Shapiro, 2007). Using longitudinal data for husbands and wives in first-time marriages, Faulkner and colleagues (Faulkner, Davey, & Davey, 2005) examined gender differences and influences on marital satisfaction and marital conflict over five years. The sample comprised 1,561 couples; on average the respondents were in their mid-forties and most had been married 16 years or more. Findings showed that wives' marital and interpersonal functioning was predictive of husbands' marital satisfaction, but not vice versa. For example, wives' depression predicted a decline in husbands' marital satisfaction, and greater well-being in wives led to greater marital satisfaction in husbands over time. The opposite, however, did not hold true. Others have found that perceived support given by their spouses was more strongly related to marital satisfaction and subjective well-being for women than for men in midlife and late life (Acitelli & Antonucci, 1994). Such findings support the early assertions of Jessie Bernard (1975) about "'his' and 'her' marriage." She argued that marriage is a qualitatively different experience for men and for women, influenced, at least in part, by perceptions of individual well-being and the meaning spouses attribute to the support they receive from one another.

Reported consistently in the marital literature is the significant positive association between satisfaction with sexual interactions and marital quality. Most findings stem from cross-sectional comparisons of couples at different life stages. One of the few longitudinal investigations of sexual satisfaction, marital quality, and marital instability was carried out with 283 middle-aged intact couples who participated in the Iowa Youth and Families Project (1989-1994) and continued participating in the Iowa Midlife Transitions Project (2001). In this study, analyses of five waves of the Iowa data (1990, 1991, 1992, 1994, and 2001) revealed initially higher levels of sexual satisfaction were found to predict an increase in marital quality, which in turn led to a decrease in marital instability over time (Yeh, Lorenz, Wickrama, Conger, & Elder, 2006). In addition, the causal sequence whereby sexual satisfaction influences marital relationships was similar for both men and women. Qualitative investigations provide further support that sexual activity and intimacy remain an important component of relationships in late life (Clarke, 2006; Hinchliff & Gott, 2004).

Daily stressors and competing demands.   Couples typically are balancing a variety of roles in their families, workplaces, and communities. Thus partners in intimate relationships need to coordinate roles and responsibilities with one another to enable both to function well in their relationship and all other domains (Sterns & Huyck, 2001). Perhaps because of competing demands as well as the amount of time they spend with one another, individuals often rate their marital and marital-like relationships more negatively and with greater ambivalence than they do their relationships with friends (Fingerman, Hay, & Birditt, 2004). Interviews with persons aged 20 to 93 (at first interview) taken 14 years apart examined the extent to which they reported that their spouse or partner, child, and best friend got on their nerves and made too many demands (Birditt, Jackey, & Antonucci, 2009). Relationships with spouses or partners were found either to be consistently negative or to increase in negativity over time. Specifically, individuals who reported having the same spouse or partner in Waves 1 and 2 rated their relationship more negatively over time. In contrast, people with a different spouse or partner in Wave 2 reported a decrease in negative relationship quality over time. The authors concluded that negative relationship quality may be more common among spouses or partners than in other relationships because they have to make decisions and deal with daily life stresses together, both of which may lead to irritation with one another.

Research shows greater conflict within marriages associated with entering parenthood. An analysis of 15 longitudinal studies on the transition to parenthood showed great consistency; approximately 40% to 70% of couples report a drop in marital quality (Gottman & Notarius, 2000). The decline was precipitous within one year after the birth of the first child as couples reverted to stereotypic gender roles, both parents were overwhelmed by the amount of housework and child care responsibilities, the fathers withdrew into outside work, and marital conversation and sexual activity decreased substantially. Umberson and colleagues (Umberson, Williams, Powers, Chen, & Campbell, 2005) found that age was associated with trajectories of change in marital quality, but the nature of this trajectory depended heavily on parental status and parenting transitions. Parenting appeared to have more costs for marriages of younger people, modest effects on marriage in midlife, and more rewards later in life. It was not simply being a parent versus not being a parent that shaped marital quality, but rather the timing of parenting transitions in the life course that played a role in shaping marital quality change. However, such changes are not universal and variations in transition patterns to and during parenthood are influenced by a number of variables in addition to age and life stage, including the availability of personal and social resources to cope with joys and challenges of parenting and shifts in the couple's household and work responsibilities and social activities.

Caring for a spouse or parent also imposes stress and competing demands on intimate relationships. Although assuming a caregiving role is less common in early adulthood, by midlife, 44% of adult children, the majority of whom are daughters, provide care for aging parents or parents-in-law (National Alliance for Caregiving, 2009). While occupying multiple roles inherently presents the potential for relationship conflict, some researchers identified positive "spillover" benefits across relationships. For example, while caregivers associated greater role conflict (e.g., competing work and caregiving demands) with greater loss of self (i.e., diminished sense of personal identity) and occupation of more roles such as spouse, parent, or employee with greater self-loss, they also associated caregiving with more self-gain or personal growth (Foley, Tung, & Mutran, 2002).

In late life, couples look to one another for help and support and, if the need arises, fulfillment of the caregiving role. As caregivers, they often find themselves assuming unfamiliar roles and responsibilities (Blieszner, Roberto, Wilcox, Barham, & Winston, 2007). These new tasks present challenges for older caregivers that may be viewed as positive when mastered but can increase stress if the sick partner is reluctant to give up responsibilities or is critical of the helping partner's performance. Most spouses with limiting physical health conditions are satisfied with the amount and type of support they receive from their partners. If they believe they are receiving more assistance than they really need, however, seemingly helpful behaviors may trigger psychological distress and marital unhappiness (Roberto, Gold, & Yorgason, 2004).

Health and psychological well-being.   Married individuals have lower rates of chronic illness, physical limitations, disability, and mortality than do persons who are not married

(Pienta, Hayward, & Jenkins, 2000). Analyses of data from the 9,195 participants in the Health and Retirement Survey (1992–2000; minimum age of 51 at first interview) revealed that marriage duration was associated with lower rates of disease for men and women (Dupre & Meadows, 2007). Specifically, health benefits of being married increase over time such that the increasing risk of disease with age occurs at a slower rate for women and men who have accumulated more married years. Conversely, evidence reveals that marital dissolution is harmful to health. Studies generally show that transitions out of marriage have a negative impact on physical health (Hemström, 1996; Wu & Hart, 2002) and psychological well-being (Barrett, 2000; Marks & Lambert, 1998). Analyses of the first three waves of data (1986, 1989, and 1994) from the Americans' Changing Lives Survey (Wave 1 age range 25–89) showed that the transition out of marriage, whether through divorce or widowhood, undermines the health of men more than women (Williams & Umberson, 2004).

Although spouse or partner relationships are most often associated with positive long-term individual well-being (Antonucci, Lansford, & Akiyama, 2001; Walen & Lachman, 2000), marriages can be distinctly happy or unhappy, leading to different marital happiness trajectories. These in turn have implications for the psychological well-being of individuals over time. Dush, Taylor, and Kroeger's (2008) analyses of data from the 20-year Marital Instability over the Life Course study (see Booth, Johnson, Amato, & Rogers, 2003), in which participants ranged in age from 16 to 55 at the time of the first interview, found that respondents in troubled relationships (i.e., low marital quality trajectory) had the lowest levels of psychological well-being over time. Although respondents in the happiest of marriages were not shielded from a decline in well-being over time, they did not decline as far as did those in the other group and they showed a decrease in depressive symptoms over time.

A meta-analysis of 93 studies revealed that marital quality and psychological well-being were positively related both concurrently and over time such that higher levels of marital quality were associated with greater individual well-being (Proulx, Helms, & Buehler, 2007). Because half of all divorces occur within the first seven years of marriage (Amato & Cheadle, 2005), and problematic processes that erode perceptions of marital quality take time to manifest themselves, the authors compared studies sampling couples who had been married fewer than eight years with those including couples in more established marriages. When controlling for all other potential moderators, the cross-sectional association between marital quality and personal well-being was stronger for marriages of fewer than eight years than for those longer in duration. However, the opposite was true for longitudinal studies, in which the association between marital quality and personal well-being was weaker for marriages of fewer than eight years duration than for longer marriages. The authors noted two main perspectives linking marital quality and psychological well-being. The stress-generation model (Davila, Bradbury, Cohan, & Tochluk, 1997) posits that when individuals with low psychological well-being encounter stressful interactions with their spouses they experience a further decline in psychological well-being. The marital discord model of depression (Beach, Katz, Kim, & Brody, 2003) hypothesizes that low-quality marriages lead to an increased risk of depression due to lack of support that spouses experience within these marriages.

As this overview of romantic relationships in adulthood shows, both stage of development (reflected in studies comparing across age categories) and marital or marital-like experience (reflected in studies comparing relationships of shorter and longer duration) influence relational interactions, effects of stressors, and personal outcomes in terms of health and well-being. We turn next to examination of the role of friendship in adults' lives.

Friendship

Prevalence. Although incidence data on marital and romantic partner relationships are relatively readily available through Census records and other national surveys, questions on friendship prevalence and interaction patterns tend to appear only in more specialized studies. However, occasional Census questions do confirm that friend relationships and regular interactions among friends are common. For example, 40% of US households report entertaining family or friends at home at least annually (U.S. Census, 2010) and an investigation of potential sources of help when in need (U.S. Census, 2003) showed that over 86% of both females and males did expect to receive assistance from significant others, including from friends (30% of females and 32% of males) as well as from relatives (45% of females and 43% of males).

Further, analysis of American adults' social networks by de Jong Gierveld and Perlman (2006) revealed that 56% of nonkin network members were friends and on average, the friendships had lasted 18 years. A nationally representative survey of 1,000 US adults showed that the average length of best friendships is 14 years with 36% of respondents reporting they had known their best friend for 20 or more years and only 15% reporting they had known their best friend for fewer than 5 years. Among the respondents, 55% were in contact with their best friend at least once a week and 91% stated they would like to go on vacation with their best friend (Fetto, 2002). Data from a small sample of older women and men revealed that respondents had between 1 and 132 friends, with an average of 30 (Blieszner, 1995). Other investigations of relationships with friends in adulthood show that the vast majority of participants respond readily about characteristics of, emotional closeness to, and myriad types of interactions with their friends (Blieszner & Adams, 1992; Dugan & Kivett, 1998). Collectively, these findings speak to the prevalence of friend ties across the years of adulthood.

Friendship interactions. Similar to romantic relationships, friendships have common characteristics yet reflect developmental and relationship stage differences. Among the most important elements of adult friendships are being comfortable enough together to engage in self-disclosure, cultivating feelings of loyalty and trust, sharing interests and values, experiencing compatibility and enjoyment of each other's company, and caring about one another (Adams, Blieszner, & de Vries, 2000; Fehr, 1996). The definition of key elements of friendship appears to be stable across adulthood, even though friend roles and relationships may change over time.

Adams and Blieszner (1994) presented a conceptual framework for friendship research that explicitly acknowledged the effects of developmental stage on friendship interaction patterns. They suggested that across the adult years, the focus of confiding and the types of shared interests and activities would shift according to individual needs. This means that whom one befriends and how friends interact are likely to differ across adulthood. For example, in young adulthood, individuals turn to friends for emotional support and advice as they make important life decisions related to beginning a career, choosing a long-term romantic partner, establishing a place in the community, and solidifying their identity. Carbery and Buhrmester (1998) demonstrated that friendships fulfill different types of needs among young adults who are single, married without children, and married with children. Trends in their data indicated that young adults in each successive family role stage relied less on friends and more on spouses for companionship, intimacy, support, and guidance. Those who were parents also secured companionship from their children, further displacing the salience of friendships in satisfying that need. The Carbery and Buhrmester (1998) findings about changes in friendship patterns across family stages were extended from dating, through parenthood, to the empty nest, in research by Kalmijn (2003). In general, the farther along the family stage continuum participants were, the more likely they were to report fewer friends, less contact with friends, and higher percentages of shared couple friendships and joint contacts with friends. These differences were pronounced in the dating-to-marriage-to-initial-parenthood stages and were less likely to continue in the later stages.

The developmental challenges of middle-aged adults pertain to advancing a career; managing complex family relationships with one's partner, children, and parents; and pursuing community and leisure interests. Hence their friends and friend interactions are likely to shift in order to provide companionship and support related to these challenges. As confirmed by Kalmijn (2003), middle-aged adults report having fewer friends and spending less time with friends than younger adults do (Adams & Blieszner, 1996), but they nevertheless consider friendships to be important and generally make the effort to sustain the most important friendship ties (Blieszner & Roberto, 2004).

As adults move into the later years, their friendships may again refocus, reflecting changes in work, family, and community activities that occur with retirement and pursuit of new leisure and volunteer interests. In a 14-year longitudinal follow-up of older women's lives and friendships, Roberto (1997) found that personal life events such as changes in marital, work, and health status affected interactions with friends. Friendship changes included aspects of face-to-face interaction that diminished over time, suggesting the potential for social support deficits. Similarly, in a 16-year, three-phase study of late-life friendship with a sample from Wales, Jerrome and Wenger (1999) found that many friendships faded away or were lost due to illness, relocation, or death. The effects of these relational changes varied, with some elders disengaging and finding contentment in a smaller network and others continuing to use social engagement skills to seek replacement friendships when needed. Coping strategies built up over a lifetime seemed to influence the relational strategies employed by people in old age. Also, friendship norms were more fluid than in earlier life; some elders made new friends with atypical partners, such as younger or opposite-sex persons, in order to sustain interesting and supportive friendships in their social networks (Blieszner, 2006).

These findings conform to the Adams and Blieszner (1994) postulation that friendships themselves are not static, but change over time. Other studies of friendships provide additional evidence. Oswald and Clark (2003) demonstrated that best friendships in high school declined in closeness and satisfaction, and required more effort to sustain them, after the friends went to college. Van Duijn, Zeggelink, Huisman, Stokman, and Wasseur (2003) investigated how students develop and sustain friendships when entering college together, focusing in particular on the structure of the social context in which these young adults are living. The investigators postulated that proximity and visible similarities (e.g., age, gender, ethnicity) contribute to potential friends being attracted to one another, but these features eventually give way to the importance of common interests, behaviors, and attitudes as friendships deepen over time. In a similar focus on friendship initiation at the other end of the adult lifespan, Shea, Thompson, and Blieszner (1988) examined the emergence of friendship in a short-term longitudinal study of older adults who had moved into a newly constructed retirement village. At Time 1, shortly after the facility opened, participants identified new acquaintances with whom they said they would like to become friends. For each potential friend, participants reported the current frequency of exchanging various forms of support and indicated their regard for each on Rubin's (1973) liking and loving scales. Four months later, participants again rated relationships with the original acquaintances who were becoming friends. All three ratings (frequency of support exchanges, liking, and loving) were significantly higher at Time 2. In response to open-ended questions, participants revealed they were more open about expressing compliments and affection with their emerging friends and had started to exchange favors or at least felt they could count on each other for help if needed. In contrast, a few participants mentioned they had not cultivated friendship with someone they originally identified as a potential friend because that person had violated a deeply held norm, such as asking to borrow money. In another study (Adams & Blieszner, 1998; Blieszner & Adams, 1998), older adults described situations with current friends that were problematic, leading to friendships fading away or being ended on purpose. As these examples show, friendship changes over time involve both growing closer and growing more distant.

Although most people consider affection, trust, and having common interests as important elements of friendship, some gender differences in perception and enactment of friend relations exist. For example, Adams and colleagues (2000) found that across subcultural groups, women tend to discuss the importance of emotional qualities and self-disclosure whereas men are more likely to mention frequency of contact and length of the relationship as important indicators of friendship. Felmlee and Muraco (2009), too, reported that women focused more on intimacy than men did, had higher expectations of friends, and were more disapproving if friends breached friendship norms. Liebler and Sandefur (2002) showed that these differences in perceptions are reflected in behavior. Women were more likely than men to exchange emotional support with their friends, whereas men were more likely than women to be low exchangers of support. Wright (1982) summarized such gender differences by suggesting that women carry out friendship face-to-face and men side-by-side. No doubt these differences emerge and persist due to lifelong socialization (Mehta & Strough, 2009). Most people meet potential new friends and cultivate friendships throughout life, but Field (1999) found that older men's desire to develop new friends declined over time, whereas older women expressed continued interest in forming new friendships. This gender difference may explain the gradual decline in number of friends among men, also noted by Field, and may reflect shifting socioemotional priorities for some older adults (Carstensen et al., 1999). Finally, the impact of friendship on well-being also differs by gender. Antonucci et al. (2001) found that women's depression and life satisfaction were strongly affected by not having a close friend in whom to confide, whereas men's depression and life satisfaction was not affected by the presence or absence of a confidant.

Friendship strains and problems.   Along with providing enjoyment and companionship, friend relationships can also be stressful. As adolescents strive to clarify their own identity, they also develop stronger norms for friendship, which may lead to more serious conflicts and friendship instability as well as deeper intimacy, compared to childhood friendships (Crosnoe, 2000). Adults, too, report troubles with friends, reflecting the same issues as adolescents mention: insufficient attention, disrespectful actions, inadequate communication, broken promises, and betrayals of trust and confidences (Hansson, Jones, & Fletcher, 1990; Moreman, 2008a).

Adams and Blieszner (1998; Blieszner & Adams, 1998) assessed detailed information about the types and predictors of friendship problems in a sample of older adults. Some friendships diminish in closeness or fade away because of changing interests, relocation, declining health of one partner, apparent jealousy over differential access to resources, or interference from other parties. Other friendship difficulties included more egregious behaviors such as overt insults and disrespect or serious betrayals. Most respondents tolerated minor irritations and personality quirks in ongoing friendships, though, and intentionally ending friendship was rarely acknowledged (Blieszner & Adams, 1998). In general, predictors of friendship problems included being female, being young-old as opposed to older, and belonging to the upper-middle class. Perhaps those with more social capital are more likely to be critical of their friends, are better at acknowledging relational problems, or are less dependent on others for their sense of worth (Adams & Blieszner, 1998).

The Birditt et al. (2009) study of close relationships described above also explored negative aspects of friendship across age groups and over time. Their results showed that older adults were less likely than middle-aged or younger adults to report that their friends were irritating or made too many demands. Respondents with different best friends at Wave 1 and Wave 2 reported less negativity over time whereas those with the same best friends at both waves did not report a change in negativity. Perhaps those with different best friends shed friendships that had any negative features and those with the same best friends sustained the friendships despite any minor annoyances. The possibility that older adults tolerate idiosyncrasies in their friends is supported by findings in the Blieszner and Adams (1998) study.

Health and psychological well-being.   As indicated previously, friends provide many kinds of support to one another, including instrumental assistance, affirmation of one's identity and worth, opportunities for interesting and enjoyable pastimes, and emotional sustenance. In fact, friends are sometimes deemed to be fictive kin (i.e., are considered to be like relatives even though they do not have blood or legal ties). When friends are viewed this way, emotional bonds may be tighter than in other friendships and these relationships may be imbued with expectations and obligations not normally associated with friendship

(Chatters, Taylor, & Jayakody, 1994). Such friendships play important roles for African Americans by extending their family networks (Chatters et al., 1994) and for gay, lesbian, bisexual, and transgender persons (Blando, 2001; Grossman, D'Augelli, & Hershberger, 2000) as well as never-married heterosexual women (McDill, Hall, & Turell, 2006) who may depend more on friends than relatives for meeting their social and emotional needs. Piercy (2000) documented the circumstances and processes under which home health care workers became friends and like-family with their clients and clients' relatives. By assuming family-like roles and responsibilities, friends foster health and well-being in much the same way that relatives do.

Even friends who are not fictive kin contribute to physical health and psychological well-being in myriad ways. Moreman (2008b) found that older women's friends helped promote good health by offering advice about diet and exercise, sharing meals, providing transportation for medical care, listening to their needs, and laughing with them. Gallant, Spitze, and Prohaska (2007) also found that friends helped foster good health in similar ways (being an exercise partner, driving, sharing information) but they further discovered that friends can interfere with health regimens, as when they tempt people to ignore dietary restrictions, discourage physical activity, offer unwanted advice, show lack of understanding, or engage in depressing conversation. In general, though, the Gallant et al. research showed that friends were more likely than not to promote and support positive self-management of chronic conditions.

Moreover, maintaining contact with friends can help thwart social isolation and feelings of loneliness common among those with chronic health problems (Roberto & Husser, 2007). People who have friends experiencing similar health problems believe their friends are more understanding of their needs than family members are, and also report that understanding friends can help distract them from their pain (Roberto & Reynolds, 2002). But if chronic health problems lead to infirmity or needs that involve too many demands deemed inappropriate by friends, those relationships can be diminished or lost (Johnson, 1993). Friends are also important sources of emotional support and social interaction for caregivers of those who are in poor physical or cognitive health, which contributes to their ability to continue caregiving and maintain their own health and well-being (Lilly, Richards, & Buckwalter, 2003).

Investigators have also studied a more indirect association of friendship with health and well-being by examining the effects of friendships on other relationships. As indicated earlier, marital bonds are more likely to be strained than friend ties, so researchers have examined whether and under what circumstances friends affect satisfaction with romantic relationships as well as personal well-being. Walen and Lachman (2000) found that for women but not men, supportive friends buffered the negative effects of partner strain on psychological well-being, as indexed by life satisfaction and positive and negative moods. They also demonstrated that for older but not young or middle-aged adults, friend support buffered the negative effects of friend strain on physical health. Proulx, Helms, Milardo, and Payne (2009) examined the issue of partner strain more deeply, focusing on the effects of friends on mitigating the harm caused by spouses who are overly critical and negative toward their partners. They hypothesized that the more often husbands treated their wives negatively, the more likely wives would be to seek support from friends. However, they found that when the husbands' negativity and interference was infrequent, friend support was positively associated with the wives' marital satisfaction, but when the husbands' criticism and lack of support was extensive, friend support did not seem to compensate for the marital negativity. These findings show that friendships can have both direct and indirect impact on personal health and well-being as well as affect dynamic processes and outcomes in other relationships.

Conclusion

This review of trends and recent research on partner and friend relationships in adulthood portrays the numerous ways that close ties differ across adulthood and influence both personal and relational development. As illustrated by this work, new conceptual and empirical approaches have emerged which hold promise for continued advancement in this area of scholarship.

Increasingly, researchers acknowledge the value of extending the lifespan development and life course perspectives beyond the individual level of analysis to the social relationship level. This approach has been used to frame analyses of the state of research as we have done here (see also Bengtson, Elder, & Putney, 2005; Lang & Fingerman, 2004; Moorman & Greenfield, 2010) as well as to provide an expanded conceptual basis for examining relationships and the persons involved in them. Theoretically, the lifespan development and life course frameworks point to the importance of considering complex intersections of (a) individual development within biological, cognitive, personality, and social domains; (b) within particular sociocultural and historical contexts; (c) while the relationships themselves are also evolving. That is, not only do partners change over time, so do their relationships, in a reciprocal set of influences (Kelley et al., 1983). External influences of social structure on partners and their relationships bear consideration, as do effects of structural features internal to the dyad or network. A comprehensive approach would encompass all forms of relational experiences and responses, including cognitive, affective, and behavioral processes and multiple phases from initiation through sustenance to ending (Adams & Blieszner, 1994). These influences and their outcomes could be investigated for a thorough understanding of relationships.

Empirically, using the lifespan and life course perspectives to guide the study of close relationships implies the need to examine change over time, including antecedents, sequences, turning points, contingencies, and consequences of personal and relational transitions. Short-term longitudinal designs are suitable for some research questions, whereas others demand longer time frames and many measurement occasions. As shown by research examples cited in this chapter, some scholars approximate analysis of change by making cross-age comparisons and by asking study participants to recall earlier stages of life or prior experiences in the focal relationship and then linking their recollections with current relational data. Such approaches are often useful for pointing to variables and findings requiring further study in longitudinal designs but they only capture perceived changes and influences on current relationships, not actual changes and influences.

Although individuals can certainly report their own relationship-related thoughts, feelings, and behaviors, designs that include dyads, triads, and more members of networks truly support a relationship level of analysis. Supplementing self-report data with behavioral observations and reports by significant others, and complementing quantitative data with analysis of responses to open-ended questions, are other methods of probing deeper into relational processes and functions. Gathering multiple types of data from multiple partners over multiple occasions presents unique challenges related to sustaining complex samples and designs. Such research is costly in time as well as money. Nevertheless, the potential reward in terms of the range and complexity of questions that can be explored is great. Studies employing developmental conceptualizations of relationships such as the Social Convoy Model (Antonucci, Langfahl, & Akiyama, 2004) and using multivariate modeling techniques for dyads and networks (e.g., Kenny, Kashy, & Cook, 2006) provide examples of designs and analytic approaches that are most likely to contribute to building knowledge about close relationships.

The literature on partner and friend relationships across the adult years is growing in both size and sophistication. Researchers are pursuing a broad array of questions and variables, including investigation of negative as well as positive dimensions of these relationships. This is an important development in the literature, because understanding more about problems can provide the basis for applied endeavors related to prevention and intervention. Although enrichment and counseling programs for romantic relationships have existed for many years, interventions targeting friendship are sparse. Early work aimed at alleviating loneliness by cultivating social skills (see Andersson, 1998 for a review) and more recent efforts have targeted older adults in need of esteem building, social integration, and emotional support. For example, Stevens, Martina, and Westerhof (2006) examined the effectiveness of a 12-week educational program aimed at helping older women cultivate friendships and become less lonely. The lessons focused on clarifying expectations for friendship, assessing the social network for current and potential friends, and establishing goals and strategies for improving existing friendships and developing new ones. Compared to a control group, women who completed the intervention reported they had developed more new friendships and made more improvements in existing friendships in the ensuing year. This research shows that learning opportunities and encouragement can, indeed, have a positive impact on close relationships. Continued efforts to extend the breadth and depth of research findings on intimate bonds will support development of other evidence-based programs for relationship enhancement and repair.

References

Acitelli, L. K., & Antonucci, T. C. (1994). Gender differences in the link between marital support and satisfaction in older couples. *Journal of Personality and Social Psychology, 67,* 688–698.

Adams, R. G., & Blieszner, R. (1994). An integrative conceptual framework for friendship research. *Journal of Social and Personal Relationships, 11,* 163–184.

Adams, R. G., & Blieszner, R. (1996). Midlife friendship patterns. In N. A. Vanzetti & S. Duck (Eds.), *A lifetime of relationships* (pp. 336–363). Pacific Grove, CA: Brooks/Cole.

Adams, R. G., & Blieszner, R. (1998). Structural predictors of problematic friendships in later life. *Personal Relationships, 5,* 439–447.

Adams, R. G., Blieszner, R., & de Vries, B. (2000). Age, gender, and study location effects on definitions of friendship in the third age. *Journal of Aging Studies, 14,* 117–133.

Amato, P. R., & Cheadle, J. (2005). The long reach of divorce: Tracking marital dissolution and child well-being across three generations. *Journal of Marriage and Family, 67,* 191–206.

Andersson, L. (1998). Loneliness research and interventions: A review of the literature. *Aging & Mental Health, 2,* 264–274.

Antonucci, T. C., Langfahl, E. S., & Akiyama, H. (2004). Relationships as outcomes and contexts. In F. R. Lang & K. L. Fingerman (Eds.), *Growing together: Personal relationships across the lifespan* (pp. 24–44). Cambridge, UK: Cambridge University Press.

Antonucci, T. C., Lansford, J. E., & Akiyama, H. (2001). Impact of positive and negative aspects of marital relationships and friendship on well-being of older adults. *Applied Developmental Science, 5,* 68–75.

Baltes, P. B. (1987). Theoretical propositions of life-span developmental psychology: On the dynamics between growth and decline. *Developmental Psychology, 23,* 611–626.

Baltes, P. B., Lindenberger, U., & Staudinger, U. M. (2006). Life span theory in developmental psychology. In W. Damon & R. M. Lerner (Eds.), *Handbook of child psychology: Vol. 1. Theoretical models of human development* (6th ed., pp. 569–664). New York: Wiley.

Barrett, A. E. (2000). Marital trajectories and mental health. *Journal of Health and Social Behavior, 41,* 451–464.

Beach, S. R. H., Katz, J., Kim, S., & Brody, G. H. (2003). Prospective effects of marital satisfaction on depressive symptoms in established marriages: A dyadic model. *Journal of Social and Personal Relationships, 20,* 355–371.

Bengtson, V. L., Elder, G. H., Jr., & Putney, N. M. (2005). The lifecourse perspective on ageing: Linked lives, timing, and history. In M. L. Johnson (Ed.), *The Cambridge handbook of age and ageing* (pp. 493–501). Cambridge, UK: Cambridge University Press.

Bernard, J. (1975). *The future of marriage.* New York: Bantam.

Birditt, K. S., Jackey, L. M. H., & Antonucci, T. C. (2009). Longitudinal patterns of negative relationship quality across adulthood. *Journal of Gerontology: Psychological Sciences, 64,* 55–64.

Blando, J. A. (2001). Twice hidden: Older gay and lesbian couples, friends, and intimacy. *Generations, 25*(2), 87–89.

Blieszner, R. (1995). Friendship processes and well-being in the later years of life: Implications for interventions. *Journal of Geriatric Psychiatry, 28,* 165–182.

Blieszner, R. (2006). A lifetime of caring: Close relationships in old age. *Personal Relationships, 13,* 1–18.

Blieszner, R., & Adams, R. G. (1992). *Adult friendship.* Newbury Park, CA: Sage.

Blieszner, R., & Adams, R. G. (1998). Problems with friends in old age. *Journal of Aging Studies, 12,* 223–238.

Blieszner, R., & Roberto, K. A. (2004). Friendship across the life span: Reciprocity in individual and relationship development. In F. R. Lang & K. L. Fingerman (Eds.), *Growing together: Personal relationships across the lifespan* (pp. 159–182). Cambridge, UK: Cambridge University Press.

Blieszner, R., Roberto, K. A., Wilcox, K. L., Barham, E. J., & Winston, B. L. (2007). Dimensions of ambiguous loss in couples coping with mild cognitive impairment. *Family Relations, 56,* 195–208.

Bookwala, J., & Jacobs, J. (2004). Age, marital processes, and depressed affect. *The Gerontologist, 44,* 328–338.

Booth, A., Johnson, D., Amato, P., & Rogers, S. (2003). *Marital instability over the life course: A six-wave panel study, 1980, 1983, 1988, 1992-1994, 1997, 2000.* (Version 1) [Data file]. Ann Arbor, MI: Inter-university Consortium for Political and Social Research.

Carbery, J., & Buhrmester, D. (1998). Friendship and need fulfillment during three phases of young adulthood. *Journal of Social and Personal Relationships, 15,* 393–409.

Carstensen, L. L., Isaacowitz, D. M., & Charles, C. T. (1999). Taking time seriously: A theory of socioemotional selectivity. *American Psychologist, 54,* 165–181.

Chatters, L. M., Taylor, R. J., & Jayakody, R. (1994). Fictive kinship relations in black extended families. *Journal of Comparative Family Studies, 25,* 297–312.

Clarke, L. H. (2006). Older women and sexuality: Experiences in marital relationships across the life course. *Canadian Journal on Aging, 25,* 129–140.

Cohn, D. (2009). *The states of marriage and divorce.* The Pew Research Center. Retrieved from http://pewresearch.org/pubs/1380/marriage-and-divorce-by-state

Collins, W. A., & Laursen, B. (2000). Adolescent relationships: The art of fugue. In C. Hendrick & S. S. Hendrick (Eds.), *Close relationships: A sourcebook* (pp. 58–69). Thousand Oaks, CA: Sage.

Crosnoe, R. (2000). Friendships in childhood and adolescence: The life course and new directions. *Social Psychology Quarterly, 63,* 377–391.

Davila, J., Bradbury, T. N., Cohan, C. L., & Tochluk, S. (1997). Marital functioning and depressive symptoms: Evidence for a stress generation model. *Journal of Personality and Social Psychology, 73,* 849–861.

de Jong Gierveld, J., & Perlman, D. (2006). Long-standing nonkin relationships of older adults in the Netherlands and the United States. *Research on Aging, 28,* 730–748.

Dugan, E., & Kivett, V. R. (1998). Implementing the Adams and Blieszner conceptual model: Predicting interactive friendship processes of older adults. *Journal of Social and Personal Relationships, 15,* 607–622.

Dupre, M. E., & Meadows, S. O. (2007). Disaggregating the effects of marital trajectories on health. *Journal of Family Issues, 28,* 623–652.

Dush, C. M. K., Taylor, M. G., & Kroeger, R. A. (2008). Marital happiness and psychological well-being across the life course. *Family Relations, 57,* 211–226.

Faulkner, R. A., Davey, M., & Davey, A. (2005). Gender-related predictors of change in marital satisfaction and marital conflict. *American Journal of Family Therapy, 33,* 61–83.

Fehr, B. (1996). *Friendship processes.* Thousand Oaks, CA: Sage.

Felmlee, D., & Muraco, A. (2009). Gender and friendship norms among older adults. *Research on Aging, 31,* 318–344.

Fetto, J. (2002, October 1). Friends forever. *American Demographics.* Retrieved from http://findarticles.com/p/articles/mi_m4021/is_2002_Oct_1/ai_92087421/?tag=content;col1

Field, D. (1999). Continuity and change in friendships in advanced old age: Findings from the Berkeley Older Generation Study. *International Journal of Aging and Human Development, 48,* 325–346.

Fingerman, K. L., Hay, E. L., & Birditt, K. S. (2004). The best of ties, the worst of ties: Close, problematic, and ambivalent social relationships. *Journal of Marriage and Family, 66,* 792–808.

Foley, K. L., Tung, H., & Mutran, E. J. (2002). Self-gain and self-loss among African American and White caregivers. *Journal of Gerontology: Social Sciences, 57,* S14–S21.

Gallant, M. P., Spitze, G. D., & Prohaska, T. R. (2007). Help or hindrance? How family and friends influence chronic illness self-management among older adults. *Research on Aging, 29,* 375–409.

Gates, G. (2009). *Same-sex spouses and unmarried partners in the American Community Survey, 2008.* The Williams Institute, UCLA. Retrieved from http://www.law.ucla.edu/williamsinstitute/pdf/ACS2008_Final%282%29.pdf

Gottman, J. M., & Notarius, C. I. (2000). Decade review: Observing marital interaction. *Journal of Marriage and the Family, 62,* 927–947.

Grossman, A. H., D'Augelli, A. R., & Hershberger, S. L. (2000). Social support networks of lesbian, gay, and bisexual adults 60 years of age and older. *Journal of Gerontology: Psychological Sciences, 55B,* P171–P179.

Hansson, R. O., Jones, W. H., & Fletcher, W. L. (1990). Troubled relationships in later life: Implications for support. *Journal of Social and Personal Relationships, 7,* 451–463.

Hemström, O. (1996). Is marital dissolution linked to differences in mortality risks for men and women? *Journal of Marriage and the Family, 58,* 366–378.

Henry, N. J. M., Berg, C. A., Smith, T. W., & Florsheim, P. (2007). Positive and negative characteristics of marital interaction and their association with marital satisfaction in middle-aged and older couples. *Psychology and Aging, 22,* 428–441.

Heyl, V., & Schmitt, M. (2007). The contribution of adult personality and recalled parent-child relations to friendships in middle and old age. *International Journal of Behavioral Development, 31,* 38–48.

Hinchliff, S., & Gott, M. (2004). Intimacy, commitment, and adaptation: Sexual relationships within long-term marriages. *Journal of Social and Personal Relationships, 21,* 595–609.

Jerrome, D., & Wenger, G. C. (1999). Stability and change in late-life friendship. *Ageing and Society, 19,* 661–676.

Johnson, C. (1993). Fairweather friends and rainy day kin: An anthropological analysis of old age friendships in the United States. *Urban Anthropology, 12,* 103–123.

Kalmijn, M. (2003). Shared friendship networks and the life course: An analysis of survey data on married and cohabiting couples. *Social Networks, 25,* 231–249.

Karney, B. R., & Bradbury, T. N. (1997). Neuroticism, marital interaction, and the trajectory of marital satisfaction. *Journal of Personality and Social Psychology, 72,* 1075–1092.

Kelley, H. H., Berscheid, E., Christensen, A., Harvey, J. H., Huston, T. L., Levinger, G., . . . Peterson, D. R. (1983). *Close relationships.* New York: Freeman.

Kenny, D. A., Kashy, D. A., & Cook, W. L. (2006). *Dyadic data analysis.* New York: Guilford Press.

Lang, F. R. (2001). Regulation of social relationships in later adulthood. *Journal of Gerontology: Psychological Sciences, 56B,* P321–P326.

Lang, F. R., & Fingerman, K. L. (Eds.). (2004). *Growing together: Personal relationships across the lifespan.* Cambridge, UK: Cambridge University Press.

Liebler, C. A., & Sandefur, G. D. (2002). Gender differences in the exchange of social support with friends, neighbors, and co-workers at midlife. *Social Science Research, 31,* 364–391.

Lilly, M. L., Richards, B. S., & Buckwalter, K. C. (2003). Friends and social support in dementia caregiving: Assessment and intervention. *Journal of Gerontological Nursing, 29,* 29–36.

Lindahl, K., Clements, M., & Markman, H. (1998). *The development of marriage: A 9-year perspective.* New York: Cambridge University Press.

Marks, N. F., & Lambert, J. D. (1998). Marital status continuity and change among young and midlife adults. *Journal of Family Issues, 19,* 652–686.

McDill, T., Hall, S. K., & Turell, S. C. (2006). Aging and creating families: Never-married heterosexual women over forty. *Journal of Women & Aging, 18,* 37–50.

Mehta, C. M., & Strough, J. (2009). Sex segregation in friendships and normative contexts across the life span. *Developmental Review, 29,* 201–220.

Moorman, S. M., & Greenfield, E. A. (2010). Personal relationships in later life. In J. C. Cavanaugh & C. K. Cavanaugh (Eds.), *Aging in America, Vol. 3: Societal issues* (pp. 20–52). Santa Barbara, CA: Praeger.

Moreman, R. D. (2008a). The downside of friendship: Sources of strain in older women's friendship. *Journal of Women & Aging, 20,* 169–187.

Moreman, R. D. (2008b). Best friends: The role of confidantes in older women's health. *Journal of Women & Aging, 20,* 149–167.

National Alliance for Caregiving. (2009). *Caregiving in the United States 2009*. Retrieved from http://assets.aarp.org/rgcenter/il/caregiving_09_fr.pdf

Oswald, D. L., & Clark, E. M. (2003). Best friends forever? High school best friendships and the transition to college. *Personal Relationships, 10*, 187–196.

Pienta, A. M., Hayward, M. D., & Jenkins, K. R. (2000). Health consequences of marriage and retirement years. *Journal of Family Issues, 21*, 559–586.

Piercy, K. W. (2000). When it's more than a job: Relationships between home health workers and their older clients. *Journal of Aging and Health, 12*, 362–387.

Proulx, C. M., Helms, H. M., & Buehler, C. (2007). Marital quality and personal well-being: A meta-analysis. *Journal of Marriage and Family, 69*, 576–593.

Proulx, C. M., Helms, H. M., Milardo, R. M., & Payne, C. C. (2009). Relational support from friends and wives' family relationships: The role of husbands' interference. *Journal of Social and Personal Relationships, 26*, 195–210.

Roberto, K. A. (1997). Qualities of older women's friendships: Stable or volatile? *International Journal of Aging and Human Development, 44*, 1–14.

Roberto, K. A., Gold, D. T., & Yorgason, J. (2004). The influence of osteoporosis on the marital relationship of older couples. *Journal of Applied Gerontology, 23*, 443–456.

Roberto, K. A., & Husser, E. K. (2007). *Social relationships: Resources and obstacles to older women's health adaptations and well-being*. In T. J. Owens & J. J. Suitor (Eds.), *Advances in life course research, Vol. 12: Interpersonal relations across the life course* (pp. 383–410). New York: Elsevier Science.

Roberto, K. A., & Reynolds, S. (2002). Older women's experiences with chronic pain: Daily challenges and self-care practices. *Journal of Women & Aging, 14*, 5–23.

Rubin, Z. (1973). *Liking and loving*. New York: Holt, Rinehart, & Winston.

Schmitt, M., Kliegel, M., & Shapiro, A. (2007). Marital interaction in middle and old age: A predictor of marital satisfaction? *International Journal of Aging and Human Development, 65*, 283–300.

Shea, L., Thompson, L., & Blieszner, R. (1988). Resources in older adults' old and new friendships. *Journal of Social and Personal Relationships, 5*, 83–96.

Snyder, D. K., Heyman, R. E., & Haynes, S. N. (2005). Evidence-based approaches to assessing couple distress. *Psychological Assessment, 17*, 288–307.

Sterns, H. L., & Huyck, M. H. (2001). The role of work in midlife. In M. E. Lachman (Ed.), *Handbook of midlife development* (pp. 447–486). New York: Wiley.

Stevens, N. L., Martina, C. M., & Westerhof, G. J. (2006). Meeting the need to belong: Predicting effects of a friendship enrichment program for older women. *The Gerontologist, 46*, 495–502.

Umberson, D., Williams, K., Powers, D. A., Chen, M. D., & Campbell, A. M. (2005). As good as it gets? A life course perspective on marital quality. *Social Forces, 85*, 487–505.

U.S. Census Bureau. (2003). Table 21 A. Help expected when in need by social characteristics: Households with expectation of help if needed, expect help from friends, expect help from family, and expect help from others: 1998. *Survey of income and program participation, 1996 panel, wave 8*. Retrieved from http://www.census.gov/population/socdemo/well-being/ppl-170/tab21A.xls - 2003-05-15

U.S. Census Bureau. (2009). America's families and living arrangements. *Current Population Survey (CPS) Reports: Families and living arrangements*. Retrieved from http://www.census.gov/population/www/socdemo/hh-fam.html

U.S. Census Bureau. (2010). Table 1203. Adult participation in selected leisure activities, by frequency: 2008. *The 2010 statistical abstract: The national data book*. Retrieved from http://www.census.gov/compendia/statab/2010/tables/10s1203.xls

van Duijn, M. A. J., Zeggelink, E. P. H., Huisman, M., Stokman, F. N., & Wasseur, F. W. (2003). Evolution of sociology freshmen into a friendship network. *Journal of Mathematical Sociology, 27*, 153–191.

Walen, H. R., & Lachman, M. E. (2000). Social support and strain from partner, family, and friends: Costs and benefits for men and women in adulthood. *Journal of Social & Personal Relationships, 17*, 5–30.

Williams, K., & Umberson, D. (2004). Marital status, marital transitions, and health: A gendered life course perspective. *Journal of Health and Social Behavior, 45*, 81–98.

Wright, P. H. (1982). Men's friendships, women's friendships and the alleged inferiority of the latter. *Sex Roles, 8*, 1–20.

Wu, Z., & Hart, R. (2002). The effects of nonmarital union transition on health. *Journal of Marriage and Family, 64*, 420–432.

Yeh, H.-C., Lorenz, F. O., Wickrama, K. A. S., Conger, R. D., & Elder, G. H., Jr., (2006). Relationships among sexual satisfaction, marital quality, and marital instability at midlife. *Journal of Family Psychology, 20*, 339–343.

20

Intergenerational Relationships and Aging

Kira S. Birditt and Elvina Wardjiman

Across the lifespan, the parent–child relationship often involves a great deal of contact, high levels of support exchange, and emotional complexity. The parent–child tie represents one of the longest-lasting social relationships (Ward & Spitze, 1992). This tie is particularly unusual because it involves people from different generations fostering a relationship considered permanent and difficult to dissolve. There is a dynamic push and pull for independence and closeness in the relationship that influences many aspects of the tie, including the support exchanged and the emotional qualities of the relationship. Indeed, parents and children often experience simultaneously intense feelings of irritation and love for one another (i.e., ambivalence) and emotional aspects of the relationship have important implications for well-being and health.

This chapter reviews the literature regarding the parent–child relationship in adulthood including the demographic trends affecting the relationship as well as three key dimensions of the tie including its structure, function, and quality. Structural aspects of the tie include coresidence, geographical proximity, and contact frequency. The function of relationships refers to the support exchanged and we discuss the types and amount of support exchanged, the predictors of support, and caregiving. Next, we review research regarding relationship quality (positive, negative, and ambivalence) and the predictors of relationship quality. Finally, we discuss the implications of the parent–child relationship for health and well-being, followed by suggestions for future research.

The Wiley-Blackwell Handbook of Adulthood and Aging, First Edition. Edited by Susan Krauss Whitbourne and Martin J. Sliwinski. © 2012 Blackwell Publishing Ltd. Published 2012 by Blackwell Publishing Ltd.

Structural Aspects of the Parent–Child Tie

We first discuss demographic changes that have affected families, followed by a review of the research on coresidence, geographical proximity, and contact frequency.

Demographic factors

Increases in life expectancy, decreases in fertility rates, and fluctuations in marriage and divorce are some of the demographic patterns affecting families. Due to industrialization and improvements in nutrition and technology, life expectancy has continued to expand throughout history (Heron et al., 2009; Kohli, Kunemund, & Ludicke, 2005; Taylor, Morin, Parker, Cohn, & Wang, 2009). A total of 8.1% of the population in 1950 was over age 65 and this percentage rose to 12.3% in 2008 (U.S. Census Bureau, 2009a). The population of older people will continue to grow over time, with the proportion of individuals over age 65 increasing by 160% and those 85 and older by 233% from 2008 to 2040 (Kinsella & He, 2009). Given these changes in life expectancy, four-generation families have become more common and relationships between parents and children last longer than ever before (Connidis, 2010; Dobriansky, Suzman, & Hodes, 2007).

Along with the increased life expectancy in the aging population comes a higher probability that individuals will experience chronic health problems (Anderson et al., 2002). A total of 62% of adults who are aged 65 and older report two or more chronic conditions (Anderson et al., 2002; Center for Disease Control and Prevention, 2009a) including heart disease, lung disease, diabetes, cancer, musculoskeletal disorders, stroke, and psychiatric disorders. A total of 49.9% of adults aged 65 and older have at least one medical condition which includes cognitive impairment, falls, incontinence, low BMI, dizziness, vision and hearing impairment, all of which are significantly associated with functional health impairments (Cigolle, Langa, Kabeto, Tian, & Blaum, 2007). Dementia has a prevalence rate of 13.9% among adults aged 71 and older and 37.4% among adults aged 90 and older (Plassman et al., 2007). The increased life expectancy and chronic illness among older adults are associated with an increase in the number of adult children providing care as well as an increase in the length of time for which caregiving is required (Family Caregiver Alliance, 2005).

The trend of increased life expectancy is occurring simultaneously with decreasing fertility rate (Center for Disease Control and Prevention, 2000; Hamilton, Martin, & Ventura, 2009). The fertility rate peaked in the post-World War II baby boom, declined dramatically until the 1970s, and has fluctuated with the economy thereafter, increasing in times of economic wealth and declining in economic recessions (Livingston & Cohn, 2010). Consequently, although older individuals today have adult children from the baby boom generation to potentially rely on in times of need, the number of adult children available to provide assistance will most likely decline over time for the baby boomers and their children.

Marriage patterns have also changed over the past few decades among both parents and children. The rate of divorce, which peaked in 1981 (Center for Disease Control and

Prevention, 2009b; S. C. Clarke, 1995), has stabilized over time. There is some evidence to suggest the decline may be due to decreases in the marriage rates, which in turn may be due in part to delays in the age of marriage and increases in cohabitation (Kreider, 2005; National Marriage Project, 2009; Snyder & Dillow, 2010; Snyder, Dillow, & Hoffman, 2009).

These trends of increased life expectancy, declines in fertility rates, and changes in marriage and divorce have led to a rise in multigenerational families that often include diverse, "blended" family forms including stepparents and stepchildren. These larger and more diverse families may serve as a resource as well as a source of strain for individuals as they age. For instance, adult children in blended families may have more family members to rely on for support in times of need. At the same time, individuals who undergo divorce may need more support due to lower psychological well-being and a loss of financial resources (Waite, Luo, & Lewin, 2009). Blended families also complicate the situation in terms of obligations to provide caregiving (Ganong & Coleman, 2006).

Coresidence, geographic proximity, and contact

Structural factors also include coresidency, geographical proximity, and contact frequency. It is becoming more common for adults in their twenties and thirties to live with their parents (U.S. Census Bureau, 2009b). According to the U.S. Census Bureau, (2009b), in 1960, a total of 52% of men and 35% of women aged 18 to 24 were living at home. In 2009, the percentage increased, with a total of 57% of men and 49% of women aged 18 to 24 living at home. Because college students who reside in dormitories are included in the category of young adults living in their parents' homes, these statistics may not be completely accurate. Nevertheless, an increasing trend involves children returning back home once they graduate from college (Mitchell, 2006). There is a need for more accurate data on these new trends among young adults.

Data on geographic proximity between parents and adult children suggest that once adult children move out, they live relatively close to one another. Unlike coresidency, trends in geographical proximity of parents and children appear to have remained stable over time. For example, more than 50% of adults reported living one hour or less from their parents in the 1990s (Lawton, Silverstein, & Bengtson, 1994). Similarly, according to the 2002 Health and Retirement Study, 51% of the respondents indicate that at least one adult child lives within 10 miles (National Institute on Aging, 2007). Likewise in Europe, parents and children appear to live relatively close; 84% of parents and adult children live within 15.5 miles from one another (Kohli, Kunemund, & Ludicke, 2005).

Throughout the world, weekly contact occurs relatively frequently between adult children and their parents (Fingerman et al., 2011; Kalmijn & De Vries, 2009). Contact frequency varies by demographics and other structural characteristics including geographical location and social roles. Parents tend to have more contact with adult children who live closer to them (Bordone, 2009). Women tend to maintain more frequent contact with their parents and adult children, especially via telephone (Taylor, Funk, Craighill, & Kennedy, 2006). Contact between adult children and fathers becomes less frequent following parental divorce (Shapiro, 2003). Married children report less contact with parents than divorced children or never married children (Bucx, van Wel, Knijn, & Hagendoorn, 2008; Sarkisian & Gerstel, 2008). Regardless of marital status, greater contact with parents occurs among adult children who have offspring of their own (Bucx et al., 2008).

Contact may be increasing over time as new ways of communicating have emerged including text messaging and use of social networking sites. The degree to which parents and children are using these new methods, and whether these forms of contact are perceived similarly as face-to-face or phone contact are unclear, but this is an excellent topic for future research. Parents and children tend to, on average, live relatively close to one another and engage in regular contact. Next, we consider what might occur during these weekly contacts in terms of support exchange.

Support Exchange in the Parent–Child Tie

Adult children and their parents serve as primary sources of social support to one another across the lifespan (Fingerman, 2001; Silverstein, Gans, & Yang, 2006; Silverstein, Parrott, & Bengtson, 1995). The majority of support travels downstream in families with parents providing more support to offspring (especially practical and financial support) than the reverse, at least until parents develop health problems and the balance starts to shift toward equilibrium or greater support given to parents (Grundy, 2005; Zarit & Eggebeen, 2002).

Types and predictors of support

There are two forms of support exchanges: tangible and intangible (Antonucci, 2001). Tangible support includes financial and practical help such as assistance with household chores and grocery shopping. Intangible support includes emotional encouragement and companionship such as listening to one another regarding problems, talking with one another about recent events, and visiting with one another socially.

Studies of support exchange in the parent–child tie often focus on the tangible form. Using the Panel Study of Income Dynamics, Schoeni and Ross (2005) found that parents of children aged 18 to 24 provide their offspring with an average of $38,000, which is about $2,200 per year. However, parents make differentiations between their children in the financial support they provide based on children's needs and their own resources. McGarry and Schoeni (1995, 1997) found that parents provide more assistance to children who have lower incomes, who are unmarried, are younger, have children, and have obtained less education. In addition, parents who have greater income, greater education, better health, and fewer children provide more financial help to their children.

These findings on tangible support are consistent with contingency theory, which suggests that family members provide support when they detect increased need such as health problems, financial hardships, and emotional needs (Eggebeen & Davey, 1998; Schoeni, 1997). It is not clear, however, from this work whether support varies by emotional factors such as relationship quality and relationship history.

In addition to financial support, parents make differentiations in other types of support provided to their children. Suitor, Pillemer, and Sechrist (2006) examined ways in which mothers differentiated the support they provide to their children including help with an illness, comfort during a personal crisis, help with chores, or financial help. Similar to the financial support literature and consistent with contingency theory, mothers appeared to respond to children's needs. Mothers provide more support to children who were daughters, unmarried, lived closer, and had poorer health. In addition, mothers provide greater support to children who provided more support to them, which is consistent with Antonucci's (1990) support bank theory. Antonucci (1990) postulated that parents and children provide lagged reciprocal support based on the amount of support they have accumulated or provided over time.

Fingerman, Miller, Birditt, and Zarit (2009) found that middle-aged parents provide frequent support to their young adult offspring, but that the frequency of support varies by support type. Parents provide intangible (emotional and listening) support an average of once a week, whereas they provide tangible support (advice, practical support, and financial help) an average of once a month to several times a year. Consistent with contingency theory, parents provided support to children with greater need (children with more problems, who were unmarried, who were younger, daughters, students, coresident children, and had offspring of their own). However, parents also provide more support to their most successful children. This finding is consistent with the intergenerational stake hypothesis (Bengtson & Kuypers, 1971), which postulates that parents feel greater investment and gain more self-worth in the relationship than do children regarding their parents. However, the situation changes when the parents become ill. In line with contingency theory, Fingerman and colleagues (2011) report that middle-aged people provide more support to their parents when their parents develop health problems.

Caregiving

Caring for individuals with mental and physical health problems involves a range of activities from performing minor daily tasks and household chores to major duties such as bathing and feeding. Older adults with health problems, especially those who are unmarried, tend to rely on their adult children for caregiving (Johnson & Wiener, 2006). One out of five adults aged 55 to 64 provide practical support to their parents or parents-in-law (Johnson & Schaner, 2005).

Although caregiving is beneficial because it reduces the likelihood of older adults having to enter a nursing home (Lo Sasso & Johnson, 2002), caregiving is often considered a harmful and long-term chronic stressor for caregivers (Zarit & Eggebeen, 2002). Caregivers often juggle multiple roles including working full-time or part-time and supporting younger adult offspring (Johnson & Lo Sasso, 2000; Johnson & Schaner, 2005). Caregiving has strong detrimental effects on psychological well-being (Pinquart, 2001) and continuous caregiver burden predicts increased depressive symptoms over time (Epstein-Lubow, Davis, Miller, & Tremont, 2008). Caregivers have poorer health than people who are not providing care (Pinquart & Sorensen, 2003; Vitaliano, Zhang, & Scanlan, 2003). Based on a meta-analysis of the literature on caregiving and health, Vitaliano and colleagues (2003) found that caregivers had higher levels of stress hormones, elevated blood pressure, elevated glucose, and compromised immune responses compared to noncaregivers. Son and colleagues (2007) found that caregivers who provide care to individuals with more behavioral problems reported poorer health and are less likely to attend to their own health compared to caregivers who provided care for individuals with fewer behavioral problems. These associations were even stronger when caregivers appraised the behavioral problems as more stressful.

There is also evidence to show that caregiving may have benefits or rewards for caregivers. For example, people who provide caregiving may feel satisfaction, pride, self-worth, and gratification (Archbold, 1983). Adult children who provide care report improvements in their relationships with parents (Hinrichsen, Hernandez, & Pollack, 1992). Studies also show that adult child caregivers report more rewards from caregiving than do spousal caregivers, perhaps because they feel less obligated to provide support and thus receive more recognition and gain greater self-worth for providing help (Raschick & Ingersoll-Dayton, 2004).

Due to increases in diverse family forms, caregiving has in some ways become more complicated. Adult children report feeling more obligated to assist their biological parents than their stepparents (Ganong & Coleman, 2006). Caregiving becomes more complicated in this context because there may be more negativity associated with providing care to people to whom there is little obligation and low levels of closeness.

Parent–Child Relationship Quality

Relationship quality includes positive and negative aspects of the relationship. Positive aspects of the relationship typically refer to the degree to which parents and children love and care for one another and understand one another.

The extent to which a relationship's quality is characterized as positive varies by characteristics of the child and the parent. Parents report greater positive relations with young adult children who do not have their own children, are employed, are married, and do not coreside with parents (Belsky, Jaffee, Caspi, Moffitt, & Silva, 2003). Suitor and Pillemer (2000) found that older mothers felt more positive about children who had involuntary problems (e.g., health problems), whereas they felt least positive about children they perceived as having voluntary problems (e.g., trouble with the law). Parents report greater positive relationship quality than children across the lifespan (Giarrusso, Feng, & Bengtson, 2004; Shapiro, 2004). Consistent with the intergenerational stake hypothesis, parents appear to be more emotionally invested in the relationship than are their offspring (Bengtson & Kuypers, 1971). In addition, parents may feel more positive about their more successful children because they gain greater feelings of self-worth from their more successful offspring (Ryff, Lee, Essex, & Schmutte, 1994).

The negative aspects of the parent–child tie often refers to the extent to which parents and children get on each other's nerves, make too many demands on one another, or are critical of one another. Mothers report more negative relationships (especially with daughters) than fathers (Fingerman, 2001; Umberson, 1992). Mothers may feel greater closeness and negativity in the relationship because they tend to have more contact and exchange more support with their children than do fathers.

Negative relationship quality also appears to decline with age. Birditt, Jackey, and Antonucci (2009) found that ratings of negativity regarding children decreased over a 12-year period among young and middle-aged adults, but not among older adults. These findings are similar to cross-sectional research indicating that older people report greater closeness and less negativity in the parent–child relationship than do younger adults (Akiyama, Antonucci, Takahashi, & Langfahl, 2003; Rossi & Rossi, 1990; Umberson, 1992). These findings may be due to age-related changes in emotion regulation as well as to changes in contact frequency as children become more independent, move out of the house, and establish their own families. Future research should examine these factors as possible explanations for longitudinal patterns of negative relationship quality.

Other studies have examined more specifically the topics that cause tensions in the relationship. Tension topics often fall into two general categories referred to as relationship-type and individual-type tensions (Birditt, Jackey, & Antonucci, 2009; Fingerman, 1996). Relationship-type tensions pertain to closeness and cohesion or lack thereof. For example, adult children may complain about parents providing unsolicited advice or about personality differences. Individual-type tensions involve problems with the behavior of one member of the dyad and include irritations regarding independence or self-care. For example, parents may express irritation with how their children manage their finances or maintain their houses.

According to the developmental schism hypothesis, parents and children experience tensions because they are at different developmental stages and have different needs (Fingerman, 1996, 2001). Parents often desire greater closeness, whereas children desire independence. These schisms lead to variations between family members in perceptions of tension topics. Fingerman (1996) found that middle-aged daughters reported their older mothers to be intrusive, which may signify mother's greater investment in the relationship. Similarly, Clarke, Preston, Raksin, and Bengtson (1999) found that mothers and fathers (mean age 62) were most upset about children's individual behaviors (habits and lifestyle choices), whereas their sons and daughters (mean age 39) were most upset about relationship-type tensions such as communication and interaction style. Birditt, Miller, Fingerman, and Lefkowitz (2009) found that mothers and fathers reported greater tension than did their children regarding individual-type tensions (e.g., finances and housekeeping). Parents may report greater individual-type tensions because they worry about their children's independence or lack thereof, or they may "reframe" problems in order to maintain positive relationship quality. Likewise, children may report more relationship-type tensions because parents desire greater closeness in the relationship.

Studies have also assessed the strategy types that parents and children use to cope with tensions in their relationship. Fingerman (1995) found that older mothers and middle-aged daughters were most likely to use constructive strategies (e.g., work with one another to find solutions, try to understand the other person's perspective) compared to avoidant (e.g., avoid talking about the topic, avoid talking to one another) and destructive (e.g., yelling, arguing). Similarly, in their study of mothers, fathers, and their adult offspring, Birditt, Rott, and Fingerman (2009) found that parents and children were most likely to cope with tensions in their relationship with constructive strategies followed by avoidant and destructive strategies. The use of destructive and avoidant strategies predicted lower relationship quality, whereas the use of constructive strategies predicted greater relationship quality. Interestingly, parents were more likely to report using constructive strategies than were offspring. Parents may use more positive strategies because they are more emotionally invested in the relationship than are their children (Bengtson & Kuypers, 1971). It is important to note that these studies were cross–sectional, so it is unclear whether relationship quality causes individuals to use different strategies or the reverse.

Ambivalence, which refers to simultaneous feelings of positive and negative quality, is also common in the parent–child tie. Up to 40 to 50% of parents and children indicate that they experience at least some mixed emotions regarding that relationship (Fingerman, Hay, & Birditt, 2004; Pillemer & Suitor, 2002). Ambivalence varies between and within families, and is most likely to occur when the balance between independence and closeness is strained (Luescher & Pillemer, 1998).

Parents tend to report greater ambivalence regarding children who have not assumed the roles associated with adulthood. Children, on the other hand, tend to experience more ambivalence when parents have health troubles or need caregiving. For example, mothers reported greater ambivalence regarding children who were unmarried, had more problems, and who they viewed as not reciprocating support (Pillemer et al., 2007). Similarly, mothers and fathers reported greater ambivalence regarding children who were invested in fewer roles (e.g., marriage, employment; Fingerman, Chen, Hay, Cichy, & Lefkowitz, 2006). Willson, Shuey, and Elder (2003) found that children reported greater feelings of ambivalence regarding mothers, and parents in poorer health who required caregiving, and with whom they had poor quality relationships earlier in life. Similarly, Fingerman et al. (2006) found that parents reported greater ambivalence when they themselves were in poorer health. It is most likely the case that children's problems and lack of social roles, as well as parents' health issues and need for caregiving, cause greater ambivalence because parents and children experience conflicting desires to help one another, while at the same time maintaining their independence. Ambivalence is caused by having two conflicting norms of behavior within the same relationship (Luescher & Pillemer, 1998).

Ambivalence also varies by generation and gender. Offspring tend to report greater feelings of ambivalence than their mothers (Willson, Shuey, Elder, & Wickrama, 2006), but lower feelings of ambivalence than their fathers (Birditt, Rott, & Fingerman, 2009). Birditt, Fingerman, and Zarit (2010) examined within-family variations in the predictors of ambivalence among mothers and fathers. Both parents reported greater ambivalence about children with less relationship success. Fathers, but not mothers, reported greater feelings of ambivalence regarding adult children with physical or emotional problems and lower career success. These findings indicate that ambivalence arises due to conflicts between independence and closeness. In addition, these findings indicated that men may be more sensitive to their children's lack of independence than women. There may be fewer variations between mothers and fathers than previously assumed.

Studies of the positive, negative, and ambivalent aspects of the parent–child tie indicate a great deal of within- and between-family variations in how parents and children feel about one another. Parents report more positivity and investment than do their children. However, parents also report feeling more tension and are more likely to use constructive strategies than their children. These seemingly contradictory findings may indicate the emotional complexity and ambivalence in this relationship, which occurs when there is imbalance in the needs for independence and closeness in the relationship. More research needs to be conducted on the emotional aspects of the relationship over time and how emotional aspects of the relationship are associated with the functional and supportive aspects of the relationship. It would be especially interesting to examine associations between relationship quality, daily contact, and support exchange between parents and children.

Effects of the Parent–Child Relationship on Health and Well-Being

Parent–child relationships are associated with a variety of outcomes for both parents and children including self-rated health, quality of life, and depressive symptoms. Studies vary in terms of the aspects of the relationship they assess as well as whether they examine the well-being of parents, adult children, or both.

Several studies have investigated the implications of support and relationship quality for parents' well-being. Silverstein and Bengtson (1991) examined the association between parents' feelings of positive relationship quality and parental mortality. Although they found no direct effect of positive relationship quality on mortality, they did find a buffering effect. Parents who were recently widowed had lower mortality rates if they had greater positive relations with offspring. Parents also report greater well-being when their children provide them with emotional support or affection (Lang & Schutze, 2002) and when they report greater positive quality relationships with children (Ryan & Willits, 2007). Byers, Levy, Allore, Bruce, and Kasl (2008) also found that parents reported fewer depressive symptoms when children relied on them for tangible support. Thus it appears that parents benefit from receiving and from giving support to their children. Parents' well-being also appears to be affected by their perceptions of how well their children are doing in their lives. Greenfield and Marks (2006) found that parents whose adult children had more problems reported lower well-being. In contrast, Ryff et al. (1994) found that parents who reported that their children were more well-adjusted (e.g., happier, satisfied with their lives) had greater levels of well-being. Interestingly, however, parents reported lower well-being when they viewed their children as better adjusted than themselves as young adults. The authors suggest that this is similar to social comparison research indicating that people report lower self-esteem after comparing themselves to more successful peers. Indeed, future work should examine whether the effects of successful offspring on well-being vary depending on whether parents compare their offspring to themselves or to other children their age.

Studies have also assessed associations between parental ambivalence and parental well-being. Ward (2008) found that parents who reported greater collective ambivalence (i.e., low quality or contact with at least some children) reported greater depression. Lowenstein (2007) examined mothers and fathers aged 75 and older in England, Norway, Germany, Spain, and Israel to determine whether their feelings of ambivalence, solidarity, and conflict predicted quality of life. In all countries, ambivalence predicted lower quality of life, whereas solidarity predicted greater quality of life. Additionally, solidarity had a greater impact on quality of life than ambivalence. Lowenstein (2007) found some interesting variations between countries in conflict and ambivalence, however. Israeli parents reported the greatest conflict in parent–child relationships whereas parents in Norway, Germany, and Spain reported the greatest ambivalence. Lowenstein (2007) suggested that the variations between countries were the result of variations in cultural norms regarding familial obligation and openness in conversation. Much more work is needed in this area, however, to understand cultural variations and the factors that account for those variations.

Parent–child relationship quality also influences adult children's well-being. Shaw, Krause, Chatters, Connell, and Ingersoll-Dayton (2004) found that adult children who reported lower parental support as children also reported greater depressive symptoms and chronic illnesses in adulthood. Umberson (1992) found that less support from mothers and greater strain with mothers and fathers were associated with greater psychological distress among adult children. It is important to note, of course, that these studies are cross-sectional. Children who report lower well-being may be more likely to view their parents in a negative light and remember their childhood experiences as having been more negative.

Other studies have examined the associations between parent–child relationship quality and well-being for both generations simultaneously. Fingerman, Pitzer, Lefkowitz, Birditt, and Mroczek (2008) assessed the associations between ambivalence and well-being among parents and offspring and found that ambivalence predicts lower psychological well-being among mothers, fathers, and offspring. Interestingly, adult children reported lower self-rated health when they had fathers who reported feeling more ambivalent about them. The authors speculated that fathers in this generation were not as involved in caring for their children as mothers and may feel uncomfortable and thus more ambivalent caring for an adult child who is ill. This finding is similar to Birditt et al.'s (2010) finding that fathers reported greater ambivalence regarding children with physical health problems. Mothers reported poorer self-rated health when children reported feeling more ambivalent about them. It is possible that children provide more care to mothers who are in poor health than to fathers and that they feel more ambivalence due to providing caregiving.

Overall, it appears that parents and their adult children have important influences on one another's physical and psychological health and well-being. More research is needed, however, on the longitudinal effects of the relationship on well-being. It is most likely that the associations between well-being and relationships are bidirectional.

Future Research Directions

There are several areas in need of further study in the parent–child tie. First, much of the research on the parent–child tie is cross-sectional and it is unclear to what extent there are causal associations between the structure, function, and quality of relationships and well-being. In order to understand the complex associations among these variables, researchers should conduct longitudinal studies of the parent–child tie. Another approach for understanding the dynamic associations between variables in the parent–child relationship may be to incorporate daily diary methods. Daily diary studies involve repeated measurements, often once a day (Almeida, 2005). Researchers could then, for example, examine whether support exchanges predict changes in daily well-being and or whether daily contacts with parents and children are associated with relationship quality and well-being.

An additional important research direction may be to include assessments of genetics and biological indicators of stress and well-being into studies of the parent–child relationship in adulthood. Research on younger children and parents indicates that gene–environment interactions have important influences on development and later health and well-being (Caspi & Moffitt, 2006). Genetic research may help us to understand the extent to which similarities between parents and children are due to genetic similarities as well as whether particular genes make individuals resilient or vulnerable to adverse parent–child relationships. Another area of potential interest is the inclusion of stress hormones into research on the parent–child tie. Adam and her colleagues have begun a very interesting program of research examining the implications of the family environment on young children's cortisol (Adam, 2004; Pendry & Adam, 2007). This research could be carried forward into adult parent–child relationships as a way to understand how daily cortisol rhythms relate to tensions. This approach would provide relevant information regarding how parent–child relationships may "get under the skin" to influence well-being and health.

Future research should also consider how parents and children are using new technology to engage in contacts and exchanges. For example, contact frequency between adult children and their parents may be facilitated by the advent of new technology including cell phones, text messaging, email, video conferencing, and social networking websites.

Conclusions

The parent–child relationship is one of the longest lasting, often enduring 60 years or more, a trend that will increase as life expectancy continues to rise. Parents and children engage in frequent contact and rely on one another for support that is both tangible and intangible. The parent–child relationship is particularly fascinating because it involves high levels of positive and negative sentiments. There is a great deal of variation within and between families in the amount of support provided and in relationship quality. It is also particularly pertinent to examine parent–child ties because they have important influences on individuals' well-being, quality of life, and longevity.

Despite the increasing momentum of research on the parent and adult child tie, there is still a great deal of work to do and many unanswered questions remain. Little knowledge exists regarding how the parent–child relationship changes longitudinally in terms of the support exchanged and the influences of this relationship on well-being. There is also little known about the influence of the parent–child tie on parents and children's biological systems beyond self-reported health. It is hoped that this chapter inspires others to contribute to this fascinating and growing field, as intergenerational relationships are such an important and influential part of life for aging adults.

References

Adam, E. K. (2004). Beyond quality: Parental and residential stability and children's adjustment. *Directions in Psychological Science, 13*, 210–213.

Akiyama, H., Antonucci, T., Takahashi, K., & Langfahl, E. S. (2003). Negative interactions in close relationships across the life span. *Journals of Gerontology: Psychological Sciences, 58*, P70–P79.

Almeida, D. M. (2005). Resilience and vulnerability to daily stressors assessed via diary methods. *Current Directions in Psychological Science, 14*, 64–68.

Anderson, G., Horvath, J., Herbert, R., Ridgway, K., Pavlovich, W., Harjai, G., . . . GYMR Public Relations., (2002). Chronic conditions: Making the case for ongoing care. Johns Hopkins University. Retrieved from http://www.rwjf.org/files/research/chronicbook2002.pdf

Antonucci, T. C. (1990). Social supports and social relationships. In R. H. Binstock & L. K. George (Eds.). *Handbook of aging and the social sciences* (3rd ed., pp. 205–226). New York: Academic Press.

Antonucci, T. C. (2001). Social relations: An examination of social networks, social support and sense of control. In J. E. Birren & K. W. Schaie (Eds.), *Handbook of the psychology of aging* (5th ed., pp. 427–453). New York: Academic Press.

Archbold, P. C. (1983). Impact of parent-caring on women. *Family Relations, 32*, 39–45.

Belsky, J., Jaffee, S., Caspi, A., Moffitt, T., & Silva, P. (2003). Intergenerational relationships in young adulthood and their life-course, mental-health, and personality correlates. *Journal of Family Psychology, 17*, 460–471.

Bengtson, V. L., & Kuypers, J. A. (1971). Generational differences and the developmental stake. *Aging and Human Development, 2*, 249–260.

Birditt, K. S., Fingerman, K. L., & Zarit, S. (2010). Adult children's problems and successes: Implications for intergenerational ambivalence. *Journals of Gerontology: Psychological Sciences, 65B*, 145–153.

Birditt, K. S., Jackey, L. M. H., & Antonucci, T. C. (2009). Longitudinal patterns of negative relationship quality across adulthood. *Journals of Gerontology: Psychological Sciences, 64B*, 55–64.

Birditt, K. S., Miller, L. M., Fingerman, K. L., & Lefkowitz, E. S. (2009). Tensions in the parent and adult child relationship: Links to solidarity and ambivalence. *Psychology and Aging, 24*, 287–295.

Birditt, K. S., Rott, L. M., & Fingerman, K. L. (2009). "If you can't say something nice, don't say anything at all": Coping with interpersonal tensions in the parent–child relationship during adulthood. *Journal of Family Psychology, 23*, 769–778.

Bordone, V. (2009). Contact and proximity of older people to their adult children: A comparison between Italy and Sweden. *Population Space Place, 15*, 359–380.

Bucx, F., van Wel, F., Knijn, T., & Hagendoorn, L. (2008). Intergenerational contact and the life course status of young adult children. *Journal of Marriage and Family, 70*, 144–157.

Byers, A. L., Levy, B. R., Allore, H. G., Bruce, M. L., & Kasl, S. V. (2008). When parents matter to their adult children: Filial reliance associated with parents' depressive symptoms. *Journal of Gerontology: Psychological Sciences and Social Sciences, 63*, 33–40.

Caspi, A., & Moffit, T. E. (2006). Gene–environment interactions in psychiatry: Joining forces with neuroscience. *Nature Reviews Neuroscience, 7*, 583–590.

Center for Disease Control and, Prevention., (2000). Live births, birth rates, and fertility rates, by race: United States, 1909-2000 (Table 1-1). Retrieved from http://www.cdc.gov/nchs/data/statab/t001x01.pdf

Center for Disease Control and Prevention (2009a). Chronic diseases: The power to prevent, the call to control. *Retrieved from* http://www.cdc.gov/chronicdisease/resources/publications/AAG/pdf/chronic.pdf

Center for Disease Control and, Prevention., (2009b). National marriage and divorce rate trends. Retrieved from http://www.cdc.gov/nchs/nvss/marriage_divorce_tables.html

Cigolle, C. T., Langa, K. M., Kabeto, M. U., Tian, Z., & Blaum, C. S. (2007). Geriatric conditions and disability: The health and retirement study. *Annals of Internal Medicine, 147*, 156–164.

Clarke, E., Preston, M., Raksin, J., & Bengtson, V. L. (1999). Types of conflict and tensions between older parents and adult children. *The Gerontologist, 39*, 261–270.

Clarke, S. C. (1995). Advance report of final divorce statistics, 1989 and 1990. *Monthly Vital Statistics Report, 43*(8), National Center for Health Statistics. Retrieved from http://www.cdc.gov/nchs/data/mvsr/supp/mv43_09s.pdf

Connidis, I. A. (2010). *Family ties and aging* (2nd ed.). Thousand Oaks, CA: Sage.

Dobriansky, P. J., Suzman, R. M., & Hodes, R. J. (2007). Why population aging matters? A global perspective. National Institute on Aging and National Institutes of Health. Retrieved from http://www.nia.nih.gov/NR/rdonlyres/9E91407E-CFE8-4903-9875-D5AA75BD1D50/0/WPAM.pdf

Eggebeen, D. J., & Davey, A. (1998). Do safety nets work? The role of anticipated help in times of need. *Journal of Marriage and the Family, 60*, 939–950.

Epstein-Lubow, G., Davis, J. D., Miller, I. W., & Tremont, G. (2008). Persisting burden predicts depressive symptoms in dementia caregivers. *Journal of Geriatric Psychiatry and Neurology, 21*, 198–203.

Family Caregiver Alliance. (2005). Fact Sheet: Selected caregiver statistics. Retrieved from http://www.caregiver.org/caregiver/jsp/content_node.jsp?nodeid=439

Fingerman, K. L. (1995). Aging mothers' and their adult daughters' perceptions of conflict behaviors. *Psychology & Aging, 10*, 639–649.

Fingerman, K. L. (1996). Sources of tension in the aging mother and adult daughter relationship. *Psychology & Aging, 11*, 591–606.

Fingerman, K. L. (2001). *Aging mothers and their adult daughters: A study in mixed emotions.* New York: Springer.

Fingerman, K. L., Chen, P. C., Hay, E. L., Cichy, K. E., & Lefkowitz, E. S. (2006). Ambivalent reactions in the parent and adult-child relationship. *Journals of Gerontology: Psychological Sciences, 61*, P152–P160.

Fingerman, K. L., Hay, E. L., & Birditt, K. S. (2004). The best of ties, the worst of ties: Close, problematic, and ambivalent relationships across the lifespan. *Journal of Marriage and Family, 66*, 792–808.

Fingerman, K., Miller, L., Birditt, K., & Zarit, S. (2009). Giving to the good and the needy: Parental support of grown children. *Journal of Marriage and Family, 71*, 1220–1233.

Fingerman, K. L., Pitzer, L. M., Chan, W., Birditt, K. S., Franks, M. M., & Zarit, S. (2011). Who gets what and why: Help middle-aged adults provide to parents and grown children. *Journal of Gerontology: Social Sciences, 66B*(1) 87–98.

Fingerman, K. L., Pitzer, L., Lefkowitz, E. S., Birditt, K. S., & Mroczek, D. (2008). Ambivalent relationship qualities between adults and their parents: Implications for both parties' well-being. *Journals of Gerontology: Psychological Sciences, 63,* P362–P371.

Ganong, L., & Coleman, M. (2006). Obligations to stepparents acquired in later life: Relationship quality and acuity of needs. *Journal of Gerontology: Social Sciences, 61B,* S80–S88.

Giarrusso, R., Feng, D., & Bengtson, V.L. (2004). The intergenerational stake over 20 years. In M. Silverstein (Ed.), *Annual Review of Gerontology and Geriatrics* (vol.24, pp. 55–76). New York: Springer.

Greenfield, E. A., & Marks, N. F. (2006). Linked lives: Adult children's problems and their parents' psychological and relational well-being. *Journal of Marriage and Family, 68,* 442–454.

Grundy, E. (2005). Reciprocity in relationships: Socio-economic and health influences on intergenerational exchanges between Third Age parents and their adult children in Great Britain. *British Journal of Sociology, 56,* 233–255.

Hamilton, B. E., Martin, J. A., & Ventura, S. J. (2009). Births: Preliminary data for 2007. *National Center for Health Statistics: National vital statistics reports, 57*(12). Retrieved from http://www.cdc.gov/nchs/data/nvsr/nvsr57/nvsr57_12.pdf

Heron, M. P., Hoyert, D. L., Murphy, S. L., Xu, J. Q., Kochanek, K. D., & Tejada-Vera, B. (2009). Deaths: Final data for 2006. *National Center for Health Statistics: National vital statistics reports, 57.* Retrieved from http://www.cdc.gov/nchs/data/nvsr/nvsr57/nvsr57_14.pdf

Hinrichsen, G., Hernandez, N., & Pollack, S. (1992). Difficulties and rewards in family care of the depressed older adult. *The Gerontologist, 32,* 486–492.

Johnson, R. W., & Lo Sasso, A. T. (2000). Parental care at midlife: Balancing work and family responsibilities near retirement. *The Urban Institute: The retirement project brief series, 9.* Retrieved from http://www.urban.org/UploadedPDF/Brief9.pdf

Johnson, R. W., & Schaner, S. G. (2005). Many older Americans engage in caregiving activities. *The retirement project: Perspectives on productive aging, 3,* 1–6. Retrieved from http://www.urban.org/UploadedPDF/311203_Perspectives3.pdf

Johnson, R. W., & Wiener, J. M. (2006). A profile of frail older Americans and their caregivers. *The Urban Institute: The retirement project.* Retrieved from http://www.urban.org/UploadedPDF/311284_older_americans.pdf

Kalmijn, M., & De Vries, J. (2009). Change and stability in parent–child contact in five Western countries. *European Journal of Population, 25,* 257–276.

Kinsella, K.& He, W. (2009). *An aging world: 2008.* Retrieved from http://www.census.gov/prod/2009pubs/p95-09-1.pdf

Kohli, M., Kunemund, H., & Ludicke., J. (2005). Family structure, proximity and contact. In A. Börsch-Supan et al. (Eds.), *Health, ageing and retirement in Europe- First results from the Survey of Health,* Ageing and Retirement in Europe (pp. 164–170). Mannheim: MEA. Retrieved from http://www.share-project.org/t3/share/uploads/tx_sharepublications/CH_4.1.pdf

Kreider, R. (2005). Number, timing, and duration of marriages and divorces: 2001. U. S. Census Bureau, *Current population reports,* P70–97. Retrieved from http://www.census.gov/prod/2005pubs/p70–97.pdf

Lang, F. R., & Schutze, Y. (2002) Adult children's supportive behaviors and older parents' subjective well-being: A developmental perspective on intergenerational relationships. *Journal of Social Issues, 58,* 661–680.

Lawton, L., Silverstein, M., & Bengtson, V. (1994). Affection, social contact, and geographic distance between adult children and their parents. *Journal of Marriage and the Family, 56*(1), 57–68.

Livingston, G., & Cohn, D. (2010). *U. S. birth rate decline linked to recession*. Pew Research Center demographic trends report. Retrieved from http://pewsocialtrends.org/assets/pdf/753-birth-rates-recession.pdf

Lo Sasso, A. T., & Johnson, R. W. (2002). Does informal care reduce nursing home admissions for the frail elderly? *Inquiry, 29*, 279–297.

Lowenstein, A. (2007). Solidarity-conflict and ambivalence: Testing two conceptual frameworks and their impact on quality of life for older family members. *Journals of Gerontology: Social Sciences, 62*, S100–S107.

Luescher, K., & Pillemer, K. (1998). Intergenerational ambivalence: A new approach to the study of parent-child relations in later life. *Journal of Marriage and the Family, 60*, 413–425.

McGarry, K., & Schoeni, R. F. (1995). Transfer behavior in the Health & Retirement Study: Measurement and the redistribution of resources within the family. *Journal of Human Resources, 30*, S184–S226.

McGarry, K., & Schoeni, R. F. (1997). Transfer behavior within the family: Results from the asset and health dynamics study. *Journal of Gerontology: Social Sciences, 52B*, 82–92.

Mitchell, B. A. (2006). *The boomerang age: Transitions to adulthood in families*. New Brunswick, NJ: Aldine Transaction.

National Institute on Aging. (2007). Family characteristics and intergenerational transfers. In F. Karp (Ed.), *Growing older in America: The health and retirement study*. Retrieved from http://www.nia.nih.gov/NR/rdonlyres/D164FE6C-C6E0-4E78-B27F-7E8D8C0FFEE5/0/HRS_Text_WEB.pdf

National Marriage Project (2009). The state of our unions: Marriage in America. University of Virginia. Retrieved from http://stateofourunions.org/2009/SOOU2009.pdf

Pendry, P., & Adam, E. K. (2007). Associations between parents' marital functioning, maternal parenting quality, maternal emotion and child cortisol levels. *International Journal of Behavioral Development, 31*, 218–231.

Pillemer, K., & Suitor, J. J. (2002). Explaining mothers' ambivalence toward their adult children. *Journal of Marriage and Family, 64*, 602–613.

Pillemer, K., Suitor, J. J., Mock, S. E., Sabir, M., Pardo, T., & Sechrist, J. (2007). Capturing the complexity of intergenerational relations: Exploring ambivalence within later-life families. *Journal of Social Issues, 63*, 775–791.

Pinquart, M. (2001). Correlates of subjective health in older adults: A meta-analysis. *Psychology and Aging, 16*, 414–426.

Pinquart, M., & Sorensen, S. (2003). Differences between caregivers and noncaregivers in psychological health and physical health: A meta-analysis, *Psychology and Aging, 18*, 250–267.

Plassman, B. L., Langa, K. M., Fisher, G. G., Heeringa, S. G., Weir, D. R., Ofstedal, M. B.,. . . Wallace, R. B. (2007). Prevalence of dementia in the United States: The aging, demographics, and memory study. *Neuroepidemiology, 29*, 125–132.

Raschick, M., & Ingersoll-Dayton, B. (2004). The costs and rewards of caregiving among aging spouses and adult children. *Family Relations, 53*, 317–325.

Rossi, A. S., & Rossi, P. H. (1990). *Of human bonding: Parent-child relations across the life-course*. New York: Aldine de Gruyter.

Ryan, A. K., & Willits, F. K. (2007). Family ties, physical health, and psychological well-being. *Journal of Aging and Health, 19*, 907–920.

Ryff, C. D., Lee, Y. H., Essex, M. J., & Schmutte, P. S. (1994). My children and me: Midlife evaluations of grown children and of self. *Psychology and Aging, 9*, 195–205.

Sarkisian, N., & Gerstel, N. (2008). Till marriage do us part: Adult children's relationships with their parents. *Journal of Marriage and Family, 70*, 360–376.

Schoeni, R. F. (1997). Private interhousehold transfers of money and time: New empirical evidence. *Review of Income and Wealth, 43,* 423–448.

Schoeni, R. F., & Ross, K. E. (2005). Material assistance from families during the transition to adulthood. In R.A. Settersten, F. F. Furstenberg, & R. G. Rumbaut (Eds.), *On the frontier of adulthood: Theory, research, and public policy* (pp. 396–417). Chicago: University of Chicago Press.

Shapiro, A. (2003). Later-life divorce and parent-adult child contact and proximity: A longitudinal analysis. *Journal of Family Issues, 24,* 264–285.

Shapiro, A. (2004). Revisiting the generation gap: Exploring the relationships of parent/adult-child dyads. *International Journal of Aging and Human Development, 58,* 127–146.

Shaw, B. A., Krause, N., Chatters, L. M., Connell, C. M., & Ingersoll-Dayton, B. (2004). Emotional support from parents early in life, aging, and health. *Psychology and Aging, 19,* 4–12.

Silverstein, M., & Bengtson, V. L. (1991). Do close parent-child relationships reduce the mortality risk of older parents? *Journal of Health and Social Behavior, 32,* 382–395.

Silverstein, M., Gans, D., & Yang, F. M. (2006). Intergenerational support to aging parents: The role of norms and needs. *Journal of Family Issues, 27,* 1068–1084.

Silverstein, M., Parrott, T. M., & Bengtson, V. L. (1995). Factors that predispose middle-aged sons and daughters to provide social support to older parents. *Journal of Marriage and Family, 57,* 465–475.

Snyder, T. D., & Dillow, S. A. (2010). *Digest of education statistics 2009 (NCES 2010-013).* Washington, DC: National Center for Education Statistics, Institute of Education Sciences, U. S. Department of Education. Retrieved from http://nces.ed.gov/pubs2010/2010013_0.pdf

Snyder, T. D., Dillow, S. A., & Hoffman, C. M. (2009). *Digest of education statistics 2008 (NCES 2009–020).* Washington, DC: National Center for Education Statistics, Institute of Education Sciences, U. S. Department of Education. Retrieved from http://nces.ed.gov/pubs2009/2009020.pdf

Son, J., Erno, A., Shea, D. G., Femia, E. E., Zarit, S. H., & Stephens, M. A. P. (2007). The caregiver stress process and health outcomes. *Journal of Aging and Health, 19,* 871–887.

Suitor, J. J., & Pillemer, K. (2000). Did mom really love you best? Developmental histories, status transitions, and parental favoritism in later life families. *Motivation and Emotion, 24*(2), 105–120.

Suitor, J. J., Pillemer, K., & Sechrist, J. (2006). Within-family differences in mothers' support to adult children. *Journal of Gerontology: Social Sciences, 61B,* S10–S17.

Taylor, P., Funk, C., Craighill, P., & Kennedy, C. (2006). Families drawn together by communication revolution. *PEW Research Center: A social trends report.* Retrieved from http://pewsocialtrends.org/assets/pdf/FamilyBonds.pdf

Taylor, P., Morin, R., Parker, K., Cohn, D., & Wang, W. (2009). Growing old in America: Expectations vs. reality. *PEW Research Center: A social & demographic trends report.* Retrieved from http://pewsocialtrends.org/assets/pdf/getting-old-in-america.pdf

Umberson, D. (1992). Relationships between adult children and their parents: Psychological consequences for both generations. *Journal of Marriage and the Family, 54,* 664–674.

U.S. Census, Bureau., (2009a). Age and sex in the United States: 2008. Retrieved from http://www.census.gov/population/www/socdemo/age/age_sex_2008.html

U.S. Census, Bureau., (2009b). Young adults living at home: 1960 to present (Table AD-1). Retrieved from www.census.gov/population/socdemo/hh-fam/ad1.xls

Vitaliano, P. P., Zhang, J., & Scanlan, J. M. (2003). Is caregiving hazardous to one's physical health? A meta-analysis. *Psychological Bulletin, 129,* 946–972.

Waite, L. J., Luo, Y., & Lewin, A. C. (2009). Marital happiness and marital stability: Consequences for psychological well-being. *Social Science Research, 38,* 201–212.

Ward, R. A. (2008). Multiple parent-adult child relations and well-being in middle and later life. *Journal of Gerontology: Social Sciences, 63B*, S239–248.

Ward, R. A., & Spitze, G. (1992). Consequences of parent-adult child coresidence: A review and research agenda. *Journal of Family Issues, 13*, 553–572.

Willson, A. E., Shuey, K. M., & Elder, G. H. (2003). Ambivalence in the relationship of adult children to aging parents and in-laws. *Journal of Marriage and Family, 65*, 1055–1072.

Willson, A. E., Shuey, K. M., Elder, G. H., & Wickrama, K. A. S. (2006). Ambivalence in mother-adult child relations: A dyadic analysis. *Social Psychology Quarterly, 69*, 235–252.

Zarit, S., & Eggebeen, D. J. (2002). Parent-child relationships in adulthood and later years. In M. Bornstein (Ed.), Handbook of parenting, Vol. 1: *Children & parenting* (2nd ed., pp. 135–161). Mahwah, NJ: Erlbaum.

21

Retirement

An Adult Development Perspective

Mo Wang

Demographic projections have shown that by 2012, nearly 20% of the total US workforce will be age 55 or older, up from just under 13% in 2000, leading to a sizable increase in the number of people who will transition into retirement in the next decade (Toossi, 2004). Similarly, 41% of the Canadian working population is expected to be between the ages of 45 and 64 by the year 2021 (Lende, 2005). In the United Kingdom, 30% of workers are already over 50 (Dixon, 2003). These labor force change patterns are also demonstrated by data from other countries and regions (e.g., European Union, Japan, China, and India; Tyers & Shi, 2007), reflecting the fact that the population as a whole is getting older due to several factors, such as the aging of the large baby boom generation, lower birth rates, and longer life expectancies (Alley & Crimmins, 2007). On the one hand, with the baby boomers reaching their retirement ages, many analysts are predicting growing labor shortages in tomorrow's workforce. In fact, according to a recent research report provided by the AARP (2005), in addition to the widely publicized shortages of nurses and other health care professionals, organizations that rely on such specially trained individuals as teachers, engineers, and many other skilled people are also starting to face significant skill shortages. On the other hand, retirement has been viewed as a major life-changing event in late life that poses significant adjustment challenges for older employees (Quick & Moen, 1998). Maladjustment to the retirement process has been shown to be associated with increased alcohol use (e.g., Perreira & Sloan, 2001) and decreased mental health (e.g., Wang, 2007).

Given the rapid aging of the labor force, employee retirement has been an important element in political, socioeconomic, and human resource areas during the past three decades. Consequently, retirement has been an interdisciplinary topic studied by researchers

The Wiley-Blackwell Handbook of Adulthood and Aging, First Edition. Edited by Susan Krauss Whitbourne and Martin J. Sliwinski. © 2012 Blackwell Publishing Ltd. Published 2012 by Blackwell Publishing Ltd.

in psychology, sociology, social work, demography, economics, and organizational sciences, to name just a few. As a result, there is a vast and diverse body of literature on retirement, both within academic circles and the popular press. In fact, a recent Google Scholar search (December, 2010) using the key word *retirement* yielded 1,040,000 hits. Using the same key word in PsycINFO database yielded 5,221 hits, while limiting the search to only peer-reviewed journal articles still yielded 3,316 hits. In the 1970s there were only 203 peer-reviewed articles for the key word *retirement* according to PsycINFO. In the 1980s the count rose to 522, in the 1990s to 680, and then in the 2000s it ballooned to 1,804. Thus it is clear that retirement is a popular topic to researchers both within and outside psychology and that it is becoming more prominent in the psychology literature (Shultz & Wang, 2011).

Research on retirement takes many forms, from in-depth qualitative interviews with retirees, to quantitative analyses of large-scale national multiwave panel studies. In addition, retirement itself can serve as a predictor (or independent variable) in attempts to understand postretirement satisfaction and adjustment. Nevertheless, more often retirement serves as the criterion (or dependent variable) where researchers attempt to predict the timing or forms of retirement. Corresponding to different types of retirement research, in a recent review, Wang and Shultz (2010) summarized four kinds of conceptualizations of retirement: retirement as decision making, retirement as an adjustment process, retirement as a career development stage, and retirement as a part of human resource management. Although a detailed discussion of these conceptualizations is beyond the scope of this chapter, what is clear is that retirement is not a single event in terms of its purpose, its content, and its consequences, but rather a complex process that older individuals go through over a period of years. This process is not only influenced by the intraindividual changes in physical, psychological, and financial conditions, but also is quickly evolving and shifting as the context in which retirement takes place changes. As a result, it may be particularly efficient and fruitful for researchers to take an adult development perspective in studying retirement, which pays specific attention to the dynamic nature, the contextual specificity, and the resource fluctuations that are manifested in the retirement process.

Therefore, the purpose of this chapter is to lay out the adult development perspective as a coherent theoretical perspective to study retirement. Specifically, I begin this chapter by deriving the definition of retirement with the adult development perspective, emphasizing the temporal view and the dynamic nature of retirement. I then review the life course perspective (e.g., Elder & Johnson, 2003; Settersten, 2003) as a major adult development theoretical framework to account for the contextual specificity of the retirement process rooted from individual life history and the temporal environment. Finally, I introduce a resource-based dynamic perspective (Wang, Henkens, & van Solinge, 2011) to provide an integrated framework to understand the impact of intraindividual changes on the retirement process. At the end of the chapter, I will highlight some methodological recommendations for applying the adult development perspective to studying retirement.

The Dynamic Nature of Retirement

As Ekerdt (2010) noted, "The designation of retirement status is famously ambiguous because there are multiple overlapping criteria by which someone might be called retired, including career cessation, reduced work effort, pension receipt, or self report" (p. 70). In fact, Denton and Spencer (2009) recently identified eight different common ways researchers from across the globe have identified individuals as retired: nonparticipation in the labor force, reduction in hours worked and/or earning, hours worked or earnings below some minimum cutoff, receipt of retirement/pension income, exit from one's main employer, change of career or employment later in life, self-assessed retirement, and some combination of the previous seven. Although how retirement was defined in the various studies reviewed by Denton and Spencer depended in large part on the research question being addressed and the researcher's discipline, a common theme of these definitions emphasizes retirement as an individual's exit from the workforce, which accompanies decreased psychological commitment to work (Wang & Shultz, 2010). This definition is consistent with the argument of life stage developmental theorists (e.g., Levinson & Levinson, 1996; Super, 1990) that retirement is a life stage that corresponds to decreased levels of physical activities and productivities, as well as lowered stress and less responsibility to others in day-to-day life.

However, adding possible confusion to this definition is the fact that individuals can "unretire" or "reretire" by rejoining the workforce and starting a new career after they retire, which is a relatively common phenomenon now (Alley & Crimmins, 2007; Wang, Adams, Beehr, & Shultz, 2009). For example, there are individuals now who retire multiple times throughout their lifetime. While starting a second career at midlife has always been common in some professions (e.g., professional sports, the military) it is now becoming the norm for many older workers, both professionals and nonprofessionals). As a result, it is not only those in their sixties and seventies who are retiring for the first time, but more and more often those in their forties and fifties (Shultz & Wang, 2008). All these suggest that it is no longer appropriate to view retirement as a single decision-making event or a static life status. Rather, retirement researchers should recognize retirement as a dynamic workforce withdrawal process that incorporates multiple stages and serves multiple functional purposes (i.e., a developmental process).

Applying this developmental view to understanding retirement, it may be particularly useful to describe and define retirement as a collection of temporally sequential phases for gradually exiting the workforce. Specifically, retirement typically begins with a somewhat distal preretirement preparation and planning phase where individuals begin to envision what their retirement might entail and begin discussing those plans with friends, family members, and colleagues. During this phase, retirees clarify their goals for retirement (e.g., enjoying leisure activities, learning new skills and knowledge, spending more time with family) and gathering resources that could help them to achieve those goals. Next, as retirement becomes more proximal, one begins the retirement decision-making process, taking into account a wide variety of factors, including the current economic and employment contexts, as well as family and personal considerations. The implicit goal for individuals during this decision-making phase is to retire at a time point (e.g., early retirement) that could maximize the psychological and economical benefits of retirement. Finally, as individuals make the transition from full-time worker to retiree, they need to begin the retirement and life adjustment process through which they get used to the changed aspects of life and achieve psychological comfort with their retirement life. This may include engaging in bridge employment (i.e., temporary or part-time work) to help smooth the transition to full retirement. It should be noted that retirees may engage in bridge employment at multiple time periods during their postretirement lives (Wang et al., 2009; Wang, Zhan, Liu, & Shultz, 2008). Therefore, the retirees' longitudinal change patterns in bridge employment status (i.e., the whole process of entering bridge employment, switching from one bridge employment status to another, and eventually exiting bridge employment into full retirement) may reflect the quality of their retirement adjustment.

Defining retirement from this temporal perspective not only allows researchers to investigate retirement as it unfolds over time from one phase to another, but also emphasizes that this process is not homogeneous across individuals. In other words, there is not a formulaic process that all individuals experience in the same lockstep way. Large variance exists in terms of how individuals act in each of those temporal phases, as well as in the consequences they experience from those temporal phases (Shultz & Wang, 2011). Further, within these broad phases, there are smaller and shorter segments that individuals go through as they approach retirement, transition through the retirement decision-making process, and begin life as a self-designated retiree. Thus researchers will often focus on a specific phase of the retirement process in a given study, all the while realizing that they are studying just one piece of the larger retirement puzzle. Finally, decomposing the retirement definition into those temporal phases also emphasizes the need to examine the interrelations among retirees' behaviors and experiences across different phases. For instance, although preretirement planning, retirement decision making, and postretirement adjustment are all experiences nested in the whole span of the retirement process, they are not separate but interrelated experiences that may influence each other in terms of the length and direction of the process (Wang & Shultz, 2010).

The Contextual Specificity of the Retirement Process

Recognizing retirement as a developmental and dynamic process, it is important to consider both the effects of context and intraindividual changes on this process. In this section, I review the life course perspective as a major adult development theoretical framework to account for the contextual specificity of the retirement process. Specifically, the life course perspective (e.g., Elder & Johnson, 2003; Settersten, 2003) draws attention to four contextual aspects of the retirement process: (a) life history (e.g., transitions and trajectories), (b) the immediate circumstance of retirement, (c) interdependence of life spheres, and (d) timing of retirement (Szinovacz, 2003).

Life history

Life history may be the most important concept in the life course framework. When considering individual development from one major life stage to another, such as retirement, the life course perspective argues that people's individual life histories influence the pathways they take to accomplish such development. These pathways include both transition (i.e., changes in status over time, such as from employment to retirement) and trajectories (i.e., life development in relatively stable statuses, such as development and adjustment in postretirement life). For the retirement process, the individual history factors may include how people dealt with previous transitions (Orel, Ford, & Brock, 2004; Settersten, 1998), their work and leisure habits (Morrow-Howell & Leon, 1988), and their previous workforce participation patterns and preferences (Appold, 2004). The general premise is that if an individual has cultivated a flexible style in dealing with previous life transitions, is less socially integrated with work, and has the attributes that help smooth and accomplish the transition, it will be more likely for this person to prepare well for the transition, engage in the transition at a more appropriate time, and achieve better outcomes of the transition (Settersten, 1998; van Solinge & Henkens, 2008). Further, these life history factors may also influence individuals' postretirement adjustment trajectories, facilitating faster adjustment to the retirement life and help retirees to achieve psychological comfort quicker (Wang, 2007).

The immediate circumstance of retirement

The life course perspective's emphasis on the immediate circumstance of retirement implies that the experience of retirement transitions and developmental trajectories are contingent on the specific circumstances under which the transition occurs. Such circumstances may include individual attributes (e.g., finance and health) and current and past work-related statuses and roles (e.g., former job attitudes, former job characteristics, and career trajectories). For example, retirees' physical health (Quick & Moen, 1998; van Solinge & Henkens, 2008), mental health (e.g., Kim & Moen, 2002; Wang, 2007), and financial status (e.g., Gall, Evans, & Howard, 1997; Quick & Moen; 1998) have been repeatedly found to be positively related to the quality of retirement transition and adjustment. Among preretirement job-related variables, retirees' work role identity (e.g., Quick & Moen, 1998; Reitzes & Mutran, 2004) has been shown to be negatively related to retirement adjustment quality, whereas work stress (e.g., Wang, 2007), psychological and physical job demands (e.g., Quick & Moen, 1998; Wang, 2007), job challenges (e.g., van Solinge & Henkens, 2008), job dissatisfaction (e.g., Wang, 2007), and unemployment before retirement (e.g., Marshall, Clarke, & Ballantyne, 2001) have been shown to be positively related to retirement transition and adjustment outcomes.

In addition, how people view their retirement also manifests an important circumstance factor of retirement. For example, if retirees recognize the continued potential for growth and renewal of careers in their retirement lives instead of viewing retirement as a career exit, they are more likely to align their career goals with their planned work and leisure activities in retirement life (Wang & Shultz, 2010). Consequently, they will be less likely to experience work role loss from retirement and enjoy better results from keeping and pursuing their career needs in retirement by developing their work-related agency efficacy (Freund & Baltes, 1998).

Interdependent life spheres

The life course perspective also recognizes that people's developmental experiences in one life sphere (e.g., postretirement life) influence and are influenced by experiences in other life spheres (e.g., marital life). According to this concept, nonwork life spheres are important for the development and dynamics in the retirement process, because they provide retirees with alternative salient identities after retirement and offer opportunities for postretirement engagement. For example, there is consistent evidence that individuals who are married and strongly identify with their family roles have more positive experience in retirement (Calasanti, 1996; Reitzes, Mutran, & Fernandez, 1996). In addition, marital problems have also been shown to enhance perceptions of retirement-related hassles (Bosse, Aldwin, Levenson, & Workman-Daniels, 1991). Further, spouses' working status, number of dependent children, and loss of a partner during the retirement transition have all been shown to relate to retirement experience. Specifically, although married retirees usually adjust better than single or widowed retirees, this beneficial effect disappears when their spouses are still working (e.g., Moen, Kim, & Hofmeister, 2001; Wang, 2007). Retirees with fewer numbers of dependent children to support (e.g., Kim & Feldman, 2000; Marshall et al., 2001) are more likely to achieve better quality of retirement adjustment. Finally, van Solinge and Henkens (2008) showed that losing a partner during the retirement transition had a negative impact on retirees' retirement satisfaction.

Besides the family life sphere, people's experiences in other nonwork life spheres, such as in community social networks, have also been shown to shape their experiences in the retirement process. For example, people who have anxiety associated with maintaining their social status and social contacts via social activities were less likely to have a good retirement transition (e.g., van Solinge & Henkens, 2008). In contrast, people who spend more time in their retirement conducting volunteer work (e.g., Dorfman & Douglas, 2005; Kim & Feldman, 2000) and nonwork-related social activities (e.g., Reeves & Darville, 1994) are more likely to achieve successful retirement transition and adjustment.

Timing of retirement

According to the life course perspective, the developmental experience of life transition is also contingent on its timing in terms of social and cultural deadlines, personal expectations, and occurrences in other life spheres. Therefore, the retirement timing is another key element to consider in the context of the retirement process. Previous research has found that role entries or exits that are experienced as "off-time" (i.e., earlier or later than is socially prescribed or personally expected) may be perceived as more stressful or disruptive than role transitions that are normatively "on-time" (George, 1993). Specifically, retiring earlier than expected has been shown to be negatively related to retirement adjustment quality (e.g., Quick & Moen, 1998; Wang, 2007). In addition, Shultz, Morton, and Weckerle (1998) found that workers who were unexpectedly forced into early retirement due to corporate restructuring experienced the off-time transition as disruptive and psychologically stressful. Further, indicating "on-time" retirement, the voluntariness of the retirement (e.g., Gall et al., 1997; Reitzes and Mutran, 2004) and the extent to which individuals are well planned for their retirement (e.g., Rosenkoeter & Garris, 2001; Wang, 2007) have been shown to be positively related to retirees' retirement satisfaction, life satisfaction, and well-being. Quick and Moen (1998) also showed that retiring for health care reasons was negatively related to retirement satisfaction.

Summary

To summarize, the life course perspective provides a useful theoretical framework to consider how the specific context may influence individuals' developmental experiences during the retirement process. The empirical findings we reviewed above generally support the utility of this theoretical framework. However, it should be noted that although the life course perspective points to a broad range of variables when it comes to understanding the contextual effects on the retirement process, it offers few concrete hypotheses regarding the underlying mechanisms of those potential effects (Szinovacz, 2003; Wang, 2007). Therefore, when drawing on this theoretical framework, researchers should also consider substantial theories that are directly related to the research questions (e.g., rational choice theory for retirement decision making, Hatcher, 2003; continuity theory for retirement adjustment, Wang, 2007) to form their empirical hypotheses.

The Impact of Intraindividual Changes on the Retirement Process

According to the adult development perspective, another key set of variables that may have important impact on the retirement process is the intraindividual changes during the same time period. Recently, Wang and colleagues (2011) have proposed a resource-based dynamic perspective to account for the effects of these intraindividual changes. In this section, we review this theoretical perspective and illustrate how it may be applied to guiding empirical studies.

According to Hobfoll (2002), resources can be broadly defined as the total capability an individual has to fulfill his or her centrally valued needs. Reviewing different types of resources studied in previous retirement research, Wang (2007) suggested that this total capability may include one's physical resources (e.g., muscle strength), cognitive resources (e.g., processing speed and working memory), motivational resources (e.g., self-efficacy), financial resources (e.g., salary and pension), social resources (e.g., social network and social support), and emotional resources (e.g., mood and affectivity). The central premise of this resource perspective for studying the retirement process is that the retirement experience can be viewed as the direct result of the individual's access to resources. Specifically, when people have higher levels of capability (i.e., resources) to fulfill needs they value in retirement, they will experience less difficulty in adjusting to retirement. On the other hand, negative changes in retirees' resources will have an adverse effect on their retirement experience. Therefore, following this perspective, when considering the intraindividual changes that may influence the retirement process, researchers may focus on examining changes that have direct impact on different types of resources.

Specifically, consistent with how the retirement process was defined earlier, the resource-based dynamic perspective argues that an individual's retirement experience is a developmental and dynamic phenomenon. During the retirement process, retirees' levels of experience may fluctuate as a function of individual resources and changes in these resources. Therefore, this perspective focuses on the underlying mechanism through which intraindividual changes have their impact. As illustrated in Figure 21.1, incorporating the resource perspective, variation in the level of positive experience (e.g., psychological well-being) along the retirement process can be viewed as a result of resource changes. In other words, if over time (e.g., t_4 to t_5 in Figure 21.1) a retiree's total resource does not change significantly (e.g., due to successfully maintaining prior lifestyles and activities), he or she may not experience significant change in psychological well-being. Alternatively, if over time (e.g., t_2 to t_3 in Figure 21.1) a retiree's total resource significantly decreases (e.g., due to losing major income source), he or she may experience negative change in psychological well-being. Further, if over time (e.g., t_1 to t_2 or t_3 to t_4 in Figure 21.1) an individual's retirement enables him or her to invest significantly more resources (e.g., due to gaining

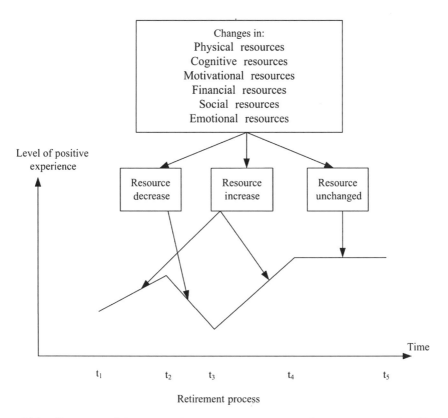

Figure 21.1 Illustration of the resource-based dynamic perspective for understanding the effects of intraindividual changes on the retirement process

cognitive resources that were previously occupied by a stressful job) in fulfilling centrally valued needs, he or she may experience positive change in psychological well-being. As such, this theoretical framework has the flexibility to accommodate a variety of longitudinal patterns for the retirement process. This significantly enriches the theoretical approach to understanding how intraindividual changes may influence one's experience during the retirement process.

Moreover, this resource-based dynamic perspective can also be linked to the life course perspective that was discussed earlier to identify contextual factors that may influence the retirement process. Specifically, similar to the life course perspective, this framework offers a large scope of antecedents that could influence various retirees' resources in the retirement process, including variables from macro level, organizational level, job level, household level, and individual level. In addition, some central constructs in the life course perspective, such as the immediate circumstance of retirement and the interdependent life spheres, can all be viewed as pointing to variables that may influence retirees' resources in different time points and aspects of the retirement process. As such, adopting the resource-based dynamic perspective may be complementary to the life course perspective in terms of integrating the examinations regarding the effects of context and intraindividual changes on the retirement process.

Finally, this resource-based dynamic perspective also provides new opportunities for us to understand other characteristics of the retirement process. For example, although other theories may provide specific predictions regarding the downward and/or upward trends in retirees' well-being change over time, they may not be as informative in terms of understanding the turning point (e.g., t_2, t_3, and t_4 in Figure 21.1) that connects two different trends (or small developmental segments) in the longitudinal retirement process. However, adopting the resource perspective, it is not difficult to hypothesize that certain individual differences (e.g., openness to change, goal orientation in retirement, and need for structure), which may impact retirees' motivational resources, and certain environmental factors (e.g., family support, community cohesiveness, and unemployment rate in the local labor market), which may impact retirees' financial and social resources, may predict how fast the turning points will be reached for retirees who experience negative change first but positive change in their well-being later. This is because these individual differences and environmental factors all facilitate retirees obtaining more resources, which make them more likely to switch from the downward trend to the upward trend. Therefore, in future studies, applying this resource-based dynamic perspective may further improve our understanding about the form and the nature of the retirement process.

So far, there exist few empirical studies that directly examine intraindividual changes in the retirement process. However, several studies (e.g., Kim & Moen, 2002; van Solinge & Henkens, 2008; Wang, 2007) have found that retirees' health decline during the retirement process had a negative impact on the retirement experience, supporting the argument of the resource-based dynamic perspective. Further, reviewing the empirical findings regarding the predictors of retirement experience during the retirement process, it is important to note that most of them are directly associated with different types of resources that retirees have during the retirement process (Wang et al., 2011). For example, retirees' physical and mental health, preretirement work stress and psychological and physical job demands, and postretirement leisure activities are associated with their physical and cognitive resources. Retirees' financial status, unemployment before retirement, number of dependent children, retirement planning, and bridge employment activities are associated with their financial resources. Retirees' marital status, spouses' working status, marital quality, and postretirement volunteer work and bridge employment are associated with their social resources. Retirees' work role identity, preretirement job dissatisfaction, and retirement motivations are associated with their motivational resources. Finally, involuntary retirement, losing one's partner during the retirement transition, and anxiety associated with the retirement transition are linked with retirees' emotional resources. All in all, these conceptual linkages between empirically identified variables and different categories of resources suggest that it is feasible to apply the resource-based dynamic perspective to account for the effects of intraindividual changes on the retirement process.

Methodological Recommendations

In this final section, I conclude this chapter by briefly summarizing the methodological recommendations for applying the adult developmental perspective to studying the retirement process. Specifically, recommendations are provided for improving designs and analytic strategies in future research aimed at better utilizing the adult developmental perspective to understand the retirement process.

In terms of research designs, the vast majority of previous studies in the field of retirement research have relied on cross-sectional designs (Wang et al., 2008). Although cross-sectional designs may be useful in establishing correlations between variables, it is difficult to make sound causal inferences based on such findings. To understand the causal mechanisms described by the adult development perspective reviewed earlier, researchers will need to understand the time sequence of the changes in variables as well as ruling out alternatives. Accordingly, it is recommended that future research use more longitudinal designs to provide more information for understanding the causal developmental processes. Specifically, improving the internal validity of the research can provide opportunities to assess the time-lagged effect between predictors and outcomes while controlling for the baseline of the outcome variables (Zhan, Wang, Liu, & Shultz, 2009). It can also help rule out the possibility of reversed causality by offering the opportunity for direct tests. Another advantage of using longitudinal designs is that they provide an examination of within-individual change trends in variables, which reveals how time influences variables of interest – the key for understanding any developmental processes.

Another methodological issue in previous retirement studies is that few of them have considered the multilevel issues embedded in their data collection and research design in understanding the developmental process of retirement. For example, among studies that measured retirees' experiences from households, few controlled for the nested effect of households. This is likely to yield inaccurate standard errors for parameter estimates, leading to the overestimation or underestimation of relationships (Wang & Shultz, 2010). Therefore, as we see more and more research examining effects of higher-level variables (e.g., regional economy and labor markets, organizational climate variables, and occupational characteristics) on individual-level retirement-related processes (e.g., retirement decision making and postretirement well-being), we recommend multilevel modeling techniques to be used to warrant achieving accurate estimates of the effects.

Further, although a large number of empirical studies have been conducted in the field of retirement, few studies have used a meta-analytic approach to quantitatively summarize and review previous findings related to the developmental experience in the retirement process (Wang et al., 2009). This may be due to the multidisciplinary nature of retirement research. Other than the field of psychology, a large volume of retirement research has been generated by the fields of sociology, gerontology, and economics. However, when reviewing retirement research articles from these fields, it is evident that few of them presented enough statistics (e.g., means, standard deviations, and correlations) that would be useful for conducting meta-analysis. Therefore, compared to other research topics in developmental psychology, it is more difficult for retirement researchers to recover enough statistical information from published studies to conduct a meta-analysis. As such, retirement researchers are recommended to be diligent in providing basic statistical information in their empirical articles to facilitate further synthesis and comparison of empirical findings.

Until recently, most studies in the field of retirement have ignored the possibility that great heterogeneity may exist in the retiree population during the dynamic process of retirement. In other words, the retiree population may consist of multiple subpopulations that are closely associated with the multiple pathways underlying the retirement processes. As Wang (2007) has shown, this heterogeneity cannot be fully accounted for by simply examining demographic differences among retirees. Therefore, traditional analyses based on separating and comparing data from multiple observed groups may not be able to sufficiently examine this heterogeneity in the retiree population. As such, future researchers are recommended to take advantage of methodological advances in latent class procedures (e.g., Wang & Bodner, 2007; Wang & Hanges, 2011). Specifically, this family of statistical procedures is capable of identifying unobserved subpopulations (i.e., latent classes) that account for the qualitative differences in configurations or temporal states among individuals. Depending on the nature of the research question, various statistical methods in latent class procedures could be used. For example, if researchers are interested in identifying retiree subpopulations that may moderate relationships between antecedents and retirement decisions, latent mixture modeling technique could be used. Alternatively, if researchers are interested in identifying retiree subpopulations that correspond to different quantitative change trajectories or qualitative status changes, growth mixture modeling and mixture latent Markov modeling could be used.

In sum, recognizing the methodological issues in previous studies, it is recommended that the general methodological goals for conducting future retirement studies with the adult development perspective include rigorously examining causal processes, incorporating and accurately estimating effects of variables from multiple levels, improving the examination on generalizability of research findings across different studies/samples, and recognizing the great heterogeneity in the retiree population. One methodological approach that may help achieve these goals is to fully utilize existing large-scale longitudinal archival data sets to conduct research using the adult development perspective. There are many unique opportunities that are afforded by using such archival data. First, it provides access to longitudinal data, which improves the rigor for testing causal process. Second, archival data sets from federally funded research often include a broad scope of variables from multiple levels that are readily examined. Third, archival data sets often have large sample sizes. This provides opportunities for conducting cross-sample validation and also helps detect unobserved subpopulations that may be small in proportion. Similarly, archival data sets that are population-representative offer more generalizability of the research findings. Finally, archival data sets from different countries and different labor sectors make it possible to conduct research across nations and labor sectors, which could help the further integration of macrolevel and microlevel variables into the examination of the retirement process.

References

AARP (2005). *The business case of workers age 50+ : Planning for tomorrow's talent needs for today's competitive environment.* Washington, DC: AARP.

Alley, D., & Crimmins, E., (2007). The demography of aging and work. In K. S., Shultz &, G. A., Adams,(Eds.), *Aging and work in the 21st century* (pp. 7–23). Mahwah, NJ: Erlbaum.

Appold, S. J. (2004). How much longer would men work if there were no employment dislocation? Estimates from cause-elimination work life tables. *Social Science Research, 33*, 660–680.

Bosse, R., Aldwin, C. M., Levenson, M. R., & Workman-Daniels, K. (1991). How stressful is retirement? Findings from the Normative Aging Study. *Journal of Gerontology: Psychological Sciences, 46*, P9–P14.

Calasanti, T. M. (1996). Gender and life satisfaction in retirement: An assessment of the male model. *Journal of Gerontology: Social Sciences, 51B*, S18–S29.

Denton, F., & Spencer, B. (2009). What is retirement? A review and assessment of alternative concepts and measures. *Canadian Journal on Aging, 28*, 63–76.

Dixon, S. (2003). Implications of population ageing for the labour market. *Labour Market Trends, 111*, 67–76.

Dorfman, L. T., & Douglas, K. (2005). Leisure and the retired professor: Occupation matters. *Educational Gerontology, 31*, 343–361.

Ekerdt, D. J. (2010). Frontiers of research on work and retirement. *Journal of Gerontology: Social Sciences, 65B*, 69–80.

Elder, G. H., & Johnson, M. K. (2003). The life course and aging: Challenges, lessons, and new directions. In R. A. Settersten, Jr. (Ed.), *Invitation to the life course: Toward new understandings of later life* (pp. 49–81). Amityville, NY: Baywood.

Freund, A. M., & Baltes, P. B. (1998). Selection, optimization, and compensation as strategies of life management: Correlations with subjective indicators of successful aging. *Psychology and Aging, 13*, 531–543.

Gall, T. L., Evans, D. R., & Howard, J. (1997). The retirement adjustment process: Changes in the well-being of male retirees across time. *Journal of Gerontology: Psychological Sciences, 52B*, P110–P117.

George, L. K. (1993). Sociological perspectives on life transitions. *Annual Review of Sociology, 19*, 353–373.

Hatcher, C. B. (2003). The economics of the retirement decision. In G. A. Adams & T. A. Beehr (Eds.), *Retirement: Reasons, processes, and results* (pp. 136–158). New York: Springer.

Hobfoll, S. E. (2002). Social and psychological resources and adaptation. *Review of General Psychology, 6*, 307–324.

Kim, S., & Feldman, D. C. (2000). Working in retirement: The antecedents of bridge employment and its consequences for quality of life in retirement. *Academy of Management Journal, 43*, 1195–1210.

Kim, J. E., & Moen, P. (2002). Retirement transitions, gender, and psychological well-being: A life-course, ecological model. *Journal of Gerontology: Psychological Sciences, 57B*, P212–P222.

Lende, T. (2005). Older workers: Opportunity or challenge? *Canadian Manager, 30*, 20–30.

Levinson, D. J., & Levinson, J. D. (1996). *The seasons of a woman's life.* New York: Knopf.

Marshall, V. W., Clarke, P. J., & Ballantyne, P. J. (2001). Instability in the retirement transition: Effects on health and well-being in a Canadian study. *Research on Aging, 23*, 379–409.

Moen, P., Kim, J. E., & Hofmeister, H. (2001). Couples' work/retirement transitions, gender, and marital quality. *Social Psychology Quarterly, 64*, 55–71.

Morrow-Howell, N., & Leon, J. (1988). Life-span determinants of work in retirement years. *International Journal of Aging & Human Development, 27*, 125–140.

Orel, N. A., Ford, R. A., & Brock, C. (2004). Women's financial planning for retirement: The impact of disruptive life events. *Journal of Women & Aging, 16*, 39–53.

Perreira, K. M., & Sloan, F. A. (2001). Life events and alcohol consumption among mature adults: A longitudinal analysis. *Journal of Studies on Alcohol, 62*, 501–508.

Quick, H. E., & Moen, P. (1998). Gender, employment, and retirement quality: A life course approach to the differential experiences of men and women. *Journal of Occupational Health Psychology, 1*, 44–64.

Reeves, J. B., & Darville, R. L. (1994). Social contact patterns and satisfaction with retirement of women in dual-career/earner families. *International Journal of Aging & Human Development, 39*, 163–175.

Reitzes, D. C., & Mutran, E. J. (2004). The transition into retirement: Stages and factors that influence retirement adjustment. *International Journal of Aging and Human Development, 59*, 63–84.

Reitzes, D. C., Mutran, E. J., & Fernandez, M. E. (1996). Preretirement influences on postretirement self-esteem. *Journal of Gerontology: Social Sciences, 51B*, S242–S249.

Rosenkoeter, M. M., & Garris, J. M. (2001). Retirement planning, use of time, and psychosocial adjustment. *Issues in Mental Health Nursing, 22*, 703–722.

Settersten, R. A. Jr., (1998). Time, age, and the transition to retirement: New evidence on life-course flexibility. *International Journal of Aging and Human Development, 47*, 177–203.

Settersten, R. A. (2003). Invitation to the life course: The promise. In R. A. Settersten, Jr. (Ed.), *Invitation to the life course: Toward new understandings of later life* (pp. 1–12). Amityville, NY: Baywood.

Shultz, K. S., Morton, K. R., & Weckerle, J. R. (1998). The influence of push and pull factors on voluntary and involuntary early retirees' retirement decision and adjustment. *Journal of Vocational Behavior, 53*, 45–57.

Shultz, K.S., & Wang, M. (2008). The changing nature of mid and late careers. In C. Wankel (Ed.), *21st century management: A reference handbook* (vol. 2, pp. 130–138). Thousand Oaks, CA: Sage.

Shultz, K. S., & Wang, M. (2011). Psychological perspectives on the changing nature of retirement. *American Psychologist, 66*(3), 170–179.

Super, C. E. (1990). A life-span, life-space approach to career development. In D. Brown (Ed.), *Career choice and development* (2nd ed., pp. 197–261). San Francisco: Jossey-Bass.

Szinovacz, M. E. (2003). Contexts and pathways: Retirement as institution, process, and experience. In G. A. Adams & T. A. Beehr (Eds.), *Retirement: Reasons, processes, and results* (pp. 6–52). New York: Springer.

Toossi, M. (2004). Labor force projections to 2012: The graying of the U. S. workforce. *Monthly Labor Review, 127*, 3–22.

Tyers, R., & Shi, Q. (2007). Demographic change and policy responses: Implications for the global economy. *World Economy, 1*, 537–566.

van Solinge, H., & Henkens, K. (2008). Adjustment to and satisfaction with retirement: Two of a kind? *Psychology and Aging, 23*, 422–434.

Wang, M. (2007). Profiling retirees in the retirement transition and adjustment process: Examining the longitudinal change patterns of retirees' psychological well-being. *Journal of Applied Psychology, 92*, 455–474.

Wang, M., Adams, G. A., Beehr, T. A., & Shultz, K. S. (2009). Career issues at the end of one's career: Bridge employment and retirement. In S. G. Baugh & S. E. Sullivan (Eds.), *Maintaining focus, energy, and options over the life span* (pp. 135–162). Charlotte, NC: Information Age Publishing.

Wang, M. & Bodner, T. E. (2007). Growth mixture modeling: Identifying and predicting unobserved subpopulations with longitudinal data. *Organizational Research Methods, 10*, 635–656.

Wang, M., & Hanges, P. (2011). Latent class procedures: Applications to organizational research. *Organizational Research Methods, 14*, 24–31.

Wang, M., Henkens, K., & van Solinge, H. (2011). Retirement adjustment: A review of theoretical and empirical advancements. *American Psychologist, 66*(3), 204–213.

Wang, M., & Shultz, K. (2010). Employee retirement: A review and recommendations for future investigation. *Journal of Management, 36*, 172–206.

Wang, M., Zhan, Y., Liu, S., & Shultz, K. (2008). Antecedents of bridge employment: A longitudinal investigation. *Journal of Applied Psychology, 93*, 818–830.

Zhan, Y., Wang, M., Liu, S., & Shultz, K. (2009). Bridge employment and retirees' health: A longitudinal investigation. *Journal of Occupational Health Psychology, 14*, 374–389.

PART VII

Well-Being and Creativity

22

Effects of Remaining Time for Psychological Well-Being and Cognition

Boo Johansson and Anne Ingeborg Berg

"The Future Acts on the Present"

In this chapter we discuss issues related to an individual's perspective of time and age-related change in later life. A main focus is on subsequent development or the ontogenetic future, that is, the question of what happens later in life. We do not only apply the typical perspective of relating late-life outcomes only to previous events and influences but rather to how life conditions and biobehavioral functioning in later life is affected by perceived and actual remaining time, that is, time to death. Our basic idea is that the unknown future in fact acts on present life and functioning.

These ideas have previously been addressed by Carstensen (2006), who claimed that subjective sense of future time becomes a better predictor than chronological age for a range of cognitive, emotional, and motivational variables. Although chronological age is accompanied by accumulated life experience it loses precision in older ages due to the fact that "degrees of freedom" for differential developmental trajectories generally increase with age. In this respect we tend to become more unlike rather than alike each other in later life.

Developmental theories generally focus on the idea that the past acts on the present and that current states of functioning can be best understood and explained by previous experiences and life circumstances. The perspective taken in this chapter is that the future also has an impact on present functioning through factual influences of the unavoidable devitalization that is the hard core of biological aging but also through ideas and expectations held by the individual. In this respect, remaining time broadly refers to

The Wiley-Blackwell Handbook of Adulthood and Aging, First Edition. Edited by Susan Krauss Whitbourne and Martin J. Sliwinski. © 2012 Blackwell Publishing Ltd. Published 2012 by Blackwell Publishing Ltd.

survival as well as late-life biobehavioral functioning of older persons. Time from birth or chronological age therefore needs to be supplemented with the ontogenetic perspective of time to death. Although these two time metrics in a way represent two sides of the same coin we claim the usefulness of both perspectives for empirical studies of developmental trajectories in later life.

Demography Gets Under the Skin – Subjective Life Expectancy

Demography is typically considered only in terms of statistics about longevity or information about the age composition of a population. From a developmental perspective, however, one may ask how we internalize these statistics into our own minds, how presented figures and information may affect us, and whether it also influences our thoughts and emotions related to our own future or remaining life.

The three major demographic factors are fertility (capability of giving new life and thereby the birth rates or input of new members into a population), mortality (death and death rates in a certain population), and migration (emigration from and immigration to a population). These factors are highly interactive and are the main determinants of the age composition in a population.

Mortality is often understood in terms of the risk of dying at certain ages or statistics about longevity. Estimates of longevity differ considerably across nations and largely reflect the overall living conditions in various regions of the world. In a recent review by Christensen, Doblhammer, Rau, and Vaupel (2009), it is estimated that most babies born from the year of 2000, in countries that already have long life expectancies, will have a chance to celebrate their 100th birthday (see Table 22.1).

The key question, however, is whether the increase in life expectancy will be accompanied by a postponement of functional limitations and disability (Christensen, Thinggaard, et al., 2009). Furthermore, there are remarkable differences in health and survival for men and women. In a review by Oksuzyan, Juel, Vaupel, and

Table 22.1 Projections of oldest age at which at least 50% of a birth cohort is still alive in eight countries. Originally appeared in Christensen, K., Doblhammer, G., Rau. R-. & Vaupel, J.W. (2009). Lancet, 3; 374 (9696): 1196–208.

	2000	2001	2002	2003	2004	2005	2006	2007
Canada	102	102	103	103	103	104	104	104
Denmark	99	99	100	100	101	101	101	101
France	102	102	103	103	103	104	104	104
Germany	99	100	100	100	101	101	101	102
Italy	102	102	102	103	103	103	104	104
Japan	104	105	105	105	106	106	106	107
UK	100	101	101	101	102	102	103	103
USA	101	102	102	103	103	103	104	104

Data are ages in years. Baseline data were obtained from the Human Mortality Database and refer to the total population of the respective countries.

Christensen (2008) they show empirical data from the Nordic countries that demonstrate "the paradox" of men being physically stronger and with fewer disabilities but at the same time having a substantially higher mortality rates at all ages compared with women. They discuss the evidence for proposed explanations based in biological, psychological, and social thinking and conclude that it is likely that there are multiple and interacting causes behind the phenomenon, including variation in genetic propensity, hormones, and immune system responses; disease patterns, lifetime exposures, and risk-taking behavior; as well as differences in seeking medical treatment and compliance with treatment regimens. The relevant question for developmental psychology is how this will affect future birth cohorts' thinking and feeling about aging and old age and whether our current understanding of development will be equally valid in future generations. For example, the current average life expectancy for newborns in the USA is about 80 for women and almost 75 for men. In 2050 the projected life expectation will be 84.3 years for women and 79.7 years in men (see Figure 22.1).

For a long time the increased likelihood of survival was mainly related to decreased risks for early life mortality, especially during the first year of life. The pronounced rectangularization of the survival curve that has occurred over time also implies that the number of remaining years to be lived has also increased at older ages. In Sweden, the average remaining life expectancy for both sexes at age 65 was about 13 years in the period 1901–1910. The corresponding figures for the period 2001–2005 were 17 years for men and more than 20 years for women.

The rectangularization of the survival curve that has occurred over years is likely to have affected personal expectations about longevity. What was expected in former generations is no longer valid. This issue is addressed in studies that have examined whether subjective

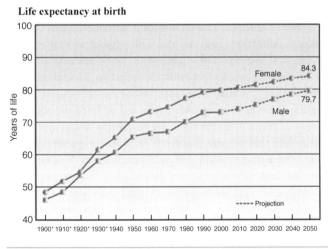

Life expectancy at birth

* Death registration area only. The death registration area increased from 10 states and the District of Columbia in 1900 to the entire United States in 1933.

Figure 22.1 Past and projected female and male life expectancy at birth, United States, 1900–2050. *Source*: U.S. Department of Commerce, Bureau of the Census.

life expectancy is related to factual survival. As stated by Perozek (2008), "old-age mortality is notoriously difficult to predict because it requires not only an understanding of the process of senescence which is influenced by genetic, environmental, and behavioural factors, but also a prediction of how these factors evolve" (p. 95). The suggested alternative for forecasting longevity may be to actually ask persons themselves to provide an estimate. The idea is that individuals are uniquely informed about their own family and genetic background as well as about previous environmental and potential risk exposures that may affect their survival – information that can be transformed into expectations about survival probabilities. This approach was empirically tested in constructions of cohort life tables that were compared with the official predictions in gender-specific life tables. Interestingly, a comparison demonstrated that these estimations were close for men but that women were less optimistic about their probability of survival. A comparable analysis by van Doorn and Kasl (1996) showed that the association between self-rated life expectancy and subsequent mortality was stronger for men than for women. They also found that self-rated life expectancy had an independent effect on mortality and that the effect of self-rated health only moderately attenuated the relationship. It seems as if individuals are using different information as a background source in making these types of self-ratings.

After a careful literature search by Mirowsky (1997), it can be said that there are still too few studies on subjective life expectancy to allow any firm conclusions about the validity of these predictions and especially about the role of contributing elements behind an individual's estimation. From a remaining lifespan perspective, demographic studies on the role of subjective life expectancy, however, need to be reviewed more in detail by taking psychological and individual characteristics into account. According to the "horizon hypothesis" proposed by Mirowsky (1997), a longer subjective life expectancy is associated with increased sense of control over one's own life. The assumption was tested on data from a US survey among individuals aged 18 and older, including more than 900 individuals older that 50. Mirowsky found that subjective life expectancy was significantly associated with higher sense of control. The relationship remained when controlling for demographics like race, sex, education, income, and widowhood, as well as adjusting for physical impairment, physical fitness, and inability to work because of a disability. Adjustment for subjective life expectancy explains the negative association between age and the sense of control that remains after adjustment for education and physical impairment. Adjusting the three factors together explained 93% of the total association between age and the sense of control, and renders the remaining association insignificant (see Figure 22.2). Studies like this suggest that sense of control represents an important psychological dimension for the understanding of perceptions about the chances to survive and the remaining time horizon.

The analyses shown in Figure 22.2 demonstrate that subjective life expectancy largely maps estimates of official life expectancies. It is also noteworthy that men seem to expect to live longer than officially estimated (about 3 years) and African Americans were even more optimistic as they expected to live 6 years longer than the actual estimates at the time for study. This optimism about survival remained also after adjustments for socioeconomic status and signs and symptoms of health.

Given the trend of an increasing life expectancy in new cohorts of older people one might assume that the expectations among younger cohorts will be even higher than

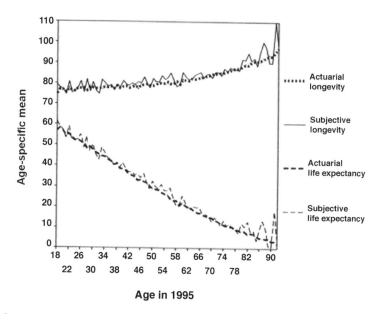

Figure 22.2 Mean subjective and actuarial longevity and life expectancy by age. *Source*: Originally appeared in Mirowsky, J. (1997) Age, subjective life expectancy, and the sense of control: the horizon hypothesis. Journal of Gerontology B: Psychological Science and Social Science, 52, 125–134.

among older birth cohorts. This idea of accounting for cohort mortality trends in the estimates was, however, not confirmed in the above analysis by Mirowsky (1999).

Increased life expectancy is typically accompanied by decreased birth rates. Together these demographics have formed a new context for aging, with a substantially increased proportion of persons of increasingly advanced ages. This changing context of aging in developed countries is illustrated by age compositions and what once used to be population pyramids, nowadays with a completely different shape. For example, the percentage of individuals 65 and older was about 6% in 1750 and 10% in 1950 in the Swedish population. The current figure is about 17% and the projection for 2030 is 23%. The most dramatic change is expected for the oldest old age segments. The ratio of people aged 20–64 to people aged 80 or more is expected to change dramatically in many countries and regions.

The substantial change of age compositions in Western countries has initiated discussions about adjusting retirement ages in line with this increased longevity. This formed the background for a study by van Solinge & Henkens (2009) in which they addressed the question whether individuals would prefer a retirement age that better fits their own life expectancy. Using data from a panel study in the Netherlands they asked older employees aged between 50 and 60 years about their expectations for survival. The first question was about their expectation that they would survive until age 75 (rated from highly unlikely to highly likely) followed by the statement "I think that my chances of living to a very old age (90 and older) are considerable," to which the participants had to respond on a scale from totally agree to totally disagree). Using these two items, van Solinge and Henkens constructed a composite scale representing subjective life expectancy. The results supported the hypothesis that expectations about remaining lifetime significantly influenced the retirement decision process. Individuals with a longer perceived future time horizon preferred later retirement. However, the differences in the time horizon did not directly influence their actual retirement plans, which suggests that legal systems and other sociocultural influences are more important in influencing actual behavior than expectations about future time horizon.

Vitality and Survival – Subjective Health

With age the likelihood for compromised health and vitality increases substantially. In the oldest-old age groups we might even find it almost impossible to identify individuals without any diagnosed diseases. For example, in a population-based sample of individuals aged 80 and older, the mean number of diagnoses defined according to World Heath Organization International Classification of Diseases (WHO-ICD) criteria (WHO, 1992) was almost seven (M = 6.7; SD = 0.3; with a range from 0–18). Only five individuals (0.7%) were found with no evidence of disease either in medical records, medication registry, and self-reports. Almost 20% were found to have 10 or more diagnoses and fewer than 10% percent had 2 or fewer diagnoses (S. E. Nilsson, Johansson, Berg, Karlsson, & McClearn, 2002). As expected, cardiovascular diseases were common: hypertension (57%), heart failure (57%), angina pectoris (26%), history of myocardial infarction (20%), and stroke (24%). The review also showed a substantial proportion with malignancy (25%), herpes zoster (23%), diabetes (17%), dizziness/vertigo (60%), problems with sleep (58%), cataract (49%), and hearing loss (61%). Only 12% were entirely free of any prescribed medication. Compromised health and comorbidities represent a major challenge both for the individual and for aging societies.

Diseases and compromised health are more or less associated with the risk of dying, and this becomes increasingly evident in later life. This idea also reflects the problems in defining health in older age. For example, according to international standards, the principle for obtaining reference values for clinical biochemical tests is to include only "disease-free subjects" and that may influence measurement values for therapies. However, this requirement becomes almost impossible to meet with advancing age. An alternative approach to defining overall health was employed in a study by S. E. Nilsson and colleagues (2003) who split their sample of individuals aged 82 and older into those who survived more and less than six years. The reference values differ considerably between groups for many of the more or less standard biochemical tests. This suggests that there are a number of subclinical changes that affect biological integrity and that are predictive of survival despite low associations with the presence of clinically manifest diseases (B.-O Nilsson et al., 2003). For example, in a number of studies of the crucial immune defense system it has been shown that certain immune system characteristics are highly related to an elevated mortality risk (Wikby, Strindhall, & Johansson, 2009).

Besides the medical and more basic biological perspective on health and vitality in aging, perceived or subjective health represents a topic of special interest from a lifespan developmental perspective. Numerous studies have shown a strong association between self-rated health and subsequent mortality. The basic message according to Jylhä (2009) is that "self-rated health, adjusted for age, shows a graded association with mortality, and that this association is usually attenuated but seldom disappears when other factors, primarily health indicators, are controlled for" (p. 311). In the discussion about subjective health and why it predicts mortality, Jylhä (2009) proposes a unified conceptual model, following a cognitive model for rational reasoning within a certain contextual framework. According to the model, individuals are likely to first ask themselves: "What constitute health and what are the relevant components of my own health?" Following a review of available sources needed to answer these broad questions, comes the question "How is my health in general, taking into consideration my age, previous health status, expectations, etc.?" The final stage of cognitive reasoning involves the decision about finding the best fit between the given options for responding (response alternatives) to the preceding assessments. Although there is an issue about the ability of a rational person to accurately rate and evaluate health, the model emphasizes that perceived health includes psychological processing of available information from internal sources ("How well does my body and mind function?") as well as from external and contextual sources (reference group comparisons and sociocultural norms influencing aspiration levels and expectations of functioning relative to own previous health and functioning). Most important, however, is the fact that subjective health cannot simply be used as a marker for more objectively defined health according to medical criteria. The weak association between subjective and objective health measures was demonstrated by Baltes and Smith in the Berlin Aging Study (2003) showing deviating trajectories of change across 25 years in four different health measures in individuals aged 70 at the first wave. Despite the marked decline in objectively measured functional health with increasing age, participants' own perception of their health was largely stable during the same time period. Moreover, participants rated their own health status higher as compared to other people at the same age. The discrepancy between subjective and objective evaluations of health also demonstrates the remarkable ability to adjust to health-related losses in late life. At the same time the ultimate question about why subjective health predicts survival largely remains to be answered and addressed to psychological science.

In a study by Berg, Hassing, Nilsson, and Johansson (2009), specific medical ICD-based diagnoses were examined for their potential relationship with self-rated health and life satisfaction in a sample of 392 cognitively intact individuals aged 80 and older. Interestingly it was found that among 25 common diagnoses, only sleeping problems, urinary incontinence, and stroke were significantly related to life satisfaction in both men and women. Men with angina pectoris and eczema were less satisfied with life compared with men without these diagnoses, whereas women with peptic ulcer were less satisfied with life compared with women without this diagnosis. Findings like this emphasizes that the perceived meaning and consequences of medical diagnoses differ among individuals and that gender may partially account for the observed variability in how certain conditions are evaluated.

Findings about subjective health reports, like all self-reports from individuals at older ages, need to take into account whether results are biased due to sample selection or the proportion of individuals actually able to reliably answer a question like: "How would your rate your overall health at present?" In the population-based sample of individuals aged 80 and older (Nilsson et al., 2002), 95% were considered to be able to provide a reliable answer to this overall question. About 60% of the men and 54% of the women stated that they were in good health. Including only those who had no signs whatsoever of cognitive impairment (57% of the total sample) did not change the proportion claiming good health.

Remaining Years – A Developmental Perspective

The lifespan perspective of human development represents a basic format for our understanding of how behavior becomes organized along the lifeline: how the past in terms of various experiences and environmental exposures, beneficial and detrimental, have affected and made a person what he or she is at present. A lifespan perspective is also helpful for our understanding of how elderly people themselves may think and act upon the present and the more or less unknown future.

At older ages we might assume that people will be less hopeful about the future, given the fact that the actual time left is becoming more and more reduced. In a population-based sample of individuals aged 80 and older, the participants were asked to respond to the following statement "During the last week I felt hopeful about the future" (item 8, CES-D scale, Radloff, 1977). The correlation with age was low ($r = -.04$) and slightly reduced when controlling for gender ($r = -.032$). Interestingly, the comparable longitudinal data showed an inverted-U trend over a 6-year period. Those who were able to respond became more hopeful about the future during the first years of the study with a modest but significant drop at the end of the study period. However, using a time-from-death design to track changes in future hope, people seemed to get slightly more hopeful about their future as they approached their time of death. One possible explanation to this seemingly paradoxical finding is that in late life the time horizons shrink, which is likely to narrow the focus down to days and weeks rather than to months and years ahead. Concern and worries about a range of future problems is possibly reduced when focus lies on aspects in the more foreseeable and predictable immediate future. See Figure 23.3.

According to the motivational theory of lifespan development by Heckhausen, Wrosch, and Schulz (2010), individuals face numerous challenges throughout the life course which activate motivational and self-regulatory processes in order to meet these challenges.

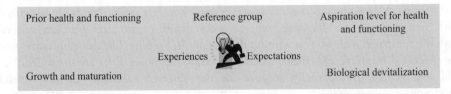

Figure 22.3   The actual position along the life line variously affect individuals thinking and feelings about past and present. Created by Boo Johansson and Anne Ingeborg Berg.

The way these challenges are met may, however, change with age in the sense that efforts to exert primary control behaviors aimed to change the environment according to one's own preferences are replaced by secondary control striving with adjustment of expectations and attributions in order to maintain control over more restricted and realistic goals that preserve psychological well-being. The functionality of this developmental pattern, seen in increased use of selective primary and secondary control and compensatory primary control strategies, is largely determined by health-related conditions and sociocultural opportunities offered for individuals in later life. The dramatic demographical changes with increased longevity and older populations have, however, changed the age-related structuring of the life course among generations. Expectations about the future are therefore likely to differ across birth cohorts and among generations in various societies.

In later life we typically expect more losses than gains in multiple domains of biobehavioral functioning. Although this gradual shift is largely out of the individual's control, we attempt to make the best out of the present for the sake of self-protection and to optimize psychological well-being (e.g., Carstensen, 2006). Depressed individuals and those with other types of compromised mental health are more prone to further decline in well-being and increased risk for morbidity and mortality.

In a population-based study of cognitively intact and mentally healthy 85-year-olds, Skoog and colleagues (1996) found that in the last month 4% had had thoughts that "life was not worth living," 4% reported "death wishes," and almost 1% expressed "thoughts of taking own life." These figures were considerably higher among those diagnosed with a mental disorder: 29% had thoughts that life was not worth living, about 28% had had death wishes, and 9% had thoughts about taking their lives, among which nearly 2% had seriously considered suicide. Women who felt that life was not worth living showed a significantly higher 3-year mortality rate compared with women without these feelings (43.2% vs. 14.2%), and it is noteworthy that this elevated mortality risk was independent of concomitant physical and mental disorders. Age identity is a topic closely related to the ontogenetic time perspective. Age identity and age perceptions were examined in relation to subjective health in a study by Demakakos, Gjonca, and Nazaroo (2007). Data from more than 8,000 men and women aged 50 and older participating in the English Longitudinal Study of Ageing (ELSA) was analyzed to examine the relationships of self-assessed health and age identity. The question about self-perceived health was formulated in the way this question has often been asked: "Would you say that your health is excellent/very good/good/fair/poor?". Answers were divided into two groups to allow a comparison between those who responded "excellent" and "very good" with the other responses. Results show that those with better perceived health also believed that entry to old age started later in life compared with those with less good subjective health.

The role of age identity was also investigated in a Finnish study by Uotinen, Rantanen, and Suutama (2005). They wanted to examine whether perceived age was directly associated with mortality independent of actual chronological age. A community sample in Finland comprising 395 men and 770 women, aged 65–84, had to answer two questions about whether they felt physically and mentally younger, the same, or older than their actual age. They found a relatively strong association between ratings of perceived physical and mental age but no evidence for gender differences. Individuals who rated their own age as older than their chronological age were also somewhat older, they had less education, more illnesses, more negative perceptions of their own health, lower cognitive status, and more depressive symptoms. This baseline data was then used to predict mortality over a 13-year period. The unadjusted relative risks, compared with those who reported a younger perceived physical age, was 2.07 (confidence interval = 1.61–2.67) for those feeling older and 1.35 (CI = 1.13–1.61) for those reporting that they felt the same as their chronological age. For perceived mental age the corresponding values was 2.05 (CI = 1.47–2.87) for those feeling older and 1.17 (CI = 0.99–1.38) for those stating a correspondence between perceived and actual age. These figures demonstrate that there is an increased risk of dying for those with an "older age identity," which is illustrated in Figure 22.4 in which these estimates were used to calculate mortality rates separately for men and women.

The prediction of mortality based on perceived mental age, however, disappeared when controlling for cognitive status, measured by a cognitive screening test. This suggests that the association between perceived mental age and mortality may be due to an increased incidence of compromised cognition and dementia among those with a mental age identity older than their age. The authors conclude that "subjective age may reflect a person's general well-being and as such the faith he or she has on [*sic*] the future" (Uotinen et al., 2005, p. 371). In another study on subjective age among noninstitutionalized individuals in Finland, Uotinen and colleagues (2006) found that the majority (53%) felt younger than their age whereas 45% felt their chronological age. Over an 8-year period about half remained in the same category while 26% had shifted into the category of feeling more youthful and 26% into the category of feeling older than their chronological age. The interesting phenomenon of getting older and feeling younger emphasizes the need to understand adjustment and coping mechanisms activated in aging.

A significant contribution to our understanding of the importance of perception of time during the lifespan is suggested by the socioemotional selectivity theory proposed by Laura Carstensen and colleagues (1999). According to her theory, with shrinking time horizons regulation of emotional states become increasingly important relative to other priorities and goals. Thus it is not so much a question of perception of age, but perception of time

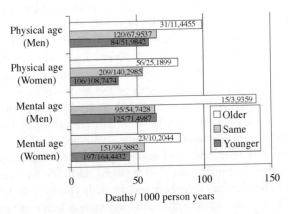

Figure 22.4   Mortality rates per 1,000 person-years in groups based on perceived age. Created by Boo Johansson and Anne Ingeborg Berg.

left to live. In a Swedish study including 453 individuals aged 80 and older, among a wide range of psychosocial and health-related variables, the social network quality was the strongest associate with life satisfaction in both women and men at the first measurement occasion, and higher levels of perceived quality of networks were also related to higher levels of life satisfaction across the study (Berg, Hoffman, Hassing, McClearn, & Johansson, 2009). The relevance of quality of social networks, in contrast to frequency of contacts, was previously confirmed in a study of old-old individuals (Newsom & Schulz, 1996). The close relationship between satisfaction with life and satisfaction with social networks points at central aspects of the topic of quality of life in old age. Socioemotional selectivity theory explains this aging-related tendency as an expression of the need for fewer and more emotionally rewarding contacts at the expense of a large social network (Carstensen, 1992). On the other hand, aging-related diseases and disability, which are exceedingly common in later life, might also explain why quality, and not quantity, of social networks gradually becomes more important to life satisfaction (Pinquart & Sörensen, 2000). As a result of health-related deterioration, people experience increased dependency on support and their social network. Frequent social contacts based on dependency do possibly meet basic practical needs, but do not necessarily correspond to the need for rewarding social interactions that contribute to quality of life. The relevance of satisfying social contacts in late life is probably an expression of both health-related dependency and, in line with socioemotional selectivity theory, a propensity to be more selective in the choice of company.

The overall devitalization that accompanies aging, and largely defines biological aging, is related to brain functioning in general and to cognitive functioning in particular, as well as to more subjective or perceived perspectives of an individual. The former can be observed in dementia and in the increased proneness to delirium or confusion. Multiple factors can overtax an individual's reserve capacity and produce changes that lower the threshold for a relatively intact cognition. A related question is how these changes are perceived by the individual and the prevailing observation of substantial interindividual differences in late-life cognitive and emotional functioning.

Cognitive Functioning – Time from Birth and Death

Memory and other cognitive abilities have been a major focus in aging research for a long time. Studies based on a longitudinal design have increased our knowledge considerably and have provided strong evidence that intraindividual trajectories may differ considerably from findings of age differences in cross-sectional studies (e.g., Schaie, 2005). The current knowledge about age-related changes in various cognitive abilities and processes is quite extensive. Most changes are in the negative direction, although certain abilities may be robust and less prone to change (Hofer & Alwin, 2008). Most previous research has related cognitive functioning to distance from birth and the neural system changes that occur with age. The developmental trajectories proposed have typically been in the format of a general decline pattern. In general, the decline is more pronounced for fluid abilities and when based on data from cross-sectional designs compared with data from longitudinal studies.

The critical question addressed in recent aging research is whether normative age-related changes only reflect an inevitable ontogenetic trajectory or whether changes are due to compromised health that potentially can be prevented and treated. Numerous health conditions and diseases are now identified for their role in partly accounting for observed declines, for example, diabetes, hypertension, cardiovascular diseases, and cancer (e.g., Anstey, Mack, & von Sanden, 2006; Hassing et al., 2002; Mezuk, 2009).

Dementia disorders represent a major public health concern largely due to demographic changes with increased longevity and greater proportions of individuals at more advanced ages with greater risk for compromised cognition (e.g., Jagger et al., 2000). Although prevalence rates for dementia tend to differ slightly across studies and countries they are typically about 5–6% among all aged 65 and older (Berr, Wancata, and Ritchie, 2005; Wancata, Börjesson-Hanson, Ostling, Sjögren, & Skoog, 2007). The rates increase substantially with increasing age, and among the very old prevalence rates are closer to and even greater than 50%, which means that half the population actually meets criteria of dementia (e.g., Andersen-Ranberg, Schrool, & Jeune, 2001; Börjesson-Hansson, Edin, Gislason, & Skoog, 2004). This is the risk scenario for an interesting study that uses a life table technique to calculate life expectancy with dementia (Nepal, Brown, & Ranmuthu-gala, 2008). Their analyses showed that an extension of life expectancy is associated with an increased likelihood for a longer period of life with dementia and that this is likely to affect women to a greater extent because they live longer. According to their calculations men are expected on average to live another 18 years from age 65, 6% of which will be with dementia. Women are expected to live for another 22 years at age 65, with a total period of about 9% with dementia. From age 85 men can expect that about 16% of their remaining life will be affected by dementia whereas the risk for women is a risk period of 25% of what, on average, will be 7 years of remaining life.

Dementia is also associated with an elevated risk of mortality. Johansson and Zarit (1997) examined the predictive power of cognitive tests for incident dementia and mortality. A sample aged 84–90 at baseline was re-examined three times over a 6-year period. As expected, those that developed dementia showed lower cognitive performance both 2 and 4 years prior to diagnosis, compared to nondemented survivors. Nonsurvivors had lower cognitive performance at prior examinations, compared to nondemented survivors. In a previous study in this oldest-old sample Johansson and Zarit (1995) also showed that there was a twofold increased mortality risk in demented subjects. They emphasized that this increased mortality risk among demented individuals counterbalances the high incidence rates in later life with the effect that prevalence rates become lower than would be the case if mortality rates were similar among demented and nondemented individuals. Findings like this suggest that impaired cognitive functioning may herald the onset of dementia and an increased mortality risk, and the lesson to be learned is that it is important to adjust or to control, not only for the effects of prevalent dementia, but also for later incidence in studies of cognition and cognitive change in later life.

A major problem in aging research is related to the previously discussed fact that morbidity and comorbidity is the rule rather than the exception at older ages. This makes it difficult to disentangle the relative contribution of compromised physical health and normative aging for cognitive functioning at older ages. The approach described above about using survival or remaining life as an index for overall health and vitality has therefore become more common in recent research. These ideas originate from observations made by Kleemeier (1962) of a pronounced decline in writing in persons who died within a 5-year period and that the complexity of writing seemed to drop within a year before death; these findings suggested that a terminal change pattern also might be seen in other cognitive abilities. Riegel and Riegel (1972) formally proposed the terminal drop or decline hypothesis for the relationship between cognitive function and remaining time to live. The initial studies usually compared performance on cognitive tests for groups of individuals with various survival times following a single measurement occasion; lower levels of cognitive function are related to an increased risk of subsequent mortality. These analyses were, however, unable to capitalize on available within-person information, that is, intraindividual change. Later longitudinal studies have largely confirmed the cognition–survival relationship by demonstrating that lower levels of cognitive function are related to an increased risk of subsequent mortality, and that cognitive decline may be driven by the same generic processes that typically devitalize an individual before death (e.g., Bäckman & MacDonald, 2006; Bosworth & Siegler, 2002). There is an ongoing discussion about the role of underlying mechanisms, as well as about methodological issues related to the longitudinal design and the use of multilevel analyses that most convincingly provide evidence that cognitive changes are related to distance from death, independent of performance levels among examined individuals (e.g., Silbereisen, 2006).

A test of the relative effects of distance from birth and distance from death was performed in a study by Thorvaldsson, Hofer, and Johansson (2006). They found that the effects of time to death were considerably greater than the effects of chronological age (see Figure 22.5). The analysis was performed in a sample which remained nondemented until their death to prevent the mortality-related effects from dementia disorders. They used a rather simple test for perceptual speed in which a person is instructed to identify figures that are identical as fast as possible, which requires discrimination between

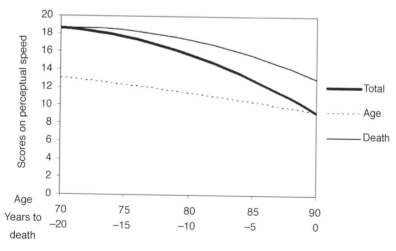

Figure 22.5 Age-based and death-based means trajectories for prototypical individuals who died at age 90 in a sample studied from age 70 in which participants remained nondemented until death. Created by Boo Johansson and Anne Ingeborg Berg.

figures before a decision. Using multilevel methods that allow the separation of within-person change from changes between individuals and controlling for chronological age, a substantial acceleration in decline was observed 14 years before death (Thorvaldsson et al., 2006).

The terminal decline hypothesis has produced questions about whether the decline varies among cognitive abilities and whether rate of change and time of onset differ for cognitive function. These questions were simultaneously addressed in another study by Thorvaldsson and colleagues (2008). Using a population-based sample followed from age 70, with more than 10 re-examinations for surviving individuals who all remained nondemented until their death, they sought to analyze whether it was possible to identify a certain time point at which an accelerated within-person change could be observed, and whether there was a difference between tests of perceptual speed, verbal meaning, and spatial ability. Analyses revealed a differential pattern for these tests. The onset of the terminal decline phase was 6–7 years for verbal ability, about 8 years for spatial ability, and almost 15 years before death in perceptual speed. This finding suggests the existence of a robust terminal decline pattern that may start long before death. The time of onset as well as the rate of decline, however, varies considerably across cognitive abilities (see Figure 22.6).

A major challenge in current research is the early identification of cognitive changes indicative of later dementia. To study this we need longitudinal samples repeatedly followed over many years. A recent study (Thorvaldsson et al., 2011) demonstrates that the time of onset and rate of acceleration of decline before dementia vary systematically along the fluid–crystallized cognitive ability continuum. An onset as early as almost 10 years before the

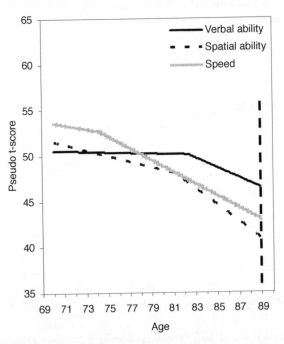

Figure 22.6   Plot of average change for the three cognitive abilities for a prototypical individual who died at age 89. Created by Boo Johansson and Anne Ingeborg Berg.

occasion at which there is evidence enough for a clinical diagnosis of dementia was observed for perceptual speed, later followed by other tests of fluid ability. Onset of dementia this early is, however, difficult due to substantial decline in normal aging before the start of the accelerated decline due to dementia. An onset and acceleration of decline in crystallized abilities are more indicative of dementia, although at a stage closer to when clinical criteria actually are met because we expect crystallized abilities to be largely preserved in later life.

The life course perspective is currently applied more often in aging research as a heuristic framework for how late-life cognitive outcomes may be related to previous interactions among genetic and various environmental influences over the life span (Kuh, 2007; Kuh, Cooper, Hardy, Guralnik, & Richards, 2009). Such a model also highlights potential reasons for interindividual differences. In a life course model genetic influences have to be considered as a robust framing system for later development. Interestingly, studies of cognitive ability in older twins have shown substantial heritability: a population estimate for the relative impact of genetic influences calculated on similarities in identical and same-sex fraternal twin pairs. A study of general and specific cognitive abilities in twin pairs 80 and older for whom neither twin had any major cognitive, sensory, or motor impairment showed that the similarities within the 110 identical pairs were significantly greater than was the case in the 130 fraternal same-sex twin pairs (McClearn et al., 1997). The estimates of heritability were 62% for general cognitive ability, 55% for verbal ability, 32% for spatial ability, 62% for speed of processing, and 52% for memory. Despite environmental influences for 80 and more years, these estimates suggest that the genetic effects on cognitive functioning are profound also in later life.

The risk for dementia is also highly influenced by genetics. In a study by Pedersen, Gatz, Berg, and Johansson (2004), a cohort of more than 600 pairs of Swedish twins aged 52–98 were investigated for their risk of developing dementia over a 5-year period. Incident cases were detected through follow-ups at 2 to 3-year intervals. About 6% of the sample was diagnosed with Alzheimer's disease. The average age of onset was estimated at age 84. Model fitting analysis showed that almost 50% of the variation in liability to Alzheimer's disease could be attributed to genetic variation. Notably, the estimates did not differ between twins younger and older than 80 years at baseline. This study provided evidence for the importance of genetic factors in late onset Alzheimer's disease, previously assumed to be less affected by genetic influences. Epidemiological studies have identified numerous environmental factors that may have a potential impact, either as neuroprotective agents or as risk factors for compromised cognitive functioning in later life. For example, education has a positive role for late-life cognition (e.g., Gatz et al., 2001). Current research is exploring the effects from various psychosocial candidates for their role to preserve functioning and prevent decline. Among these are earlier work exposures and intellectual demands (Finkel, Gatz, & Pedersen, 2009), leisure time activities, as well as lifestyles differing in physical activity and nutritional habits (see e.g., Fratiglioni & Qiu, 2009; Hendrie et al. 2006).

The increased vulnerability for cognitive impairment in older individuals often becomes evident following various major life events and in hospital settings. It is frequently observed in relation to surgery and in intensive care. Pisani and colleagues (2009) examined the association between number of days of delirium when in an intensive care unit (ICU) with subsequent mortality in a patient population of 300 consecutive admissions of those 60 years and older. After adjusting for covariates, including age, severity of illness, comorbid conditions, psychoactive medication use, and baseline cognitive and functional status, number of days with ICU delirium was found to be significantly associated with time to death within a 1-year period. The finding of delirium as a significant predictor of mortality is confirmed in many other studies (e.g., Kiely et al., 2009). Dementia is also a major risk factor for delirium. Although the remaining brain reserve in dementia affects the clinical expression of impairments, the efficiency by which individuals use cognitive strategies to cope with their pathology is also of importance for their actual functioning in early stages of the disease (e.g., Kolanowski, Fick, Clare, Therrien, & Gill, 2010). Recent research has emphasized the role of this cognitive reserve by which pathology becomes modified through lifelong experiences of everyday cognitive demands, education, and other influences that may have a neuroprotective effect (see Stern, 2002).

A lesson to be learned from several longitudinal studies and clinical experience is that older individuals in fact can maintain and even improve their functioning although population average trajectories tend to make us less optimistic about recovery and preserved cognition.

Subjective Well-Being – Time from Birth and Death

With age and generation our time perspective is likely to change. The increasing number of years that an individual can expect to live nowadays has dramatically changed within a few generations. Our age identity – the way we view our own age or subjective age – may make people in their seventies consider themselves as being in midlife. The "future of aging" may still be far away. Compared with young adulthood, in which individuals may almost consider themselves immortal, with age we are likely to become more aware of the fact that the future is shorter. The question is how these experiences may affect our emotional states and other aspects of psychological well-being.

In recent research this distance-from-death hypothesis has been incorporated into empirical studies. In an already classical study, Lewy, Slade, Kunkel, and Kasl (2002) found that longevity is increased by positive self-perceptions of aging and that this effect remained after controlling for the effects of chronological age, gender, socioeconomic status, loneliness, and functional health. Individuals with more positive self-perceptions of aging (PSPA), measured up to 23 years earlier, lived 7.5 years longer than those with less positive self-perceptions (see Figure 22.7).

Subjective well-being, and in particular life satisfaction, has earlier been found to be fairly stable across life (Costa et al., 1987). Longitudinal studies including individuals aged 80 and older, however, have actually demonstrated a decrease in life satisfaction in very old age (Berg et al., 2009; Mroczek & Spiro, 2005). These findings challenged the previously recognized paradox of lifespan stability in happiness; that is, despite all losses that come with increasing age we are still happy. The conclusion to be drawn is that the load from health-related and psychosocial losses escalate at these ages and pose a negative impact on well-being.

For a long time chronological age has been the almost solely used index to which developmental changes are related. In early life this is less of a problem, but in later life distance from birth gradually becomes less informative. The heterogeneity in health and

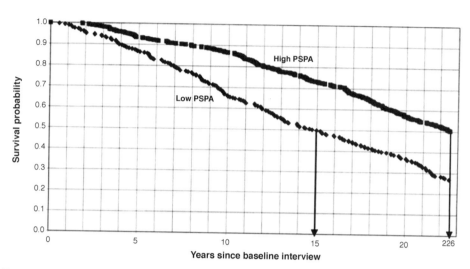

Figure 22.7 Self-perceptions of aging and survival. *Source*: Originally appeared in Lewy, B.R., Slade, M.D., Kunkel, S.R., & Kasl, S.V. (2002). Longevity increased by positive self-perceptions of aging. Journal of personality and social psychology, 83, 261–270. Copyright APA 2002.

functioning in older individuals has recently drawn attention to the need for alternative and more appropriate time metrics to understand as well as measure change in subjective well-being and life satisfaction.

In contrast to studies of younger populations, mortality and pathology-related processes accompany and influence age-graded processes which need to be taken into account in the study of late-life development requiring adaptation to bodily changes as well as to changes in the external environment of very old individuals (Baltes & Smith, 1997; S. Berg, 1996). Consequently, chronological-age-related changes in life satisfaction also incorporate effects of mortality-related processes, given that individuals aged 80 and older are close to their average life expectancy. These aging-specific circumstances suggest that a distance-from-death time metric can be more valid in the study also of continuity and change in emotions and late-life psychological well-being.

Mroczek and Spiro (2005) found that individuals who would die within one year showed a steeper decline in life satisfaction. That change in life satisfaction was related to distance from death was further confirmed by Gerstorf, Ram, Röcke, Lindenberger, & Smith (2008) who applied a time-to-death metric in their study. They also identified a terminal decline 4 years prior to death. Berg, Thorvaldsson, Hassing, & Johansson (2011) also found that changes in well-being were better accounted for in growth curve models using the time-from-death metric compared to chronological age or time-in-study. In these studies the change related to death could not be related to health status or changes in health. Thus the outcome of an age-related decline may conceal an underlying and more powerful influence: In samples of individuals aged 80 and older an increasing proportion are in fact approaching their actual point of death. In this respect the impact of impending death processes may increasingly intervene with chronological age. Level and changes in satisfaction in the oldest-old population are probably related to mortality and morbidity but the nature of the relationship is assumed to become an area for intense investigation in the years to come.

Palgi and colleagues (2010) contributed to this research with a study in which they examined change in subjective well-being and subjective health in relation to distance from death in a longitudinal sample drawn from the National Population Registry in Israel. At the start, initially 75–95 year olds were interviewed at three occasions between 1989 and 2002. In 2009 most of the individuals were deceased. Growth curve models were used to fit each measure of well-being and health with chronological age and time to death. Analysis revealed that the time metric of distance from death was a superior marker for change compared with age. They controlled for physical and cognitive functioning and background characteristics such as chronological age at interviews, gender, education, marital status, place of residency and whether persons were born in or outside Israel; they found that the pattern remained for subjective well-being but not for subjective health.

Another approach for studying the potential impact of the largely unknown future is to interview individuals about their ideas and expectations of the future. In a study by Cheng, Fung, and Chan (2009), they examined whether having a negative expectation of the future may protect well-being in old age. Participants were 200 individuals aged 60 and older who rated their current and future selves in the physical and social domains twice over a 12-month period. They found that future self was positively related to well-being concurrently, but negatively related to well-being 12 months later after a control for current symptoms and current self. Those who underestimated their future selves had higher well-being 12 months later than did those who overestimated their future selves. The authors conclude that we tend to actively construct representations of the future that are consistent with the normative age-related declines and losses, so that the effects of these declines and losses are lessened when they actually occur. In this anticipatory way we may prepare and protect ourselves for the unknown future of age-related loss and devitalization.

An interesting parallel in this context are the studies reported by Van Boven and Ashworth (2007). They conducted five experiments to examine the role and intensity of emotions in thinking about the past, the present, and the future. The results provide evidence for more intense emotions during anticipation of an upcoming event than for a retrospective evaluation of the event. This finding was confirmed for positive as well as negative events, for routine and more hypothetical events. The experiments indicate that there is a tendency to expect future emotions to be more intense than remembered past emotions having been. The researchers conclude that anticipation seems to be more evocative than retrospective thinking about an event. This tendency has interesting implications for our understanding of the willingness to experience an unknown future that we hope to be better than the past.

Although we often tend to separate the focus on cognition and psychological well-being in research studies, there are several changes and conditions in which it becomes evident that the two domains are closely related. For example, a question often addressed is about how individuals themselves react to cognitive change and decline. Are changes in mood and depressive symptoms indicative of later cognitive decline and dementia?

Brommelhoff and colleagues (2009) addressed the questions of whether a history of depression is associated with an increased risk of dementia, and whether a first depressive episode earlier in life is associated with increased dementia risk, or whether only depressive episodes close in time to dementia onset are related to dementia. They used a population-based sample of twins providing information about depressive episodes from national hospital discharge registries, medical history, and medical records. Dementia in the sample was diagnosed according to clinical routines using information from neuropsychological test, medical examination, and informant data. The case–control design showed that those with recent registry-identified depression were almost four times more likely than those with no registry-identified depression history to have dementia. Notably, depression earlier in life was not associated with an elevated dementia risk. Analyses based on a case-control design showed that those with recent registry-identified depression were 3.9 times more likely than those with no registry-identified depression history to have dementia, whereas depression earlier in life was not associated with dementia risk. It is concluded that late-life depression for many individuals may be a prodrome condition rather than a risk factor for dementia (Brommelhoff et al., 2009). Findings like this emphasize that individuals may be emotionally affected by subsequent changes, perhaps even long before it is obvious for others that the individual experiences cognitive decline that later will develop into dementia.

Studies of metamemory – knowledge about ones own memory – in relation to continuity or later change in memory capacity represents another line of research that aims to bridge the domains of cognitive functioning and self-perceived functioning. Studies on this relationship have usually demonstrated rather low associations, which suggest that our ability to accurately evaluate own performance is limited and influenced by many other factors than actual performance (e.g., psychological well-being, depression, neuroticism, and feeling of self-control often contribute to self-evaluations and memory complaints; Derouesne, Lacomblez, Thibault, & LePoncin, 1999; Frerichs & Tuokko, 2006; Kliegel et al., 2005; Verhaeghen et al., 2000). In recent years there has been a discussion about whether metamemory relates to executive functioning and whether the low association can be explained by the decline in executive-frontal functioning typically observed in aging. A recent study, however, suggests that subjective memory may be a better indicator among individuals with possible incipient cognitive impairment because those who experience cognitive decline in early stages may have heightened their insight into own memory functioning (Cook & Marsiske, 2006). Along the same line, Johansson, Allen-Burge, and Zarit (1997) investigated whether self-evaluation of memory is an indicator of concurrent, retrospective, or future decline in memory functioning in a longitudinal population-based sample of oldest-old individuals. They found that self-reported decline over a 2-year period was associated with actual decline in some memory tests. Self-evaluations also predicted decline on specific tests of memory over 2 years and subsequent diagnosis of dementia after 2 and 4 years. The amount of variance accounted for by self-evaluations, however, was relatively small, suggesting that complaints reflect different processes, only one of which is the pathological decline involved in dementia.

Biopsychosocial Integration of Late Life Emotions and Thinking

The lifespan perspective, and especially the study of late-life development, provides numerous arguments and empirical data for the integration of biological, psychological, and sociocultural elements into a comprehensive general biopsychosocial framework. There is also a need to realize that distance from birth is likely to become less of concern in late life than the time that actually remains. For a young "immortal" person the future may seem almost infinite compared to an oldest old individual who realizes that the future means a limited time and who experiences changes in the internal bodily environment, physical and cognitive functioning, and can report major sociocultural changes and age-graded events that have provided impetus that the meaning of remaining time differs along the lifeline. The meaning of the notion of *carpe diem* is therefore likely to differ for a young and an old person. The psychological perspectives of older individuals may in this sense provide arguments for the evaluation of alternative models for their explanatory role in our understanding of well-being and cognitive functioning in late life. Recent research provides evidence to supplement and even to replace the traditional time metrics of distance from birth with a metric based on remaining time or time to death, whether factual or perceived. Not only at the individual level, but also from a societal perspective, there seems to be a tendency to de-emphasize chronological age for criteria more directly related to capacities and functioning. We may therefore expect concepts like the "third and fourth age" to become more common because these concepts do in fact refer to autonomy and the actual capacity to manage everyday life in later life, independent of actual age.

A model for the integration of psychological and social characteristics suggested by Gerstorf, Smith, and Baltes (2006) may serve as guideline for future research of late-life emotional and cognitive health. Instead of using the standard design focusing on interrelationships among variables, they employed cluster analysis in their proposed systemic-wholistic model for the study of differential aging. They studied late-life trajectories over a 6-year period in a sample drawn from the Berlin Aging Study. At baseline, three subgroups were identified with distinct within-person psychological profiles across cognitive, personality, and social integration constructs defined as overall positive profile ($n = 61$), overall average profile ($n = 28$), and high cognition, low self and social profile ($n = 41$). Interestingly, the subgroups differed in level and slope of change and in two major outcomes. The overall positive profile subgroup reported higher well-being over a 6-year interval and lived longer than members of other subgroups after the end of the study. The study has contributed to the understanding of effects of patterns of hetero-geneity in health, social, and psychological functioning in aging populations. The use of real-life individual uniqueness as reflected in functioning across multiple coinciding domains could improve the ecological validity of future research on late life.

A recent study by Orth, Trzesniewski, and Robins (2010) examined the development of self-esteem in adulthood and aging. Using a cohort-sequential design, including four measurement occasions over a 16-year period, they investigated age-related changes in more than 3,000 individuals aged 25 to over 100. Their main finding was that of an overall trajectory showing an increase in younger adulthood and with a peak at about 60 years of age followed by a decline thereafter. Notably, they found no cohort differences but self-esteem was higher in men (especially at younger ages) and among those with better education (fairly stable across ages). The authors suggest that lower socioeconomic status and compromised physical health at older ages may account for decline in self-esteem in late life. A study like this provides support for an understanding of psychological phenomena like self-esteem within the broader context of potentially modifiable effects of biological health and sociocultural conditions. Although most studies on aging currently are focusing on continuity and change in selected variables of gerontological relevance by using more advanced statistical methods that allow us to simultaneously examine interindividual differences and intraindividual changes, it is also necessary to remind ourselves about the obvious fact that we are not aging as variables but as whole individuals in a certain sociocultural context. The microperspective on mechanisms for age-related change in biological systems tends to neglect the macro effects from differential environmental influences that operate from conception. At the same time there is a risk that a macroperspective of human aging avoids the understanding of biological limitations and the genetic influences that variously contribute to survival and functioning in later life. In the same way as biodemography, for example, tries to integrate studies of aging populations with biological sciences (i.e., "demography gets under the skin"), critical or humanistic gerontology (e.g., Estes & Phillipson, 2007) emphasizes that aging also represents a social construction based on values, culture, and political forces that allocates beneficial conditions variously because of age and in relation to gender, class, and ethnicity. Patterns of such age stratification become evident in status and prestige of older individuals across societies and cultures. From a developmental perspective these patterns are internalized over the lifespan and affect our perceptions and expectations of becoming older and also how we tend to evaluate our thinking and psychological well-being as older individuals.

A biopsychosocial perspective of aging is not simply a summary of observations of biological, psychological, and social changes associated with distance from birth and death, but requires an integrative model for the understanding of how these variables are interrelated and operate both at the individual level and in various populations in producing normative patterns of change as well as substantial interindividual differences over time.

Acknowledgment

The authors are grateful for constructive comments from Marcus Praetorius on draft versions of this chapter.

References

Anderson-Ranberg, K., Schrool, M., & Jeune, B. (2001). Healthy centenarians do not exist, but autonomous centenarians do: A population-based study of morbidity among Danish centenarians. *Journal of American Geriatric Society, 49,* 900–908.

Anstey, K. J., Mack, H. A., & von Sanden, C. (2006). The relationship between cognition and mortality in patients with stroke, coronary heart disease, or cancer. *European Psychologist, 11,* 182–195.

Bäckman, L., & MacDonald, W. S. (2006). Death and cognition. Viewing a 1962 concept through 2006 spectacles. Introduction to the special section "Death and Cognition." *European Psychologist, 11,* 161–163.

Baltes, P., & Smith, J. (1997). A systemic-wholistic view of psychological functions in very old age: Introduction to a collection of articles from the Berlin Aging Study. *Psychology and Aging, 12,* 395–409.

Baltes, P., & Smith, J. (2003). New frontiers of in the future of aging: From successful aging of the young old to the dilemmas of the fourth age. *Gerontology, 49,* 123–135.

Berg, A. I., Hassing, L. B., Nilsson, S. E., & Johansson, B. (2009). "As long as I'm in good health." The relationship between medical diagnoses and life satisfaction in the oldest-old. *Aging Clinical and Experimental Research, 21,* 307–313.

Berg, A. I., Hoffman, L., Hassing, L. B., McClearn, G. E., & Johansson, B. (2009). What matters, and what matters most, for change in life satisfaction in the oldest-old? A study over 6 years among individuals 80 + . *Aging and Mental Health, 13,* 191–201.

Berg, A. I., Thorvaldsson, V., Hassing, L. B., & Johansson, B. (2011). Personality and personal control matters for life satisfaction in the oldest-old. *European Journal of Ageing.* doi: 10.1007/s10433-011-0181-9.

Berg, S., (1996). Aging, behavior, and terminal decline. In J. E. Birren & K. W., Schaie (Eds.), *Handbook of the psychology of aging* (4th ed., pp. 323–337). New York: Academic Press.

Berr, C., Wancata, J., & Ritchie, K. (2005). Prevalence of dementia in Europe. *European Neuropsychopharmacology, 15,* 463–471.

Bosworth, H. B., & Siegler, I. C. (2002). Terminal change in cognitive function: An updated review of longitudinal studies. *Experimental Aging Research, 28,* 299–315.

Brommelhoff, J. A., Gatz, M. Johansson, B., McArdle, J. J., Fratiglioni, L., & Pedersen, N. L. (2009). Depression as a risk factor or prodromal feature for dementia? Findings in apopulation-based sample of Swedish twins. *Psychology and Aging, 24,* 373–384.

Börjesson-Hansson, A., Edin, E., Gislason, T., & Skoog, I. (2004). The prevalence of dementia in 95 year olds. *Neurology, 63,* 2436–2438.

Carstensen, L. L. (1992). Social and emotional patterns in adulthood: Support for socioemotional selectivity theory. *Psychology and Aging, 7,* 331–338.

Carstensen, L. L. (2006). The influence of a sense of time on human development. *Science, 312* (5782): 1913–1915.

Carstensen, L. L., Isaacowitz, D. M., & Charles, S. T. (1999). Taking time seriously: A theory of socioemotional selectivity. *American Psychologist, 54,* 165–181.

Cheng, S. T., Fung, H. H., & Chan, A. C. (2009). Self-perception and psychological well-being: The benefits of foreseeing a worse future. *Psychology and Aging, 24,* 623–633.

Christensen, K., Doblhammer, G., Rau. R., & Vaupel, J.W. (2009). Ageing populations: The challenges ahead. *Lancet, 374*(9696), 1196–1208.

Christensen, K., Thinggaard, M., McGue, M., Rexbye, H., Hjelborg, J.V., Aviv, A., . . . Vaupel, J. W. (2009) Perceived age as clinically useful biomarker of ageing: Cohort study. *British Medical Journal, 339,* b5262.

Cook, S., & Marsiske, M. (2006). Subjective memory beliefs and cognitive performance innormal and mildly impaired older adults. *Aging and Mental Health, 10,* 413–423.

Costa, P. T., McCrae, R. R., & Zonderman, A. B. (1987).Environmental and dispositional influences on well-being: Longitudinal follow-up of an American national sample. *British Journal of Psychology, 78,* 299–306.

Demakakos, P., Gjonca, E., & Nazroo, J. (2007). Age identity, age perceptions, and health: Evidence from the English longitudinal study of ageing. *Annals of New York Academy of Sciences, 1114,* 279–287.

Derouesne, C., Lacomblez, L, Thibault, S., & LePoncin, M. (1999). Memory complaints in young and elderly subjects. *International Journal of Geriatric Psychiatry, 14,* 291–301.

Estes, C. L., & Phillipson, C. (2007). Critical gerontology. In J. E. Birren (Ed.), *Encyclopaedia of gerontology* (2nd ed., pp. 330–336). New York: Elsevier.

Finkel, D., Andel, Gatz, M., Pedersen, N. L. (2009). The role of occupational complexity in trajectories of cognitive aging before and after retirement. *Psychology and Aging, 24,* 563–573.

Fratiglioni, L., & Qiu, C. (2009). Prevention of common neurodegenerative disorders in the elderly. *Experimental Gerontology, 44,* 46–50.

Frerichs, R. J., & Tuokko, H. A. (2006). Reliable change scores and their relation to perceived change in memory: Implications for the diagnosis of mild cognitive impairment. *Archives of Clinical Neuropsychology, 21,* 109–115.

Gatz, M., Svedberg, P., Pedersen, N. L., Mortimer, J. A., Berg, S., & Johansson, B. (2001). Education and the risk of Alzheimer's disease: Findings from the study of dementia in Swedish twins. *Journals of Gerontology B: Psychological Sciences & Social Sciences, 56,* 292–300. Erratum in: *Journals of Gerontology B: Psychological Sciences & Social Sciences, 2004, 59,* 34.

Gerstorf, D., Ram, N., Röcke, C., Lindenberger, U., & Smith, J. (2008). Decline in life satisfaction in old age: Longitudinal evidence for links to distance-to-death. *Psychology and Aging, 23,* 154–168.

Gerstorf, D., Smith, J., & Baltes, P. B. (2006). A systemic-wholistic approach to differential aging: Longitudinal findings from the Berlin Aging Study. *Psychology and Aging, 21,* 645–663.

Hassing, L. B., Johansson, B., Berg, S., Nilsson, S. E., Pedersen, N. L., Hofer, S. M., & McClearn, G. (2002). Terminal decline and markers of cerebrovascular and cardiovascular disease: Findings from a longitudinal study of the oldest old. *Journal of Gerontology: Psychological Sciences, 57B,* 268–276.

Heckhausen, J., Wrosch, C. & Schulz, R. (2010). A motivational theory of life-span development. *Psychological Review, 117,* 32–60.

Hendrie, H. H., Albert, M. S., Butters, M. A., Gao, S., Knopman, D. S., Launer, L. J., . . . Wagster, M.V. (2006). The NIH cognitive and emotional health project. Report of the critical evaluation study committee. *Alzheimer & Dementia, 2,* 12–32.

Hofer, S. M. & Alwin, D. F. (Eds.) (2008). *Handbook of cognitive aging. Interdisciplinary perspectives.* Thousand Oaks, CA: Sage.

Jagger, C., Andersen, K., Breteler, M. M., Copeland, J. R., Helmer, C., Baldereschi, M. . . . Launer, L. J. (2000). Prognosis with dementia in Europe: A collaborative study of population-based cohorts. Neurologic Diseases in the Elderly Research Group. *Neurology. 54*(11 Suppl. 5), S16–S20.

Johansson, B., Allen-Burge, R., & Zarit, S. H. (1997). Self-reports on memory functioning in a longitudinal study of the oldest old: Relation to current, prospective, and retrospective performance. *Journal of Gerontology: Psychological Science, 52,* 139–146.

Johansson, B., & Zarit, S. H. (1995). Prevalence and incidence of dementia in the oldest-old: A study of a population-based sample of 84-90 year olds in Sweden. *International Journal of Geriatric Psychiatry, 10,* 359–366.

Johansson, B., & Zarit, S. H. (1997). Early cognitive markers of the incidence of dementia and mortality: A longitudinal population-based study of the oldest-old. *International Journal of Geriatric Psychiatry, 12,* 53–59.

Jylhä, M. (2009). What is self-rated health and why does it predict mortality? Towards a unified conceptual model. *Social Science & Medicine, 69,* 307–316.

Kiely, D. K., Marcantonio, E. R., Inouye, S. K., Shaffer, M. L., Bergmann, M. A., Yang, F. M, . . . Jones, R. N. (2009). Persistent delirium predicts greater mortality. *Journal of the American Geriatrics Society, 57,* 55–61.

Kleemeier, R.W. (1962) Intellectual changes in the senium. *Proceedings of the American Statistical Association, 1,* 290–295.

Kliegel, M., Jäger, T., Phillips, L. H., Federspiel, E., Imfeld, A., Keller, M., & Zimprich, D. (2005). Effects of sad mood on time-based prospective memory. *Cognition and Emotion, 19,* 1199–1213.

Kolanowski, A. M., Fick, D. M., Clare, L., Therrien, B., & Gill, D.J. (2010). An intervention for delirium superimposed on dementia-based cognitive reserve theory. *Aging and Mental Health, 14* (2), 232–242.

Kuh, D. (2007). A life course approach to healthy aging, frailty, and capability. *Journal of Gerontology, Series A: Biological Sciences and Medical Sciences, 62,* 717–721.

Kuh, D., Cooper, R., Hardy, R., Guralnik, J., & Richards, M. (2009). Lifetime cognitive performance is associated with midlife physical performance in a prospective national birth cohort study. *Psychosomatic Medicine, 71,* 38–48.

Lewy, B. R., Slade, M. D., Kunkel, S. R., & Kasl, S. V. (2002). Longevity increased by positive self-perceptions of aging. *Journal of Personality and Social Psychology, 83,* 261–270.

McClearn, G. E., Johansson, B., Berg, S., Pedersen, N. L., Ahern, F., Petrill, S. A., & Plomin, R. (1997). Substantial genetic influence on cognitive abilities in twins 80 or more years old. *Science, 278,* 1383–1387.

Mezuk, B. (2009). Epidemiology of diabetes and cardiovascular disease. The emergence of health disparities over the life span. *Annual Review of Gerontology and Geriatrics, 29,* 77–98.

Mirowsky, J. (1997) Age, subjective life expectancy, and the sense of control: The horizon hypothesis. *Journal of Gerontology, Series B: Psychological Science and Social Science, 52,* 125–134.

Mirowsky, J. (1999) Subjective life expectancy in the US: Correspondence to actuarial estimates by age, sex and race. *Social Science & Medicine, 49,* 967–979.

Mroczek, D. K., & Spiro, A. (2005). Changes in life satisfaction during adulthood: Findings from the veterans affairs normative aging study. *Journal of Personality and Social Psychology, 88,* 189–202.

Nepal, B., Brown, L., & Ranmuthugala, G. (2008). Years of life lived with and without dementia in Australia, 2004-2006: A population health measure. *Australian and New Zealand Journal of Public Health, 32,* 565–568.

Newsom, J. T., & Schulz, R. (1996). Social support as a mediator in the relation between functional status and quality of life in older adults. *Psychology and Aging, 11,* 34–44.

Nilsson, B-O., Ernerudh, J., Johansson, B., Evrin, P.-E., Löfgren, S., Ferguson, F., & Wikby, A. (2003). Morbidity does not influence the T-cell immune risk phenotype in the elderly: Findings in the Swedish NONA Immune Study using sample selection protocols. *Mechanisms of Ageing and Development, 124,* 469–476.

Nilsson, S. E., Evrin, P. E., Tryding, N., Berg, S., McClearn, G., & Johansson B. (2003). Biochemical values in persons older than 82 years of age: Report from a population-based study of twins. *Scandinavian Journal of Clinical and Laboratory Investigation, 63,* 1–13.

Nilsson, S. E., Johansson, B., Berg, S., Karlsson, D., & McClearn, G. E. (2002). A comparison of diagnosis capture from medical records, self-reports, and drug registrations: A study in individuals 80 years and older. *Aging, Clinical & Experimental Research, 14,* 178–184.

Oksuzyan, A., Juel, K., Vaupel, J. W., & Christensen, K. (2008). Men: Good health and high mortality. Sex differences in health and aging. *Aging Clinical and Experimental Research, 20,* 91–102.

Orth, U., Trzesniewski, K. H., & Robins, R. W. (2010). Self-esteem development from young adulthood to old age: A cohort-sequential longitudinal study. *Journal of Personality and Social Psychology, 98,* 645–658.

Palgi, Y., Shrira, A., Ben-Ezra, M., Spalter, T., Shmotkin, D., & Kavé, G., (2010): Delineating terminal change in subjective well-being and subjective health. *Journals of Gerontology, Series B: Psychological Sciences and Social Sciences, 65B,* 61–64.

Pedersen, N. L., Gatz, M., Berg, S., & Johansson, B. (2004). How heritable is Alzheimer's disease late in life? Findings from Swedish twins. *Annals of Neurology, 55,* 180–185.

Perozek, M. (2008) Using subjective expectations to forecast longevity: Do survey respondents know something we don't know? *Demography, 45,* 95–113.

Pinquart, M., & Sörensen, S. (2000). Influences of socioeconomic status, social network, and competence on subjective well-being in later life: A meta-analysis. *Psychology and Aging, 15,* 187–224.

Pisani, M. A., Kong, S. Y., Kasl, S. V., Murphy, T. E., Araujo, K. L., & Van Ness, P. H. (2009). Days of delirium are associated with 1-year mortality in an older intensive care unit population. *American Journal of Respiratory and Critical Care Medicine, 1*(180), 1092–1097.

Radloff, L. S. (1977). The CES-D Scale: A self-report depression scale for research in the general population. *Applied Psychological Measurement, 1,* 385–401.

Riegel, K. F., & Riegel, R.M. (1972). Development, drop, and death. *Developmental Psychology, 6,* 309–316.

Schaie, K.W. (2005). What can we learn from longitudinal studies of adult development? *Research Human Development, 2,* 133–158.

Silbereisen, R. K. (Ed.). (2006). Death and cognition (Special issue) *European Psychologist, 11.*

Skoog, I., Aevarsson, O., Beskow, J., Larsson, L., Palsson, S., Waern, M., . . . Östling, S. (1996). Suicidal feelings in a population sample of nondemented 85-year-olds. *American Journal of Psychiatry, 153,* 1015–1020.

Stern,Y. (2002). What is cognitive reserve? Theory and research application of the reserve concept. *Journal of the International Neuropsychological Society, 8,* 751–757.

Thorvaldsson, V., Hofer, S., & Johansson, B. (2006). Aging and late-life terminal decline in perceptual speed: A comparison of alternative modelling approaches. *European Psychologist, 11,* 196–203.

Thorvaldsson, V., Hofer, S. M., Berg, S., Skoog, I., Sacuiu, S., & Johansson, B. (2008). Onset of terminal decline in cognitive abilities in individuals without dementia, *Neurology, 71,* 882–887.

Thorvaldsson, V., MacDonald, S.W.S., Fratiglioni, L., Winblad, B., Kivipelto, M., Jonsson Laukka, E., . . . Bäckman, L. (2011). Onset and rate of cognitive change before dementia diagnosis: Findings from two Swedish population-based longitudinal studies. *Journal of the International Neuropsychological Society, 17,* 154–162.

Uotinen, V., Rantanen, T., & Suutama, T. (2005). Perceived age as a predictor of old age mortality: A 13-year prospective study. *Age and Ageing, 34,* 368–372.

Uotinen, V., Rantanen, T., Suutama, T., & Ruoppila, I. (2006). Change in subjective age among older people over an eight-year follow-up: "Getting older and feeling younger?" *Experimental Aging Research, 32,* 381–393.

Van Boven, L. & Ashworth, L. (2007). Looking forward, looking back: Anticipation is more evocative than retrospection. *Journal of Experimental Psychology: General, 136,* 289–300.

Van Doorn, C., & Kasl, S.V. (1998). Can parental longevity and self-rated life expectancy predict mortality among older persons? Results from an Australian cohort. *Journals of Gerontology Series B: Psychological Sciences & Social Sciences, 53,* 28–34.

Van Solinge, H. & Henkens, K (2009). Living longer, working longer? The impact of subjective life expectancy on retirement intentions and behaviour. *European Journal of Public Health, 20,* 47–51.

Verhaeghen, P., Geraerts, N., & Marcoen, A. (2000). Memory complaints, coping, and well-being in old age: A systemic approach. *Gerontologist, 40,* 540–548.

Wancata, J., Börjesson-Hanson, A., Ostling, S., Sjögren, K., & Skoog, I. (2007). Diagnostic criteria influence dementia prevalence. *American Journal of Geriatric Psychiatry, 15,* 1034–1054.

Wikby, A., Strindhall, J., & Johansson, B. (2009). The immune risk profile and associated parameters in late life: Lessons form the OCTO and NONA longitudinal studies. In T. Fulop, T., C. Franxeschi, K. Hirokawa, & G. Pawelec (Eds.), *Handbook on immunosenescence. Basic understanding and clinical applications* (pp. 3–28). New York: Springer.

World Health Organization (WHO) (1992). *ICD-10: International Statistical Classification of Diseases and Health Problems* (10th revised ed.). Geneva: Author.

23

Successful Aging

Colin A. Depp, Ipsit V. Vahia, and Dilip V. Jeste

Introduction

While much of the focus of geriatrics and gerontology has been on identifying and treating "pathological aging," the diseases and disabilities that are associated with aging, a smaller body of work has focused on what defines and determines successful or healthy aging. The public health relevance of this body of work is coming into sharper focus as the wave of "baby boomers" has just begun to transition into older adulthood. The broad purpose of the literature on successful aging is to identify what characteristics are associated with living well into older age. At the same time, there are an increasing number of interventions that are aimed at altering the course of normal aging, and thus are geared toward lengthening the human healthspan. In this chapter, we review the historical conceptualization of successful aging, leading to a review of current controversies in the definition of the term. We then describe recent work on the biological, psychological, and social determinants of positive outcomes in later life, and we conclude with a review of interventions that may increase the likelihood of successful aging.

Historical Perspectives

Although the quest for immortality has long been of intensive human interest, the concept of "successful" or "healthy" aging as an explicit focus of clinical research has emerged only in the past 100 years. Nevertheless, historical views on aging provide some frame of reference for today's debates on the determinants of positive outcomes in aging.

The Wiley-Blackwell Handbook of Adulthood and Aging, First Edition. Edited by Susan Krauss Whitbourne and Martin J. Sliwinski. © 2012 Blackwell Publishing Ltd. Published 2012 by Blackwell Publishing Ltd.

During the emergence of Western medicine in ancient Greece, the conceptualization of aging was that of a systemic illness or disease. Based largely upon the humoral theory, it was believed that aging was associated with a drying and cooling of the body. The metaphor used to depict aging was that of a lamp running out of oil. Aristotle and Galen were leading proponents of this view, and the depletion of vitality seemed to extend to all aspects of behavior. Aristotle was notably unkind when describing older adults in *Rhetoric*, II, 13: "They are small-minded, because they have been humbled by life; their desires are set upon nothing more exalted or extraordinary than what will help them keep alive." Therefore the view of aging was that of a *cause* of disease, and perhaps the only way to reduce its effects was to live healthfully in younger life so as to forestall the inevitable decline presumed to accompany aging.

A contrasting, and more contemporary, view of aging was proposed by the Roman statesman Cicero in 44 BCE. Cicero's brief essay, *Cato Maior De Senectute* (translated as *On Old Age*; Cicero, 1909), provides a systematic set of counterpoints to many of the prevailing assumptions about aging. Importantly, the essay refutes claims that the phenotypes associated with older age were *caused* by older age. Additionally, the concept of potential behavioral influences on later life, and even neuroplasticity, was introduced. The idea of selection, later raised by contemporary gerontologists, was also depicted, in that performance on some tasks was maintained, particularly the important ones. Another concept raised by Cicero was the influence of society in facilitating positive aging. For example, he urged that older adults who could no longer complete physically challenging tasks could fulfill important advisory roles. Cicero also depicted emotional maturity as a strength of aging, with older age associated with diminished carnal desires of youth that served to facilitate greater capacity to pursue virtuous lives. Therefore Cicero's view of aging was less that of a causal process in disease, and more consistent with a series of losses and gains, the course of which could be altered by an individual's choices and behaviors, along with society's capacity to support new roles. The debate between whether the changes seen in aging are intractable or whether plasticity is retained is evident in more modern authors – for instance, one can contrast the views of Sigmund Freud (1924) who claimed that near the age of 50, the "elasticity of mental processes" is no longer present (Freud, 1924) with that of the malleable lifespan development view of Erikson (1993), who believed that life at middle age was still capable of stimulating surprises and discoveries.

Sociological and psychological theories

One of the first references to the term "successful aging" was in 1961, in an editorial published in the first issue of the pre-eminent journal *Gerontologist* (Havighurst, 1961). Written by journal editor Robert Havighurst, the essay claimed that it was a central task for gerontologists to research and promote successful aging, which was defined, at least temporarily, as "getting a maximum of satisfaction and happiness out of life" (p. 8). Following this article came a number of multidimensional, and largely sociological, theories that, while not explicitly describing successful aging, depicted what positive outcomes in later life might entail. The disengagement theory described the process of withdrawal from active pursuits as older individuals changed roles and prepared for disability and death (Cumming & Henry, 1961). Although this theory was not prescriptive, as disengagement was seen as neither good nor bad, it did raise a number of opposing views. In sharp contrast were activity theory (Lemon, Bengtson, & Petersen, 1972), which encouraged society's role in promoting social and recreational activities in older adults, and continuity theory (Atchley, 1989), enhancing the capacity of older adults to carry forward roles and activities from middle age. Each of these theories grappled with what factors might produce positive trajectories in later life across emotional, social, and behavioral phenotypes. These theories also described a role for how society can facilitate or place barriers in the attainment of positive outcomes.

Shifting from sociological to psychological theories, several decades later Baltes and Lang (1997) described successful aging in terms of behavioral processes aimed at adaptation to losses of function. They described successful aging as entailing selection, optimization, and compensation (SOC). Selection refers to reduction of the range of activities to a smaller set, optimization pertains to practice and repetition enhancing performance in the selected behaviors, and compensation refers to behavioral adaptations to better facilitate the behavior in light of age related changes. In Baltes and colleagues' longitudinal Berlin Aging Study, older adults who reported engaging in selection, optimization, and compensation reported greater well-being on follow-up assessment (Baltes & Lang, 1997). The SOC theory remains powerful in that it explains the processes related to adaptation, and, in contrast to some of the broader sociological theories described earlier, allowed for more testable hypotheses.

At the same time as Baltes' work, epidemiological theories grappled with the ramifications of population aging. An important concept, and one that is relevant for successful aging, is compression of morbidity, described by Fries (1980). The essence of this theory is that biomedical advances that work to extend the lifespan must accompany complementary extension of the "healthspan" – the ideal aging population scenario is thus to reduce the number of years spent disabled prior to death, which in addition to lost well-being produces great societal costs. Life extension without commensurate increases in the healthspan would increase the number of years of disability. Thus Fries advocated for gauging interventions on their capacity to lengthen the healthspan rather than, or at least in addition to, the lifespan. Much of the later work on successful aging aims at defining and operationalizing the contributors to the healthspan.

Defining successful aging: Quantitative Studies

The basis of much of the recent work on successful aging is that of Rowe and Kahn (1987), who proposed a number of lasting concepts. One is that aging can be characterized as on a continuum, ranging from pathological aging to normal aging to successful aging. Rowe and Kahn argued that the vast majority of the effort of biomedical researchers had been on delineating pathological from normal aging, and that serious research effort should be aimed at discovering what separated successful from normal aging.

Two important outcomes from Rowe and Kahn's work were an operational definition of successful aging and a cohort study. The authors define successful aging as involving three necessary components: (a) freedom from disease and disability, (b) high cognitive and physical functioning, and (c) social engagement, which was divided into participation in social relationships and productive activities. The MacArthur Successful Aging Cohort study followed over 1,000 older adults who met all of these criteria at the outset of the study, examining the predictors of maintenance of successful aging in numerous publications (Rowe & Kahn, 1997).

Since the Rowe and Kahn paper in 1987, there have been a number of studies that have provided an operationalized definition of successful aging and assessed the prevalence and predictors of successful aging in samples of older adults. Depp and Jeste (2006) reviewed 28 studies that included samples of at least 100 older adults and had provided a multidimensional definition either categorizing individuals as successfully aging or employing a continuous indicator of successful aging.

A key finding from this review was that there was surprisingly little agreement among researchers as to what successful aging comprises; in fact, in 28 studies there were 29 unique definitions of successful aging. As to the components of successful aging, the most commonly employed was freedom from physical disability/disease (appearing in 25 studies). No other component – including cognitive ability, well-being, and social engagement – appeared in more than half of the studies. All told, the median proportion of those sampled who met the various criteria for successful aging was 35%, ranging from less than 1% to 96%. Therefore the body of work that has sought to define successful aging is limited by a lack of agreement on the definition of the outcome, which of course makes understanding its predictors more difficult. Nevertheless, the most common statistically significant predictors of successful aging were largely those associated with better physical functioning – younger age, freedom from diabetes, and not smoking.

Since the Depp and Jeste review (2006), recent initiatives have strived to provide more emphasis on cognitive and emotional health in later life, given that most studies had focused on physical health. The Cognitive and Emotional Health Project sponsored by the U.S. National Institute of Health has begun to attempt to operationalize and study cognitive and emotional "success" in older age – they define cognitive health as:

> the development and preservation of the multidimensional cognitive structure that allows the older adult to maintain social connectedness, an ongoing sense of purpose, and the abilities to function independently, to permit functional recovery from illness or injury, and to cope with residual functional deficits. (Hendrie et al., 2006, p. 13)

Future work will develop a "toolbox" and common measures to be used in studies so as to facilitate comparability among research studies.

Defining successful aging: Qualitative Studies

A smaller set of studies has taken a different approach to identifying a definition of successful aging – asking older adults what they believe to be the meaning of the term. Qualitative methods employed in this effort include focus groups, individual interviews, and surveys in which preferences are ranked or rated. Von Faber and colleagues (2001) conducted a mixed method study in which they examined the prevalence and predictors of a definition of successful aging faithful to the Rowe and Kahn criteria. They also employed personal interviews asking for participants' views on successful aging. What Von Faber et al. (2001) found, and what is echoed in later qualitative interview studies, is that the majority of older adults believe themselves to be aging well. In fact, Montross et al. (2006) asked 206 older adults to rate themselves on a scale of 0 to 10 from least to most successful. The median response was 8 out of 10. Thus there is an apparent discrepancy between older adults' tendency to self-report that they are aging well, even though many would not meet researcher-based definitions of successful aging proposed in the studies described above.

Why are older adults inclined to believe they are aging well? Qualitative interviews reveal that older adults are describing a somewhat different phenomenon when they refer to successful aging. In contrast to the emphasis on freedom from disability or disease, older adults are more likely to depict successful aging with regard to positive psychological factors, such as positive attitudes. In addition, older adults are more likely to describe successful aging in terms of adaptation and compensation to diseases and disabilities, factors which rarely appeared in the operational definitions of successful aging employed in quantitative studies.

Another finding from qualitative studies of successful aging is that the definition of successful aging is likely to be culture-bound. Phelan, Anderson, LaCroix, and Larson (2004) conducted a survey study of older adults who were Japanese natives, Japanese Americans, and Caucasian Americans, asking participants to rate the importance of various factors related to successful aging. What they found is that, while there are many similarities in the perceived level of importance of aspects of successful aging, Caucasian Americans rated "independence" as more important than did Japanese Americans.

Summary

Tracing the history of successful aging, there has been great interest in the subject yet there remains no consensual definition of successful aging. Nevertheless, there are several notable areas of agreement. It is generally agreed that successful aging embodies more than longevity, and that the healthspan, however defined, is a critical target for public health efforts and intervention. The constituents of the healthspan vis à vis successful aging are multidimensional, encompassing phenotypes of physical health and functional abilities, as well as cognitive and emotional health, along with social engagement. In addition, psychological and behavioral processes, such as resilience and adaptability, appear to facilitate the maintenance of successful aging. Much of what has been studied thus far in regard to successful aging has focused on freedom from physical disability and illness, although recent work has begun to more intensively study the predictors of cognitive and emotional health. On balance, there remains a long-standing debate between models of successful aging that emphasize maintenance of gains made in earlier life (e.g., retaining cognitive abilities) versus theories where the emphasis is on the capacity of older adults to adapt to disabilities and illnesses. This divergence is particularly evident when one compares researcher-based definitions of successful aging and that of older adults – epidemiological studies typically emphasize levels of abilities whereas older people emphasize adaptation, and, likely as a result, most older adults believe they are aging well. There is clearly much more work to be done in regard to defining successful aging, in particular creating a common set of phenotypes and measurement tools to aid in this process.

Determinants of Successful Aging

Notwithstanding the difficulty in arriving at a definition of successful aging, there are a number of recent findings that help to explain the determinants of positive outcomes in later life. In this section, we provide an overview of the impact of various factors, from genes to psychological factors on successful aging.

Genes and basic physiological processes

The influence of genes on aging-related phenotypes is a burgeoning field of inquiry, with insights derived from an ever-expanding array of methods (Glatt, Chayavichitsilp, Depp, Schork, & Jeste, 2007). The heredity of phenotypes is typically assessed by way of twin studies, estimating the proportion of variation attributed to genetic and environmental factors. In regard to aging, most studies have focused on the heritability of longevity, and the general estimate is that about 20–30% of variation in the lifespan can be attributed to additive genetic factors (Christensen, Johnson, & Vaupel, 2006). A recent study estimated the heritability of functional outcomes in older veterans similar to that associated with longevity, at approximately 21% (Gurland, Page, & Plassman, 2004). In contrast to other phenotypes, such as cognitive ability (∼50%) and height (∼90%), the lifespan and perhaps the healthspan may be less determined solely by genetic factors.

Other genetic studies have examined the role of genetic variation in age-related phenotypes, typically through candidate gene studies using the case-control design. Typical studies might contrast the presence of allelic variations in older adults who are free of cognitive impairment with younger adults or older adults who are exhibiting greater age-related decline. Alternatively, genome-wide scans have been used to examine the relationship between the entire genome contrasting different groups. A review by Glatt et al. (2007) identified six genes that appeared to vary by successful aging groupings: APOE, GSTT1, IL6, IL10, PON1, and SIRT3. Thus there are some candidate genetic markers that pertain to successful aging phenotypes, which interestingly are also implicated in age-related changes such as cognitive decline and inflammation.

However, there are some important points in interpreting aging in light of genetic variation. For one, Kirkwood and Austad (2000) point out that much of aging occurs after the age of maximum reproduction, leaving what has been called a "selection shadow" – the diseases (or positive phenotypes) of aging may thus be less susceptible to evolutionary pressure as a result. Another finding is that, while it is sensible to assume that genetic influences decline with age and the accompanying accumulation of experiences and injuries, the influence of genes may not decline linearly across the lifespan. Genetic variation among the oldest-old, those older than age 90, may actually be lower, perhaps as a result of attrition. Therefore, even though it is safe to expect that genetics will provide remarkable insights into successful aging in the future, unraveling the influence of genes on healthy aging is a formidable task.

One route to improving the definition of successful aging may be to focus on intermediate phenotypes, in particular biological markers of fundamental aging processes that can be measured across species and in subgroups of older adults. A key finding in recent years has been the observation that a portion of the chromosome, the telomere, seems to provide an indication of basic cellular aging. In work that earned them a Nobel prize, Epel and colleagues (2004) have shown that a shorter telomere is associated with psychosocial stress and putative accelerated aging. In addition, even among centenarians, older adults who exemplify healthy aging, the presence of longer telomeres was associated with lower rates of diabetes, better cognitive functioning, and less disability (Atzmon et al., 2010). The importance of this finding is that fundamental processes in aging may better reflect and enable monitoring the multidimensional phenotypes of successful aging, which may facilitate interventions designed to directly alter telomeres and other basic processes.

Neurobiological factors

Cognitive health in later life is of great interest in an era when Alzheimer's disease (AD) has become one of the 10 most common causes of death. Key concepts that relate to successful cognitive aging are brain reserve and cognitive reserve (Stern, 2009). As one enters older age, brain reserve can be characterized by the integrity of the neurobiological structures that one possesses. Thus brain reserve is a "passive" model of cognitive health, such that at the same rate of neural deterioration, greater brain reserve would delay the time at which one crosses a threshold at which cognitive impairment is evident. Evidence in support of brain reserve is the relationship between early educational attainment and delay of onset of AD.

In contrast, cognitive reserve is an "active" model of maintaining cognitive health, in which brain plasticity aids in maintaining efficiency of neural processes to compensate for neurobiological changes. Evidence supporting cognitive reserve includes the observations through functional neuroimaging indicating greater bilateral activation of the brain among high-performing older adults – in other words, older adults who did better on cognitive tasks seemed to use more of their brains than did younger adults (Cabeza, Anderson, Locantore, & McIntosh, 2002). Related to cognitive reserve is the evidence that rates of engagement in cognitively stimulating activities may be associated with lower rates of cognitive decline (i.e., the "use it or lose it" phenomenon). It is important to note that cognitive reserve and brain reserve are not incompatible – both contribute to maintaining cognitive health, yet the strategies to increase either type of reserve might be somewhat different. In this manner, there are parallels between models of successful aging that emphasize resources brought to older age versus adaptation.

Psychological factors

Positive psychological constructs have been a focus in literature on successful aging, in particular mastery, self-efficacy, wisdom, and resilience. Mastery refers to a global sense of control over one's future and life circumstances. Low mastery would therefore imply a fatalistic sense of a predetermined future. Individuals with high mastery have a sense of control over events in their daily living and tend to believe that they can solve problems that arise in their lives (Pearlin & Schooler, 1978). Self-efficacy (Bandura, 1997), in contrast, is most often related to a specific task or domain, though it may also represent a more universal trait (Berry & West, 1993; Rodin & McAvay, 1992; Sherer et al., 1982).

In healthy older adults, a high sense of mastery is associated with fewer anxiety symptoms (Mehta et al., 2003; Pudrovska, Schieman, Pearlin, & Nguyen, 2005). Conversely, low levels of mastery have been associated with greater depressive symptoms in healthy older adults (Pudrovska et al., 2005) and in those with severe arthritis (Penninx et al., 1997). Furthermore, high mastery has also been shown to protect against the negative impact of economic hardship (Pudrovska et al., 2005) and the effect of deteriorating health (Jonker, Comijs, Knipscheer, & Deeg, 2009). A high level of general self-efficacy has been associated with improved quality of life (Kostka & Jachimowicz, 2010), less loneliness, and less psychological distress in older adults (Fry & Debats, 2002). Self-efficacy for managing instrumental daily activities has been found to correlate with better cognitive functioning (Seeman, Rodin, & Albert, 1993) and better maintenance of cognitive performance in elderly men (Seeman, McAvay, Merrill, Albert, & Rodin, 1996).

Higher personal mastery and self-efficacy also appear to have a positive impact on biological and physiological outcomes. In healthy older women, mastery was found to be associated with lower levels of salivary cortisol and proinflammatory cytokines, decreased cardiovascular risk, and longer duration of REM sleep (Ryff, Singer, & Dienberg Love, 2004). In a population of older caregivers (i.e., persons with high levels of stress), higher mastery has been found to protect against stress-related decreases in immune function (Mausbach et al., 2008), stress-related increases in sympathetic arousal (Roepke et al., 2008), and stress-induced depressive symptoms (Mausbach et al., 2007). Greater self-efficacy may also promote adherence to healthy behaviors such as adoption and maintenance of regular exercise (Ardelt, 2003).

In contrast to mastery and self-efficacy, wisdom is a relatively new area of research, although the association with aging has held since ancient times. While wisdom was initially thought of as simply expert comprehensive knowledge, current definitions incorporate social and emotional aspects. Ancient and modern definitions are more similar than different. Comparing definitions in recent research (based on Western philosophy) to the definition of wisdom in the *Bhagavad Gita*, an ancient Indian text that is approximately 2,500 years old, Jeste and Vahia (2008) noted the similarities in the concepts of wisdom from these two bodies of literature.

More recently, a possible neurobiological basis for wisdom has been proposed (Meeks & Jeste, 2009). The prospective model conceptualizes that the lateral prefrontal cortex (PFC), especially the dorsolateral PFC, works in concert with dorsal anterior cingulated cortex, orbitofrontal cortex, and medial prefrontal cortex to exert an important inhibitory effect on several brain areas associated with emotionality and immediate reward dependence (e.g., amygdala, ventral striatum). Based on this model a rational/analytical aspect of wisdom possibly operates in synergy with a more emotion-based subcomponent, including prosocial attitudes and behaviors.

One operationalized model of wisdom is the three-dimensional model proposed by Clayton and Birren (1980) and refined by Ardelt (2003), which divides wisdom into cognitive, affective, and reflective domains. This model describes a wise person as one who can simultaneously demonstrate cognitive qualities (i.e., expert knowledge, reasoning ability, problem solving/decision making), affective qualities (i.e., positive emotions, fewer negative emotions, ability to regulate emotion), and reflective qualities (i.e., ability to overcome subjective perspectives and accept other views, including contradictory ones). The 3-Dimensional Wisdom Scale (3D-WS) is a self-rated quantitative measure of wisdom developed using this model, and has been demonstrated to be valid and reliable (Mattson, Chan, & Duan, 2002).

Using the Delphi method, Jeste and colleagues (2010) characterized wisdom as a uniquely human but rare personal quality, which can be learned and measured, and increases with age through advanced cognitive and emotional development that is experience-driven. At the same time, the authors noted that wisdom was not expected to increase by taking medication. It appears that the process of becoming "wise" begins in childhood (Sternberg & Jordan, 2005). It remains unclear whether aging itself is associated with wisdom but acquiring wisdom with age is dependent on opportunities to gather experiences, the nature of those experiences, and the ability to learn from such experiences. Based on recent advances in our understanding of wisdom and its underlying mechanisms, as well as the availability of measures such as the 3D-WS, it is likely that wisdom may become the focus of increased attention in the future.

Resilience is understood in physiological terms as the ability to return to homeostasis in the presence of stressful experiences that would be expected to bring about negative effects (Rutter, 2006). The interest in resilience in regard to aging relates to the consistent observation that older adults, on average, are able to maintain levels of subjective well-being, despite increasing biological vulnerabilities to stressors.

In physiologic terms, the response to chronic stress is called allostatic load (McEwen, 2003). Allostatic load is operationalized as a cumulative index comprising biomarkers of cardiovascular, immune, and hypthothamalmic-pituitary-adrenal axis overactivation. Resilient individuals may then be identified by low levels of allostatic load in the presence of chronic stressors. There is considerable literature on physiological effects of stress, animal models, and the genetic, cellular, and neural systems involved in resilience. One consistent finding is that, during and after experiencing adversity-related stress, more resilient individuals appear to experience more positive emotions and maintain optimism than less resilient individuals. Resilient individuals demonstrate active, problem-focused coping (rather than avoidant or passive coping). Physiologically, resilience may be characterized by reduced levels of stress hormones such as cortisol. Neuropeptide Y and dehydroepiandrosterone are also thought to be protective by reducing autonomic stress response. Therefore a second conclusion is that resilience appears to be an active physiological process, not simply a function of attenuated stress response, and one that integrates a complex physiological system (Charney, 2004).

An extremely limited body of work has investigated the expression of resilience in older adults. In one sample, predictors of resilience included higher educational attainment, and greater social support (Loucks, Berkman, Gruenewald, & Seeman, 2006). Resilience was associated with higher levels of optimism and more positive attitudes towards aging.

Spirituality

In recent years, there has been a growing interest in understanding the role of spirituality and religious practices in relation to mental health and well-being. A discussion of the differences between spirituality and religiosity, and a complete appraisal of all literature in this area, is beyond the scope of this chapter, so we have restricted our focus to the impact of religiosity/spirituality on physical, psychological, and cognitive functioning in older adults.

Reflecting the lack of consensus in definitions of spirituality and religiosity, there have been few measures that comprehensively encompass the multiple domains of spirituality and religiosity, and reflecting this, several models have been proposed to explain the role of spirituality and religion and aging. Crowther, Parker, Achenbaum, Larimore, and Koenig (2002) have proposed an amendment to Rowe and Kahn's model of successful aging, to include the construct of positive spirituality. A number of studies indicate an association of religious involvement with longevity (Glass, de Leon, Marottoli, & Berkman, 1999), better adaptation to medical illness (Ell, Nishimoto, Morvay, Mantell, & Hamovitch, 1989), greater resilience (Vahia et al., 2011) and improved health behaviors such as lower rates of smoking and alcohol use (Koenig et al., 1998). Some authors have suggested a role for spirituality in health promotion (Crowther et al., 2002). The association between spirituality/religion and cognitive function may be the best studied – van Ness and Kasl (2003) and Hill and colleagues (Hill, Burdette, Angel, & Angel, 2006) demonstrated that people who attend religious services more frequently demonstrated slower rates of age-related cognitive decline. A significant limitation of most studies is that they are restricted to specific clinical populations (e.g., cancer patients, persons with chronic pain). In a study of spirituality in community-dwelling older women, Vahia and colleagues (2011) have noted that greater spirituality was associated with greater resilience as well as lower income and education levels. Precise correlates of spirituality/religiosity may be dependent to some extent on the nature of the study sample, yet there is some compelling evidence across samples that spiritual health could be included under the umbrella of successful aging.

Summary

The determinants of successful aging are clearly varied, ranging from basic biological building blocks to esoteric psychological constructs like wisdom. Some of the key themes from the above are that there is no single gene or psychological trait that predicts who will age well; rather there is a complex interaction between physiological resources and psychological and behavioral processes that regulate biological systems. For example, some early-life determinants, like education, may build up the brain's resources upon entering later life. Other determinants, such as resilience, may serve to protect the brain from damage caused by stress. Still other behaviors help the brain compensate for losses by promoting plasticity and recruitment of other brain regions to maintain task performance. Unraveling this complex set of determinants is a major challenge, yet some of the more exciting findings are the promise of biological markers, such as telomeres, which appear to some extent to indicate both the cumulative effects of life stress as well as the rate of aging.

Another recurring theme is that positive psychological factors, such as personal mastery, are inversely correlated with physiological processes associated with age-related diseases such as inflammation. Thus one can imagine interventions developed to address the basic biology of aging, such as altering telomere shortening so as to promote longevity (note that treatments are being developed to hasten telomere shortening in cancer cells). On the other hand, cognitive and behavioral treatments that target factors such as personal mastery or resilience may influence these basic biological processes.

Finally, placing these individual-level determinants in the context of social networks has been a major recent advance. Recent work has indicated that some of the determinants of successful aging, including health behaviors and even happiness, may spread among social networks as if by contagion (Christakis & Fowler, 2007). Therefore it is best to imagine the determinants of successful aging as part of a system that links genes, attitudes, and beliefs, and the broader social environment – a system we are just beginning to unravel.

Interventions to Increase Successful Aging

From all of the work described above in quantifying and predicting successful aging, a logical question is: What is the evidence for interventions to increase the likelihood of aging well? A number of determinants of successful aging described above are modifiable, and the extent to which the course of normal aging can be altered by interventions is just beginning to be researched extensively. There are clearly many products that are marketed toward healthy aging, such as brain games, vitamins, and many others; the claims of many of these products often overstate the benefits. As noted by Salthouse (2006), while many interventions may produce temporary effects, altering the *rate* of aging-related trajectories such as cognitive decline is a much higher bar that is rarely, if ever, reached. Nevertheless, there are some exciting findings that suggest that the healthspan may be more malleable than previously believed.

Dietary restriction

The most frequently studied intervention in relation to lifespan extension is dietary restriction. Mice who are subjected to dietary intake of approximately two-thirds of ad libitum diets tend to live longer than mice that can feed freely; in some studies the effect is up to a 40% extension of lifespan. The lifespan-extending effect of dietary restriction is evident in primates as well, although not to the same extent as in mice. Other phenotypes of aging are also apparently less evident in dietary-restricted animals, with lower musculoskeletal indicators of aging as well as neuroprotective effects. The exact mechanisms of caloric restriction remain unknown, but are obviously an area of keen interest given the magnitude of effects seen. It is believed that alteration to metabolism may reduce oxidative damage, enabling the preservation of functioning. Some trials in humans show indicators of benefit of caloric restriction, although the challenge remains to make such a diet palatable. Nevertheless, caloric restriction represents one of the most promising avenues for learning about how the lifespan might be extended, and human trials have shown promising results.

Physical activity

There is good reason why physical activity is such a focus of public health efforts in aging. Greater participation in physical activity is linked with better bone health, markers of physiological aging, and lower rates of cardiovascular disease (Kramer, Erickson, & Colcombe, 2006). In addition, physical activity is associated with lower rates of depression as well as higher cognitive functioning in older adults, evidenced in longitudinal studies, including the MacArthur successful aging cohort. Importantly, positive effects of physical activity appear to be attainable among older adults who initiate exercise programs in later life. In one randomized controlled trial of aerobic exercise among sedentary older adults, those assigned to the exercise group experienced clinically significant gains in cognitive functioning as measured by neuropsychological tests. On structural neuroimaging, increases were also seen in brain volumes. In another clinical trial, older adults with major depression were assigned to either receive an antidepressant, an exercise program, or both (Blumenthal et al., 1999). The results found similar response rates in the antidepressant and exercise conditions, with some evidence for more lasting benefit among older adults who sustained exercise. Despite these broad benefits of physical activity, the proportion of older adults who meet U.S. Centers for Disease Control guidelines for physical activity is approximately 22% (moderate exercise for at least 30 minutes at least five times per week or vigorous exercise three times a week for at least 20 minutes) (National Institute of Aging, 2010). Older women are the segment of the population with the lowest rates of exercise participation. Barriers to exercise can be overcome by addressing structural barriers to physical activity and home-based exercise. One recent pilot study indicated that exergames – videogames that produce physical activity – may offer promise in this regard (Rosenberg et al., 2010).

Cognitive interventions

As cognitive stimulation is associated with lower rates of cognitive impairment, there have been a number of studies that have examined the impact of cognitive remediation in improving cognitive abilities in older adults. There are several avenues to cognitive remediation – cognitive training, which aims at restoring cognitive abilities by engaging in activities that tax memory and other cognitive domains (e.g., games aimed at increasing processing speed); compensatory training, which teaches skills in making cognitive processes more efficient (e.g., note taking, reducing distractions); and cognitive stimulation, which provides more naturalistic opportunities that tax cognitive abilities (e.g., acting). As far as the effectiveness of these approaches, the ACTIVE trial has been extremely informative (Willis et al., 2006). The largest clinical trial to date, the ACTIVE trial enrolled over 3,000 older adults who were randomly assigned to one of four different kinds of cognitive training or a control condition. Gains in cognitive abilities were seen at 2- and 5-year follow-up. However, these improvements were primarily restricted to the cognitive domain that was trained upon – therefore, performance gains did not necessarily generalize to other cognitive domains that were not trained. Moreover, the effects on distal outcomes, performance on functional tasks, were more subtle. Nevertheless, the effects seen show promise that cognitive training in generally cognitively healthy older adults can have long-lasting effects. There are a number of cognitive training programs that are available to consumers on home computers, the evidence for which is mixed. Some programs have been evaluated in randomized clinical trials and were associated with positive effects, while others do not appear to be associated with research.

There are a number of innovative approaches that employ structured yet naturalistic cognitively demanding activities to improve cognitive abilities in older adults. Standardized programs evaluated in randomized controlled trials have employed activities such as acting, narrative writing, or problem solving in groups (Stine-Morrow, Parisi, Morrow, Greene, & Park, 2007; Carlson et al., 2008). While these programs do not directly target practicing cognitive skills, the tasks involved in these activities demand social interaction, memory, problem solving, and planning. Additionally, an intergenerational program, Experience Corps, pairing volunteer older adults with school-age children, has shown both improved scholastic performance among children and better performance on cognitive tests in the older adult volunteers. Although probing the mechanisms of these interventions is more difficult when compared to traditional cognitive training, the appeal of nontraditional approaches to cognitive remediation is that they have the additional benefit of meaningful activity, social interaction, and pleasurable activity.

Finally, other recent trends in cognitive remediation include combining physical and cognitive activity in the same intervention. Additionally, there are a number of existing and upcoming pharmacologic approaches that are aimed at cognitive enhancement in people who are generally healthy, with recent debate as to ethical and societal implications of cognitive enhancement.

Enhancing attitudes toward aging

Attitude towards aging incorporates self-perception of aging, cultural and personal beliefs about aging, age identity, as well as physical and other psychological factors. Evidence from the medical, psychology, sociology and gerontology literature indicates several adverse consequences of negative attitudes towards aging. In her extensive work, Levy (2003) has identified associations between negative attitudes towards aging and greater morbidity (e.g., more hearing, cognitive, and mood disturbances, poorer function, and higher mortality rates than those with more positive views of their aging. Although there is relatively little in the way of an evidence base for interventions to enhance attitudes toward aging, Levy and colleagues (e.g., Levy, Ashman, & Dror, 1999) have conducted a number of remarkable studies that indicate that when older adults are exposed to positive stereotypes about aging (e.g., being wise, learned) versus negative ones (e.g., being infirm), objective performance on physical tasks such as walking or handwriting are affected. It is believed that older (and younger) adults maintain stereotypes that once activated through experimental manipulation, impact performance on daily tasks. These findings hint that efforts to alter public attitudes toward aging could positively alter the course of aging.

"Antiaging" interventions

As the evidence base for interventions such as physical activity has expanded, there has been a corollary growth recently in the industry of "antiaging" products. These products are of multiple types and include vitamins and other nutritional supplements, "superfoods," and various types of hormones. While their growth has been supported by aggressive marketing campaigns, there remains a dearth of valid and reliable scientific evidence demonstrating their efficacy and safety. Many of the claims made by proponents of antiaging therapies are not subjected to randomized controlled trials, in part because they are not regulated by the U.S. Food and Drug Administration (FDA) as drugs. There are concerns about health risks associated with some antiaging therapies and even if other antiaging therapies are benign, it has also been suggested that use of these products may distract older adults from engaging in established healthy behavior such as exercise and caloric restriction (Perls, 2004).

Conclusion

Even if we do not yet have a definitive recipe for successful aging, there appear to be a number of compelling approaches to lengthening the healthspan. Among the most exciting recent findings to emerge is that older people seem to benefit from interventions aimed at increasing physical and brain fitness, challenging earlier assumptions about the intractability of age-related phenotypes. To be sure, aging remains a great mystery, with as yet no satisfactory explanation for fundamental questions such as why we even age at all. Nevertheless, the recent findings about the basic physiological processes involved in aging suggest that diseases of aging share underlying causes, and there is some suggestion that interventions to retard aging may also share fundamental mechanisms. Mattson and Magnus (2006) have argued that caloric restriction, physical activity, and cognitive stimulation may share a common pathway to stimulating neurogenesis. Even though on the surface these interventions involve widely different behaviors, each is a mild stressor that leads the brain to produce neurotrophic factors – a process called hormesis. The more that the phenotypes of aging can be linked with fundamental physiological processes, interventions can be developed to directly target these complicated pathways to the maintenance of cognitive, emotional, and physical health in later life.

We conclude with a note about the scale of the opportunity of altering trajectories toward successful aging. Today, there are more people older than 65 than children younger than 14 for the first time in recorded history. In the developed world, the leading causes of death and years of life due to disability are now almost exclusively age-associated, compared to one hundred years ago when infectious diseases were leading causes of our demise. Therefore, aging has been called the number one public health issue we face (Cutler & Mattson, 2006). The gaps between the prevalence of protective factors against age-associated illnesses (e.g., physical activity, social engagement) and risk factors for age-associated illnesses (e.g., sedentary behavior, depression) are a critical challenge for public health efforts. One projection states that if the rates of diabetes and obesity continue to increase, the gains achieved in mean lifespan will decelerate in the coming decades. Recent work by our group suggests that older adults may spend about 25% of their waking time watching television, more than double the rate in younger adults – yet, older adults actually enjoyed TV less than did younger people (Depp, Schkade, Thompson, & Jeste, 2010). Thus the pessimistic view is that despite the accumulation of data suggesting that aging-related phenotypes can be altered, the prevalence of risk factors for aging-related illnesses increases. The optimistic view is that there is an immense and growing reservoir of opportunity to increase the likelihood of successful aging, however defined, through basic biological science and behavioral and social change.

References

Ardelt, M. (2003). Empirical assessment of a three-dimensional wisdom scale. *Research on Aging, 25*(3), 275–324.

Atchley, R. C. (1989). A continuity theory of normal aging. *Gerontologist, 29*(2), 183–190.

Atzmon, G., Cho, M., Cawthon, R. M., Budagov, T., Katz, M., Yang, X., ... Suh, Y. (2010). Genetic variation in human telomerase is associated with telomere length in Ashkenazi centenarians. *Proceedings of the National Academy of Sciences, 107*(Suppl. 1), 1710–1717.

Baltes, M. M., & Lang, F. R. (1997). Everyday functioning and successful aging: The impact of resources. *Psychology and Aging, 12*(3), 433–443.

Bandura, A. (1997). *Self-efficacy: The exercise of control.* New York: Freeman.

Berry, J. M., & West, R. L. (1993). Cognitive self-efficacy in relation to personal mastery and goal setting across the life span. *International Journal of Behavioral Development, 16*(2), 351–379.

Blumenthal, J. A., Babyak, M. A., Moore, K. A., Craighead, W. E., Herman, S., Khatri, P., ... Krishnan, K. R. (1999). Effects of exercise training on older patients with major depression. *Archives of Internal Medicine, 159*(19), 2349–2356.

Cabeza, R., Anderson, N. D., Locantore, J. K., & McIntosh, A. R. (2002). Aging gracefully: Compensatory brain activity in high-performing older adults. *Neuroimage, 17*(3), 1394–1402.

Carlson, M. C., Saczynski, J. S., Rebok, G. W., Seeman, T., Glass, T. A., McGill, S., ... Fried, L. P. (2008). Exploring the effects of an "everyday" activity program on executive function and memory in older adults: Experience Corps. *Gerontologist, 48*(6), 793–801.

Charney, D. S. (2004). Psychobiological mechanisms of resilience and vulnerability: Implications for successful adaptation to extreme stress. *Focus, 2*(3), 368–391.

Christakis, N. A., & Fowler, J. H. (2007). The spread of obesity in a large social network over 32 years. *New England Journal of Medicine, 357*(4), 370–379.

Christensen, K., Johnson, T. E., & Vaupel, J. W. (2006). The quest for genetic determinants of human longevity: Challenges and insights. *Nature Reviews Genetics, 7*(6), 436–448.

Cicero, M. (1909). *On old age* (Harvard Classics, vol. 9). New York: P. F. Collier.

Clayton, V., & Birren, J. (1980). The development of wisdom across the life-span: A reexamination of an ancient topic. In P. Baltes & O. Brim (Eds.), *Life-span development and behavior* (pp. 103–135). New York: Academic Press.

Crowther, M. R., Parker, M. W., Achenbaum, W. A., Larimore, W. L., & Koenig, H. G. (2002). Rowe and Kahn's model of successful aging revisited. *The Gerontologist, 42*(5), 613–620.

Cumming, E., & Henry, W. E. (1961). *Growing old: The process of disengagement.* New York: Basic Books.

Cutler, R. G., & Mattson, M. P. (2006). The adversities of aging. *Ageing Research Reviews, 5*(3), 221–238.

Depp, C. A., & Jeste, D. V. (2006). Definitions and predictors of successful aging: A comprehensive review of larger quantitative studies. *American Journal of Geriatric Psychiatry, 14*(1), 6–20.

Depp, C. A., Schkade, D. A., Thompson, W. K., & Jeste, D. V. (2010). Age, affective experience, and television use. *American Journal of Preventive Medicine, 39*(2), 173–178.

Ell, K., Nishimoto, R., Morvay, T., Mantell, J., & Hamovitch, M. (1989). A longitudinal analysis of psychological adaptation among survivors of cancer. *Cancer, 63*(2), 406–413.

Epel, E. S., Blackburn, E. H., Lin, J., Dhabhar, F. S., Adler, N. E., Morrow, J. D., & Cawthon, R. M. (2004). Accelerated telomere shortening in response to life stress. *Proceedings of the National Academy of Science of the United States of America, 101*(49), 17312–17315.

Erickson, E. (1993). *Childhood and society*. New York: W.W. Norton.

Freud, S. (1924). *On psychotherapy*. London: Hogarth Press.

Fries, J. F. (1980). Aging, natural death, and the compression of morbidity. *New England Journal of Medicine, 303*(3), 130–135.

Fry, P., & Debats, D. (2002). Self-efficacy beliefs as predictors of loneliness and psychological distress in older adults. *International Journal of Aging and Human Development, 55*(3), 233–269.

Glass, T. A., de Leon, C. M., Marottoli, R. A., & Berkman, L. F. (1999). Population based study of social and productive activities as predictors of survival among elderly Americans. *British Medical Journal, 319*(7208), 478–483.

Glatt, S. J., Chayavichitsilp, P., Depp, C., Schork, N. J., & Jeste, D. V. (2007). Successful aging: From phenotype to genotype. *Biological Psychiatry, 62*(4), 282–293.

Gurland, B. J., Page, W. F., & Plassman, B. L. (2004). A twin study of the genetic contribution to age-related functional impairment. *Journals of Gerontology, Series A: Biological and Medical Sciences, 59*(8), 859–863.

Havighurst, R. (1961). Successful aging. *Gerontologist, 1*(1), 8–13.

Hendrie, H., Albert, M., Butters, M., Gao, S., Knopman, D., Launer, L., …. Wagster, M. V. (2006). The NIH Cognitive and Emotional Health Project: Report of the Critical Evaluation Study Committee. *Alzheimer's and Dementia, 2*(1), 12–32.

Hill, T. D., Burdette, A. M., Angel, J. L., & Angel, R. J. (2006). Religious attendance and cognitive functioning among older Mexican Americans. *Journals of Gerontology, Series B: Psychological Sciences and Social Sciences, 61*(1), P3–P9.

Jeste, D. V., Ardelt, M., Blazer, D., Kraemer, H. C., Vaillant, G., & Meeks, T. W. (2010). Expert consensus on characteristics of wisdom: A Delphi method study. *The Gerontologist, 50*(5), 668–680.

Jeste, D. V., & Vahia, I. V. (2008). Comparison of the conceptualization of wisdom in ancient Indian literature with modern views: Focus on the Bhagavad Gita. *Psychiatry, 71*(3), 197–209.

Jonker, A. A. G. C., Comijs, H. C., Knipscheer, K. C. P. M., & Deeg, D. J. H. (2009). The role of coping resources on change in well-being during persistent health decline. *Journal of Aging and Health, 21*(8), 1063–1082.

Kirkwood, T. B., & Austad, S. N. (2000). Why do we age? *Nature, 408*(6809), 233–238.

Koenig, H. G., George, L. K., Cohen, H. J., Hays, J. C., Larson, D. B., & Blazer, D. G. (1998). The relationship between religious activities and cigarette smoking in older adults. *Journals of Gerontology, Series A: Biological Sciences and Medical Sciences, 53A*(6), M426–M434.

Kostka, T., & Jachimowicz, V. (2010). Relationship of quality of life to dispositional optimism, health locus of control and self-efficacy in older subjects living in different environments. *Quality of Life Research, 19*(3), 351–361.

Kramer, A., Erickson, K. I., & Colcombe, S. J. (2006). Exercise, cognition and the aging brain. *Journal of Applied Physiology, 101*(4), 1237–1242.

Lemon, B. W., Bengtson, V. L., & Petersen, J. A. (1972). An exploration of the activity theory of aging: Activity types and life expectation among in-movers to a retirement community. *Journal of Gerontology, 27*(4), 511–523.

Levy, B. R. (2003). Mind matters: Cognitive and physical effects of aging self-stereotypes. *Journals of Gerontology, Series B: Psychological Science and Social Science, 58*(4), P203–P211.

Levy, B. R., Ashman, O., & Dror, I. (1999). To be or not to be: The effects of aging stereotypes on the will to live. *Omega (Westport), 40*(3), 409–420.

Loucks, E. B., Berkman, L. F., Gruenewald, T. L., & Seeman, T. E. (2006). Relation of social integration to inflammatory marker concentrations in men and women 70–79 years. *American Journal of Cardiology, 97*(7), 1010–1016.

Mattson, M. P., Chan, S. L., & Duan, W. (2002). Modification of brain aging and neurodegenerative disorders by genes, diet, and behavior. *Physiological Reviews, 82*(3), 637–672.

Mattson, M. P., & Magnus, T. (2006). Ageing and neuronal vulnerability. *Nature Reviews Neuroscience, 7*(4), 278–294.

Mausbach, B. T., Patterson, T. L., Von Känel, R., Mills, P. J., Dimsdale, J. E., Ancoli-Israel, S., & Grant, I. (2007). The attenuating effect of personal mastery on the relations between stress and Alzheimer caregiver health: A five-year longitudinal analysis. *Aging & Mental Health, 11*(6), 637–644.

Mausbach, B. T., Von Känel, R., Patterson, T. L., Dimsdale, J. E., Depp, C. A., Aschbacher, K., . . . Grant, I. (2008). The moderating effect of personal mastery and the relations between stress and Plasminogen Activator Inhibitor-1 (PAI-1) antigen. *Health Psychology, 27*(2), S172–S179.

McEwen, B. S. (2003). Interacting mediators of allostasis and allostatic load: Towards an understanding of resilience in aging. *Metabolism, 52*(Suppl. 2), 10–16.

Meeks, T. W., & Jeste, D. V. (2009). Neurobiology of wisdom: A literature overview. *Archives of General Psychiatry, 66*(4), 355–365.

Mehta, K. M., Simonsick, E. M., Penninx, B. W. J. H., Schulz, R., Rubin, S. M., Satterfield, S., & Yaffe, K. (2003). Prevalence and correlates of anxiety symptoms in well-functioning older adults: Findings from the health aging and body composition study. *Journal of the American Geriatrics Society, 51*(4), 499–504.

Montross, L. P., Depp, C., Daly, J., Reichstadt, J., Golshan, S., Moore, D., . . . Jeste, D.V. (2006). Correlates of self-rated successful aging among community-dwelling older adults. *American Journal of Geriatric Psychiatry, 14*, 43–51.

National Institute of Aging. (2010). *Older Americans 2010: Key indicators of well-being.* Retrieved from http://www.agingstats.gov/agingstatsdotnet/Main_Site/Data/2010_Documents/Docs/OA_2010. pdf

Pearlin, L. I., & Schooler, C. (1978). The structure of coping. *Journal of Health and Social Behavior, 19*(1), 2–21.

Penninx, B. W. J. H., van Tilburg, T., Kriegsman, D. M. W., Deeg, D. J. H., Boeke, A. J. P., & van Eijk, J. T. M. (1997). Effects of social support and personal coping resources on mortality in older age: The Longitudinal Aging Study Amsterdam. *American Journal of Epidemiology, 146*(6), 510–519.

Perls, T. T. (2004). Anti-aging quackery: Human growth hormone and tricks of the trade–more dangerous than ever. *Journals of Gerontology, Series A: Biological Sciences and Medical Sciences, 59*(7), 682–691.

Phelan, E. A., Anderson, L. A., LaCroix, A. Z., & Larson, E. B. (2004). Older adults' views of "successful aging" – how do they compare with researchers' definitions? *Journal of the American Geriatrics Society, 52*(2), 211–216.

Pudrovska, T., Schieman, S., Pearlin, L. I., & Nguyen, K. (2005). The sense of mastery as a mediator and moderator in the association between economic hardship and health in late life. *Journal of Aging and Health, 17*(5), 634–660.

Rodin, J., & McAvay, G. (1992). Determinants of change in perceived health in a longitudinal study of older adults. *Journal of Gerontology, 47*(6), P373–P384.

Roepke, S. K., Mausbach, B. T., Aschbacher, K., Ziegler, M. G., Dimsdale, J. E., Mills, P. J., . . . Grant, I. (2008). Personal mastery is associated with reduced sympathetic arousal in stressed Alzheimer caregivers. *American Journal of Geriatric Psychiatry, 16*(4), 310–317.

Rosenberg, D., Depp, C. A., Vahia, I. V., Reichstadt, J., Palmer, B. W., Kerr, J., . . . Jeste, D. V. (2010). Exergames for subsyndromal depression in older adults: A pilot study of a novel intervention. *American Journal of Geriatric Psychiatry, 18*(3), 221–226.

Rowe, J. W., & Kahn, R. L. (1987). Human aging: Usual and successful. *Science, 237*(4811), 143–149.

Rowe, J. W., & Kahn, R. L. (1997). Successful aging. *Gerontologist, 37*(4), 433–440.

Rutter, M. (2006). Implications of resilience concepts for scientific understanding. *Annals of the New York Academy of Sciences, 1094*(1), 1–12.

Ryff, C. D., Singer, B. H., & Dienberg Love, G. (2004). Positive health: Connecting well-being with biology. *Philosophical Transactions of the Royal Society, B: Biological Sciences, 359*(1449), 1383–94.

Salthouse, T. A. (2006). Mental exercise and mental aging. *Perspectives on Psychological Science, 1*(1), 68–87.

Seeman, T., McAvay, G., Merrill, S., Albert, M., & Rodin, J. (1996). Self-efficacy beliefs and change in cognitive performance: MacArthur studies of successful aging. *Psychology and Aging, 11*(3), 538–551.

Seeman, T. E., Rodin, J., & Albert, M. (1993). Self-efficacy and cognitive performance in high-functioning older individuals. *Journal of Aging and Health, 5*(4), 455–474.

Sherer, M., Maddux, J., Mercadante, B., Prentice-Dunn, S., Jacobs, B., & Rogers, R. (1982). The self-efficacy scale: Construction and validation. *Psychological Reports, 51*, 663–671.

Stern, Y. (2009). Cognitive reserve. *Neuropsychologia, 47*(10), 2015–2028.

Sternberg, R., & Jordan, J. (2005). *A handbook of wisdom: Psychological perspectives.* New York: Cambridge University Press.

Stine-Morrow, E. A., Parisi, J. M., Morrow, D. G., Greene, J., & Park, D. C. (2007). An engagement model of cognitive optimization through adulthood. *Journals of Gerontology, Series B: Psychological Science and Social Science, 62* (Spec No. 1), 62–69.

Vahia, I. V., Depp, C. A., Palmer, B. W., Fellows, I., Golshan, S., Thompson, W., . . . Jeste, D. V. (2011). Correlates of spirituality in older women. *Aging & Mental Health, 15*(1), 97–102.

Van Ness, P. H., & Kasl, S. V. (2003). Religion and cognitive dysfunction in an elderly cohort. *Journals of Gerontology, Series B: Psychological Sciences and Social Sciences, 58*(1), S21–S29.

von Faber, M., Bootsma-van der Wiel, A., van Exel, E., Gussekloo, J., Lagaay, A. M., van Dongen, E., . . . Westendorp, R. G. (2001). Successful aging in the oldest old: Who can be characterized as successfully aged? *Archives of Internal Medicine, 161*(22), 2694–2700.

Willis, S. L., Tennstedt, S. L., Marsiske, M., Ball, K., Elias, J., Koepke, K. M., . . . Wright, E. (2006). Long-term effects of cognitive training on everyday functional outcomes in older adults. *Jama, 296*(23), 2805–2814.

24

Creative Productivity and Aging

An Age Decrement – or Not?

Dean Keith Simonton

Introduction

Pop quiz: Who conducted the very first empirical study in developmental psychology? By "empirical" I mean that a developmental question was systematically addressed by collecting suitable data and by subjecting those data to appropriate statistical analyses. Was it G. Stanley Hall, James Mark Baldwin, or perhaps even Charles Darwin? No, the earliest bona fide developmental inquiry was published by Adolphe Quételet in 1835. This Belgian mathematician and scientist is better known for introducing the normal distribution into the study of human individual differences – with the associated concept of the "average person" (*l'homme moyen*). Yet he also collected and analyzed data on longitudinal changes. In particular, Quételet examined the agewise distribution of the plays created by leading French and English dramatists. His goal was to assess the relation between age and creativity, where the latter was gauged by the output of creative products. Hence the subject of this chapter, as indicated by the chapter's title, can be easily considered the first substantive question in developmental psychology to be subjected to a scientific response. Indeed, so thorough were Quételet's data analyses that his 1835 results were unsurpassed for well over a century, and his principal conclusions are still valid today.

This is not to say that the issue was not addressed by subsequent researchers. Beard (1874) returned to the question some decades later, but adopted a qualitative approach. However, it was not until the late 1940s that the topic again became the subject of quantitative research. More specifically, Harvey Lehman made the topic the basis for a

The Wiley-Blackwell Handbook of Adulthood and Aging, First Edition. Edited by Susan Krauss Whitbourne and Martin J. Sliwinski. © 2012 Blackwell Publishing Ltd. Published 2012 by Blackwell Publishing Ltd.

lifelong research program, beginning with a paper on the relation between age and creative output in literature, including English drama (Lehman & Heidler, 1949). After conducting similar studies with respect to other domains of creativity, Lehman compiled the findings in his 1953 *Age and Achievement*. Although this book has often been viewed as his magnum opus, it is important to note that Lehman continued to carry out empirical investigations on this question (e.g., Lehman, 1958, 1960, 1962, 1963, 1965), some even appearing after his death in 1965 (e.g., Lehman, 1966a, 1966b).

Unfortunately, Lehman (1953) was evidently unaware of Quételet's (1835/1968) prior research. Consequently, Lehman's methods are actually less sophisticated than Quételet's were. These methodological inadequacies became the target of many critics (e.g., Cole, 1979; Dennis, 1954c, 1956a, 1956b; Lindauer, 2003). Although most of these criticisms were justified (but see Lehman, 1956), subsequent research has introduced methods far more sophisticated than even Quételet could envision (Kozbelt, 2008a; Simonton, 1988a, 1997; Zickar & Slaughter, 1999). These methods include multivariate analyses, structural equation models, cross-sectional time-series analyses, and hierarchical linear and nonlinear models. Furthermore, the topic seems to have attracted increased interest over the years, an expansion that may reflect the increasing number of baby-boomers who are reaching retirement age. Thus it is timely to offer here an update on what we have learned about the age–output relationship over the past 175 years. This review will focus on whether or not creative productivity displays an age decrement in the latter part of life. Not only is this question the one that sparks the most controversy, but it also may have the most practical consequences (see, e.g., Kim, 2003).

The chapter begins with the basic empirical findings, and then examines the methodological issues and substantive interpretations associated with those findings. It closes with a discussion of whether the age decrement is inevitable. If not, what factors counteract its appearance?

Empirical Findings

The central results can be grouped into three categories: (a) the typical age curve, (b) interdisciplinary contrasts in that curve, and (c) individual differences in that curve.

Typical age curve

All of the early research on the age–output relationship adopted the same basic procedure that Quételet introduced in 1835 (e.g., Dennis, 1966; Lehman, 1953; cf. Cole, 1979). First, a sample of creative individuals and their creative products was assembled from biographies, histories, bibliographies, or other reference works. Second, the products were dated and then the creator's age calculated by subtracting his or her date of birth. Finally, the products were tabulated into consecutive age periods, such as 5- or 10-year intervals (e.g., 20–24, 25–29, 30–34, . . .). These tabulations may undergo a modest transformation, such as dividing by the length of the age period to yield the annual output rate.

With or without a transformation, the tabulations aggregate the output of all creators active in a given age period.

This aggregation has the advantage that it yields a statistical average that removes the idiosyncrasies in any given creative career. These idiosyncrasies may be due to such extraneous events as the outbreak of war, the death of a loved one, changes in employment, physical illness, and the like. Because such "random shocks" would cancel out when averaged across all creators in the sample, the result will be a smoother curve representing the overall career trajectory. Of course, the curve is smoothed even more by using 10- or 5-year periods rather than annual tabulations.

It should also be noted that Quételet's (1835/1968) general procedure is superior to studies that assess the age–productivity relation using cross-sectional data (e.g., Bayer & Dutton, 1977). The latter confound age effects with cohort effects (cf. Levin & Stephan, 1991). Insofar as the sample is heterogeneous regarding year of birth, this method also avoids period effects, that is, the impact of major historical events, such as World War II or the Great Depression (Simonton, 1985).

For the most part, research using the above procedure arrives at consistent results, namely, that creative productivity is a nonmonotonic, single-peaked function of age (Simonton, 1988a). Typically, output will rise rapidly to a maximum output period in the late thirties or early forties, after which a gradual decline sets in. The postpeak decrement will tend to approach some nonzero asymptote such that output in the seventies or even eighties is at about half the level seen at the career peak. So in that sense, the age decrement is substantial. Even so, output in these final decades will often surpass output in the twenties (Dennis, 1966; cf. Horner, Rushton, & Vernon, 1986). Hence, creators toward the close of their careers may still be more productive than those creators who are just beginning their careers.

Figure 24.1 illustrates the typical age curve. Here the curve is defined in terms of the annual output rate, which reaches its peak somewhere between four and five creative products per year. In addition, for reasons that will become more clear later, the horizontal axis has been transformed from chronological age to career age. That is, under the assumption that the career began at age 20, then 20 years was subtracted from the actual age. Once the independent variable is translated into these terms, then we can see more easily that the productive peak tends to appear around 20 years into the career.

Interdisciplinary contrasts

The previous description of the typical career trajectory dates back to Quételet (1835/1968). Nonetheless, Quételet only studied creative productivity in the single domain of drama. When Lehman and Heidler (1949) addressed the topic over a century later, they looked at several forms of literary creativity besides drama, including various kinds of poetry as well as novels. They found that the career peaks differed according to the domain of creative achievement. For example, poets tend to produce their best work at younger ages than do novelists, a finding that has been replicated both cross-culturally and transhistorically (Simonton, 1975a, 2007b). Nor is literature the only domain where the age curve depends on the particular type of creativity (Dennis, 1966; Lehman, 1953;

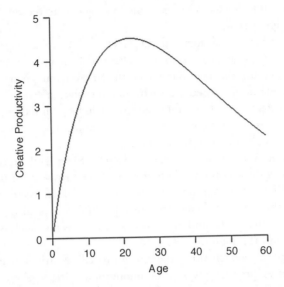

Figure 24.1   Typical curve representing the relation between creative productivity as a function of age where the latter has been converted into career age, assuming that the career began at age 20. The vertical axis represents the expected annual output rate. Created by Dean Keith Simonton

Simonton, 1988a, 1997). For instance, career trajectories in the sciences are markedly contingent on the specific discipline in which creativity takes place (Cole, 1979; Dennis, 1966; Kyvik, 1990a; Levin & Stephan, 1989, 1991; Simonton, 1991a). As an example, creators in pure mathematics attain their career acme at younger ages than creators in the earth sciences do (cf. Levin & Stephan, 1990; Stern, 1978).

These interdisciplinary contrasts have important implications for the age-decrement issue. In some fields, the peak occurs so late, and the decline is so minimal, that it is hardly appropriate to speak of a drop in creative productivity with age. For example, historians and philosophers may reach their peak output when they are in their sixties, and their productivity in their seventies can still surpass what they produced in the first few decades of their careers (Dennis, 1966; cf. Kyvik, 1990a). As we will see multiple times throughout this chapter, these interdisciplinary contrasts are by no means the only factor that can effectively obliterate the age decrement.

Individual differences

It cannot be overemphasized that the foregoing conclusions are predicated on aggregating productivity data across large samples of creative individuals. As Quetélet (1835/1968) noted long ago, individual differences are always substantial; besides the mean of the cross-sectional distribution representing the "average person," we also have to report the standard deviation representing the dispersion around that central tendency. The same applies to the creative productivity of the "average 40 year old" or the "average 70 year old." There will be error bars around the expected value for each age period. Lehman

(1953) was certainly aware of this fact, for he devotes two chapters to giving examples of exceptions to the rule. One chapter lists great achievements by exceptionally young thinkers and the other great achievements by exceptionally old thinkers.

Many of these discrepancies may be attributed to some of the random shocks mentioned earlier. Later we will also document some of the extrinsic factors that impinge on a creator's output as his or her life unfolds. Nevertheless, a major part of the individual differences may be credited to intrinsic and systematic factors. Of the latter factors, two are most critical: age at career onset and output rate.

Age at career onset. It has already been stated that the curve in Figure 24.1 depicted creative productivity as a function of career age. In other words, age at career onset was subtracted from chronological age. This transformation was implemented because the longitudinal function is most accurately expressed in this manner (Simonton, 1988a, 1997). As an example, the location of the career peak is determined more by how long a creator has been active in a given domain than his or her actual chronological age. To be sure, in most instances chronological and career age will be highly correlated (e.g., Bayer & Dutton, 1977; Over, 1989). The high correlation results from the fact that most people begin their careers at roughly the same time. In most academic fields, the onset is determined by the typical age at which individuals in a given field receive the higher degrees necessary for full-time positions. For this reason, career age may be calculated as years since doctorate (e.g., Lyons, 1968; Messerli, 1988). Whatever the details, because people can still differ regarding when in their lives they receive the requisite certification, some allowance must be made for this variation. This provision becomes especially crucial for those persons who entered a field unusually late, perhaps as the result of a career change.

Individual differences in age at career onset have profound repercussions for the anticipated age decrement (Simonton, 1991a, 1991b, 1997). In Figure 24.1 this age was optimistically set at 20 years, but it could just as well be put at 30 or 40 years of age. If the maximum output rate appears approximately 20 years after the career begins, then the peaks would be shifted to 50 or 60 years of age. Better yet, when the career optima appear so late in life, the creator's death will more likely intercede before the postpeak decrement becomes at all conspicuous. Instead of productivity declining to half of the career maximum, the decline might only be 25% or less. And, again, such late-blooming creators will be more productive in their final years than many of their far younger colleagues just launching their careers.

Although I have specified age at career onset as an individual-difference factor, it must be admitted that this variable may reflect historical and cross-cultural circumstances. Sometimes creators can complete the training or education at relatively young ages, whereas at other times creators will have to wait longer before these prerequisites are usually met (Pressey & Combs, 1943; Wray, 2009). Additionally, different domains will differ in how fast creators in those domains can initiate their careers (Roe, 1953; Zuckerman & Merton, 1972). For instance, physicists are likely to complete their doctoral training at younger ages than psychologists do, giving physicists a head start on their career trajectories.

Output rate. When output is aggregated across a large number of creators, the resulting timewise tabulations obscure a vital fact: Creators very immensely in their productivity, whether on an annual or lifetime basis (Cole & Cole, 1973; Simonton, 1997). Some are extremely prolific, whereas others are "one-idea" people at best (cf. Kozbelt, 2008b). One might think that this output rate is normally distributed across creative individuals, but this is far from the case. The actual distribution is highly skewed, with a long upper tail (e.g., Huber 1999; Lotka, 1926; Price, 1963; Shockley 1957; Simon 1955; Sutter & Kocher, 2001). So skewed is the cross-sectional distribution for total lifetime output that the mode is a single product per person (Dennis, 1955), and the mean number of lifetime contributions across all creators may range between three and four (Wray, 2010). This means that for the vast majority of creators, Figure 24.1 would make no sense. The typical creators would have one 5- or 10-year age period in which they made their lone contribution, and the rest of the age periods would have zero values. Although there would be some tendency for the single product to occur at about career age 20, it would not have to be so. In fact, output for such low-output creators distributes in an almost random fashion over the course of their careers (Huber, 1998a, 1998b, 2000, 2001; Huber & Wagner-Döbler, 2001a, 2001b).

Although one-product creators constitute the plurality, the creators at the upper tail of the distribution easily compensate (Dennis, 1954a, 1954b, 1955). Indeed, the persons who make up the top 10% in total lifetime output can sometimes be credited with about half of all the products contributed to a given field. To put this disparity in context, the bottom half of the distribution is only responsible for about 15% of the total output. That amounts to an almost complete reversal of fortunes. Moreover, for the highly prolific elite, the typical curve seen in Figure 24.1 applies quite nicely (Simonton, 2004a, 2010). They are highly productive early in their careers, highly productive at the career peaks, and highly productive at the end of their careers. The shape of the individual career trajectory therefore closely parallels that for the aggregated data. The only real divergence is that the amplitude of the curve will be heightened. Annual output may peak at 10 products instead of being between four and five.

The implications for the age-decrement question should now be patent: Creators who reside at the upper tail of the productivity distribution are more productive in the last years of their lives than most creators are for their entire lives. In rough terms, a creator at the top of the distribution who is entering his or her final career decade can be expected to equal the entire career output of dozens upon dozens of creators who sit at the bottom of the distribution. Stated more abstractly, cross-sectional variation in creative productivity swamps longitudinal fluctuations in creative productivity (Over, 1982b, 1982c; see also Christensen & Jacomb, 1992). For samples showing sufficient cross-sectional variation, age will account for less than 10% of the total variance (e.g., Levin & Stephan, 1989; Over, 1982c; see also Bayer & Dutton, 1977; Horner et al., 1986; cf. Kozbelt, 2008a). Accordingly, individual differences in productivity at the beginning of a creator's career are usually much better predictors of his or her productivity at the end of the career than is age per se (Simonton, 1997; see also Lehman, 1946; cf. Kaufman & Gentile, 2002). The most prolific creators start early and end late.

The existence of these late-life products is critical to understanding creativity across the lifespan. In the arts, at least, the products will often undergo a qualitative change that sets them apart from earlier work created by the same persons (Lindauer, 1993a; Munsterberg, 1983; Simonton, 1989b). These "swan songs" or products in an "old-age style" may not necessarily represent a creator's "best work," but they still will provide a fitting finale to an artist's life and career. Composer's swan songs, for instance, tend to be shorter in duration, with more accessible thematic content, and yet with greater aesthetic significance (Simonton, 1989b). Operating on the principle of "less is more," these last testaments feature an artistic elegance that sets them apart.

Methodological Issues

It was remarked earlier that Lehman's (1953) methods were subjected to severe criticism. Almost all of these criticisms concentrated on the age decrement, arguing instead that it was an artifact. Probably three criticisms stand out above them all: aggregation error, augmented competition, and the quality–quantity connection.

Aggregation error

As said before, by counting productivity across large numbers of individuals, we obtained a smoother age curve. Various personal idiosyncrasies cancel out. Yet not all idiosyncrasies are thus removed. On the contrary, some quirks will actually become amplified through aggregation. One case in point is the impact of lifespan. Not everybody lives to the same ripe old age. Some can even die at a tragically young age. So what happens when we aggregate creative products into consecutive 5- or 10-year age periods? Because fewer creators are alive in the later periods, say the sixties, fewer products will be counted in those periods. Only the earliest periods, like the twenties, will have all creators included in the tabulations. It immediately follows that (a) the peak output period might be shifted toward earlier ages, and (b) the postpeak downturn will be far steeper than holds for any individual creator. Even worse, an age decrement would appear in the aggregated data even if not one single creator exhibited such a drop in his or her own career. The error introduced by aggregation may not only bias the results, but also generate artifactual results (Simonton, 1988a).

Amazingly, Quételet (1835/1968) was aware of this potential artifact, and so added a correction. This allowed him to show that even after adjusting for the number of creators alive in a given age period (namely the average output per creator per time unit), the decline still emerged. Yet when Lehman began his investigations, he blithely published his tabulations and figures without imposing this correction, opening himself up to severe criticism (Lehman & Heidler, 1949; but see Lehman, 1951). Dennis (1956a), one of those major critics, devised his own solution, different than Quételet's. Specifically, Dennis (1966) confined his samples to creators who had lived to become sexagenarians, a solution that required a draconian reduction in the number of cases investigated (see also Crozier, 1999). Naturally, with the advent of modern multivariate techniques, these makeshift adjustments are no longer necessary. It is now possible to retain the full sample and still control for differential life spans (e.g., Kozbelt, 2008a; Simonton, 1977a, 1985; Zickar & Slaughter, 1999). When researchers do so, they still find a diminished but still present age decrement (Kozbelt, 2008a; Simonton, 1977a, 1985; see also Simonton, 2007a, 2007b). Just as significant is the fact that the expected career peaks appear somewhat later than reported in the bulk of Lehman's (1953) research. The shift toward later peaks appears greatest for creators who have the shortest life expectancies, such as poets and mathematicians (Kaufman, 2003; Simonton, 1975a, 1991a).

Before continuing, it should be mentioned that aggregation error can introduce other artifacts besides an exaggerated postpeak decline (Simonton, 1988a). One example is what happens if the sample of creators is highly variable with respect to age at career onset but their products are tabulated into age periods defined by chronological rather than career age. In that case, assuming that age at career onset is normally distributed, the prepeak portion of the curve will more likely be convex rather than concave as shown in Figure 24.1 (Simonton, 1984b). A second example is what occurs if an investigator tabulates creative output from domains that feature contrasting career trajectories, such as both poets and novelists or both pure mathematicians and applied mathematicians. The result will be a bimodal ("saddle shaped") distribution with two peaks, despite the fact that all of the contributing data exhibit single-peaked functions (see, e.g., Cole, 1979; Dennis, 1966; Lehman, 1953; cf. Bayer & Dutton, 1977).

Augmented competition

Just a couple of years before Lehman initiated his research on the age–productivity relation, he published an investigation showing that the number of creative products contributed to a given domain in a given historical period has grown exponentially over time (Lehman, 1947). This finding has been replicated many times across many disciplines and even civilizations (e.g., Murray, 2003; Price, 1963; Simonton, 1975b, 1988b, 1992a). In large part, this exponential growth in overall cultural output reflects the exponential growth in the general population. Yet sometimes the expansion in certain creative domains is faster than the general increase. A case in point is creative productivity in the scientific disciplines. This growth has been so spectacular that in the 1960s it could be said "that 80 to 90 percent of all the scientists who have ever lived are alive now" (Price, 1963, p. 1).

Ironically, Lehman did not realize that this growth could induce an artifactual age decrement in his data (Simonton, 1988a). This artifact emerges because as creators progress through their careers, they face increasingly more competition from younger creators just entering the field. Thus older scientists may find it harder to publish their work in the same journals that used to accept their submitted manuscripts quite readily. Of course, one can argue that journals could gradually expand their page count allotments to keep up with the enhanced submissions. But without directly controlling for this potentially confounding factor, we can never know for sure. In addition, when the raw lists of creative products are taken out of reference works, such as biographical dictionaries and encyclopedias, we have no way of ensuring that the coverage of more recent works keeps pace with the total output (Dennis, 1958).

Even so, there are two reasons to believe that augmented competition cannot completely account for the observed age decrement (Simonton, 1988a). First, when studies introduce controls for this factor, the age decrement still appears (e.g., Simonton,

1977a). Second, the decrement still appears in those domains of creativity where the number of active creators has declined, such as opera (Simonton, 2000). Still, we certainly need additional empirical studies to assess the precise degree to which augmented competition affects the postpeak decline. Because psychologists tend to focus on individual creativity, they tend to ignore this contextual influence.

Quality–quantity connection

Creative products vary greatly in quality (Simonton, 2010). This variation is perhaps most apparent in the number of citations received by scientific journal articles. Although some articles can receive thousands of citations, other articles are completely ignored: Almost half of all publications are never cited at all (Redner, 1998). This phenomenal variation then raises the issue of what should be tabulated in the consecutive age periods. Should we count total quantity of output independent of quality, or should we count only the high-impact products, such as scientific breakthroughs or artistic masterpieces. Many early researchers chose the latter course (e.g., Lehman, 1953), and were severely criticized for the practice (e.g., Bullough, Bullough, & Mauro, 1978; Dennis, 1954c, 1956a). Subsequent researchers were more likely to count total output regardless of quality (e.g., Dennis, 1966; Over, 1982b, 1982c). The latter course of action was particularly favored by investigators who examined creative productivity in academic settings (e.g., Bridgwater, Walsh, & Walkenbach, 1982; Levin & Stephan, 1989, 1991).

It should be obvious that an even better solution would be to take both quantity and quality into consideration (e.g., Cole, 1979; Simonton, 1977a, 1985). It turns out that there are two main ways to accomplish this integration: We can scrutinize (a) the aggregate-level relation between quantity and quality or (b) the product-level relation between quality and age.

Aggregate-level relation between quantity and quality.   The most obvious solution is just to stratify the output of creators in the sample into high-quality and low-quality products, create two independent tabulations, and then correlate the two (Simonton, 1988a). Surprisingly, the first researcher to conduct such an empirical inquiry was none other than Quételet (1835/1968). Indeed, he broke the tabulations down into three levels of quality and showed that the three separate series pretty much agree, except that the age decrement starts somewhat later for the lower-quality products. Subsequent researchers have also shown that the periods in which creators produce the greatest number of minor works also tend to be the periods in which they produce the greatest number of major works (e.g., Simonton, 1977a, 1985). This positive quality–quantity relation has then inspired two additional issues: (a) How does the quality ratio change with age? (b) What is the longitudinal location of career landmarks?

The quality ratio is the ratio of major works per age period to the total works produced during the same age period (Simonton, 1988a, 1997). Even if quantity and quality are positively related, this ratio may be either positive, negative, zero, or adopt some curvilinear form. This question is highly relevant to the age-decrement question because it is possible that declines in output quantity are compensated by increases in the quality ratio. Although the earliest research on this question suggested that this quality ratio displayed no systematic change with age, but rather fluctuated randomly across the career course (Simonton, 1977a, 1985; see also Over, 1988, 1989), recent research provides at least some instances where the quality ratio may either increase (Hass & Weisberg, 2009; Kozbelt, 2005) or at least display a curvilinear single-peaked age function (Kozbelt, 2008a). What is known for sure is that the quality ratio normally does not decline monotonically with age, even if output quantity does fall off (Over, 1988, 1989).

On the issue of longitudinal location of career landmarks, given a set of major works for a given creator, we can single out three as constituting career landmarks (Raskin, 1936; Simonton, 1991a, 2007a; Zusne, 1976). These three are the first major work, the single best work, and the last major work. Lesser works will usually appear before the first career landmark and after the last career landmark, as well as fill the intervals between these two landmarks. In theory, it is conceivable that the three landmarks collapse into just two: Either the first or the last landmark may also represent the creator's single best work. Nevertheless, empirical research using samples of hundreds and even thousands of creators have consistently indicated that the single best work tends to appear about midway between the first and last major works (Simonton, 1997, 2007a). If anything, the best work occurs somewhat closer to the first landmark, particularly if control is introduced for differential lifespan, which has a major impact on the expected age of last major work (Lindauer, 1993b; Simonton, 1991a, 1991b, 2007a; Zusne, 1976). Significantly, the agewise location of the three landmarks closely tracks that for total output (Simonton, 1997). The age at best work appears at or a little after the age for maximum output, and the age for last major work appears later when the age decrement in total output is the most minimal. Interestingly, contrary to common conjecture (e.g., Kuhn, 1970), even scientific breakthroughs are more likely to be made by creators who are mid-career (Wray, 2003, 2004; but see Dietrich & Srinivasan, 2007, for a differing view).

It is worth pointing out that studies of career landmarks use individuals as the unit of analysis rather than aggregated age periods. Such units enable researchers to introduce controls for other variables not possible otherwise. As seen in the next section, this reduction can be continued a step farther.

Product-level relation between quality and age.   Rather than treat quality as a categorical variable, it can be viewed as a numerical variable. After evaluating the differential quality of all works produced by a sample of creative individuals, the investigator can then examine how variation in quality changes as a function of chronological or career age (e.g., Simonton, 1980; 1986). Here the primary unit of analysis is the creative product, but the product is nested within creators, indicating that the optimal analytical strategy is to use hierarchical models (e.g., Zickar & Slaughter, 1999), although the earlier research used less than optimal multiple regression models that ignored this hierarchical structure (e.g., Simonton, 1980). In any case, the research indicates that the differential quality of creative products tends to be a curvilinear, single-peaked function of age. So an age decrement still appears. Even so, the career trajectories for subsets of creators can depart conspicuously from this general trend (Zickar & Slaughter, 1999). Some creators may have their best work occur early in their careers, whereas other creators may produce their best work toward the end of their careers. It is also of interest that some creators display an upturn in quality as they approach the final years of their lives (Simonton, 1989b). These creative resurgences will sometimes show up in aggregate data as well, implying that the phenomenon is by no means rare (Bayer & Dutton, 1977; Davis, 1953; Haefele, 1962). Beyond doubt, creative decline is statistical rather than deterministic.

Substantive Interpretations

All told, the empirical literature suggests that an age decrement is very real. Exceptions do exist, and sometimes the decline can be reversed, but the decrement represents an empirical generalization as robust as can be expected in the behavioral sciences (Simonton, 1988a, 1997). Indeed, how many findings in developmental psychology can be said to have survived 175 years of empirical scrutiny? So the question now becomes: Why does it appear? After all, if creativity were merely a form of domain-specific expertise, we should even expect a decline (Simonton, 2000). Even if total output might drop off over the years, that drop does not necessitate a corresponding loss in quality. Quite the contrary, the quality ratio as well as differential product quality should remain positively monotonic even while reaching an asymptote. Furthermore, the single best work should then appear close to – if not being actually identical to – the last major work. Yet this placement of the last two career landmarks is the exception rather than the rule. Most often, the best work is more proximate to the first major work than to the last major work.

The culprits behind the decrement can be roughly grouped into two categories of factors: extrinsic and intrinsic (Simonton, 1988a). Extrinsic factors entail any variables that bear no immediate connection with the creative process but that could still impede the process. Lehman (1953) provided a long list of possible circumstances that might interfere with creativity in the latter part of life, and some of these extrinsic factors have been investigated in subsequent empirical research (e.g., Hargens, McCann, & Reskin, 1978; Horner, Murray, & Rushton, 1994; Kanazawa, 2000; Kyvik, 1990b; McDowell, 1982; Simonton, 1977a). These inhibitory conditions include increased physical illness, marital or family distractions, and professional or administrative responsibilities. Although it cannot be doubted that these and other extrinsic factors can undermine creative productivity in the later years, it is equally clear that they cannot provide the whole story. The postpeak decline still occurs even after making adjustments for these extraneous influences.

As a result, it is essential to consider intrinsic factors (Simonton, 1988a). By intrinsic I mean influences that bear an intimate connection with the creative process and person. The following four explanations or sets of explanations fall into this second class.

Beard (1874) offered the earliest intrinsic theory. According to this theory, creative output is a function of enthusiasm and experience. Enthusiasm provides the motivation, and experience offers the expertise. Where experience increases over the course of a career, enthusiasm steadily declines. The career peak indicates the point where these two contrary trend lines meet, producing the highest level of both enthusiasm and experience. Products prior to this peak tend to be more original than competent, whereas those emerging in the postpeak period tend to be increasingly routine, proficient, but unsurprising (cf. Mumford, 1984). One positive feature of this theory is that it can help explain interdisciplinary contrasts in the career peak (Simonton, 1988a). Distinct domains may require a different mix of enthusiasm and experience. For example, poets may depend more on the former, novelists on the latter.

In the second explanation, creativity is associated with individual-difference variables that display distinctive trends across the lifespan. As a consequence, the age decrement may merely reflect these longitudinal changes. Two examples will suffice. First, creativity is positively correlated with the capacity for divergent thinking (Carson, Peterson, & Higgins, 2005), yet the latter capacity tends to decline with age, especially after about age 40 (McCrae, Arenberg, & Costa, 1987). Insofar as divergent thinking requires fluid rather than crystallized intelligence, then the decline in creativity may be tracking longitudinal decrements in fluid intelligence (cf. Dietrich & Srinivasan, 2007; Horn & Cattell, 1967; Schaie, 1994). Second, creativity is positively associated with openness to experience, one of the Big-Five Personality Factors (Carson et al., 2005; Feist, 1998), a supportive trait that may also decline in the latter part of life (Lucas & Donnellan, 2009). This negative trend for openness parallels research showing that scientists are sometimes inclined to become less receptive to new ideas in the latter part of their careers (Hull, Tessner, & Diamond, 1978; Sulloway, 1996; cf. Messerli, 1988). It should be observed that divergent thinking and openness, besides being correlated with creativity, are also correlated with each other (McCrae, 1987).

The third explanation takes an economic approach. Some researchers have attempted to explicate creativity in economic terms (e.g., Rubenson & Runco, 1992; Sternberg & Lubart, 1991), so it should not be surprising that some economists have attempted to explain the age–productivity relation. For instance, Diamond (1984, 1986) treats the problem in terms of investment in human capital, an investment that will tend to diminish as creators age because the possibility of recouping the investment declines with the proximity of death (see also Levin & Stephan, 1991). Most recently, Galenson (2001, 2005) has argued for the existence of two alternative creative life cycles. On the one hand are the conceptual creators, or "young geniuses," who tend to peak early and rapidly decline, and who are prone to be most famous for one or two breakthrough works. On the other hand are the experimental creators, or "old masters," who develop very slowly, peaking late in life, and becoming best known for a body of work rather than isolated masterworks. This distinction has consequences regarding how much their respective paintings fetch when sold in open auctions (cf. Hellmanzik, 2009). Although Galenson originally confined his theory to painters (Galenson, 2001), he subsequently applied the theory to all major forms of creativity, including the sciences (Galenson, 2005; Weisberg & Galenson, 2005).

Finally, Simonton (1984b, 1997) has developed a complex mathematical model on the age–productivity relation that is predicated on a two-step mechanism. First, each individual begins with a certain quantity of creative potential that is progressively transformed into ideas-in-progress through the ideation process. Second, the ideas-in-progress are then transformed into overt products through the elaboration process. This model leads to some highly specific predictions not only about total output across the lifespan (Simonton, 1984b, 1989a), but also regarding the longitudinal placement of the three career landmarks (Simonton, 1991a, 1991b, 1992b, 2007a). It also accounts for both individual differences (Simonton, 1991a, 1992b, 2007a) and interdisciplinary contrasts (Simonton, 1989a, 1991a, 1997). At present, it is fair to say that it provides the most comprehensive and precise model currently available. It has the added advantage that it can be integrated with even broader combinatorial models that can account for other features of creativity and discovery (Simonton, 2010). Yet it also posits that creative potential is converted into creative products faster than that potential can be replenished, hence generating a postpeak decline.

Needless to say, the above four explanatory perspectives do not have to be mutually exclusive. For example, perhaps longitudinal trends in human capital and creative potential might be highly congruent, and both might be partially contingent on longitudinal shifts in openness or divergent thinking. Alternatively, the diverse explanations might make independent contributions to explaining the phenomenon. For instance, Simonton (2007b) was able to show that the difference in career peaks between poets and novelists predicted by his mathematical model were orthogonal to Galenson's (2005) contrast between conceptualists and experimentalists. Poets can be either conceptual or experimental, and the same holds for novelists, meaning that an experimental poet can peak later than a conceptual novelist.

Is the Age Decrement Inexorable?

For those creators who are already past the supposed productive peak in Figure 24.1, the postpeak decline will have personal meaning. Nobody wants to be perceived as "over the hill" or "running out of steam." Nonetheless, when we scrutinize the literature more carefully, we must realize that the picture is not nearly so dismal as some might infer (Simonton, 1990).

Let us begin by recognizing that many extrinsic factors that impinge on creativity in the later years of life have had their impact severely reduced. Courtesy of modern healthcare, creators can live longer, healthier, and hence more productive lives. For instance, the life expectancies of 696 classical composers from the Renaissance to the 20th century increased 4.75 years per century, an increase that directly affected the expected length of their creative careers (Simonton, 1977b; see also Simonton, 1991a). In addition, creators, like other people, are probably having smaller families, and find it easier to obtain childcare for the children they do have, thereby reducing the adverse effect of becoming a parent. These facts taken together, creative individuals probably have a longer "empty nest" period in which they can devote fuller time to their scientific or artistic progeny. Furthermore, with the advent of modern research universities and institutions, fellowships and grants, sabbatical leaves and clerical support, and various other resources designed to support creative productivity – such as computers and the internet – it is reasonable to suppose that the age decrement today should be far smaller than that seen in the days when the "lone genius" really had to do it all alone and in isolation.

Having more leisure for engaging in productive endeavors means more than merely spending more time at the writing desk, easel, or lab bench. Creative persons then have the opportunity to pursue wide interests, including extensive reading and exploring the internet, allowing them to maintain the openness to experience that is associated with creativity. With less urgency imposed on continued output, creators can also work on multiple projects. Besides providing a creative outlet when an obstacle intrudes on a given project, such a working style permits "cross-talk" between different projects. Sometimes the solution to one problem is found in the solution of a seemingly unrelated problem (Simonton, 2004a).

Finally, we have to consider the fact that creators operate in a social context (Simonton, 1984a, 1992c). This context includes role models and mentors, collaborators, associates, rivals, and students or apprentices. These relationships can enhance creative productivity beyond what could be anticipated were the creativity to take place in isolation. Of special interest is the increasingly collaborative nature of creativity. Although collaboration is most conspicuous in the sciences (Over, 1982a; Smart & Bayer, 1986; Zuckermann & Merton, 1973), it also appears in the arts, such as architecture, theater, dance, cinema, and video games (Ferriani, Corrado, & Boschetti, 2005; Sawyer, 2007; Simonton, 2004b). In collaborative creativity, new ideas emerge out of the dynamic interaction of individual minds. Because not all collaborative groups are equally creative, it is necessary to inquire about the characteristics of highly creative collaborations. In general, such groups are most creative when they are highly heterogeneous with respect to various professional and demographic attributes (Andrews, 1979; Nemeth & Nemeth-Brown, 2003; Page, 2007). Among those attributes is age. Highly creative groups contain a mix of apprentices and masters, those just starting out and those who have been around for a long time. This cohort diversity helps both the young and the old overcome their agewise liabilities. In terms of Beard's (1874) two-factor theory, the young can bring enthusiasm to the table, while the old contribute the experience. The two interacting together produces creativity that neither could generate alone. These various collaborative forces may explain why recent research finds that the age decrement in scientific output has itself declined, if it shows up at all (Feist, 2006; Gingras, Lariviere, Macaluso, & Robitaille, 2008; Kyvik & Olsen, 2008).

In sum, although the age decrement is real, the downturn is not inexorable. Various factors can not only ameliorate the decline, but even turn it around. In the latter instance, some creators end their careers at the top of their game.

References

Andrews, F. M. (Ed.). (1979). *Scientific productivity: The effectiveness of research groups in six countries*. Cambridge, UK: Cambridge University Press.

Bayer, A. E., & Dutton, J. E. (1977). Career age and research-professional activities of academic scientists. *Journal of Higher Education, 48,* 259–282.

Beard, G. M. (1874). *Legal responsibility in old age*. New York: Russell.

Bridgwater, C. A., Walsh, J. A., & Walkenbach, J. (1982). Pretenure and posttenure productivity trends of academic psychologists. *American Psychologist, 37,* 236–238.

Bullough, V. L., Bullough, B., & Mauro, M. (1978). Age and achievement: A dissenting view. *Gerontologist, 18,* 584–587.

Carson, S., Peterson, J. B., & Higgins, D. M. (2005). Reliability, validity, and factor structure of the Creative Achievement Questionnaire. *Creativity Research Journal, 17,* 37–50.

Christensen, H., & Jacomb, P. A. (1992). The lifetime productivity of eminent Australian academics. *International Journal of Geriatric Psychiatry, 7,* 681–686.

Cole, S. (1979). Age and scientific performance. *American Journal of Sociology, 84,* 958–977.

Cole, S., & Cole, J. R. (1973). *Social stratification in science.* Chicago: University of Chicago Press.

Crozier, W. R. (1999). Age and individual differences in artistic productivity: Trends within a sample of British novelists. *Creativity Research Journal, 12,* 197–204.

Davis, R. A. (1953). Note on age and productive scholarship of a university faculty. *Journal of Applied Psychology, 38,* 318–319.

Dennis, W. (1954a). Bibliographies of eminent scientists. *Scientific Monthly, 79,* 180–183.

Dennis, W. (1954b). Productivity among American psychologists. *American Psychologist, 9,* 191–194.

Dennis, W. (1954c). Review of age and achievement. *Psychological Bulletin, 51,* 306–308.

Dennis, W. (1955). Variations in productivity among creative workers. *Scientific Monthly, 80,* 277–278.

Dennis, W. (1956a). Age and achievement: A critique. *Journal of Gerontology, 9,* 465–467.

Dennis, W. (1956b) Age and productivity among scientists. *Science, 123,* 724–725.

Dennis, W. (1958). The age decrement in outstanding scientific contributions: Fact or artifact? *American Psychologist, 13,* 457–460.

Dennis, W. (1966). Creative productivity between the ages of 20 and 80 years. *Journal of Gerontology, 21,* 1–8.

Diamond, A. M. (1984). An economic model of the life-cycle research productivity of scientists. *Scientometrics, 6,* 189–196.

Diamond, A. M., Jr. (1986). The life-cycle research productivity of mathematicians and scientists. *Journal of Gerontology, 41,* 520–525.

Dietrich, A., & Srinivasan, N. (2007). The optimal age to start a revolution. *Journal of Creative Behavior, 41,* 54–74.

Feist, G. J. (1998). A meta-analysis of personality in scientific and artistic creativity. *Personality and Social Psychology Review, 2,* 290–309.

Feist, G. J. (2006). The development of scientific talent in Westinghouse Finalists and members of the National Academy of Sciences. *Journal of Adult Development, 13,* 23–35.

Ferriani, S., Corrado, R., & Boschetti, C. (2005). Organizational learning under organizational impermanence: Collaborative ties in film project firms. *Journal of Management and Governance, 9,* 257–285.

Galenson, D. W. (2001). *Painting outside the lines: Patterns of creativity in modern art.* Cambridge, MA: Harvard University Press.

Galenson, D. W. (2005). *Old masters and young geniuses: The two life cycles of artistic creativity.* Princeton, NJ: Princeton University Press.

Gingras, Y., Lariviere, V., Macaluso, B., & Robitaille, J.-P. (2008). The effect of aging on researchers' publication and citation patterns. *PLoS ONE, 3,* 1–8.

Haefele, J. W. (1962). *Creativity and innovation.* New York: Reinhold.

Hargens, L. L., McCann, J. C., & Reskin, B. F. (1978). Productivity and reproductivity: Fertility and professional achievement among research scientists. *Social Forces, 57,* 154–163.

Hass, R. W., & Weisberg, R. W. (2009). Career development in two seminal American songwriters: A test of the equal odds rule. *Creativity Research Journal, 21,* 183–190.

Hellmanzik, C. (2009). Artistic styles: Revisiting the analysis of modern artists' careers. *Journal of Cultural Economics, 33,* 201–232.

Horn, J. L., & Cattell, R. B. (1967). Age differences in fluid and crystallized intelligence. *Acta Psychologica, 26,* 107–129.

Horner, K. L., Murray, H. G., & Rushton, J. P. (1994). Aging and administration in academic psychologists. *Social Behavior and Personality, 22,* 343–346.

Horner, K. L., Rushton, J. P., & Vernon, P. A. (1986). Relation between aging and research productivity of academic psychologists. *Psychology and Aging, 1,* 319–324.

Huber, J. C. (1998a). Invention and inventivity as a special kind of creativity, with implications for general creativity. *Journal of Creative Behavior, 32,* 58–72.

Huber, J. C. (1998b). Invention and inventivity is a random, Poisson process: A potential guide to analysis of general creativity. *Creativity Research Journal, 11,* 231–241.

Huber, J. C. (1999). Inventive productivity and the statistics of exceedances. *Scientometrics, 45,* 33–53.

Huber, J. C. (2000). A statistical analysis of special cases of creativity. *Journal of Creative Behavior, 34,* 203–225.

Huber, J. C. (2001). A new method for analyzing scientific productivity. *Journal of the American Society for Information Science and Technology, 52,* 1089–1099.

Huber, J. C., & Wagner-Döbler, R. (2001a). Scientific production: A statistical analysis of authors in mathematical logic. *Scientometrics, 50,* 323–337.

Huber, J. C., & Wagner-Döbler, R. (2001b). Scientific production: A statistical analysis of authors in physics, 1800-1900. *Scientometrics, 50,* 437–453.

Hull, D. L., Tessner, P. D., & Diamond, A. M. (1978). Planck's principle: Do younger scientists accept new scientific ideas with greater alacrity than older scientists? *Science, 202,* 717–723.

Kanazawa, S. (2000). Scientific discoveries as cultural displays: A further test of Miller's courtship model. *Evolution and Human Behavior, 21,* 317–321.

Kaufman, J. C. (2003). The cost of the muse: Poets die young. *Death Studies, 27,* 813–821.

Kaufman, J. C., & Gentile, C. A. (2002). The will, the wit, the judgement: The importance of an early start in productive and successful creative writing. *High Ability Studies, 13,* 115–123.

Kim, S. (2003). The impact of research productivity on early retirement of university professors. *Industrial Relations, 42,* 106–125.

Kozbelt, A. (2005). Factors affecting aesthetic success and improvement in creativity: A case study of musical genres in Mozart. *Psychology of Music, 33,* 235–255.

Kozbelt, A. (2008a). Longitudinal hit ratios of classical composers: Reconciling "Darwinian" and expertise acquisition perspectives on lifespan creativity. *Psychology of Aesthetics, Creativity, and the Arts, 2,* 221–235.

Kozbelt, A. (2008b). One-hit wonders in classical music: Evidence and (partial) explanations for an early career peak. *Creativity Research Journal, 20,* 179–195.

Kuhn, T. S. (1970). *The structure of scientific revolutions* (2nd ed.). Chicago: University of Chicago Press.

Kyvik, S. (1990a). Age and scientific productivity: Differences between fields of learning. *Higher Education, 19,* 37–55.

Kyvik, S. (1990b). Motherhood and scientific productivity. *Social Studies of Science, 20,* 149–160.

Kyvik, S. & Olsen, T. B. (2008). Does the aging of tenured academic staff affect the research performance of universities? *Scientometrics, 76,* 439–455.

Lehman, H. C. (1946). Age of starting to contribute versus total creative output. *Journal of Applied Psychology, 30,* 460–480.

Lehman, H. C. (1947). The exponential increase of man's cultural output. *Social Forces, 25,* 281–290.

Lehman, H. C. (1951). Average age at time of achievement vs. longevity. *American Journal of Psychology, 64,* 534–547.

Lehman, H. C. (1953). *Age and achievement.* Princeton, NJ: Princeton University Press.

Lehman, H. C. (1956). Reply to Dennis' critique of Age and Achievement. *Journal of Gerontology, 11,* 128–134. Lehman, H. C. (1958). The chemist's most creative years. *Science, 127,* 1213–1222.

Lehman, H. C. (1960). Age and outstanding achievement in creative chemistry. *Geriatrics, 15,* 19–37.

Lehman, H. C. (1962). More about age and achievement. *Gerontologist, 2,* 141–148.

Lehman, H. C. (1963). Chronological age versus present-day contributions to medical progress. *Gerontologist, 3,* 71–75.

Lehman, H. C. (1965). The production of masterworks prior to age 30. *Gerontologist, 5,* 24–30.

Lehman, H. C. (1966a). The most creative years of engineers and other technologists. *Journal of Genetic Psychology, 108,* 263–270.

Lehman, H. C. (1966b). The psychologist's most creative years. *American Psychologist, 21,* 363–369.

Lehman, H. C., & Heidler, J. B. (1949). Chronological age vs. quality of literary output. *American Journal of Psychology, 62,* 75–89.

Levin, S. G., & Stephan, P. E. (1989). Age and research productivity of academic scientists. *Research in Higher Education, 30,* 531–549.

Levin, S. G., & Stephan, P. E. (1990). Publishing productivity in the earth sciences. *Eos, 71,* 1173–1182.

Levin, S. G., & Stephan, P. E. (1991). Research productivity over the life cycle: Evidence for academic scientists. *American Economic Review, 81,* 114–132.

Lindauer, M. S. (1993a). The old-age style and its artists. *Empirical Studies and the Arts, 11,* 135–146.

Lindauer, M. S. (1993b). The span of creativity among long-lived historical artists. *Creativity Research Journal, 6,* 231–239.

Lindauer, M. S. (2003). *Aging, creativity, and art: A positive perspective on late-life development.* New York: Kluwer Academic.

Lotka, A. J. (1926). The frequency distribution of scientific productivity. *Journal of the Washington Academy of Sciences, 16,* 317–323.

Lucas, R. E., & Donnellan, M. B. (2009). Age differences in personality: Evidence from a nationally representative Australian sample. *Developmental Psychology, 45,* 1353–1363.

Lyons, J. (1968). Chronological age, professional age, and eminence in psychology. *American Psychologist, 23,* 371–374.

McCrae, R. R. (1987). Creativity, divergent thinking, and openness to experience. *Journal of Personality and Social Psychology, 52,* 1258–1265.

McCrae, R. R., Arenberg, D., & Costa, P. T. (1987). Declines in divergent thinking with age: Cross-sectional, longitudinal, and cross-sequential analyses. *Psychology and Aging, 2,* 130–136.

McDowell, J. M. (1982). Obsolescence of knowledge and career publication profiles: Some evidence of differences among fields in costs of interrupted careers. *American Economic Review, 72,* 752–768.

Messerli, P. (1988). Age differences in the reception of new scientific theories: The case of plate tectonics theory. *Social Studies of Science, 18,* 91–112.

Mumford, M. D. (1984). Age and outstanding occupational achievement: Lehman revisited. *Journal of Vocational Behavior, 25,* 225–244.

Munsterberg, H. (1983). *The crown of life: Artistic creativity in old age.* San Diego, CA: Harcourt-Brace-Jovanovich.

Murray, C. (2003). *Human accomplishment: The pursuit of excellence in the arts and sciences, 800 B.C. to 1950.* New York: HarperCollins.

Nemeth, C. J., & Nemeth-Brown, B. (2003). Better than individuals? The potential benefits of dissent and diversity. In P. B. Paulus & B. A. Nijstad (Eds.), *Group creativity: Innovation through collaboration* (pp. 63–84). New York: Oxford University Press.

Over, R. (1982a). Collaborative research and publication in psychology. *American Psychologist, 37*, 996–1001.

Over, R. (1982b). Does research productivity decline with age? *Higher Education, 11*, 511–520.

Over, R. (1982c). Is age a good predictor of research productivity? *Australian Psychologist, 17*, 129–139.

Over, R. (1988). Does scholarly impact decline with age? *Scientometrics, 13*, 215–223.

Over, R. (1989). Age and scholarly impact. *Psychology and Aging, 4*, 222–225.

Page, S. E. (2007). *Difference: How the power of diversity creates better groups, firms, schools, and societies.* Princeton, NJ: Princeton University Press.

Pressey, S. L., & Combs, A. (1943). Acceleration and age of productivity. *Educational Research Bulletin, 22*, 191–196.

Price, D. (1963). *Little science, big science.* New York: Columbia University Press.

Quételet, A. (1968). *A treatise on man and the development of his faculties.* New York: Franklin. (Reprint of 1842 Edinburgh translation of 1835 French original)

Raskin, E. A. (1936). Comparison of scientific and literary ability: A biographical study of eminent scientists and men of letters of the nineteenth century. *Journal of Abnormal and Social Psychology, 31*, 20–35.

Redner, S. (1998). How popular is your paper? An empirical study of the citation distribution. *European Physical Journal B, 4*, 131–134.

Roe, A. (1953). *The making of a scientist.* New York: Dodd, Mead.

Rubenson, D. L., & Runco, M. A. (1992). The psychoeconomic approach to creativity. *New Ideas in Psychology, 10*, 131–147.

Sawyer, R. K. (2007). *Group genius: The creative power of collaboration.* New York: Basic Books.

Schaie, K.W. (1994).The course of adult intellectual ability. *American Psychologist, 49*, 304–313.

Shockley, W. (1957). On the statistics of individual variations of productivity in research laboratories. *Proceedings of the Institute of Radio Engineers, 45*, 279–290.

Simon, H. A. (1955). On a class of skew distribution functions. *Biometrika, 42*, 425–440.

Simonton, D. K. (1975a). Age and literary creativity: A cross-cultural and transhistorical survey. *Journal of Cross-Cultural Psychology, 6*, 259–277.

Simonton, D. K. (1975b). Sociocultural context of individual creativity: A transhistorical time-series analysis. *Journal of Personality and Social Psychology, 32*, 1119–1133.

Simonton, D. K. (1977a). Creative productivity, age, and stress: A biographical time-series analysis of 10 classical composers. *Journal of Personality and Social Psychology, 35*, 791–804.

Simonton, D. K. (1977b). Eminence, creativity, and geographic marginality: A recursive structural equation model. *Journal of Personality and Social Psychology, 35*, 805–816.

Simonton, D. K. (1980). Thematic fame, melodic originality, and musical zeitgeist: A biographical and transhistorical content analysis. *Journal of Personality and Social Psychology, 38*, 972–983.

Simonton, D. K. (1984a). Artistic creativity and interpersonal relationships across and within generations. *Journal of Personality and Social Psychology, 46*, 1273–1286.

Simonton, D. K. (1984b). Creative productivity and age: A mathematical model based on a two-step cognitive process. *Developmental Review, 4*, 77–111.

Simonton, D. K. (1985). Quality, quantity, and age: The careers of 10 distinguished psychologists. *International Journal of Aging and Human Development, 21*, 241–254.

Simonton, D. K. (1986). Popularity, content, and context in 37 Shakespeare plays. *Poetics, 15*, 493–510.

Simonton, D. K. (1988a). Age and outstanding achievement: What do we know after a century of research. *Psychological Bulletin, 104,* 251–267.

Simonton, D. K. (1988b). Galtonian genius, Kroeberian configurations, and emulation: A generational time-series analysis of Chinese civilization. *Journal of Personality and Social Psychology, 55,* 230–238.

Simonton, D. K. (1989a). Age and creative productivity: Nonlinear estimation of an information-processing model. *International Journal of Aging and Human Development, 29,* 23–37.

Simonton, D. K. (1989b). The swan-song phenomenon: Last-works effects for 172 classical composers. *Psychology and Aging, 4,* 42–47.

Simonton, D. K. (1990). Creativity in the later years: Optimistic prospects for achievement. *Gerontologist, 30,* 626–631.

Simonton, D. K. (1991a). Career landmarks in science: Individual differences and interdisciplinary contrasts. *Developmental Psychology, 27,* 119–130.

Simonton, D. K. (1991b). Emergence and realization of genius: The lives and works of 120 classical composers. *Journal of Personality and Social Psychology, 61,* 829–840.

Simonton, D. K. (1992a). Gender and genius in Japan: Feminine eminence in masculine culture. *Sex Roles, 27,* 101–119.

Simonton, D. K. (1992b). Leaders of American psychology, 1879–1967: Career development, creative output, and professional achievement. *Journal of Personality and Social Psychology, 62,* 5–17.

Simonton, D. K. (1992c). The social context of career success and course for 2,026 scientists and inventors. *Personality and Social Psychology Bulletin, 18,* 452–463.

Simonton, D. K. (1997). Creative productivity: a predictive and explanatory model of career trajectories and landmarks. *Psychological Review, 104,* 66–89.

Simonton, D. K. (2000). Creative development as acquired expertise: Theoretical issues and an empirical test. *Developmental Review, 20,* 283–318.

Simonton, D. K. (2004a). *Creativity in science: Chance, logic, genius, and zeitgeist.* Cambridge, UK: Cambridge University Press.

Simonton, D. K. (2004b). Group artistic creativity: Creative clusters and cinematic success in 1,327 feature films. *Journal of Applied Social Psychology, 34,* 1494–1520.

Simonton, D. K. (2007a). Cinema composers: Career trajectories for creative productivity in film music. *Psychology of Aesthetics, Creativity, and the Arts, 1,* 160–169.

Simonton, D. K. (2007b). Creative life cycles in literature: Poets versus novelists or conceptualists versus experimentalists? *Psychology of Aesthetics, Creativity, and the Arts, 1,* 133–139.

Simonton, D. K. (2010). Creativity as blind-variation and selective-retention: Constrained combinatorial models of exceptional creativity. *Physics of Life Reviews, 7,* 156–179.

Smart, J. C., & Bayer, A. E. (1986). Author collaboration and impact: A note on citation rates of single and multiple authored articles. *Scientometrics, 10,* 297–305.

Stern, N. (1978). Age and achievement in mathematics: A case-study in the sociology of science. *Social Studies of Science, 8,* 127–140.

Sternberg, R. J., & Lubart, T. I. (1991). An investment theory of creativity and its development. *Human Development, 34,* 1–31.

Sulloway, F. J. (1996). *Born to rebel: Birth order, family dynamics, and creative lives.* New York: Pantheon.

Sutter, M., & Kocher, M. G. (2001). Power laws of research output: Evidence for journals of economics. *Scientometrics, 51,* 405–414.

Weisberg, B. A., & Galenson, D. W. (2005). Creative careers: The life cycles of Nobel laureates in economics. Working Paper 11799, National Bureau of Economic Research. Retrieved from http://papers.nber.org/papers

Wray, K. B. (2003). Is science really a young man's game? *Social Studies of Science, 33,* 137–149.

Wray, K. B. (2004). An examination of the contribution of young scientist in new fields. *Scientometrics, 61,* 117–128.

Wray, K. B. (2009). Did professionalization afford better opportunities for young scientists? *Scientometrics, 81*(3), 757–764.

Wray, K. B. (2010). Rethinking the size of scientific specialties: Correcting Price's estimate. *Scientometrics, 83*(2), 471–446.

Zickar, M. J, & Slaughter, J. E. (1999). Examining creative performance over time using hierarchical linear modeling: An illustration using film directors. *Human Performance, 12,* 211–230.

Zuckermann, H., & Merton, R. K. (1973). Age, aging and age structure in science. In R. K. Merton, *The sociology of science* (pp. 497–559). Chicago: University of Chicago Press.

Zuckerman, H., & Merton, R. K. (1972). Age, aging, and age structure in science. In M. W. Riley, M. Johnson, & A. Foner (Eds.), *Aging and society: Vol. 3. A sociology of age stratification* (pp. 292–356). New York: Russell Sage Foundation.

Zusne, L. (1976). Age and achievement in psychology: The harmonic mean as a model. *American Psychologist, 31,* 805–807.

Author Index

aan het Rot, M. 280
Aartsen, M. J. 245
Abbott, R. D. 109
Abeles, N. 277
Abraham, J. 7
Abrams, R. C. 313, 315, 318
Achenbaum, W. A. 468
Acitelli, L. K. 383, 384
Ackerman, B. P. 247
Ackerman, P. L. 255
Adam, E. K. 409
Adams, D. R. 137
Adams, G. A. 418
Adams, G. R. 213
Adams, R. G. 387, 388, 389, 390
Ader, R. 7
Adler, N. E. 12, 39
Agrigoroaei, S. 261, 361
Agronick, G. S. 224, 228
Agronin, M. E. 313, 315, 316
Akiyama, H. 338, 386, 393, 405
Akwin, D. F. 443
Al-Aidroos, N. 159

Albert, M. S. 85, 199, 466
Albert, S. M. 337
Albertson, S. A. 176
Albuquerque, P. B. 277
Aldwin, C. M. 81, 421
Aleman, A. 181, 366
Alexopoulous, G. S. 276, 277, 281, 282
Alfeeli, A. 6
Allaire, J. C. 190, 193, 195, 196, 197, 198, 199, 200, 241
Allard, E. S. 243
Allen-Burge, R. 451
Alley, D. 7, 416, 418
Allore, H. G. 104, 407
Almeida, D. 12, 80, 197, 239, 241, 264, 359, 409
Alonso, Y. 6
Alwin, D. F. 12, 76, 174
Amato, P. R. 33, 386
Ames, A. 318
Ames, D. 275, 335
Amrhein, P. C. 261
Anas, A. P. 371

The Wiley-Blackwell Handbook of Adulthood and Aging, First Edition. Edited by Susan Krauss Whitbourne and Martin J. Sliwinski. © 2012 Blackwell Publishing Ltd. Published 2012 by Blackwell Publishing Ltd.

Subject Index

3-Dimensional Wisdom Scale   467

AARC *see* awareness of age-related change
ABI *see* ankle-brachial blood pressure index
ability dedifferentiation   147
ability tests   195–6
academic performance   260
accelerated aging   97, 112, 465
accommodation   265–6
accuracy scoring   193
acetylcholine   294
acetylcholinesterase   294
achieved identity   213
achievement motivation   259–60, 264
achievement striving   259
activated long-term memory   161
active concern   218
active life engagement   4
ACTIVE Study   148, 470–1
activities of daily living   37, 86, 110,
   336–7
   see also daily living tasks; instrumental
   activities of daily living

activity
   aging and   xx, 3, 97, 104–5, 262–3, 470
   as marker of frailty   103
   bone health and   470
   cancer and   107
   cardiometabolic risk and   112
   cardiovascular disease and   40, 470
   cardiovascular fitness and   181
   cardiovascular risk factors and   104–5, 110
   chronic conditions and   112
   cognitive decline and   109
   cognitive functioning and   109, 112, 470
   colon cancer and   105
   coronary heart disease and   105–9
   dementia and   105, 109, 301, 308, 447
   depression and   470
   diabetes and   105
   disability and   109, 110, 112
   guidelines   112
   hypertension and   105
   longevity and   105
   memory and   181
   mortality and   43, 105–10